Perspectives
on the
Christian Reformed Church

John Henry Kromminga

Perspectives
on the
Christian Reformed Church

Studies in Its History, Theology, and Ecumenicity

Presented in Honor of
John Henry Kromminga
At His Retirement as President
of Calvin Theological Seminary

Peter De Klerk and Richard R. De Ridder, *Editors*

BAKER BOOK HOUSE
Grand Rapids, Michigan 49506

ISBN: 0-8010-2934-1

Library of Congress
Card Catalog Number: 83-072234

"A Bibliography of John Henry Kromminga" is an updated version of the bibliography which appeared in *A Bibliography of the Writings of the Professors of Calvin Theological Seminary,* copyright 1980 by Peter De Klerk and published by Calvin Theological Seminary, Grand Rapids, Michigan

Printed in the United States of America

≡ Contents

6

PART TWO Studies in Theology

PART THREE Studies in Ecumenicity

Contributors

Harry R. Boer is Minister Emeritus of the Christian Reformed Church, resident of Grand Rapids, Michigan

John H. Bratt is Professor Emeritus of Religion and Theology at Calvin College, Grand Rapids, Michigan

Herbert J. Brinks is Professor of History at Calvin College, Grand Rapids, Michigan

Donald J. Bruggink is Professor of Historical Theology at Western Theological Seminary, Holland, Michigan

Elton J. Bruins is Professor of Religion at Hope College, Holland, Michigan

Peter De Klerk is Theological Librarian at Calvin Theological Seminary, Grand Rapids, Michigan

Richard R. De Ridder is Professor of Church Polity and Church Administration at Calvin Theological Seminary, Grand Rapids, Michigan

I. John Hesselink, Jr., is President and Professor of Theology at Western Theological Seminary, Holland, Michigan

Anthony A. Hoekema is Professor Emeritus of Systematic Theology at Calvin Theological Seminary, Grand Rapids, Michigan

Fred H. Klooster is Professor of Systematic Theology at Calvin Theological Seminary, Grand Rapids, Michigan

Carl G. Kromminga is Professor of Practical Theology at Calvin Theological Seminary, Grand Rapids, Michigan

Doede Nauta is Professor Emeritus of Church History at the Free University, Amsterdam, The Netherlands

Lubbertus Oostendorp is Professor Emeritus of Theology at Reformed Bible College, Grand Rapids, Michigan

Klaas Runia is Professor of Practical Theology at the Theological School of the Gereformeerde Kerken in Nederland, Kampen, The Netherlands

Paul G. Schrotenboer is General Secretary of the Reformed Ecumenical Synod, Grand Rapids, Michigan

Harvey A. Smit is Director of Education, Board of Publications of the Christian Reformed Church in North America, Grand Rapids, Michigan

Willem van 't Spijker is Professor of Church History and Church Polity at the Theological School of the Christelijke Gereformeerde Kerken in Nederland, Apeldoorn, The Netherlands

Henry Stob is Professor Emeritus of Philosophical and Moral Theology at Calvin Theological Seminary, Grand Rapids, Michigan

Henry Zwaanstra is Professor of Historical Theology at Calvin Theological Seminary, Grand Rapids, Michigan

Foreword

In all the years since its founding as a denomination in 1857 the Christian Reformed Church has produced only a small number of leaders who may legitimately be called "churchmen." Dr. John H. Kromminga must be numbered among them. His distinctive talents as pastor, scholar, professor, and ecumenist have been widely acclaimed and appreciated beyond the confines of the denomination of which he has been a lifelong member. Although he has worn many "hats" in the years he served his denomination, they were always worn in that beautiful and appropriate way which blended the heart of a pastor, the mind of the scholar, and the life-style of a Christian. His colleagues, students, and friends were the beneficiaries in a very special way of this combination.

This collection of essays in honor of John Kromminga was prepared to commemorate his ministry in the Christian Reformed Church in North America. The occasion of his retirement as President of Calvin Theological Seminary in Grand Rapids, Michigan, was deemed an appropriate time in which to present this volume to him.

The essays are grouped into three classifications: historical, theological, and ecumenical. Each category is intended to address issues in these areas of specialty because John Kromminga's interests and contributions find their focus in all of them.

The project was begun in 1979 and was initiated by Mr. Peter De Klerk, Theological Librarian of Calvin Theological Seminary. Dr. David E. Holwerda, a Professor in the Religion and Theology Department of Calvin College, originally participated in the planning process. When illness made it necessary for him to curtail his work, Dr. Richard R. De Ridder, a Professor of Calvin Theological Seminary, joined with Mr. De Klerk as co-editor. Together they completed the project.

Special appreciation is expressed to the authors for their contributions, which together constitute a remarkable unity while avoiding overlapping of subject matter. We regret that although Dr. Ford Lewis Battles was asked to submit an essay, he died before he was able to do so. In some of the essays additional footnotes have been supplied by the editors in order to complete or supplement the documentation by the authors.

The editors also acknowledge with appreciation the splendid and ready cooperation of Mr. Herman Baker and his staff at Baker Book House for their partnership in the publication and distribution of this volume. The services of student assistants, secretaries, and others are likewise appreciated. Special thanks is due Rev. Martin Geleynse for his translation of the essay contributed by Dr. Doede Nauta, and to Dr. Ralph W. Vunderink for his translation of the essay contributed by Dr. Willem van 't Spijker. Peter De Klerk updated his bibliography of John Kromminga's writings originally published in the volume, *A Bibliography of the Writings of the Professors of Calvin Theological Seminary* (Grand Rapids: Calvin Theological Seminary, 1980).

Above all we thank God for all that he has given us in John Kromminga. We trust that this memorial will in its own way give expression to our thankfulness for God's multiplied blessing to the church and society when he raised up John Kromminga for his kingdom in such a time as this.

John Henry Kromminga

Church Historian, Theological Educator, and Churchman

Carl G. Kromminga

John Henry Kromminga's service as a "churchman" is the core of his career in the Christian ministry. In him the "church historian" and "theological educator" both existed in service to the "churchman," since both were constantly pressed into the service of the Christian Reformed Church in North America (hereafter CRC). As a church historian, he pursued his discipline not for the sake of pure scholarship, but in service to the church. As a theological educator, he immersed himself in teaching and administration, convinced that denominationally sponsored and confessionally directed seminary education was crucial to the vitality of the church's life and witness. Both the course of his life and a dominant concern in his theological thought demonstrate that Kromminga's full energies were devoted to the service of the church.

Kromminga's life and career bear the mark of a churchman. He was reared in the family of a church historian, theological educator, and churchman. He was born to Diedrich and Katherine Kromminga on August 25, 1918, the third child of four, in Grundy Center, Iowa. At the time his father was teaching in Grundy College, established by Reformed Christians largely of Ostfrisian origin. In 1922 Diedrich returned to the pastorate by accepting the call to serve the Peoria CRC, Peoria, Iowa. There Kromminga began his formal education in the Christian grade school. When his father accepted the call to serve the Neland Avenue CRC, Grand Rapids, Michigan, in 1926, Kromminga entered the Christian grade school system in that city. In 1928 Diedrich Kromminga was elected to serve as Professor

11

of Church History at Calvin Theological Seminary, a post he held until his
death in 1947. Consequently, most of Kromminga's pre-doctoral education
was acquired in Grand Rapids: at Oakdale Christian School, Christian High
School, Calvin College, and Calvin Theological Seminary.

Although he was destined to follow in his father's footsteps, he was not
the product of a hot-house piety. His Christian convictions were formed
and matured with a healthy seriousness which did not preclude the
enjoyment of good times and the expression of a fine sense of humor. He
was a hard-playing, fun-loving youth, sociable, musically inclined, loyal,
and persistent. He was a voracious reader, but by no means a recluse. As he
matured he developed his gifts for clear composition, effective speaking,
and creative writing.

In 1942 Kromminga was accepted into a doctoral program in Church
History at Princeton Theological Seminary under the supervision of Professor Lefferts A. Loetscher. After one year of full-time residency at Princeton, he married Claire Ottenhoff of Hinsdale, Illinois, and they moved to
the Newton CRC, Newton, New Jersey, where he began a pastorate in a
newly organized CRC congregation. In the course of time John and Claire
Kromminga became the parents of two daughters and a son. Kromminga
received his doctorate in theology in 1948 during his pastorate in the Des
Plaines CRC, Des Plaines, Illinois. In 1952, while serving the First CRC of
Grand Haven, Michigan, he was named to the chair of Church History at
Calvin Theological Seminary by the CRC Synod. In 1956 he was elected
President of the Seminary and for the rest of his career he served in that
post while continuing to teach in the Department of Historical Theology.

Various other denominational duties and assignments give evidence
that Kromminga was primarily a scholar and educator in the service of the
church. He was chairman of the executive committee named by the CRC
Synod to plan, promote, and guide the celebration of the denomination's
centennial in 1957. For more than a decade he served on a committee
charged with the task of thoroughly revising the Church Order. He was
delegated to the meetings of the Reformed Ecumenical Synod in Edinburgh, Scotland, in 1953 and in Potchefstroom, South Africa, in 1958. He
served as an official observer at the Fifth Assembly of the World Council of
Churches (hereafter WCC) held in Nairobi, Kenya, in 1975. These and
numerous other assignments clearly establish the fact that Kromminga
was, as preacher, scholar, and educator, a man wholly involved in service to
the church.

As with his life and career, Kromminga's theological thought and expression reflects one basic concern which is crucial to the vitality of a
Reformed church in the modern world. He repeatedly and in many ways
expresses his basic conviction that loyalty to the truth of God's Word and
relevance to contemporary society are not inherently in conflict. It is not a

matter of either-or, either fidelity to the Truth or relevance to the contemporary scene. In fact, both elements are essential to the church's obedient life in the world. The Truth must serve the times, but the deepest need of the times is the need for God's Truth. Again, Truth which hides from contemporary issues becomes dead orthodoxy, while orthodoxy which allows its essence to be altered by the times ceases to be teaching of the Truth. How can the twin evils of dead orthodoxy and truth-compromising modernity be avoided? How can the church obey the call to timely witness without losing the Truth in the process? This theme of relevant orthodoxy and its attendant dangers appears regularly in Kromminga's writings. It dominates his concern, from his doctoral study of the CRC to his latest writings.

The conviction that God has committed to a specific denomination a sacred trust which must be guarded and maintained, come what may, is common to all groups which secede for doctrinal reasons from established or main-line churches. But in the history of such groups critical points are reached at which a decision must be made on the question whether the group is called simply to preserve and conserve the Truth until Jesus returns, or called to risk investing the deposit of Truth in the hope of gaining larger return for the Lord. Kromminga refused to see preservation and investment in terms of either-or. Midway in his career, as he assumed the presidency of Calvin Theological Seminary with permanent tenure, he put the matter this way:

> Having faced the great challenge of our times, the orthodox church has a twofold task by way of response. One may speak of that task in terms of home work versus field work; deeper roots versus broader horizons; understanding of the heritage versus communicating it; doctrinal knowledge versus missionary zeal. However the duality is put, it is important to remember both parts. It is essential to the discharge of either responsibility to be working at the other as well. It is a fact theoretically simple but often forgotten that there is no communicating the Christian heritage unless it is understood. It is less obvious and perhaps less logical, but in the nature of the case no less true that there is no understanding of *this* heritage without communicating it. God has given His treasures for use and for increase. Wrapping them in a napkin is a denial of their value, and the consequences of such denial are certain and devastating.[1]

The lines of this struggle to understand and practice both faithfulness to the Truth and obedience to the call to witness go back to the beginning of Kromminga's ministry. In the later 1940s and early 1950s he was a regular contributor of Scripture meditations to *The Christian Labor Herald*, the

---

1. John H. Kromminga, *Teaching Theology in an Era of Change*, Inaugural Address Delivered in Calvin Seminary Chapel (Grand Rapids: Calvin Theological Seminary, 1963), pp. 15–16.

official publication of the Christian Labor Association. In those meditations he repeatedly stressed the theme of strength through fidelity to ideals. Not numerical growth and bigness but faithfulness to the biblical principles relative to labor and witness to such principles was the calling of Christian labor in this land.[2]

These notes were sounded, to be sure, in the interest of encouraging and promoting a minority labor movement. A "minority" denomination is in a somewhat different position. In fact, the members of the Christian Labor Association were a minority of the laboring people in a minority denomination! But the dynamics and spirit of a confessional kingdom organization and a secessionist church are similar. A willingness to suffer indignity and to endure scorn for the sake of Christ mark both.

When it came to the church, however, Kromminga sensed the danger of failing to distinguish between a secessionist and a sectarian stance. The CRC had carefully guarded its identity in the Truth. Kromminga vigorously affirmed that it was called to continue to do so. But already in 1950 he clearly saw and warned against the kind of fear of new ideas that would produce heresy-hunting and premature condemnation of new thought. Actions of that kind would "stifle progressive thought among [the church's] members and leaders, and stunt her own growth."[3]

The move from pastorate to seminary caused some shifts in Kromminga's perspectives and emphases, but not in his basic conviction. In addition, his role as chairman of the Centennial Committee re-enforced his concern to help the church face the challenge of communicating a vital orthodoxy to the world around her without a concomitant loss of distinctiveness. He deeply shared the sense of privilege and mission expressed in the centennial motto, "God's favor is our challenge," and he was deeply grateful for the honor of promoting and overseeing the erection of the new seminary building on the Knollcrest campus, in which that motto is given brick-and-mortar expression.

This sense of obligation placed on tradition by contemporary opportunities shaped Kromminga's approach to his new assignment as President of Calvin Theological Seminary in 1956. Theological education, he affirmed, is to serve the church—not only the CRC but, ultimately, the whole church of Christ. Calvin Seminary can best render that service by unashamedly and wholeheartedly engaging in *denominational* theological education. And that education will best serve both ends if it is not so classical that it

2. John H. Kromminga, "Great Power for Little Things," (Zechariah 4:6) *The Christian Labor Herald* 10 (March 1949): 3. Cf. also "What Are We Working for?" (John 18:36) *The Christian Labor Herald* 10 (November 1949): 3.

3. John H. Kromminga, "Guarding the Truth," (Problems Facing the Church) *The Young Calvinist* 31 (December 1950): 9.

ignores change, nor so ultramodern that it loses its theological essence.[4] A similar emphasis appears in his inaugural address in 1963. He admitted that close ties between church and school created problems, and asserted that these problems were particularly of the type which concern the vitality of the seminary's address to the times. But this did not make him retreat from the position that close ties between church and school are good for a theology concerned with being relevant.

> If we are asked whether theology's concern for the world is best expressed in a divinity school unconnected with a church or in a denominational seminary, we choose unhesitatingly for the latter. The address of the Christian faith to modern unbelief is the church's address; there is much in the current ecumenical re-emphasis on the church to bear this out. The concerns of the church are the concerns of the seminary. The work of the seminary is one important aspect of the work of the church. The study of theology is not properly carried out in abstraction, but in deep involvement in the life and work of the Church of Jesus Christ.[5]

The lively ecumenical activity in the worldwide church in the late 1950s and early 1960s doubtless stimulated Kromminga to reflect more intensively on the massive question of the nature of the church and the more limited but equally knotty problem of the ecumenical calling of the CRC. In the late 1940s and early 1950s he had favored continued participation by the CRC in the National Association of Evangelicals, and he continued to write from time to time on the church's ecumenical responsibilities. But in the 1960s the seeds of ecumenical reflection found in earlier writings came to full flower. In this period, his teaching for three months in Korea, his service on various contact committees of the CRC, his participation in the work of the executive committee of the American Association of Theological Schools, and his other wideranging extradenominational contacts doubtless served to intensify his interest in the ecumenical movement and to enrich his teaching on the subject. His sabbatical study carried on at Cambridge, England, in 1968–69 resulted in the publication in 1970 of a study of the ecumenical movement entitled *All One Body We.*[6]

In a sense, the tension between maintaining denominational orthodoxy and ministering Christianly to a world in rapid change is a small-screen version of the tension projected in large-screen dimensions by the relationship between present-day evangelicalism and ecumenism, particularly ecumenism as represented by the WCC. But only in a sense, since orthodoxy cannot simply be equated with evangelicalism nor Christian ministry

---

4. John H. Kromminga, "Doing the Work of the Lord," *The Banner* 91 (1956): 1161, 1180–1181.

5. Kromminga, *Teaching Theology,* p. 4.

6. John H. Kromminga, *All One Body We,* The Doctrine of the Church in Ecumenical Perspective (Grand Rapids: Eerdmans, 1970).

to the times with ecumenism. The Bible's teaching on the unity of the church, to which ecumenism makes constant appeal, proves an embarrassment to institutionally fissiparous evangelicalism. On the other hand, the address of the WCC to the burning issues of the age often appears to be rooted more in secular humanist presuppositions than in the Christian Faith. Bible-committed and socially concerned evangelicals are therefore confronted with a dilemma: How can evangelical churches witness to their times from the Scriptures in a way which does not compromise but express their unity with God's people everywhere? To many evangelicals, membership in the WCC is in itself a compromise with apostasy. But other evangelicals feel uncomfortable with a position outside the forum of the WCC, where evangelical witness can be made and some evangelical direction may possibly be given. And this discomfort becomes especially acute because the WCC seems to speak out on all the important issues of the day—war and peace, nuclear proliferation, economic injustice, human rights, etc.—while evangelicalism stands almost mute or hopelessly divided over against these enormous issues.

Although Kromminga was not prepared to urge the CRC to full membership in the WCC, he had great sympathy for the position that effective evangelical witness could be made from within the WCC. In 1970 he stressed the need for evangelicals to speak with a united voice even if they were to testify to and about the ecumenical movement from the outside.[7] Subsequently, he assessed the impact of the more unified speaking of evangelicals, particularly at Lausanne, Switzerland, in 1974, on the words and works of the WCC meeting at Nairobi in 1975. His evaluation of the evangelical influence on the ecumenical movement as evidenced by events at Nairobi is generally positive. In summary he wrote:

> But there is at least some reason for gratification in the way in which the two groups, evangelicals and ecumenicals, addressed each other and listened to each other. Some commonness of purpose, despite all qualifications, emerged from their dealings with each other. If this kind of mutual respect and attention to each other continues, it can only serve to the enrichment of both parties. And particularly if both will . . . use this experience to learn to listen better to the Lord, there is no telling what the benefits may be.[8]

Here Kromminga reveals again the basis for his conviction that the dilemma of orthodoxy versus relevance need not continue to immobilize evangelical and confessional churches. The dilemma is overcome through

---

7. Ibid., pp. 213–214.
8. John H. Kromminga, "Evangelical Influence on the Ecumenical Movement," *Calvin Theological Journal* 11 (1976): 180.

full-orbed obedience by the whole church to the whole Word of God, in faith and confidence that the Lord still leads by his Word and Spirit.

Concurrently with this ecumenical concern, Kromminga was compelled to face internal problems in the CRC's address to the challenges of modernity. For example, early in his presidency he became directly involved in a discussion of the validity and viability of using the term "infallible" to describe the Bible, and he had to defend himself against formal accusations which were leveled against him because of his stance on that issue. Indirectly this dispute contributed to a series of forward-looking synodical studies and reports on the nature of Scripture, and the scope and nature of its authority.

Kromminga's own positions on various matters of controversy within the CRC were often inferred—sometimes quite erroneously—from the positions taken by certain of his colleagues on these issues. Toward the close of his presidency it became apparent that the seminary sorely needed to be in more open and continuous communication with the denomination at large if it were to retain and in some instances regain the church's confidence. In addressing this problem, Kromminga wished to maintain the healthy tension between traditional accents and free inquiry as the faculty members in their respective fields attempted to relate Scripture to current issues in a vital way. He sought the advice and participation of the faculty in plans for fuller and ongoing communication between school and church. It became increasingly apparent that the seminary had to assume a larger part of the traditional role which over the years it had somewhat relinquished in favor of speaking to the broader areas of theological scholarship. It had to serve as teacher not only to the church's ministry but also to the church in its total membership. But the complexion of the church which now required such instruction was vastly different from that of the church which had earlier sought and cherished leadership from a small and respected corps of professors. The church which now needed to be reached in open conversation and by forthright yet patient teaching was in the 1980s a church which embraced many and varied emphases. It was a United States-Canadian-Dutch-background church which included Native American, Oriental, Black, Hispanic, and other minorities, a church crisscrossed by various currents of progressivism, traditionalism, mild charismaticism, and fundamentalism. The address by Reformed tradition to environment which Kromminga had consistently fostered as church historian, theological educator, and churchman had borne abundant fruit. Now a new form of the challenge had emerged, that of helping a church, which had become increasingly pluralistic through vital contact with its environment, be a church whose diversity-in-unity could increasingly serve the cause of Christ on new horizons while maintaining vital union with its Reformed roots.

At the end of his regular ministry in church and school Kromminga devoted his energies to serious curriculum review and to the question of minority theological education as well as to the problem of open communication with the denomination as a whole. The responsibility for giving leadership in relating sacred tradition to changing times and ideas in the life of the church would now pass to other hands. But future attempts by the CRC to cope with this concern for vital and viable Reformed witness in a complex and changing world—a complexity and changeableness which the Lord's Church in mission is bound to reflect—will always bear the imprint of Kromminga's thought and action. His greatest comfort relative to this continuing mission of paramount importance lay in the fact that the Son of God continues to be the life and Lord of his church, and that the gates of hell shall, for that reason, prove ineffective against her.

PART ONE

Studies in History

1

Ostfrisians in Two Worlds[1]
Herbert J. Brinks

Situated in the northwest corner of West Germany, Ostfriesland presently contains but five Old Reformed (Altreformierte) congregations with a combined membership of about 1200.[2] Though always miniscule, this segment of the Reformed faith has produced a remarkable number of important ministers and theologians, including several who emigrated to North America, where their influence has been especially pronounced in the Christian Reformed Church in North America (hereafter CRC), the German Presbyterian Church, and the Reformed Church in America (hereafter RCA).[3] The Ostfrisian contingent of the CRC has manifested a persisting loyalty to the denomination of its native German province where devotion to mission work and ecclesiastical independence has sustained the witness of the Old Reformed Church (hereafter ORC) through the turmoils of heightened nationalism and two World Wars.

Ostfrisian-Americans, in shaping their New World communities to the cultural contours of their German birthplaces, behaved like many other

1. Funding for the research which made this contribution possible was provided by a 1980 Fullbright-Hays Fellowship and additional assistance from the Calvin Foundation. This contribution was first presented at the Third Conference on Dutch-American Studies sponsored by the Association for the Advancement of Dutch-American Studies in Pella, Iowa, on October 9, 1981.

2. *Jaarboek 1982* van de Gereformeerde Kerken in Nederland (Goes: Oosterbaan & le Cointre, 1982), p. 55.

3. The Kromminga family has been especially significant in the history of the CRC. Diedrich, who at the age of twelve, immigrated with his parents to Lincoln Center, Iowa, in 1891, was Professor of Historical Theology at Calvin Theological Seminary from 1928 to 1947. During the following decade his two sons were appointed to that school's faculty: John in 1952 (who has been President since 1956) and Carl in 1954. The German Presbyterian Seminary of Dubuque, Iowa, acquired Nicholas M. Steffens in 1895, but his most notable service (with Western Theological Seminary of the RCA) occurred from 1884 to 1895 and again from 1903 to 1912. Steffens' son Cornelius carried the family name back to Dubuque as the President of the German Presbyterian Seminary in 1908.

immigrants, but the Ostfrisians were not content, however, to maintain fossilized reconstructions, for they sought to structure their New World institutions with constant reference to transitions occuring within the churches and schools of their homeland, and until the outbreak of World War II their cultural models lay across the Atlantic. Though they affiliated with the largely Netherlandic CRC, the Ostfrisians poured most of their energy into the creation of a quasi-independent subculture characterized by an increasing dependence on the German language and the erection of an academic institution, Grundy College and Seminary.

Despite their separation, the Ostfrisians of both worlds maintained intricate cultural connections, even including an intensification of German nationalism from 1890 to 1930. Language usage symptomized this development, for during the 1890s the Ostfrisians of both worlds, who had always used German and Dutch, adopted high German as their official language. For example, the minutes of the Bunde CRC of Bunde, Minnesota, though written in Dutch until 1895, were thereafter inscribed in German, and that by the same secretary. Thirty-eight years later, and long after the German language purge of World War I, Bunde's church records were first kept in English.[4]

The two obvious vehicles of Germanization within the Ostfrisian-American community were the steady arrival of German-trained pastors and the distribution of the *Grensbode,* a periodical published by the German border churches.[5] From these sources the discussions and debates

---

4. The pattern of language usage in Classis Ost Friesland varied considerably as the chart below indicates.

Language Usage in the Minutes of Churches Founded Prior to 1900*

Name of Church	Period of Dutch Language Use	Period of German Language Use	English
Ackley, IA	1868–1936		1936
Bunde, MN	1887–1895	1895–1933	1933
Emden, MN**	1917–1934	1890–1917	1934
Lincoln Center, IA		1882–1939	1939
Ostfriesland, IA		1896–1935	1935
Parkersburg, IA		1891–1942	1942
Ridott, IL	1866–1905	1905–1935	1935
Wellsburg, IA***	1867–1920	1920–1934	1934
Wright/Kanawha, IA	1897–1910	1910–1932	1932

*Egbert Kolthoff, "Etwas von den deutschen Gemeinde der christ. reformirten Kirche in Amerika," *Grensbode* 20 (9 November 1902): 3–4, reported that of ten Ostfrisian churches in North America, five used German and Dutch, while five others used German exclusively.

**This curious reversal (German-Dutch-English) was probably a wartime expedient to avoid anti-German persecution.

***Obo Haupt, the secretary for the Wellsburg CRC, kept the minutes successively in Dutch, German, and English. He, like most of the ministers and many parishioners in Classis Ost Friesland, were tri-lingual. Unfortunately this phenomenon diminished and disappeared after World War II.

5. The ORC, concentrated in the province of Ostfriesland and the Graafschap Bentheim of Germany, lost a large percentage of its ministers to emigration. Thirty percent of the pastorate from Ostfriesland

occurring in Germany spread quickly to the immigrant community. Thus, the immigrants were well informed of the movements which were reshaping their birthplaces, and as their native province became more clearly identified with German cultural unity, the Stateside community followed suite.

The most persisting problem for the ORC concerned its own identity, for, clustered as it is along the Dutch borders of two German provinces, the ORC has frequently been described as more Dutch than German. This ambiguous status was further complicated by the denomination's close association with the orthodox Reformed churches of the Netherlands.[6] But

---

and 15 percent from Bentheim were drawn to the New World. Several of the denomination's native sons were also attracted to the Netherlands, but the most astounding number of migrants consisted of those 52 percent who came from the Netherlands to serve the border churches briefly before returning to a life-long career in the Netherlands. These transients, who were not significant leaders but departing native sons, seriously depleted the ranks of intellect by drifting to the Netherlands or sailing to the New World. In short, the ORC suffered a very serious "brain drain" during the 19th century.

Immigrant Ministers from the ORC to the CRC in North America

Name	Date of Immigration		Destination
J. B. De Beer*	1866	CRC	Holland/Niekerk, MI
Klaas B. Weiland	1868	CRC	Ridott, IL
Nicholas M. Steffens**	1872	RCA	Silver Creek, IL
Gerrit K. Hemkes	1877	CRC	Vriesland, MI
Jan H. Vos	1881	CRC	Grand Rapids, MI
Willem R. Smidt	1882	CRC	Ridott, IL
John Plesscher	1885	CRC	Lincoln Center, IA
Herman Potgeter	1889	CRC	Ridott, IL
Jan H. Schultz	1892	CRC	Bunde, MN
Hendericus Beuker	1893	CRC	Muskegon, MI
Frederick Schuurmann	1912	CRC	Emden, MI

The data for this table was gathered from the various *Yearbooks* of the CRC and *Honderd Veertig Jaar Gemeenten en Predikanten van de Gereformeerde Kerken in Nederland* (Leusden: Algemeen Bureau van de Gereformeerde Kerken in Nederland, 1974), together with church report columns in the *Grensbode* 1883–1900.

*J. B. De Beer served congregations in both the CRC and RCA but returned to the Netherlands in 1880.

**Although he disagreed with the CRC's justification for denominational separation, Steffens was highly regarded in the CRC and a frequent contributor to its periodicals. Steffens also served the German Presbyterians in Iowa for several years.

6. Both Hendericus Beuker, who wrote *Tubantiana, Iets over de Regeering in Staat en Kerk van het Graafschap Bentheim, van af de Hervorming tot op Onzen Tijd* (Kampen: J. H. Kok, 1897) and Jan Schoemaker who wrote *Geschiedenis der Oud Gereformeerde Kerk in het Graafschap Bentheim en het Vorstendom Ostfriesland* (Hardenberg: A. Kropveld, 1900) carefully delineated the German origins of the denomination. During this same era Lieuwe Bouma, Egbert Kolthoff, and Johannes Jäger contributed a series of lengthy articles in the *Grensbode* (Lieuwe Bouma, "De Oud-Geref. Kerken," *Grensbode* 15 (19 September 1897):2, (3 October 1897):3, (17 October 1897):1–2, (31 October 1897):1–2, (14 November 1897):2–3, (12 December 1897):1–2; 16 (9 Januari 1898):3–4; Egbert Kolthoff, "Duitsche Invloeden op de Gereformeerde Kerken der Graafschap," *Grensbode* 16 (26 Juni 1898):2–3, (24 Juli 1898):3, (7 Augustus 1898):2, (21 Augustus 1898):2; Johannes Jäger, "Rechte der Kirche innerhalb des Staates," *Der Grenzbote* 37 (24 Mai 1919):4, which discussed the independent origins of the secession in Germany. On the matter

during the 1880s the ORC sought to establish a more precise identity, and the publication of its biweekly *Grensbode* in 1883 provided a vehicle for discussing the denomination's peculiar status and future.

Leaders who sought to highlight the church's independent identity found their most convincing evidence in regional history which they interpreted to demonstrate that the ORC had remained faithful to the doctrines and polity of the Reformation, while the established Reformed Church of Germany had not only faltered in doctrine but had also sacrificed its independence to retain official status and financial advantages from the government.[7] Consequently the history of the Reformation and its subsequent decline in Ostfriesland became a crucial ingredient in the ORC's justification for secession. Further, the public pronouncements of discontent which led to the schism of the 1840s became pivotal in the new denomination's arsenal of self-defense.

In 1837 Reemt W. Duin wrote a pamphlet[8] that contained the foundational analysis upon which the ORC built its historical argument. Modeling his pamphlet on the Old Testament's jeremiad, he declared that Emden had been among the most blessed and early adherents of the Reformation with a provincially supported Lutheran Church dating from 1519. Duin records further that as Emden's theologians adopted the teachings of John Calvin, the city became a center of Calvinist influence whose leaders included the exiled Polish reformer, John à Lasco. In addition, Emden's leading theologians had participated in the Synod of Dordrecht, and one of these, Daniel B. Eilshemius, together with Eduard Meiners, had written the Emden Catechism, which not only preceded that of Heidelberg, but was, in some respects, superior to its more famous successor. Reaping the fruit of these

---

of ecclesiastical identity the authors sought to clarify the misconceptions of the denomination's friends in the Netherlands and of their antagonists in Germany. The writing of Lieuwe Bouma, "De Heerlijkheid van Christus," *Grensbode* 16 (12 Juni 1898):1–2, illustrates a common Dutch assumption that the ORC had grown directly from the spread of the Dutch secession into Germany. Thus Bouma argued for close relationships between the seceded German and Dutch churches. In Germany this same misperception created barriers which made it difficult for native Germans to take the ORC seriously, for it was perceived as a foreign institution, more Dutch than German. Consequently, Kolthoff and the other church historians sought to highlight the life and works of Jan B. Sundag, Harm H. Schoemaker, and Reemt W. Duin, all of whom had protested liberal preaching in the established church without knowledge of similar movements in the Netherlands. Both Sundag and Schoemaker had initiated conventicles prior to visits by Netherlandic ministers such as Albertus C. Van Raalte and Hendrik de Cock.

7. Menno Smid's *Ostfriesische Kirchengeschichte*, vol. 6 of Jannes Ohling, *Ostfriesland im Schutze des Deiches*, Beiträge zur Kultur- und Wirtschaftsgeschichte des Ostfriesischen Küstenlandes (Pewsum: Deichacht Krummhörn, 1974), pp. 453–463, contains the history of ecclesiastical consolidation among the Reformed churches of Ostfriesland. The ORC, which opposed this process, argued that the state church had given up its Presbyterian polity and independence for economic support. Hendericus Beuker, "Pastor Hölscher en de Oudgereformeerden," *Grensbode* 1 (15 Augustus 1883):1–2, (1 September 1883):2–3, (15 September 1883):2–3, (1 October 1883):2–4, (15 October 1883):2–3, (1 November 1883):3–4, (15 November 1883):4, (15 December 1883):3–4, stated the case for this view.

8. Reemt W. Duin, *Emdens en Oostvrieslands geestelijk Hoerdom*, of Ontrouw aan den God der Vaderen, Opengelegd en Aangedrongen (Amsterdam: J. J. Hamelau Tacke, 1837).

early blessings, Emden and its neighboring villages flourished under the pure gospel until the end of the eighteenth century when false prophets began to preach and publicize the doctrines of general salvation and human goodness.

Duin found the influence of the "New Light" or Enlightenment so pervasive during the early decades of the nineteenth century that few pulpits proclaimed the old truths of sin and free grace. Even worse, attempts to acquire orthodox ministers from the Netherlands were thwarted by governmental restrictions, including the requirement that the established Reformed Churches of Ostfriesland abandon the Dutch language by beginning to preach in high German on at least one Sunday of each month. This, according to Duin, stemmed from a Lutheran conspiracy designed to destroy the international character of the German Reformed Church. To stem the tide of enlightenment theology, Duin wrote, besides the one mentioned above, a second pamphlet[9] in 1838, which identified both the wayward teachings and practices of the established church. But Duin aimed his sharpest barbs at Helias Meder's Catechism, which had generally replaced the Emden Catechism. Because it contained Remonstrant or Arminian viewpoints Duin suggested that, "On a pleasant evening," his readers would do well "to take Meder's book, together with a Psalm or hymnbook to a spot designated for public burning. Then when you have a good fire going, tear Meder's catechism to shreds and throw it into the fire. Meanwhile, you can sing Psalm 68 or Hymn 156."[10]

Duin and his ascerbic pamphlets gained immediate notoriety, together with an official reprimand which eventually cost him his ministerial status in Ostfriesland. As he was under censure, Duin could no longer serve the established church, and he then accepted a position among the religious seceders in the Netherlands. There he served the churches in the Province of Friesland until his contentious behavior resulted in disciplinary censure. He returned to Ostfriesland in 1840 where he continued to criticize the established church until his death in 1844.[11]

9. Reemt W. Duin, *Rondborstige Protestatie of Ernstige en Vrijmoedig Betuiging tegen het Schromelijk Verval in de Leer en de Tucht der Gereformeerde Kerk te Emden en in Geheel Oostvriesland,* Gedaan in Naam van al Degenen, die, in Onze Stad en in Ons Land, de Zuivere Gereformeerde Kerkleer, Volgens de Beste Belijdenissen der Gereformeerde Kerke van Harte zijn Toegedaan (Amsterdam: J. J. Hamelau Tacke, 1838), registers twenty-eight items of protest concerning the teaching and practice of both the churches and schools of Ostfriesland.

10. Duin, *Emdens en Oostvrieslands geestelijk Hoerdom,* pp. 67–68.

11. Only scant biographical information is available for Duin's career, but his influence came primarily through the widespread reading of his pamphlets. He was, it seems, unsuited for the ordinary pastorate as his first efforts of that sort in Veenhusen, Germany, ended in failure. His pastoral career in Friesland, the Netherlands, also terminated amid controversy. The records indicate that Duin was an unreasonable autocrat who dismissed elders and deacons for slight disagreements. Then, too, Duin argued with Simon van Velzen, his only colleague in Friesland. Duin joined Hendrik P. Scholte in criticizing van Velzen's emphasis on divine election and reprobation, and Duin also favored the use of hymn singing in worship services, a practice which had been heatedly castigated among the Dutch

The ease with which Duin circulated among both the Dutch and German dissenters stems from a long history of interrelationship between Ostfriesland and the northern provinces of the Netherlands. These connections are apparent in early regional narratives which place Ostfriesland in a conglomerate of Frisian tribes located along the island fringes of the North Sea. During the twelfth century these groups clustered in the three Northern provinces of Friesland, Groningen, and Ostfriesland, and for juridical purposes they formed a loose union known as the "Upstalboom." The cities and villages of the whole region looked to this institution for the settlement of local disputes until the tribes began to distinguish themselves along more clearly provincial lines. While the Province of Groningen grew more dependent on its urban center, Ostfriesland developed greater cohesion from its attachment to several leading families.

Ostfriesland became part of the Holy Roman Empire in 1464 when the local nobleman, Ulrich Cirksena, solidified his authority by pledging fealty to Emperor Frederick III. Nonetheless Ostfriesland remained largely uninvolved in the Spanish, French, and Austrian struggles for dynastic dominance throughout the 16th and 17th centuries. Finally, in 1744, during the reign of Frederick the Great, Ostfriesland became united with Prussia. Still this political link did not restrict the exchange of cultural influences across the German-Dutch border, an influence which was particularly evident in religious affairs.

In the Netherlands the Protestant Reformation struggled under official repression and persecution until 1580 when, with the Union of Utrecht, the Reformed faith gained official status. However, during the previous sixty years, Emden had become a city of refuge for many Calvinists from the Netherlands. Already in 1524 Count Edzard I had invited Georg Aportanus from Zwolle to institute Calvinism in Ostfriesland, and in 1594, when Groningen joined the Union of Utrecht, ministers from Ostfriesland provided religious services across the border. Following its establishment in 1614, the University of Groningen became the religious center of the Reformed community in Ostfriesland, Groningen, Drenthe, and for much of Graafschap Bentheim. Then, as scientific theology began to dominate the University of Groningen toward the end of the eighteenth century, the

---

seceders. It is worth noting that Duin and the seceders of Ostfriesland did not experience the anti-hymn movement in Germany. Consequently, when the Ostfrisians immigrated to North America and joined the CRC, the Ostfrisians acquired an exemption in 1888 from the CRC general ban on hymn singing for worship services. Duin's "soft" view of election, coupled with other controversies, made for a brief and troubled tenure in Friesland. He returned to Ostfriesland under censure in 1840 and remained there until his death in 1844. Data on Duin's career can be gathered from Smid, *Ostfriesische Kirchengeschichte*, pp. 405, 534–536, and 538. J. Wesselings, *De Afscheiding van 1834 in Friesland*, Vol. 1 (Groningen: De Vuurbaak, 1980), pp. 59, 107, contains several references to Duin, but the author promises a fuller account of Duin's career in a forthcoming volume. The Hendrik de Cock papers, in the Archives of the Gereformeerde Kerken in Nederland, recently moved to the Dienstcentrum in Leusden, the Netherlands, contain a brief account of Duin's troubled career in the Netherlands.

university's graduates carried the critical methods of the Enlightenment into their sermons and catechetical instruction.[12] These developments inspired Duin's pamphleteering.

Quite naturally then, Duin's pamphlets were printed in Dutch because the Reformed churches of Ostfriesland not only preferred Dutch, but they identified German with the Lutheran Church, and until the onset of German unification and nationalism under Otto von Bismarck Calvinism and the Dutch language seemed indivisible for the Reformed churches of Ostfriesland. However, during the 1880s German nationalism ejected the neighboring Dutch tongue from the schools and churches of the province. But since the seceded ORC was not bound to ecclesiastical rules designated for the established church, the seceders continued using Dutch long after the established church had adopted high German. Nonetheless, by the 1890s the seceders had also begun to adopt German, for, since the local schools no longer used Dutch, that language became progressively artificial for the children and young people of the church.

In its publications, preaching, and seminary instruction, the ORC became bilingual during the 1890s and exclusively German by 1915. That this transition occurred so gradually reflected divisions within the denomination, for while the congregations in Ostfriesland had long favored the adoption of German, the Graafschap Bentheim segment of the Church had stronger links with the Netherlands, and these congregations were reluctant to scuttle the Dutch language.[13] The two decades of linguistic transition in the ORC were accompanied by a vigorous discussion of the denomination's history, which, going beyond Duin's analysis, sought a specifically German origin and denominational purpose. Thus, the Germanization of the ORC became the topic of many articles in the *Grensbode* and the theme for a regional conference in 1898.

Presenting the case for the continued and accelerated growth of German identity, Egbert Kolthoff declared that the German reformation had predated the Dutch reformation in both its Lutheran and Reformed phases, but more significantly that the nineteenth-century origins of the ORC were indigenous. While admitting that the 1834 revival in the Netherlands had spread beneficial influences across the border, Kolthoff pointed to Germans like Duin, Harm H. Schoemaker, and Jan B. Sundag who had planted the seeds of reform without foreign inspiration or assistance.[14]

---

12. W. J. Formsma, "De Historische Betrekkingen tussen Groningen en Oost Friesland," *Groningse Volksalmanak voor her Jaar 1955* (Groningen: B. van der Kamp, 1955), pp. 1–13; J. J. Boer, *Ubbo Emmius en Oost-Friesland* (Groningen: J. B. Wolters' Uitgevers-Maatschappij, 1936), pp. 4–40; Marshall Dill, Jr., *Germany*, A Modern History (Ann Arbor: The University of Michigan Press, 1970), pp. 45–68.

13. Johannes Jäger, "Die Zukunft unsrer theol. Schule," *Grensbode* 18 (2 September 1900):1–3; Johannes Jäger, "Warum muss der Grensbode Deutsch sein," *Grensbode* 28 (19 Februari 1910):3. The minutes of the Classis, the Curatorium of the Seminary, and the *Grensbode* were all written and printed in German by 1915.

14. Egbert Kolthoff, "Conferentie te Emlichheim," *Grensbode* 16 (12 Juni 1898):2–4, reported the debates of the conference.

Clearly, then, the border churches could not be identified as the mere backwash of a Netherlandic revival. Kolthoff argued further that while the ORC had always been bilingual, the church's witness in Germany required an increasingly exclusive use of the national language.

Supporting Kolthoff's position, Jan Schoemaker asserted that the border people were unmistakably German and that the use of their national language neither could nor should be restrained. But Schoemaker also feared the liberal influences of the German schools which, he argued, could be curbed best by using the orthodox theological schools in the Netherlands. The debate, then, did not center on the relative merits of German and Dutch, because both the ministers and parishioners realized that the declining use of Dutch along the border could not be reversed. Instead, the church feared the inroads of liberalism as a by-product of Germanization, and thus the issue focused on several proposals involving an expansion or alteration of the church's educational program. Kolthoff suggested that the church expand its theological school in Emden, which would reduce dependence on the Netherlands while simultaneously enlarging the orthodox witness of the ORC in Germany.[15]

In 1900 the denomination's theology teacher and leading intellect joined the discussion of Germanization. Trained in a German mission school, Johannes Jäger had accepted a joint appointment as the denomination's theological professor and part-time pastor in 1880. Coming to the denomination from a small village west of Köln, in the Rhine Province, Jäger had little sympathy for Ostfriesland's attachment to the Dutch language or for the church's ambiguous identity. He sought to convince its members that their primary tasks lay within the German borders.[16]

Formulating both a theoretic and practical foundation for his views, the professor declared that although Christ's church knew no national boundaries, its members were not alike, for if that were the case, they could learn nothing from each other. Furthermore, since God had given each folk and nation peculiar gifts and characteristics, the cultural conditioning which these peculiarities produced in the church could not be ignored. While heartily endorsing the unifying bonds of Presbyterian polity shared throughout Europe, England, and North America, Jäger insisted that each denomination was obligated to witness within its own culture. And since the ORC had always been either Hanoverian[17] or Prussian, the obligation to maintain a truly Reformed witness in Germany stood paramount—a task which could be achieved best by a clergy trained in Germany for Germany.

15. Ibid.
16. Johannes Jäger, "Die Zukunft unsrer theol. Schule," *Grensbode* 18 (24 Juni 1900):2–3, (8 Juli 1900):1–3, (22 Juli 1900):2–3, (5 Augustus 1900):2–3, (19 Augustus 1900):2–3, (2 September 1900):1–3, (16 September 1900):1–3, (30 September 1900):2–4, wrote about the future of the Theological School. In this series Jäger sets forth his justification for the Germanization of the ORC.
17. Prior to German unification, Graafschap Bentheim had been part of the Hanoverian regions of Germany.

Pointing to the denomination's experience with its Dutch-trained pastorate, Jäger gently exposed the long-standing flaws which had resulted from sending their sons across the border for theological education. It was painfully clear that the best of their students and pastors (Jan Bavinck, Hendericus Beuker, Jan H. Vos, Jan Schoemaker, Herman Potgeter, Jan H. Schultz, and Nicholas M. Steffens) were lured to larger churches in the Netherlands. This, Jäger asserted, resulted from an education which had weaned the students away from their native culture and people. On the other hand, the services of Dutch pastors in Germany were frequently of short duration and generally ineffectual.

Jäger had little patience with the language issue, as in his view it was inexcusable for a church to inhibit its impact by using a foreign tongue. The argument that the survival of the miniscule ORC required stronger ties with the Netherlands was, by his lights, evidence of too little faith. Had not lonely reformers like Luther and Calvin demonstrated that God's work bore no relationship to numerical strength? Could He not also use a small but faithful ORC? The answers were obvious, but, he added, "We must be prepared to serve our region, and how can we do that if we are virtually strangers among our own neighbors?"[18]

Jäger, Kolthoff, and the other advocates of Germanization discovered a particularly instructive analogy for the ORC in the experiences of North America's immigrants, and they frequently examined the patterns of cultural adjustment occurring among their acquaintances in the New World. Thus, when Abraham Kuyper advised his Dutch-American admirers to learn English in order to infuse their adopted culture with Reformed principles, Kolthoff redirected this advice to the ORC, which, he argued, had a similar obligation in German culture.[19] Although the *Grensbode* contained many reports on American church life, its editors kept particular watch over the Ostfrisian communities in Iowa, Illinois, and Minnesota because, in addition to their familial connections, the two groups shared a large number of ecclesiastical similarities.

That the Ostfrisians on both sides of the Atlantic experienced parallel histories was no mere coincidence, because the stateside group sought assiduously to draw its leaders and inspiration from the homeland. The intensity of this attachment is evident in the efforts of the American communities to acquire ministers from Ostfriesland. Of the fourteen German ministers who served the ORC in that province between 1854 and 1900, ten received calls from the Ostfrisian-Americans, and seven responded favorably.[20]

18. Jäger, "Zukunft unsrer theol. Schule," *Grensbode* 18 (5 Augustus 1900):2–3.
19. Egbert Kolthoff, "Kirchliche Nachrichten," *Grensbode* 18 (13 Mei 1900):2.
20. From the fourteen "German" pastors I have excluded three who either died or left the ministry during their first assignment, and five others (Jan Bakker, G. Kramer, Fake Moet, H. Volten, and Gerrit van Groningen), who provided short term service to Ostfriesland before returning to life-long careers in

Emigration affected the Neermoor congregation with exceptional force as more than a third of that church's parishioners had gone to North America by the 1880s. This loss crippled the church to such an extent that it could no longer support a pastor, and thus between 1885 and 1888 Neermoor shared the services of Herman Potgeter with the neighboring congregation of Ihrhove. But that arrangement terminated when Potgeter accepted a call to Ridott, Illinois, in 1889.[21] Neermoor's first pastor, Nicholas M. Steffens, left East Friesland in 1872 and became an important leader in the RCA, while the ministers, Klaas B. Weiland, John Plesscher, Herman Potgeter, Gerrit K. Hemkes and Frederick Schuurmann formed a virtual procession leading from the German border to the CRC. There they were particularly influential in the Ostfrisian segment of the denomination. Although the Neermoor church suffered the greatest loss of members and leaders, the other four churches were similarly afflicted, as each gave one or more of their pastors to the immigrants of Illinois, Iowa, and Minnesota.

Conscious of their origins, the Midwestern Ostfrisians gained permission from the CRC to organize an ethnically defined Classis in 1896. Though geographic proximity ordinarily structures the organization of a classis, the Classis of Ost Friesland reached across the boundaries of three states, an arrangement which both recognized and fostered the growth of a German subculture within a Dutch-American subculture.[22] But even that curious identity drew sustenance from the German border where the ORC maintained similar ties in the Gereformeerde Kerken in Nederland while searching simultaneously for a German identity at home. In this and nearly every other respect the Ostfrisian-Americans sought to duplicate the ecclesiastical shape of their native province.

Despite, or perhaps because of their increasing Germanization, the Ostfrisian immigrants did influence the CRC, for they have been justifiably

the Netherlands. Thus, of a pastorate with a clearly Ostfrisian orientation, 50 percent emigrated, and the best of those who remained (Jäger, Lambert Stroeven, Kolthoff) were frequently called to join the American community. Indeed it is possible to conclude that the Ostfrisian contingent of the ORC in North America has far surpassed its parental body. The immigrants not only acquired the core of its pastorate from Ostfriesland, but their membership outnumbers their mother churches by nearly a three to one ratio. According to the *Yearbook 1982* of the Christian Reformed Church (Grand Rapids: Board of Publications, 1982) the Ostfrisian churches contain some 3,500 souls while the German churches number about 1,200. See also footnote 2.

21. Minutes and Membership Records of the Neermoor congregation in Ostfriesland, 1861–1905, in the archives of the Neermoor church in Germany. The specific notation of Plesscher's emigration is from the minutes of July 5, 1885. Additional data can be gathered from *Honderd Veertig Jaar Gemeenten en Predikanten.* I will note here my gratitude to Gerrit Jan Beuker, Pastor of the ORC in Uelsen, Germany. He provided access to the Neermoor records and those of all the churches used in this study. Furthermore, his assistance in acquiring printed sources such as the *Grensbode (Der Grenzbote)* was crucial to this research.

22. Wayne Brouwer, in his series, "The German Element in the CRC," *The Banner* 115 (April 11, 1980):10–12, (April 18, 1980):14–15, (April 25, 1980):14–16, (May 2, 1980):17–19, (May 9, 1980):14–15, (May 16, 1980):16–18, (May 23, 1980):18–20, provides a detailed account of the origin and growth of the German subculture within the CRC.

credited with spearheading the growth of mission activity in the denomi-nation. The CRC's annual mission festivals, for example, first appeared during the 1890s as regional events among the Ostfrisians. But these occa-sions, devoted to inspirational speeches, picnicking, and the collection of funds, had already been institutionalized among the ORCs during the 1880s. Thus the vigorous support of mission work, which characterized the Ostfrisian community in both worlds, originated in Europe,[23] and it can also be traced to the influence of Jäger. Trained as a foreign missionary, Jäger was the ORC's theology instructor at the Theological School at Emden from 1880 to 1925, and his concept of pastoral duty combined congregational service with regional evangelism. When he sought increased support for the denominational school at Emden, he frequently cited the achievements of the alumni of the Emden school who served beyond the borders of the ORC.[24] The greatest number of these were working among the Ostfrisian-Americans, where mission activity among other German Americans had become a primary objective.

Jäger, then, provided intellectual leadership to an international com-munity of Ostfrisians, and his success in leading the Emden school inspired the Iowa immigrants to organize a similar institution. Indeed, the rationale for founding Grundy College, Grundy Center, Iowa, came largely from Jäger's defense of the Emden school as both institutions were declared necessary to provide a German-preaching clergy for a German-speaking constituency. While this objective seems both logical and necessary for a church in Germany, its appearance among Ostfrisian-Americans, many of whom had been using Dutch for three decades, requires further comment.

As the desire for a college using German as the language of instruction intensified among the Ostfrisians near the turn of the century, Henry C. Bode became the leading advocate of the institution. He defended the proposed school by pointing to the spiritual needs of a large German-speaking minority in North America, and he argued that this 10 percent segment of the American populace contained magnificent opportunities for home mission work.[25] Then, in 1912, when Classis Ost Friesland ap-pointed a committee to investigate the feasibility of organizing the school, Henry Beets, editor of the CRC's English-language periodical, *The Banner,* supported the venture vigorously.

---

23. H. Wilms, "Weleerwaarde Heer!" *Grensbode* 1 (31 Maart 1883):4, makes note of an annual festival with guest speakers, and a holiday atmosphere.

24. In his autobiographic sketch, Johannes Jäger devotes much attention to his youthful desire to become a missionary. A copy of this document, acquired from Enno Jaeger of Hamburg, Germany, is in the Colonial Origins Collection of the Calvin Library. While attempting to justify the continued existence of the denomination's seminary in Emden, Jäger, "Einiges zur Erlauterung unserer Schulfrage," *Grens-bode* 20 (31 August 1902):2–3, cited the potential benefits of the school for Germany but also for the Netherlands and North America.

25. Henry C. Bode, "De Beteekenis van het Duitsche Element voor Onze Kerk," *De Gereformeerde Amerikaan* 7 (1903):276–277.

Beets declared that the "German element" of the church needed a school like that which Jäger headed in Emden. According to Beets, theological schools served their churches best when located amid their constitutents, and since the distantly located denominational seminary in Grand Rapids used Dutch and English as the languages of instruction, the Ostfrisians received significantly diminished benefits from the distantly located seminary. In addition, a German school in Iowa would educate pastors with a greater understanding of their prospective parishioners, and while still in school, the students could fill the region's vacant pulpits and augment the home mission efforts within the larger German-American community.[26]

Beets' enthusiasm for what he labeled the "German element" in the CRC had been evident in his frequent praise of their "missionary zeal," but he also wrote historical sketches and editorials extolling the origins of the ORC. Attention of this sort created good will between the two groups, and much of Beets' writing was reprinted in *Der Grenzbote* (with the January 6, 1912, issue the Dutch title of the periodical was changed to German). The decisions of the CRC's bi-annual synods, along with information about its ministers and educators were regularly publicized throughout the ORCs on the German border. Thus, when the folk from this region emigrated, they were inclined to join the church of Beets.[27] Always an aggressive proponent of the CRC, with much concern for its continued growth, Beets was not minded to alienate prospective members from Germany by publicizing the differences between the Ostfrisian and Dutch segments of the CRC.

The most notable of these differences was the absence of the Christian day school among the Ostfrisians, a feature shaped again by Old World traditions. Arriving in the Midwest between 1850 and 1890, the border people from Germany discovered little difference between public education

---

26. Henry Beets, "That German Theological School," *The Banner* 47 (1912):620–621. Earlier that year, Henry Beets, "News from the Old Reformed Churches of Bentheim and East Friesland," *The Banner* 47 (1912):315, featured the ORC Seminary in Emden. Using the arrival at Emden, Minnesota, of the Reverend Frederick Schuurmann from Campen, Ostfriesland, to highlight Jäger's work, Beets noted that the Emden school has benefited the CRC by training a number of its prominent ministers. Throughout his editorship of *The Banner*, 1904–1928, Beets devoted more than forty articles to discuss and report on the "German Element" in the CRC.

27. Henry Bode's article, "De Beteekenis van het Duitsche Element voor Onze Kerk," was reprinted in *Grensbode* 21 (30 Augustus 1903):4, and beginning in 1911, when plans for establishing a German Seminary in Iowa were announced, Beets' supportive reportage of that effort found constant space in the columns of *Grensbode*. From its inception *Grensbode* had lavished attention on the immigrated border people. Pastors who left for North America provided lengthy reports on their travels and the ecclesiastical conditions of the churches they served or visited. Greetings from American family branches were transmitted in pastoral letters and the activities of the CRC's biennial synods received full reports in *Grensbode*. Concerning a German Theological School in North America, Egbert Kolthoff, "De Duitsche Theologische School der Christ. Geref. Gemeenten in Amerika, *Der Grenzbote* 30 (9 November 1912):3, editorialized, "It is too bad that we are divided by the ocean and that we cannot join forces with them in support of the theological school."

in Germany and North America, since both, with ample opportunity for religious instruction and devotional exercises, were essentially Christian. It seemed obvious then that public education in North America could satisfy the religious requirements of the community. By contrast, to both the German and American situations, public education in the Netherlands had been shorn of ecclesiastical influences during the revolutionary era which began in 1780, and orthodox groups in the Netherlands responded to that development by organizing independent Christian schools. Influenced deeply by the ideas of Kuyper during the 1880s, these schools acquired an increasingly complicated theoretical foundation which featured the importance of Christian interpretations for all subjects. Neutral or secular knowledge had no place in the system. Thus, when Kuyper's American disciples could find no satisfactory American parallel to their native institution, they organized private schools to duplicate those which they had cherished in the Netherlands.[28]

While the absence of this particular Kuyperian influence among the Germans did not lead to denominational conflict, it did release the Ostfrisians from the financial obligations required by a private school system, and they were able to expend their energies and resources in other directions. Together with its support of mission work, the "German Element" rallied around its most cherished ideal, the organization of Grundy College.

Grundy College and Seminary, which flourished between 1916 and 1934, offered a preparatory, college, and seminary curriculum with a faculty selected from the most prominent Ostfrisian ministers. The core of this staff, William Bode, John Timmerman, and Diedrich Kromminga, had been leaders in the Classis Ost Friesland and frequent contributors to its periodical, *Der Reformierte Bote*. But after hopeful beginnings, the school suffered economic setbacks and it failed to gain financial support throughout the denomination. One by one the faculty slipped away and in 1934, amid the Great Depression, Grundy College disbanded.[29] Thus, the most

28. While writing about the secularization of the Dutch schools, Hendericus Beuker, "Vrije Scholen," *Grensbode* 2 (16 Januarij 1884):3, declared: "In the public schools of the Netherlands the Bible is a forbidden book.... Fortunately we do not yet have such a problem here in Prussia.... In our Protestant schools the Bible not only may, but must be used in the schools. Some free thinkers do indeed try to initiate godless schools here, but they have not yet succeeded. We must thank the Lord that things are still different here than in the Netherlands." Egbert Kolthoff in his editorial, "Die freie christliche Schule in Holland," *Der Grenzbote* 37 (19 Juli 1919):3, repeated again this general assessment. The rationale for establishing Dutch-American Christian Schools, is most particularly explained by Peter Ekster, "De Christelijke School aan Sigsbee en Baxter Straten in Grand Rapids," *De Gereformeerde Amerikaan* 19 (1915):215–220. For earlier views favoring church schools as a vehicle for retaining the use of Dutch in church worship and instruction, see Douwe J. Van der Werp, "Onderwijs en Opvoeding van de Kinderen der Gemeente," *De Wachter* 3 (6 Mei 1870):2; and especially the editorial by Geert E. Boer, "Hollandsch Onderwijs," *De Wachter* 8 (16 September 1875):1, which argues for Dutch language instruction to facilitate parental supervision of the educational process and to preserve the "beautiful language of the Dutch nation and culture."

29. Brouwer, "German Element in the CRC: The School," *The Banner* 115 (May 23, 1980):18–20. For an assessment of Grundy College's twilight dilemma see Henry J. Kuiper, "Grundy College and Hull Academy, *The Banner* 66 (1931):645.

visible symbol of the Ostfrisian community faded from the landscape, but some of its leaders[30] over the years were drawn to prominent positions in other parts of the CRC.

With the demise of Grundy College in 1934 and the adverse impact of Adolf Hitler on all things German, the Ostfrisians of the CRC have avoided public declarations of their German identity. Yet, recently they have shared in North America's ongoing revival of ethnicity, and their enthusiastic response to a 1981 series of articles in *The Banner*, entitled "The German Element in the CRC," indicates a continued empathy for their European traditions. It may be safe to assume that a revitalization of Ostfrisian ethnicity can only be temporary and nostalgic, but we cannot be certain. Nonetheless, an ethnic folk whose country tombstones record expectations of eternal life successively in Dutch, German, and English should keep faith with their ancestral heritage.

30. Of the Grundy College faculty, John J. Timmerman (at Grundy, 1932–1934), William T. Radius (at Grundy, 1929–1930), and Jan William Kingma (at Grundy, 1931–1934) became professors at Calvin College in Grand Rapids. Another of their colleagues, Henry Schultze (at Grundy, 1920–1924), served as president of Calvin College from 1940–1951. Thereafter he joined Calvin Theological Seminary faculty where both William H. Rutgers (at Grundy, 1930–1933) and Diedrich H. Kromminga (at Grundy, 1916–1922) had also migrated from Grundy College and Seminary. Another prominent teacher Frederick H. Wezeman (at Grundy, 1921–1927), moved from Grundy College to Chicago Christian High School, Chicago, where his teaching resulted in controversy. Later he served as the President of Northwestern College in Orange City, Iowa.

2

Ecclesiastical Architecture in the Christian Reformed Church
Donald J. Bruggink

The trauma of the Eighty Years' War (1568–1648) resulted in an iconoclasm so pervasive that two centuries later the Dutch who came to North America seemed innocent of the impact of their architecture upon their worship. The result was an immediate Americanization of their architecture, which soon began to Americanize their worship.

The ferment of reformation was slow in gaining momentum in the Low Countries, in part because of the earlier reform movement of Geert Groote and the Brethren of the Common Life. When reform did begin to gain ground, it included the usual manifestations of iconoclasm which were also usually the last straw in the effort of the magistrate to be tolerant. Iconoclasm was certainly nothing new to the church. It constituted one of the most ferocious struggles of Eastern Christendom in the sixth and seventh centuries, but from it the church emerged with its theology and institutions intact—and with its images soon restored. Latin Christendom, while not a participant in that upheaval, had nonetheless its own mild iconoclastic experiences during the Middle Ages, sometimes led by monastic reform groups such as the Cistercians. With the Reformation, however, the political situation which encouraged and allowed the realization of reform efforts in Germany, Switzerland, Scotland, and subsequently in the Netherlands, also resulted in the division of the church into Catholic and Protestant. Although the struggles may have been more bloody during the Thirty Years' War in Germany, nowhere were they more protracted than in the war of independence of the Netherlands, where for eighty years the struggle went on against the power of Spain. The trauma began in the war between the Netherlands and Spain, but that war was inseparable in the

mind of the Reformed with the struggle against Catholicism, and of iconoclasm against idolatry.[1]

For the Reformed Churches of the Netherlands the iconoclasm which
had helped to precipitate the war for independence and became a matter
of doctrine during that struggle resulted in the cleansing of the churches
not only of their statues and paintings, but also the whitewashing of the
walls to cover their frescoes. The abundance of pre-Reformation religious
houses, each with its own place of worship, and the extant village and city
churches meant a plethora of church structures which, together with the
depletion of the population as a result of the war, limited the need for
church building for over a century.[2]

Architecturally, the buildings remained as they were except for the iconographic purge and the reorientation of the structure for the purposes of
Reformed worship. Where the pulpit was already so positioned that the
congregation could easily gather around and hear the Word proclaimed,
the pulpit frequently remained in its place. The elimination of the monks,
canons, and priests meant that the choir stalls in the nave became superfluous, lacking the personnel to worship God three, five, or seven times in
the daily offices. The reform of worship meant not only the removal of the
priest, but of his altar and the sacrifice of the mass. In their place came
those who ministered at the table where Christ's people celebrated the
Lord's Supper. In those churches where there was an adequate apse or
choir, the stalls for the clergy were frequently removed and for occasions
of the celebration of the Supper tables were set up that all might gather
around the "Lord's board." This custom of sitting at table for the celebration of the Lord's Supper was common practice in both the Netherlands
and in Scotland. In Scotland it died out in the mid-nineteenth century; in
the Netherlands it persists to this day. Smaller country and village churches
were usually also of such size that there was no problem in finding space
within the commodious brick walls not only to hear the Word, but also to
celebrate the Lord's Supper about a table.

Those churches which were built after the Reformation were marked
by creative architecture which purposed to bring as large a number of the
congregation into proximity with the pulpit as was possible. The new
church at Willemstad (1596) was an octagon.[3] The large Westerkerk in

   1. The depth of that iconoclasm has an interesting reflex, as seen by the fact that the colleges of both
the Christian Reformed Church in North America and the Reformed Church in America, while excelling
in the musical arts virtually from their inception, had no viable departments of the visual arts until the
middle of the twentieth century. Calvin College officially established its art department in 1965.
   2. For a history of the major churches built after the Reformation in the Netherlands see Jan N.
Bakhuizen van den Brink, "De Tegenwoordige Toestand van den Kerkbouw en zijn Geschiedenis" in
Protestantsche Kerkbouw, Een Bundel Studies onder Redactie van Jan N. Bakhuizen van den Brink
(Arnhem: S. Gouda Quint—D. Brouwer en Zoon, 1946), pp. 7–55.
   3. Gustaf Hamberg, *Tempelbygge för Protestanter,* Arkitekturhistoriska Studier i Äldre Reformert
och Evangelisk-Luthersk Miljö (Stockholm: Svenska Kyrkans Diakonistyrelses Bokförlag, 1955), p. 81. Cf.
Bakhuizen van den Brink, "Tegenwoordige Toestand van den Kerkbouw," p. 22, Plate II.

Amsterdam (1620–31), while rectangular, located its pulpit equidistant between the two far ends of the building.[4] The Noorderkerk in Amsterdam (1620–23) had a Greek cross plan with the pulpit on one of the interior corners.[5] The Marekerk in Leiden (1639) was octagonal with a central drum supported by a circle of pillars. The pulpit was forward between two of the pillars.[6] Similarly, with an octagonal central drum above a Greek cross plan was the Kapel in Renswoude.[7] The Nieuwe Kerk in Haarlem (1650) was a square with the freestanding pulpit centrally located a third of the distance forward from the wall,[8] an arrangement similar to the Ooster-kerk in Amsterdam.[9] The church in Oudshoorn was also a square but with the pulpit against one wall.[10] Most spectacular of all was the Nieuwe Kerk in the Hague (1702) with six conjoined octagons. This might also be described as a rectangular church surrounded by six contiguous bays, or the conjunction of two diamond-shaped halves with the pulpit at the central intersection—perhaps the most brilliant architectural *tour de force* to bring a maximum number of auditors into close proximity to the pulpit with neither pillars nor balconies to separate parishioners.[11] All of these churches had enough area free of fixed pews to accommodate tables for the Lord's Supper.

This was the aniconic-architectural inheritance of the seceders of 1834. One of the most prominent leaders, Hendrik de Cock, was pastor in the village church of Ulrum, Groningen, a brick structure which had been standing for centuries. It now had a pulpit affixed to the middle of the side wall, and there was room for the celebration of the Supper. Our more immediate predecessor, Albertus Christiaan Van Raalte, was never ordained to the ministry of the Nederlandse Hervormde Kerk, and thus never had a church structure. Like his fellow secessionists, he preached to his followers in homes or barns (one of which is still shown near the village of Ommen, Overijsel, being located on land, the owner of which had inherited certain medieval rights, which enabled the seceders to worship there relatively immune from governmental harassment).

No pictures have come to hand of the first church built by these seceders, but it is instructive to note that the church built in the 1920s by the Gereformeerde Kerk in Ommen is in no way different stylistically, nor in

4. Ibid., pp. 92–96; Bakhuizen van den Brink, "Tegenwoordige Toestand van den Kerkbouw," p. 22, Plate I.

5. Ibid., pp. 96–98; Bakhuizen van den Brink, "Tegenwoordige Toestand van den Kerkbouw," p. 23, Plate V.

6. Ibid., pp. 104–107; Bakhuizen van den Brink, "Tegenwoordige Toestand van den Kerkbouw," pp. 25–27, Plates X and XI.

7. Ibid., pp. 107–108.

8. Ibid., pp. 110–112; Bakhuizen van den Brink, "Tegenwoordige Toestand van den Kerkbouw," p. 24, Plates VI, VII, and VIII.

9. Ibid., pp. 113–115; Bakhuizen van den Brink, "Tegenwoordige Toestand van den Kerkbouw," p. 24.

10. Ibid., p. 113.

11. Ibid., pp. 117–121; Bakhuizen van den Brink, "Tegenwoordige Toestand van den Kerkbouw," p. 23.

terms of liturgical appointment, than its counterparts in the Nederlandse Hervormde Kerk. It would be a mistake to assert that the seceders of 1834 or their successors in the Gereformeerde Kerken in Nederland did not care about church architecture. It would be more accurate to say that the hostility to iconography inherited from the Reformation before and during the Dutch War for Independence had so desensitized them to the iconographic possibilities of church architecture that the building of a church was not considered an iconographic exercise in worship and doctrine. If the hypothesis is true, it will be especially hard to prove, for disinterest in the iconography of architecture has allowed the raw data to go unanalyzed. Until there has been a congregation by congregation analysis of the Afscheiding and the Doleantie church buildings, the above must remain what it is: a hypothesis with a very high probability of truth, but one which is nonetheless unproven.

As groups of seceders under such pastors as Van Raalte came to North America, the trauma of the Afscheiding in the Netherlands (later fed by the Doleantie) made it difficult to work with a church of similar doctrine but thoroughly Americanized piety—especially in the controverted matter of hymns. The overarching concern which distinguished the Christian Reformed Church in North America (hereafter CRC) from the Reformed Church in America (hereafter RCA) during the latter half of the nineteenth century was its concern to be true to its Calvinistic and Dutch heritage, of which being for Psalms and against hymns was a serious part—although only a part. As Henry Zwaanstra has so ably pointed out, those Dutch into the 1890s were "almost unanimous in their opinion that the American churches and social life harbored dangers which, if not exposed and effectively resisted, would eventually lead to the destruction of the church."[12] However, their pervading iconoclasm was such, that even in the midst of a determined effort to stay Dutch, both religiously and ethnically, one is struck with the fact that there is absolutely no attempt made to be Dutch in church architecture![13]

The prevailing architecture of the nineteenth-century CRCs can be best described as "pioneer colonial." It was quintessentially American and was common wherever churches were built on the frontier: a simple rectangle with pitched roof, with a small steeple perched on one end (or in cases of greater affluence, with a small tower which served as an entryway at

12. Henry Zwaanstra, *Reformed Thought and Experience in a New World*, A Study of the Christian Reformed Church and its American Environment 1890–1918 (Kampen: J. H. Kok, 1973), p. 38.
13. It is not until the 1960s, among a very few Canadian churches, that one can detect Dutch architectural influences in the sense of the use of very high walls, *25th Anniversary Directory*, Rehoboth Christian Reformed Church, Bowmanville, Ontario [Bowmanville: Rehoboth Christian Reformed Church, 1975, p. 24], large pulpits, *Newmarket* Christian Reformed Church, Thanksgiving Service and Dedication Program, February 28th, 1969 [Newmarket: Christian Reformed Church, 1969, p. 8] and sometimes a sounding board, *Newmarket* CRC [p. 8] and *25 Years*, First Christian Reformed Church, Guelph, Ontario, 1953–1978 [Guelph: First Christian Reformed Church, 1978, p. 28].

ground level and as a belfry at the upper level, and was surmounted by a small steeple).[14] The structure was invariably of balloon frame construction [the technique of framing with thin wood (2" x 4" or 2" x 6") developed in the 1830s in North America] with board siding painted white. It was used by all denominations, with Methodists erecting more of this type than any other group, if for no other reason than that Methodists were building more churches during the nineteenth century than any other group.

Next in popularity was "pioneer gothic," again a balloon frame structure, this time with an essentially square plan, spanned by intersecting ridge-poles carrying pitched roofs. The plan could be described as a Greek cross plan, but it never was that. The windows sometimes had pointed arches, and were often filled with colored art glass. It should be added that often rural congregations have repeated the same "pioneer colonial/gothic" style through a second or third building right up to the present time.

Not all of the church buildings of the CRC in the nineteenth century were of the humble varieties described above. Within those cities enjoying a large Dutch population one frequently found churches which were very substantial and occasionally spectacular. The LaGrave Avenue CRC of Grand Rapids built in 1888 was an absolutely splendid brick structure, essentially Gothic, but with a marvelous tower showing some Italianate influences.[15]

However, whether we think of the humble "pioneer colonial" of the poor or the majestic brick structures of the well-to-do, the fact remains that these churches were American in style. Dutch iconoclasm was so deep-seated that in the midst of attempting to remain culturally and ethnically Dutch, and thoroughly Calvinistic, they were from the very beginning American in their church architecture.[16]

The two possible exceptions to the above hypothesis were in the Spring Street CRC and the Eastern Avenue CRC, both of Grand Rapids. Externally, the style of the former was an elegant, slightly Victorian adaptation of colonial design, done in brick. The clock in the tower might be interpreted as a Dutch influence, but clocks in church steeples had precedent in American church architecture as well. Inside, one finds a double-decker pulpit. From the lower pulpit the voorzanger would have led the singing; or an

14. Cf. John Veillette and Gary White, *Early Indian Village Churches*, Wooden Frontier Architecture in British Columbia (Vancouver: University of British Columbia Press, 1977).

15. *Thinking on God's Lovingkindness*, Souvenir of the Quarter-Centennial Celebration of the La Grave Avenue Christian Reformed Church, Grand Rapids, Michigan, February 24 A.D. 1887–February 22 and 23, 1912 (Grand Rapids: H. Verhaar, 1912), p. 2. This building was replaced with a new structure in 1960.

16. This hypotheses is confirmed by an excellent study done by Linda Jasperse. Her conclusion is similarly that "the Dutch Christian Reformed Church members were building according to the predominant Protestant church style of their day." "It becomes apparent that Christian Reformed church buildings are, to varying extents, modeled after the main currents in American architecture." Linda Jasperse, "The Christian Reformed Church: An Architectural Study" (History Seminar Paper, Calvin College, 1978), pp. 2, 6.

elder, lacking ordination, would have read the sermon. From the higher pulpit the ordained minister would have proclaimed God's Word. However, while this arrangement was common in eighteenth-century America as well as in the Netherlands, when the Spring Street CRC was remodeled prior to 1907, it was brought into conformity with late nineteenth-century American standards: the familiar flat platform with a reader's desk (pulpit) center stage forward.[17]

While the first structure of the Eastern Avenue CRC was a balloon frame, "pioneer colonial" church of unrecorded interior appointment, the second building of 1887 boasted a double-decker pulpit, complete with sounding board. In and of itself, neither this type of pulpit, nor its sounding board was peculiarly Dutch.[18] Both were found in Colonial New England, the Middle Colonies, and the Virginia Colonies. While in Eastern Avenue CRC its use was consonant with Dutch practice, similar practices had prevailed in Colonial America.

> Two prominent stairways led to the high pulpit. Above the pulpit there was a sounding board with a circular window on which stood an oil lamp to light the pulpit. Below stood a reader's lectern. . . . at first there was no organ, *Voorzinger* [sic] Veltkamp had the full responsibility to lead the congregation in singing the well known Dutch psalms.[19]

In addition to the use of the low pulpit by the *voorzanger,* it was also used by the *voorlezer:* "Elders were also used in the time of the low pulpit as readers of the Word. This reflected their role in the teaching task of the church."[20]

As in Spring Street CRC, when Eastern Avenue CRC was remodeled its liturgical appointments were brought into conformity with late nineteenth-century American models.

If one accepts the original interiors of these two churches as intentionally Dutch, then they represent the exceptions which prove the rule. They can, of course, also be legitimately interpreted as following conservative

17. *One Hundredth Anniversary 1857–1957,* First Christian Reformed Church, Organized March 19, 1857, Grand Rapids, Michigan [Grand Rapids: First Christian Reformed Church, 1957], pp. 22, 42, 47.

18. David Wynbeek, "75 Years on Eastern Avenue," in *75 Years on Eastern Avenue,* Diamond Jubilee of the Eastern Avenue Christian Reformed Church, Grand Rapids, Michigan, September fifteen, nineteen hundred fifty-four [Grand Rapids: Eerdmans, 1954], p. 11. More unusual than its double decker pulpit is Eastern Avenue CRC's excellence in publishing commemorative histories! Almost invariably commemorative booklets are a chronicle of ministers and a collection of pictures, mostly contemporary with the publication of the booklet. Eastern Avenue CRC, both in its *75 Years on Eastern Avenue,* as well in its later *100 Years in the Covenant,* Eastern Avenue Christian Reformed Church, Grand Rapids, Michigan, 1879–1979 (Dallas: Taylor Publishing Co., 1979), represent excellent congregational histories. These two volumes are easily the richest single congregational source on worship practice. Special appreciation must go to Case H. Vink for his chapter entitled "Eastern's People in Worship" (pp. 77–84) in the latter volume.

19. Wynbeek, "75 Years on Eastern Avenue," p. 11.

20. Vink, "Eastern's People in Worship," p. 78.

(i.e., eighteenth-century) American models. In any case, the general hypothesis is reinforced by the fact that both churches were remodeled to the then-contemporary American low-church, Protestant liturgical styles.

Another type of evidence of iconoclasm in the church architecture of the CRC becomes apparent when searching the picture file, commemorative booklets, and newspaper clippings in the Colonial Origins Collection of Heritage Hall in the Calvin library: the general disinterest in architecture. That exemplifies itself first of all in the paucity of references in all three of the above categories, the commemorative booklets of the Eastern Avenue CRC being the sole major exception. The picture file is obviously composed of those photos which have come to hand, as are the commemorative booklets, of which there is a considerably larger percentage included. Newspaper clippings are the result solely of the interest of individuals whose collections of papers have found their way to the Colonial Origins Collection. The above is not intended to denigrate that collection or those who have so assiduously compiled this archival treasure. It is simply to note that the contents accurately reflect the general disinterest of the church in architecture, which is another way of offering evidence in favor of the original thesis that the iconoclasm of the Reformation is still making itself felt in terms of the church architecture of the CRC.

In the commemorative booklets themselves, this disinterest is once more reflected. The booklet of the Beaverdam CRC of Beaverdam, Michigan, contains more information than most when it records as its total contribution on the subject that there was a building committee to supervise the work, and "Josiah Westrate was asked to prepare a plan."[21] In most commemorative booklets, even of city churches with very substantial brick gothic structures, one finds it difficult to find the date of their construction in the midst of the narrative describing the ministers who served the church. Even of such splendid edifices as Spring Street CRC and La Grave Avenue CRC, while there must surely have been considerable pride and satisfaction in these fine buildings, one finds little comment about them in the records.

This phenomena continues into the first half of the twentieth century. For example, the Bethel CRC of Grand Rapids, built in 1913, was architecturally avant-garde, both in style and construction.[22] The architectural principles for such a building had been adumbrated but a few years earlier in Louis Sullivan's "Ornament in Architecture"[23] and was soon to be manifested in Europe under such descriptions as "De Stijl" or "L'Esprit Nouveau." Stylistically, it can be compared to work done by Adolf Loos

21. *Seventy-fifth Anniversary* of the Beaverdam Christian Reformed Church, 1882–1957, Friday, April 26, 1957 [Beaverdam: Christian Reformed Church, 1957], p. 15.

22. *Silver Anniversary and Souvenir Booklet* of the Bethel Christian Reformed Church, March 13, 1913–March 13, 1938 [Grand Rapids: Bethel Christian Reformed Church, 1938], p. 4.

23. Louis H. Sullivan, "Ornament in Architecture," *Engineering Magazine*, August 1892.

around 1910. It is a church built within three years of Loos' Steiner House in Vienna (which is still published in architectural histories),[24] but there is no evidence that either the congregation or its commentators was aware of its significance either then or at any time since. In the commemorative booklets of the church there is not even an attempt to describe the architecture, let alone an awareness of its importance. It is recorded only that it has been refurbished and repainted. Among the treasures of the church are listed its Bibles and its communion linen; nothing is said of the architecture of the church.

In articles contemporary with the building of Bethel CRC, a newspaper clipping notes that Pierre Lindhout was the architect, and Henry Beets observes that it was "built of reinforced concrete with tile and brick facing," had a round dome, an octagonal shape, seated 700, was built on a steep hillside, had a basement, sub-basement and sub-sub-basement, and cost $15,000.[25] In terms of the development of international architectural style, Bethel was probably the most significant CRC built during the first hundred years of the denomination, but that fact seems to have escaped everyone!

A search of the subject card catalogue of the Colonial Origins Collection shows how unimportant the visual as a means of communication was in the CRC. Under the subject heading *Architecture* one is advised to see *Buildings* or *Church Architecture*, the former also leading to the latter. In addition to being advised to check *Art; Christian Art and Symbolism; Theology, Practical;* and *Christian Reformed Church, Architecture;* the sole item of significance is the recently written paper by Linda Jasperse. Under *Art*, there are all sorts of notes from the papers of Henry J. Van Andel in connection with his art courses at Calvin College, but the only architectural reference is to a brochure advertising a book on the Christian altar. Attempting to find architectural information through card catalogue references to liturgical furniture, one finds under *Baptism* no reference to fonts (and nothing under *Fonts*), but many articles concerning who is to be baptized and its significance. Similarly, *Pulpit* turns up no architectural references; nor does *Lord's Supper*—except through the question of the serving of communion. Similarly, the subject *Choir* offers no materials as to its placement. What does become very apparent during such a search of the card file is that just as church commemorative booklets were concerned with their ministers rather than their buildings, so the literary documents that make up the Colonial Origins Collection are concerned with theology. Even as it touches choirs or sacraments, it is the theology of the issue with which there is concern, never the symbol.

---

24. Banister Fletcher, *A History of Architecture on the Comparative Method.* Revised by R. A. Cordingley (London: University of London, the Athlone Press, 1963), p. 1072.
25. Henry Beets, "Grand Rapids Notes," *The Banner* 48 (1913):481.

Similarly, under the headings *Worship* or *Liturgy*, which lead one to the finely crafted lectures of Hendericus Beuker,[26] William W. Heyns,[27] or Samuel Volbeda,[28] one finds the focus on theology, rather than action. In one of the very few references to symbolism by the latter professor he says, "Now it should also be observed that the employment of symbolism in worship is fraught with danger."[29] The symbolism of which Volbeda speaks is the raising of the hands in the salutation. It is also interesting to note that unlike the works of Beuker and Heyns, which are primarily selective histories of worship, Volbeda is speaking to the issue of the CRC liturgy of 1928. In 118 pages of single-spaced typewritten 8½ x 11 pages his lectures take us only through the Penitential Prayer in the Service of Reconciliation, which is the second part of a five-part Liturgy of the Word. The weekly celebration of the sacrament, or for that matter any celebration of any sacrament, is never mentioned in this otherwise erudite and well-researched tome. The iconoclasm of the sixteenth century was so fixed in the fires of the Dutch War of Independence and religious reformation that three centuries later the inheritors of that ethnic and religious tradition could build churches without awareness of their communicative impact, either theologically or ethnically. The style was purely American, built by a people who understood themselves to be trying to be faithful to their Dutch-Calvinistic heritage. Their interests, even when they built well, were not in the buildings but upon the minister who preached the Word; and what they wrote about was theology. Even when they wrote of liturgy and sacraments, they wrote theology; they wrote about words, not about the nature of visual communication in architecture and symbol.

Without the question ever having been raised for discussion, the iconoclasm of the Dutch Reformation and the subsequent history of the seceders, augmented by the Doleantie, had effectively emphasized the role of the church building as that of meeting house.[30] In meeting God in worship, the mystery lay in the Word and in the sense of God's presence, in which architecture played no intended symbolic part. Insofar as the furniture of liturgy communicated anything, it was the result of its utilitarian use for worship, the relative unimportance of which was usually assumed. Let us consider this in terms of the means of grace, Word and sacrament, and the congregation's response in praise.

26. Hendericus Beuker, *Liturgiek* (Grand Rapids: Theologische School, 1898?) 70 leaves (Mimeographed Class Notes).

27. William W. Heyns, *Liturgiek*, Ten Dienste van de Studenten van de Theologische School der Christelijke Gereformeerde Kerk te Grand Rapids, Michigan (Holland: H. Holkeboer, 1903).

28. Samuel Volbeda, *The Liturgy*, or the Program of public Worship (Grand Rapids: Calvin Theological Seminary, 1928), 118 leaves (Mimeographed Class Notes).

29. Ibid., p. 49.

30. See the excellent discussion of church as meeting house in Harold W. Turner, *From Temple to Meeting House*, The Phenomenology and Theology of Places of Worship, Religion and Society, 16 (The Hague: Mouton Publishers, 1979).

The sign and seal of the sacrament of baptism confronted the synods of the CRC over seventy times during its first century,[31] but at no time was the sacrament as sign, per se (i.e., its value as symbol), ever considered; nor at any time, either in synodical or in other writings, have I found consideration given to the symbolism of the font. Architecturally, the above lack of emphasis is usually reflected in the church, for it is seldom that one can visually identify the font in those interior pictures found in the Heritage Hall picture file or the commemorative booklets.[32]

Just as there were no references to fonts in the *Index of Synodical Decisions*, the *Revised Church Order Commentary*,[33] or the subject card catalogue of the Colonial Origins Collection, so too there is no mention of the Lord's Table. There is, however, in the discussion of the Communion cups a few oblique references to the way in which Communion was celebrated which give some indication that the iconoclasm of the Reformation, transferred to the New World by the seceders, resulted in a lack of sensitivity for symbol which allowed marked changes in sacramental practice on two counts.

The issue which brought the sacramental practice before the Church was the question of the continued use of the common cup. It first appears in the papers of Beets in 1916,[34] then in two of his editorials and his response to two letters in *The Banner*.[35] Strangely, a typescript titled "Editorials," but dated January 14, 1918, 1:30 P.M., and signed, is also found in his papers.[36] By 1920[37] the issue had made its way to the floor of Synod, where it reappeared in 1930[38] and 1934.[39] The issue was of sufficiently serious moment that when James A. Brouwer of Holland, Michigan, wrote to Beets asking about the dates of his earlier articles in *The Banner*, the good editor took the time to refer him not only to the articles but to rehearse the

31. *Index of Synodical Decisions, 1857–1962* (Grand Rapids: Christian Reformed Church in North America, 1965), pp. 20–21.

32. The exceptions are the previously mentioned Canadian churches, together with such a fine and notable American exception as the University Hills CRC of Farmington, Michigan, Carl H. Droppers, architect.

33. Idzerd Van Dellen and Martin Monsma, *The Revised Church Order Commentary*, An Explanation of the Church Order of the Christian Reformed Church (Grand Rapids: Zondervan Publishing House, 1967).

34. Papers of Henry Beets, Colonial Origins Collection, Folder 20, a typed note labeled C.A.P., February 1, 1916.

35. Henry Beets, "Individual Communion Cups?" *The Banner* 52 (1917): 644–646, 660–661, 706, 732; Simon Lieffers, "Individual Cup Movement Attributed to Pride," *The Banner* 52 (1917):706; Fred Warners, "Individual Cup Arguments Weighed and Found Wanting (?)," *The Banner* 52 (1917):732.

36. Papers of Henry Beets, Folder 20.

37. *Acta der Synode 1920* van de Christelijke Gereformeerde Kerk Gehouden van 16 tot 30 Juni, 1920, te Grand Rapids, Michigan (Grand Rapids: M. Hoffius, Printer, 1920), p. 31 (Art. 26).

38. *Acta der Synode 1930* van de Christelijke Gereformeerde Kerk Gehouden van 11 Juni tot 27 Juni, 1930, te Grand Rapids, Michigan (Grand Rapids: Grand Rapids Printing Co., 1930).

39. *Acts of Synod 1934* of the Christian Reformed Church in Session from June 12 to June 29, 1934, at Grand Rapids, Michigan (Grand Rapids: Grand Rapids Printing Co., 1934).

argument as well as adding new information in a three-page single-spaced letter dated December 5, 1924.[40]

What had raised the issue after almost two millenia of the common cup? Evidently the wide dissemination of the knowledge of germs, which in turn encouraged a greater fastidiousness of eating and drinking habits, which in turn was reinforced by the great flu epidemics of 1918–19. It is interesting that in 1916 Beets does not have a great deal of patience with multiple cups, citing "saving time" as the principal excuse for their use. By 1917, 1918, and 1924 his principal argument concerns sanitation: medical sources have proven that diseases, "including syphilis, are transmissible by one drinking vessel . . . and we all know how frequently these diseases exist among us.[41]

While the change from the common to individual cups appeared before Synod on several occasions, it repeatedly refused to make any other rule than to insist that either way of communing was acceptable and that individual consistories would have to make the final decision for their congregations. What is interesting, within the context of our discussion, is the argumentation by which the members of the CRC, who so valued their Calvinistic tradition, as well as their Dutch inheritance, could change their way of celebrating the sacrament with such relative ease. In the case of Beets, his notes of February 1, 1916, appear to be reflections in which he is trying to find his own mind on the matter. He lists twelve changes in the celebration of Communion, the last being multiplying the number of cups, all of which have taken place without destroying the sacrament.[42] In his typescript of January 14, 1918, he reiterates this argument and then cites Herman Bavinck's distinction[43] between the essence and integrity of the sacrament, arguing that one or many cups is not of the essence of the sacrament. Note that the argument concerning the cups is not carried on in terms of symbol, history, or psychology. Instead, theological distinctions are used to justify a change for the sake of hygiene. It is very true that many other low-church protestants also made the change from the common to individual cups, but that is precisely part of the hypothesis: in terms of iconography (architecture or symbol) the CRC underwent almost immediate Americanization as the result of its iconoclastic inheritance.

An even more phenomenal transition occurred with reference to the Lord's Supper, wherein the Americanization occurred with such unthinking ease that it did not even generate enough discussion to reach the floor of synod: the transition from partaking of the Lord's Supper by going

---

40. Papers of Henry Beets, Folder 56.

41. A long list of other diseases follows during the first ellipses, but the sentence probably indicates that even editors should edit their own material. Papers of Henry Beets, Folder 20, item dated January 14, 1918.

42. See footnote 35.

43. Herman Bavinck, "Het Avondmaal en de Zieken," *De Wachter* 48 (17 November 1915):2.

forward to sit at table to the American low-church custom of remaining seated in the pews. In northwest Iowa, many older Reformed people can still remember having sat at table for Communion. My mother could still remember the practice as a girl in the RCA church of Oostburg, Wisconsin, around the turn of the century. In the East there are still a few RCA churches going back to the seventeenth century that mark their Dutch heritage by celebrating at table once a year, and in the Virgin Islands, the Dutch Reformed Church still has pews near the front of the church where boards can be flipped up to form a narrow table.

Yet, in the CRC the transition was made from the common Dutch practice, which went back to the Reformation, of being seated at table for Communion, to being seated in the pews, without the matter once being referred to Synod: an incredible example of the Americanization of a central sacramental gesture. That it could happen is evidence that this symbolic action connected with the sacrament had also suffered the general iconoclasm of symbol, and thus readily succumbed to a new American practice.[44] Nor did this change cause even enough argument to find its way into the subject card catalogue of the Colonial Origins Collection. One learns of the transition taking place quite by accident in the notes of Beets, when in the early months of 1916 he is first trying to come to a position concerning the Communion cups. In his list of twelve changes in Communion, after (1) time of year; (2) time of day; (3) elimination of foot washing; (4) no couches; (5) leavened bread; in number 6 he notes, *"Tables have been abolished* in many Protestant churches, some of them Christian Reformed. No special protest is heard against their departure from the old way. Why no Tables? Lack of time or room? But provision *could* be made if wanted!"[45]

Architecturally, the practice of sitting for Communion seems seldom to have visually manifested itself. In searching the picture file in the Colonial Origins Collection and the commemorative booklets, there are no churches built prior to 1960 which have tables other than the little on-the-floor-in-front-of-the-pulpit tables common to all low-church American Protestants. Even more unusual, when one considers that the practice of sitting for Communion must have been almost universal into at least the beginning of the twentieth century, was the fact that few churches seem to have left a *commodious* space for such celebration. In the pictures of the Ninth Street CRC of Holland, Michigan,[46] as well as in the Spring Street CRC,[47] there is a

44. This is all the more remarkable when one considers the pitch of feelings that could be aroused in other areas of church life. Henry Beets, for example, received a letter dated April 10, 1923, from the frequent correspondent in Chicago who could end his letter by insisting, "In conclusion, one of the following supposition [sic] is true. De [sic] clergy of to day, in general, is a fraud, a lie, a humbug, acomonflage [sic], and represent fully and truly the priesthood of Jesus' time, or the writer is as blind as a brickbat. . . ." Papers of Henry Beets, Folder 39.

45. Papers of Henry Beets, Folder 20 (underling and punctuation by Beets).

46. *One Hundredth Anniversary* of the Ninth Street Congregation, Holland, Michigan 1847–1947 [Holland: Ninth Street Christian Reformed Church, 1947], p. 35.

47. Picture in Colonial Origins Collection of Heritage Hall, Calvin Library.

row of chairs in front of the first row of pews, but even allowing for the flexibility of space created by that single row of chairs, the place for the communion table must have been very limited. With this lack of architectural provision for the sacrament, it is no wonder that Idzerd Van Dellen and Martin Monsma, writing in 1941, could still remember that, "In certain large churches even a few years ago as many as twelve or more distinct tables or administrations occurred in one communion service."[48]

In the liturgical expression of the Lord's Supper the early triumph of the Americanization of church architecture was inexorably also Americanizing a worship practice held since the Reformation. The inconvenience of celebrating at a table in those cramped areas, tightly hemmed in by pews, with the resulting multiplication of tables (i.e., administrations) led to the early demise of this time-honored Reformation practice of liturgical celebration. While the insensitivity to the impact of architecture upon matters theological and liturgical had occasioned the immediate acceptance of American architectural styles and arrangements, this same insensitivity to the importance of symbol allowed the CRC to abandon a sacramental practice of great historic and psychological import without even leaving traces of a struggle. Beets answered his own rhetorical question, "Why no tables? Lack of time or room? But provision *could* be made if wanted?"[49]

It should be noted that in the Netherlands the custom of sitting at table for Communion continues, and in most of the churches built since World War II the architects have been at great pains to provide adequate room, spatially and psychologically, for such celebration of the sacrament.[50] The influence of those contemporary Dutch churches, together with the literature which has accompanied them, has made itself felt in at least a few recent CRCs, which will be discussed later.

The only area where liturgical precedent held its own architecturally was in the matter of the choir. To the extent that choirs were rejected, choir lofts were also rejected. On this issue the CRC Synod had spoken with considerable clarity. As late as 1930 the synod had reaffirmed that it "discourages choir singing as a distinct element of public worship.[51] It was only in 1926 that the synod had allowed the question of choirs to be a matter to be decided by local consistories.[52] Prior to that time the synod had

48. Idzerd Van Dellen and Martin Monsma, *The Church Order Commentary,* Being a Brief Explanation of the Church Order of the Christian Reformed Church (Grand Rapids: Zondervan Publishing House, 1941), p. 260; also in Van Dellen and Monsma, *Revised Church Order Commentary,* p. 241.

49. Papers of Henry Beets, Folder 20, February 1, 1916.

50. See Donald J. Bruggink and Carl H. Droppers, *Christ and Architecture,* Building Presbyterian/Reformed Churches (Grand Rapids: Eerdmans, 1965) and W. J. G. van Mourik, *Hervormde Kerkbouw na 1945* ('s-Gravenhage: Boekencentrum, 1957).

51. *Acta der Synode 1930,* p. 101 (Art. 90).

52. *Acta der Synode 1926* van de Christelijke Gereformeerde Kerk Gehouden van 9 Juni tot 28 Junie, 1926, te Englewood, Chicago, Illinois (Grand Rapids: Grand Rapids Printing Co., 1926), p. 69 (Art. 57).

"opposed the use of all church choirs which sang alone, though permitting the employment of a choir to lead congregational singing."[53]

Once the matter of the choir was left to local consistorial option, synodical discouragement failed in its effectiveness. Once again, Americanization was pressing hard upon the CRC. "Choir singing in the services of worship was recognized by the members of the Christian Reformed Church as 'American.' Rev. Jan K. Van Baalen even argued that '*worship without a choir is simply un-American, foreign,*' and the practice of having church choirs was essential for the growth of the CRC."[54] However, the impact of tradition is still measurable. In his survey of 1972 (which gained a 70 percent response in questionnaires mailed to all ministers of CRCs)[55] Bertus F. Polman found that only 35.2 percent of CRCs used choirs regularly, while 21.2 percent never used a choir in services of public worship.[56] With over a fifth of all CRCs still having no need for a choir loft, one does, in this instance, find the liturgical practices faithfully reflected in church architecture. The picture file and the commemorative booklets alike reveal churches that are American in everything, the choir loft excepted. It should be noted that the absence of a choir loft imposed no problems of either architectural style or design to American architects. In many churches the ancient practice of having the choir in the balcony still prevailed (as it continues to do in many Lutheran churches to the present). Architects built nineteenth-century churches with room for choirs in the balcony and in front in lofts behind the minister; for Anglo-Catholics they soon learned how to put them in split chancels. For CRCs it was simply a matter of not putting a choir anywhere.

There were, of course, those avant-garde churches which had choir lofts, and presumably choirs at a very early date. Presumably they either took refuge in Calvin's, and later the 1904 Synod's, dicta that choirs could be used to lead congregational singing, or, perhaps the congregations were of such wealth and power that no one wished to raise the issue. In any case, when the magnificent brick structure of the La Grave Avenue CRC was dedicated in 1888, it had its organ in the corner, alongside the shallow apse for the pulpit, and immediately in front of the organ it had room for a choir!

The question must be raised, however, as to why choirs, or the lack of them, left their architectural impact while the Lord's Supper did not? The answer lies in their perceived relative importance, which was in turn associated with word and symbols. In his discussion of the attempted liturgical

53. Bertus Frederick Polman, "Church Music & Liturgy in the Christian Reformed Church of [sic] North America" (Ph.D. dissertation, University of Minnesota, 1980), pp. 81–82. See also *Acts of Synod 1904*, pp. 41–42 Art. 125).

54. Ibid., p. 83; see Jan Karel Van Baalen, *The Pound in a Napkin*, A Plea for Better Church Music (Grand Rapids: Eerdmans, 1939), p. 43.

55. Polman, "Church Music & Liturgy," pp. 175–176.

56. Ibid., p. 232.

reforms of 1928, Polman observes that in liturgical battles ". . . virtually no concern for the celebration of the Lord's Supper" is manifested.[57] In fact, "Calvin's ideal of weekly preaching and weekly communion . . . was not even mentioned once."[58] The Lord's Supper was a symbolic act, and the iconoclasm of the Dutch Reformation relegated symbolism to relative unimportance. As long as the theological essence of the Supper, i.e., its doctrine, remained pure, even practices held since the Reformation were easily washed away in the process of Americanization. But choirs were a matter of Word—the sung Word, but Word nonetheless. The Afscheiding of 1834 had focused on the hymns King William's department of worship sought to force upon the church, and the seceders had left that church singing their Psalms. Similarly, when in North America, Van Raalte led his seceders into a union with the RCA, the element in the worship of that church with which they were disquieted was the seemingly indiscriminate singing of hymns. After the organization of a non hymn-singing church, consistories soon became aware that singing groups all too easily began singing other than the Psalms. Thus, at the Spring Street CRC, which boasted the very first choral society (*zangvereniging*) in 1874, the consistory in 1880 refused the use of the church to "the local singing society on the grounds that they were singing hymns."[59]

While it is very easy for those thoroughly enmeshed in American ecclesiastical practice to treat this argumentation lightly, it is, I am convinced, correct. Choirs and hymns do pose a threat to good theology. In that perception the CRC has been correct. In maintaining a high degree of uniformity in the use of a synodically approved book of psalms and hymns (96.7 percent of all congregations responding [70 percent] use the *Psalter Hymnal* of 1959; 1.3 percent use that of 1934; while another 5.7 percent use the Dutch *Psalmboek & Gezangen*)[60] the CRC has achieved a degree of musical control rare in American Protestantism. The variety of hymnals and song books used as supplements, as well as in Sunday Schools and societies, together with the feeling of 77.5 percent of the clergy that their training in hymnody and the use of the *Psalter Hymnal* was "poor" indicates an advised concern.[61] To the degree that choirs sing what may be popular (e.g., Bill Gaither) they can be theologically subversive. The fathers should not be scorned for their concern with music. For the future, however, sound musical and theological education would seem to be the way to exercise that concern, rather than by a proscription which seems less and less effective.

All of this is not to say that the sacrament should not be viewed with

57. Ibid., p. 92.
58. Ibid.
59. Ibid., pp. 78–79.
60. Ibid., p. 240.
61. Ibid., pp. 239–240.

equal concern—although Polman's questionnaires make it only too plain that it is not.[62] It helps to explain, however, why the question of choirs leaves its architectural mark: choirs were associated directly, and indirectly (through their influence on the use of hymnody) with the Word and its faithful communication. Sacraments, especially in the symbolic nature of their celebration (seen in isolation from the theology of the sacraments) were regarded with a disinterest born of long accepted iconoclasm.

The intense theological concern exercised in the Netherlands in the church building boom following World War II, together with the propagation of similar concerns in this country in *Christ and Architecture*[63] has resulted in considerable tension in many church building programs since the late 60s. On one hand, the high level of theological literacy, sophistication, and seriousness within the CRC has resulted in intense theological concern in many congregations to build appropriately. On the other hand, the strong sense of tradition, which operates both within the context of theological justification, and in the context of past happenstance, makes significant church building difficult.

An example of the above took place in the 60s in the architectural design for the Shawnee Park CRC of Grand Rapids by Glenn A. Vander Sluis, project architect for Daverman Associates. His design, enthusiastically endorsed by the building committee under the leadership of Earl Ophoff, was the finest architectural expression of the Reformed faith which I have yet seen for a CRC or RCA church. By a narrow margin of three votes it was rejected by the congregation. In addition to unease concerning the lack of familiarity of design, the chief theological critique was by a person who repeatedly insisted that the large communion table, made of wood, on legs, surrounded by chairs, in the midst of the congregation, was Roman Catholic! The theological/architectural accuracy of the architect and building committee came in conflict with tradition as perceived by a segment of the congregation.

Sometimes less ambitious architectural attempts have received more kindly congregational treatment. In the Peace CRC of South Holland, Illinois, an exterior appearance familiar to midwestern suburbia nonetheless contains a very thoughtful interior worship space with simple but dignified liturgical furniture emphasizing the sacraments as well as the Word; a seating plan "gathering" the congregation about the means of grace and an organ and choir augmenting the congregation (as the Synod of 1904 desired) from the rear.

Another Peace CRC, this one in Cedar Rapids, Iowa, has also sought a proper emphasis on both Word and sacraments, while at the same time maintaining the flexibility of their building through the use of movable seating.

62. Ibid., pp. 91–92. Cf. p. 235.
63. Bruggink and Droppers, *Christ and Architecture*.

An excellent example of the creative wedding of site, exterior form and liturgy is in the Ferrysburg CRC of Ferrysburg, Michigan by an architect who has at least been allowed a message, if not his name, in the dedicatory folder (iconoclasm strikes again?). Located on the north slope of a rolling sand dune the form of the fan-shaped church projects up and away from the slope, its sanctuary roof culminating in a large vertical light scope. Inside, the congregation is gathered in radial seating under the fan, focused on Word and sacraments, raised slightly above floor level and flooded with natural light from above. Unfortunately, piano and organ console clutter the front, although they are kept below the level of the sacraments.

More iconographically emphatic than the Ferrysburg CRC is the University Hills CRC of Farmington, Michigan. A happy combination of a daring building committee, with its pastor, Jay Harold Ellens, giving strong leadership, and with a creative architect, Carl H. Droppers, all combined to make a very strong and appropriate architectural statement about the Reformed faith on a very limited budget. The triangular-shaped church forms the base for a very high steeple, bearing a cross—the building giving three-dimensional reality to the cross-on-triangle emblem of the CRC. Two low sidewalls of the triangle contain rooms for support services and education, the latter open through glass walls to the sanctuary for congregational overflow. In the sanctuary, the peak of the triangle is directly above the baptismal font, which repeats the triangular form and allows the families of the covenant to stand together in the midst of the people of the covenant for baptism. A large pulpit, with sounding board, stands midway between two corners, but away from the side wall, while between pulpit and side wall runs a very long communion table almost the length of the wall. The overall plan, the flexible seating, and the liturgical furniture offer a very strong statement of the Reformed faith and encourage not only intellectual but physical interaction in worship, which includes a return to the traditional Dutch practice of sitting at table for the Lord's Supper.

It is unfortunate that the resources are not available for a proper assessment of contemporary CRCs. Remaining iconoclasm is still sufficiently strong so that no one is rigorously compiling architectural archival material, nor, judging by the many gaps in the collection, are churches particularly zealous in providing materials of architectural content. Hopefully, as interest in the iconography of church architecture increases, students will not only continue to be encouraged to do papers on church architecture, but will also be urged to do both surveys and critiques of the churches in their classes, while archivists will receive a better response in their effort to collect photographs of both contemporary and older churches. A mutually beneficial relationship might be encouraged where architects would receive proper recognition for their church work through sharing copies of their architectural photos (well labeled with the name of both firm and project architect) for archival preservation. Where such architectural photos are not available, most congregations have competent amateur photographers who would be pleased to do a photographic essay on their church. It is only as we learn where our finest churches have been built and are able to discuss them that we can learn from one another.

The CRC has a rich heritage in articulate theological discussion. Its iconoclastic inheritance resulted in the early (in fact, immediate) Americanization of their architecture, with its influence upon the Americanization of its worship as well. With the renaissance of interest in worship and the recommended models of the Liturgical Committee, firmly grounded in the principles of Calvin and, in turn, of the early church, it is to be hoped that iconoclasm can be tempered at least to the point where it is recognized that building must be done intentionally in such a way that church architecture will be in conformity to our Reformed theology and will enhance our worship of Almighty God.

3

The Masonic Controversy in Holland, Michigan, 1879–1882

Elton J. Bruins

The Reformed Church in America[1] (hereafter RCA), founded by Dutch settlers on Manhattan Island, New York, in 1628, has endured a series of controversies and subsequent secessions related to the question of adaptation to the American culture and society. The Coetus-Conferentie controversy in the fourth decade of the eighteenth century was a debate about the formation of an American classis[2] which would give the Dutch Reformed churches (RCA) an ecclesiastical organization of their own. The "American" party argued that an American classis would enable the American Dutch Church (RCA) to conduct some of its own affairs (the most crucial being the right to ordain its own candidates for the ministry) without having to get permission from the Amsterdam Classis in the Netherlands every time it wanted to act.

The next issue which disrupted the Dutch Reformed Church was the charge by some ministers that the Dutch Reformed Church was adopting certain American theological deviations called Hopkinsianism,[3] which allegedly espoused a doctrine of general atonement, and not remaining true to the doctrine of the Synod of Dort (1618–19). This controversy resulted in the secession of several New Jersey and New York congregations in 1822 and the formation of the True Reformed Protestant Dutch Church.

---

1. The title of the Reformed Church in America prior to 1867 was the Reformed Protestant Dutch Church. During the entire history of this denomination it is commonly referred to as the Dutch Reformed Church.

2. A classis is composed of a number of Reformed congregations in a given geographical area.

3. See Dick L. Van Halsema, "Hopkins, Hackensack, and Haan," *The Reformed Journal* 7 (January 1957):7–9, for information of and evaluation of this issue.

A third controversy, this one among some of the recently arrived Dutch immigrants in Holland, Michigan, resulted in the Secession of 1857 and the organization of the Ware Hollandsch Gereformeerde Kerk (the original name of the CRC). Encouraged by the Reverend Albertus C. Van Raalte, the founder of Holland, and the pastor of the First Reformed Church, the immigrants who had formed the Classis of Holland in 1848 united with the old Dutch Reformed Church in New York and New Jersey in 1850. Subsequently, a few churches in the Classis of Holland determined that the Dutch Reformed Church was too American and seceded to found what later would be called the Christian Reformed Church in North America (hereafter CRC),[4] a totally Netherlands-oriented denomination.

However, the Americanization issue was not settled for the Midwestern Dutch immigrant churches with the Secession of 1857 and the formation of the CRC. The majority of the Dutch immigrant churches that stemmed from the 1847 immigration to the Middle West[5] under the direction of Van Raalte in Michigan and the Reverend Hendrik P. Scholte, the founder of Pella, Iowa, remained with the RCA. The founders of the CRC were unhappy dissidents who were not joined by many other Dutch immigrants during the 1857–1880 period. The majority of the Dutch immigrant Reformed congregations in Michigan, Illinois, Wisconsin, and Iowa simply learned to live with sister congregations in New York and New Jersey, many of which had, over the course of 250 years, fully adapted to the American religious and cultural scene.

For various reasons, the union between the old Dutch immigrants in the eastern part of the United States of America and the new Dutch immigrants of the Middle West was never completely happy. But under the leadership of Van Raalte the interests of the two groups were melded, and Van Raalte was able to channel gifts and monies from the eastern churches to the Middle West to aid the new Dutch immigrant congregations. Eastern money helped to establish the Pioneer School in Holland in 1851, to build churches such as the Pillar Church in Holland, and to develop Hope College in Holland, which was chartered in 1866. Scholte never united with the Dutch Reformed Church but most of his followers in Iowa did. Moreover, the churches of the East and the Dutch Reformed churches of the West joined in efforts to evangelize the world during the period of growing interest in foreign missions which swept the American churches in the nineteenth century.

However, the community of interests between the eastern and western churches of the RCA between 1868 and 1880 was severely jarred by an unusually difficult dispute concerning membership in secret societies, the

4. This name was adopted in 1890.
5. The best study on the subject of Dutch immigration to the Middle West is Henry S. Lucas, *Netherlanders in America*, Dutch Immigration to the United States and Canada, 1789–1950, University of Michigan Publications, 21 (Ann Arbor: The University of Michigan Press, 1955).

lodge of the Freemasons in particular. Although Calvinist churches in Europe and North America were opposed to Freemasonry in general, the RCA in New York and New Jersey had, during its process of Americanization in the eighteenth century, accepted the lodge as part of American society, and many of its members joined the lodge as a matter of course. The new Dutch immigrants of the nineteenth century, fresh from the Netherlands, were unanimous in the opinion that Freemasonry was an anti-Christian organization and that membership in the lodge or in any secret society should be forbidden. The western churches believed, further, that members of churches who were Freemasons should be disciplined and expelled if they did not resign their lodge membership. The issue proved so divisive and so difficult to settle that a new secession from the RCA resulted in 1882. The impact of this secession was equal to that of 1822 and greater than that of the Secession of 1857.

To understand the issues which led to the Secession of 1882, it is necessary to understand the nature of Freemasonry and the reasons why the mainstream American Protestant churches, including the RCA, were able to accept lodge membership as a support of Christianity and not as an opponent. Freemasonry was founded in England in 1717.[6] It derived from the masons' guilds which had existed for centuries and which had built the cathedrals of Europe. However, beginning in 1717, the guilds developed into lodges which accepted members interested in history, philosophy, and science as well, and the lodges became speculative organizations rather than operative ones. To be an "accepted" mason, one did not have to be a working mason. Instead, the guild became a fraternal and social organization with its own myth, symbolism, and ritual along speculative lines; in

6. For general background on Freemasonry in Europe and the United States of America, see J. Fletcher Brennan, *A General History of Freemasonry*, Based upon the Ancient Documents Relating to, and the Monuments Erected by This Fraternity, From Its Foundation in the Year 715 B.C. to the Present Time (Cincinnati: American Masonic Publishing Association, 1871); Elijah Alfred Coil, *The Relation of the Liberal Churches and the Fraternal Orders* (Boston: American Unitarian Association, 1927). Ninth printing; David B. Davis, "Some Themes of Counter-subversion; An Analysis of Anti-Masonic, Anti-Catholic, and Anti-Mormon Literature," *The Mississippi Valley Historical Review* 47 (1960/61):205–224; James Dewar, *The Unlocked Secret: Freemasonry Examined* (London: William Kimber, 1966); Charles Grandison Finney, *The Character, Claims and Practical Workings of Freemasonry* (Chicago: National Christian Association, 1913); Walton Hannah, *Darkness Visible*, A Revelation and Interpretation of Freemasonry (London: Augustine Press, 1952); Melvin M. Johnson, *The Beginnings of Freemasonry in America*, Containing a Reference to All That Is Known of FREEMASONRY in the Western Hemisphere Prior to 1750, and Short Sketches of the Lives of Some of the Provincial Grand Masters (New York: George H. Doran Co., 1924); Jacob Katz, *Jews and Freemasons in Europe, 1723–1939* (Cambridge: Harvard University Press, 1970); Dorothy Ann Lipson, *Freemasonry in Federalist Connecticut* (Princeton: Princeton University Press, 1977); Gustavus Myers, *History of the Bigotry in the United States*, Ed. and rev. by Henry M. Christman (New York: Capricorn Books, 1960); Gerard M. Van Pernis, *Masonry, Antithesis of the Christ*, A Study of Free Masonry in the Light of the Word of God, Also Tested by the Reformed Standards, Especially Designed for Consistories (Grand Rapids: Eerdmans, 1932); Nesta Helen Webster, *Secret Societies and Subversive Movements* (London: Boswell Printing and Publishing Co., 1928). Fourth edition; William Joseph Whalen, *Christianity and American Freemasonry* (Milwaukee: The Bruce Publishing Co., 1958).

actuality, the lodge was a child of the Enlightenment. The lodge of Free-masons affirmed a religious and moral universalism and had a universally shared apprehension of evil.[7]

Freemasonry spread rapidly into Europe and to North America. The first lodge in the Netherlands was founded in 1725 at the Hague,[8] although the Calvinist clergy were hostile to it, and forty-six more lodges had been established by 1871. Because of England's ties with North America, the lodge was immediately exported to the American colonies. As a young man, Benjamin Franklin joined the lodge in 1731.[9] By 1800, many thousands of men in North America had become Masons, and Freemasonry and other lodges had become a vital part of the American social structure and a recognized part of society. According to Dorothy Lipson the lodge "offered the many pleasures of fraternal conviviality."[10] Nor was the lodge seen as inimical to the interests of American Christianity, although in the case of men like Franklin, who were not church members, the lodge fulfilled a religious function.

Since the lodge was seen primarily as a fraternal and social organization, many men who were Christians joined the lodges and personally experienced no conflicts between lodge values and ideas and their Christian beliefs and value systems. In time, the clergy even gave its blessing to fraternal organizations such as Freemasonry. For instance, Ashbel Baldwin, a Congregational clergyman in Connecticut, became the chaplain of the Grand Lodge of the state in 1797.[11] A son of Jonathan Edwards, the great theologian of the eighteenth century, also served as a grand master of the Connecticut lodge. The Universalist clergy were the first to join the lodges in Connecticut, but as Congregationalist clergy also joined, people concluded that men in good standing in their churches could join the lodges in good conscience.[12] For Christians, the "Great Light" or source of truth in Masonry was the Bible, and the Bible was considered the basis for Masonic myth and ritual. One thing the clergymen affiliated with lodges insisted on was that the morality which Masonry affirmed was the morality which Christianity had affirmed. By 1800, Freemasonry was for the most part a widely accepted institution in North America, highly regarded by many and, according to Masons, not considered to conflict with basic Christianity.

Masonry's wide acceptance in North America, however, does not mean that it did not engender opposition.[13] There has always been in American

7. Lipson, *Freemasonry in Federalist Connecticut*, p. 41.
8. Brennan, *General History of Freemasonry*, p. 123.
9. David Freeman Hawke, *Franklin* (New York: Harper and Row, 1976), p. 44.
10. Lipson, *Freemasonry in Federalist Connecticut*, p. 9.
11. Ibid., p. 92.
12. Ibid., pp. 125–129.
13. Ibid., p. 127.

society an undercurrent of opposition to secret societies and to Freemasonry in particular. Opposition to the lodge of Freemasons built up for both theological reasons and social reasons. Outsiders perceived the secrecy of the lodge as hostile, and there was an inherent elitism in lodge membership:[14] men of the higher social and economic class were more likely to be members of lodges than those from the lower class. But opposition built for religious reasons, too. The orthodox clergymen in Connecticut, for instance, believed that Masonry was at odds with Calvinism and held that some members used the lodge as a surrogate religion.[15] Such men refused to accept Masons into the church and for similar theological reasons, the Roman Catholic Church had banned the Masonic order in Europe shortly after its formation in 1717.[16]

The first major outburst of opposition to Freemasonry in North America occurred in 1826 as a reaction to the abduction and presumed murder of William Morgan of western New York.[17] A former Mason, Morgan announced an exposé of Freemasonry and disappeared soon after. He was never seen alive again and his body was never found. His abductors were members of the Freemasons, but they received only very light sentences from a jury composed of Masons. The scandalous affair crystallized the opposition to Masonry, and by 1828 a formal anti-Masonry movement, combining an evangelical impulse with political action, had been organized. The movement became a political party, and many anti-Masonic publications sprang up. The movement was active for about five years.

The RCA in New York and New Jersey paid no formal attention to anti-Masonry. A committee of the General Synod reported annually that it deplored the decline of the Sabbath in American life and the rise of intemperance, but there is no evidence in the minutes of the General Synod or Particular Synods that there was any sympathy with the anti-Masonic movement in the later part of the 1820s.[18] At the same time, the dissident True Reformed Protestant Dutch Church which had originated in the Secession of 1822 went on record very clearly in response to the Morgan affair. Masonry was to be condemned, and membership in the lodge was not to be permitted among members of the denomination.[19] Since this new

14. Ibid., p. 9.

15. Ibid., p. 120.

16. In 1738 Pope Benedict XIV renewed the bull of excommunication that Clement XII had issued against the Freemasons. Brennan, *General History of Freemasonry*, p. 320.

17. Lipson, *Freemasonry in Federalist Connecticut*, pp. 267–273, gives a thorough account of this event.

18. Article XVII in the General Synod's *Acts* was entitled, "Prevailing Sins." See, e.g., The *Acts* and Proceedings of the [Twenty-second] General Synod of the Reformed Dutch Church in North America, at New York, June, 1829 (New York: Vanderpool & Cole, Printers, 1829), p. 204 (Art. 17). Freemasonry was never mentioned nor was it alluded to in the synodical reports on the state of the church.

19. A full account of their action is worth noting: "The Committee on the subject of Freemasonry ask leave to report—Your Committee are aware, that the Masonic Institutions and Principles have lately attracted much public attention in this country; several pamphlets and books on the subject, have been

denomination was clearly opposed to the RCA, from which it had seceded, this action can also be interpreted as a reaction to the RCA, which had not condemned Masonry and had remained silent about the scandalous Morgan affair. Given the magnitude of the opposition to Masonry, the failure of the RCA to mention Morgan's murder at the synodical level suggests that it had already become so Americanized that it could not publicly condemn membership in an organization which many of its members had joined.[20] When the question of membership in the lodge did reach the General Synod of the RCA in 1868, the attitude of the eastern churches toward the lodge prevailed: the lodge was not viewed as anti-Christian but compatible with Christianity, and membership in the lodge was left to the individual's conscience.

Therefore, the issue of Freemasonry had not been mentioned at all when the Dutch immigrant churches in Michigan united with the RCA in 1850. The new Dutch immigrants had come to North America with the attitude generally held in the Netherlands that membership in the lodge was a sin and assumed that the RCA in the East was of the same mind. Van Raalte had rightly assured his people that the old RCA in the East was not touched by the liberalism which plagued the Nederlandse Hervormde Kerk in the Netherlands and that the piety of the churches in the East was very similar to that of the colonists in Holland.

But as the old RCA in the East and the new RCA in the West came to know each other better, differences due to the Americanization process in the East began to appear. One of them was the attitude toward the lodge. The first mention of the lodge issue was made in the Classis of Holland in 1853. The classis made quick work of the issue and said that because Masonry was among the works of darkness it was "thus unlawful for a

---

published, professing to reveal the nature and tendency of its secrets. Among these publications, 'Bernard's Light on Masonry,' holds a conspicuous place. The members of the masonic fraternity appear to be numerous in every part of the United States; belonging to every class in society, whether civil or religious, and some of the highest standing. As to the civil, or political character of the institution, we deem it not necessary, at present, to make any remarks; but as to the *religious* nature and pretensions of this mysterious association, as far as revealed, we think it demands the attention of the Synod. The Masonic Society professes to find its foundation in the sacred volume;—to have an intimate relation with Solomon's Temple; and to be a religious fraternity—a household of faith—a band of mystic brethren. Examining it in this light, we find the religion of the Association to be a mixture of Paganism and Mohammedanism, with the corruptions of Judaism and Christianity; for many professed Christians, many Papists, Jews, and even Gentiles, are found in its communion. We also find, that it perverts the meaning and use of the Bible, is full of names of blasphemy, and administers illegal, profane, and horrible oaths. We are decidedly of this opinion, that no true Christian can, consistently with his profession, to be a free and accepted mason—and that the ministers and members of our true Reformed Dutch Church can have no fellowship with this fraternity." The *Acts* and Proceedings of the General Synod of the True Reformed Dutch Church in the United States of America, at Hackensack, June, 1831 (New York: Dewey's Press, 1831), pp. 10–11.

20. Peter Hoekstra, "The American Revolt against Freemasonry," *The Reformed Journal* 9 (April 1959):20, did not get this straight. He credited the Dutch Reformed Church (RCA) with this action.

[church] member" to belong to a Masonic lodge.[21] There were no lengthy debates, no majority and minority opinions, and no reference to the attitude on Freemasonry in the denomination. This was a local matter, and the Classis of Holland expressed the traditional European and Dutch attitudes.

Henry Beets, an eminent historian of the CRC, claimed that Freemasonry was one of the formal causes for a group of people leaving the RCA in 1857 and organizing a new denomination for Dutch immigrants.[22] This was not the case, however. The formal reasons that gave rise to the secession were that hymns were acceptable for use in the RCA, that non-Reformed Protestants were accepted at the Lord's Supper in some RCA churches in the East and that the preaching of the Heidelberg Catechism and regular house visitation by ministers and elders was falling into disuse in the RCA.[23] Masonry was not listed in the complaint to the classis. Within a decade, however, the infant CRC took formal action against membership in the lodge.

The actual controversy about Masonry began in earnest in 1867 when the CRC officially banned membership in the lodge by synodical order just as its sister, the True Reformed Protestant Dutch Church, in the East, had done in 1831.[24] The Midwestern Dutch immigrant churches of the RCA were not about to suffer by comparison with the CRC, so in 1868 the Classis of Wisconsin, under the leadership of John H. Karsten, Herman Stobbelaar, and Hendrik G. Klyn [Kleyn], sent a memorial to the General Synod of the RCA, asking the synod to declare that membership in the church and the lodge were incompatible and to condemn Masonry. The General Synod voted to take no action by a vote of 89 to 19. Van Raalte, Jacob and John Vander Meulen (the sons of the founder of Zeeland, Michigan, Cornelius Vander Meulen) and Karsten all voted with the small minority.[25]

The Midwestern Dutch immigrant churches soon confirmed their representatives' opposition to the General Synod's ruling. In 1869 the Classis of Holland and the Classis of Wisconsin went to the General Synod with overtures reaffirming their position of 1868; the synod referred the matter to a committee for further consideration.[26] In 1870, the General Synod

21. *Classis Holland:* Minutes 1848–1858, Tr. by a Joint Committee of the Christian Reformed Church and the Reformed Church in America (Grand Rapids: The Grand Rapids Printing Co., 1943), p. 144.

22. Henry Beets, *The Christian Reformed Church in North America,* Its History, Schools, Missions, Creed and Liturgy, Distinctive Principles and Practices and its Church Government (Grand Rapids: Eastern Avenue Book Store, 1923), p. 47.

23. *Classis Holland,* p. 242.

24. "Notulen van de Klassikale Vergadering van 20 Februari 1867," *Minutes of the Highest Assembly of the Christian Reformed Church, 1857–1880* (Grand Rapids: Calvin Theological Seminary, 1937), p. 77 (Art. 15).

25. The *Acts* and Proceedings of the [Sixty-second] General Synod of the Reformed Church in America, 1868 (New York: Board of Publication of the Reformed Church, 1868), p. 463.

26. The *Acts* and Proceedings of the [Sixty-third] General Synod of the Reformed Church in America, 1869 (New York: Board of Publication of the Reformed Church, 1869), p. 662.

made itself very clear on the issue: membership in a secret society, they declared, was not a good practice; church members should not belong. This statement was clearly a concession to the protesters from the West for many members of the General Synod were undoubtedly Masons. But the synod declared further that it could not and would not rule that membership in the lodge was to be forbidden by church law. In explaining its thinking, the General Synod maintained that if it had disallowed membership in the lodge, it would have set up a new test of membership and, moreover, have interfered with consistorial privileges; only the local consistory admitted new members, and it alone had the prerogative to decide who could be a member of the church and who could not.[27] The General Synod has never budged from this position, leaving it to the consistory to declare whether membership in the lodge was compatible or incompatible with membership in the local church.

Most of the Dutch immigrant churches in the Middle West accepted this ruling, and consistories continued to ban Masons from church membership as they would have done had they still been in the Netherlands. Even though Van Raalte voted against the action of the synod in 1868, he later declared that membership in the lodge was a matter for discipline only if the church members lived in such a manner as to give cause for disciplinary action.[28] Clearly Van Raalte had Americanized his attitude toward Freemasonry. He did not like the Freemasons and would never have joined the lodge himself, but after 1868 he no longer voiced the traditional Dutch opposition to Masonry and demonstrated an ability to live with the decision of the General Synod of 1870.

In view of the immensity of the eruption over Masonry in 1880, it is strange that this bitter disruption had not occurred in 1870 or earlier in 1868 when the issue first reached the synodical level and before the immigrant churches in the Middle West had adapted still more to the American scene. Apparently the difference was the living presence of Van Raalte himself. Although he had retired from his pastorate at the First Reformed Church of Holland in 1866, he remained active in the affairs of the Classis of Holland and the Particular Synod of Chicago and encouraged further Dutch immigration to North America, such as the new colony in Amelia,

27. The minute reads as follows: "Our brethren are evidently sincere and earnest in their convictions. They are greatly perplexed on account of what they perceive to be a serious evil in the Church, and they have done well to state their difficulties. We cannot think, however, that they expect from Synod such a deliverance as would authorize Consistories to exclude Free Masons from church fellowship, for this would be to establish a new and unauthorized test of membership in the Christian Church, and would interfere with consistorial prerogatives." The *Acts* and Proceedings of the [Sixty-fourth] General Synod of the Reformed Church in America, 1870 (New York: Board of Publication of the Reformed Church, 1870), pp. 96–97.

28. Henry Elias Dosker, *Levensschets van Dr. A. C. Van Raalte* (Een Man, Krachtig in Woorden en Werken). Een der Vaders der "Scheiding" in Nederland en Stichter der Hollandsche Koloniën in den Staat Michigan, Noord Amerika (Nijkerk: C. C. Callenbach, 1893), p. 331.

Virginia, settled between 1868 and 1871.[29] Van Raalte remained the titular leader of the Dutch immigrant settlements in western Michigan until the time of his death on November 7, 1876. His very presence kept the lid on the simmering Masonic controversy and prevented it from boiling over into the controversy it became from 1879 to 1882.

The controversy simmered during the 1870s, and the discontent with the synodical actions of 1868, 1869, and 1870 never died out. In 1874 Gerrit Van Schelven, the astute editor of the *Holland City News* and a leader in the Holland community, reported that First Reformed Church of Holland, Van Raalte's former congregation, had discovered two Masons in its membership. The editor then went on to say disconsolately that "this is the beginning of an unpleasant controversy."[30] Van Schelven did not realize how prophetic he was. For there soon followed a series of unfortunate incidents which precluded a peaceful solution to the Masonry question over which the eastern and western churches were at great odds. Van Raalte's moderating presence was gone after 1876.

About the same time, Hope College, the institution which Van Raalte had founded and which was so useful to the Dutch immigrant churches, began to suffer severe reverses due to the poor management of its financial resources under the direction of President Philip Phelps.[31] In 1877 Phelps was relieved of the presidency, and in the same year the General Synod declared that theological education, begun in 1866, could no longer continue at Hope College because of the poor financial base of the college. Training young immigrant men for the ministry of the Midwestern churches was extremely crucial to the life of the RCA in the Middle West, but in an effort to save the college, the General Synod jettisoned theological education. The immigrant churches regarded this action a "Masonic plot." G. Henry Mandeville, an eastern RCA clergyman and secretary of the Board of Education of the RCA, was appointed provisional president of the college to guide the institution through its crisis. The question of membership in the lodge was raised with his appointment. Either because he was a Mason or because of the majority vote of the General Synod a decade earlier, the typical Dutch immigrant response to the crisis at Hope College was that Masons were at the bottom of the problem![32] This

29. This colonization attempt was a failure, and Van Raalte lost some of his prestige in this unfortunate venture.

30. Gerrit Van Schelven, "Editorial," *Holland City News*, May 23, 1874, p. 4.

31. Wynand Wichers, *A Century of Hope, 1866–1966* (Grand Rapids: Eerdmans, 1968), pp. 108–111.

32. This was reported in the *Holland City News*, September 6, 1879, p. 1. The charge was made by an A. Feenstra in his letter which had appeared in *De Hope* on July 23, 1879. For the most part, *De Hope*, the paper published by Hope College for the Midwestern Dutch immigrant community, kept a very low profile during the Masonic controversy. Wichers claimed that it was under orders not to publish "abusive" articles. Wichers, *Century of Hope*, p. 109. This policy was quite different from *De Wachter's* because that publication and *De Grondwet* did everything possible to enflame the situation. In addition, Cornelius Doesburg, the editor of *De Hope*, was an alleged Mason, one of the two who were members of First Reformed Church. Miss Ruth Keppel, a student of local history, said that Doesburg was a Mason. Conversation of the author with Miss Keppel, August 5, 1980.

simplistic conclusion indicated that Holland had become a fertile field for controversy.

To the great dismay of Van Schelven, who knew that Van Raalte would never have condoned the invitation, the Pillar Church,[33] which in April of 1879 had dedicated a beautiful black marble plaque to Van Raalte's memory,[34] invited an ex-Mason, Edmond Ronayne, to lecture on the supposed evils of Masonry.[35] Ronayne, who lived in Chicago, devoted all his efforts to fighting the lodge and had published a book against Masonry that same year: *The Master's Carpet; or Masonry and Baal Worship Identical.*[36] The title of the book left no doubt as to his position, and it was this book that led to an invitation to come to Holland in June, 1879, to inform the members of the RCA about Freemasonry and reinforce what they already knew about its "evils." Since Ronayne compared Masonry with the Roman Catholic Church, he was sure to have a good audience in Holland because in the Dutch immigrant mind there was little doubt as to which institution was worse.

The itinerant lecturer declared unequivocally that these two religious systems "must without question be the 'doctrine' and worship of demons."[37] But he focused on the evils of Freemasonry and not on "Romanism" while in Holland. Freemasonry, he claimed, conducted "abominable, wicked, degrading ceremonies." It was incomprehensible, he continued, how any respectable man could join a lodge in view of what the lodge stood for and in view of the similarity between ceremonies it conducted and the Baal worship reported in the Bible. Moreover, like Romanism, Masonry was a religious system that demanded "blind unquestioning obedience to all its laws, rules, and edicts, whether 'right or wrong.'"[38] Not only should laymen refrain from joining the lodge, but any clergyman who became a member should be suspended from the ministry. Ronayne's message was considered "gospel" by the Holland churches, and the smoldering embers burning for years now flared into a major fire.

The churches responded to Ronayne's challenge immediately by petitioning the Classis of Holland to take action. At that time, the two leading

33. A popular designation for the edifice of First Reformed Church.

34. The event was reported by Gerritt Van Schelven, "Editorial," *Holland City News,* April 26, 1879, p. 4.

35. Van Schelven made this editorial comment on May 31, 1879 about Ronayne's impending visit: "We see it announced in the city papers that there will be held an exposition of the secrets of Freemasonry, by Mr. Edmond Ronayne, in the First Reformed Church, on the 3d, 4th and 5th days of June next. If that man does it, he makes a perjurer of himself, and how a perjurer can get permission to pollute *that* church—to say the least—marks an epoch in the history of it. It is an astounding piece of news to us, and it seems very inconsistent with its previous history." Gerrit Van Schelven, "Editorial," *Holland City News,* May 31, 1879, p. 5.

36. Edmond Ronayne, *The Master's Carpet; or Masonry and Baal-Worship Identical. Reviewing the Similarity between Masonry, Romanism and "the Mysteries" and Comparing the Whole with the Bible* (Chicago: Press of Streich Brothers, 1879).

37. Ibid., p. vii.

38. Ibid., p. 69.

ministers in the Classis, the Reverend Roelof Pieters of the First Reformed Church of Holland, and the Reverend Nicholas M. Steffens of the First Reformed Church of Zeeland, the largest and oldest churches in the classis, were, fortunately, president and stated clerk, respectively. Had Pieters not died during surgery the following February, he would probably have been a conservative throughout the controversy. However, Pieters seems to have been irenic and reasonable in comparison with the contentious elder of the First Reformed Church, Teunis Keppel, who led the laity in the First Church and became the *de facto* leader of the congregation after the death of Pieters. Pieters' premature death at a crucial period in the burgeoning controversy was a great loss to the First Reformed Church, the Classis of Holland, and the RCA. Steffens, a moderate in the controversy, favored the General Synod position of 1870.

Beginning on September 3, 1879, a special meeting before its regular fall meeting, the classis met to deal with petitions urging the congregations to take action against Masonry and to begin a new movement in the RCA against membership in a secret society. The committee on overtures and judicial business made its report at this meeting and set the course of action for the classis:

> To your committee three communications were referred, out of which the following appears: The First Church of Holland feels itself called upon to contend with the evil of Secret Societies, also found in our denomination, and requests Classis to take suitable and effective measures to this end.
>
> The Church of Fynaart finding that one of its members belongs to two of this [sic] Societies, viz. those of Freemasonry and Odd Fellowship [sic] is busied at present by means of Christian discipline to save that brother and to purify the Church, and requests that Classis, whose duty it is, to watch on [sic] the peace and prosperity of the Churches, and who have a general Supervising power in cases of appeal over the acts and proceedings of the consistories within their bounds, take into consideration the propriety of expressing itself in regard to this general deceptive evil.[39]

The congregation of North Holland called Freemasonry a great sin "which may not be tacitly forborn in the Church of God," but "on the other hand it admonishes against imprudent and unchristian action which would further the greater sin of contention and division." Membership in a secret society was, in short, an evil but schism was a still greater evil.[40]

The Classis of Holland disliked Masonry as an institution, but the question was how to deal with it. Classis agreed with the 1870 decision of the General Synod that the consistory had the right to expel a member if, after

---

39. Minutes of the Classis of Holland, September 3, 1879, pp. 280–281. The unpublished minutes of the classis are in the Archives of Western Theological Seminary, Holland, Michigan.
40. Ibid., p. 281.

a proper period of prayer and pastoral concern, he did not discontinue his membership in the lodge. The report of the overtures and judicial committee mentioned further problems, however. Because the denomination did not ban membership in the secret society wholesale, the consistories which disapproved of Masonry found it difficult to discipline members and cast them out of the church, for other consistories would gladly accept such individuals into their fellowship. In addition, the action of the General Synod prevented a "hearty fellowship in the denomination." That is to say, the Dutch immigrant churches in the West could not experience full fellowship in the denomination with the eastern brethren if membership in the lodge were tolerated. Also, the Classis of Wisconsin thought it offensive to the conscience of the people who opposed Masonry to attend General Synod and receive Communion at the hands of ministers and elders who disagreed with them and who might even be members of the lodge.[41] The vote of the Classis of Holland to memorialize General Synod again on the question of Masonry passed by a vote of 16 to 6. The minority of six, led by Steffens, disliked secret societies but maintained that the General Synod's position of 1870 was true to the Reformed-Presbyterian system of church polity. Since the majority view prevailed, a committee was appointed to prepare the new materials for presentation to the June, 1880, meeting of the General Synod. Pieters was the chairman; Steffens and Peter Lepeltak, a moderate and a conservative, were the other two ministers; two elders completed the five member committee. Keppel was not appointed to the committee.

During the period between September 3, 1879, and April 7–9, 1880, when the committee reported, Pieters died, but a full report had been prepared for the classis. It took three major sittings for the classis to review the document and vote 23–3 in favor of the report. The conservatives had won, and 3500 copies of the report were ordered and distributed to the churches before the meeting of the General Synod in June. During the same period, September to June, the entire Midwestern Dutch immigrant community became involved in the controversy. When the General Synod convened in June of 1880, it had memorials not only from the Classis of Holland, but also from the Classis of Grand River (which included the Grand Haven and Grand Rapids RCA churches), the Classis of Illinois (which represented the American non-immigrant RCA churches in Illinois), and the Classis of Wisconsin which represented the Dutch immigrant RCA churches of Illinois, Iowa, and Wisconsin.

The overture and memorial from the Classis of Wisconsin, by far the most articulate, was undoubtedly composed by Karsten, a veteran fighter

41. "A Memorial on the Subject Freemasonry to the General Synod of the Reformed Dutch Church in America to Meet in Brooklyn June 2nd 1880 Presented by the Classis of Wisconsin and Her Action of April 22d 1880." The attitudes toward Masonry were identical in the Classes of Holland and Wisconsin.

against Masonry. It was deemed to be the most representative of the anti-Masonic overtures, so Synod dealt with it directly. The overture from Wisconsin included the usual diatribes against Freemasonry (e.g., that it was "the child of darkness and communistic"),[42] but the overture also included a novel theme: Freemasonry was "anti-Republican, anti-Christian and anti-Reformed."

Masonry was clearly anti-Christian because it had no Savior and was universalistic in its approach to religious truth. It was anti-Reformed because it disagreed with the Heidelberg Catechism and taught another way to salvation than Jesus Christ. But the principal emphasis of the document was that Freemasonry was anti-Republican because it was "contrary to the spirit of American institutions." The Masons promoted political preferment of fellow members, a practice contrary to American democratic principles.

After the document concluded its doctrinaire position, it turned to a major problem facing the Dutch immigrant churches. If the General Synod did not reverse its decision of 1870 and take a position agreeing with the position of the Midwestern Dutch immigrants, the Midwestern church was severely threatened by a loss of members, not from the impending secession (which did take place) but from a loss of "the new Dutch immigrants from the Netherlands coming now in large numbers [who] may unite with the 'True Reformed Church' [CRC] in this land instead of the Reformed Church." The RCA Dutch immigrant churches wanted the immigrants now coming to North America in such great numbers to unite with them and increase the borders of their kingdom in the Midwest and not join the despised dissidents[43] of that time, the CRC, now for the first time openly acknowledged as a threat. Nor was this an idle, politically-inspired threat. For through its publication *De Wachter,* the CRC was proclaiming openly that the RCA was an impure church and toleration of Masons only the final sign of its degradation.

The General Synod of 1880 knew that there was much agitation on the question of membership in the secret society, so it took the overtures seriously and debated them at length. The outcome was the same as in 1870, but this time the synod spoke to the issue clearly and directly in an attempt to show the classes in the West that it took the overtures seriously:

> . . . no communicant members, and no minister of the Reformed Church in America ought to unite with or to remain in any society or institution, whether secret or open, whose principles and practices are anti-Christian, or

---

42. Ibid. The document does not have pagination.

43. The word "dissident" is used in a derogatory manner here, but Henry Beets, *The Christian Reformed Church,* Its Roots, History, Schools and Mission Work, A.D. 1857 to 1946 (Grand Rapids: Baker, 1946), p. 81, also referred to the early members of his church as "some reactionary, over-conservative in the group."

contrary to the faith and practice of the Church to which he belongs. . . . this Synod solemnly believes and declares that any system of religion or morals whose tendency is to hide our Savior, or to supplant the religion of which He is the founder, should receive no countenance from his professed followers. . . . That this Synod also advises Consistories and Classes of the Church to be very kind and forbearing, and strictly constitutional in their dealings with individuals on this subject, and that they be and are hereby affectionately cautioned against setting up any new or unauthorized tests of communion in the Christian Church.[44]

This firm but irenic statement was the official position of the synod and would remain so in spite of repeated attempts of the same classes to reverse the decision in the 1880s and 1890s.

The decision of the General Synod is misleading, however, because it does not reflect the full debate that took place at the 1880 Synod. The eastern majority was fully Americanized in its attitudes toward Masonry and lost patience with the minority of the delegates from the West. Dr. Elbert S. Porter of the Williamsburgh RCA, Williamsburgh, New York, the leading spokesman in the synod for the policy enunciated in 1870, was as articulate and firm in his defense of Masonry as Karsten of the Alto RCA, Alto, Wisconsin, was in his attack. The words of Porter as reported in the Brooklyn papers typify the attitudes of the eastern RCA members at that time:

I am a Mason; but being a Mason I am also a minister of the Lord Jesus Christ. I was born and educated in the Reformed Dutch Church; I have been a pastor of the church all the years since I was licensed to preach. I have never been out of the harness. I hope I am a Christian while I am a Mason, and a Royal Arch Mason of the Seventh Degree. I never believed there was an institution in the world superior to the Church to which I belong. My Christian brother (a member of the synod from the West) said that he would not belong to an institution which was not founded by God.[45]

Porter then made a joke out of his Christian brother's remarks by asking, "Was he a Democrat or a Republican?" The reporter of the Brooklyn paper reported that "laughter" followed that question. But since Porter did not want to seem flippant, he continued: "I belong to a lodge which meets on Court street [in Brooklyn]; nine-tenths of the members of my lodge are members of churches—ministers, deacons, elders,, vestrymen, etc. The issue presented is, can we circumscribe the consciences of other

44. The *Acts* and Proceedings of the Seventy-fourth General Synod of the Reformed Church in America, Convened in Regular Session in the City of Brooklyn, New York, June, 1880 (New York: Board of Publication of the Reformed Church in America, 1880), p. 536.

45. Newspaper clippings in the Archives of the RCA, the Dutch Church Room, Sage Library of the New Brunswick Theological Seminary, New Brunswick, New Jersey.

people."[46] Throughout his extensive remarks Porter simply expounded the traditional American understanding of the lodge membership as he and the church members he knew had experienced it.

The ruling of the 1880 General Synod (which basically affirmed the position taken in 1870) coincided with the minority opinion in the Classis of Holland, but the synodical decision solved no problems for the Midwestern classes, particularly the Classis of Holland. The troubles now increased with intensity. At the meeting of the Classis of Holland, September 8–10, 1880, the churches of the classis made clear their disapproval of the synodical decision. The synod still had not outlawed Masonry. At its October 6, 1880, meeting, the classis went on record that "public opinion has almost universally interpreted General Synod's actions as a decision that Masons were to be allowed in the communion of the Reformed Church." Synod, the Classis of Holland continued, had provided no help to consistories trying to "purify the church of this evil."[47] A minority in the classis surely realized that synod's actions had been misconstrued, but most members of the Holland churches saw the issue in this light. The classis went on record by a vote of 17 to 5 as disagreeing with the action of the General Synod, clearly determined to show the member churches that it was opposed to the action of the synod (even though it could not do anything about it). Dissatisfaction and discontent were now rampant throughout Dutch immigrant churches of the Middle West, and the Classis of Wisconsin went on record against the action of the synod in its meeting of April 20, 1881.[48]

Worst of all, not only were members leaving RCA congregations and joining the CRC, but they were not taking their membership papers with them, adding insult to the injury of secession and schism. Those congregations in the RCA which did attempt to discipline Masons often found that offending members simply left the RCA congregations which prohibited Masons and joined ones that did not. The primary example was right in Holland, where, despite the resentment of the Dutch churches, the Second [Hope] Reformed Church, founded by English-speaking Hope College faculty who had come from the East, accepted members of secret societies in its fellowship.[49]

The Dutch immigrant classes continued to press for action against Masonry in succeeding years, but the General Synod would never again discuss the Masonic issue in any detail. As a sop to the suffering churches in the West, the General Synod decided to meet in the West for the first time and convened in Grand Rapids in June of 1884, at which time the

---

46. Ibid.
47. Minutes of the Classis of Holland, October 6, 1880, pp. 380–381.
48. Another memorial to the General Synod, now in the Archives of the RCA, New Brunswick.
49. *Holland City News*, June 10, 1876, p. 5, reported that the Oddfellows Lodge was in charge of the funeral service for Alderman John Aling at Second [Hope] Reformed Church.

delegates traveled to Holland to see Hope College and to take a large offering of $3100 to build a home for the president of the college.[50]

In spite of repeated attempts to get the General Synod to change its mind, the focus of classical action was now simply to prevent wholesale secession of RCA churches and members to the CRC. At the October 21, 1881, session of the Classis of Holland, the majority of members in the churches of Saugatuck and East Saugatuck, led by the Reverend John C. Groeneveld, left the RCA.[51] Classis met repeatedly that fall to stanch the exodus of members from the RCA: September 7, 1881; October 21, 1881; November 2, 1881; and November 16–18, 1881. At the November 16 meeting, the classis resolved once again to admit no Masons to membership in the classis but also resolved to stay with the RCA.[52] Yet at the same time the classis expressed its deep disappointment that the General Synod had not spoken more plainly on the "sinfulness of Freemasonry."

The next three sessions of the classis were occupied with Groeneveld's trial on the charge of schism. At the meeting of January 18, 1882, he was suspended by the narrow vote of 9 to 8![53] This vote must be interpreted as a protest against the action of the General Synod. Keppel and the Reverend Adrian Zwemer, who had risen to leadership in the classis, were among those who voted not to suspend Groeneveld. Here was a very divided classis; it was opposed to Masonry but barely had the heart to suspend a person who had seceded from the classis to demonstrate his dissatisfaction with synod's decision on Masonry.

After this vote, the Secession of 1882 began in earnest. At a meeting of the congregation of the Pillar Church on February 27, 1882, the congregation voted 86 to 18 to leave the RCA.[54] The Graafschap congregation and its minster, Zwemer, left the RCA on the next day. To deal with the schism, the classis called a meeting for March 1, 1882, at the Pillar Church, but when the members arrived at the First Reformed Church, Elder Keppel locked the church and refused the classis entrance. This was a harsh experience for a battered classis, but it was not so bad as the reports, in the *New York Sun* and *New York Herald*, that a major fracas had occurred at this church.[55] Instead, the classis adjourned peacefully and met at the nearby

---

50. Wichers, *Century of Hope*, pp. 112–113.

51. Minutes of the Classis of Holland, October 21, 1881, p. 469. East Saugatuck was called Fynaart at that period of time.

52. Minutes of the Classis of Holland, November 16, 1881, p. 493. Hope RCA of Holland was a member of the Classis of Michigan, however, and was not affected by the ban.

53. Minutes of the Classis of Holland, January 18, 1882, p. 532.

54. As reported to the Classis, Minutes of the Classis of Holland, March 1, 1882, pp. 545–548. First Church reported that a large majority of eighty-six men (since women did not have voting privileges at the time) approved breaking the ecclesiastical relationship with the Reformed Church. Eighteen men opposed the secession, but First Church consistory did not report this.

55. *The Banner of Truth*, the official publication of the True Reformed Dutch Church in New York and New Jersey, had little love, of course, for the RCA, but it did want to set the record straight: "The accounts which many, perhaps, have seen in the *Sun* and *Herald* of difficulties in the First Reformed

Third Reformed Church. A major concern was how to shepherd the small minority that wanted to continue the existence of the First Reformed Church congregation as an RCA Church.

The roll call of delegates for the March 1, 1882, meeting revealed a decimated classis. The stated clerk, Zwemer, had defected. Four congregations had seceded. Several churches were unrepresented. Yet one decision made at this unhappy session was to counsel the minority of the Pillar Church "not to resort to forcible seizure of the property." However, in the following year a legal battle was joined when the minority sued to regain the property of the church. The courts found against the minority, and thus the historic Pillar Church was lost to the RCA.[56] The minority then built a new building at the other corner of the same block on Ninth Street, but through the decades the cry has gone from one generation of RCA members to the next: "They stole our church!" The final blow came when the seceded congregation united with the CRC.[57] But after the loss of First Reformed Church, the worst was over, and the troubles subsided. The Secession of 1882 was over.

Certain conclusions can be drawn from the experience that the RCA had as a result of the Secession of 1882. Although the RCA leaders in the Midwest tended to minimize the effect of the 1882 secession,[58] it was far more hurtful and damaging to the RCA, especially its Dutch immigrant wing, than the 1857 secession had been. The most injurious aspect of the Secession of 1882 was that the RCA lost the recognition of the mother church in the Netherlands, the Christelijke Gereformeerde Kerk in Nederland (hereafter CGKN), out of which Van Raalte, Scholte, and so many of their followers had come. From 1850 on, the CGKN had given its blessing to the RCA and from 1857 to 1882, it had considered the CRC a dissident

---

Church of Holland, Mich., seems to have been exaggerated, and to be misunderstood by many—'A personal fist fight,' 'The Riot Act Read,' etc. The fact appears to be these: The members of that congregation at a public meeting, had voted 84 [sic] for and 18 against resigning their membership and connection with the Reformed Church. An extra Classis attempted to meet in the church-house, presumably to take possession and discipline the 84, among which were the consistory. The trustees refused to open the doors, and, of course, a crowd gathered around the grounds. After some wordy contention the Classis adjourned to another church to transact their business, and steps have been taken peaceably to effect the division of the church property. This is entirely distinct from the Christian or True Reformed Dutch Church in the West." *The Banner of Truth* 16 (1881/82):159.

56. The record of this lawsuit is in the Archives of the Netherlands Museum in Holland.

57. As bitter as the loss of the Pillar Church was to the RCA, the CRC gladly received that congregation into the fold. Beets, *Christian Reformed Church*, p. 81, ". . . last but not least [in the number of congregations which joined the CRC during the controversy] December 3, 1884, the First Church of Holland, Van Raalte's old congregation, with its monumental 'pillar church,' was joyfully received into the Christian Reformed fellowship."

58. Gerhard De Jonge, in his essay, "Secession Movements," wrote, "the movement was not a success," (p. 32) and "The addition of more than a thousand members [to the Christian Reformed Church] was not to be despised" (p. 33). This typed manuscript without any further information as to institution and date is in the Archives of Western Theological Seminary in Holland. In general, the essay is an excellent summary of the Secession of 1882.

group that had lacked sufficient reason for seceding in 1857. The Masonic controversy changed all that. In 1882, the Synod of the CGKN withdrew its blessing from the RCA and gave it to the CRC.[59] The long range effect of this action is incalculable, but it had to be considerable. After 1882, most of the new immigrants from the Netherlands joined the CRC instead of the RCA.[60]

The statistics of the CRC show the benefit of official recognition by the CGKN. In 1880, at the beginning of the Masonic controversy, the CRC had 4 classes, 12,201 members, 39 congregations, and 19 ministers. By 1890, it had grown to 7 classes, 37,834 members, 96 congregations, and 55 ministers. In 1900, the CRC numbered 144 congregations and 47,349 souls.

The CRC was clearly the beneficiary of the Secession of 1882. The RCA tended to minimize the rush of members to the CRC; Gerhard De Jonge, a leading RCA minister, concluded that only 1,000 members left the RCA, and RCA statistics for the Synod of Chicago show a net loss of 500 members between 1880 and 1884 when the great defections took place. The net loss appeared low because the RCA was also growing rapidly at this time, and its numerical recovery after the controversy was very rapid; and some members did return to the RCA, the most notable being Zwemer who brought his congregation back with him. But the direct membership loss of 1,000 adults actually represented many more people because non-communicant members are not included in this tally. In actuality, at least one-tenth of the membership of the Particular Synod of Chicago which represented the Classes of Michigan, Illinois, Holland, Grand River, and Wisconsin was lost during the bitter controversy. Classis of Holland alone had a loss of 1,622 persons between 1880 and 1884. Not many congregations left *en masse* as did First of Holland, East Saugatuck, Saugatuck, Fourth of Grand Rapids, and Graafschap, but eleven new CRC congregations were organized from individual members who left various RCA churches: Second of Grand Haven; North Street of Zeeland; Montague; Drenthe; Zutphen; Beaverdam; Fremont I; Spring Lake; Harderwijk of Holland; Overisel; and Alto, Wisconsin.[61] Of the ministers who left the RCA, the greatest loss was the Reverend Lammert J. Hulst who led the majority of members out of the Fourth Reformed Church in Grand Rapids and into the newly organized congregation of Coldbrook. By 1884, he was president

59. Beets, *Christian Reformed Church in North America*, p. 79.

60. Elton J. Bruins, "Immigration," in *Piety and Patriotism*, Bicentennial Studies of the Reformed Church in America, 1776–1976, ed. James W. Van Hoeven, The Historical Series of the Reformed Church in America, 4 (Grand Rapids: Eerdmans, 1976), pp. 70–71; Beets, *Christian Reformed Church in North America*, p. 73, mentioned that 85,517 Netherlanders came to North America between 1880 and 1900. The RCA statistics are found in the *Acts RCA 1880*, p. 532 and the *Acts* and Proceedings of the Seventy-eighth Regular Session of the General Synod of the Reformed Church in America, convened at Grand Rapids, Michigan, June, 1884 (New York: Board of Publication of the Reformed Church in America, 1884), p. 499.

61. Beets, *Christian Reformed Church in North America*, pp. 77–79.

of the Synod of the CRC and later the editor of *De Wachter*, the official publication of the CRC.[62]

It is also clear that if the CRC had not been organized in 1857, it would have been organized in 1882. By 1882 it was no longer possible to avoid a definite decision about what adaptation could be made to the American scene. The CRC insisted that its policy was the safest and purest. Americanization was to be resisted as much as possible in denominational life. It saw accommodation to the American scene as a threat to its doctrinal position and its purity as a denomination.[63] The Masonic controversy clearly demonstrated to the CRC that the RCA had failed to remain a pure church and that the Dutch immigrant congregations had compromised their souls by remaining with the RCA. Schism was clearly justified. Those in the RCA who regarded schism as the greater sin made their peace with the RCA and stayed within it. In spite of his leadership of the anti-Masonic faction of the RCA, Karsten never seceded, nor did the congregations he served in Wisconsin. Karsten and people like him stayed with the RCA grudgingly, for they could not see their way to schism. The Dutch immigrant churches which stayed with the RCA had Van Raalte on their side, and in time they had the great Reformed Church leader in the Netherlands, Abraham Kuyper, on their side, for in the 1890s, Kuyper adopted a position on Masonry similar to Van Raalte's.[64]

After 1882, the RCA in the Middle West was forced to take another look at the young CRC which was now developing into a sturdy denomination and demanding at least a grudging respect. Bitterness between the two denominations endured well into the twentieth century, and ill feeling is still not entirely overcome, but the dissident group of 1857 now had to be regarded a full-fledged denomination in the very areas where the RCA had held sway, for in nearly every Dutch immigrant community in the Middle West a CRC was erected, often only a short distance from the RCA and vice versa. After the Secession of 1882, the RCA took a self-congratulatory view toward the CRC, noting that the people who left the RCA brought new ideas and fresh air into the CRC and crediting the new members from the RCA with reviving the Sunday school and the cause of missions in the CRC.[65]

62. Jacob G. Vanden Bosch, "Lammert Jan Hulst," *The Reformed Journal* 7 (December 1957):17–21.

63. See Henry Zwaanstra, *Reformed Thought and Experience in a New World*, A Study of the Christian Reformed Church and Its American Environment 1890–1918 (Kampen: J. H. Kok, 1973), for a thorough and scholarly discussion of the question of how the CRC handled the Americanization process during that period. The work by John H. Kromminga, *The Christian Reformed Church*, A Study in Orthodoxy (Grand Rapids: Baker, 1949), is equally helpful on this subject.

64. Zwaanstra, *Reformed Thought and Experience*, p. 8.

65. One could expect such a chauvinistic attitude from someone in the RCA like Gerhard de Jonge, "Secession Movement," p. 33, who said, "Best of all, the new blood that entered the Christian Reformed Church in 1882, became the cause of liberation from the bondage of a sickly conservatism. Then their Sunday Schools began, then the spirit of Missions began to work, then higher education took its start. Then that Church began to be more liberal, lost its clannish exclusivism. Why the influx of the seceders

Overall, the Secession of 1882 made clear the direction both churches were going to take. The RCA in the Middle West despised Masonry but hated schism more. It would declare an uneasy peace with the denomination it had joined in 1850 yet forge ahead, hoping that more Dutch immigrants would join it but certainly continuing the process of Americanization as rapidly as feasible despite the even more rapid loss of many Dutch-minded members. The CRC had finally won a place in the sun, and its future was assured. It now had its own school, its own publication, *De Wachter*, and a clear, set policy for all Dutch immigrants; it would clearly carry out the policies of the CGKN and adapt to the American way in a manner that would not endanger its doctrinal and ecclesiastical purity.[66]

---

of 1882 has all but swept away, every ground on which the secession of 1857 rested, and transformed that to such an extent that the fathers would not be able to recognize their church in the church of today." Beets, *Christian Reformed Church*, p. 81, essentially agreed with De Jonge: "This accession [of 1882] . . . meant the infusion into the denominational body of precious life blood, that of a progressive element, with broader vision than some of the people of the older organization had ever had."

66. Other useful works on the Masonic controversy and the Secession of 1882 are: *The Christian Intelligencer*, the official publication of the Reformed Church; Henry E. Dosker, "In Memorian," in Nicholas H. Dosker, *De Hollandsche Gereformeerde Kerk in Amerika* (Nijmegen: P. J. Milborn, 1888), pp. vii–xv. The material in the book was first published chapter by chapter in *De Hope* after the secession from July 1882 to May 1884; Roelof T. Kuiper, *A Voice from America about America* (Grand Rapids: Eerdmans, 1970); The personal papers of Albertus Pieters and John H. Karsten in the Archives of Western Theological Seminary in Holland.

4

The Ecclesiastical Struggles of the Rilland and Crook Christian Reformed Churches in Colorado in 1893

A History

Peter De Klerk

In the summer of 1892 De Nederlandsch-Amerikaansche Land-en Emigratie-Maatschappij (hereafter NALEM), located in Utrecht, Domsteeg 8, issued a well-written and persuasive brochure entitled *De Emigratie van Landbouwers naar Noord-Amerika*, promoting emigration, especially of farmers and laborers, to the San Luis Valley, Colorado, North America.[1] The prevalent depressed economic conditions in the Netherlands that year resulted in a meager livelihood for farmers and laborers,[2] hence there was a great interest[3] in the NALEM brochure when it was offered as early as July 1892 through advertisements[4] in Christian daily and weekly newspapers. The brochure, among other things, described the San Luis Valley (where NALEM had bought 15,000 acres of land with an option to buy

---

1. *De Emigratie van Landbouwers naar Noord-Amerika, San Luis Vallei, Staat Colorado* [Utrecht: De Nederlandsch-Amerikaansche Land- en Emigratie-Maatschappij, 1892].
2. Jan van Boven, "De Emigratie van Landbouwers naar Noord-Amerika," *De Oranjevaan* 12 (23 Juli 1892):1.
3. *De Protestantsche Noordbrabanter* 14 (1 October 1892):2 (News item).
4. Advertisements offering the brochure were found in several daily and weekly newspapers, e.g., *De Oranjevaan* 12 (23 Juli 1892):4; *De Protestantsche Noordbrabanter* 13 (6 Augustus 1892):1; *De Standaard* 21 (15 Augustus 1892):4. There were eighteen advertisements placed in *De Standaard* between August 15, 1892, and January 16, 1893.

30,000 more)[5] as very fertile.[6] Through hard work in the first few years, the farmers could earn enough money, it said, to pay all their annual obligations and still have some cash left at the end of the year.[7]

On August 17, 1892, NALEM was incorporated as a limited company within the laws of the Kingdom of the Netherlands by Frederik C. P. Boterhoven de Haan, notary, who resided in Amsterdam.[8] Albertus Zoutman, 21 years old, is reported to have bought 375,000 guilders' worth of shares in the company,[9] and he seemed to have been the prime mover in its establishment.[10] Zoutman, however, is not known to have been a rich man, was often penniless, and frequently had to borrow money.[11] He spent about half a year during 1891 in Denver on account of his health and during his second stay there in 1892 he visualized the emigration of Hollanders to the San Luis Valley.[12] His persuasiveness enabled him to recruit some genteel persons as officers of this company, though they had not the vaguest notion as to what emigration demanded, and knew even less about farming. But the names of these "well-known" officers served as an effective cover, and Zoutman made good use of them.[13] The incorporation papers of NALEM list three prominent officers on the Board of Directors: as president, Maarten Noordtzij, Professor of Semitic languages in the Theologische School at Kampen; as secretary, Karel de Vidal St. Germain, Superintendent of the Municipal Buildings in Kampen; and Jan de Boer, landowner and assessor of the Township of Almkerk. The real power of NALEM, however, resided in Zoutman, manager and authorized agent in Colorado; the other manager, Pieter T. Dekker, was in charge of the Utrecht office.[14] The brochure included the names of the two other executives of NALEM: Cornelis W. Van der Hoogt, who was entrusted with the supervision and control over management of NALEM, and Willem C. Van Dusseldorp, in charge of the corporation's office of information in Alamosa, Colorado.[15]

5. "Statuten der Naamlooze Vennootschap: Nederlandsch-Amerikaansche Land- en Emigratie-Maatschappij" *Nederlandsche Staats-Courant*, 8 September 1892, pp. [6–8]; *Emigratie van Landbouwers naar Noord-Amerika*, pp. 5–6; "Hollanders reach Alamosa" *The Denver Republican*, December 1, 1892, p. 2.

6. *Emigratie van Landbouwers naar Noord-Amerika*, p. 5.

7. Ibid., pp. 32–33.

8. "Statuten der Naamlooze Vennootschap," pp. [6–8].

9. Ibid.

10. "Emigratie III," *De Protestantsche Noordbrabanter* 13 (17 September 1892):1; *The Antonito Ledger* 1 (December 17, 1892):4 (News item).

11. "Boldest of Swindles," *The Denver Republican*, December 12, 1892, pp. 1–2.

12. This information is based on the annotations made by Gijsbert van Tienhoven, Minister of Foreign Affairs of the Netherlands.

13. Jan van Boven, *De Eerste Hollandsche Nederzetting in Colorado*, en het Optreden der Nederlandsch-Amerikaansche Land- en Emigratie-Maatschappij van Nabij Beschouwd (Utrecht: H. Honig, 1893), pp. 2–3.

14. "Statuten der Naamlooze Vennootschap," pp. [6–8].

15. *Emigratie van Landbouwers naar Noord-Amerika*, p. i.

About thirty families and thirty-three single persons[16] (totaling about two hundred men, women and children) were the first to respond to the NALEM promotion advocating the start of a new life in the San Luis Valley. This first group boarded the steamship "Dubbeldam" in Amsterdam on November 12, 1892. Their expectations for this dreamland were at a high pitch, for Zoutman and Van der Hoogt had heightened their excitement on every possible occasion.[17] Their excitement about their new environment was further promoted on their arrival in Alamosa on November 30, 1892. The citizens of this city had prepared a lavish meal for them, a welcome respite after their long journey.[18] Having stayed overnight in several municipal buildings in Alamosa and at the homes of citizens, the Hollanders on the morning of December 1, 1892, took a special train[19] to their final destination, a place known as Willis Switch, four or five miles west of Alamosa. Here two hastily and poorly constructed wooden buildings, each measuring 36 x 60 feet and two stories high, had been erected to house the two hundred persons.[20] The flimsy condition of these homes, along with the poor quality of the soil and other such circumstances, brought home to the immigrants the stark and painful reality that the dazzling prospects described in the brochure were directly opposed to the facts. First, the brochure described the region as "the Italy of western North America,"[21] with comfortable summers and winters, never too warm nor too cold.[22] The truth was otherwise. On the night of December 8, 1892, the thermometer measured 18°F and -30°F on December 17.[23] Second, the brochure indicated that NALEM had bought land in the blooming State of Colorado under the most favorable circumstances and only after a long, precise, and expert investigation.[24] Upon arrival in the San Luis Valley the immigrants learned that NALEM had only an option to buy the 15,000 acres which it had claimed to have bought from the Empire Land and Canal Company (hereafter ELaCaC),[25] of which Theodore C. Henry was president. It had deposited $1,000 for these acres with Stuart O. Henry, Theodore's brother, in Paris on August 1, 1892.[26] The second payment of $5,000 had fallen due on

---

16. See Appendix for their names under the ship "Dubbeldam."

17. Cornelius A. Sluijs, "Brieven uit Amerika," *Enkhuizer Courant* 23 (28 December 1892):2–3.

18. Cornelius A. Sluijs, "Brieven uit Amerika," *Enkhuizer Courant* 23 (30 December 1892):2; Bastiaan Van der Wel, "Een Brief," *De Protestantsche Noordbrabanter* 14 (31 December 1892):2–3.

19. "The Dutch Have Come," *The Alamosa Independent-Journal* 8 (December 1, 1892):3.

20. "Hollanders Arrive in Alamosa," *The Antonito Ledger* 1 (December 3, 1892):4; Samuel Hartog, "Uit Colorado," *De Grondwet* 33 (7 Maart 1893):10.

21. *Emigratie van Landbouwers naar Noord-Amerika,* p. 8.

22. Ibid., p. 7.

23. "Boldest of Swindles," pp. 1–2; Van Boven, *Eerste Hollandsche Nederzetting in Colorado,* pp. 12–13.

24. *Emigratie van Landbouwers naar Noord-Amerika,* pp. 5–6.

25. Van Boven, *Eerste Hollandsche Nederzetting in Colorado,* pp. 19–20.

26. "Verslag van de Buitengewone Vergadering van Aandeelhouders en Commissarissen der Ned. Amer. Land- en Emigratie-Maatschappij te Utrecht den 23 Feb. '93, met Verkort Rapport van Prof. Noordzij [sic] over Zijn Verrichten in Noord-Amerika" *De Hope* 27 (19 April 1893):6; "Boldest of Swindles," pp. 1–2.

December 1, 1892, but had not been paid when the immigrants arrived in the valley.[27] It also became known that NALEM intended to sell the land for $26.00 per acre, which it had bought for $11.25 per acre.[28] Third, the brochure described that only cultivated land had been bought so the farmers could count on a good crop in the first year.[29] Actually many sections of land were still prairie and much of it unsuitable for cultivation because of the hilly condition of the land.[30] Fourth, the brochure claimed that all the vegetables of Europe could be raised in the valley, but in fact the short growing season and cold nights of the valley made the farming of such tender vegetables impossible.[31] Fifth, many families had been privately assured by Zoutman and Van der Hoogt that homes would be ready for occupation upon their arrival. Only two small homes were available for immediate occupancy, while all the other families had to stay in the two newly erected buildings.[32] These very drafty and uncomfortable structures[33] soon became known as the "Emigrant Houses."

Providing for the daily needs of close to two hundred persons requires a good deal of planning and supervision. Such planning was absent. Meals were not ready on time or not available at all; drinking water was scarce—if available. These deficiencies only aggravated the already tense situation brought on by the unhappy predicament in which the immigrants found themselves. They were also in a foreign country whose language they could neither speak nor understand. Everything had sounded so beautiful back in the Netherlands, but now they felt swindled, robbed, and betrayed.[34]

In addition, the immigrants lacked a spiritual leader to guide and help them through this difficult and troublesome period. It had, however, been reported that it was NALEM's intention to take a pastor along to minister to them during their voyage and their stay in the San Luis Valley. The Reverend Kornelis van Goor of Gorinchem was requested to shepherd the Hollanders to and in their new abode. Since van Goor felt that the request had not come through the proper ecclesiastical channels, and was therefore not an official, ecclesiastically correct call, he declined it.[35] The need for a pastor was probably more acutely felt when scarlet fever and diphtheria

---

27. "Boldest of Swindles," pp. 1–2; Van Boven, *Eerste Hollandsche Nederzetting in Colorado*, p. 37.
28. "Boldest of Swindles," pp. 1–2; Van Boven, *Eerste Hollandsche Nederzetting in Colorado*, pp. 25–26.
29. *Emigratie van Landbouwers naar Noord-Amerika*, p. 6; Van Boven, *Eerste Hollandsche Nederzetting in Colorado*, p. 21.
30. *Emigratie van Landbouwers naar Noord-Amerika*, p. 6; Van Boven, *Eerste Hollandsche Nederzetting in Colorado*, p. 20.
31. *Emigratie van Landbouwers naar Noord-Amerika*, p. 6; Van Boven, *Eerste Hollandsche Nederzetting in Colorado*, p. 21.
32. *Emigratie van Landbouwers naar Noord-Amerika*, p. 6; Van Boven, *Eerste Hollandsche Nederzetting in Colorado*, p. 21.
33. "Een Brief" *Middelburgsche Courant*, 20 Januari 1893, p. 1.
34. Van Boven, *Eerste Hollandsche Nederzetting in Colorado*, pp. 11–15.
35. "De Nieuwe Hollandsche Kolonie in Colorado," *De Grondwet* 33 (27 December 1892):1.

broke out in the Emigrant Houses, mostly among the children. Eleven of these children succumbed to these diseases by the middle of January, 1893.[36] It was with good reason that Maude Ermine Eubank, the nurse who assisted Dr. Jonathan Gale in caring for the sick, wrote: "They [i.e., the immigrants in the Emigrant Houses] were packed in these rooms like sardines in a box."[37] It is therefore understandable that under these conditions contagious diseases continued to spread rapidly until the sick were finally quarantined in railroad cars.[38]

In spite of the fact that no minister was present to give guidance and to preach to them, the colonists, faithful to their tradition, held two worship services in the Emigrant Houses on their first Sunday in their new fatherland, the fourth of December, 1892.[39] Both morning and evening services were held under the leadership of Arnaud J. Van Lummel, one of the colonists. In the morning service he exhorted on the words found in Joshua 24:15, ". . . choose for yourselves this day whom you will serve, whether the gods your forefathers served beyond the River, or the gods of the Amorites, in whose land you are living. But as for me and my household, we will serve the Lord" (NIV).[40] When there were no classical appointments, Van Lummel, who later was elected elder and clerk of the Rilland Christian Reformed Church (hereafter CRC), continued to exhort the colonists in the morning worship services[41] until he left the colony in August, 1893.[42] At the second worship services, which were later held in the afternoon instead of in the evening, the catechism sermons of George F. Gezelle Meerburg were read by either Lambertus Verburg or Harm Mulder, both of whom later became elders in the Rilland CRC.[43]

In the afternoon of December 4, Van der Hoogt conducted a Sunday school for the children in the Emigrant Houses.[44] After the evening worship service, a meeting for all the men of the colony was called. At this meeting two committees were appointed: the first to look into the formation of a church, and the second to work toward the establishment of a Christian school with Feike Zijlstra, one of the colonists, as its teacher.[45] With regard to the formation of a church, Andries Hof, one of the colonists and later an elder and clerk of the Bethel CRC of Crook, Colorado, recalled that Van der Hoogt had related to them his correspondence with the Reverend

36. Van Boven, *Eerste Hollandsche Nederzetting in Colorado*, p. 51.
37. Maude Ermine Eubank, "An Interesting Letter," *The Alamosa Independent-Journal* 8 (January 19, 1893):3.
38. *The Denver Republican*, December 21, 1892, p. 6 (News item).
39. "De Eerste Indrukken in de San Louis Vallei" *De Zeeuw* 7 (2 Januari 1893):1.
40. Peter G. Vos, "Een Brief," *De Protestantsche Noordbrabanter* 14 (31 December 1892):2–3.
41. Rilland CRC, Notulen van de Kerkeraadsvergadering van 10 Februari 1893.
42. *The Alamosa Independent-Journal* 9 (September 21, 1893):5 (News item).
43. Rilland CRC, Notulen van de Kerkeraadsvergadering van 10 Februari 1893.
44. Vos, "Brief," pp. 2–3.
45. "Eerste Indrukken in de San Louis Vallei," p. 1.

Rense H. Joldersma, Superintendent of Western Missions of the Reformed Church in America (hereafter RCA), who was thinking of coming to the colony and eventually organizing a Reformed Church. Some of the colonists objected to this procedure. They wanted to know a little more about this church before they would join it. Van der Hoogt countered that several ministers of the Christelijke Gereformeerde Kerk in Nederland were serving in the RCA, and he saw no reason, therefore, for the colonists' hesitation. When the colonists suggested affiliation with the CRC, Van der Hoogt steered the conversation either back to the RCA or the Presbyterian Church, for he did not want to have anything to do with the CRC.[46]

No evidence exists that Joldersma ever paid the colonists in the San Luis Valley a visit. He himself admitted that he shied away from visiting them on account of the difficulties that had arisen between NALEM and ELaCaC.[47] The distressing events concerning the colonists were reported in many American newspapers. These circumstances may not have stirred the heart of Joldersma, but they did move the Reverend Arie J. Vanden Heuvel of the Rotterdam (now Dispatch) CRC in Kansas when he read about it in the papers. He promptly related his concern about the welfare of the colonists in a letter and offered any material assistance that was needed.[48] Jan Van Boven, who accompanied the colonists in order to form an impartial opinion about the suitability of the valley for emigration and to report his findings to NALEM in Utrecht,[49] received Vanden Heuvel's letter on December 31, 1892. Van Boven, deeply moved with the sympathy expressed in this letter, answered Vanden Heuvel that, since the writing of the newspaper reports, the situation in the colony was much improved. He was able to report that the sick were on their way to recovery and that the colonists were settled on land of much better quality than that offered by NALEM. But he also said that additional aid was required.[50] With Van Boven's letter in hand, the consistory of the Rotterdam CRC called a congregational meeting on Thursday, January 5, 1893, to consider what kind of ministry they could provide to the colonists in the San Luis Valley. When the letter was read at this meeting, it was decided to forward it to the Home Missions Board of the CRC. Vanden Heuvel's request that he be allowed to go to the colony was denied.[51] Four days later the consistory of Rotterdam CRC overturned the decision of the congregation and permitted Vanden Heuvel to go to the San Luis Valley but with the understanding that the Home Missions Board would bear the accrued expenses. The consistory also

46. Andries J. Hof, "De Kolonie in Crook, Colorado," *De Grondwet* 33 (22 Augustus 1893):5.

47. Rense H. Joldersma, "Een Bezoek aan de Hollanders in Logan Co., Colorado," *De Hope* 27 (12 April 1893):5.

48. Van Boven, *Eerste Hollandsche Nederzetting in Colorado*, pp. 62–63.

49. Jan van Boven, "Colorado," *De Zeeuw* 7 (25 Maart 1893):5.

50. Van Boven, *Eerste Hollandsche Nederzetting in Colorado*, pp. 62–63.

51. Dispatch CRC, Notulen van de Gemeente Vergadering van 5 Januari 1893.

judged that Van Boven's letter should not be forwarded to the Home Missions Board.[52] A special relationship between the colonists and Vanden Heuvel began with this, his first visit to Colorado. He showed himself to be a faithful servant who was able to comfort and proclaim the Word of God to the people.[53] He also became a sounding board for many of the colonists, and in this way, was able to resolve many problems and difficulties.[54]

Vanden Heuvel arrived in Alamosa on January 18, 1893, for a three-week stay and was greeted at the railroad station by Van Dusseldorp, an old friend from the Netherlands. On their way to the Empire Farm, where the colonists had bought land, about six or seven miles south of Alamosa, Vanden Heuvel was asked to conduct a worship service that evening.[55] The service was to be held in a white schoolhouse which formed the center for the colonists of the Empire Farm. This schoolhouse, with its little steeple and slanted roof, served as the group's place of worship, and later as the Christian school building.[56] The evening in the schoolhouse began with a time of fellowship, followed by reports on their unfortunate situation and a discussion of their future as colonists, as well as their church relationship. So much other business demanded attention, that Vanden Heuvel never did get around to conducting the evening worship![57] Van Boven was present at this gathering, though the next day he intended to return to the Netherlands via Minnesota and Michigan, where he wanted to visit relatives and friends.[58] He read a letter from Joldersma in which the latter offered his ministerial services. Naturally, the discussion soon centered on the question as to which denomination to affiliate with, and whether they wanted to be organized as a congregation. The pros and cons of the RCA and the CRC were discussed. Some said that Noordtzij had advised several of the colonists to affiliate with the RCA. This had also been the recommendation of Vander Hoogt. Since the colonists of the Empire Farm had lost respect for Noordtzij, the question of denominational affiliation received very close scrutiny. No final decision about affiliation was made at this meeting, however.[59]

The next afternoon, a memorial service was held for the eleven children who had died of scarlet fever and diphtheria in the latter part of December, 1892, and in the early part of January, 1893, and for the elderly grandmother, Johanna Ballast, who died soon after her arrival in the San Luis Valley. The sermon text which Vanden Heuvel chose for this special service

52. Dispatch CRC, Notulen van de Kerkeraadsvergadering van 9 Januari 1893.
53. Van Boven, *Eerste Hollandsche Nederzetting in Colorado*, p. 63.
54. Arie J. Vanden Heuvel, "Onze Gemeente Rilland," *De Wachter* 25 (8 Februari 1893):3.
55. Ibid.
56. Samuel Hartog, "Brieven uit Colorado," *De Zeeuw* 7 (30 September 1893):1.
57. Vanden Heuvel, "Onze Gemeente Rilland," p. 3.
58. Ibid.; *San Luis Valley Courier* 4 (January 21, 1893):1 (News item).
59. Vanden Heuvel, "Onze Gemeente Rilland," p. 3.

was Ecclesiastes 12:5a, "When men are afraid of heights and of dangers in the street" (NIV).[60]

A few days later, on Saturday afternoon, January 20, 1893, a public meeting was called in the schoolhouse to discuss further with which denomination to affiliate. In order to make the decisions of this assembly binding, Vanden Heuvel suggested the election of a president and secretary. Those present elected Vanden Heuvel as president and Douwe Sjaardema, a colonist, as secretary. Only two main items were on the agenda: first, the question whether to organize a congregation, and second, with which denomination to affiliate. Without a dissenting vote the first question was answered in the affirmative. With one dissenting vote, but without any discussion, the colonists of the Empire Farm decided to affiliate with the CRC. A letter requesting the Classical Committee of Classis Iowa of the CRC for permission to organize as a congregation was drawn up at this meeting and mailed. Furthermore, three trustees were instructed to structure the congregation according to the laws of the State of Colorado. It was also decided to name the congregation the "Rilland Christian Reformed Church." Rilland was the name of the town where Van Boven was born and had lived, and so the church's name honored the man who had done so much for the colonists in their first days in Colorado. The name *Rilland* won out over the name *Utrecht*, the city where NALEM had its headquarters.[61]

The next day, Sunday, Vanden Heuvel preached twice in the schoolhouse for the colonists, who felt a real need for the preaching of God's Word. Their departure from the Old Country, their shattered dreams of an assured and promising future in North America, and their loved ones torn from their hearts by death, made the colonists' desire more than ever to hear and to listen to the proclamation of the Word.[62] Vanden Heuvel preached again for them on Thursday afternoon, January 26, 1893.[63] While Vanden Heuvel waited for word of confirmation from the Classical Committee for the organization of the Rilland congregation, he visited and talked with the colonists of the Empire Farm.[64] Noordtzij showed appreciation for the work that Vanden Heuvel was doing among the colonists on the Empire Farm, even though he criticized him for not showing any concern for those who were left in the Emigrant Houses.[65]

Vanden Heuvel announced during the Thursday afternoon service that there would be another public meeting on Saturday, January 28, 1893, to discuss further several ecclesiastical matters. This turned out to be a really

60. Ibid.
61. Rilland CRC, Notulen van de Openbare Vergadering van 20 Januari 1893.
62. Vanden Heuvel, "Onze Gemeente Rilland," p. 3.
63. Arie J. Vanden Heuvel, "Rilland," *De Wachter* 26 (1 Maart 1893):3.
64. Vanden Heuvel, "Onze Gemeente Rilland," p. 3.
65. *The Alamosa Independent-Journal* 8 (January 26, 1893):3 (New item).

lively meeting. While the meeting (again held in the schoolhouse) was in session and chaired by Vanden Heuvel, representatives of NALEM, such as Noordtzij, Vander Hoogt and Zoutman, with their lawyer, H. E. Luthe, disrupted the deliberations of the colonists of the Empire Farm by entering the schoolhouse.[66] The previous day these men had returned from a visit to the Platte Valley in Northeastern Colorado, where they had bought 32,000 acres of land.[67] Their sole purpose in being present was to persuade as many Empire Farm colonists as possible to go with them to the Platte Valley. The dialogue of the advantages and disadvantages must have been a very lively one, for the colonists of the Empire Farm, due to their past experiences with NALEM, did not trust the promises of these representatives anymore, and they made that known.[68] The question of ecclesiastical affiliation must also have entered the conversation with Noordtzij. Vanden Heuvel probably confronted Noordtzij as to why he had recommended to several colonists that they join the RCA instead of the CRC, since Vanden Heuvel brought up the whole question of Freemasonry in the RCA with Noordtzij.[69] Noordtzij, although he was against Freemasonry, admitted that he had never thought much about Freemasonry when he was in Colorado. He also more or less denied that he had recommended that the colonists join the RCA rather than the CRC.[70] This was hotly contested by Vanden Heuvel and others.[71] Interestingly, *The Alamosa Independent-Journal,* a weekly, printed an extract of a letter of Noordtzij in which he said: "That we have not neglected the spiritual welfare of our people is evident from the fact that last November Mr. Vander Hoogt requested Reverend Jolgersma [sic] of the Dutch Reform [sic] Church to charge himself with the spiritual interests of our people."[72]

Noordtzij and associates continued their conversations with several families the next day, and were able to persuade five more families along with a few bachelors, to go with those who were still in the Emigrant Houses to the Platte Valley.[73] Vanden Heuvel expressed his indignation that they had to do this business on the Sabbath day, for he had missed several of these families in the worship services that day.[74] The colonists of the Emigrant

---

66. Vanden Heuvel, "Rilland," p. 3; "Hollanders' Hegira," *San Luis Valley Courier* 4 (February 4, 1893):1.

67. *The Alamosa Independent-Journal* 8 (February 2, 1893):3 (News item); "The Dutch Colony," *The Denver Republican,* January 29, 1893, p. 8.

68. Vanden Heuvel, "Rilland," p. 3.

69. Maarten Noordtzij, "WEw. Heer K[laas] Kuiper," *De Bazuin* 41 (7 April 1893):3; also in *De Wachter* 26 (3 Mei 1893):1.

70. Ibid.

71. Vanden Heuvel, "Onze Gemeente Rilland," p. 3; Evert Bos, "Een en Ander," *De Wachter* 26 (1 Maart 1893):1–2.

72. *The Alamosa Independent-Journal* 8 (January 26, 1893):3 (News item).

73. Vanden Heuvel, "Rilland," p. 3.

74. Ibid.

Houses left the Alamosa area for the Crook region by train on Tuesday, January 31, 1893.[75]

Feeling content that NALEM was still alive, Noordtzij departed for the Netherlands, arriving in Kampen on March 1, 1893.[76] He regretted that his teaching duties in the Theologische School at Kampen prevented him from staying any longer in North America. Moreover, he had to skip a visit to Grand Rapids, Michigan, where he intended, as he wrote, "to press the brethren there a warm hand."[77] But "the brethren there" were somewhat perturbed that he had not visited Western Michigan while he was in North America.[78]

Vanden Heuvel's departure from the San Luis Valley was drawing near. The Rotterdam CRC consistory had given him permission to spend two Sundays in Rilland,[79] and it was now nearly three weeks that he had labored among the colonists. Since no communication had yet been received from the Classical Committee concerning the organization of a CRC congregation, and Vanden Heuvel could stay no longer to finalize it, another public meeting was held on February 6, 1893, to decide whether to continue making preparations for eventual organization or to make Rilland a home mission station. The latter option was chosen[80] and they proceeded with the election of elders and deacons. Chosen as elders were: Harm Mulder, Arnaud J. Van Lummel, and Lambertus Verburg; as deacons: Douwe Sjaardema and Jan Van Dalen.[81]

The long-awaited letter of the Classical Committee, with its approval to organize, finally came two days later, the day that Vanden Heuvel was going to preach his farewell sermon. Since most of the preliminary work had already been taken care of, it was only a matter of the installation of the three elders and two deacons to make the Rilland CRC a reality. The usual procedure of having the names of the candidates for elder and deacon announced in two previous worship services was waived so that Vanden Heuvel could install them into their offices. After he had preached the sermon, they were duly installed.[82] Vanden Heuvel's parting words were based on Mark 9:50, "Have salt in yourselves, and be at peace with each other" (NIV).[83] The consistory met immediately after the service to sign the "Eed Formulier" (Form of Subscription) and to elect a president (Lambertus Verburg) and a clerk (Arnaud J. Van Lummel).[84] And so Vanden

75. *The Alamosa Independent-Journal* 8 (February 2, 1893):3 (News item); "Hollanders' Hegira," p. 1.
76. Maarten Noordtzij, "Emigratie naar Noord-Amerika," *De Zeeuw* 7 (4 Maart 1893):2.
77. Noordtzij, "WEw. Heer K. Kuiper," p. 1.
78. Geert E. Boer, "Aan Mijn Vriend L. in Nederland," *De Wachter* 25 (22 Februari 1893):1.
79. Dispatch CRC, Notulen van de Kerkeraadsvergadering van 9 Januari 1893.
80. Rilland CRC, Notulen van de Openbare Vergadering van 6 Februari 1893; Hartog, "Uit Colorado," p. 10.
81. Rilland CRC, Notulen van de Openbare Vergadering van 6 Februari 1893.
82. Douwe Sjaardema, "Rilland, Conejos Co., Colorado," *De Wachter* 26 (1 Maart 1893):2.
83. Vanden Heuvel, "Rilland," p. 2.
84. Rilland CRC, Notulen van de Openbare Vergadering van 8 Februari 1893.

Heuvel's first stay in Rilland came to an end. In the three week period he conducted worship services, administered the Lord's Supper and baptism, held a memorial service, visited the bereaved and the needy, and organized a CRC congregation.

Another noteworthy event took place in Rilland on February 13, 1893, with the opening of the Christian school. As noted earlier, already on their first Sunday in the San Luis Valley the colonists had named a committee for the establishment of a Christian school with Feike Zijlstra as its teacher.[85] This dream was realized when Zijlstra was granted a temporary certificate by the county superintendent to teach[86] and the school was opened with an appropriate ceremony.[87] Since Zijlstra knew the English language reasonably well,[88] the pupils, about thirty-five in number,[89] were taught the various subjects in English.[90] Apparently Zijlstra was not only a likable person but also an excellent teacher, for the children enjoyed going to school.[91]

NALEM was unable to obtain a clear title to the land in the Alamosa area that it claimed to have bought from ELaCaC, since Henry, ELaCaC's president, wanted to make certain that the stock of NALEM was good before he would be willing to exchange ELaCaC stock for that of NALEM as a partial payment. He repeatedly requested the representatives of NALEM, Vander Hoogt and Zoutman, either to show their books, giving evidence that the $200,000, on which NALEM was capitalized, had been paid up or to prove that their stock was good.[92] The representatives of NALEM refused to comply with Henry's requests, claiming that he had no right to make such demands, for the contract with ELaCaC did not stipulate an investigation into the private affairs of NALEM.[93] Noordtzij, probably not having been told the true situation by his representatives, believed Henry to be a "scoundrel" and his company to be insolvent,[94] but while in Colorado he made no effort to see Henry at his Denver office to find out for himself what was wrong. He had been advised, however, to talk with Henry personally to learn first-hand the true state of affairs.[95] Noordtzij, not knowing the English language, could have talked with Henry through an interpreter. He had taken along an interpreter, Gerhard J. D. Aalders,[96] one of his

85. "Eerste Indrukken in de San Louis Vallei," p. 1.
86. "New Netherland Items," *San Luis Valley Courier* 5 (February 25, 1893):4.
87. *De Zeeuw* 7 (4 Maart 1893):1 (News item).
88. "Work for 500 Men," *The Rocky Mountain News*, December 27, 1892, p. 8.
89. "Brieven uit Colorado," *De Zeeuw* 7 (5 September 1893):2.
90. Hartog, "Brieven uit Colorado," p. 1.
91. Ibid.
92. "Boldest of Swindles," pp. 1–2.
93. Ibid.
94. "A Letter" dated January 1893 forwarded to Dr. Abraham Kuyper by Maarten Noordtzij from Denver, Colorado.
95. Van Boven, *Eerste Hollandsche Nederzetting in Colorado*, pp. 56–57.
96. "Investigating the Trouble," *The Alamosa Independent-Journal* 8 (January 12, 1893):4.

students, who had been a businessman in London before he enrolled in the Theologische School at Kampen.[97]

Noordtzij had arrived in Alamosa from the Netherlands on January 12, 1893.[98] After having acquainted himself for a few days with the situation in the colony, he left for Denver.[99] There he conferred with John P. Brockway, NALEM's attorney, and with David H. Waite, the Governor of Colorado, who was naturally concerned about the plight of the colonists. Waite suggested that there was plenty of government land available in the northeastern part of the state.[100] Being pleased with the climatic conditions and with the soil of Colorado, Noordtzij preferred to have a colony in this state rather than in any other.[101] A party of four, Noordtzij, Vander Hoogt, Zoutman[102] and a colonist from the Emigrant Houses, Cornelius A. Sluijs,[103] went to see the Platte Valley, which Waite had suggested as a possible settlement for the colonists.[104] There they investigated very carefully, as they had done in the San Luis Valley: soil, products, yield, prices, and the water canal with its reservoirs and its irrigation. From this investigation they decided that this location was a more suitable area to start a colony than the one in the San Luis Valley.[105] From a Denver syndicate NALEM bought 32,000 acres of land for $450,000[106] on January 26, 1893, and was given the right to possess it immediately, so that they could immediately start building homes and barns on the land.[107] After returning to Alamosa the next day, Noordtzij and company lobbied hard, contacting each family in the San Luis Valley personally and writing to those working in the mountains. They praised the Platte Valley over the San Luis Valley.[108] Without making the necessary provisions for lodging, thirteen families and a few young men[109] left by a special train for Crook on January 31, 1893. The fare was paid for by NALEM.[110]

The new colonists from the Netherlands were also now directed to the Platte Valley instead of the San Luis Valley.[111]

97. Gerhard Ch. Aalders, "Ds. Gerhard Jean Daniel Aalders (17 Juni 1855–8 September 1926)," in *Jaarboekje Ten Dienste van de Gereformeerde Kerken in Nederland 1927* (Goes: Oosterbaan & Le Cointre, 1927), pp. 353–355.

98. "Investigating the Trouble," p. 4.

99. "President Noordtzy [sic] arrives," *San Luis Valley Courier* 4 (January 21, 1893):1.

100. "Verslag van de Buitengewone Vergadering van Aandeelhouders," p. 6.

101. "Mr. Nordtzy [sic] returns," *The Denver Republican*, January 19, 1893, p. 6.

102. "Dutch Colony," p. 8.

103. Cornelius A. Sluijs, "Brieven uit Amerika," *Enkhuizer Courant* 24 (17 Februari 1893):2–3.

104. "Verslag van de Buitengewone Vergadering van Aandeelhouders," p. 6.

105. Ibid.

106. "Dutch Colony," p. 8.

107. "Verslag van de Buitengewone Vergadering van Aandeelhouders," p. 6.

108. Ibid.

109. See Appendix for the persons who left for Crook. They are listed under the ship "Dubbeldam," and are identified by an asterisk.

110. "Verslag van de Buitengewone Vergadering van Aandeelhouders," p. 6.

111. See Appendix for those persons who arrived in Crook from the Netherlands.

With a population of about 175 persons, Crook did not have much extra housing space available, so the colonists from Alamosa had to stay in railroad cars owned by the Union Pacific and arranged on a side track.[112] Until suitable homes were located or new ones built, families remained in the railroad cars, some for a short time, others, for many weeks. Meals were prepared in one of the railroad cars which was outfitted with kitchen facilities.[113] By July, 1893, there were still about nine families who did not have a home of their own. Four lived together in one home; the rest lived with other families.[114] The dwellings of all of the colonists were spread over a large area, some of them as far away as Iliff, sixteen miles southwest, and others as far away as Red Lion, eight miles northeast of Crook.[115] During this period Zoutman, the manager, lived in a tent near the realroad station in Crook.[116] Vander Hoogt, on business in Grand Rapids, visited with Joldersma, the superintendent of Western Missions of the RCA. He again did his best to persuade Joldersma to organize a Reformed Church in Colorado, but now in Crook.[117] It took Joldersma another month to visit the colonists in Crook, and he preached for them on March 26 and Easter Sunday, April 2, 1893.[118] Not since their first weeks in Colorado, except for the Sunday in January, 1893, when Noordtzij had preached for them in the Emigrant Houses, had these colonists heard any preaching or received a visit from a minister.[119] It was, therefore, a blessed experience not only to listen to his preaching but also to talk directly with him.[120] On his way to the April meeting of the Iowa classis of the RCA, Joldersma pressed his cause hard, telling the colonists that if they would not sign now, they would have to wait until the September meeting of classis to get a petition for organization of a Reformed Church approved. He was able to secure the signatures of twenty-nine families.[121] A few of the colonists let it be known, however, that they were not in complete agreement with this action, and he must regard the petition null and void if they discovered that Joldersma's denomination was not the Reformed Church which acted in accordance with the Word of God and the three Forms of Unity[122] (the Belgic Confession, the Heidelberg Catechism, and the Canons of Dort).

112. "New Netherland Items," p. 4.
113. Maarten Noordtzij, "Waarde Redactie," *De Protestantsche Noordbrabanter* 14 (18 Maart 1893):3; Cornelius A. Sluijs, "Brieven uit Amerika," *Enkhuizer Courant* 24 (1 Maart 1893):2–3.
114. Andries J. Hof, "Aan Rev. C. Bode," *De Wachter* 26 (16 Augustus 1893):3.
115. Andries J. Hof, "Rev. C. Bode," *De Wachter* 26 (2 Augustus 1893):3.
116. This information is taken from the testimony of Cornelius J. Driscoll in the divorce proceedings of Neeltje Vander Hoogt Roest vs. Cornelis Willem Vander Hoogt in the District Court of Arapahoe County, State of Colorado. This testimony is dated November 9, 1893.
117. R. Kanters, "De Hollanders in Colorado," *De Hope* 27 (1 Maart 1893):8.
118. Cornelis W. Vander Hoogt, "Zeer Geachte Heer Kanters," *De Hope* 27 (12 April 1893):5.
119. Bastiaan Vander Wel, "Een Brief," *De Protestantsche Noordbrabanter* 14 (8 April 1893):4; Johannes De Kruijter, "Uit Crook, Colorado," *De Hope* 27 (19 April 1893):5.
120. Vander Hoogt, "Zeer Geachte Heer Kanters," p. 5; De Kruijter, "Uit Crook, Colorado," p. 5.
121. James F. Zwemer, "A Bit of History," *The Christian Intelligencer* 64 (1893):898.
122. Hof, "Kolonie in Crook," p. 5.

The March 29, 1893, issue of the weekly, *De Hope*,[123] in a way answered their concern, for it indicated that Freemasonry was not a censurable sin which they regarded as in diametrical opposition to the Word of God.[124] A visit by the Reverend Henry Bode, a classical home missionary of the CRC, gave the colonists a chance to ask him some questions and to hear the other side of the issues that concerned them. He had visited the colonists of the Empire Farm and also had preached for them on April 23, 1893. Since he was on his way to the Classis Iowa meeting of the CRC to be held in Orange City, Iowa, on May 2 and 3, 1893, he visited the colonists in the Crook area. On April 30, 1893, he preached for them and carried with him to the classis meeting a petition signed by the heads of twenty families requesting to be organized as a CRC congregation.[125] This was a second request for organization as a congregation, but the first to the CRC. Aware of their previous action, the colonists forwarded a letter to the Stated Clerk of Classis Iowa of the RCA, the Reverend James F. Zwemer, indicating that they were withdrawing their petition for organization as a congregation of the RCA.[126]

Classis Iowa of the RCA met in Pella, Iowa, on April 12 and 13, 1893, where the petition from the Crook colonists for the organization of a Reformed Church was received and approved. Upon the recommendation of the Committee of Church Extension, the Reverends Peter De Pree and Peter Lepeltak were appointed to visit the colonists at their earliest opportunity and to oversee their eventual ecclesiastical organization. By correspondence De Pree made arrangements with the leading parties at Crook that he would conduct religious services on Sunday, May 14, 1893. Lepeltak would join him on Wednesday, May 17, for the actual organization and would remain there through Sunday, May 21, to complete the organization.[127]

At the meeting of Classis Iowa of the CRC, Bode reported on his work as Home Missionary and about his recent visits to the Colonists on the Empire Farm (the Rilland CRC) and those in Crook. He also related to the ecclesiastical body the concerns of the Crook colonists about the visit of Joldersma, about the pressure he had put on the colonists to sign the petition, and about the withdrawal letter which the colonists had forwarded to Zwemer.[128] Then he presented to Classis the petition of the Crook colonists for organization as a Christian Reformed Church. This

123. "Dr. Kuypers Verklaring aangaande zijne Artikelen over Vrijmetselarij," *De Hope* 27 (29 Maart 1893):4.

124. Hof, "Kolonie in Crook," p. 5.

125. Ibid.

126. Ibid., "Classis Iowa" (RCA), *De Hope* 27 (3 Mei 1893):4.

127. Classis Iowa of the RCA, Minutes of September 13 and 14, 1893. See also De Pree's report in *The Christian Intelligencer* 64 (1893):898.

128. Henry Bode, "Nalezing," *De Wachter* 26 (4 October 1893):3; Classis Iowa of the CRC, Notulen van 3 en 4 Mei 1893.

petition was approved. The Reverend Evert Breen of the Firth CRC, Nebraska, was given full authorization by classis and appointed to go to Crook "as soon as possible" to organize the faithful there as a CRC congregation.[129]

The letter which the colonists of Crook had sent to Zwemer terminating the relationship with the RCA never reached De Pree. Unaware of what had happened in Crook in the meantime, he left his hometown, Pella, Iowa, for Crook on May 12, 1893, so that he could lead the Sunday services there and prepare the colonists for the organization of a Reformed Church as he had previously arranged.[130] Breen, following the instruction of Classis Iowa to go "as soon as possible" to Crook, was also on his way to fulfill his task. It so happened that Breen and De Pree, both on their way to Crook, met face to face on the train between Julesburg and Crook on Saturday, May 13, 1893. In his conversation with Breen, De Pree heard for the first time the turnabout that had taken place concerning ecclesiastical affiliation.[131]

Breen, who had traveled about 450 miles to get to Crook, conducted three worship services in one of the homes of the colonists on May 14, 1893. The following Wednesday, the same day that De Pree had planned to organize a Reformed Church, Breen organized the Bethel Christian Reformed Church of Crook. After the preaching of the sermon those present elected Kier Koster, Andries J. Hof, and Jan B. Walhof as elders, and Adriaan Gunst and Evert Ten Napel as deacons. The consistory elected Walhof as president, and Hof as clerk.[132] The next day the Bethel CRC was incorporated under the laws of the State of Colorado.[133]

After his encounter with Breen, De Pree continued his journey to Crook, and upon his arrival there the painful truth was confirmed by the nine heads of families who had not signed the second petition[134] and by others who rather "unceremoniously" informed him that the services of the RCA Classical Committee were no longer wanted.[135] That De Pree was an embittered man appeared in the way he pursued the matter. He gave two reasons why the change from the RCA to CRC had taken place. First, he branded Bode as "an intruder" in a field that already "through the voice of the people in fact" was surrendered to the RCA. Second, he labeled a letter from Professor Gerrit K. Hemkes, which he claimed had circulated among

---

129. Classis Iowa of the CRC, Notulen van 3 en 4 Mei 1893.

130. Peter De Pree, "De opbrekende Hollandsche Kolonie te Crook, in Colorado," *De Hope* 27 (2 Augustus 1893):1–2.

131. Ibid.

132. Evert Breen, "Onze Gemeente Bethel," *De Wachter* 26 (31 Mei 1893):2.

133. "Articles of Incorporation" of the HOLLAND CHRISTIAN REFORMED CHURCH dated May 18, 1893, filed with the County Clerk of Logan County, State of Colorado. The "Articles of Incorporation" were signed by Andries J. Hof, Dirk Swier, Kier Coster, Frederik Aué, Cornelis J. Kooiman, Adriaan Gunst, Rijk Van Voorst, Jacob Vander Klooster, Pieter Kragt, Willem H. Van Schooneveld, Leendert Van Staalduinen, Jan B. Walhof, Koop Drok, Evert Ten Napel, and Jan Van Wijk, Czoon.

134. De Pree, "Opbrekende Hollandsche Kolonie te Crook," pp. 1–2.

135. Classis Iowa of the RCA, Minutes of September 13 and 14, 1893.

the colonists, as "low, slanderous, and wicked."[136] This letter of Hemkes was by then in his hands. The circulation of Hemkes' letter among the colonists, as De Pree alleged, had been angrily disputed by Hof. He himself had never seen the letter, nor did he know which colonists had read it. He also felt, therefore, that Hemkes' letter had no calculable influence on the colonists' decision to join the CRC instead of the RCA, as De Pree had written.[137] The entire letter of Hemkes was subsequently published by De Pree with his comments,[138] and it was part of his report to the September meeting of Classis Iowa of the RCA.[139]

What had happened was that soon after the visit of Joldersma to the Crook area at the end of March and the beginning of April, the colonist Kier Koster (who had arrived there in March 1893 from the Netherlands and who had not signed the petition for the organization of a Reformed Church) had written a letter to his friend, J. Stevens, in Grand Rapids, requesting information about the RCA. Koster also asked Stevens to show his answer to a minister of the CRC and ask for his signature.[140] Stevens, an elder in Grandville Avenue CRC, asked Hemkes, Professor of Historical Theology in the Theological School at Grand Rapids, whether he would be willing to answer Koster's inquiries. Hemkes consented.[141] In his reply, Hemkes gave, among other things, illustrations from history about the dissatisfaction in the RCA: the secession of 1822 due to the existence of Arminian views, the Union of Classis Holland with the RCA in 1850, and the secession of four congregations in 1857.[142]

When De Pree presented his report to the September Classis, the committee which had been appointed at the April meeting of Classis to oversee the organization of a Reformed Church in Crook recommended that the report of the committee be published as part of the classical minutes. This was approved.[143] (De Pree had already written about Hemkes' letter in the August 30, 1893, issue of *De Hope.*) The committee also expressed special concern for the statement in Hemkes' letter that the Reverend Isaac N. Wyckoff had offered a bribe to persuade the leaders of Classis Holland to unite with the RCA. The statement in question read: "... that if the Hollanders unite they will then get $200 for a missionary and aid to build churches, and for the support of ministers."[144] The committee considered these to be false and slanderous charges and demanded that Hemkes retract these

136. De Pree, "Opbrekende Hollandsche Kolonie te Crook," pp. 1–2.
137. Hof, "Kolonie in Crook," p. 5.
138. Peter De Pree, "De Berucht Geworden Brief van Prof. G. Hemkes aan de (Vroegere) Colorado Kolonisten," *De Hope* 27 (30 Augustus 1893):2.
139. Classis Iowa of the RCA, Minutes of September 13 and 14, 1893.
140. Gerrit K. Hemkes, "Gemeente Stichting te Crook, Colo.," *De Wachter* 26 (16 Augustus 1893):2–3.
141. Ibid.
142. De Pree, "Berucht Geworden Brief van Prof. G. Hemkes," p. 2.
143. Classis Iowa of the RCA, Minutes of September 13 and 14, 1893.
144. Ibid.

allegations and insinuations against the leaders of the RCA in the columns of *De Hope* and *De Wachter*.[145] Hemkes responded. He stated that he would not put something on paper without being certain of the facts. His proof that Wyckoff had offered $200 to the leaders of the Holland Classis was taken from Tede Ulberg's reminiscence published in 1882.[146] Ulberg wrote:

> In 1849 the ministers Maarten A. Ypma, A. C. van Raalte, and I. N. Wyckoff came to us. We were pleased to see Dominie Wyckoff because we knew him so well from our daily relations with him in Albany. He posed the question whether the people would want to join the Dutch Reformed Church? To that question at first no answer was made. "Our church offers advantages," he declared. "You still are in your youth, but when you arrive at your mature years if you are not pleased with the union, you can extend a brotherly hand and stand by yourselves. You are in need of a visiting missionary pastor, you can invite one from Holland or from any other place. Our Board will provide $200 for that purpose, and, if the congregation can contribute something, the object will be attained more easily."[147]

Hemkes' reply appeared in the October 11, 1893, issue of *De Wachter*, but *De Hope* chose not to publish it, although Hemkes had requested them to do so.[148] The Stated Clerk of Classis Iowa of the RCA, Zwemer, added a postscript to his classical report of the September meeting which read as follows: "Professor Hemkes has attempted a so-called defense of his statement, based upon the hearsay testimony of one long since dead, and who died outside of the communion of our Church."[149] This dispute raged on long after the colonists from the Crook area had been resettled, mostly in Iowa.

Soon after the organization of the CRC congregation in Crook, the situation of the colonists grew very bleak. Vander Hoogt and Zoutman were given leave in the latter part of April,[150] and a certain C. J. Heijblom, who was working in the office of NALEM in Crook at that time, was placed in charge of the colonists.[151] The news from the Netherlands concerning NALEM was bad, for NALEM was undergoing liquidation. No more money could be expected from NALEM to support a colony in Colorado. No

145. Zwemer, "Bit of History," p. 975.

146. Gerrit K. Hemkes, "Aan de Eerw. Classis der Ref. Church, Die Gehouden Zal Worden te Orange City, Iowa," *De Wachter* 26 (11 October 1893):2–3.

147. Tede Ulberg, "Tede Ulberg's Notes on the First Settlers in the Dutch Kolonie in Michigan," in *Dutch Immigrant Memoirs and Related Writings*, Selected and Arranged for Publication by Henry S. Lucas (Assen: van Gorcum & Co., G. A. Hak & H. J. Prakke, 1955), Vol. I, pp. 272–289. Dutch Text entitled "Uit de Portefeuille van de Eerste Settlers in de Hollandsche Kolonie in Michigan," in *Jaarboekje voor de Hollandsche Christelijke Gereformeerde Kerk in Noord Amerika voor het Jaar* 1883 (Grand Rapids: D. J. Doornink, 1882), pp. 65–79.

148. Hemkes, "Eerw. Classis der Ref. Church," pp. 2–3.

149. Zwemer, "Bit of History," p. 975.

150. Breen, "Onze Gemeente Bethel," p. 2.

151. Cornelius A. Sluijs, "Brieven uit Amerika," *Enkhuizer Courant* 24 (4 October 1893):2.

income could be expected from the crops, for there were no crops. Most of the crops had dried up for lack of water. With no money, a colonist could not buy provisions for himself and his family. Starvation lay on the doorsteps. Desperate messages were placed in the American Dutch language church papers for financial assistance. Two student pastors, Gerrit Berkhof of the CRC and Herman Vander Ploeg of the RCA, ministered in the Crook area and did most of the work to get these colonists resettled.[152] The first family left the Crook area around July 13, 1893,[153] and the last one resettled around August 3, 1893.[154] Only four families remained in the Platte Valley, though very soon two of these left also: one family left for Michigan; a second went back to the Netherlands in the beginning of 1894. The third family left for Maxwell City, New Mexico, after having farmed for nearly five years in the Iliff area. The fourth family trekked to Montana at a later date.[155]

When the Crook CRC congregation broke up, no one imagined that by the end of the year the colonists of the Empire Farm would find themselves in a similar situation.

The failure of the colonization plan and of the efforts to keep the project alive was quite a difficult fact for Vanden Heuvel to swallow. As a counselor of the Rilland CRC, he had had a warm heart for the spiritual and material needs of the colonists of the Empire Farm. Confidently, he had expected that there would be a future for them in the San Luis Valley.[156]

Fulfilling a classical appointment, Vanden Heuvel returned to the San Luis Valley with an assignment to be with the colonists of the Empire Farm for three Sundays. During his stay, he presided over four consistory meetings. In the fourth and last meeting, August 30, 1893, he proposed the formation of a company for promoting emigration of Hollanders to the valley. He also presented to the consistory a draft of articles for incorporating such a company and a draft of a contract with ELaCaC for buying land and for obtaining water rights. Both drafts were endorsed by the consistory.[157]

The new colonization company was incorporated under the laws of the State of Colorado on October 3, 1893, with the name of "The Holland-San Luis Valley Colonization Company of Colorado." The officers of this company were: Lambertus Verburg, president; Samuel Hartog, administrator;

152. Henry Bode and Gerrit Berkhof, "Eene Stem uit Colorado, Eene Noodkreet om Hulp," *De Wachter* 26 (26 Juli 1893):1; Herman Vander Ploeg, "Een Stem uit Colorado, Eene Noodkreet om Hulp," *De Hope* 27 (26 Juli 1893):5.

153. "De Hollanders in Colorado," *De Grondwet* 33 (25 Juli 1893):5.

154. *De Volksvriend* 19 (10 Augustus 1893):5 (News item).

155. "Een Brief," dated Juli 18, 1928, forwarded to Nanne Groot Szoon by Cornelius A. Sluijs from Lynden, Washington.

156. Arie J. Vanden Heuvel, "Brief," *De Standaard*, 30 December 1893, p. 2.

157. Rilland CRC, Notulen van de Kerkeraadsvergadering van 30 Augustus 1893.

Douwe Sjaardema, treasurer; Cornelius Kloosterman and Johannes Oranje, managers.[158]

Through a letter sent to several newspapers in the Netherlands, the officers of this new company explained the purpose and goals of their colonizing endeavors.[159] They also advertised that Theodore C. Henry, the president of ELaCaC and his secretary, R. A. Van Angelbeek, were on their way to the Netherlands and would be available for consultation at the "Hotel Adrian," located in the Kalverstraat in Amsterdam.[160]

Recognizing a business opportunity in selling land and water rights to new colonists from the Netherlands, Henry offered $800 per year to the consistory of the Rilland CRC for two years as a contribution to the salary of a minister. In his letter Henry specified, however, that the minister had to be Vanden Heuvel, and only after he accepted the call, would the consistory receive $800 for the first year, and a second $800 for the next year. Not wishing to reject this offer, the consistory decided to accept it and to start into motion the procedure for calling a minister.[161]

The idea of a new colonizing effort to the San Luis Valley was received with mixed feelings in the Netherlands. It was not easy for the Hollanders to comprehend why the colonists organized an emigration company before the results of the immigrants' harvest were known. Was there really a future for them in the valley? The immigrants' letters never revealed that.[162] And why had they engaged Henry, who was labeled as a land speculator in the Netherlands,[163] and Van Angelbeek, who was not to be trusted and about whom they could not say a kind word?[164]

On October 25, 1893, Henry and Van Angelbeek left New York for the Netherlands.[165] Henry carried with him excellent credentials provided by the colonizing company, the consistory of the Rilland CRC, Charles D. Hayt, Judge of the Supreme Court of Colorado, and Davis H. Waite, Governor of Colorado.[166] His stay in the Netherlands was of short duration, however,

---

158. "Articles of Incorporation" of THE HOLLAND–SAN LUIS VALLEY COLONIZATION COMPANY OF COLORADO dated October 3, 1893 filed with the Secretary of State of the State of Colorado (Denver).

159. "De Hollandsche Kolonisatie-Vereeniging (San Luis Valley)," De Standaard, 24 October 1893, pp. 2–3; also in De Protestantsche Noordbrabanter 15 (28 October 1893):2 and in De Zeeuw 8 (21 October 1893):1.

160. "Colorado," De Zeeuw 8 (11 November 1893):1; "Colorado," De Standaard, 22 November 1893, p. 1.

161. Rilland CRC, Notulen van de Kerkeraadsvergadering van 9 October 1893.

162. A. de Boer, "Emigratie en Nog Iets," De Standaard, 30 October 1893, p. 6.

163. Iman G. J. van den Bosch, "Emigratie naar de San-Luis Vallei," Middelburgsche Courant, 20 Januari 1893, p. 1; 21 Januari 1893, p. 1; also in Maandblad van de Vereeniging van Oud-Leerlingen der Rijks Landbouwschool 5 (1892/93):100–104; Iman G. J. van den Bosch, "Nog Eens de Emigratie naar de San-Luis-Vallei," Maandblad van de Vereeniging van Oud-Leerlingen der Rijks Landbouwschool 5 (1892/93):122–124.

164. "Colorado," De Zeeuw 8 (11 November 1893):1.

165. Ibid.

166. Een Hollandsche Kolonie in het Rotsgebergte van Noord-Amerika, San Luis Vallei, Colorado (Rotterdam: T. van Weemt, 1893), pp. 28–32.

and he quickly returned to New York via Paris. The reasons for his abrupt departure were: first, that he found there very little sympathy for emigration to Colorado, and second, and more important, that the situation on the Empire Farm had taken a different turn. The news had reached Henry that the colonists were very dissatisfied with the harvest and that they wanted to leave the valley. A longer stay in the Netherlands would, therefore, be futile for him.[167] When the summer rains had drenched their fields and had started to give new life to their crops, the colonists of the Empire Farm were enormously heartened, so that their expectations for a promising harvest were unquestionably improved.[168] But the harvest did not give the yield that was anticipated. With depressed wheat prices, the colonists lost their hope for the future. Their discontent of a few months ago arose with greater force; they were convinced that no bread and cheese could be earned in the San Luis Valley. In the end, they were eager to leave the valley and to leave their bitter and sorrowful memories behind.[169]

In a letter to Breen, the consistory of the Rilland CRC gives five reasons why it felt that the colonists should leave the valley:

1. The soil is too poor to expect a bounteous harvest and besides the alkali in the soil spoils a good deal of the yield.
2. We are forced to sell our products to the Alamosa Milling & Elevator Company, the only market-place in town, and we are thus dependent on the arbitrariness of its management.
3. We live here among Americans who chase their horses, cows and pigs into our fields, so that these animals graze everything, even the fodder meant for our cattle, without being able to do much about it.
4. There is some uncertainty as to whether we are able to get sufficient water for irrigation the following year, since a good share of the main water canal has been seized by others.
5. There is no industry here, where we can find work for extra income. Our income is, therefore, totally dependent on the farm. The proceeds of the farm are not sufficient to pay our debts, interest, etc. and to provide us with our daily need.[170]

Shortly after the fall meeting of Classis Iowa of the CRC, a special classical meeting at which not all the congregations were represented, was held again in Orange City on November 22, 1893. The main item on the agenda was to discuss the situation of the colonists of the Rilland CRC. The Reverend Evert Bos of the Luctor CRC of Luctor, Kansas, fulfilling a

167. "De Hollandsche Kolonie Rilland in Colorado," *De Protestantsche Noordbrabanter* 15 (2 December 1893):1; "Colorado," *De Zeeuw* 8 (2 December 1893):1.
168. "Uit Alamosa, Colo.," *De Volksvriend* 19 (31 Augustus 1893):8; "Brieven uit Colorado," *De Zeeuw* 7 (5 September 1893):2.
169. Samuel Hartog, "De Hollandsche Kolonie in Colorado," *De Grondwet* 34 (5 December 1893):4.
170. Rilland CRC, Notulen van de Kerkeraadsvergadering van 28 November 1893.

classical appointment, ministered there for a few weeks. In a letter that was read in the session of Classis he described the deplorable circumstances in which the colonists found themselves. Only a few families wanted to stay, but all the others desired to leave the valley. Bos consequently suggested that the families be relocated to Luctor and that the Luctor CRC congregation through special collections throughout the denomination be reimbursed for the incurred expenses. Classis did not go along with this suggestion. It decided to distribute the families among the different congregations of the Iowa Classis. This decision was made with the understanding that the congregations themselves would bear the costs of supporting the families. The families, along with the single persons, were resettled in Iowa, Kansas, and Nebraska.[171]

After the first disappointments, the promising new beginnings of the Dutch immigrants at the Empire Farm ended in dismal failure a year later. Except for a few, most of these immigrants not only lost all their capital, but also incurred great debts in the "Paradise of Colorado," the "Italy of western North America."[172] The clever advertising campaign of Vander Hoogt and Zoutman transformed in imagination, not reality, the naked, wind-swept expanse into a prosperous countryside, where, according to Zoutman, "the most ignorant pagan would fall on his knees adoring its grandeur."[173] Only the Adolph Heersink family stayed behind in 1893 in this valley, where their descendants are still living. Naturally the resettled immigrants picked up the pieces in their new environments. Many of them prospered and with their descendants took their places in the religious life of the RCA and CRC in North America.

Appendix: A List of Immigrants in Alamosa and Crook, Colorado in 1892–93

No complete record of the Dutch immigrants who had been in Alamosa and Crook, Colorado, in 1892–93 is available. Nor is there a complete record of those who moved from Alamosa to Crook on January 31, 1893 (identified in the following list by an asterisk). Names of immigrants who were in the San Luis Valley and the Platte Valley have been gleaned from passenger lists of the ships of the Holland American Line arriving in New York City from December 1892 through June 1893, from naturalization records and court records (such as land deeds and civil suits), from newspaper accounts, and from civil records in the city halls of the cities in the Netherlands from which the immigrants hailed. More research has yet to be done

171. Classis Iowa of the CRC, Notulen van 22 November 1893.
172. "Colorado," *De Zeeuw* 8 (2 December 1893):1; *Emigratie van Landbouwers naar Noord-Amerika*, p. 8.
173. Van Boven, *Eerste Hollandsche Nederzetting in Colorado*, p. 11; Henry S. Lucas, *Netherlanders in America*, Dutch Immigration to the United States and Canada, 1789–1950, University of Michigan Publications, History and Political Science, 21 (Ann Arbor: The University of Michigan Press, 1955), p. 431.

on the accuracy of the last and Christian names. The author would appreciate
receiving any information which the reader might have concerning the immigrants
who came under the auspices of NALEM to the two valleys in Colorado in 1892–93.

Immigrants Destined for Alamosa, Colorado

Ship: Dubbeldam
Arrival New York: November 26, 1892

Aardema, Liekele Marcus
Ballast, Dirk*
  Van Randen, Ypkje* (Mrs.)
  Child: Johanna Egberdina*
Ballast, Johanna Alida Moritz (Mrs.)
  (died in Alamosa)
Bleijenberg, Stephanus*
Boon, Thijs Oostenraad
Bout, Hendrik Pieter*
Boute, Theodoor Jurgen
Boxum, Harm
Boxum, Jan
Bruintjes, Andries
Brune, Evert
Davidse, Salomon
De Bondt, Joost*
  Reedijk, Adriana Anthonia* (Mrs.)
De Greeuw, Jacques Louis
De Jong, Roelof*
  ?, Anna* (Mrs.)
  Children: Cornelia*
           Gerardus*
           Elisabeth*
           Johannes*
           Johanna (died in Alamosa?)
           Cornelis (died in Alamosa?)
           Gelde (died in Alamosa?)
Dekker, Frederik
De Kruijter, Johannes*
  Remijn, Catharina* (Mrs.)
  Children: Wilhelmina Maria
              (died in Alamosa)
           Nicolaas*
           Johannes*
           Hermanus*
           Pieter Johannes*
           Adriaan*
           Jacobus*
           Janna*
Driesen, Hendrik

Evers, Hendrik A.*
  ?, A.* (Mrs.)
  Children: Emma*
           Mina*
Gunst, Adriaan*
  Van der Klooster, Willemina* (Mrs.)
  Children: Anthonie Johannes*
           Johannes Nathan*
           Thona*
           Willem*
Hartog, Samuel
  Oranje, Pieternella (Mrs.)
  Children: Neeltje
           Jacoba Adriana
           Maria
           Leendert
           Pieternella (died in Alamosa)
Heersink, Adolph
  Barink, Grada Johanna (Mrs.)
  Children: Jan Willem
           Albertus Wilhelmus
           Hendrik
           Gradus Johannes
           Gezina Aleida
           Johanna Antonia
           Adolf
Hof, Andries J.*
  Van der Woude, Jantje* (Mrs.)
  Children: Jantje (died in Alamosa)
           Jantje* (born in Alamosa)
Hols[t], Jacob*
  Wichhart, Cornelia* (Mrs.)
  Children: Willem
           Berendina*
           Gijsbert*
           Cornelis*
           Aaltje*
           Maaike*
           Karel*
           Jacob*
           Cornelia*
Jongerius, Gerrit*

*moved from Alamosa to Crook, Colorado, on January 31, 1893.

Kloosterman, Cornelis
  Vette, Dina (Mrs.)
    Children: Cornelis
            Gommert
            Daniel Gerard
            Jacoba Margaretha
            Adriana Paulina
            Elizabeth
            Geertruida
            Catharina
Kragt, Pieter*
  Wydenes, Aagje* (Mrs.)
    Children: Dina*
            Cornelis*
            Pieter*
            Jacob*
            Jan*
            Jaapje*
Moerman, Cornelis
  Zuydweg, Sarah (Mrs.)
    Children: Adriana
            Jannetje
            Cornelis
Monsma, Marten Jans
Oranje, Jacobus
Oranje, Johannes
    Children: Adriana
            Maria Geertruida
            Jacobus
Oranje, Neeltje
Penny, Abraham*
Pluister, Albert
Porma, Maaike (Mrs. K. Otten)
Sjaardema, Douwe
  Van Dijk, Catherine (Mrs.)
    Children: Jouke
            Akke
            Libbelina Catharina
            (One born in Alamosa?)
Sluijs, Cornelis*
  Vriend, Dina* (Mrs.)
    Children: Grietje*
            Jan*
            Antje*
            Dina*
            Arien*
            Pietertje (died in Alamosa)
Teunissen, Teunis
  Verhaaf, Sibelia Antje (Mrs.)
Uit den Boogaart, Hannes*
    Children: Johannes*
            Jan*

Van Dalen, Gerrit
  Rook, Geesje (Mrs.)
Van Dalen, Jan
Van de Kieft, Jan Maas*
Van de Kieft, Lubbert*
Van der Beek, Jan
  De Pender, Helena (Mrs.)
    Children: Gerrit
            Hendrikus
            Helena
            Teunis
            Govert
            Bastiaan
            Jenneke
            Jan
            Teuntje
            (One born in Alamosa?)
            (One died in Alamosa)
Van der Kaaij, Dirk
Van der Klooster, Jacob*
Van der Linde, Leendert*
  Kole, Janna* (Mrs.)
    Children: Willemina Josina*
            Maria Willemina*
            Willem*
            Adriana*
            Antonia*
            Leonard C. (born in Crook)
Van der Wel, Bastiaan*
  Lankhaar, Cornelia* (Mrs.)
    Children: Marigje*
            Teuntje*
            Pieter*
Van Lummel, Arnaud Johan
  Rougoor, Elisabeth (Mrs.)
    Children: Gerrit Jan Colenbrander
            Derk Adolf Colenbrander
            Hendrik Colenbrander
            Aleida Johanna Colenbrander
            Hendrik Johan Van Lummel
Verburg, Lambertus
  Porma, Cornelia (Mrs.)
    Children: Jetje
            Pieter
            Marie
            Lambertus
Verhoef, Willem
Vos, Peter Gerrit
  Nederveen, Anneke (Mrs.)
    Children: Krijn Bastiaan
            Maria Wouterina
            Adriaan

Weidenaar, Hollechien
  Children: Geesien
            Hollechien
Wichhart, Derk*
  Van Rees, Maaike* (Mrs.)
  Children: Hendrina*
            Evert*
            Geertruida*
            Derk*
            Maaike*
            Willem*
            (One died in Alamosa)
Winter, Evert
Zandbergen, Hendrikus
Zwier, Jan
  De Jong, Wijntje (Mrs.)
  Children: Daniel
            Trijntje
            Simon
            Aafje
            Jantje
Zwier, Simon
Zijlstra, Feike
  Hoitsma, Grietje (Mrs.)
  Child: Klaaske (died in Alamosa)
Zijlstra, Rein

Ship: Obdam
Arrival New York: January 13, 1893

Mulder, Harm
  Child: Willem Stuart (stepson)

Ship: Rotterdam
Arrival New York: March 24, 1893

Boone, Adriaan
Cornelissen, Johannes
Louws, Jan
  Louwerse, Pieternella (Mrs.)
  Children: Pieter
            Anna Jacoba
Schütte, Derk
  Rook, Annigje (Mrs.)
  Children: Hilligje
            Willem
            Jan
            Koopje
            Geuje
            Piet
            Jan
            Derk

Ship: Dubbeldam
Arrival New York: April 12, 1893

Aalbers, Marinus
  Hols[t], Hendrina (Mrs.)
  Children: Gerrit
            Jacobus

Ship: Maasdam
Arrival New York: May 31, 1893

Heslinga, Gjalt
Molenaar, Klaaske
Polderboer, Youke
  Schulstra, Willemke (Mrs.)
  Children: Auke
            Lutske
            Trinke
            Napke
            IJke
Schoutema, Akke
  (Mrs. Gerben Westerbaan Van Dijk)
Sjaardema, Freerk
  Van Dijk, Oetske (Mrs.)
  Children: Sibbeltje
            Gerben Frederik
Van Dalen, Gerrit Jan
Van Dalen, Jan
Van Dijk, Meine

Ship: Amsterdam
Arrival New York: June 12, 1893

Schipper, Johan
  ?, Gezina (Mrs.)
Sjaardema, Franke
  ?, Jenna (Mrs.)
  Children: Janke
            Jouke
            Amkje
Van der Bij, Jan
Wicherus, Johan
Wichhart, Willem

Also in Alamosa, arrival date unknown:

Wichhart, Christiaan
  Cooke, Maria (Mrs.)
  Children: Catharina
            Hendrika
            Cornelia
            Jacob
            Maria
            Christina
            Cornelia Berendina

Immigrants Destined for Crook, Colorado

Ship: Spaarndam
Arrival New York: February 4, 1893

Heusinkveld, Hendrik Willem
  Velthorst, Hendrika Gertruida (Mrs.)
  Children: Gerrit
    Alida Gerharda
    Hendrik Gerard
    (born in Crook)
Hoftijzer, Arend Jan
Westerveld, Gerrit Jan
  Oosterink, Derkje (Mrs.)
  Children: Harmina Catharina
    Gerrit Jan
    Everdina Geertruida
    Drika Johanna
    Johanna Willemina

Ship: Maasdam
Arrival New York: March 9, 1893

Aué, Frederik
  Dix, Suzanna (Mrs.)
  Children: Hermina Johanna
    Jan Frederik
    Johanna Christina
    Christiaan
    Frederik Cornelis
Coster, Kier
  Kooiker, Klaasje (Mrs.)
  Children: Hendrik
    Stijntje
Den Ouden, Johannes
Hulst, Harm
  Wind, Hilligje (Mrs.)
  Children: Klaasje
    Lubbertus
    Gerard
    Klaas Hermanus
    Hendrik Christiaan
Kooiman, Cornelis
  Swier, Antje (Mrs.)
  Children: Wilhelmina
    Klaasje
    Trijntje
Molenaar, Aaltje
Mulder, nee Wiechers, Geziena (Mrs.)
  Children: Gerhard Johannes Stuart
    Arend Mulder (stepson)

Swier, Dirk
  Zwier, Aaltje (Mrs.)
  Children: Dieuwertje
    Trijntje
    Antje
    Cornelia
    Gerritje
    Aafje
Van der Veen, Rinse
  ?, Rinske (Mrs.)
  Children: Wiebrechje T.
    Evert M.
Van Staalduinen, Arie
Van Staalduinen, Leendert
Van 't Sant, Gerrit Nicolaas
Van Voorst, Rijk
  Beumer, Hermina (Mrs.)
  Children: Rijk
    Hendrika
    Petronella
    Gerrit Jan
    Gijsbertus
Van Wijk, Jan
  Van 't Sant, Neeltje Dirkje (Mrs.)
  Children: Cornelis
    Antonie Adriaan
Zomermaand, Egbert
  ?, Sientje (Mrs.)
  Child: Anntje
Zwier, Pieter**
  Zwier, Neeltje** (Mrs.)
  Child: Trijntje**

Ship: Edam
Arrival New York: May 2, 1893

Bleijenberg,
  Helena Catharina De Haan (Mrs.)
Drok, Koop
  Ten Napel, Neeltje (Mrs.)
  Children: Jantje
    Hendrikje
Schelling, Cornelis
Ten Napel, Evert
  De Vries, Pietertjen
  Children: Hermanus Jacobus
    Harm
    Hendrik

**moved from Crook to Alamosa, Colorado

Uit den Boogaart, nee Van Es, Martha (Mrs.)
   Children: Adriaantje
           Elisabeth Johanna
           Martha
           Albert
           Leendert
           Willem
Van Schooneveld, Willeminus Hendrikus
Smits, Wilhelmina (Mrs.)
   Children: Willem Johannes Leonardus
           Daniel
Walhof, Jan Barend
   Children: Carel Alexander
           Peter Evert

Ship: Obdam
Arrival New York: May 25, 1893

De Haan, Jansje
Van der Werff, Jan Sjierks
?, Grietje (Mrs.)
   Children: Sjerk
           Jacobus

Also in Crook, arrival date unknown

Brem, C. J. L.
Des Tombe, Frederik Willem
Groen, Roelof
Kalkman, Pieter
Keijzer, Fredrik Willem

With the Holland-American Land- and
   Immigration Company:

Heijblom, C. J.
Roest, Johanna Isaaca
Van Boven, Jan (returned to the Nether-
   lands in January 1893)
Van der Hoogt, Cornelis Willem
   Roest, Neeltje (Mrs.)
Van Dusseldorp, Willem Cornelis and wife
Zoutman, Albertus

5

The Americanization of Hendrik Peter Scholte
Lubbertus Oostendorp

Hendrik Peter Scholte was no average American immigrant. He was much more affluent than most of them. His role as a leader of a group of religious pilgrims makes his contributions and plans significant for the student of the Dutch colonies in North America. However, we should not too readily simply link him with Albertus Christiaan Van Raalte. In spite of basic similarities, there are some radical differences between the leader of the Pella, Iowa, colony and the leader of the group which settled in Holland, Michigan. While Van Raalte's story is fairly well known, Scholte's is less well known, so that he may be called "the lost leader." It was Scholte who influenced Van Raalte to join the Afscheiding of 1834 in the Netherlands.

Charming and talented as he was, Scholte also had a fatal independence which caused tragic breaches between him and the movements which he led. This was sadly true both of his church leadership in the Netherlands and his relation to his colony in North America.

The Scholtes escaped the many difficulties, danger, and trials which poorer immigrants had to endure. While the members of the flock were experiencing the long days of crossing the Atlantic in sailing ships, the pastor and his family made the crossing in thirteen days in the steamship "Sarah Sands."[1]

With Van Raalte, Scholte had been encouraging the seceders to migrate

---

1. Henry S. Lucas, *Netherlanders in America*, Dutch Immigration to the United States and Canada, 1789–1950, University of Michigan Publications, History and Political Science, 21 (Ann Arbor: The University of Michigan Press, 1955), p. 165.

to North America. Although he himself had suffered fines and imprison-
ment for being a leader in the Afscheiding, he hesitated for some time to
recommend leaving the homeland. Among the four to five thousand persons who left the established church in the Afscheiding, there were very
few who were wealthy. Although religious persecution had largely ceased,
a good deal of economic and social prejudice against the seceders remained. It took little persuasion to bring about a mass movement of about
two thousand seceders who were ready to migrate to North America. Religious, social, and economic motives were so deeply interwoven in their
reasons for emigrating that these motives must be considered as a combination of causes for the emigration rather than a single cause. Significantly, the immigrants of 1847 and for several years thereafter were very
largely seceders and they were concentrated in the settlements in Michigan and Iowa.

Apparently the difficulties which kept these people from leaving the
Netherlands were removed by the formation of an immigration society.
Objections among the seceders to emigrating were thus met by the assurance that they could form a colony in North America. Many who did not
have the money to undertake the journey from their own resources were
assisted financially by others. Moreover, the fears of getting lost in North
America were met by the assurance that their church would go with them.

Most prominent among the professed motives of Scholte, which he
made known in various articles in his magazine, *De Reformatie*,[2] and in
various other pamphlets, was the desire to help the oppressed seceders.
Their future in the Netherlands seemed to him very dim, especially eco-
nomically, but also religiously and politically.[3] Less obvious was the sense
of frustration with certain fellow seceders with whom he had been at odds
for several years. In fact, some of the leaders had broken fellowship with
him and his congregation in 1844 because Scholte had made concessions
to the government concerning the name and claim of the secession
churches. This alienated men like Hendrik de Cock and Simon van Velzen,
who continued to press for the right to be recognized as the true Reformed
Church in the Netherlands. Moreover, Scholte was experimenting with new
church orders which differed from the Church Order of Dort. Last but not
least, through contact with John N. Darby he had become a dispensational
premillenarian.[4] Thus among many of the seceders he was considered
persona non grata. It is remarkable that the differences among the seceders

2. *De Reformatie*. Tijdschrift ter Bevordering van Gods Koningrijk in Nederland, 1837–1847. Series 1,
vol. 1–8; series 2, vol. 1–8; series 3, vol. 1–3.

3. Lucas, *Netherlanders in America*, p. 164.

4. Lubbertus Oostendorp, *H.P. Scholte*, Leader of the Secession of 1834 and Founder of Pella (Franeker: T. Wever, 1964), pp. 137–140.

seemed to be forgotten or at best obscured in the common movement for emigration.

The mystery of motives deepens when we consider the voice of prophecy. The time had come, so thought Scholte, to seek a refuge from impending doom! In the name "Pella" Scholte memorialized the Iowa city as a "place of refuge." After all, Pella was the city to which the Christians fled before the destruction of Jerusalem in 70 A.D.. For most of the distressed immigrants this might have meant only refuge from the persecution and oppression which they had lately endured in the Netherlands. Not so for Scholte! For him, North America offered shelter from the impending doom prophetically pronounced on all of Europe.[5] With the Swiss theologian Alexandre R. Vinet, he considered Europe to be under the judgments pronounced in the Book of Revelation upon the Roman Empire. Moreover, the basic reason for this judgment was the effort of Rome and her successors to control the church. Thus from Constantine to King William I the earthly rulers had made themselves worthy of doom. But God would provide a "Pella" for his people! And North America could be such a place because it was never part of the Roman empire nor had it tried to control the church.[6]

For the second wife, Maria Scholte, the move to America proved difficult. Her story had been portrayed quite accurately under the title, *A Stranger in a Strange Land*.[7] Her father did not want her to leave her homeland and quarreled with his son-in-law about it.[8] It was rumored that she refused to go and had to be bribed by promises of prosperity and the right to take her sister, Hubertina Krantz, along. For Scholte himself this rather common problem of migration continued to plague him in the colony. It did not help the leader to have a wife whose highly cultured training contrasted sharply with life on the prairie. How largely the domestic situation caused trouble in the colony is hard to evaluate. It certainly was a factor, and it is significant that after Scholte's death Mrs. Scholte remarried and moved to New York.[9]

Nothing would seem more natural than the facile Americanization of Scholte. Seldom had an immigrant been more determined to make the transition quickly and completely. He eagerly wished the same for the colony. But could he realistically expect to find a Dutch settlement becoming Americanized so readily?

5. Oostendorp, *Scholte*, pp. 151–152. See also Hendrik P. Scholte, *Tweede Stem uit Iowa* ('s Bosch: H. Palier en Zoon, 1848), p. 21.

6. Ibid., pp. 151–152.

7. Leonora Scholte, *A Stranger in a Strange Land*, Romance in Pella History (Iowa City: The State Historical Society of Iowa, 1939). See also note in Oostendorp, *Scholte*, p. 149.

8. Lucas, *Netherlanders in America*, p. 164.

9. Scholte, *Stranger in a Strange Land*, p. 83.

About his own preparation for Americanization it should be noted that he not only spoke English well, but that he had accepted some American ideals. In seeking to establish a free church in the Netherlands, he had fought valiantly for the freedom of the church from all state control. He had developed his theory of the separation of church and state, having written a book on the subject, *Kerk en Staat.*[10] Several of his fellow seceders still held to the idea of state support for the church. But he was eager to live under a constitution which guaranteed the separation of church and state.

In fact, he had become acquainted with the New England experiment with religious intolerance, having studied Robert Baird's book, *Religion in America.*[11] Baird had bemoaned the ill effects of theocracy in the Puritan settlements. Scholte agreed with him and intended to avoid any such error in his colony. Pella was planned by Scholte to be an "open city."

Scholte also had some definite ideas about the church in the new country. Some of the Dutch colonies consisted of congregations which were literally transposed to North America with their pastors and elders. Such was the case of Cornelius Vander Meulen in Zeeland, Michigan.[12] This was not strictly true of Van Raalte. Both he and Scholte sort of "fell into" the position of pastor of the church of the colony. However, Scholte wanted a new church in a new country.

Influenced by the independentism of Darby and the congregationalism of Baird, he advocated a new beginning for the church in the colony. He even prevailed on the Utrecht group to adopt a resolution stating that they would be guided only by the Word of God and have a form of government most nearly agreeing with congregationalism.[13] He envisaged North America as a place where the congregation might form itself as it saw fit. Such was his vision of a free church, liberated not only from the state but from all denominational traditions.

Scholte's plans were evidently not shared by all the leaders, and certainly not by many of the colonists. The range of resistance to Americanization varied with various groups and individuals. Deliberate efforts were made to keep the settlements Dutch in membership, language, and customs. Some of the churches, such as the Christian Reformed Church (hereafter CRC) in 1857, considered themselves transplants of the seceder churches in the Netherlands. Others like Van Raalte and a majority of the Holland

10. Hendrik P. Scholte, *Kerk en Staat* (Amsterdam: Hoogmaker & Co., 1844).

11. Robert Baird, *Religion in America,* or, An Account of the Origin, Relation to the State, and Present Condition of the Evangelical Churches in the United States with Notices of the Unevangelical Denominations (New York: Harper & Brothers, 1856).

12. Diedrich H. Kromminga, *The Christian Reformed Tradition,* From the Reformation till the Present (Grand Rapids: Eerdmans, 1943), p. 99.

13. Oostendorp, *Scholte,* p. 153.

settlers were willing to join the Reformed Church in America (hereafter RCA). The RCA had become quite Americanized in the eastern states. The relationship, however, was not very close and the Holland colony remained something of a Dutch island for many years.[14]

It was, however, not Scholte's intention that Pella should remain such an "island of Hollanders." As much as he himself was determined to become an English-speaking American, so too he made every effort to make Pella an American town. In fact Pella's population was 50 percent non-Dutch in 1857.[15] The Pella church, too, was to take on a form which would free it from any dependence on the churches in The Netherlands and make it independent from any denominational ties. Scholte had been invited to join the RCA when he met its leaders while passing through New York in 1847, but he had firmly rejected their overtures.[16] His would be a new church, completely free, the "Christian Church of Pella."

It should be noted that Scholte's premillenial theology and undenominational church polity were several decades too early for ready acceptance by the Dutch settlers in North America. Through his writings he did influence a CRC minister, Harry Bultema. By the 1920s this belated disciple found a more congenial soil in North America for the dispensationalism of Scholte.[17]

Meanwhile, Scholte was enthusiastically proceeding with the Americanization of the settlement. By a special act of the Iowa legislature, the people of Pella were given a kind of "halfway" citizenship. This allowed them both to serve in and vote for local offices. Their leader was soon moving easily among the rich and powerful of Iowa. He stressed the need for learning English, especially in school. Since he owned the whole town of Pella, he encouraged Americans to buy lots there. He was especially eager to bring in American businessmen. In this he succeeded only too well, for in a thoughtless moment he sold the lot on the city square, which had been set aside for a church, to two American businessmen. This wilful act caused much trouble in Pella![18]

Scholte continued to express his optimism that Pella would soon be a large Americanized city. To help matters along he began on February 1,

---

14. Herman Harmelink III, *Ecumenism and the Reformed Church*, The Historical Series of the Reformed Church in America, 1 (Grand Rapids: Eerdmans, 1968); Elton J. Bruins, *The Americanization of a Congregation*, A History of the Third Reformed Church of Holland, Michigan, The Historical Series of the Reformed Church in America, 2 (Grand Rapids: Eerdmans, 1970), pp. 40–46.

15. Oostendorp, *Scholte*, pp. 172–173.

16. Ibid., pp. 160–161. See also Hendrik P. Scholte, *Eene Stem uit Pella* (Amsterdam: Hoogkamer & Compe., 1848), pp. 10–11.

17. Ibid., pp. 190–191. Harry Bultema made such a study while in Pella, wrote in manuscript a life of Scholte and told me that Scholte influenced his theology which led to a break with the CRC and the founding of the Berean Church in Muskegon in 1918.

18. Ibid., p. 173.

1855, to publish an English paper, *The Pella Gazette*. It was financed largely by himself and ceased publication on February 22, 1860. He used the paper mainly to keep the citizens of Pella abreast of things happening in the American world and to influence them politically.[19]

Very early he plunged into the mainstream of American politics. Angered by the anti-immigrant stand of the "Know-Nothing" party, he became in 1856 a forceful advocate of the Democratic party.[20] He wrote a small book (in English) in modified defense of the right of states in the matter of slavery.[21] On a whirlwind tour of Holland, Grand Rapids, and Kalamazoo, Michigan, in 1856, he made quite an impression upon the immigrants. He suddenly seemed to sense the evils of slavery and of the Democratic position and as a result he became in 1860 a strong advocate for Abraham Lincoln. The value of his support is clearly evidenced by the fact that he was delegated from Iowa to the national convention which nominated Abraham Lincoln. This was a truly remarkable Americanization of the Dutch seceder minister.[22]

A great change had no doubt taken place in Scholte. As a young man he had been a committed and favorite follower of the Dutch poet, Isaäc da Costa. He was even one of the circle of friends of the poet and was invited to his readings. This friendship cooled when Scholte chose in favor of the Afscheiding while da Costa stood against it. But da Costa had great influence in forming the world view of his ardent pupil. Da Costa was the man of the *Bezwaren Tegen den Geest der Eeuw*.[23] He was a leader among the counter-revolutionary group. He reacted against all that the French Revolution stood for. This meant that he was against democracy, the franchise, etc. He was for the restoration of church and state under the monarchy. To appreciate fully the long journey Scholte had made we must remember that at one time he had been a strong conservative![24] Later some of this wore off under the influence of Darby and others. How amazing it is to hear the Americanized Scholte in a Fourth of July speech praising his new homeland. With all the exuberance of a patriot he now predicts that "soon this great democracy will blend with the glorious millenium.'"[25]

North America dealt kindly with Scholte. He prospered financially and had a show-case mansion with acres of beautiful gardens. People came for miles to see the place and especially the gardens. North America had

19. Ibid., p. 183.
20. Ibid., p. 184.
21. Hendrik P. Scholte, *American Slavery in Reference to the Present Agitation in the United States* (Pella: The Gazette Book and Job Office, 1856).
22. Oostendorp, *Scholte*, pp. 184–185.
23. Isaäc da Costa, *Bezwaren tegen den Geest der Eeuw* (Leyden: Herdingh en Zoon, 1823).
24. Oostendorp, *Scholte*, pp. 33–36.
25. Ibid., p. 189.

become for him in many ways the land of freedom. Not the least was the freedom to extend his activities far beyond those of a preacher. It must have been for him a heady wine, this opportunity to try his hand at many ventures. He became a banker, businessman, real estate speculator, publisher, politician, and an attorney. As an attorney he had even taken a divorce case! But ultimately he paid a heavy price for all this exciting freedom. His business deals (e.g., selling the church lot) brought him into deep trouble with the church. His sudden change from being a Democrat to becoming a Republican created many enemies for him in Democratic Pella. His move to bring a Baptist college into the city (later Central College) made people suspicious of his theological soundness. And the basically Reformed people of Pella soon tired of the way he ran his independent church. Nor were the Dutchmen too eager to be Americanized![26]

Pella reacted. It reaffirmed both its Reformed and Dutch ways. Having a preacher who took no salary proved less a blessing than it would seem. It meant he could engage in all kinds of labors besides the ministry and neglect the church. By 1854 the break between preacher and church was final and in 1856 the church invited Van Raalte to come from Holland, Michigan, and lead them into the RCA.[27]

Scholte formed and personally built a building for his own little church and preached for it until his death in 1868. Tension continued to mount between the leader and the town of Pella. After the Civil War he was able to restore some of his popularity when he gave free lots in Pella to 129 returning veterans. But once more there were differences and even lawsuits. As more immigrants arrived, the proportion of non-Dutch persons in Pella became negligible. Pella became a Dutch island in North America!

Meanwhile, Scholte's relationship with the city which he had helped found became more and more strained. Not only were there quarrels about the "church lot" but even a lawsuit about the ownership and use of the city square. Scholte maintained that it still belonged to him. The court agreed but restricted his use of it.[28] His relation with the seceders who remained in the Netherlands had not improved. Rather the leaders in the Netherlands were becoming loathe to recommend Pella as a haven for the immigrants. Among the colonists in Michigan men spoke of the evils of the "Scholte spirit."

Just when and why it happened, we do not know. A great change came over Scholte. Shortly after the end of the Civil War the enthusiastic optimism about North America seemed gone. The hope for an ideal American church had faded. North America was regarded by him as being full of pious frauds, and its preachers were "ecclesiastical charlatans" and "clerical

26. Ibid., pp. 174–175.
27. Ibid.
28. Ibid., p. 173.

humbugs." Perhaps the disillusion was due to some knowledge of the greed and graft that characterized the administration of President Ulysses S. Grant. But something seems to have changed in the mind of Scholte himself.

It seems as though he had abandoned his counter-revolutionary stand when he had been swept along in the stream of the American dream. In fact, he had modified the pessimistic side of his premillenial view by excepting North America from the nations under the devil's rule. As stated above, his Fourth of July oration had even envisaged the American nation as "blending with the glorious millenium."[29] But all that changed. Symptomatic of the transformation is his return to writing in Dutch. From September 1866 until his death in August 1868 he published a little paper called *De Toekomst.*[30]

Sobriety returned to Scholte after the Civil War. By 1866 the enthusiastic immigrant found North America no better than the rest of the world, although he still warned against alliances with any area once part of the Roman Empire. With characteristic premillenarian pessimism, he mocked the New England experiment to establish the kingdom in this age and in this world.[31] Least of all could anything be expected from American democracy. A kingless state will never rule the world.[32] Echoes of Willem Bilderdijk's suspicion of popular sovereignty and the ideology of da Costa are here clearly mixed with the new eschatology. Scholte considered the whole church to be a bankrupt Babylonian confusion[33] and expected the Jews to evangelize the world in the kingdom age. Thus any optimism about missions or Christian action faded. He continued to defend infant baptism as being based on the covenant,[34] preached soundly Reformed doctrine and hated all Arminianism. In this way he escaped some of the radicalism of certain forms of dispensationalism.

"My kingdom is not of this world" was the recurring theme of *De Toekomst.* "Come, Lord Jesus!" was the constant prayer of Scholte. Since he presents no systematic development of his eschatology, it is impossible to reconstruct its details. The articles "God's Different Dispensations,"[35] "The Congregation Taken Away Before the Last Judgment,"[36] and "My

29. Ibid., p. 189.

30. *De Toekomst.* Ed. Hendrik P. Scholte (Pella: Henry Hospers Uitgever, 1866/68).

31. Hendrik P. Scholte, "De Pelgrims in Nieuw Engeland," *De Toekomst* 1 (November 1866):2.

32. Hendrik P. Scholte, "De Christen in de Wereld," *De Toekomst* 1 (October 1866):3.

33. Hendrik P. Scholte, "Verschillende Bedeelingen Gods," *De Toekomst* 2 (1867/68):11.

34. Hendrik P. Scholte, "Kerkelijk Lidmaatschap," *De Toekomst* 2 (1867/68):129–136; Hendrik P. Scholte, "Geheiligd in Christus," *De Toekomst* 2 (1867/68):171–176. Also a manuscript of Scholte papers defending his truly Reformed stand on infant baptism.

35. Scholte, "Verschillende Bedeelingen Gods," pp. 4–13.

36. Hendrik P. Scholte, "De Gemeente Weggenomen voor de Laatste Oordeelen," *De Toekomst* 2 (1867/68):13–16, 17–22, 33–38.

Kingdom Is Not of This World"[37] contain his viewpoints on the return of the Jews to Palestine, the rapture of the church, great tribulation for the Jews, a thousand-year kingdom, and the literal fulfillment of prophecy. The editor warned against the Adventists, against setting a time for the Lord's coming, and against identifying Napoleon III with the Antichrist. These faulty reckonings were not to be used, he wrote, to disparage the study of prophecy.

Scholte recognized that only a few Christians seemed interested in eschatology. He rejoiced in the publishing of a little premillenarian book, *Christocracy*, by two ministers of the RCA, John Terhume and William R. Gordon.[38] The heated discussion in that denomination about dropping "Dutch" from the name, he saw as symptomatic of a low spiritual level.[39] His sharpest criticism was of Joseph F. Berg of New Brunswick Theological Seminary for holding the stone in Daniel's vision to be American democracy. Why not pray, "Your Republic come," he suggested.[40] For all forms of secularized, optimistic postmillenarianism within American liberalism he had only contempt.

He also had contempt for the Freemasons,[41] but most of all for the Ware Hollandsche Gereformeerde Kerk, that is, the CRC. A glance at *De Wachter*, newly issued publication of that denomination, brought back bitter memories and touched off a bitter blast aimed at all the seceders in North America. He would rather have joined the RCA than this group. Had they not belittled Anthony Brummelkamp, in whose shade none of them could stand? As for this Wilhelmus H. Van Leeuwen with the letters "v.d.m." behind his name, let all know the v.d.m. stands for "verleiders der menschen." Scholte fumed, "We cannot conclude any different than that the denomination which deceives itself and others with the title 'Ware Gereformeerde Kerk' is the most wicked district in the contemporary Babylon, with its choking atmosphere destroying the spiritual life and hindering spiritual maturity in grace, or as Jodocus van Lodenstein said, 'a lantern without light, and a temple without God.'"[42]

This bitter blast became his "swan song." The same issue of *De Wachter* which replied to his diatribe carried the notice, "H. P. Scholte Is Dead." A heart attack brought the end on August 25, 1868.[43] With unusual charity a contributor dismissed the bitter attack as due to "Scholte's idea that all

37. Hendrik P. Scholte, "Mijn Koningrijk Is Niet van Deze Wereld," *De Toekomst* 2 (1867/68):152–159.
38. Hendrik P. Scholte, "Tijdsbepaling," *De Toekomst* 2 (1867/68):165; John Terhume and William R. Gordon, *Christocracy*, or, Essays on the Coming and Kingdom of Christ. With Answers to the Principal Objections of Post-millenarians (New York: A. Lloyd, 1867).
39. Hendrik P. Scholte, "Inleiding," *De Toekomst* 2 (1867/68):1–3.
40. Scholte, "Tijdsbepaling," p. 165.
41. Hendrik P. Scholte, "Vrijmetselarij," *De Toekomst* 2 (1867/68):187.
42. Hendrik P. Scholte, "De Wachter," *De Toekomst* 2 (1867/68):185–187.
43. *De Wachter* 1 (11 September 1868):4.

churches were Babylon" and expressed a debt of gratitude for what the leader of the Afscheiding had done in his better days.[44]

The notes of his swan song faded away. Perhaps it was just as well, for no one seemed to be listening. There was still the Scholte church, of course, but less than one-tenth of the three thousand inhabitants of Pella were members of it. The city fathers passed a resolution to honor the leader of the Colony. Various newspapers in North America and the Netherlands carried the news of his death. His words had already ceased to bear weight.

For many of his poor contemporaries, the other-worldliness in the last years of the life of the preacher-turned-banker had a hollow ring. He who disappointed the hopes of "het Reveil" led and quarreled with the Afscheiding, and cocaptained the migration, founded and failed the colony. The greatest and most disillusioned politician of the immigrants died virtually alone, a stranger in a strange land.

Perhaps his life was mostly failure. Certainly his leadership faltered time and again. But there was also a kind of consistency in his inconsistency; nobility and idealism redeemed a seeming pragmatism. His willful character, combined with economic independence and ready rationalization, made him careless of his friends and colleagues. There is no evidence that he ever accepted correction or admitted he was wrong. More basically his Reveil individualism, biblicism and romantic idealism unfit him for bondage to crowd, creed, or custom. A man of less conviction would have compromised at many of the crises of his life. He preferred to follow the gleam wherever it led. Perhaps this too is a kind of greatness![45]

---

44. "Nog eens aan Ds. de Beij," *De Wachter* 1 (11 September, 1868):4.

45. The influence of Scholte in the theology and church life of the Dutch colonies in North America took a most unexpected course. Since he made no provision for a school to train future ministers and since he was part of no denomination, it seemed that his direct influence ended with the early demise of the Scholte church in Pella. Many years later, Bultema, interested in the life and teaching of Scholte, became the leader of a premillenial movement of considerable influence in the 1920s. In several personal conversations with Harry Bultema, the leader of the Berean Church of Muskegon, I was assured that he had been deeply influenced by the writings of Scholte. Undoubtedly there have been others, especially around Pella, who were impressed by the views of Scholte. Henry Beets was also fond of Scholte and helped me with many materials about him.

6

≡ Grundy College: 1916–1934

Henry Zwaanstra

The establishment of Grundy College belongs to the period of the hyphenated American in our national life. Prior to World War I the Christian Reformed Church in North America (hereafter CRC) consisted of two ethnically distinct and culturally self-conscious groups. The larger group was of Dutch ancestry, the smaller German. Both groups wished to retain in North America and in the CRC their inherited ethnic character traits, languages, and cultures.

The German contingent emigrated from Ostfriesland, a province in the Northwest corner of Germany. In North America these German immigrants settled in rural areas in Illinois, Iowa, and Minnesota. Central Iowa, particularly the vicinity of Grundy Center, was the area of greatest concentration. Being German-speaking, these immigrants formed a separate classis in the CRC: Classis Ost Friesland.

From the beginning the churches of Classis Ost Friesland experienced difficulty in procuring ministers for their congregations. In 1883 the synod of the CRC advised them to seek help from the Theological School of the Old Reformed Church at Veldhausen, Graafschap, Bentheim in Germany.[1] Three years later, when the Old Reformed Church in Germany asked for financial assistance, the synod of the CRC recommended that an offering be taken for the school at Veldhausen. Recognized needs of the German-speaking congregations here influenced the decision to aid the brethren in Germany.[2]

1. *Handelingen* van de Synodale Vergadering der Hollandsche Christelijke Gereformeerde Kerk Gehouden te Grand Rapids, Michigan den 23 Mei en Volgende Dagen 1883 (Holland: De Wachter Drukkerij, 1883), p. 24 (Art. 68).
2. *Handelingen* van de Synodale Vergadering der Hollandsche Christelijke Gereformeerde Kerk in

That Veldhausen could not meet the demands of an expanding German constituency in North America became increasingly apparent. In 1894 Classis Iowa asked Calvin College and Seminary to provide prospective ministers for their congregations with more instruction in German. The Calvin Board of Trustees and faculty told the classis that at that time the College and Seminary did not have the resources to offer more German.[3] In 1902 it was Classis Ost Friesland, constituted (1896–98) out of some of the churches of Classis Iowa which urgently requested an increase in instruction in German at the denominational school in Grand Rapids.[4] The impatience of German-speaking congregations prompted Classis Ost Friesland to ask the next synod for permission to open its own theological school. Although the request received public support in the church press,[5] the synod was not ready to endorse it. The synod did, however, acknowledge the special needs of its German churches and with the help of the classis promised to meet these needs through Calvin Theological Seminary.[6]

In 1907 Henry Beets, the editor of *The Banner,* suggested that the CRC people of German ancestry start a small secondary school and entrust the literary education of their students to a teacher from their own community. Beets believed that this would prepare the way for a reasonable request for a theological seminary like Dubuque, the theological school of the German Presbyterians. If the classis could guarantee the salary of a theological professor, Beets said he saw no reason why the synod would not appoint one. Beets was convinced that the CRC had to have such a seminary if the church's ministry among the German immigrants was to grow as it should. He was no less certain that Classis Ost Friesland should take the initiative.[7] Nine years later the classis took the initiative on a somewhat larger scale than Beets had modestly suggested.

Christian Reformed College and Seminary
Under the Supervision of Classis Ost Friesland:
1916-1920

In March 1916 Lincoln Center CRC of Lincoln Center, Iowa, where William Bode was stationed as a home missionary, asked Classis Ost Friesland

---

de Vereenigde Staten van Noord Amerika, Gehouden te Grand Rapids, Michigan, den 9den Juni, en Volgende Dagen, 1886 (Holland: De Wachter Drukkerij, 1886), p. 36 (Art. 113).

3. *Acta van de Synode* der Hollandsche Christelijke Gereformeerde Kerk in Amerika Gehouden te Grand Rapids, Michigan in 1894 (Grand Rapids: J. B. Hulst, 1894), p. 31 (Art. 70).

4. *Acta der Synode* van de Christelijke Gereformeerde Kerk in Amerika Gehouden te Holland, Michigan van 18 tot 27 Juni, 1902 (Holland: H. Holkeboer, 1902), pp. 20–26 (Art. 39).

5. "Classis East Friesland Notes," *The Banner of Truth* 39 (1904):108.

6. *Acta der Synode* van de Christelijke Gereformeerde Kerk Gehouden te Holland, Michigan 14 Juni, en Volgende Dagen, 1904 (Holland: H. Holkeboer, 1904), p. 25 (Art. 87).

7. Henry Beets, "East Friesland's Problem," *The Banner* 42 (1907):221.

to "undertake ways and means to further the German work." What Lincoln Center apparently had specifically in mind with the request was taking an option to purchase an available building for the purpose of opening a school. A committee with Bode as chairman was appointed to investigate the matter.[8]

Before the results of the investigation were presented to the classis they were evidently reported in *The Banner.* The April 27, 1916, issue of *The Banner* featured the McKinley Public High School in Grundy Center, Iowa, on its front page. In a news item from Classis Ost Friesland it was reported that the committee had already obtained an option to purchase the property, appraised at $25,000, for $7,500. The news item further stated that Bode had been appointed educational secretary, that $2,500 had already been pledged for the school by the Commercial Club in Grundy Center, and that another $2,200 had been promised by other interested parties. According to the news release Bode was planning to visit all the consistories in the classis and, accompanied by a consistory member from each church, would be going house to house soliciting support for the school.[9]

In the same issue of *The Banner* Beets gave his enthusiastic endorsement to the contemplated undertaking and with much animation argued the case for a German institution of higher learning. In his judgment the CRC's work among German immigrants in the West was bleeding to death for lack of an institution of higher education. Unless such an institution were established, Beets predicted, the German congregations would dwindle away as had those of the True Reformed Protestant Dutch Church in the East. The lack of a central rallying point, a school to furnish leaders for the congregations and pastors for the pulpits, was the main reason for the earlier decline of these congregations in the East.[10] Moreover, the history of the German Presbyterian College in Dubuque, Iowa, and other similar schools demonstrated that a group of churches could be built up around the nucleus of an educational institution. Beets said the present bloodletting resulted from the fact that other denominations were drawing the more ambitious and intelligent young people away from the German CRCs and were furnishing preachers for new immigrant settlements in the West.

The arguments used by the Synod of 1904 to counteract the opening of a separate seminary for educating ministers for the German congregations, Beets said, looked quite good on paper, but in reality had little value. The preparation of an acceptable and effective ministry for the German

---

8. Minutes of Classis Ost Friesland, March 21 and 22, 1916.

9. "East Friesland Items," *The Banner* 51 (1916):275.

10. The reference is to a group of English-speaking churches that had seceded from the Reformed Protestant Dutch Church in 1822. In 1890 these churches (Classis Hackensack) joined the CRC. Unfortunately the union was not a mutually satisfying and happy one. In 1908, all except three of these churches voted to dissolve the union with the CRC.

churches required much more than studying German as a course of instruction. It demanded a German environment, constant training in the German language, German literature and history, and a continuous imbibing of the spirit that made Germany so great. Because the Dutch language and culture were so prominent in the CRC students of German ancestry had to struggle to remain true to their own people and to retain the desire to minister to them rather than to Dutch congregations.

Beets also argued the case for other than ethnic reasons. Going to Calvin College from Iowa was not so easy as it looked, especially in view of the competition offered by other schools. The Presbyterians were planting high schools, colleges and seminaries throughout the country. The Reformed Church in America (hereafter RCA) had Rutgers College in New Brunswick, New Jersey, Hope College in Holland, Michigan, as well as Central College in Pella, Iowa. The RCA west of Chicago was no larger than the CRC and it would soon have four institutions of higher learning west of Chicago, while the CRC had none.

Beets' final argument was really an affirmation of the indispensability of Christian higher education for CRC young people. To leave them uneducated was to condemn them to remain "hewers of wood and drawers of water." Without the necessary institutions of higher learning the CRC could never fulfill its unique calling to leaven North America with a Calvinistic view of life and the world. If the young people were trained in other institutions, they would either leave the CRC, robbing it of its precious life-blood, or they would remain with the church and taint its blood with liberal, or at least uncalvinistic, religious ideas. Beets urged the brethren from Ost Friesland "to strike on the anvil unitedly and continually while the iron was hot!"[11]

A special meeting of Classis Ost Friesland was called to consider the recommendations of the committee appointed in March 1916.[12] The meeting was held May 2 and 3, 1916, at Lincoln Center. The Reverend Cornelius Bode, the father of William Bode, was elected chairman. Henry C. Bode, also a son of Cornelius Bode and pastor of the Ridott CRC of Ridott, Illinois, served as secretary pro tem. Sessions held the first day were devoted to a discussion of the recommendations presented by the committee. The kind of school being contemplated and its location were discussed. Bode related his experiences and expressed the hope that the classis would adopt the recommendations. According to the minutes the matter was looked at from every angle and considered in detail. All were given the time they needed to express themselves wholly and completely. The crucial

11. Henry Beets, "A School in Grundy County, Iowa," *The Banner* 51 (1916):268–269. Beets did not identify the four institutions of higher education of the RCA west of Chicago.

12. The delegates to classis probably did not have the opportunity to read the April 27, 1916, issue of *The Banner* prior to the meeting.

decision was finally taken. The secretary simply recorded, ". . . earlier thoughts descend and a hopeful future appears, we can finally say, with faith and trust in God, we can dare this step: namely we can make this move in Grundy Center and erect this school provided Bode is ready to dedicate himself to it."[13] Bode was then offered an appointment, without official title, at a salary of $1,500. Not unlike Martin Luther, the doctor asked for time to think it over. To the joy of everyone he accepted the appointment the next morning. A committee was then appointed to assist Bode in implementing the decision of the previous day. In the afternoon the classis recessed for a sightseeing tour of Grundy Center and the McKinley High School. After the visit Henry Bode, in the presence of the other delegates, pledged a respectable amount of money to the new school.[14]

The news of the classis' decision was heralded in the local press. Both *The Grundy Center Democrat* and *The Grundy Center Republican* carried the announcement. The papers reported that Bode had been the unanimous choice for president of the new college. According to *The Grundy Center Democrat* Bode's selection was especially pleasing to the people of Grundy Center where his enthusiasm, energy, good fellowship, and business capacity were so well known.[15]

In his time Bode was probably the best educated minister in the CRC. After studying at Dubuque and Penn colleges, he received an A.B. degree from Haverford College in 1899. In 1902 he graduated from Calvin Seminary and became a candidate for the ministry in the CRC. Bode served the Woden CRC of Woden, Iowa, and the Burton Heights CRC of Grand Rapids, Michigan, before enrolling in a program of graduate studies at the University of Chicago in 1910. After being declared a candidate for the Ph.D. degree in Philosophy, Bode returned to the study of theology. In 1913 he was awarded a doctorate in Sacred Theology at Temple University, Philadelphia. Bode then became a home missionary, organizing churches among German immigrants in central Iowa.[16]

After the May, 1916, meeting of Classis Ost Friesland Bode went right to work. Stationery for the new school was immediately printed. The heading read: "Christian Reformed College Under the Auspices and Supervision of Classis Ost (East) Friesland, Rev. Dr. W. Bode, President." Members of an advisory board were also listed on the letterhead.[17]

In a letter to Beets dated May 12, 1916, Bode expressed appreciation for Beets' letters and writings. He told Beets "what a comfort it was, when in

---

13. Minutes of Classis Ost Friesland, May 2 and 3, 1916.
14. Ibid. Diedrich H. Kromminga represented the Ackley, Iowa, church at the meeting of classis.
15. *The Grundy Center Democrat*, May 4, 1916, and *The Grundy Center Republican*, May 4, 1916.
16. *Grundy Center Messenger*, Catalog Edition, 1930–1931, p. 3, and Henry Beets, "In Memoriam," *The Banner* 76 (1941):1070.
17. Diedrich H. Kromminga was also a member of the Advisory Board.

the lonely hours of the night the words of Beets spurred me on in this gigantic task." Bode also briefly reported the progress of his work. A Mr. T. Abkes of the Ackley CRC of Ackley, Iowa, a former elder and widower of eighty-two years, contributed $25,000. Bode described him as "a good, grand old man full of the fear of God, awaiting the hope of Israel." Bode thought the college would bear Abkes' name.[18] Another unidentified man offered to give property valued at $10,000. In addition to these commitments Bode already had two donations of $1,000. Thirteen contributions of $500 and some smaller gifts, making a total of $46,500. "What the Lord can do with His people!" Bode exclaimed.[19]

The synod of the CRC, meeting in June 1916, had on its agenda an overture from Classis Ost Friesland requesting a grant of $2,000 for the establishment of a "German School" and asking the synod to relieve the churches of the classis from the obligation to pay the quota for Calvin College and Seminary. The synodical advisory committee recommended granting the $2,000 but did not favor canceling the quota. The committee was not ready to endorse the quota request because it was not able to judge precisely what kind of school the classis intended to establish. The committee said that it did not appear that Ost Friesland would have a college and seminary. Quotas should not be canceled in those areas where Christian high schools were erected. The synod did not accept the advice of its committee. It rather decided conditionally to grant the classis' request and appointed a committee to investigate the basis and constitution of the school. Only if the committee had no objections could the promised $2,000 be paid from the treasury of the denominational school, Calvin College and Seminary. Synod's committee was also asked, with the assistance of Classis Ost Friesland, to prepare a regulatory statement which would indicate and determine the relationship between the denomination and the school under consideration at Grundy Center. The committee was to report the result of its work to the next synod. The synod also agreed to release the Ost Friesland churches from the obligation to pay the assessment for the denominational school, but only until the next meeting of synod.[20]

18. An article on the establishment of the new college also appeared in one of Grand Rapids newspapers. Beets may well have been the informer. The article in the newspaper stated that the college would be known as Abkes College. According to the report CRC people were displeased with the idea of naming the school after a man because he gave a large financial contribution. The practice was considered not only in flat contradiction with the scriptural rule that the left hand should not know what the right hand does, but it was also contrary to the church's customs. The newspaper article concluded by saying: "Local people have no grudge against the Iowa people at all for doing what they have done in establishing this college, and especially Calvin College will be glad to have a friend in the Middle West." Clipping from a Grand Rapids newspaper, Beets Collection, Colonial Origins, Calvin Library (Folder 20).

19. Letter to Henry Beets, May 12, 1916, Beets Collection (Folder 20).

20. *Acta der Synode 1916* van de Christelijke Gereformeerde Kerk Gehouden van 21 tot 30 Juni 1916 te Grand Rapids, Michigan (Holland: Holland Printing Co., 1916), pp. 32–34 (Art. 33).

While the synod was proceeding cautiously Bode was forging ahead rapidly, recruiting faculty[21] and students and soliciting funds[22] in preparation for the opening of the school in the fall. The August 31, 1916, issue of *The Banner* announced the opening and dedication of the "Christian Reformed College, Grundy Center, Iowa," on October 4.

The announcement presented a comprehensive and ambitious instructional program with no less than seven departments or courses of study:

1. Sub-Preparatory Department, for those who had not yet finished the eighth grade.
2. Academy (high school), a four-year course of study, preparatory for college.
3. College, for the 1916–1917 academic year, with only the freshman course being offered.
4. Divinity Department, a three-year course of study in preparation for the Christian ministry (most of the work in this department was to be done in the German language).
5. Musical Department.
6. Special Evening Classes, especially in German.
7. Special Winter Course, to be offered as a sort of Winter Interim.

According to the "Announcement," the aim of the school was: "Coeducational, thorough training, Christian teaching, upholding the Reformed

---

21. Rev. John Timmerman from Orange City, Iowa, was offered an appointment to teach theology. A letter to Beets indicates that he experienced considerable difficulty and engaged in much soul-searching before accepting the appointment. Because the letter provides an excellent commentary on the spiritual and human dimensions of the history of Grundy College most of it is reproduced as written.

"My dear Brother:

Thank you for your interest in my call from Grundy Center, IA. You have a full share in this latest development of the German work. The Germans will not forget their noble Dutch champion without fear and without reproach! But I was not going to pay you compliments now, but to tell you about the great straits into which this call has put me. I do not know what the Lord wants me to do! Aside from the question of my ability or rather *in*ability, which in itself would be serious enough already, there are so many other questions, I cannot solve. Can the school have a future? With pl. ms. 400 families sustaining it? May we expect theol. students right along from such a small field? Will there be fields for candidates every year? Can the institution be financed? Will the prophecies of ministers that are telling me, the school will be a failure, not come true? May I leave my present field, where people desire to keep me very much for such problematical work? Then again is this movement not from the Lord? What if I decline? My dear Brother, it is too much for me! I took another week to decide and I feel that I cannot decide. May the Lord have mercy upon me and direct my path. Please pray for me. . . ."

Letter to Beets, August 8, 1916, Beets Collection (Folder 20).

22. In a letter to Beets dated August 26, 1916, Bode again thanked Beets for his letters, public writing and inspiration. Bode then said, "Can't you go out later on a tour in behalf of our college for an old fashioned campaign for a Holland chair? If you could do this, say next year, perhaps we could put you in it. Meanwhile, may the Lord bless us." Letter to Beets, August 26, 1916, Beets Collection.

Standards, German as a specialty, competent instructors, fitting for life's service, and preparation for the Christian ministry."[23]

On October 4, 1916, the school was dedicated. In the afternoon, Bode spoke on "Our Movement," greetings were received from Classes Orange City and Sioux Center,[24] and then Cornelius Bode installed Dr. William Bode, the Reverends John Timmerman, and Diedrich H. Kromminga as Professors of Theology. In the evening, Bode spoke on "Coming to Grundy" and greetings were received from Classis Pella and the Board of Trustees of Calvin College and Seminary. Professor Kromminga also gave an address.[25]

President Bode was immensely successful in recruiting a faculty. The school opened with eight full-time professors whose assignments were as follows: William Bode: Old Testament and Missions; John Timmerman: Dogmatics, Homiletics, and German; Diedrich H. Kromminga: New Testament, Greek, and German; Lylas King: Latin and English; Minette Schulte: Music; A. Clevering: Science; W. G. Strack: Mathematics; and O. G. Poppen: History.[26] Bode was only somewhat less successful in attracting students. Although there are no official admission records, eighty-one students probably enrolled during the 1916–1917 academic year.[27] The first faculty meeting was held October 5, 1916. The minutes of this and subsequent meetings are recorded in beautiful English in the handwriting of Professor Kromminga.

From the beginning, Sunday worship services were held on campus, a German service in the morning and a Dutch one in the afternoon. Later biweekly Sunday evening services in English were added for students who could not benefit from German or Dutch sermons.[28] On October 31, 1916, College Church was organized. Comprised primarily of students and faculty members and their families, College Church never became a flourishing congregation. It was always financially dependent on Classis Ost Friesland and frequently had difficulty raising the money to pay the modest rent for using the college's facilities.[29]

In spite of the ominous clouds and forebodings of World War I and the depression which forced an early closing and the canceling of com-

23. "Christian Reformed College, Grundy Center, Iowa," *The Banner* 51 (1916):549.

24. Representatives and supporters of Grundy College later argued that the presence of delegates and official greetings at the dedication service committed the classes represented to support the school.

25. Dedication of Christian Reformed College and Installation of Theological Professors, Grundy Center, Iowa, October 4, 1916 (Dedication program).

26. Ibid.

27. The names of eighty-one students were listed in the *Announcement* of the Christian Reformed College and Seminary, a sort of college catalog for the 1917–1918 academic year.

28. Grundy Faculty Minutes, September 7, 1917.

29. Grundy Board Minutes, June 2, 1925, and January 26, 1926. Grundy College Church existed from 1916 to 1941.

mencement in the spring of 1917, Grundy College did surprisingly well during the first years of its existence.[30] A second year of college study was added in the fall of 1917. Probably to enhance the academic prestige of the fledgling institution, the school awarded its first degrees to the theology professors, Timmerman (M.A.) and Kromminga (A.B.).[31] Students completing the theological course of studies were given A.B. degrees; those finishing the two-year college course were granted "Associate of Arts" degrees. Over the years, in addition to Timmerman and Kromminga, Grundy College awarded A.B. degrees to J. B. Frerichs, J. Masselink, and O. Poppen (1918),[32] Herman Schultz (1919),[33] and John G. Plesscher and William Masselink (1920).[34]

Although the school still had no official and permanent name,[35] it was advertised and presented to the public as "The Christian Reformed College and Seminary, Grundy Center, Iowa." The advertisements and announcements described Grundy Center as a beautiful little city of sixteen hundred inhabitants surrounded by one of the most prosperous farming districts in the world. It was conveniently located, had paved streets and a fine library. Grundy Center was a clean town, an ideal place for a college offering all the advantages, but without the temptations, of a large city. The school was publicized as the institution of higher learning for CRC young people in the West. Only students of good repute were encouraged to apply for admission and degrees were to be awarded only to those who demonstrated intellectual ability and moral character. Parents were assured that all students were under strict discipline and consequently they could "feel perfectly safe" in sending their children to "Grundy."[36]

At "Grundy" discipline *was* strict. The programs and activities of all

30. Grundy Faculty Minutes, May 1, and 11, 1917.

31. On April 13, 1917, the faculty decided to request the board to confer on Professor Timmerman an honorary M.A. degree. Timmerman then closed the meeting with prayer. Kromminga had to work for his degree. With the assistance of Professor Clevering, Kromminga completed a course in physics. Upon the recommendation of the faculty, the board granted him an A.B. degree. Grundy Faculty Minutes, October 20, 1916, April 13, 1917, and May 1, 1917. See Board decisions reported to the Faculty which were recorded with the Grundy Faculty Minutes of May 11, 1917.

32. Commencement Program, 1918.

33. There is no official record indicating that Schultz received the degree. He did, however, complete the theological course of studies and was examined for candidacy. Presumably he graduated and was awarded a degree. Grundy Faculty Minutes, June 17, 1919.

34. Commencement Program, 1920. Later, Edward Masselink, who supplemented his Grundy work with courses at the University of Chicago, frequently requested the faculty and board to grant him an A.B. degree. Masselink even argued that he was promised the degree. For his benefit the board informed Princeton Seminary that he had completed work equivalent to a four-year college course and that when, and if, Grundy College was able to give such a degree, he would be given one. Grundy Faculty Minutes, February 2, 1923, and May 5, 1924; Grundy Board Minutes, February 8, 1923, and June 3, 1924, and February 3, 1925.

35. Grundy Faculty Minutes, April 13, 1917.

36. *Announcement, 1917–1918;* "Christian Reformed College and Seminary," *Bugle 1919,* p. 5; and *Grundy College Announcements, 1923–1924,* pp. 8–9.

student organizations had to be approved by the faculty. The faculty even approved the school colors. No social functions could be held on Monday, Tuesday, Wednesday, or Thursday evenings. Dormitory residents had to observe a 7:00 o'clock curfew. The faculty forbade students to attend theaters, pool halls, and other places of amusement.[37]

At student initiative an athletic association was formed in 1917, and a basketball game played with Grundy Center High School.[38] The faculty made a diligent, but eventually futile effort to establish an unrealistic dress code for the team. The suits had to extend to the knees; the jerseys could not be narrow across the shoulders nor wide open at the arms. Boys who failed to meet these requirements had to wear summer underwear under their suits. When it was learned that suits in accordance with the requirements laid down by the faculty were not on the market, an effort was made to get such suits made to order. Manufacturing companies evidently were unable to fill the order. The faculty disciplinarian was finally asked to find out what kind of suits were available and to require the boys to wear the kind that were in his judgment the most decent.[39]

Over the years student interest in competitive sports, especially basketball, increased. The faculty, however, made a strenuous effort to hold the line. Since in the faculty's judgment competitive games had a tendency to absorb the energy of the participants, the faculty passed a resolution forbidding games outside of Grundy Center.[40] The students, however, continued to agitate for permission to participate. In response to a petition signed by a majority of the students, the faculty capitulated and granted the basketball team permission to play with schools outside Grundy Center provided that no more than one game per month was scheduled, that each player had at least a B- average, and that the games were held on Friday afternoon or evening. In capitulating the faculty assumed no responsibility for the games and reserved for itself the right to retract without previous notice the permission granted should the faculty consider the games detrimental either to the students or the school.[41] In later years basketball under coach Benjamin Janssen became an accepted part of Grundy College's extra-curricular program.[42]

From its founding Grundy College sought to train its students in the arts of rhetoric and public speaking. Students and faculty members formed a society for the purpose of promoting skill and freedom in public address.

37. Grundy Faculty Minutes, February 22, 1918; March 6, 1918; September 13, 1918; February 13, 1919; January 16, 1920; and January 3, 1921.

38. "Athletics," *The Bugle* 1 (November 1917):58.

39. Grundy Faculty Minutes, February 22, 1918; September 13, 1918; and September 2, 1921.

40. Ibid., January 3, 1921.

41. Ibid., December 18, 1922, and October 19, 1923.

42. Ibid., November 27, 1927; October 26, 1928; and March 1, 1929.

At society meetings students presented sermons, essays, and orations. All faculty members, and students who were appointed for the occasion, criticized the students' addresses and performance. Every third sermon delivered by a theological student had to be in the English language.[43] The society soon was given the name *Fare Fac*. *The Bugle*, the school annual of Grundy College, originated with *Fare Fac*. Later, probably due to increased anglicanization, *Fare Fac* became the "Sunrise Society," a society whose specific purpose was to develop the art of speaking and debating.[44] Every year graduating students were required to write an essay and give an oration. The Board of Directors itself evaluated the students' literary work. Commencement programs regularly featured orations by members of the graduating classses. The faculty somewhat sporadically sponsored oratorical contests.[45]

In June 1917 Bode sent out a letter addressed to "Kind Friends." After again briefly indicating the unique character and purpose of the school and recounting God's blessings upon it during the first year, Bode said that the same faith underlying the founding of the school had led to a decision to build a boys' dormitory to accommodate the many students contemplating enrolling in the fall. Bode then made a plea for money and invited his readers to join in the "noble work for the Master" by means of a contribution. The letter, somewhat intimidatingly, stated the consequences if the necessary funds were not made available.[46]

At a public ceremony on August 11, 1917, the cornerstone of the boys' dormitory was laid. The Reverend Gerhard L. Hoefker of Wellsburg, Iowa, gave an address in German; Beets gave one in English.[47] The new dormitory was a very substantial four-story brick building with 66 rooms, a gymnasium, and dining facilities in the basement. It was erected at a cost of approximately $100,000. Grundy Center contributed $5,000; Classis Ost Friesland underwrote the rest. The money to cover the construction costs evidently came pouring in. Less than a year later only a little debt remained on the building.[48]

Almost every piece of publicity that came from the pen of Bode and from the school in Grundy Center included pleas for funds and prayers, especially funds. Bode offered to name the new dormitory after a wealthy contributor; friends and supporters of the school were encouraged to

43. Ibid., October 20, 1916, and November 3, 1916.

44. "Fare Fac," *The Bugle* 1 (November 1917):51–52, and *Grundy College Announcements*, 1923–1924, p. 11.

45. Grundy Faculty Minutes, May 11, 1923; June 4, 1923; March 7, 1924; March 29, 1927; and October 7, 1927.

46. Letter of Bode, June 15, 1917.

47. Program for the Laying of the Corner Stone, August 11, 1917.

48. William Bode, "Our Dormitory," *The Bugle* 1 (November 1917):45–46, and Classis Ost Friesland, *Historische Toelichting*, 1918, pp. 1–4.

cover the costs for educating a Christian young man for the ministry.[49] A "Perpetuate Memory Club" was formed to create an endowment fund. In 1917 forty-one people decided to perpetuate their memory by contributing $500 or more.[50]

The apparent initial success of the German school was greeted with considerably more enthusiasm in Classis Ost Friesland than in the CRC at large. The Board of Trustees of Calvin College and Seminary reported to the Synod of 1918 that many concerned parties had called the board's attention to the manner in which the school at Grundy Center attempted to acquire students and financial support outside Classis Ost Friesland. The board urged the synod to take the necessary measures to avoid competition between the two schools. The board also called the synod's attention to the fact that two schools were now training candidates for the ministry in the CRC, and to the fact that the Grundy Center school did not stand under the supervision of the churches collectively as was the case with the denominational school in Grand Rapids.[51]

The committee appointed by the Synod of 1916 to examine the basis of the school in Grundy Center and to draw up a regulatory statement determining the relationship between the new school and the CRC reported that it had found nothing objectionable in the basis of the school. The school was based on the Holy Scriptures and the confessional standards of the Reformed churches. The committee further observed that the school arose very rapidly and already had a complete high school, a two-year college course of study, and a three-year theological department. Unfortunately, the committee with the assistance of Classis Ost Friesland had not succeeded in formulating a statement outlining the relationship between the school in Grundy Center and the denomination. This failure resulted from two different interpretations of the decisions of the previous synod. According to the one interpretation the Synod of 1916 was fully aware of Classis Ost Friesland's intention to establish a complete college and seminary for the German-speaking churches and had endorsed and attached itself to the new school. If this interpretation were true, the committee said a constitution like the one for the denominational school in Grand Rapids should be formulated for the school in Grundy Center. According to the other interpretation the Synod of 1916 had not yet endorsed and attached itself to the Grundy Center school. The previous synod had temporarily withheld judgment and appointed the committee to advise the Synod of 1918 on the desirability of and reasonableness of the school Ost Friesland envisioned. The committee judiciously withheld judgment on whether or

49. Bode, "Our Dormitory," pp. 45–46.
50. *Announcement*, 1917.
51. Report of the Calvin Board of Trustees, May 28–30, 1918.

not the new school should become a denominational institution leaving the matter entirely to the wisdom of the synod.[52]

Anticipating difficulty, Classis Ost Friesland published in the Dutch language a defense of its school under the title, "Historical Explanation." The apology, also printed in the *Acts of Synod 1918* as appendix XVI, was intended to illumine the delegates to synod. The "Historical Explanation" highlighted the role of divine providence and suppressed the human factor in the establishment of the school. The school came into existence unexpectedly under the Lord's providential guidance. "After serious reflection and fervent prayer, the classis thought it saw here [Grundy Center] an open door and could not do otherwise than to follow the direction in which God was pointing his finger." Under God's blessing the work progressed beyond all expectation. The classis contended that the Synod of 1916 knew very well what the classis had in mind: a school to train ministers for German congregations. Moreover the classis did not believe its action was contrary to sound Reformed Church polity and thought it had the right to request the church to recognize its school, that is, if the synod thought that the school had not yet been approved. The classis did not wish to act arbitrarily or contrary to the judgment of synod. It was, however, convinced that closing the theological department would be a great loss which could never be restored. Under the present circumstances, the classis said, it did not have the courage to close the seminary because the money collected and given had been for training ministers. It was, however, willing to accept stipulations and limitations prescribed by synod, such as to allow only students of German ancestry who were committed to serving German congregations to study theology. And finally, Ost Friesland said that it was willing to place the entire school under synodical jurisdiction as long as the original purpose of the institution was not lost.[53]

Once again, two quite different opinions and sets of recommendations came out of the synodical advisory committee. Reviewing the matter as it presently came before the synod, the majority stated that shortly after the conclusion of the previous synod, Classis Ost Friesland established not only a high school, but also a college and seminary. Before the synodical committee even had a chance to meet, professors were appointed and began teaching. The speed with which the movement progressed evoked surprise and widespread astonishment in the church. In the opinion of the majority, the original request from Ost Friesland was very vague and unclear. The majority, however, admitted that the Synod of 1916 to a certain extent agreed to the founding of a German school by exempting the classis from

52. "Report of Committee Regarding the School at Grundy Center," *Agendum* voor de Synode der Christelijke Gereformeerde Kerk, te Vergaderen te Grand Rapids, Michigan 19 Juni en Volgende Dagen (Holland: Holland Printing Co., 1918), pp. 16-17.
53. Classis Ost Friesland, *Historische Toelichting*, 1918.

paying the quota and by conditionally promising $2,000. Nevertheless, the previous synod obviously did not expect that a college and seminary would soon come into existence. The present confusion, the majority contended, was due to the fact that Classis Ost Friesland failed to declare, and the Synod of 1916 failed to ask, precisely what kind of school was to be established. History had now shown what Ost Friesland had in mind. History had also shown what the CRC desired.

According to the majority the synod now faced the problem of "double training" for the ministry, a problem imposed on the church by the all too hasty action of Classis Ost Friesland. To solve the problem the majority recommended that the synod instruct Classis Ost Friesland to discontinue its seminary. In support of its recommendation the majority argued that the denominational bond uniting all the churches and classes prohibited a classis from establishing a separate theological school alongside a denominational seminary supported by all the churches. If a second seminary were needed, then not a classis but the church as a whole should take the matter in hand. The majority also expressed the opinion that a seminary for Classis Ost Friesland would not promote denominational unity and cooperation, but just the opposite when the church desperately needed unity in order to fulfill its calling in North America. What Classis Ost Friesland itself needed was oneness with the entire denomination, not a seminary of its own. The German language and customs were considerations of decreasing importance which could not and must not be allowed to warrant the classis having its own theological school. And finally the majority, forthrightly although uncharitably, argued that it was absurd for a classis the size of Ost Friesland with only 404 families and 13 congregations, some of which were too small to support a minister, to presume that it needed a school to train its own ministers.

Since the CRC had its own college in Grand Rapids and since the college at Grundy Center, as well as the seminary at Grundy Center, was and was intended to be an institution of the denomination, the majority said a college for Classis Ost Friesland was burdened with the same objections as a seminary. They therefore advised the synod to instruct the classis to disband its college. Two arguments were presented in support of the recommendation. The first was that Classis Ost Friesland itself argued that the college was necessary only because the seminary was necessary. The second was that a college exclusively for the churches in Classis Ost Friesland made no sense. Even the classis recognized this fact and consequently advertised the college as a school for the entire West. All sorts of sordid and damaging results, the majority presumed, would inevitably arise from a college in the West. A college there could now survive only at the expense of Calvin. At that time, the majority thought, all the denomination's resources should be used to maintain and expand Calvin College.[54]

Hoefker, a delegate from Classis Ost Friesland, submitted a minority report. Hoefker took serious exception to the majority report. In his judgment the majority report did not sufficiently reckon with the historical fact that the school in Grundy Center had already existed for two years. Moreover, it onesidedly freed the synod of any responsibility for the school in Grundy Center even though the decisions of the Synod of 1916 had powerfully aided the establishment and development of the institution. The advice to disband the school immediately, Hoefker said, did not sufficiently take into consideration the classis' obligations to the people who contributed the money, the theological professors, or the students already studying theology. Hoefker wanted the synod to declare that the Synod of 1916 was partially responsible for the present flourishing condition of the school in Grundy Center because it endorsed the founding of the school and in this way promoted its initial growth. He also asked the synod to continue the entire school because Calvin College and Seminary had never adequately prepared anyone for ministry in German congregations. Finally, Hoefker requested that should the synod wish to terminate the seminary, the decision to do so be postponed until 1920 because Classis Ost Friesland could not immediately close the seminary.[55]

The Synod of 1918 advised Classis Ost Friesland to disband its seminary. In order to enable students presently enrolled to graduate, the synod allowed the theological department at Grundy College to continue two more years. The synod also agreed to continue to subsidize the school in the amount of $2,000 for another two years. Regarding the college at Grundy Center, the synod said that it did not want another denominational college and therefore urged Classis Ost Friesland to abandon its college. While acknowledging the right of God's people in the West to establish a college, the synod strongly advised against establishing one at that time because the denomination's resources were limited and Calvin College needed what was available.[56]

Bode was not ready to concede to the wishes of the synod and to abandon his school. During the summer of 1918 he made a tour of the western classes to rally support. Beets again applauded his efforts and frankly and sincerely expressed the wish that the people in the West would "pull together, a long pull and a strong one and continue the good work," so that a denominational college might be obtained in Grundy Center.[57]

---

54. *Acta der Synode 1918* van de Christelijke Gereformeerde Kerk Gehouden van 19 tot 29 Juni, 1918 te Grand Rapids, Michigan (Grand Rapids: Christelijke Gereformeerde Kerk, 1918), pp. 67–74 (Art. 59).
55. Ibid.
56. Ibid., pp. 89–90 (Art. 75).
57. Henry Beets, "The Grundy Center School: A Plea for It," *The Banner* 53 (1918):688–690.

During the 1918–1919 academic year approximately one hundred students studied at Grundy College.[58] Although enrollment figures were not regularly recorded and reported, in subsequent years the size of the student body stabilized at a little more than one hundred students. Other than an influenza epidemic in the fall of 1918, necessitating a temporary closing of the school, there are few noteworthy events to record.[59] In the spring of 1920 Timmerman decided to go East, leaving the school for a pastorate in Paterson, New Jersey.[60] Financially, the college and seminary must have immediately felt the impact of the decision of the Synod of 1918. In 1918 only two parties decided to perpetuate their memory by contributing $500 and joining the "Club."[61]

In 1920 Classis Ost Friesland asked the synod to reconsider the decisions of the previous synod. The classis reaffirmed its incontestable right to have its own school to train ministers. The classis said that discontinuing the theological department would be a severe blow to the school and the German congregations. In the opinion of the classis forcing the seminary to close would not promote denominational unity but would only further dissatisfaction and disunity. The synodical advisory committee again produced majority and minority reports. The majority simply advised the synod not to reconsider the matter because Classis Ost Friesland had failed to prove that the grounds on which the decision of the Synod of 1918 obviously rested were untenable.

Professor A. Clevering, a delegate from Ost Friesland, submitted a minority report. Although Clevering's report contained nothing new, it was a well-constructed piece, cogently and forcefully presenting the case for the classis. The request and conflicting reports evoked an animated discussion in which the Reverend John J. Hiemenga, President of Calvin College, and Bode participated. After the debate the synod decided to refer Classis Ost Friesland's request to a special committee. The committee was asked to formulate recommendations that would, as much as possible, remove the objections of the classis to the decision of the previous synod and that would provide a consensus of opinion that could be implemented. Presidents Bode and Hiemenga were appointed to the committee.[62]

Sensing the synod's desire for unity both within the church and for the training of its ministers, the committee, without assuming the responsibility

58. *Announcement,* 1918–1919.
59. Grundy Faculty Minutes, December 17, 1918.
60. Ibid., April 9, 1920.
61. *Announcement,* 1918–1919. Cf. footnote 50.
62. *Acta der Synode 1920* van de Christelijke Gereformeerde Kerk Gehouden van 16 tot 30 Juni, 1920 te Grand Rapids, Michigan (Grand Rapids: M. Hoffius, 1920), pp. 31–35 (Art. 28).

for the decision of the Synod of 1918, judged that it was not desirable to have a theological seminary in Grundy Center. Yet at the same time the committee thought the synod should try to meet the special needs of Classis Ost Friesland, especially since in its judgment the Synod of 1916 was to a certain degree responsible for the existence of the school in Grundy Center. The committee asked Bode and Hiemenga to draw up a plan which would both insure unity in ministerial training and meet the particular needs of the German churches. Hiemenga later said that he first proposed to Bode that the synod appoint Bode to Calvin Seminary to teach theology for German-speaking students. Bode did not want this. Hiemenga then proposed that Bode take his place as President of Calvin College.[63] Again Bode said No. Hiemenga's third proposal was that the synod itself provide a two-year Seminary Preparatory Course beyond the high school level at Grundy College.[64] This proposal, formulated by both presidents and approved by the other members of the committee and the delegates from Ost Friesland, was presented to the synod and unanimously adopted. According to the proposal, technically called "Basis of Agreement," and later popularly known as "the Compromise," the Seminary Preparatory Course was to be designed by the Board of Trustees in consultation with the Executive Committee of the Board of Directors of the school in Grundy Center. Two professors, who would also be members of the Grundy College faculty, were to be appointed to teach the course of study. Their appointment was to be by the Grundy College Board, subject to the approval of the Trustees of Calvin College and Seminary. The Seminary Preparatory Course was to be financed by the Board of Trustees.

The Compromise also called for the formation of a junior college in Grundy Center. A committee of six, consisting of the Presidents Bode and Hiemenga and two board members from each school, was to work out the details and outline the relationship between the junior college and Calvin College and Seminary. Subject to the conditions already stated, the supervision of the entire educational enterprise at Grundy Center was to remain with the faculty and president.

Under the terms of the Compromise, Classis Ost Friesland had to sacrifice its seminary program and Grundy College had to promise not to expand its junior college until Calvin College had at least three graduate departments. Unity had presumably been achieved.[65]

---

63. Why not? Bode had been a college president longer than Hiemenga. Hiemenga became the first president of Calvin College in 1919.

64. John J. Hiemenga, "De Zaak Grundy Center II," *De Wachter* 55 (8 Februari 1922):10.

65. *Acta der Synode 1920*, pp. 62–65 (Art. 40). At the closing session of the synod, the Reverend William P. Van Wijk, President of the 1920 Synod, expressed the wish that the synod would be known in history as the "Unity Synod."

Grundy College: 1920-1934

Classis Ost Friesland temporarily accepted the decisions of the Synod of 1920, but under protest. In compliance with the terms of the Compromise, the theological department was discontinued.[66] With the opening of the new school year, Kromminga was assigned to teach Ancient, Medieval, and Modern History, and courses in Dutch, Greek, and Calvinism.[67] Henry Schultze, a native son, was added to the teaching staff in 1920.[68]

The synodical committee mandated to implement the Compromise met on November 30, 1920. Jacob Manni and Idzerd Van Dellen represented the Calvin Board of Trustees; Henry Ahuis and Henry C. Bode were the representatives of Classis Ost Friesland. Bode informed the committee that the assignment of all the work in the Seminary Preparatory Course to just two professors was impractical and infeasible. The minutes indicate that Hiemenga assured Bode that the work could be distributed among various professors. The committee proposed that Bode, Kromminga, Schultze and Bajema be appointed to the Seminary Preparatory Department. The committee also decided that $4,500 should be paid annually to cover the costs of the preparatory course and that this sum should be forwarded to the college as soon as the Executive Committee of the Calvin Board of Trustees approved the appointment of the four professors. Bode undoubtedly surprised the representatives of the Board of Trustees and Hiemenga with the news that the school would probably be transferred to a society in the near future. The synodical committee, therefore, did not deal with the other points of the Compromise but decided to consider them later at a meeting to be called sometime in March by the secretary, Van Dellen.[69]

Before the synodical committee met, plans had already been made to organize a society and transfer the school from the classis to the new society.[70] On December 8, 1920, an impressive group of forty-three delegates, coming from various places in the states of Iowa, Minnesota, North Dakota, and Illinois, assembled in Grundy Center. Professors Kromminga and Bajema represented Grundy College. Bode gave an introductory address, laying special stress on God's blessings in the founding, growth,

---

66. Minutes of the Calvin Board of Trustees, June 1, 1921, and *Agendum* voor de Synode der Christelijke Gereformeerde Kerk te Vergaderen te Orange City, Iowa, 21 Juni en Volgende Dagen, 1922 (Grand Rapids: M. Hoffius, Printer, 1922), p. 2. Presumably the meeting was not too cordial. Hiemenga later reported that he had persistently asked Bode how much of the preparatory course was taught in German. Bode just as persistently refused to answer the question.

67. Grundy Faculty Minutes, August 9, 1920.

68. Ibid., September 17, 1920.

69. The Minutes of the meeting are reproduced in "Appel van Classis Ostfriesland . . . ," *Agendum Synode* 1922, pp. 21–22 (Rapport III) and John J. Hiemenga, "De Zaak Grundy Center III," *De Wachter* 55 (15 Februari 1922):6.

70. Grundy Faculty Minutes, November 26, 1920.

and development of the school. He also reported on the financial condition of the institution. The property was appraised at about $200,000. The school had other assets worth $19,055.82. The total indebtedness was only $16,200.[71]

Representatives of Classis Ost Friesland presented proposals which were to serve as a Basis of Agreement between the classis and the society. According to the "Agreement," the society was to be based on the Word of God as expressed in the confessional standards of the Reformed churches. Provision had to be made for the special needs of the classis by retaining a German department and offering suitable courses necessary for students preparing for the ministry. The society was also to assume the present debt, honor existing contracts, and keep the buildings insured and in good repair. In case Classis Ost Friesland decided to reopen the seminary, the classis was to have its present rights and privileges restored. If in the future the society failed or was dissolved, the property would revert to the classis.[72]

A "Draft Constitution" was also submitted and tentatively adopted. According to the constitution the society was to be called, "The Society for Secondary and Higher Education on a Reformed Basis in the West." Its stated purpose was to assume and maintain the school at Grundy Center. A Board of Directors consisting of eight members was elected at the meeting on December 8. Bode was appointed to the board as a member ex officio.[73]

The first meeting of the Board of Directors was held February 8, 1921. At this meeting "Grundy College" was adopted as the official name of the school, and "Articles of Incorporation" were drawn up and adopted. The board also passed a resolution expressing its sympathy to Kromminga and his family who were under quarantine for scarlet fever. To help defray expenses the board gave the Krommingas $50. In response to a question raised by a church, the board stated that all its actions were in harmony with synodical decisions and that the same would be true in the future.[74]

The synodical committee did not meet again in March at the call of Van Dellen. Late in February the Compromise of 1920 began to come unraveled when a representative group of the members of the Calvin Board of Trustees decided that the full board should hear the report of its delegation.[75] Consequently, the payment of the promised subsidy for Grundy College was also postponed. After a lengthy and evidently animated discussion, the Calvin Board of Trustees in June 1921 decided to

71. Grundy College Society Minutes, December 8, 1920.
72. Ibid.
73. *Voorloopig Reglement*, Grundy College Society Minutes, December 8, 1920.
74. Grundy Board Minutes, February 8–9, 1921.
75. Minutes of the *Curatorium Contractum* of Calvin Board of Trustees, February 22, 1921.

appoint a committee to investigate whether or not Grundy College had satisfied the conditions of the Compromise adopted by the Synod of 1920. Should the committee find that the synodical stipulations had indeed been met, then the board would meet its obligation and pay the $4,500. Three members of the board, Van Dellen, Jacob Mulder, and William Stuart, protested the decision because in their judgment it did not take into consideration the generally favorable progress report of the synodical committee, and because it did not specifically indicate what the objections were that needed to be investigated and on the basis of which the subsidy was being withheld. Van Dellen attached a note of explanation to his protest expressing the opinion that the board's decision made it impossible for the synodical committee to act because the investigating committee had to report to the Calvin Board of Trustees before anything could be done. Hiemenga, Manni, and Ralph Haan, the latter obviously replacing Van Dellen, were appointed to do the investigating.[76] Shortly after the June 1921, meeting of the Calvin Board of Trustees a committee of Classis Ost Friesland informed the investigating committee that it could not be officially received before the denomination lived up to its part of the Compromise of 1920.[77]

Being deprived of the denominational subsidy, the financial condition of Grundy College began to deteriorate in the fall of 1921.[78] The cost of making a frame house purchased in 1920 into an attractive, modern, eleven-room girls' dormitory, were considerably larger than had originally been anticipated.[79] In an effort to obtain financial relief, Bode sent a letter to CRC consistories stating the reason for the financial distress and requesting that a collection be taken for Grundy College. He also published in the *Grundy College Messenger*, a periodical edited by Kromminga, an

76. Minutes of the Calvin Board of Trustees, June 9, 1921. In a letter to Bode, Beets said that he had talked to some members of the board yesterday (the same day that the board decided to appoint the investigating committee) and told them that Bode had made a mistake by not keeping his school as a seminary and college. He told them, "We ought to look twenty-five or fifty years ahead." Beets also informed Bode that the news had it that he expected to open a seminary soon and perhaps have the East Friesian churches leave the denomination. Bode quickly responded to Beets. Bode said he was surprised at the information the letter contained. He had no knowledge whatsoever on the subject other than that the churches were abiding by the resolutions of the synod. Of course, if support was refused, he did not know what might happen. People were watching the eastern movement, a euphemism for Grand Rapids, very closely. Bode said there was no truth in the statement either that the East Friesian churches were intending to leave the denomination. Somebody evidently wanted to put them in a bad light. Letter of Beets to Bode, June 10, 1921, and Letter of Bode to Beets, June 13, 1921. Beets Collection.

77. "Appel van Classis Ostfriesland . . . ," *Agendum Synode 1922*, pp. 23–24. The classical committee also appointed a committee including Bode and Kromminga to meet with the investigating committee in an informal way. According to Kromminga the committee of the Calvin Board of Trustees did not come to Grundy Center until October 1921. Diedrich H. Kromminga, "Op de Lange Baan Schuiven," *Onze Toekomst* 26 (20 Januari 1922):11. There is no record of a meeting between the investigating committee and the classical committee.

78. Grundy Faculty Minutes, November 18, 1921.

79. Grundy Board Minutes, January 31, 1922.

"Open Letter to J. Manni," the President of the Calvin Board of Trustees.[80] In the "Open Letter" Bode sharply criticized the Calvin Board of Trustees for their failure to implement the Compromise and to pay the promised $4,500. Bode's letters provoked an extraordinarily acrimonious and passionate public airing of the issues. Manni, who said he was shocked by the harshness and crassness with which Bode expressed himself, attempted to give a reasonable explanation for the Calvin Board of Trustees' action.[81] Kromminga articulately and passionately defended the position of Classis Ost Friesland and Grundy College.

Kromminga's ire and indignation were directly aimed at the Calvin Board of Trustees for appointing a committee of investigation rather than following through with the implementation of the Compromise of 1920. By its action the Calvin Board of Trustees had shoved the synodical committee aside and rendered it impotent. They had broken and rendered worthless the Compromise which Kromminga considered a contract between Classis Ost Friesland and the synod. Kromminga was simply outraged that this was done on the basis of "some objections," mere rumors, and suspicions of dishonesty without supporting evidence. He forthrightly stated that in his judgment the only objections the Calvin Board of Trustees had were to the Compromise itself. That the Calvin Board of Trustees did not want the Compromise was now apparent and publicly confessed. If the Calvin Board of Trustees were allowed to dispose of the Compromise, the consequences for Grundy College were clear and certain: Death! Kromminga said he would rather die immediately than suffer persecution for years.[82]

Under the existing circumstances, Kromminga said, synod would either have to condemn the action of the Calvin Board of Trustees and hand over the money or things would return to the *status quo ante,* that is, Classis Ost Friesland would again have the right to its own seminary and the Grundy College Society would have the right freely to develop the college as it pleased. Either the Compromise held or the old rights returned. Kromminga said he preferred the latter.[83]

Kromminga made no effort to conceal the fact that he was extremely angry and personally felt deeply hurt. He said he could understand and tolerate the fact that in some parts of the denomination there was no love

80. Unfortunately, neither of these letters are available. Barend K. Kuiper, editor of *De Wachter* at that time, refused to publish Bode's "Open Letter" because it was judged to be a protest for the synod and protests were not to be published. Barend K. Kuiper, "Geen Monopolie," *De Wachter* 55 (1 Februari 1922):6.

81. Jacob Manni, "Het Besluit van het Curatorium in Zake Grundy Center," *De Wachter* 55 (4 Januari 1922):7.

82. Diedrich H. Kromminga, "De Regeling Gestaakt," *Onze Toekomst* 26 (Januari 1922):2; Kromminga, "Op de Lange Baan Schuiven," p. 11.

83. Diedrich H. Kromminga, "Dr. Bode's Gewraakt Verzoek," *Onze Toekomst* 26 (25 Januari 1922):10.

for Grundy College. What he could not tolerate, however, was that some people in order to get what they wanted repeatedly painted Grundy College black. This had been done from the beginning. Kromminga said that he would not object if there had been grounds for doing this, but since it had been done without reason, it hurt. According to the professor, the Synod of 1920 made a new and hopeful beginning. A compromise was entered: the seminary had to be closed but the rest of the school was to receive recognition and support. "Fortunately," Kromminga said, "we at last knew where we were and peace had come." But no, the Calvin Board of Trustees was still there and the Calvin Board of Trustees did not really want what the synod wanted. The Calvin Board of Trustees did this simply by denying the classis its rights. By not carrying out their own task, the Calvin Board of Trustees got what they wanted. And all this was done by accusing the brothers in Grundy Center of dishonesty. That hurt! Kromminga concluded by saying that in order to put aside the bitterness he felt, he was considering devoting his time and energy to the pastoral care of a small congregation and letting the larger life of the denomination run its course. "But what," Kromminga asked, "would happen if the present evil were allowed to persist?" Kromminga thought that he was not the only one who felt this way. "Woe to our churchly life!" he said.[84]

Hiemenga entered the fray as the defender of the Calvin Board of Trustees' position and action. Not the Calvin Board of Trustees but Bode started the new and threatening storm. In Hiemenga's opinion both Bode and Kromminga had mistakenly given the impression that Grundy College was unjustly treated and that dishonorable motives and practice played a role. Hiemenga said the issue was very simply whether or not Grundy College had kept the agreement and satisfied the conditions of the Compromise of 1920. He boldly stated that Grundy College had not entirely kept the agreement.[85]

Hiemenga was evidently a strict constructionist, Bode a loose one. According to Hiemenga Classis Ost Friesland had always argued the case for a school of its own on the basis of its "special needs." He understood these needs to be German.[86] Regrettably the Synod in 1920 did not specify what precisely was meant by "special needs." Hiemenga was now sorry that he had not persisted in demanding a careful definition and specification of these needs when the agreement was originally negotiated. If the Seminary Preparatory Course at Grundy College were taught in German,

---

84. Ibid., p. 11. Six days later the Grundy College Board of Directors thanked Professor Kromminga for his valuable articles explaining the exact situation in the school controversy. Grundy Board Minutes, January 31, 1922.

85. John J. Hiemenga, "De Zaak Grundy Center IV," *De Wachter* 55 (22 Februari 1922):7.

86. In Hiemenga's series of articles the word *Duitsch* (German), obviously for emphasis, always appears in bold type.

Hiemenga said, there would be no difficulty. From public announcements, however, it was apparent that only one lecture hour was given in German, and only three courses were offered in the German language and literature at Grundy College while Calvin College offered five such courses.

Hiemenga asserted that Grundy College had not in fact kept the Compromise of 1920. Grundy College's Seminary Preparatory Course had not been outlined and arranged by a committee of the Calvin Board of Trustees nor did it entirely correspond with the same course taught at Calvin College as had been specified in the Compromise. The Compromise also called for the appointment of two professors, not four. And the representatives of Grundy College never discussed with the synodical committee how their institution was to be organized as a junior college. On the contrary, the leaders at Grundy College transferred the school to a society so that one party to the contract no longer existed, asserting their Seminary Preparatory Course was under the supervision of Classis Ost Friesland rather than the synod, and in public representing their institution as a complete four-year college.[87]

The personality clashes and hassling over the specific terms of the Compromise were really only incidental to more fundamental and conflicting visions for Christian higher education in the CRC.

Hiemenga wanted the denomination unitedly to invest all of its intellectual and financial resources in a single distinguished institution of higher learning where young people from the East and the West could receive the best education possible. He said little schools and colleges without recognition were a waste of money. And Calvin College was not yet what Hiemenga wanted it to be and thought it should be. In Hiemenga's judgment the synod had clearly and repeatedly said that it did not desire a second college. He bluntly stated that if the brothers in Grundy Center did not want a school such as the one outlined in the Compromise and desired to proceed on their own, then they should not be surprised if they met with opposition. The opposition, Hiemenga insisted, was not due to lack of love, but due to conviction.[88] Kromminga meant what he said. At its January 31, 1922, meeting, the Grundy Board of Directors received from the professor a lengthy letter of resignation. From the board's response, the specific content of the letter can be surmised. Kromminga was unhappy with his teaching assignment.[89] He also evidently anticipated that the position he took as a member of the committee investigating the teaching of Ralph Janssen would have an adverse effect on Grundy College.[90] Although it is

87. Hiemenga, "Zaak Grundy Center II," p. 10; Hiemenga, "De Zaak Grundy Center III," p. 6.

88. Hiemenga, "Zaak Grundy Center IV," p. 7.

89. After being away to study, Bajema objected to having to teach Rural Education and two Dutch courses. The Dutch courses were assigned to Kromminga. Grundy Faculty Minutes, December 16, 1921.

90. Ralph Janssen was Professor of Old Testament at Calvin Seminary. Kromminga represented the

impossible to determine the precise nature of the problem, Kromminga's sermons were giving him difficulty. In response to the letter, the board passed a series of resolutions obviously intended to persuade Kromminga to withdraw his resignation. The board expressed its full confidence in the professor and his teaching. It also acknowledged that the present distribution of work among the professors was unfair to Kromminga and promised to arrange a better and more equitable division of labor. The board assured Kromminga that his presence at the college was not detrimental but rather a blessing and an asset. Since the resolution of the Janssen case was still pending, the board said that it could not pass judgment on the matter, but that it had full confidence in Kromminga and believed him to be a man who would stand for the truth. The problem with the sermons was lightly dismissed. The board simply did not feel the force of the arguments. Finally, the board called attention to a petition, signed by all available students, requesting Kromminga to stay. The board devoted most of the day to cordial discussions with Kromminga regarding the matters raised in his letter and the board's response to them. Kromminga could not, however, be persuaded to withdraw his resignation, and the board could not bring itself to comply with his request. The board finally decided to table the matter.[91]

Kromminga soon received a call from the Edgerton CRC of Edgerton, Minnesota. The faculty relieved him of his teaching assignment in Dutch and urged him to stay. He declined the call.[92] Not long afterward, however, he was asked to become the pastor of the Peoria CRC of Peoria, Iowa. This call he accepted. As secretary of the faculty he attached the following note to the minutes of the April 28, 1922, meeting: "This finishes my work in this line. God bless the School and the Faculty!"[93]

In March 1922, Classis Ost Friesland sent a communication to the Calvin Board of Trustees, registering its objections to the appointment of the investigating committee and criticizing the Calvin Board of Trustees for failing to pay the subsidy according to the terms of the Compromise of 1920. The classis accused the Calvin Board of Trustees of obstructing the

---

minority position on the investigating committee. Kromminga was not exactly a defender of Janssen. He considered the man himself a riddle. Kromminga was, however, concerned to bring fairness and truth into the controversy. That Janssen tried to "explain away the supernatural character of Revelation," Kromminga vigorously denied. Kromminga also felt the Calvin Board of Trustees was treating Janssen the same way it was treating Grundy College: unjustly. Kromminga, "Dr. Bode's Gewraakt Verzoek," p. 11; Diedrich H. Kromminga, "Waarde Redacteur," *Onze Toekomst* 26 (5 April 1922):9–10; Diedrich H. Kromminga, "Geachte Br. van Lonkhuyzen," *Onze Toekomst* 26 (3 Mei 1922):9.

91. Grundy Board Minutes, January 31, 1922.

92. Grundy Faculty Minutes, March 9, 1922, and March 31, 1922.

93. After serving the Peoria CRC of Peoria, Iowa (1922–1926), and the Neland Avenue CRC of Grand Rapids (1926–1928), Kromminga was appointed Professor of Historical Theology at Calvin Seminary where he remained until his death in 1947.

implementation of the synodical agreement and of making cooperation impossible. Consequently the classis declared itself no longer bound to the terms of the agreement and free, should it decide to do so, to expand its junior college and to reopen the seminary. Ost Friesland also informed the Calvin Board of Trustees that unless its grievances were satisfied, it would appeal the matter to the synod.[94]

In order to remove the present difficulties between the Calvin Board of Trustees and Classis Ost Friesland prior to the meeting of synod, the Calvin Board of Trustees decided to send Manni, Van Dellen, and Hiemenga, its original synodical committee, to meet with a committee of the classis.[95] The two committees evidently met early in May. "On board a shaking train," Van Dellen informed the Secretary of the Calvin Board of Trustees, John Dolfin, that "the meeting was a complete failure because the brethren Hiemenga and Manni seemingly did not want to make an attempt to come to a compromise."[96]

Classis Ost Friesland kept its promise and submitted an appeal to the Synod of 1922 against the actions of the Calvin Board of Trustees. The synodical advisory committee attempted to state as succinctly as possible the differences between Classis Ost Friesland and the Calvin Board of Trustees. The classis insisted that it had satisfied all the conditions of the previous synod; the Calvin Board of Trustees argued that the classis had met only one of the requirements, the closing of the seminary. According to the advisory committee the central point at issue in the controversy was whether or not the Seminary Preparatory Course at Grundy College had to be taught primarily in the German language. The Calvin Board of Trustees argued that the "special needs of Classis East Friesland" was the presupposition on which the Compromise was based and that these presumed needs had always been represented by the classis as preparation for the ministry of the Word in the German language. Consequently the Calvin Board of Trustees' main objection to the preparatory course of studies presently being offered at Grundy College was that it was not taught in the German language but was only a duplicate of the same course available at Calvin College. The classis did not agree. In its opinion the Seminary Preparatory Course did not have to be taught in German nor did the Compromise require that it be offered in German. The classis admitted that during the last two years German had been placed in the background because of the new situation brought about by the war.[97]

---

94. "Appel van Classis Ostfriesland . . . ," *Agendum Synode 1922*, pp. 24–26.

95. Minutes of the Calvin Board of Trustees, March 22–29, 1922.

96. Letter of Van Dellen to Dolfin, May 5, 1927, Reports to the Calvin Board of Trustees, 1922, Colonial Origins Collection.

97. *Acta der Synode 1922* van de Christelijke Gereformeerde Kerk Gehouden van 21 Juni tot 5 Juli, 1922 te Orange City, Iowa (Grand Rapids: Grand Rapids Printing Co., 1922), pp. 19–23 (Art. 19). World War I

The synod consistently supported both the judgment and actions of the Calvin Board of Trustees. Classis Ost Friesland did not receive a single word of commendation. Even though the synod judged that classis had not satisfied the conditions of the Compromise of 1920, it, nevertheless, in order to avoid even the appearance of unfairness or lack of friendliness, decided to give Grundy College $9,000 subsidy, $4,500 for each of the last two years. The synod, however, decided not to give Grundy College any more financial subsidy in the future. With this decision the CRC terminated all past, and closed the door to all future, official connections with Grundy College.[98]

In the spring of 1922 Grundy College was accredited as a junior college by the State of Iowa.[99] After the Synod of 1922 adjourned a special meeting of the Grundy Board of Directors was held in Orange City, Iowa, where the synod had assembled. At this meeting the board decided not to reopen the seminary immediately as some had urged but to put the matter on the agenda of a later meeting. The board did, however, decide to offer a third year of college instruction.[100] At a faculty meeting held in September Bode somewhat optimistically advised the faculty to be on the lookout for a forthcoming board announcement to expand the college to a four-year course of study and to reopen the seminary.[101] The board was more cautious than Bode anticipated. It did, however, pass a resolution to recommend to the Grundy College Society that a Theological Department again be opened in the fall and that this department serve as the fourth year of a college degree program. The resolution was then referred to the various local societies and to Classis Ost Friesland for comment and reactions.[102] Presumably it was not favorably received, since the proposal was never formally presented to the society. Upon the recommendation of the board the society in June 1923 unanimously adopted a resolution to complete the college by adding a fourth year of instruction. The board and the faculty were commissioned to develop the necessary curriculum and to expand the teaaching staff.[103]

---

greatly hastened the Americanization of ethnic groups. People of German ancestry especially felt the impact of the war on their ethnic identity and perhaps nowhere was this more true than in Iowa. During the war, Governor Harding decreed that only English could be used in all public addresses, speech in public places, and instruction given in the schools.

98. Ibid., p. 24 (Art. 20). Classis Ost Friesland, for moral and financial reasons asked the next synod for permission to give the portion of the denominational quota designated for Calvin College to Grundy College. The synod did not grant the request. *Acta der Synode 1924* van de Christelijke Gereformeerde Kerk Gehouden van 18 Juni tot 8 Juli, 1924 te Kalamazoo, Michigan (Grand Rapids: Grand Rapids Printing Co., 1924), pp. 26–27 (Art. 30).

99. Grundy Board Minutes, June 6, 1922.

100. Ibid., June 28, 1922.

101. Grundy Faculty Minutes, September 11, 1922.

102. Grundy Board Minutes, November 2, 1922, and February 8, 1923.

103. Ibid., June 5, 1923, and Grundy College Society Minutes, June 6, 1923.

The expansion of the college into a four-year degree granting institution proved more difficult than had been anticipated. Reality chastened the vision. The faculty advised the board first to devise a plan to provide the necessary funds to support a complete college program. Since the president was encumbered with the care of too many administrative details, the faculty recommended the appointment of a business manager so that Bode could devote himself to educational policies and to the development of the school. The faculty also urged the board immediately to introduce a laboratory-taught chemistry course, to expand the library facilities and holdings, and to fill the vacancy on the staff recently created by Schultze's acceptance of a call to the Sherman Street CRC of Grand Rapids.[104]

Although the board endorsed these faculty proposals and committees were appointed to carry them out,[105] a year later the feasibility of a four-year program was still being investigated and the three-year college course had not yet been approved by the state.[106] At an informal meeting held in August 1925 Bode informed the faculty that the state Board of Examiners did not accredit the third-year study course because there were only two students in the program and because the college did not have the equipment required for teaching natural science.[107] Later a faculty committee met with representatives of the state board to discuss accreditation. The results of the meeting were discouraging.[108] In January the board rescinded all previous decisions to establish a three-year college course.[109] At the society meeting held in June Bode reported that the board had dropped the third year of study largely because of the "friction which it created among our people especially in the East."[110]

The Grundy College Society never was a very effective instrument for either the maintenance or promotion of the college. The society was organized in local groups or chapters of dues-paying members. A general society meeting of delegates from the local societies was held annually in June in conjunction with the commencement exercises. Delegates to the annual meeting received reports from and acted on recommendations presented by the Grundy Board of Directors. The election of board members was probably the most important item on the agenda of the meetings of the general society. The first general society meeting was the best-attended and most prestigious of the annual meetings.

104. Grundy Faculty Minutes, February 15, 1924; Grundy Board Minutes, February 20, 1924. Professor Schultze later taught theology at Calvin Seminary (1926–1942; 1951–1959). He also served as President of Calvin College (1940–1951).

105. Grundy Board Minutes, February 20, 1924.

106. Grundy Faculty Minutes, February 3, 1925, and Grundy Board Minutes February 3–4, 1925.

107. Grundy Faculty Minutes, August 17, 1925.

108. Ibid., November 18, 1925.

109. Grundy Board Minutes, January 26 and 27, 1926.

110. Grundy College Society Minutes, June 3, 1926.

The number of delegates present and the amount of business conducted at these meetings gradually decreased. After 1927 the minutes do not even list the names of the delegates. The last meeting, for which the minutes are exceedingly brief and uninformative, was held in 1929. The declining vitality of the general society meetings probably reflected the inertness of the local societies. Recognizing that the local societies were dying out, the board proposed that the consistories of the CRCs in Classis Ost Friesland and in other classes which were favorably disposed to the school be required to function as societies and send delegates to the annual meeting.[111]

Unfortunately for Grundy College the Board of Directors was a weak and ineffectual body. Since Bode was himself a member of the board and prepared its agendas, the board was too dependent on him. Once an unsuccessful effort was made to remove Bode from the board.[112] The college had no regular procedures for appointing professors and the board's role in this important matter was minimal. Bode, sometimes in consultation with members of the Executive Committee, chose whom he wanted and then submitted the name to board members individually for their approval. There is reason to believe that Bode sometimes at his own initiative and without previous interview made appointments to the teaching staff. Absenteeism at board meetings was common and increased as the years passed. To compensate for the loss of society interest and support, the Grundy Board of Directors was eventually increased from 8 to 14 members in the hope that more board members would generate more enthusiasm for the college.[113]

Bode indisputably possessed the necessary intellectual gifts and breadth of vision to be a college president. Unfortunately, he was not a good administrator. Repeatedly and over extended periods of time faculty committees failed to report on cursory and mundane as well as more complicated and difficult matters.[114] For long intervals, the faculty did not meet on a regular basis, but informal faculty meetings were hastily called to deal with routine matters that could no longer be neglected or postponed.

Between 1921 and 1925 three new faculty members were added to Grundy College. In 1921 Frederick H. Wezeman joined the staff bringing along an impressive list of academic degrees, B.S., L.L.B., and B.D. He was soon appointed Vice-President of the College. Early in 1925 he became the pastor of College Church, while continuing to carry a reduced teaching

---

111. Grundy Board Minutes, June 3, 1929.
112. Grundy College Society Minutes, June 3, 1926.
113. Grundy Board Minutes, June 3, 1929.
114. For example, the committee appointed to investigate how the students' academic records should be kept did not report for more than two years. When the committee did report, it informed the faculty that record cards had already been procured.

load at the college. The following year Wezeman's credentials became even more impressive when he was awarded a doctorate in Jurisprudence.[115] In 1925 Lillian Drake and Henry J. Kuiper, whose specialty was education, began teaching careers at Grundy College.[116]

From the summer of 1924 to the fall of 1927 the Grundy College faculty was plagued by internal conflict and serious morale problems, eventually reaching crisis proportions. A summer course was offered for the first time in 1924. Income from tuition was not enough to pay the summer salaries promised to Professors Bajema, Clevering, Plesscher, and Wezeman, and the school treasury was too depleted to provide the necessary additional funds.

Before Plesscher was reappointed he had to assure the board that his attitude toward the school was satisfactory.[117] Unhappiness prompted Jakob Bajema to resign from an important faculty committee.[118] Just before Christmas in 1925 Professors Bajema, Clevering, Kuiper, and Plesscher submitted a "letter of grievances" to the faculty. Official minutes nowhere indicate precisely what these grievances or charges were. They were apparently very serious. The faculty postponed action on the letter until after the holiday recess.[119] At a faculty meeting held on January 6, 1926, Bode protested that the previous meeting was illegal and proceeded to read his answer to the letter of the four professors. Two days later the faculty decided that both the professors' letter and the president's answer to it were to be withdrawn. According to the record this was done to the mutual satisfaction of the parties involved.[120] At a faculty meeting held on January 13, 1926, the minutes of the January 8 meeting were approved. The mutual satisfaction was, however, short-lived. Just before the adjournment of the next faculty meeting held on January 22, Bode protested that the faculty minutes of January 8 were incomplete. He argued that the minutes should read, "with apology from the side of those who signed the letter of grievances."[121]

The Board of Directors meeting on January 26 had on its agenda a list of grievances presented by Bajema, Clevering, and Plesscher, a reply to these grievances from Bode, a letter of recommendations regarding the matter from Professor Kuiper, and a petition supporting the President signed by forty-six students. The board, in the absence of Bode, first tentatively formulated a series of propositions intended to resolve the conflict. The four

115. Grundy Faculty Minutes, September 7, 1921, and Grundy Board Minutes, February 3 and 4, 1925, and January 26 and 27, 1926.

116. Grundy Faculty Minutes, May 25, 1925, and November 17, 1925.

117. Grundy Board Minutes, February 3 and 4, 1925.

118. Grundy Faculty Minutes, August 17, 1925, and November 17, 1925.

119. Ibid., December 23, 1925.

120. Ibid., January 6, 1926, and January 8, 1926.

121. Ibid., January 22, 1926.

professors, Bajema, Clevering, Plesscher, and Kuiper, some individually and some under protest, then appeared before the board. After talking to the professors the board met with the entire faculty to discuss the conflict. According to the record the faculty members involved expressed regret that the situation had reached such a crisis and acknowledged that they had erred in procedure. The board finally decided to retain Bode as President. The faculty members were urged to do their utmost to rectify the hurt the school had suffered, to maintain the peace and prosperity of the school by hearty cooperation, and because of the deep personal wounds that had been inflicted to make all possible amends. Whether or not there was any connection between the board's action to resolve the controversy in the faculty and the next item on the agenda is not clear. But in order to dispel rumors concerning the mismanagement of school funds, the board adopted a resolution declaring that there was no foundation for or truth whatsoever in the report circulating that college money had been misappropriated by anyone connected with the college.[122] Plesscher soon received and accepted a call to become the pastor of the Ridott CRC of Ridott, Illinois.[123]

When the Grundy Board of Directors met in April to deal especially with reappointments, Bode regretfully informed the board that the attitude of some of the professors toward him had not changed after the January meeting, but had become worse. Unless a definite change took place with those professors, Bode said cooperation with them would be impossible. Clevering was asked to give an account for his unfriendly and independent attitude. After the meeting with Clevering, Bode handed the board a letter of resignation. After long and serious discussion the board decided to remain with the decision of the January meeting and not to accept the president's resignation. Bajema was then called in and asked to answer for his attitude toward Bode. The board decided not to reappoint Bajema and Clevering.[124]

The faculty was extremely unhappy with the board's decision. In the absence of Bode, the faculty discussed a resolution expressing the opinion that serious injustice had been done to Clevering and Bajema. It also urgently requested the board seriously to reconsider its decision. A role call vote was finally taken. Except for Wezeman, who refused to vote, and King, who cast a conditionally affirmative vote, all the professors voted in favor of the resolution.[125]

Bajema made no effort to be reinstated, but rather joined Plesscher in a request for prompt payment of overdue salary. Through the mediation of

122. Grundy Board Minutes, January 26 and 27, 1926.
123. He was examined for ordination at the March 2–4, 1926, meeting of Classis Ost Friesland.
124. Grundy Board Minutes, April 29 and 30, 1926.
125. Grundy Faculty Minutes, May 7, 1926.

Wezeman, Clevering and Bode were at least temporarily reconciled. Clevering confessed his previous errors, including delinquency in church attendance, and promised the board that he would pray for grace to work in harmony with Bode. The board was satisfied and reappointed Clevering for one year. Bajema and Plesscher were not quite so successful in getting what they wanted. The board decided to insert in the minutes of its January meeting a statement indicating that the salaries for the summer session in 1924 were to be paid by promissory notes.[126] Clevering evidently had second thoughts. After ten years of teaching service he resigned shortly before the beginning of the new school year.[127]

After the crisis of 1926 Grundy College had increasing difficulty acquiring and retaining faculty members. La Vern Morrison, John Primus, and William Landsiedal began teaching in the fall of 1926.[128] Primus and Landsiedal left after one year. Wezeman accepted an appointment to become principal of Chicago Christian High School in May 1927.[129] In September 1927 Benjamin J. Janssen was welcomed to the faculty.[130] The following spring Lylas King, after twelve years of teaching service, was unexpectedly removed from the faculty by death.[131] In the fall of 1928 three new faculty members were added: Ursala Athenstadt, Meindert De Jong, and G. Ramaker.[132] De Jong did not last long. Before the middle of October, he was gone, reportedly without having given official notice of his departure.[133] Fanny Potgieter taught the second semester in De Jong's place.[134] William T. Radius and his wife Marianne joined the staff in September 1929 and remained for only one year.[135]

Money, or rather the lack of it, was Grundy College's most pressing and debilitating problem. The very brief financial reports available in the board minutes and annual minutes of the general society meetings do not give a clear and probably not a very honest picture of the college's ongoing fiscal condition. The reports submitted to the board and the society gave a

---

126. Grundy Board Minutes, June 2, 1926. Less than a year later Rev. Plesscher died. His widow requested the unpaid salary of her deceased husband. The board asked her to accept interest-bearing bonds instead of the salary. Grundy Board Minutes, May 31, 1927. The financially hardpressed widow preferred cash. On February 1, 1928, the board decided to send her a token payment of $25.
127. Grundy Board Minutes, January 25, 1927. Clevering regularly served as an elder in Grundy College Church. He was the secretary of the consistory until September 1926. At the November congregational meeting that year, he announced that he did not wish to serve another term as elder. On August 12, 1927, Clevering asked to have his membership transferred to the Presbyterian Church in Grundy Center because he no longer felt at home in Grundy College Church.
128. Grundy Faculty Minutes, September 6, 1926.
129. Ibid., May 18 and 30, 1927.
130. Ibid., September 2, 1927.
131. Ibid., April 13, 1928.
132. Ibid., September 28, 1928.
133. Ibid., October 15, 1928, and Grundy Board Minutes, January 29, 1929.
134. Grundy Board Minutes, January 29, 1929.
135. Grundy Faculty Minutes, September 3, 1929.

generally favorable impression, with receipts equal to disbursements, and the indebtedness, although gradually increasing, appeared manageable. A careful and critical reading of the data, however, suggests that there were present and potential problems. Cash on hand was consistently less than $100. The college's most serious problem was that never more than one-third and sometimes as little as one-fourth of operating revenues came from student tuition and payments for board and room. During the severe economic depression the situation could not be corrected simply by an increase in tuition. The students were poor and frequently behind on their payments. The Grundy College Society through gifts and membership dues regularly contributed a little over one-third of annual income. The rest of the money to defray expenses had to be raised from other sources.

A clearer and more honest picture of the school's consistently deplorable financial condition can be drawn from faculty and board minutes. Promised salary increases were postponed, faculty members frequently requested pay increases, sometimes to cover unexpected costs due to illness in the family, and, most seriously, the school treasury defaulted on the regular payment of faculty salaries.[136] Salary arrearages at the end of the 1925–1926 academic year were calculated at approximately $8,163.10.[137] Faculty members were often given promissory notes for unpaid salary.

Almost every conceivable means was explored to raise money and secure solvency. The board, somewhat indiscreetly, authorized Bode, as long as he was treasurer, to borrow from the banks.[138] An Educational Secretary, Luke Brinks, was engaged as early as August 1922 to solicit funds and students for the school. Brinks was succeeded by George Schultz, and Schultz in turn by Elbert Van Maanen, who was given the title of Field Secretary.

In November 1924 Bode launched a new endowment fund campaign. The program asked subscribers to sign a note promising to pay Grundy College $100 on or before ten years after the date the note was signed. Until the note was paid, the signatory was obligated to pay interest annually at the rate of 5 percent.[139] Soon after contributions to the endowment fund were received, the board decided to transfer the money to the operating account and to place notes for an equivalent amount in the endowment fund.[140]

136. Cf. Faculty Statement to the board. Ibid., February 3, 1925.

137. This is the only such figure recorded in the official minutes. Grundy College Society Meeting Minutes, June 3, 1926.

138. Grundy Board Minutes, February 20, 1924.

139. Bode offered a note to Beets. Beets did not subscribe because he did not like to sign a note. He did, however, save $100 "for the good purpose" and sent Bode a check for that amount. Letter to Bode, April 7, 1925, Beets Collection.

140. Grundy Board Minutes, February 3 and 4, 1925.

At the request of the board, representatives of the William L. Steele Associates, a financial advisory agency, met with the board in April 1926. The board, however, was not yet ready to buy the firm's services. Instead the board authorized Van Maanen to sell unsecured Grundy College bonds with a face value of $1,500. In order to secure a more permanent appointment as Field Secretary, Van Maanen had to demonstrate his effectiveness as a fundraiser and seller of bonds. At the same meeting President Bode was asked to explore the possibility of getting a loan from a certain church finance company in Nashville, Tennessee[141] and authorized, if necessary, to pledge the college property as security. In September 1926 Grundy College borrowed $30,000 through a mortgage bond issue secured with college property. The money was used to pay indebtedness and to cover present operating costs.[142] Van Maanen was very successful in selling bonds. The school's total debt, however, was increasing.[143] When bonds reached maturity and some bond- and noteholders became uneasy about the security of their investments, pressure again mounted on the treasury. In February 1928 the board announced a fund drive in Grundy County to raise $25,000.[144] The results were never reported. Again Bode was authorized to go to the bank and to execute a mortgage on the property in the amount of $25,000.[145] The money was used to retire bonds and to pay other debts. Nothing was left over for operating costs.

As the college's financial situation worsened, Bode and the board resorted to more extreme and desperate fundraising measures. In April 1928 Bode sent a letter to CRCs, asking for help. In the letter Bode said that the College's present financial difficulties were the direct result of the unfavorable judgment of the synod in 1922. If the Compromise of 1920 had remained in force, he said, the church would now owe Grundy College $27,000.[146] At the suggestion of the board, Bode and E. Joling went to Grand Rapids to ask Jelle Hekman, the prosperous owner of the flourishing Hekman Biscuit Company, for a contribution.[147] The board also authorized Bode to engage a solicitor in addition to Van Maanen on the 25 percent commission basis. In spite of the school's rapidly deteriorating financial condition the board's vision remained incredibly optimistic. On June 3, 1929, the board authorized its Executive Committee to proceed with plans to build a new gymnasium provided sufficient funds could be raised from outside sources.[148]

141. Ibid., April 29 and 30, 1926.

142. Minutes of the Joint Finance and Executive Committee meeting, September 3, 1926.

143. Grundy Board Minutes, May 31, 1927.

144. Ibid., February 1, 1928.

145. Ibid.

146. Letter of Bode to the churches, April 14, 1928, Beets Collection (Folder 94).

147. Minutes of the Finance and Executive Committee, October 24, 1928. Some months later, Hekman gave the school $300. Minutes of the Finance and Executive Committee, May 14, 1929.

148. Grundy Board Minutes, June 3, 1929.

During the decade of the 1920s an exceedingly competitive and acrimonious relationship existed between Grundy College and Western Christian High School, founded in 1918 in Hull, Iowa. Animosity surfaced when Grundy College's solicitor made a foray into territory in northwest Iowa claimed by Western. The response was swift and biting. Grundy College was sarcastically depicted as a wretched brute under the leadership of unprincipled people with evil intentions concealed in their hearts and greediness sparkling from their eyes.[149] To relieve the tension between the two schools and their respective boards the Board of Directors of Grundy College drew up a plan of cooperation calling for mutual commitments to work for unity in Christian secondary and higher education in the West. Both schools were also to pledge themselves to avoid conflict in soliciting either funds or students.[150] The plan was ignored in Hull and never implemented in Grundy Center. For some years intermittent correspondence was carried on between representatives of the two schools, but personal animosities and institutional competitiveness precluded the possibility of genuine cooperation or a combined effort.[151]

The deepening depression and mounting debts[152] brought representatives of Grundy College and Western to the bargaining table to discuss a merger of the two institutions in the fall of 1929. Delegations from each school presented proposals for amalgamating the two schools. The proposals were mutually exclusive and diametrically opposed. The delegates from Grundy College somewhat unhistorically recommended a return to the situation that obtained before Western came into existence, with one institution for Christian higher education in the West, located in Grundy Center. The representatives from Hull argued that a Christian high school should be located where interest in Christian education was the greatest. Consequently the only logical place for such a school was in Sioux County. There 1800 children were already attending Christian grade schools.

Since the establishment of a Christian junior college was being discussed in northwest Iowa, the delegation from Hull came to the meeting with clearly formulated opinions on this subject, too. They candidly stated that two Christian junior colleges in the West, supported by the same constituency, made no sense. In their opinion a Christian junior college

149. John B. Van den Hoek, "Western Academy, Hull, Iowa, II" *De Wachter* 55 (15 November 1922):10–11, and a newspaper clipping in Grundy College Papers, Colonial Origins Collection.

150. Grundy Board Minutes, February 20, 1924, and June 3, 1924.

151. In a letter to Beets, Bode said, "A few leaders out West have, as far as I have been able to see, started the Western movement just to break Grundy. . . . we have tried in so many ways to get next to them and the only thing we get is mud slinging and opposition, and evil reports such that if you would believe them we would be the most insane people in the world as well as unreligious and that from brethren who claim to have a divine calling. How these brethren ever dare to broadcast the lies they do, I do not know." Letter to Beets, October 16, 1924, Beets Collection (Folder 54).

152. Western Christian High School had $70,000 debt at the time.

ought to be located in the same place as the Christian high school and for the same reasons. The representative from Hull, therefore, proposed that the Grundy College Society and the society of Western Christian High School merge, assume the debt of both institutions, and dispose of the Grundy College buildings and grounds.[153]

In order to remove the impasse, the Grundy College board suggested that through proper ecclesiastical channels the present differences of opinion be referred to the synod of the CRC for adjudication and resolution. Underlying this proposal was the conviction that a merger of the two existing schools was highly desirable, if not absolutely necessary, and the assumption that the CRC could perhaps be induced to support and maintain a denominational school in the West. Very specifically, the Grundy College board recommended that an overture be drafted asking the synod to assume the responsibility for Christian secondary and higher education in the West. Both Western Christian High School and Grundy College would offer their properties to the denomination with the request that the synod, after careful study and review, decide where its school should be located. The societies and boards of both institutions were to acquiesce in the synod's decisions and disposition of the matter.[154]

Western's board did not respond favorably to this proposal either. As consistent followers of Abraham Kuyper, the spokesmen from Hull were for reasons of principle convinced that the church and Christian education were fundamentally distinct and separate areas of human life and activity. They therefore objected to presenting an overture to synod because the problems and issues involved were not ecclesiastical in nature. They also somewhat uncharitably rendered the opinion that the choice of Grundy Center as the location for a Christian institution of higher learning had not been the best. Moreover the churches in that area had not demonstrated sufficient interest in Christian education. Consequently, Grundy College, as they saw it, had no future. The only way to achieve unity and to promote Christian education in the West was by way of their original proposal.[155]

In January 1929 Bode again resigned. Since the board was not very well represented, action on the resignation was postponed.[156] Six months later the board, by ballot, unanimously voted not to accept Bode's resignation.[157]

In the presence of an obviously weakened president, the faculty appointed a committee consisting of Professors Kuiper, Janssen, and Radius to meet with the Executive Committee of the board to discuss educational

153. Grundy Board Minutes, November 12, 1929, and Grundy College Papers.
154. Grundy Board Minutes, January 29, 1930.
155. Ibid., February 18, 1930, February 26, 1930, and March 26, 1930.
156. Ibid., January 29, 1929.
157. Ibid., June 3, 1929.

policies.[158] Later Radius and Kuiper presented proposals to the board for
resolving the difficulties with Hull and a plan for reorganizing the college.
The board was willing to listen, but took no formal action on these proposals.[159] The professors were evidently discouraged by the board's com-
placency and indecision. Radius and his wife allowed their terms of
appointment to expire and the board made no formal effort to retain them.
Kuiper resigned from the faculty.[160] After resigning, Kuiper evidently had
second thoughts or anticipated difficulty in finding employment. Before
offering him a reappointment, the board examined him regarding his attitude toward the college. Kuiper promised to work wholeheartedly for the
school and was reappointed, but for only one year.[161] The personal damage
was, however, irreparable and less than a month later Kuiper declined the
reappointment.[162]

On March 17, 1930, Bode appeared before the consistory of College
Church with an overture to be submitted first to Classis Ost Friesland and
then passed on to synod. The overture briefly reviewed the decisions of the
Synods of 1920 and 1922, and indicated the detrimental effects the actions
especially of the Synod of 1922 had on both Grundy College and Calvin
College and Seminary, since for these reasons many of the churches in
Classis Ost Friesland refused to pay the portion of the denominational
quota designated for Calvin College and Seminary. Because of this twofold
ill-effect the overture asked that the matter be reopened and a committee
appointed to confer with Classis Ost Friesland so that an amiable solution
might be found.[163] Two days later the classis adopted the overture.[164] This
overture originating with Bode was one of his last desperate efforts to save
the college before his departure.

On March 26, 1930, Bode requested and was granted by the board what
technically was called a "leave of absence" but was in fact a resignation.
The board immediately decided to appoint a committee to inform the
ministers of Classes Pella and Ost Friesland that the college needed someone to replace Bode. The committee was also mandated to explain to the
ministers that Grundy College could not merge with Western on Western's
terms and that the continuation of the college required the united effort
and support of all. In order to stabilize the faltering institution and shore up
its credibility the board decided to issue a public announcement to be

158. Grundy Faculty Minutes, October 25, 1929.
159. Grundy Board Minutes, January 29, 1930, and February 18, 1930.
160. Ibid., February 26, 1930. William T. Radius later became Professor of Classical Languages at
Calvin College where he remained until retirement.
161. Ibid., April 23, 1930.
162. Ibid., May 28, 1930.
163. Consistory Minutes of Grundy College Church, March 17, 1930.
164. Minutes of Classis Ost Friesland, March 18–19, 1930. The synod showed no sympathy whatsoever for the overture.

formulated by Bode. The announcement asserted that Grundy students would have no difficulty transferring credits to state educational institutions and that the board would endeavor to obtain a full staff of qualified teachers for the coming year. It was also stated that the enrollment and financial condition of the college were practically what they had been for years.[165] Less than a month after these decisions were taken Bode was literally given his credentials. He was released from presidential duties and temporarily asked to assist Van Maanen. The board urged Bode and Van Maanen to sell as many Grundy College bonds as they could.[166]

William H. Rutgers assumed the presidency of Grundy College in the fall of 1930. He was given an impossible assignment. In addition to being a college president and professor, Rutgers, for financial reasons, was called to be the pastor both of College Church and the Holland CRC of Holland, Iowa. Rutgers' salary was set at $2,200.[167] The two churches were responsible for $1,200: each church contributing $300 from its membership, and Classis Ost Friesland raising the remaining $600.[168]

In September 1930 Benjamin J. Janssen, Ursula Athenstadt, John C. Primus, and Sadie Kuiper joined Rutgers on the faculty.[169] Miss Athenstadt resigned during the school year and Sadie Kuiper and Janssen terminated their services at the end of the 1930–1931 academic year. Erna Landsiedel and Jan William Kingma began teaching in the fall of 1931. Klaas J. Stratemeier and John J. Timmerman, son of the former theological professor, joined the staff a year later. Jacob Heerema taught at Grundy College during the 1933–1934 academic year, and Gertrude Dresselhuis was evidently added to the faculty sometime in 1934.[170]

Under the Rutgers administration the Grundy College faculty was a weak and uninfluential body. The faculty records are poor and extremely brief. Most of the faculty meetings were special or informal ones, called to deal with some pressing need. After September 1, 1931, the official minutes were written on loose-leaf tablet paper. Matters pertaining to educational policies are noticeably absent.

Rutgers attempted to expand the college's base of support by enlisting the cooperation of other evangelical churches in the vicinity of Grundy Center. To facilitate this effort a new constitution was drafted and later

165. Grundy Board Minutes, March 26, 1930.

166. Ibid., April 23, 1930. At the September meeting of Classis Ost Friesland, Bode represented the church in Bunde, Minnesota. He continued to serve as the pastor of the Bunde Church until retirement in 1937. Bode died October 22, 1941.

167. Ibid., May 28, 1930.

168. Consistory Minutes of Grundy College Church, September 9, 1930, and September 10, 1930.

169. Grundy College Messenger, Catalog edition, 1930–1931.

170. It is very difficult to determine precisely who was teaching and what at any given time. The faculty minutes do not list the names of the professors, and the appointments and resignations of the professors are not always recorded in the minutes of the Board of Directors.

adopted. While still expressing loyalty to the confessional standards of the Reformed churches, the new constitution self-consciously pushed the school in a decidedly fundamentalist and anti-modernist direction. The Word of God, understood as a supernatural revelation, verbally and plenarily inspired, was made the foundational article of faith in the revised constitution. The new constitution explicitly affirmed as fundamental articles of faith, creation, substitutionary atonement, the resurrection, ascension, and return of Christ, the necessity of rebirth, and the resurrection of the body. Since Christianity was being assailed and its historic foundations challenged by humanism, the college's aim and purpose, according to the revised constitution, was to preserve the faith and to stem the onrushing tide of modernism.[171]

No small part of Rutgers' time and energy were expended on financial problems. Students, faculty members, and Grundy College creditors all suffered as the great depression took its toll and the school became insolvent. Tuition was reduced and in some cases even waived for students who simply could not pay. Late in 1932 student debt to the school amounted to $1,552.14.[172]

For faculty members, non-payment of salary and salary arrearages were circumstances of life and employment.[173] A year after severing connections with the college Bode accepted unsecured college bonds and a multigraph machine appraised at $100 for unpaid salary.[174] After a little more than one year of service, the school owed Rutgers $1,200.[175] Other faculty members found themselves in the same situation and had little choice but to accept the bonds offered them by the board in place of salary. One faculty member, however, resisted the board's practice. After resigning from the faculty, Erna Landsiedel retained an attorney and sued the college for back salary with interest.[176] To add insult to injury the board appointed a committee to investigate the faculty's loyalty to the institution and to the Christian foundation on which it stood. Faculty members were asked whether they still subscribed to the principles on which the college was based and whether they put forth a serious effort to inculcate these principles in their teaching. All of them said Yes.[177]

Numerous fund-raising programs were initiated to restore solvency to the financially troubled institution. President Rutgers visited meetings of

171. Constitution of Grundy College, Board Minutes, April 26, 1932.
172. Grundy Faculty Minutes, May 31, 1932, and Grundy Board Minutes, December 20, 1932.
173. Grundy Board Minutes, February 24, 1931, and April 26, 1932.
174. Ibid., July 1, 1931.
175. Ibid., September 2, 1931.
176. Executive Committee Minutes, August 25, 1933, and Grundy Board Minutes, September 12, 1933.
177. Report of the Committee to the Board. The specific date is not indicated, but the interrogation took place during the spring of 1932.

classes where he gave candid reports on the college's financial problems and requested special collections. The churches of Classis Ost Friesland designated their Thanksgiving Day offerings for the college.[178] Locally the board sponsored a Rally Day[179] and later Grundy College Week, a campaign that raised a modest $125.[180] Rutgers and representatives of the board visited prominent industrialists in the State of Iowa such as Maytag, Rawleigh, and McNess in the hope that one of them might make a sizeable contribution and save the institution from bankruptcy. The college received some sympathy from these men but no money.[181]

Cost-saving as well as fund-raising measures were also introduced. When Van Maanen resigned as Field Secretary, Peter De Groot assumed the position strictly on a commission basis. To reduce operating costs the Boys' Dormitory was closed and regular janitorial services discontinued. Students were employed to do the cleaning for as little as 15¢ an hour.[182] And, for financial reasons, basketball was eliminated.[183]

Kind women from the town and county organized a food plan and collected canned food to feed students who could not afford to pay both board and room.[184] The students also did what they could to alleviate the desperate situation. They prayed.[185]

Eventually the college had to face its creditors. The Austinville Bank was requested to accept bonds in place of an overdue note.[186] Bond and noteholders were first informed of the college's inability to pay the interest.[187] Later when the bonds reached maturity, the board extended the date on them another ten years. The board also asked the bondholders voluntarily to reduce the face value of their bonds and to donate the interest due on them to the college. Some bonds were graciously returned to the school; other were bought back at 20 percent of face value.[188] In the spring of 1933 the sheriff served notice on Grundy College to pay notes due to the First National Bank of Grundy Center in the amount of $5,900. No one, however, appeared in District Court to contest the notes because the college had no reason for not paying them other than lack of funds.[189]

After reporting to the Grundy Board of Directors that no one had

178. Grundy Board Minutes, February 24, 1931, and September 2, 1931.
179. Ibid., February 24, 1931.
180. Ibid., April 7, 1933.
181. Ibid., December 20, 1932, and April 7, 1933.
182. Ibid., December 10, 1931, April 26, 1932, and December 20, 1932.
183. Ibid., October 19, 1932.
184. *Yearbook of Grundy Junior College and Senior Academy*, 1933–1934, p. 8.
185. The Grundy College Prayer League was well-attended by the students. *Grundy College Catalog* 1933–1934, p. 7.
186. Grundy Board Minutes, February 24, 1931.
187. Ibid., December 10, 1931, and October 19, 1932.
188. Ibid., December 20, 1932.
189. Ibid., April 7, 1933, and April 20, 1933.

appeared in the District Court, the affable Rutgers informed the board that although he had enjoyed the work at Grundy College, he had accepted a call to become pastor of the Cicero CRC of Cicero, Illinois. The board accepted his resignation "with deep regret." The question whether or not to continue could no longer be postponed. The board decided to send a letter to the remaining members of the almost defunct Grundy College Society, indicating the school's need in the present time of distress and specifically asking them whether or not the college should continue.[190]

The response from the society members was mixed, giving the board no clear direction. After much serious deliberation and an extended consultation with the faculty the board decided to continue the college on the basis of a plan proposed by the faculty. The plan called for an administrative reorganization, with the faculty virtually assuming all the responsibility for the services and management of the institution. Salaries were to be paid every two weeks, if money was available.[191] In keeping with this decision, the board in September 1933 rented the college buildings and equipment to the faculty until June 1, 1934, for a fee of one dollar.[192]

How effective the new administrative organization was or could have been is impossible to determine. Board records during 1934, however, suggest that the board was becoming increasingly unstable. Some of its decisions and actions appear inconsistent if not contradictory. In January the board decided again to assume complete control of the institution.[193] In March it informed faculty members that they should not attend board meetings unless they were requested to be present.[194] And then, in April the board gave the chairman of the faculty, Jan William Kingma, authority to control and direct the educational program of the college.[195] In February all faculty members were reappointed.[196] In May the board appointed a committee to draw up a set of questions to be put to each member of the faculty.[197] Primus, Kingma, and Dresselhuis satisfied the board immediately and were reappointed.[198] Heerema was not reappointed. Timmerman was reappointed but only after his reappointment had been reconsidered.[199] On August 2, 1934, the board decided to continue the school. Then at the

190. Ibid., April 20, 1933. In 1944 Rutgers became Professor of Systematic Theology at Calvin Theological Seminary. In 1952 he returned to the pastoral ministry.

191. Ibid., May 15, 1933, and May 16, 1933.

192. Ibid., September 12, 1933.

193. Ibid., January 31, 1934.

194. Ibid., March 19, 1934.

195. Ibid., April 30, 1934.

196. Ibid., February 21, 1934.

197. Ibid., May 21, 1934.

198. Ibid., May 23, 1934.

199. Ibid., May 28, 1934. Professor Timmerman informed the author that he was unaware of these board proceedings. He had, however, been told that the board had some difficulty with the fact that he was unmarried.

same meeting it issued a quit claim deed to Classis Ost Friesland.[200] Without an official notice of closing, Grundy College did not open in the fall of 1934. The minutes of Classis Ost Friesland indicate that the board of Grundy College resigned and that consequently the property reverted to the classis.[201]

The subsequent history of Grundy College is a story of lingering dreams and deteriorating property. In March 1935 Classis Ost Friesland appointed members, including William Bode, to a "Board of the Christian Reformed College and Seminary."[202] Upon the recommendation of the newly established board, the classis adopted a three-step course of action: 1) to establish legal possession of the Grundy College property, 2) to make an out of court settlement with all creditors on a percentage basis, perhaps twenty cents on the dollar, and 3) to make plans for reopening the school.[203] The first step was accomplished in March 1937, when the classis again gained legal possession of the property free of debt.[204] No serious effort was ever made to implement the second step. The third step received more attention. The classis attempted to generate interest in a Christian junior college movement and invited other classes of the CRC to participate.[205]

The college grounds were literally let out to pasture. When, however, the privilege was abused, the sheriff was asked to serve a notice to remove the cattle.[206] Unidentified persons from Western and Pella Christian High Schools and from the Sully and Peoria Christian schools removed equipment from the abandoned College Building, leaving the board in the unenviable position of having to negotiate a price for the confiscated goods after they had been taken.[207] Again the sheriff's services were enlisted to protect the building against intruders and the county attorney's advice was sought in preparing court orders to retrieve stolen goods.[208] Without authorization families moved into the dormitories. The board was willing to let them stay if one member of the family was a confessing member of the CRC and if the occupants paid a token fee each month for rent. This privilege, too, was abused and notices eventually had to be served to vacate the rooms.[209]

The old boiler in the College Building was sold for iron to support the war effort.[210] In April 1945 the College Building itself was sold for $250 to

200. Ibid., August 2, 1934.
201. Minutes of Classis Ost Friesland, September 25 and 26, 1934.
202. Ibid., March 27, 1935. Five negative votes were recorded.
203. Ibid., September 24 and 25, 1935.
204. Ibid., March 16, 17, and 18, 1937.
205. Ibid., September 15, 1937, and September 13, 1938.
206. Classical Board Minutes, May 6, 1935, and March 18, 1940.
207. Ibid., September 14, 1943.
208. Ibid., March 14, 1939.
209. Ibid., September 12, 1938, and January 25, 1940.
210. Ibid., March 17, 1942.

the Excelsior Christian School Society for building material on the condition that the society would clean up the debris and fill the hole level with the ground. Almost a year later the debris had not been picked up and the hole remained hazardously open.[211] The Girls' Dormitory was sold at public auction for $500.[212] After unsuccessful efforts to give the Boys' Dormitory to the Grundy Center Hospital Board, to the supervisors of the local old people's home, and to the Lincoln Center CRC for building material, Joe and Marvin Graves bought it for $5,200.[213]

Upon the recommendation of the classical board all funds of the Christian Reformed College and Seminary were placed in a trust fund later to be used for higher Christian education in Classis Ost Friesland.[214] On November 9, 1970, the Secretary of State of the State of Iowa issued notice that the corporate period of Grundy College Society would expire on February 17, 1971.[215]

211. Ibid., April 16, 1945, and March 19, 1946.
212. Ibid., February 26, 1946.
213. Ibid., January 23, 1950; February 20, 1950; and March 13, 1950.
214. Ibid., August 28, 1950, and November 21, 1950.
215. Notice of Expiration, November 9, 1970.

PART TWO

Studies in Theology

7

The Premillennial Eschatology of Diedrich Hinrich Kromminga

Harry R. Boer

Before anyone elected or appointed to hold office in the Christian Reformed Church in North America (hereafter CRC) can enter upon the discharge of his duties he must sign the "Form of Subscription," a document which states, among other things, "We, the undersigned ... declare by this our subscription that we heartily believe and are persuaded that all the articles and points of doctrine [in the three official creeds of the CRC] do fully agree with the Word of God."[1] The seriousness with which the "Form of Subscription" has been taken in the CRC was fully reflected in the life and ministry of Diedrich H. Kromminga, Professor of Historical Theology at Calvin Theological Seminary from 1928 to his death in 1947, and the father of John H. Kromminga in whose honor the contributions comprising this volume have been written.

For the most part premillennialism cannot be harmonized with the official Reformed creedal basis. Article 37 of the Belgic Confession, one of the three official creeds of the CRC, teaches "... we believe ... that, when the time appointed by the Lord . . . is come and the number of the elect complete . . . our Lord Jesus Christ will come from heaven . . . to declare Himself Judge of the living and the dead." For Kromminga the critical phrase in the statement was "and the number of the elect complete."[2] This confessional assertion effectively bars belief in the return of Christ before a

---

1. "Form of Subscription" in *Psalter Hymnal*, Doctrinal Standards and Liturgy of the Christian Reformed Church (Grand Rapids: Board of Publications of the Christian Reformed Church, 1976), p. 117.
2. "Confession of Faith" in *Psalter Hymnal*, p. 89.

millennial period in the course of which men will be brought to Christ to complete the fullness of the church and thereby the fullness of the elect.

Kromminga discharged his office with distinction, but under the heavy burden of never being able to express the strong conviction that the return of Christ would effect a profound alteration in the life of mankind.

He held this conviction in terms of a magisterial eschatological vision to which he had been led by scrupulous study both of Scripture and of the history of millennial thought in the Christian church. In 1945 he published *The Millennium in the Church,*[3] subtitled "Studies in the History of Christian Chiliasm." It was, as the book jacket correctly stated, "a comprehensive study of the millennium concept as found in ancient, medieval and modern thought." Kromminga had hoped that the contents of the *The Millennium,*[4] published posthumously and discussed in this contribution, would form the last two chapters of *The Millennium in the Church.* The realization that this would not be allowed by the "Form of Subscription," however, led him to publish *The Millennium in the Church* without them.

Convinced that he should not let things rest at that inconclusive point, he appealed in that same year to the denominational synod but at a far more fundamental level. He asked the synod to show him where in Scripture it is taught that all the elect will have been gathered in when Christ returns. From June 1945 to June 1947 the synodical concern with Kromminga's understanding of the millennium was shunted from committee to committee which drew from him at last an official expression of his disillusionment with the church's faithfulness to its promise given in the "Form of Subscription" to *examine* and to *judge* officially submitted objections to the teaching of the creeds. With his death in 1947 all further concern for his views ceased. The concrete opportunity which the CRC had to enrich its own eschatological insights, little articulated or reflected on as they were by a study of Kromminga's eschatological views, was thus surrendered.

It would appear from the author's preface to *The Millennium*[5] that prior to his death he had prepared the two chapters in question for separate publication. It appeared in 1948. An intimation of the theological loneliness in which he had lived for more than three decades is found at the close of the book, where he writes, ". . . I know from experience what it means, when for long years one is rather completely shut up with his own ideas without the opportunity of controlling them by discussion with others."[6]

---

3. Diedrich H. Kromminga, *The Millennium in the Church,* Studies in the History of Christian Chiliasm (Grand Rapids: Eerdmans, 1945).

4. Diedrich H. Kromminga, *The Millennium,* Its Nature, Function, and Relation to the Consummation of the World (Grand Rapids: Eerdmans, 1948).

5. Ibid., p. 7.

6. Ibid., p. 106.

The inability of Kromminga to publish his eschatological views in *The Millennium in the Church* in 1945, leading three years later to their separate publication is, in the end, more gain than loss. The former volume is a distinctly historical study. It was the author's purpose to "trace briefly the history of Christian chiliasm."[7] Having earlier observed, ". . . it will not surprise, that upon closer inspection the eschatological problem turns out to be a most complicated problem, for which the most varied solutions have been proposed,"[8] he expresses the hope that after finishing the historical review "it may be possible to take up the eschatological puzzle anew for another attempt at its solution."[9] This he undertook to do in *The Millennium*. It is a distinctly theological and exegetical effort and therefore deserved publication as a separate study rather than as an appendage to the history.

This contribution sets forth salient features of Kromminga's conception. The writer is not without his reservations on the views which he reports, but these are mainly presented in a final section.

The suspicion with which premillennialism has been regarded in the Reformed tradition arises to no small extent from the doctrinal aberrations that have so often attended it. In the judgment of Kromminga these centered basically in divergence from the biblical doctrine of the covenant of grace. He firmly believed that the doctrine of the covenant was essential in maintaining the integrity of the Reformed conception of salvation. The unity of the covenant extends from the fall of Adam to the consummation of history. In the midst of its administration stands the incarnation of the Son of God which, while dividing covenant history into the Old and the New Testament dispensations, also holds them in inseparable unity. This is a central theme in his understanding of the millennium and it effectively excludes any form of dispensational premillennialism from the whole of his theological vision. With equal firmness, however, he believed that the biblical data require a premillennial eschatology and that this, far from threatening the Reformed covenantal conception, would be fully in harmony with it.

A second major feature of Kromminga's theology is his insistence on grounding it solidly on an exegetical basis. It is questionable whether any eschatology can escape the danger of speculation. In its nature eschatology is futuristic. It seeks to illumine the End which, while here in principle, is also emphatically not-yet. This invites the putting together of exegetical data in a manner that may not prove ultimately to have been justified. A

---

7. Kromminga, *Millennium in the Church*, p. 27.
8. Ibid., p. 18.
9. Ibid., p. 27.

careful reading of *The Millennium*, however, cannot fail to leave the impression that Kromminga has been at great pains to stay within the parameters set by the data with which Scripture provided him. These data, moreover, he uses with surprising insight and originality, and with a power altogether wanting in traditional Reformed amillennial exposition.

We undertake therefore a description of a premillennial eschatology which fully adheres to Reformed integrity, on the one hand, while being devoutly faithful to the demands of exegetical integrity, on the other. Faithfulness to these desiderata does not in itself guarantee a full-orbed reflection of biblical teaching, but it does require respect for and careful listening to the articulation of the resultant eschatological vision.

The sweep of Kromminga's conception is majestic. It extends back to creation itself and to the earliest history of the race of man, and climaxes in the revelation at the end of time of the new heaven and the new earth. The millennium is therefore not an appendage to but rather an integral part of the entire historical process. The author discerns a closing period in human history, which finds a remarkably corresponding opening period at the beginning of the historical process. The correspondence is not a parallel one in the sense that what is first in the opening period finds a corresponding feature in the first phase of the closing period, and so on to the end, but rather the reverse. The primordial beginning of the opening period is the creation of heaven and earth; the climactic end of the closing period is the revelation of the new heaven and the new earth. The opening period moves from the glory of creation down through the fall of man to the near disintegration of the race at Babel; the closing period moves progressively upward from the destruction of the great harlot in Babylon (cf. Babel) to glory restored in the disclosure of the new creation.

As Kromminga sees them, each of the two movements contains seven steps. These he presents not so much as two precisely corresponding systems moving respectively in opposite orders of descent from and return to creation glory, but as two distinctly discernible periods containing eminently striking parallel phenomena which responsible reading of the Bible may not ignore. Both Irenaeus and Tertullian, Kromminga writes, "had the idea that it was a matter of equity or propriety, that the saints should enjoy a kind of triumph in the same world in which they now suffer."[10] This theme Kromminga develops in depth.

The seven parallels which he discerns,[11] are as follows:[12]

10. Kromminga, *Millennium*, p. 48.
11. Ibid., pp. 46–47.
12. The schematization is mine. It is done in the interest of clarity which does not come to its rights in the presentation in the book.

I	**II**
1. Creation of heaven and earth	7a. Babylon, the great harlot, destroyed
2. Fall of Man	6b. Armageddon: rebellious combination against God destroyed
3. Race separates into Cainites and Sethites	5c. Nations freed from deception of Satan by his being bound
4. The separation removed by intermarriage	4d. Racial homogeneity removed by the preaching of the gospel
5. God terminates the striving of his Spirit with mankind	3e. Gog-Magog versus the saints and the holy city
6. Antediluvian race destroyed except Noah and his family	2f. Judgment of the Great White Throne
7. Confusion of tongues of Babel	1g. New heaven and new earth

We can best compare these columns by distinguishing between their qualitative and chronological aspects. Qualitatively, the process listed under I is one of degeneration; the process listed under II is one of return to integrity. To understand the relevant parallelism of column II great allowance must of course be made for the vast complexities introduced by historical developments that took place between the confusion of tongues at Babel in I/7 and the destruction of Babylon and its harlot queen in II/7. When that is done, it is perceived that the return to integrity repeats in reverse order a parallel stage of the degenerative process. This becomes evident when any number in column I is compared with its corresponding number in column II.

The chronological order of II is obviously the same as that of I. This is indicated by the *a* to *g* sequence. Were it not too cumbersome this could perhaps best be indicated by printing both columns in one vertical list with the history of Abraham to Christ and that of the church after Christ, and their contextualization in world history, inserted in the list between I/7 and II/7a.

The millennium falls wholly within the limits indicated by column II. After human pride and wantonness reach both their height of achievement and nadir of iniquity, the Babyonian world power is destroyed and Christ returns from heaven as the rider on the white horse to slay the host led by the beast and his prophet. He thereupon binds Satan and initiates the millennium by raising the believing dead and rapturing them to heaven together with transformed living believers, to reign with him in it. The millennium is concluded by the defeat of Gog and Magog, the destruction of Satan, and the judgment of the Great White Throne. Thereupon the revelation of the new heaven and the new earth ushers in the eternal state of bliss and glory.

The author is at pains to emphasize that the closing stage (period II) grows out of its preceding history just as the history following upon the pre-Abrahamic stage (period I) grew directly out of that initial stage of human history. The historical line extending from creation to the end of the final period of history is therefore continuous. As the Bible does not suggest that, in spite of profound divine intervention, there is historical discontinuity between the history leading to the confusion of tongues of Babel and the history following it, so there is, notwithstanding Christ's mighty deeds in introducing the millennium, a wholly continuous procession between our present history and the reign of Christ and the saints in that final period called the millennium. The thousand-year period will therefore not be lived in some strange, other-worldly, wholly new awareness and environment. It will be this world and this humanity carrying on to the end, living on the same street as before the rapture, marrying, procreating, working, worshiping, and continuing to make significant history. All this, however, will be done under conditions of justice and restraint on sin never before experienced in the history of man.

With these general observations before us we must now more particularly concern ourselves with the nature of the millennial period.

Kromminga conceives of the successive visions of Revelation 12:1–21:27 as presenting a "continuous historical trail"[13] from the incarnation of Christ to the consummation of the age. The New Testament period is divided into two closely related but nevertheless distinct stages: that of the church and that of the kingdom. The former constitutes the period from the incarnation to the return of Christ; the latter constitutes the millennial period. Far from the one excluding the other, the kingdom is in the church stage and the church in the kingdom stage. The two are named as they are in terms of emphasis and prominence rather than in terms of mutual exclusion. The New Testament period is therefore organically one from incarnation to consummation.

The church, in her "age," lives in a historical context which is dominated by three fateful developments. The overrunning of the Western Roman empire by the barbarians during the fifth century and the Islamic military and religious sweep of North Africa and the Middle East during the seventh century brought to an end the old world, whose series of great civilizations had climaxed in that of the Graeco-Roman. In the course of their occupation of Europe the barbarians performed a further function. They laid the basis for the rise and development of European nationalism. Out of the

13. Kromminga, *Millennium*, p. 30.

resulting national states emerged a "resurgence of Imperialism among the Christian nations that sprang from the barbarian invaders upon the ruins of the ancient world."[14] This development Kromminga calls "the greatest Woe of Satan's deception of the nations by the beast and the false prophet."[15] Out of the resulting national states has emerged the capitalistic-colonialistic civilization that has characterized the modern period.

These three historic developments, that is, the barbarian tide, the Islamic conquests, and the rise of the great national states in capitalist-colonial form, the author sees prefigured in the Book of Revelation in the fifth, sixth, and seventh trumpet blasts in the second cycle of judgments as recorded in chapter nine and further in chapter thirteen where the awesome power of the beast and the false prophet are revealed. This latter phase is still in effect and is working out the consequences of its scientific, religious, political, social, and educational anti-Christian bias. "It may well be, that the developments which we have witnessed in recent years both within the various national units and on the international scale toward totalitarianism and a superstate are providentially preparing the world and race for subjection to such a rule of Christ as the only solution of its problems and the only salvation from otherwise certain ruin."[16] It may be observed that in the course of the thirty-five years since the writing of these words, world events have, if anything, accentuated their seriousness.

How must we conceive of this "rule of Christ?"

The battle of Armageddon—whatever the form that may take—will destroy the now prevailing anti-Christian power and this destruction will be climaxed in the binding of Satan. At the same time, the basic structure of human society will remain unchanged. The daily life of its people in economic, political, social, religious, and educational contexts will continue. Vast changes will indeed have come about by the introduction of the millennium, but they will have come about *within* the existing structure of society and *within* the existing flow of history. "It should be noted that in such a millennium the ordinary processes of human life and society will run their natural course; nor is there in the millennial picture any indication to the contrary, nor any indication of special privileges of some kind for any one national or racial group above the others."[17] Also, the millennium does not call for the "conversion of a great mass of mankind. . . . The removal of Satan's ability to deceive the nations in no wise removes the godlessness of the natural unregenerate human heart. . . . What emerges at the close of the millennial period is just a final regrouping of the human race purely along the . . . lines of the antithesis spoken of in Gen. 3:15, as

14. Ibid., pp. 24–25.
15. Ibid., p. 26.
16. Ibid., pp. 66–67.
17. Ibid., pp. 54–55.

intended by God from the first. That antithesis . . . will find its perfect social embodiment at the end of our human earthly history."[18]

It was the dream of the men of Babel to keep mankind socially one, a desire naturally flowing from the divinely given racial unity of humanity. This intent God frustrated by the confusion of tongues. The obstacle raised by the phenomenon of linguistic diversity has never wholly exterminated in the mind of man the ideal of a social unification of the race. This, however, cannot take place so long as there is a basic religious diversity. The persecution of the early church did not destroy its propagation of the gospel with its inherent religious antithesis. The conquests of Islam isolated Christianity in Europe, but it burst out of this in the seventeenth century and this in turn laid the basis for the world-wide missionary proclamation of the gospel. In contemporary society Satan seeks through the forces represented by the beast and the false prophet to oppose to true religion a secularism that has no serious place for God. This is the threat of the modern age. It seeks to replace religion by a vast activity in the improvement of society and the amelioration of suffering. At the same time, on the political, economic, and military fronts, super-power rivalry has centrally in it the possibility of mutual destruction. Such is the world that Satan with the help of the beast and the false prophet has brought into being. It is the conquest of such a world that Armageddon envisions and it is such a world in which Christ, after the conquest, will set up his kingdom.

It is an irony that Satan's efforts to remove the antithesis in his present assault on the Christian faith will indeed lead to the unplanned realization of this aim at the beginning of the millennium. When Armageddon has destroyed the hosts of his human allies and the beast and the false prophet have been cast into the lake of everlasting fire, Satan himself lying bound in the bottomless pit, the religious and social antithesis arising out of the gospel will for a time have ceased to exist. But this will be the result of a divine, not a satanic act. The rapture following upon Armageddon and the binding of Satan will have removed all true believers from the earth. Religiously, therefore, however the forms in which it manifests itself may vary, the whole of the remaining mankind will live in a state of unbelief. This, however, will be a transition rather than an abiding phenomenon. The gospel has not been withdrawn, the knowledge of salvation still exists, the church remains, and true faith will again manifest itself. As a result, the antithesis will again become a dividing factor in society and for the first time in history the pro-Christian forces will have, as it were, a built in advantage over the enemies of the gospel. For in spite of the continuity in the flow of history, there will be new factors governing the life of man in the millennium which will give to it its distinctive character.

18. Ibid., pp. 68–69.

The banishment of Satan alone from the life of man frees that life from a circumambient atmosphere the relief of which we can hardly imagine. In addition to this negative gain there is the powerfully positive element of the reign of Christ and the saints over the millennial society. Since the glorified saints are not on the earth, and since the normal social, economic, political, and other processes continue, it can only be assumed that the manifestation of Christ's power, in ways not revealed, leads to such restraint on sin as to bring into being a society that is honest and clean in comparison with what had existed before. The new situation will bring into being a new moral climate which will, at least initially, be born from common rather than from special grace. The legislative, administrative, and judicial arms of government will, more than in the past, be tilted toward the good. Soon the church, revitalized by true faith, will exert an uncommon influence on the society. There may not arise a Christian majority, but there will be a "moral majority." It is after this fashion that we must understand Christ and the saints as ruling "with a rod of iron" (Rev. 12:5; 19:15). Out of this situation and specifically under the preaching of the gospel believers will emerge whose election had not yet taken "historical and subjective effect in their regeneration and conversion."[19]

These several considerations underline the crucial development that will be basically characteristic of the millennium. It is the process of *differentiation* between believers and unbelievers in the course of which the antithesis set by God himself between the seed of the woman and the seed of the serpent will find its fullest expression. The amalgamation of the Sethites with the Cainites, the "sons of God" with the "daughters of men" in the antediluvian period resulting in the well-nigh complete apostasy of mankind from God, finds that remarkable opposite development in the millennial period, which the nature of the antithesis as it were calls for. After Armageddon there remains a society that is characterized by a "religious similarity or homogeneity which puts all those nations on the same level, just as the present dechristianization of the so-called Christian nations is rapidly bringing them close to the religious condition of those non-Christian nations which are no longer unaware of the Gospel of Christ but have not nationally accepted it."[20] On comparing this condition with what is found at the close of the millennium, "the idea at once suggests itself that the millennium is to serve the purpose of *undoing* the amalgamation of the nations of the earth in *the spiritual apostasy* which the dominance of modern imperialism together with a Christless education and an apostatizing church has brought upon us today."[21] At the end of the millennium this

19. Ibid., p. 39.
20. Ibid., p. 53.
21. Ibid., pp. 53–54.

amalgamation will have been broken up into "two well-defined and sharply contrasting groups."[22] namely the camp of the saints and the beloved city, and the followers of Gog and Magog.

Kromminga is not unaware of the problem posed by the place of the Jews in the millennium. He acknowledges the special attention which prophecy accords them, particularly in Romans 9–11, but finds himself unable to crystallize the scriptural data into a definite pattern or picture. Perhaps God has laid away for them some particular service to be rendered in the millennium, but he puts this forward only tentatively.[23] He concludes, ". . . the Word of God is not clear on national promises for the Jews which they shall enjoy [in the millennium] in distinction from the spiritual Israel, while it is clear on the unity of all God's redeemed people of all ages and climes and races."[24]

The question arises: precisely how does Kromminga conceive of the role of the risen and transformed saints in the millennium? With this subject he concerns himself in the last third of the book in the chapter entitled "The Resurrection and the Judgment." In it data from the Book of Revelation recede into the background and diverse passages from the gospels and the epistles are powerfully brought to the fore. Central features in the treatment of the texts thus adduced are the time-extensive character of judgment in the course of the millennium, the role of the raptured saints in it, and the judgment of the great white throne, which is the final prelude to the revelation of the new heaven and the new earth. These we must now briefly characterize.

The dominating feature in the third and final section of Kromminga's exposition is the role in the millennium of the saints that have been raised, transformed, and raptured. They are together with Christ and with him rule the world in the millennial period. On the earth, life continues with all its characteristic activities and processes. A visitor driving through any town would see nothing abnormal in its life. Behind this continuity, however, there lies a vast discontinuity. The church is as much on the earth as before, but initially it has only non-raptured and therefore merely nominal members. The evil influences that emanated from Satan as Prince of the world are no longer felt for he lies bound in a bottomless pit and is cut off from all communication with mankind. A new power center for good now exists in the form of a raised and raptured humanity which joins with Christ to govern the earth. Sin is still a powerful reality, for the heart of man is as yet unchanged. But far more than before it is under restraint, whereas

22. Ibid., p. 54.
23. Ibid., p. 55.
24. Ibid., p. 74.

the good now exists in a context of less restraint and therefore greater freedom and it is encouraged to express itself in all aspects of life. As a result there will have come into being a wholly new spiritual dimension in the life of man.

This new and powerful development will have the effect of bringing to clear manifestation, gradually but effectively, what had always been obscured in human history in considerable degree, namely the antithesis between believers and unbelievers, specifically the distinction between the seed of the woman and the seed of the serpent as prophesied in Genesis 3:15. The millennium begins with a complete though doubtless varied religious homogeneity as an unregenerate mankind; it ends in a complete religious separation between the "camp of the saints and the beloved city," on the one hand, and the "nations" inspired by Satan and led by Gog and Magog whose number is like the sand of the sea, on the other.

Between this initially unbelieving uniformity and the final complete antithesis between believers and unbelievers, that is, during the extent of the millennium, the glorified saints fulfill their distinctive function. This task is that of judging the human society then on earth and of the history that brought them to that point in time. Every believer will doubtless have his or her specific assignment, but the judgment will essentially be a corporate one. Not only will specific evil-doers be plucked out of society, but also all *skandala*, i.e., things that offend. Both "offenders and offences will be removed, and that remaining world and society is evidently the kingdom over which Christ and his saints will rule.[25] Not only men will be judged, therefore, but also movements and institutions, i.e., the corporate as well as the individual side of life, together with "the concrete things which they have brought about."[26] "The great positive end which the judgment of the world by the believers with Christ serves is no doubt the establishment of a common opinion about the historical past of our race in that redeemed society of the new world that is to come."[27] This common opinion the saints and Christ will reach on basis of their own "conscientiously fair scrutiny of the facts."[28]

In view of the human instrumentality that is to be used to form this evaluation of history, one wonders how this can be done when the unbelieving dead shall not be judged until the close of the millennium in the assize of the great white throne. If the meaning of history is to be fairly determined by human agents while many who have played so large, indeed major, roles in the eventuation of the facts of history remain absent and as yet unjudged, how must this "fair" evaluation be understood? Were the

25. Ibid., p. 98.
26. Ibid., p. 93.
27. Ibid.
28. Ibid., p. 94.

judgment to be rendered on the basis of God's omniscience, this reservation would be out of place, but if the new humanity is to do the judging, it would seem to require the presence of the unbelieving as well as the believing segment of mankind.

Another area in which Kromminga's view is not wholly clear is the position of the church and her evangelism in the millennium. To the church itself there is little reference in the book. Such as there is, is mainly concerned to show the continuity of the church in the millennium as evidence of the continuity of the covenant.[29] The silence is not altogether surprising. The church that is left after the rapture consists wholly of nominal members. Indeed there is very little reference in the entire discussion to the true believers who emerge in the course of the millennium. Yet they are definitely to come into being. At the end of the millennium the antithesis between believers and unbelievers will not only be clear, but will be more distinct, more open, than at any time in previous human history. The impression is left that the antithesis, although very clear, will also be very one-sided so far as numbers of people in its two respective component parts are concerned, nations and people like the sand of the sea innumerable on the one hand, and a camp and a city on the other.

Even so, a major problem emerges here. The judgment of the great white throne, Kromminga holds, involves only unbelievers. The book of life, however, is opened in that judgment. All are condemned whose name are not written in it. But what of those whose names are written in it? The first resurrection and the rapture account for all who believed up to the time of Christ's return to establish the millennium. That leaves only those believers to be accounted for who came to faith in the course of millennial history. Their number, according to the expectation of Kromminga, should not be inconsiderable. He conceives of a possible Christianization of "the rest of the world" both comparable to and far exceeding the past Christianization of Europe and North America, a development so extensive as "to dwarf" all earlier differences in extent between successive periods in the history of the church.[30] While such Christianization "by no means involves the universal conversion and salvation of every individual," it certainly would seem to involve, in the course of the thousand years, a vast multitude of true believers.[31]

It is therefore surprising to read that in the final judgment of the great white throne there will be "few if any" believers there.[32] The mystery is resolved by the author's suggestion of a return in the millennium "of the

29. Ibid., pp. 62–65.
30. Ibid., p. 51.
31. Ibid., p. 52.
32. Ibid., p. 84.

longevity that marked the ante-diluvian race"(Gen. 5),[33] and the further possibility that "in fact, death might not touch the believers till they all together pass on to glory when the fire from heaven shall defeat the last assault on them and shall consume those who stage it."[34] But this would definitely run contrary to the earlier posited assumption that in the millennium "the ordinary processes of human life and society will run their natural course."[35] The return to longevity and the cessation of death, doubly so when they are limited to believers, certainly will introduce factors into human life that are not explainable from the prior flow of history as it will continue in the millennium "very much in the usual non-miraculous way."[36]

As one reads and rereads Kromminga's eschatological exposition, he is struck by two opposite yet related emphases. One is that he regards his expectation of a millennial reign of Christ and the saints as thoroughly scriptural. On this he is firm and uncompromising. The other emphasis is that much in his exposition is negotiable. Again and again conclusions are acknowledged to be tentative and uncertain, that they are in need of further examination. Not least, he invites proponents of other eschatological views to enter into discussion to test the validity of his claims.[37]

I feel, therefore, that in presenting some critical notes as a conclusion of this essay, I am acting wholly within the spirit of Kromminga's final legacy to the church.

True criticism is appreciative as well as stricturing in character. In my judgment, Kromminga has made a remarkable contribution in an area in which Reformed theology has been unproductive, not to say sterile. This has had far-reaching effect on the pastoral ministry of the church. It is virtually limited to the comfort given by the hope of eternal life with God and his Christ in heaven. The central thrust of eschatology, however, does not lie in eternity but in time. This is well conveyed by the more popular designation of eschatology, namely the doctrine of "the last things," that is, the last drama or dramas in man's earthly history. This vacuum or near vacuum Kromminga fills with fascinating perspectives concerning things that are to come, and not a few of these invite search for horizons not explored by the book. He has presented an eschatological vision that is profound in character, theologically and religiously refreshing, exegetically well fortified, and doctrinally wholly compatible with the genius of the Reformed faith.

33. Ibid., p. 60.
34. Ibid.
35. Ibid., p. 54.
36. Ibid., p. 99.
37. See especially pp. 106–107.

The central conception of the book moves commandingly from creation to consummation, from the defeat and failure of the first Adam to the conquest and abiding success of the last. In doing so he discloses prospects that have never been seriously contemplated in mainline Reformed theology. They center around the expectation of a final era in human history, comparable in antithetical order to the first era in human history, in which faith shall be so dominant and influential in the affairs of men as almost to negate its manifested power in any previous era. It will be a power to be reckoned with not only religiously but also in the affairs of the economy, politics, international relations, education, the home, indeed, in the whole of life. It will have the ability, after the binding of Satan, to bind also the aggressive exploitative, demoralizing, and other negative proclivities of the human spirit. This power, emanating from Christ and the saints, will be channeled not only through believers but also through institutions, notably the institution of government, which leads to the characterization of this binding and restraint as a reigning "with a rod of iron."

In the judgment of the saints at Christ's return, in the governing of millennial mankind, in the judgment of all history that preceded the millennium, and finally in the judgment of all unbelievers in the retribution meted out from the great white throne, a full reckoning will take place with respect to the whole of humanity from the beginning to the end of time. When the revelation of the new heaven and the new earth at long last shall usher in the fulness of the eternal state, there will be no loose ends left hanging, no wrong unredressed, no right unrecognized or unrewarded.

Such are the pluses of Kromminga's eschatological vision, and they are massive. There are, however, also minuses, and these, too, are not inconsiderable. This contribution is aimed at the exposition of a particular understanding of the millennium. This has to some extent been done, but in the doing of it questions inevitably arose which require recognition. Some have already been noted, and there is little room left in the allotted space to do more than that with others. I mention the following problems as deserving of critical attention.

First, the argument of the book is predicated to no small extent on the validity of a Euro-centered conception of history. This history is in the New Testament period of the church, dominated by three crucially significant negative developments. These are the contents of the fifth, sixth, and seventh trumpet blasts in the second of the three cycles of judgment (the seven seals, chapters 5 and 6; the seven trumpets, chapters 8 and 9; and the seven plagues, chapters 15 and 16) that the Book of Revelation details. The fifth trumpet represents the barbarian conquest of the Roman empire; the sixth represents the limiting of European power by the rise of the impenetrable barriers created by the rise of Islam. These both bring to an end the old order of great empires, on the one hand, and effectively limited the outreach of the church on the other. The seventh trumpet represents the modern period of European colonial capitalistic domination and the rise of the super-states. It is this latter development that reveals the bankruptcy of human wisdom and might and, as it were, calls for the initiation of the millennium if mankind is not to destroy itself. Africa is mentioned nowhere in the book and Asia is referred to only tangentially. Both, however, are implicitly destined for a great Christian future. When Christianity virtually died out in North Africa and the Levant, Europe became the sole trustee of the gospel, broadening its trusteeship in the course of the years by its extensions to the Americas, South Africa, Australia, and New Zealand. Meanwhile, it brought into being through the missionary outreach of the church a vast Christian base in Africa and substantial outposts in the Orient.

Is it not possible that European Christianity will atrophy while the church in Africa blossoms with the Orient following later? Such a development would not, from Kromminga's point of view, require the intervention of Christ's millennial reign. But is it realistic to entertain such a possibility? Is it not conceivable that under the aegis of Western power the degeneration of society and its self-made potential for the destruction of society has advanced so far that there is no longer adequate time or opportunity to evangelize the Orient and that this must therefore await the millennium? Is this not a far more conceivable possibility today than it was when some forty years ago Kromminga wrote his book?

Second, the question of interpretation raised above is further deepened by the highly symbolical character of the Book of Revelation and the bearing of this on the meaning of the fifth, sixth, and seventh trumpets in the second cycle of judgments. With what exegetical or prophetical justification is the barbarian invasion declared to be the fulfillment of the fifth seal, and the Islamic conquests that of the sixth? This question is even more applicable to the fulfillment of the seventh trumpet blast. It would seem to be exegetically very questionable that the seventh trumpet can with exegetical legitimacy be made to apply to the appearance of the two beasts in Revelation 13, and similarly that these two beasts find their fulfillment in the modern captitalistic-colonial period and the rise of the super-states. Their immediate reference in the Book of Revelation is to the Roman empire. Does not the seventh trumpet more reasonably refer to the judgment of the seven bowls of the wrath of God in chapters 15 and 16? As the judgments of the seven trumpet blasts arose out the opening of the seventh seal (8:1), do not the judgments of the seven plagues or bowls of wrath arise out of the seventh trumpet (11:15) with an excursus of chapters 12, 13, and 14 between it and its effectuation in chapters 15 and 16? In 10:7 John writes that "in the days of the trumpet call to be sounded by the seventh angel, the mystery of God as he announced to his servants the prophets should be fulfilled," and in 15:1 John presents the vision of "seven angels with seven plagues, which are the last, for with them the wrath of God is ended." The question arises, therefore, whether the three cycles of judgment in the Book of Revelation are not representative of judgments that are always suspended above the ways of man in his sinful rebellious-ness against God. Is it appropriate to single out three judgments in the second of three cycles of judgment to indicate specific historical phe-nomena while the other eighteen judgments are given no particular meaning?

Third, it cannot escape the notice of the careful reader that in the exten-sive use Kromminga makes of Matthew 24 and 25, he makes only one cursory reference to 25:31–46. This section also speaks of a "throne" judg-ment. It is a "glorious throne" rather than a "great white throne" before which judgment takes place, but so similar is the one reference to the other that one looks at first glance for an identity of reference. Matthew, however, speaks of a simultaneous judgment of believers and unbelievers. In Kromminga's judgment there is no possibility of such a contemporaneity in God's judgment on mankind. There is no indication in Matthew 25 of a judgment in which believers and unbelievers are separated from each other to receive separate judgments pursuant to wholly separate group resurrections, and also distant from each other by the long period of time represented by the millennium. Nevertheless, Matthew 25:31–46 is an important part of the available data and must somehow be related exegeti-cally to the whole complex of data adduced by Kromminga.

Fourth, the explicit basis for a doctrine of the millennium is found exclu-sively in Revelation 20:1–10, that is in the very last part of the last book in the Bible. It can be inferred in earlier references in the New Testament, and there may be discernible a marked correspondence between Genesis 1–11 and Revelation 17–21, as we have seen. Kromminga draws both of these inferential conclusions with great skill. But in the end, all these inferences must find their legitimation in the first ten verses of Revelation 20. Without them, the many references adduced cannot become inferences. Here we must face the fact that the Book of Revelation in its totality is a highly symbolical book. That the symbolism has historical meaning can hardly be questioned, but what in the symbolism refers to history, past, present, or future, and what represents purely figurative framework for the historical symbolism is doubtless one of the prime hermeneutical problems in the book. Consider only two details in the whole: first, do the martyrs who are raised in the first resurrection (Rev. 20:4), second part, represent all believ-ers in all ages before the millennium, or do they represent *martyrs*, that is to say, those who have suffered physically for the sake of Christ as such suffering is prominently portrayed in the whole of the Book of Revelation? Second, in Revelation 20:4 there is reference to thrones on which were seated "those to whom judgment (*krima*) was committed." Are these the same as the souls in the remainder of the verse who reign (*basileuo*) with Christ? Kromminga assumes that they are and that the *judgment* rendered by the first group is the same as the *reigning* exercised by the second group. but there would seem to be as much room for uncertainty here as for positive interpretation.

The study of Kromminga's book raises with striking force the possible relevance of the words of I Peter 1:10–12: "The prophets who prophesied of the grace that was to be yours searched and inquired about this salvation; they inquired what person or time was indicated by the Spirit of Christ within them when predicting the sufferings of Christ and the subsequent glory" (RSV). And again: ". . . things into which angels long to look" (RSV). It seemed to me that it is precisely in that way that Kromminga "searched and inquired" and "longed to look." As inadequate and unclear as were the searchings and inquiries of the prophets of the Old Testament to understand the impending developments leading to and through the church of the New Testament, so inadequate and unclear it may well be that Kromminga's searchings and inquiries necessarily had to be. But as the prophets sensed something crucial and majestic about to eventuate in the unfolding redemptive process, so Kromminga leaves the impression of having seen something very big and profoundly meaningful about to burst into history that has eluded Reformed theologians.

More than that, is it not altogether possible that the inadequate and uncrystalized insight of the prophets of the old dispensation about the next great step to be taken in the history of redemption is similarly characteristic of the writers of the New Testament in seeking to apprehend the succession of events and their meaning that will conclude the New Testament dispensation and usher in the eternal order? May not the unexplicated vagueness of apparently significant statements have led Kromminga to discern an order in them which in its very nature is immature and rudimentary? As it is only in the incarnate and risen Christ that we can rightly read the Old Testament prophecies about him, may it not also be true that only in the returned Christ we shall rightly understand these elementary revelations that now appear to be beyond our power to comprehend in their fulness of meaning and proper sequential order of a new age that is to be?

The virtue of Kromminga's contribution is that he has alerted us to eschatological possibilities in a manner and on a scale that the Reformed tradition up to now has not taken into account. Most especially an appreciation of Kromminga's eschatological vision should raise the question by what legitimate rationale can public discussion of it be ecclesiastically prohibited.

8

Lifetime Tenure of Ministers in Reformed Church Polity

Richard R. De Ridder

It is entirely appropriate that a study in the area of Reformed church polity should be included in a volume honoring the many contributions of John H. Kromminga to the life and development of the Christian Reformed Church in North America (hereafter CRC). Included among his contributions was the significant role he served in the lengthy process that led to the revision and adoption of the CRC's Revised Church Order in 1965. Kromminga was among the initial appointees to the Committee for Revision of the Church Order in 1951, serving first as secretary of the committee (1951–1956), and after that, because of the press of duties as seminary president, as the committee's chairman (until 1965).[1]

Tenure of Office Bearers in General

The CRC has never officially addressed the question of the tenure of its office bearers and apart from brief mention in Church Order Commentaries very little has been written on the subject. Past assumptions seem rather to have been accepted uncritically. In recent years certain church order changes have been adopted with respect to the offices recognized by the CRC (minister of the Word, elder, deacon, and evangelist) which have implications for the way in which such tenure is understood by the CRC,

---

1. *Acts of Synod 1951* of the Christian Reformed Church, June 13 to June 26, 1951, at Calvin College, Grand Rapids, Michigan (Grand Rapids: Christian Reformed Publishing House, 1951), p. 101 (Art. 171); *Acts of Synod 1957,* Centennial Year of the Christian Reformed Church, June 12 to June 26, 1957, at Calvin College, Grand Rapids, Michigan (Grand Rapids: Christian Reformed Publishing House, 1957), p. 399 (Suppl. 33).

but these changes were made without reflection regarding what these implications are.[2] Greater attention has been paid to the question of tenure with respect to the offices of elder and deacon than to that of ministers of the Word.[3] Elders and deacons are now said to be ordained at the beginning of each term of service, while the ordination of an evangelist is limited to the time in which he serves a specific emerging congregation and ceases as soon as that emerging church is organized.

This review will be confined to the subject of the tenure of the minister of the Word.

The question of the lifetime tenure of ministers has become more acute in recent years in the light of the number of terminations of the ministerial status of ministers as well as the increasing number of ministers who are engaged in functions other than service as pastors of local congregations.[4] The question whether all such "specialized ministries" are legitimate definitions of the meaning of the office of minister continues to be raised.

Reformed churches have always held that with the exception of those called to specialized ministerial functions (e.g., missionaries, teachers, executive secretaries, etc.) the church does not extend ordination nor does it permit a minister to retain his ordination unless he has a call to a specific pastorate or serves in an approved function judged to be "consistent with the calling of a minister of the Word."[5] No one is presumed to be truly

2. *Acts of Synod 1965*, June 9 to June 17, 1965, at Dordt College, Sioux Center, Iowa (Grand Rapids: Christian Reformed Publishing House, 1965), p. 58 (Art. 85; C.O. Art. 4); Ibid., p. 61 (Art. 94; C.O. Arts. 11–13; *Acts of Synod 1978*, June 13 to 22, 1978, at Calvin College, Grand Rapids, Michigan (Grand Rapids: Board of Publications of the Christian Reformed Church, 1978), pp. 46–47 (Art. 37; C.O. Arts. 11–14); *Acts of Synod 1979*, June 12 to 22, 1979, at Calvin College, Grand Rapids, Michigan (Grand Rapids: Board of Publications of the Christian Reformed Church, 1979), p. 66 (Art. 59; C.O. Art. 23).

3. *Acts of Synod 1965*, p. 113. (C.O. Art. 24b). In the early churches constituting Classis Holland (which later united with the Reformed Church in America and from which the Christian Reformed Church separated in 1857) the question of the tenure of elders and deacons was raised on a number of occasions. *Classis Holland*, Minutes 1848–1858, tr. by a Joint Committee of the Christian Reformed Church and the Reformed Church in America (Grand Rapids: Grand Rapids Printing Co., 1943), p. 20 (Art. 8), p. 58 (Art. 5).

4. Termination of the ministerial status of pastors includes resignations, release from ministry to enter a nonministerial position, termination due to lack of a call over an extended period of years, as well as deposition. At the same time the percentage of nonretired ministers not serving as pastors of congregations continues to increase. Using the official statistics of the annual *Yearbook* of the Christian Reformed Church, 1952, 1962, 1972, 1982 (Grand Rapids: Christian Reformed Publishing House), the following decadal figures are interesting.

Year	No. of ministers (nonretired)	No. of ministers not serving as pastors of local congregations	% of ministers not serving as pastors of local congregations
1952	354	74	21%
1962	637	174	27%
1972	855	254	30%
1982	1052	349	33%
1983	1037	380	37%

5. William P. Brink and Richard R. De Ridder, *Manual of Christian Reformed Church Government 1980* (Grand Rapids: Board of Publications of the Christian Reformed Church, 1980), p. 76 (C.O. Art. 12).

called of God in the Reformed tradition unless he, the denomination, and the local congregation all agree that he is called by God to be a minister and this is confirmed through a call from a local congregation. The essence of ministry (office) according to Reformed polity lies in election or calling to a particular office. There is an essential difference in this regard in that Reformed church polity differs from Presbyterian polity. In Presbyterian polity the essence of the minister's call lies in his ordination rather than in his call or election. In the Reformed tradition ordination is an adjunct to and consummation of the ministerial call, whereas to Presbyterians election (calling) only provides the opportunity to exercise one's official authority over those who chose him.[6] Ordination is, therefore, for life in Presbyterian polity unless for very exceptional cause it is terminated.

Roman Catholic polity likewise maintains that once a person has received an office he never loses it. Church censure does not take away a person's office even if he makes himself totally unworthy to exercise that office. One only loses the right to exercise his office.[7]

Lifetime Tenure of Ministers

Lifetime tenure as an assumption applying to the clergy of the church arose quite early in the development of the post-New Testament era. Although our scant knowledge of the actual developments that led to the introduction of a full-time clergy keeps us from being too dogmatic about this specific issue, the canons of the various councils and synods of the western church to the time of the Reformation give us a clear picture as to what the church expected of its clergy. Repeated provisions of the developing body of canon law forbade the clergy to leave their office. They were required to devote full time to their ministry and were not permitted to engage in "secular" work. Nor were they permitted to leave their ministry for a secular vocation or transfer their labors to another congregation or diocese without permission.[8]

Reformed church polity has tended in recent years to place greater emphasis on function, thereby tying office and function much more closely together than had previously been true in the western tradition. This is also the thrust of the report on "Ecclesiastical Office and Ordination" to the

6. Harry G. Goodykoontz, *The Minister in the Reformed Tradition* (Richmond: John Knox Press, 1963), pp. 114–115, cites a number of commentators on church polity anent this point.

7. *Acts of Synod 1973,* June 12 to 22, 1973, at Calvin College, Grand Rapids, Michigan (Grand Rapids: Board of Publications of the Christian Reformed Church, 1973), pp. 678–679 (Report 44).

8. Henry J. Schroeder, *Disciplinary Decrees of the General Councils,* Text, Translation, and Commentary (St. Louis: B. Herder Co., 1937). It is interesting to compare these canons with early Reformed church orders and to note how many of the practices of the early and even medieval church were incorporated into the developing Reformed church polity. There is probably less that is new than what reflects centuries-old concepts and rules.

1973 Synod of the CRC.[9] With the Reformation and the establishment of the protestant church, church polity among the Reformed churches began a new, but not a historically fully independent era. This was so because the church was convinced that there must be room in its polity for adjustment to historical circumstances—in Calvin's words, "as the need of the times demands."[10] The Church Order of the Synod of Dort (1618–19) stated this principle even more clearly in Article 86: "These articles relating to the lawful order of the church . . . (if the profit of the church demand otherwise) may and ought to be altered, augmented, or diminished."[11] It is regrettable that the Revised Church Order of 1965 of the CRC reduced this to the simple statement that "The Church Order . . . shall be faithfully observed, and any revision thereof shall be made only by Synod."[12] Even though the Committee for the Revision of the Church Order reported that the article (as proposed and later adopted) continues "the provisions now expressed in the final article of our (former) Church Order" and is essentially "expressive of the same principles and provisions," this is obviously not quite so clear, as a cursory reading of both versions demonstrates.[13] The principle expressed in the Church Order of the Synod of Dort (1618–19) is important in that it does not regard Church Order as static but dynamic. Only when Scripture itself speaks to a matter is any part of it unchangeable.

The question concerning lifetime tenure of ministers has been posed and answered in various ways in the Reformed tradition in which the CRC stands. Sometimes the answer was given in terms of the minister being "bound to the service of the church for life,"[14] while at other times it was answered in terms of his ordination vows in that he must understand that he is committing himself to a lifetime of service to the church (sometimes this was understood to mean the congregation in which he was ordained).[15]

9. *Acts of Synod 1973*, pp. 635–716 (Report 44).

10. Ibid., cited in this report, p. 684.

11. Brink and De Ridder, *Manual*, p. 334.

12. Ibid.

13. Ibid., p. 335; *Acts of Synod 1962*, June 13 to 22, 1962, at Calvin College, Grand Rapids, Michigan (Grand Rapids: Christian Reformed Publishing House, 1962), p. 411 (Suppl. 33).

14. *Acta der Synode 1920* van de Christelijke Gereformeerde Kerk Gehouden van 16 tot 30 Juni, 1920, te Grand Rapids, Michigan (Grand Rapids: M. Hoffius, 1920), pp. 146–147. This translation is the official English version of the 1914 Church Order [cf. *Acts der Synode 1914* van de Christelijke Gereformeerde Kerk Gehouden van 17 tot 25 Juni, 1914, te Roseland, Chicago, Illinois (Grand Rapids: Grand Rapids Printing Co., 1914), pp. 54–57] was also translated into English in a slightly different version in 1916. *Acta der Synode* van de Christelijke Gereformeerde Kerk Gehouden van 21 tot 30 Juni, 1916, te Grand Rapids, Michigan (Holland: Holland Printing Co., 1916), p. 114.

15. *Acta der Synode 1920*, pp. 146–147. These articles of the CRC's pre-1965 Church Order stated, "A Minister, once lawfully called, may not leave the congregation with which he is connected, to accept a call elsewhere . . ." (C.O. Art. 10); and "Inasmuch as a Minister of the Word, once lawfully called, as described above, is bound to the service of the Church for life, he is not allowed to enter upon a secular vocation . . ." (C.O. Art. 12). The Church Order of the Synod of Paris, Art. 12, is cited from Harm Bouwman, *Gereformeerd Kerkrecht*, 2 vols. (Kampen: J. H. Kok, 1928), vol. 1, pp. 460–461.

In more recent years the Church Order states that a minister, "once law-fully called, may not forsake his office."[16] Generally, however, the Reformed churches have recognized that this ideal cannot always be realized and have provided ways by which a minister may be honorably released from his office (or permitted to accept a call to another congregation).[17]

The matter of lifetime tenure, while not always specifically mentioned, has been closely tied to other matters concerning ministers. Ministerial salaries, retirement, pensions for ministers, their widows and orphans, even discipline (suspension and deposition) figure in this. For example: while the CRC's present Church Order (Art. 89a) speaks of "neglect or abuse of office,"[18] the pre-1965 Church Order listed among the gross sins "worthy of being punished with suspension or deposition from office" what it de-scribes as "faithless desertion of office or intrusion upon that of another" (C.O. Art. 80).[19] Although there have been varied understandings as to the application of these matters, all commentators are agreed that the basic assumption common to all was that a minister, once lawfully called and ordained, binds himself to serve the church for his entire lifetime.

The Background

The background of this understanding (regulation) is to be found in the early centuries of the establishment and organizational development of the Christian church and of its offices. Although some, even among more recent church order commentators, seek to defend the proposition of life-time tenure from Scripture, this attempt is less than convincing.[20]

Examples of this reasoning are found in the commentaries of the Reverend John L. Schaver and Professor Martin Monsma. Both appear to be citing a similar authority or else are interdependent. Schaver writes: "To the support of a life tenure for the ministry it may be urged that for this office there is required 'all our love, John 21:15–17, II Cor. 5:14; all our time, John 9:4; all our willingness to serve, Luke 9:62, I Cor. 9:16, 17; all our endurance, II Tim. 4:1–5, 10; and our whole separation unto and devotion to this work, Rom. 1:1, Acts 15:26.'"[21] Similarly, Monsma writes: "Scripture also indicates that the service of the Word demands our undivided love (John

<hr>

16. Brink and De Ridder, *Manual,* p. 85 (C.O. Art. 14).
17. Ibid., pp. 85–86.
18. Ibid., p. 320.
19. *Acta der Synode 1916,* p. 125 (C.O. Art. 80).
20. E.g., Martin Monsma, *The New Revised Church Order Commentary,* A Brief Explanation of the Church Order of the Christian Reformed Church (Grand Rapids: Zondervan Publishing House, 1967), pp. 65–66; William W. Heyns, *Kybernetiek,* Een Handboek voor de Kerkregeering (Grand Rapids: Calvin Theological Seminary, 1910), pp. 112–115; John L. Schaver, *The Polity of the Churches,* Concerns all the Churches of Christendom, 2 vols., (Chicago: Church Polity Press, 1947), vol. 1, pp. 124–125; Bouwman, *Gereformeerd Kerkrecht,* vol. 1, pp. 460–466.
21. Schaver, *Polity of the Churches,* vol. 1, p. 125.

21:15-17; II Cor. 5:14), our full time (John 9:4), our readiness of will (I Cor. 9:16, 17), our unfailing perseverance (II Tim. 4:1-6), and our complete separation unto the work (Rom. 1:1)."[22]

The report to the 1973 Synod on "Ecclesiastical Office and Ordination" specifically challenged this assumption, as did the synodical study committee on revision of Church Order Articles 11 to 14.[23]

The first reference to the concept of lifetime tenure was made by the Synod of Paris, 1559, of the French Reformed Church. In that Church Order the statement was simply made that "he who has once been elected to the office of the Minister of the Word must understand that he was elected to be a minister for his entire lifetime."

> Art. 12: Ceux qui sont esleus une fois au ministere de la parole doivent entendre, qu'ils sont esleus pour estre ministre toute leur vie (zij, die eenmaal gekozen zijn tot den dienst des Woords, moeten weten, dat zij gekozen zijn om dienaar te blijven gedurende geheel hun leven).[24]

It wasn't until 1578 that reference to this matter appeared in the emerging church orders of the Dutch churches. At that time the Synod of Dordrecht 1578 declared that "whereas the ministers are bound to their ministry for their entire life, so also it is not permissible for them to enter a secular vocation or to forsake their office, as though they had no congregation to serve...." This synod made provision for ministers who because of sickness or old age could no longer perform the functions of a minister to retain "the honor and title of a minister" (but not the office!). It also refused to allow persons who "had no congregation to serve" to continue to hold the office of minister.[25]

The National Synod of Middelburg 1581 provided that "a Minister of the Word being lawfully called is bound to the Church of Christ for life," and

22. Monsma, *New Revised Church Order Commentary*, p. 65.

23. *Acts of Synod 1973*, pp. 689-690; *Acts of Synod 1978*, June 13 to 22, 1978, at Calvin College, Grand Rapids, Michigan (Grand Rapids: Board of Publications of the Christian Reformed Church, 1978), pp. 45-47, 481.

24. Bouwman, *Gereformeerd Kerkrecht*, vol. 1, pp. 460-466.

25. The following references through the Synod of Dort (1618-19) can be found in Petrus Biesterveld and Herman H. Kuyper, *Kerkelijk Handboekje, Bevattende de Bepalingen der Nederlandsche Synoden en Andere Stukken van Beteekenis voor de Regeering der Kerken* (Kampen: J. H. Bos, 1905). See "De Acta der Nationale Synode van Dordrecht van 1578, p. 98 (Art. 7). "Dewyle de Dienaers haer leuen lanck aen haren dienste verbonden syn, soo en isset niet gheoorloft datse hen tot eenen anderen staet des leuens begheuen, ofte oock haren dienst onderlaten, ten ware dat sy gheen ghemeynte en hadde om te bedienen, Ende soo het gheschiedde dat sy door ouderdom ofte sieckte onbequaem wierden tot oeffeninghe hares dienst, soo sullen sy nochtans dies niet te min de eere ende den naem eenes Dienaers behouden. Ende op dat sy den ouerighen tyt hares leuens eerlick toebrenghen moghen, soo sullen sy van den Kercken versorght werden. Soo sy oock om dese ofte eenighe andere oorsaken haren dienst voor eenen tyt nalaten moeten, soo sullen sy nochtans hen tot allen tyden der beroepinghe der ghemeynte onderwerpen. Ende het en betaemt neimant van deen plaetse tot dander te reysen om te predicken dewyle het ampt der Apostelen ende Euangelisten voor langhen tyt in der ghemeynten Godes opghehouden is." Also, Art. 12 of this same Synod.

forbade the minister from forsaking his office in the congregation he served.[26] The change from "bound to the ministry" (Dordrecht 1578) to "bound to the Church of Christ" (Middelburg 1581) is interesting to note.

The National Synod of 's-Gravenhage 1586 had a still different formulation. This synod made a few changes in this article. It declared that "whereas a Minister of the Word once lawfully called as above is bound for his lifetime to the service of the church (kerkendienst), so also it is not permissible for him to enter into a secular vocation."[27] This provision was taken over word for word by the Synod of Dort (1618–19).[28] And that is what the Church Order of the CRC provided until the Revised Church Order was adopted in 1965.[29]

The pre-1965 Church Order stated in Article 12:

Inasmuch as a Minister of the Word, once lawfully called, is bound to the service of the church for life, he is not allowed to enter upon a secular vocation except for such weighty reasons as shall receive the approval of the classis.[30]

The 1965 Revised Church Order states in Article 14:

a. A Minister of the Word shall not leave the congregation with which he is connected for another church without the consent of the consistory.
b. A Minister of the Word, once lawfully called, may not forsake his office. He may, however, be released from office to enter upon a non-ministerial vocation for such weighty reasons as shall receive the approval of the classis with the concurring advice of the synodical deputies.[31]

The Gereformeerde Kerken in Nederland (hereafter GKN) have amended this article to read: "A Minister of the Word is not free to lay aside his office.

26. Ibid., "Kerkenordening der Nationale Middelburgsche Synode van 1581," p. 144 (Art. 6). "Een Dienaer des Woordts wettelick beroepen zijnde is aen der Kercke Christi zijn leuen lanck verbonden, alsoo dat hij soo langhe de Ghemeijnte staet, dewelcke hij dient, zijnen Dienst niet onderlaten, noch eenighe andere beroepinghe des leuens aenveerden mach, sonder het oordeel des particulieren Sijnodi."
27. Ibid., "Kerkenordening der Nationale Synode van 's-Gravenhage van 1586," p. 194 (Art. 10). "De wyle een Dienaer des Worts eens wettelijken als bouen beropen synde sijn leuen lanck aenden kerkendienst verbonden is, soo sal hem niet gheoorloeft sijn hem tot eenen andren staet des leuens te begheuen, Ten sij om groote ende wichtighe oorsake daer van de Classis kennisse nemen ende oordeelen sal."
28. Ibid., "Kerkenordening van de Nationale Synode van Dordrecht van 1618–19," p. 229 (Art. 12). "Dewijle een Dienaer des Woordts eens wettelijck, als bouen, beroepen zijnde, syn leven langh aenden Kercken-dienst verbonden is, soo sal hem niet geoorloft zijn hem tot eenen anderen staet des levens te begheven: ten zy om groote ende wightighe oorsaken, daer van de Classe kennisse nemen ende oordeelen sal."
29. Acta der Synode 1914, pp. 54–55 (Art. 12). "Dewijl een Dienaar des Woords, eens wettelijk als boven beroepen zijnde, zijn leven lang aan den Kerkedienst verbonden is, zoo zal hem niet geoorloofd zijn, zich tot eenen anderen staat des levens te begeven; tenzij om groote en gewichtige oorzaken, waarvan de Classe kennis nemen en oordeelen zal."
30. Acta der Synode 1916, p. 114 (Bijlage XIV).
31. Acts of Synod 1965, p. 61 (Art. 94).

He can only become free from his office to enter a secular vocation when the consistory and the classis, with the cooperation and approval of the deputies of the particular synod, judge that compelling and weighty reasons exist for this."[32]

One must bear in mind that very few ministers retired in early days. It was understood that a minister, unless otherwise prevented, would continue to serve until the end of his life. The period of retirement (if this happened) was very short. It was, therefore, possible for the church orders to specify that the last church a minister served must provide "honorably for his support and that of his dependents." This provision, strangely enough, is still retained in the CRC Church Order, Art. 18b, even though this support is now provided through a denominational pension fund and retired ministers are permitted (even encouraged) to transfer their ministerial credentials to a congregation in the place of their retirement![33]

In the sixteenth century widows and orphans of ministers were not always well cared for. At times the retired minister was regarded as being without a fixed charge and hence principially not eligible for support. There was no pension fund. In the CRC it is only in recent years that the present concept regarding ministers' pensions has changed radically (and even now is not an acceptable principle to many as overtures to synod indicate). The present basis of our pension system, while declared by synod to be "mandated by Scripture," is hardly so except by a stretch of the imagination.[34] It would be far better (and more accurate) to affirm simply that our society being what it is that it is proper and right to provide pensions for our ministers and that "the cost of providing retirement benefits . . . is incurred while he is in active service."[35] It is only in comparatively recent years that retirement from the ministry may occur on the basis of age alone without other compelling factors. In the earlier years of the CRC retirement was rare and a large proportion of our ministers never retired. Today, many retired ministers enjoy several years of good health and perform many valuable services to the church after their retirement.

The Church Order of the Christian Reformed Church

As noted above, the provisions of the Synod of Dort (1618–19) with respect to lifetime service were until 1965 a part of the Church Order of the

---

32. Doede Nauta, *Verklaring van de Kerkorde van de Gereformeerde Kerken in Nederland* (Kampen: J. H. Kok, 1971, p. 80. "Art. 14: Het zal aan een dienaar des Woords niet vrijstaan zijn ambt neer te leggen. Hij kan slechts van zijn ambt worden ontheven, om zich tot een andere staat des levens te begeven, indien de kerkeraad en de classis, met medewerking en goedvinden van de door de particuliere synode aangewezen deputaten, oordelen dat daarvoor bijzondere en gewichtige redenen zijn."

33. *Acts of Synod 1979*, p. 105 (Art. 92); Brink and De Ridder, *Manual*, p. 99.

34. This statement, found in the *Acts of Synod 1979*, p. 105, is no more convincing than the so-called biblical proofs for lifetime service (see footnotes 20 and 21).

35. *Acts of Synod 1979*, p. 105 (Art. 92).

CRC. However, a subtle and unchallenged change was proposed and adopted in the 1965 Revised Church Order. Early proposals of the Committee for Revision retained the article as it was from the time of the Synod of Dort (1618–19).[36] Without explanation (was this perhaps influenced by the revision of the GKN?) the proposed article as re-stated by the committee became: "A Minister of the Word, once lawfully called, may not forsake his office."[37] This statement, as adopted by the CRC Synod of 1965, remained unchanged when the article was amended in 1978.[38]

The study committee which in 1978 proposed the revisions of Church Order Articles 11 to 14 reflected on the question whether provision should be made for those who for legitimate reasons wish to leave the ministry of the Word temporarily for other occupations. The committee wrote:

> ... we know of no biblical warrant for requiring that the ministry of the Word be "for life," whereas the offices of elder and deacon are not. A second reason is that there are *numerous* Christian occupations that can be well served by a person with theological training and ministerial experience, but that are not ecclesiastical in nature and are not directly related to the purpose and primary task of the ministry of the Word. Let us be clear about this matter! Just because a (former) minister of the Word is able to do a job does not automatically make that job either ecclesiastical or directly related to the purpose and primary task of the ministerial office.
>
> As a matter of fact, in frequent instances we think it would be appropriate and even helpful if a minister of the Word could honorably and without prejudice set aside his ordination for a specific time (such as two years minimum, five years maximum) while he engage(s) in an occupation that [does] not satisfy the requirements of Articles 11–13 as proposed. Essentially such action is no different than in the case of elders and deacons who conclude a term of service on the consistory, only to be reelected and installed at a later date. When the other assignment is completed, the (former) minister could then follow the appropriate steps for returning to a ministerial vocation.[39]

In commenting as it did the study committee was in agreement with the comments of the 1973 study committee report on "Ecclesiastical Office and Ordination." In that report this comment was made:

> Reformed church order makes ministry a lifelong occupation while requiring periodic retirement from office by elders and deacons. Commentators

36. *Acts of Synod 1957,* p. 403 (C.O. Art. 11; Suppl. 33). The Synod of 1965 did not accede to an overture requesting a change in the heading of Section IB of the Church Order to read "The Ministers of the Word and Sacraments," and retained the title "Minister of the Word." *Acts of Synod 1965,* pp. 58, 446.

37. *Acts of Synod 1960,* June 8 to 21, 1960, at Calvin College, Grand Rapids, Michigan (Grand Rapids: Christian Reformed Publishing House, 1960), p. 144 (C.O. Art. 14; Report 1).

38. *Acts of Synod 1978,* p. 47 (Art. 37).

39. Ibid., pp. 479–480 (Report 30).

on this distinction seek to give it a biblical basis. Jansen (p. 56)—followed by Van Dellen and Monsma (p. 65)—buttresses the argument for lifelong ministry as follows:

> ... Yet we hold that a minister is bound to the service of the church for life. Why? In the first place because this is biblical. Even in the Old Testament days Elijah, Isaiah, Jeremiah, and other prophets were called to the ministry for life. The disciples also and the apostles and evangelists were "separated" unto their ministry, not temporarily, but permanently, for life. . . .

> Scripture also indicates that the service of the Word demands our undivided love (John 21:15–17; II Cor. 5:14), our full time (John 9:4), our readiness of will (I Cor. 9:16, 17), our unfailing perseverance (II Tim. 4:1–6), and our complete separation unto the work (Rom. 1:1).

But with respect to elders it is argued that the absence of scriptural stipulations leaves the churches free to regulate this matter according to their best interests (Jansen, p. 128; Van Dellen and Monsma, p. 94). Even if one grants the relevance of the scriptural citations given above, the question must be faced why the same passages do not apply to elders and deacons as well. Were not priests and kings also called to office for life in the Old Testament? And do the New Testament texts cited prove, upon examination, to apply only to the ministry of the Word, or to all of Christian service?

The danger does not lie in making distinctions as to term of office, but in misapplying scriptural proof to support these distinctions. A distinction between the term of office of a minister and an elder or deacon may be defended on practical grounds. The length of preparation for the ministry argues for a long-term commitment to it. The demands of time and the necessity of earning a living may speak for periodic retirement of elders and deacons. But the introduction of biblical arguments for the distinction comes dangerously close to recognizing a priestly or clerical class in the church, and to reviving the Roman Catholic idea that ordination confers an indelible character on its recipient. Furthermore, this sort of argumentation is rendered suspect by the fact that in the New Testament those servants whom we now call ministers are described as elders who labor in the Word and in teaching (I Tim. 5:17).[40]

Conclusions and Observations

It would appear that the CRC is for traditional reasons still committed to the concept of lifetime commitment to the ministry of the Word on the part of a candidate seeking admission to that ministry. Additionally, the Revised Church Order of 1965, written as it was under the restrictive mandate given by the Synod of 1952 to the Committee for Revision and only partially aware of the rapid changes through which the CRC was about to pass, is hardly adequate any longer for our contemporary situation. It cries out for a new revision in terms of the principle of the Church

---

40. *Acts of Synod 1973*, pp. 679–680 (Report 44).

Order of the Synod of Dort (1618–19) that "when the profit of the church demands" these articles "may and ought to be altered, amended, or diminished."[41] The fact that in the short span of seventeen years (1965–82) no less than twenty-three amendments have been made to the 1965 Revised Church Order, two proposed changes await ratification by synod, and a number of articles have been modified to fit the particular situation of CRC Classis Red Mesa, demonstrates how important it is that a coherent, unified, but not piecemeal, revision is necessary. When this takes place, attention will have to be given to changes respecting the tenure of ministers.

Not so many years ago foreign missionaries were recruited with the understanding that such ministry was a lifetime commitment on the part of the missionary candidate to missionary service. This is no longer so. It is interesting to speculate whether a candidate would be admitted to the ministry of the Word if at his classical examination he would say, "I intend to remain a minister for at least ten years, but I will always keep my options open to other areas of Christian vocation as fits my gifts and my understanding as to where I can best employ them."

While there seems to have been little erosion in the church's expectation with reference to the candidate's commitment to lifetime service, there seems also to be little awareness as to the subtle but significant changes in the church's dealing with its ministers. Poor health in addition to age is no longer a required basis for eligibility to retire from ministry. More adequate pension provisions encourage retirement at the approved age (generally automatically approved at age 65, but may be approved at age 62). An increasing number of ministers request and are granted release from their office in order to enter other, equally valid, vocations but which are not directly related to the definition of the ministerial task.[42] Return to ministry is, however, not easily accomplished once one has accepted employment in another vocation.

At the same time greater concern must be shown by the church for its ministers. New opportunities, personal advancement, family circumstances,

---

41. *Acts of Synod 1952* of the Christian Reformed Church in Session from June 11 to 25, 1952, at Calvin College, Grand Rapids, Michigan (Grand Rapids: Christian Reformed Publishing House, 1952), p. 35 (Art. 92). The mandate of synod was adopted upon the recommendation of the Committee for Revision of the Church Order and provided such directives as these: ". . . the proposed revision shall seek to retain the venerable Church Order of Dordt (1618–19) as to its general order and the number of articles. . . . All needless changes shall be studiously avoided. . . . In so far as situations of sufficient importance have arisen in the life of the churches which are not covered by the rules of the present Church Order, the proposed revision may include additions to certain relevant articles, as long as these are in accordance with the Scriptures, our Reformed principles and present established ecclesiastical practice. There [are] developments . . . re Missions, Church Extension, etc., which may require a certain amount of regulation by the Church Order."

42. For statistical information and suggested revisions of the Church Order see Report 35 of the Healing Ministries Committee to the 1982 Synod. *Acts of Synod 1982*, June 8 to 17, 1982, at Calvin College, Grand Rapids, Michigan (Grand Rapids: Board of Publications of the Christian Reformed Church, 1982), pp. 581–589 (Report 35).

interest and ability to use one's talents in a variety of vocations during one's lifetime are all considered normal and acceptable options for professional persons and members of the church to change their vocation. Why not for ministers? The fact that more than one-third of the ministers of the CRC now serve in noncongregational positions (the euphemism is "specialized ministries") and that this percentage continues to increase indicates that the church itself has become quite ambiguous as to what constitutes being a minister of the Word.[43]

The way to release from and return to ministry should, of course, only be done for valid reasons. The church should never stigmatize a person who sees and accepts the challenge to work in his Lord's vineyard in other ways than as a minister. Perhaps we still operate, admittedly unconsciously, too much with remnants of conceptions of the meanings of office and ordination which are neither scripturally valid nor in harmony with Reformation insights and today's needs. Very likely the concepts "religious vs. secular," or "clergy vs. laity" also have some influence here.

This is not intended to call into question the appropriateness of an individual's personal commitment to lifetime service. That is a matter between a minister and his Lord. It is rather intended to call into question the church's own response when, having once certified that one has the requisite gifts and having defined a call to ministry, it demands in addition that this call is for life, without any turning away. In fact, when because of circumstances (e.g., completion of a leave of absence, termination of one's ministry in a local congregation for specific reasons, completion of an assignment such as missionary service, as well as no reappointment to a specialized ministry) a minister does not receive a call, the church itself takes the initiative to terminate his status! When such a person terminates a specific ministry and does not receive a call, it is not unusual but grossly unjust for members to be suspicious as to whether he is in fact unqualified, that there is some fault in his character, or that he lacks essential gifts for ministry.

A final comment needs to be made with reference to the implications this has for the call a congregation extends to a minister. Interestingly, the majority of ministers in specialized ministries serve under contracts which (at least initially or for the first few reappointments) specify a limited number of years. Foreign and home missionaries, teachers, seminary professors, denominational executives and appointees all are called under contractual arrangements that specifically limit the length of the appointment. At the conclusion of each appointment (or reappointment) both the person and agency reserve the right to terminate the relationship or mutu-

---

43. See footnote 11 for a statistical summary.

ally agree to its continuation. Attempts have been made to endorse this form of contract (for that is in essence what a letter of call is) to ministers serving as pastors of congregations. These attempts have met, strangely enough, with opposition and even express refusal to give endorsement when the advice of classis was requested. Meanwhile, situations in which pastors and congregations are incompatible, or whose relationship is such that the minister is no longer able to use his gifts fruitfully in a particular place, continue to multiply, and both congregation and pastor are needlessly and unwisely required to continue the relationship until it deteriorates irreparably or a call finally comes which mercifully releases them from further obligation to each other. In not a few instances the reputation of a talented minister has been so tainted that his future effectiveness is rendered suspect in the entire denomination.

We must recognize the necessity and wisdom that underlie the provisions of the early Reformed synods and that of the Church Order of the Synod of Dort (1618–19). The provisions fit that day and time. Church polity, as observed earlier, is not static. The temptation to make abiding principles out of our fathers' expedients must be resisted. Church polity cannot be treated or dealt with in the same manner as Scripture and doctrines are. We need to be responsive in our day to the needs of the church today.

To summarize, it must be observed that a person whose personal call to ministry is confirmed by a call from the church ought not take such a call lightly. The call to office in the church is not the same as entering into some other vocation, even though the call to every Christian is to a sacred work under the Lordship of Jesus Christ. Nowhere does Scripture imply that these two forms of service to God are the same. Scripture rather emphasizes the special nature of a call to office (function) in the church.

At the same time a person once called and ordained to office may not leave that office on his own initiative. The Church Order provides for honorable release from office, as noted above, for "weighty reasons" of which consistory, classis, and synodical deputies must be informed and must judge. Acceptance of office involves a solemn commitment to Christ and the church which ought not be terminated simply on a personal whim, fancy, or desire. There must be valid reasons and of sufficient weight to which one appeals when making a request for release.

Although it is right to assume that a candidate for ministry accepts that ministry with a strong personal commitment to lifetime service, changing times and circumstances may for sufficient reasons make reevaluation of that commitment necessary. No stigma should be attached to this.

Finally, the church will have to come to grips with the questions relating to the definition as to what vocations are consistent with the calling of a minister. The present trend is to be very lenient as to the areas of vocation ministers may choose to enter apart from the pastorate of a congregation. The report of the study committee stated this succinctly: "Just because a (former) minister of the Word is able to do a job does not automatically make that job either ecclesiastical or directly related to the purpose and primary task of the ministerial office."[44]

44. *Acts of Synod 1978*, p. 480.

9

≡ The Christian Reformed Church and the Covenant

Anthony A. Hoekema

The doctrine of the covenant of grace has been an important aspect of the teaching and life of the Christian Reformed Church in North America (hereafter CRC) from its very beginning. It may well be said that this doctrine is one of the distinctive teachings of this denomination, basic to its conception of the church, the sacraments, the family, the Christian life, and Christian education. It is probably indicative of the importance of the covenant concept in its thinking that the CRC measures the size of its congregations in terms of families rather than individuals.

Though definitions of the covenant of grace vary from author to author, as we shall see, we may think of the covenant of grace as that gracious arrangement which God establishes with believers and their children in which God promises them salvation through faith in Christ, and requires of them a life of faith and obedience.

The Covenant of Grace in Our Doctrinal Standards

References to the covenant of grace in our doctrinal standards are few but significant. Article 34 of the Belgic Confession affirms that the infants of believers "ought to be baptized and sealed with the sign of the covenant, as the children in Israel formerly were circumcised upon the same promises which are made unto our children."[1] Question 74 of the Heidelberg Catechism, "Should infants, too, be baptized?," is answered as follows: "Yes.

---

1. "Belgic Confession," in *Ecumenical Creeds and Reformed Confessions* (Grand Rapids: Board of Publications of the Christian Reformed Church, 1979), p. 81.

Infants as well as adults are in God's covenant and are his people. . . . Therefore, by baptism, the mark of the covenant, infants should be received into the Christian Church. . . ."[2] Further, answer 82 states that the covenant of God would be dishonored if people are admitted to the Lord's Supper who by their confession and life show themselves to be unbelieving and ungodly.[3]

A very important statement about the significance of the covenant is found in the Canons of Dort (chap. I, par. 17): "Since we are to judge of the will of God from His Word, which testifies that the children of believers are holy, not by nature, but in virtue of the covenant of grace, in which they together with the parents are comprehended, godly parents ought not to doubt the election and salvation of their children whom it pleases God to call out of this life in their infancy."[4] The covenant is also referred to in chapter II, paragraph 8, where it is said that "Christ by the blood of the cross . . . confirmed the new covenant." There are other references to the covenant in the Rejection of Errors (chap. II, par. 2, 4, 5; chap. V, par. 1).[5]

Significant Contributions to the Doctrine of the Covenant of Grace

What follows is a review of teachings on the covenant of grace found in books written by CRC authors from 1893 to 1974. To be sure, much material on the covenant of grace can be found in CRC and related periodicals like *The Banner, De Gereformeerde Amerikaan* and *De Wachter.* Because of limitations of space and time, however, this material has not been consulted. It is hoped that what is presented in this section will give the reader a good account of the major emphases in covenant teaching found in the history of the CRC.

We begin with Geerhardus Vos, who was Professor of Systematic and Exegetical Theology at Calvin Theological Seminary from 1888 to 1893. It may be noted that already in 1891 Vos indicated his interest in the covenant of grace by lecturing at the seminary on the topic *De Verbondsleer in de Gereformeerde Theologie.*[6] His teachings on the covenant of grace are, however, more fully set forth in his *Dogmatiek,*[7] originally distributed in mimeographed form between 1888 and 1893.

We note first that according to Vos there was, in addition to the covenant of grace, a so-called "covenant of redemption" and a "covenant of works."

2. "The Heidelberg Catechism," in *Ecumenical Creeds and Reformed Confessions,* p. 34.

3. Ibid., p. 40.

4. "Canons of Dort," in *Ecumenical Creeds and Reformed Confessions,* p. 88.

5. Ibid., pp. 48–49, 63.

6. Geerhardus Vos, *De Verbondsleer in de Gereformeerde Theologie,* Rede bij het Overdragen van het Rectoraat aan de Theologische School te Grand Rapids, Michigan (Grand Rapids: "Democrat" Drukpers, 1891).

7. Geerhardus Vos, *Dogmatiek,* 5 vol. in 3. (Grand Rapids: Calvin Theological Seminary, 1910).

The covenant of redemption may be defined as follows: "The agreement between the Father, giving the Son as Head and Redeemer of the elect, and the Son, voluntarily taking the place of those whom the Father had given Him."[8] This covenant was thought of as having been drawn up prior to creation, and as being the eternal foundation for the covenant of grace and the guarantee of its execution.[9]

By the covenant of works is meant the covenant between God and unfallen man in which man is threatened by death if he disobeys the command not to eat of the fruit of the forbidden tree and, by implication, is promised eternal life if he continues to obey God. Maintaining that there is a close connection between the covenant of works and the covenant of grace, Vos devotes several pages to a discussion of the covenant of works.[10]

There has been much discussion about whether the covenant of grace is unilateral (one-sided) or bilateral (two-sided). Vos holds that the covenant of grace is unilateral in the sense that God has originated it. However, he continues, the covenant is also bilateral in the sense that there are two parties in it, and in the sense that man appears in the covenant as believing and turning to God.[11] It is clear, therefore, that Vos understands the covenant of grace as involving both the sovereign grace of God and the responsible activity of man. God, to be sure, takes the initiative in establishing the covenant of grace with fallen man, but it is essential to the covenant relationship that God requires those with whom he makes the covenant to be faithful and obedient covenant partners.

There has also been much discussion about the question of whether the covenant of grace is conditional or unconditional. Vos holds that the covenant is not conditional in the sense that there is in it any condition with meritorious value, or in the sense that what is asked of man in the covenant must be fulfilled in his own strength. But the covenant of grace is conditional as concerns its completion and its final blessings. We may speak of faith as a condition in the covenant in the sense that the exercise of faith is the only way along which one can come to conscious enjoyment of the blessings of the covenant.[12] Vos adds that if there were no conditions in the covenant of grace there would be no room in it for threatenings, such as we find in the Bible. Also, if there were no conditions, only God would be bound by the covenant and not man; but then the covenantal character of the covenant of grace would be lost.[13]

Perhaps one of Vos' most important contributions is what he has to say about the so-called dual aspect of the covenant. One of the problems

---

8. Louis Berkhof, *Systematic Theology* (Grand Rapids: Eerdmans, 1938), p. 271.
9. Vos, *Dogmatiek*, Deel 2, *Anthropologie*, pp. 94–95.
10. Ibid., pp. 34–39, 43–52, 95–96.
11. Ibid., p. 85.
12. Ibid., p. 115.
13. Ibid., p. 117.

involved in the doctrine of the covenant is the question of the relationship between membership in the covenant of grace and divine election (that is, God's choosing in Christ from eternity of those who are to be saved). In one sense membership in the covenant of grace is restricted to the elect, since only the elect enjoy the fellowship with God which is the heart or essence of the covenant. In another sense, however, membership in the covenant of grace includes more than the elect, since many members of the covenant (through birth from believing parents) never arrive at true covenant fellowship.[14] The great difficulty in the doctrine of the covenant of grace, Vos asserts, is the problem of reconciling these two sides of the covenant.[15]

To face this difficulty properly, and to meet the problem which it presents, continues Vos, we must distinguish between two senses in which we can think or speak of the covenant of grace. We may think of the covenant first of all as a "relationship" (sometimes called a "legal relationship"), a bond between two parties, with conditions on both sides. The covenant in this sense exists even when nothing has been done to realize its goal. It then exists only as a relationship, as something which ought to be. Persons who live under such a bond are in the covenant, since they find themselves under the reciprocal stipulations of the covenant.[16]

In the second place, we may think of the covenant as a fellowship. In this sense the covenant does not concern primarily what ought to be, but what actually is. Every covenant in the first sense looks forward to and is intended to become a covenant in this second sense: a "living fellowship," or a "fellowship of life."

Only those who are true believers can be said to be in the covenant of grace in this latter sense.

Actually, if one has been born of believing parents, one is first *under* the covenant (the covenant as relationship) and then *in* the covenant (the covenant as fellowship). Such a person is first under the promise and requirement of the covenant, and then he enters into the blessings of the covenant.[17]

This distinction can throw light on many points. It can throw light, for example, on the question: who is in the covenant of grace? If we look at the legal-relationship aspect of the covenant—that is, if it be asked, of whom can it be expected that they will live the covenant life, the answer is: of all who through profession of faith or through birth have become covenant members; in other words, of believers and their children. If, on the other hand, we look at the essential side of the covenant—that is, if it be asked, in

14. Ibid., p. 126.
15. Ibid., p. 101.
16. Ibid., p. 106.
17. Ibid., p. 108.

whom has this legal relationship become a living fellowship, the answer is: in all who have been regenerated, have faith, and are living for God.[18]

The presumption is that the children of the covenant who are in the covenant relationship will also be led into the fellowship of the covenant. Hence we say: of those who are born under the covenant it is not only demanded with double force that they repent and believe, but it is also expected and prayed for with double confidence that they will be regenerated so that they will be enabled to repent and believe.[19]

Only in this way can we maintain the organic connection between being under the covenant and being in the covenant, between the covenant relationship and the covenant fellowship. The first is, as it were, the shadow cast by the second. The covenant relationship into which a child of believing parents is born is the image and likeness of the covenant fellowship in which he is later expected to live. Being under the covenant, therefore, not only precedes the covenant fellowship in the case of believers' children, but is also instrumental in bringing it about.[20]

It will be noted that Vos' distinction between covenant relationship and covenant fellowship does full justice both to the sovereignty of God and the responsibility of man in the covenant of grace. The distinction avoids the one-sidedness of saying that only the elect are members of the covenant of grace, and leaves room for the reality of covenant breaking.

Another significant contribution to the doctrine of the covenant of grace by a CRC author was made by Menno J. Bosma in his *Exposition of Reformed Doctrine*.[21]

Bosma defines the covenant of grace as follows: "It is the gracious agreement between God and his people, whereby God promises them complete salvation in the way of faith, and they accept this in faith."[22] Though various modes of administration in the covenant of grace are distinguished, it is maintained that the covenant is the same in Old Testament and New Testament times.[23] Like Vos, Bosma also speaks of a covenant of redemption between the Father and the Son from eternity, but distinguishes between this covenant and the covenant of grace.[24]

On the question of membership in the covenant of grace, Bosma's position is similar to that of Vos. Bosma distinguishes between an outward and inward side of the covenant of grace, or between the covenant of grace as a judicial relationship and as a vital or living fellowship.[25] He gives biblical

18. Ibid., p. 107.
19. Ibid., p. 111.
20. Ibid.
21. Menno John Bosma, *Exposition of Reformed Doctrine*, A Popular Explanation of the Most Essential Teachings of the Reformed Churches, 4th ed. (Grand Rapids: Smitter Book Co., 1927).
22. Ibid., p. 111.
23. Ibid., p. 119.
24. Ibid., pp. 121–123.
25. Ibid., p. 127.

evidence for the contention that all children of believers are in the covenant of grace in some sense, calling this grouping of believers and their children "the circle of the covenant."[26] Though only God can enable man to believe, yet mere passivity is wrong; covenant children must turn to the Lord in repentance and faith, trusting that God will enable them so to turn.[27]

Bosma mentions three results of stressing the doctrine of the covenant of grace: first, this doctrine recognizes God's sovereign grace as the source of all spiritual blessing; second, this doctrine implies that we must seek to live as God's partners in every area of life; and third, the doctrine of the covenant underscores the necessity for the Christian training of children in the home, the church, and the school.[28]

We turn next to William W. Heyns, who was Professor of Practical Theology at Calvin Theological Seminary from 1902 to 1926, and whose covenantal views were quite influential in the CRC of his day. He set forth his views on the covenant of grace in his *Gereformeerde Geloofsleer.*[29] This book was translated into English and published ten years later under the title, *Manual of Reformed Doctrine.*[30]

Like Vos, Heyns teaches both a covenant of redemption from eternity[31] and a covenant of works. He discusses both the importance of the latter covenant and its relation to the covenant of grace.[32] Whereas the covenant of works had a head (namely Adam) who acted for all those whom he represented, Heyns insists that the covenant of grace has no representing covenant head who acts and decides for all the covenant members. He elaborates on this point by saying, ". . . accepting and keeping or breaking the Covenant of Grace is for each covenant member a personal matter."[33] Membership in the covenant of grace, therefore, does not guarantee salvation, since there is the possibility of covenant breaking.[34]

Heyns defines the covenant of grace as follows: "The Covenant of Grace is that special institution for the salvation of man in which the Triune God binds Himself with a covenant and an oath to believers and their seed, to be their God: their Father, their Redeemer, and their Sanctifier, and binds them to Himself to be His own and to serve Him, thus insuring their salvation, unless they break the Covenant by unbelief and disobedience."[35]

26. Ibid., pp. 126, 129.
27. Ibid., p. 130.
28. Ibid., pp. 132–133.
29. William W. Heyns, *Gereformeerde Geloofsleer,* Voor de Literarische Klassen van de Theologische School en Calvin College te Grand Rapids, Michigan (Grand Rapids: Eerdmans-Sevensma Co., 1916).
30. William W. Heyns, *Manual of Reformed Doctrine* (Grand Rapids: Eerdmans, 1926).
31. Ibid., pp. 53–54.
32. Ibid., pp. 69–72.
33. Ibid., p. 125.
34. Ibid., p. 71.
35. Ibid., p. 125.

More briefly expressed, the covenant of grace is defined as "the promise of salvation in the form of a covenant."[36]

As is clear from the above definitions, Heyns does not wish to describe the covenant of grace as including only the elect. His objections to this view are as follows: If one thinks of the covenant of grace as established only with the elect, the character of the covenant of grace is totally changed, for then there can be no possibility of covenant breaking. Further, the covenant of grace is then deprived of its objectivity, since one cannot know whether one's children are covenant members or not. Again, if only the elect are in the covenant, one cannot administer baptism to the infants of believers.[37]

In distinction from Vos and Bosma, Heyns does not wish to speak of distinctions within the membership of the covenant of grace. He rejects, for example, the distinction between an internal and an external covenant. Since he defines the covenant as "the promise of salvation in the form of a covenant,"[38] he holds that the covenant of grace has the same meaning for all its members. Some covenant members accept the covenant promise and are saved, whereas others break the covenant and are lost.[39]

According to Heyns, God has given to the promise of salvation the binding form of a covenant, of a covenant confirmed with an oath and witnessed and sealed with sacraments. The purpose of the covenant is the encouragement and strengthening of faith. The obligation of the covenant is faith and obedience. Covenant members, however, cannot fulfill these covenant obligations in their own strength. In this respect also the covenant shows itself to be a covenant of grace, in that the covenant God himself will grant to covenant members the strength to fulfill these obligations.[40] It will be observed that, while Heyns does not deny the sovereignty of God in the covenant and the impossibility of fulfilling covenant requirements apart from God's sovereign grace, there is a strong emphasis in his covenant doctrine on the responsibility of man in the covenant and on the real possibility of covenant breaking.

We look next at the covenantal views of John Van Lonkhuyzen, set forth in his book, *Heilig Zaad*.[41] Van Lonkhuyzen, a follower of Abraham Kuyper, saw the covenant of grace as having been established with Christ as the Head of the elect, and with his people in him.[42] The covenant of grace, he

---

36. Ibid.
37. Ibid., p. 143.
38. Ibid., p. 125.
39. Ibid., pp. 145–146.
40. Ibid., p. 139.
41. John Van Lonkhuyzen, *Heilig Zaad*, Verhandelingen over den Heiligen Doop (Grand Rapids: Eerdmans-Sevensma Co., 1916).
42. Ibid., pp. 21–22.

holds, is the means whereby God carries out his counsel of election; it is the stream through which he brings grace to his elect.[43]

He rejects the distinction between an external and an internal covenant of grace, but for reasons different than those of Heyns. For Van Lonkhuyzen the only covenant is an internal covenant—a covenant whose true membership is restricted to the elect. Those who are not elect, he says, may be found in the revelation of the covenant in history but are not part of its essence. Such people are then false covenant members or hypocrites.[44]

Heyns had said that the sacraments seal the promises of the covenant of grace. Van Lonkhuyzen, however, following Kuyper, holds that the sacraments seal not only the promises but the actual benefits of the covenant, such as regeneration, faith, and forgiveness.[45] How, then, can one baptize the infants of believers, who cannot yet exercise faith? The answer is that the seed of faith can be implanted into the hearts of little children.[46] Following Kuyper's teaching on the possibility of "slumbering regeneration," Van Lonkhuyzen holds that the seed of faith given to a child presumably before baptism may lie dormant for many years and not be revealed in the form of actual faith until late in the life of a covenant child.[47] Christian parents are to presume that their children are regenerated and elect unless and until the opposite appears.[48]

A strong reaction against Van Lonkhuyzen's covenantal views appeared in a book published the following year by Lammert J. Hulst, a minister in the CRC, entitled *Kentering in de Verbondsleer.*[49] The shift which Hulst was describing was being looked at by many in the Reformed churches. Van Lonkhuyzen was one among others who saw the covenant of grace as including only the elect. This conception, in which the doctrine of the covenant of grace is dominated by the doctrine of election, was not found in the Reformers, but has been influential in churches of Reformed persuasion since the seventeenth century.

Hulst strongly opposes the understanding of the covenant of grace as including only the elect. For, he says, this conception of the covenant goes contrary to Deuteronomy 29:29, "The secret things belong to the Lord our God; but the things that are revealed belong to us and to our children . . ." (RSV). Further, this conception does not do justice to the reality of covenant breaking, which is clearly taught in Scripture. For, if only the elect are in the covenant of grace, how could anyone in the covenant become a

---

43. Ibid., p. 20.
44. Ibid., p. 22.
45. Ibid., p. 37.
46. Ibid., p. 63.
47. Ibid., p. 81.
48. Ibid., p. 69.
49. Lammert Jan Hulst, *Kentering in de Verbondsleer* (Holland: Holland Printing Co., 1917).

covenant breaker? On the basis of the covenantal view in question, such covenant breaking would involve the possibility that God could change his decree and that those who are elect could fall away from the faith.[50] A further objection to the covenantal view being criticized is that it would take away all comfort from believing parents whose children have died in infancy, since one could not determine whether these infants were elect and were therefore truly in the covenant (and therefore saved) or not.[51]

In his definition of the covenant of grace, Hulst follows Heyns, indicating that the understanding of the covenant of grace conveyed in this definition is quite different from that of the view he has been criticizing.[52]

Hulst maintains that the shift in the doctrine of the covenant came in the seventeenth century, after the Synod of Dort. At that time many Reformed theologians began to teach that the covenant of grace was established either with the elect, or with Christ as the head and representative of the elect. This view, Hulst insists, does not do justice to Scripture, since it puts the nonelect outside of the covenant of grace, whereas Scripture puts the Ishmaels and the Esaus within the covenant.[53]

The promise of the covenant, so writes Hulst, is the same as the promise of the gospel. In distinction from Van Lonkhuyzen, Hulst holds that the sacrament of baptism confirms, not the possession of the spiritual blessings of the covenant, but the promise that the person baptized will possess these blessings if he or she turns to God in repentance and faith.[54]

In short, what Hulst asks the church to give up is not the doctrine of election but rather the domination of the doctrine of the covenant of grace by the doctrine of election. He pleads with his brothers in the church that they may come to see the scripturalness of the position that the covenant of grace was established with Abraham and his seed, and therefore with us and our children.[55]

Foppe M. Ten Hoor was Professor of Systematic Theology at Calvin Theological Seminary from 1900 to 1924. In his *Compendium der Gereformeerde Dogmatiek*[56] he sets forth views on the covenant of grace which generally follow the line of Heyns and Hulst. He makes the point that we may not abstractly deduce the doctrine of the covenant of grace from the doctrine of election, adding that we may never fully understand the relationship between these two.[57] Ten Hoor insists that the covenant of grace

50. Ibid., p. 14.
51. Ibid., p. 19.
52. Ibid., p. 18.
53. Ibid., pp. 24–26.
54. Ibid., p. 45.
55. Ibid.
56. Foppe Martin Ten Hoor, *Compendium der Gereformeerde Dogmatiek,* Een Leidraad voor Studenten in de Theologie (Holland: A. Ten Hoor, 1922).
57. Ibid., pp. 119–120.

includes more than the elect, since nonelect people may be in the covenant all their lives.[58]

Being in the covenant, Ten Hoor continues, is by itself no absolute guarantee of salvation; God has not established a covenant which includes only elect and regenerate people. In the present dispensation the covenant is relative and mixed; it includes nonelect and unregenerate people. By way of proof he adduces Scripture passages showing that the covenant can be broken; this could not happen, however, if these covenant-breakers were not in some sense covenant members. Only in the life to come will the covenant of grace be absolute and unmixed.[59]

The mixed condition of the covenant of grace in this dispensation has led theologians to make various distinctions within the covenant. Ten Hoor rejects the distinction between an internal and an external covenant, since this gives the impression that God has made only an external covenant with some of his people.[60] He favors a distinction similar to that made by Vos: between the covenant of grace as a "legal bond" (*rechtsverbintenis*) and a "fellowship of life" (*levensgemeenschap*).[61] Though he is willing to recognize this kind of distinction, however, Ten Hoor insists that there is only one covenant of grace.[62]

Ten Hoor claims that Christ is never called the head of the covenant of grace in Scripture. Since Christ is our surety in the covenant of works, taking the place of Adam by his perfect obedience and substitutionary suffering, he is the Mediator of the covenant of grace.[63] Neither is it correct to say that Christ is the second party in the covenant of grace; the covenant of grace has been established with believers and their children.[64]

The unbelief of a covenant member does not set him outside of the covenant of grace. A disobedient covenant member cannot cancel God's being bound to him. Only God can do this, on the Day of Judgment.[65]

Ten Hoor prefers not to speak of conditions in the covenant of grace, because of the possibility that the word may be interpreted in an Arminian way. He does teach, however, that the covenant includes both promises and requirements. Some say that the difference between the covenant of works and the covenant of grace is that the former involves promises and requirements, whereas the latter involves neither. But Ten Hoor insists that both the covenant of works and the covenant of grace include promises and requirements. But there is a difference. In the covenant of works the requirement precedes the promise, and must be fulfilled by man in his own

58. Ibid., pp. 135, 140.
59. Ibid., pp. 147–148.
60. Ibid., p. 148.
61. Ibid., p. 122; cf. p. 178.
62. Ibid., p. 154.
63. Ibid., p. 136.
64. Ibid., p. 147.
65. Ibid., pp. 153–154.

strength. In the covenant of grace, however, the promise precedes the
requirement: the covenant member receives the right to the blessings of
the covenant through the promise, and is enabled to fulfill the covenant
requirement through the strength given by God's grace.[66] In this way Ten
Hoor tries to do justice both to man's inability by nature and to his responsibility to do God's will as a partner in the covenant of grace.[67]

We turn next to the covenantal teachings of Louis Berkhof, who was
Professor of Systematic Theology at Calvin Theological Seminary from
1926 to 1944. These teachings were first set forth in the first volume of his
Reformed Dogmatics.[68] Berkhof teaches both the covenant of redemption
from eternity,[69] holding that this covenant is the eternal prototype and the
firm foundation for the covenant of grace,[70] and the covenant of works,[71]
maintaining that this covenant still has significance for us today, since
Christ fulfilled the obligations of the covenant of works for his people.[72] In
agreement with Heyns and Ten Hoor, Berkhof avers that Christ is not the
head of the covenant of grace but its Mediator.[73]

When we ask about Berkhof's definition of the covenant of grace, we
face a problem. The definition reads as follows: "That gracious agreement
between the offended God and the offending but elect sinner, in which God
promises salvation through faith in Christ, and the sinner accepts this
believingly, promising a life of faith and obedience."[74] What is puzzling
about this definition is the description of the second party as "the offending
but *elect* sinner." Does this imply that Berkhof sees no room in the covenant of grace for any but the elect? No; it becomes clear from his discussion of the dual aspect of the covenant that Berkhof recognizes a wider
aspect of the covenant than the one given in his definition. According to
this wider aspect the covenant of grace has been established with believers
and their children, and thus includes some who are not regenerate and
some who are not elect. It would seem, therefore, that in his definition
Berkhof is describing the covenant in its essential and most profound
sense—the sense in which the covenant extends no further than those in
whom the covenant blessings are fully realized. But he grants that the
covenant may also be thought of in a wider sense.

In connection with the contents of the covenant of grace, Berkhof

---

66. Ibid., p. 157.
67. Ibid., p. 165.
68. Louis Berkhof, *Reformed Dogmatics*, 2 vol. (Grand Rapids: Eerdmans, 1932); revised and
enlarged edition entitled *Systematic Theology* (Grand Rapids: Eerdmans, 1938). The pages of the 1938
edition are added in parenthesis.
69. Ibid., pp. 247–256 (pp. 265–271).
70. Ibid., p. 255 (p. 270).
71. Ibid., pp. 200–206 (pp. 211–218).
72. Ibid., p. 206 (p. 218).
73. Ibid., pp. 270–721 (pp. 282–283).
74. Ibid., p. 261 (p. 277).

speaks of the promises of God and the response of man. The central covenant promise is that God will be the God of his people, but this promise includes the promise of temporal blessings, of justification, of the Spirit, and of final glorification.[75] Under the response of man, trustful love and saving faith in Christ are mentioned.[76]

Berkhof teaches that the covenant of grace is both conditional and unconditional. In a fashion reminiscent of Vos, Berkhof argues that the covenant of grace is unconditional in the following senses: there is in it no condition which can be called meritorious, there is no condition in the covenant which man must perform in his own strength, and there are covenantal blessings whose reception is not dependent on a condition.[77] But the covenant may be called conditional in the following senses: the covenant of grace is conditional on the suretyship of Jesus Christ, the first conscious entrance into the covenant as a fellowship of life is conditional on faith (which is, however, a gift of God), and the further unfolding and completion of the life of the covenant is conditional on sanctification.[78]

With respect to the dual aspect of the covenant of grace, Berkhof also follows Vos. After rejecting a number of distinctions which have been made within the covenant of grace, Berkhof expresses a preference for Vos' distinction between the covenant as a "legal relationship" (in which sense it includes believers and their children) and as a "fellowship of life" (in which sense it includes only the elect).[79] Further implications of this distinction are worked out pretty much along the lines laid down by Vos. In connection with this distinction, Berkhof states that there may be not merely a temporary but a final breaking of the covenant, though there is no falling away of the saints.[80]

Berkhof discusses the various historical phases of the covenant of grace, such as the first revelation of the covenant in Genesis 3:15, the covenant with Noah, the covenant with Abraham, the Sinaitic covenant, and the New Testament dispensation of the covenant. Though recognizing certain differences between these various phases, he insists that the covenant of grace is basically the same throughout its history, though its administration varies.[81]

By way of summary, Berkhof represents a mediating position on the covenant of grace, which avoids the onesidedness of men like Kuyper and Van Lonkhuyzen, and follows generally the position of Herman Bavinck,[82] Vos, Heyns, and Ten Hoor.

75. Ibid., pp. 261–262 (p. 277).
76. Ibid., p. 262 (p. 277).
77. Ibid., p. 266 (p. 280).
78. Ibid., pp. 266–267 (pp. 280–281).
79. Ibid., pp. 272–280 (pp. 284–289).
80. Ibid., p. 280 (p. 289).
81. Ibid., pp. 281–294; see also pp. 264–265 (pp. 290–301; see also pp. 279–280).
82. See Anthony A. Hoekema, "Herman Bavinck's Doctrine of the Covenant" (Th.D. Dissertation, Princeton Theological Seminary, 1953).

In 1932 William Hendriksen published a small book entitled *The Covenant of Grace*.[83] Basically, Hendriksen's position is the same as Berkhof's. Hendriksen defines the covenant of grace as "a legal arrangement which has for its purpose the establishment of friendship in its fullest scope."[84] It is said that in one sense only the elect are in the covenant of grace, whereas in another sense the covenant includes believers and their children.[85] In a concluding chapter Hendriksen sets forth the comfort of the covenant of grace for those who accept their covenant obligation.[86]

Another minister of the CRC, George W. Hylkema, issued and distributed a mimeographed study on the covenant of grace entitled *God's Covenant with Man*, which was published posthumously.[87] In this study he expressed dissatisfaction with some common ideas about the covenant. For one thing, he felt that the doctrine of the covenant of grace had been developed too much under the dominating influence of the doctrine of predestination. For another thing, he believed that the forensic or legal aspect of the covenant had been stressed too exclusively, in distinction from the role of the covenant in determining and shaping our Christian life-style.[88] He also criticized the idea that the covenant was thought of primarily as a means of bringing people to salvation.[89]

What is lacking in these concepts, Hylkema maintains, is the thought that the covenant binds persons together for the achievement of a common purpose.[90] The doctrine of the covenant properly understood answers the question: How does God propose to use his saved people?

Hylkema finds the key to the meaning of the covenant in the idea of partnership. He therefore defines the covenant of grace as follows: "The covenant is that tie brought about by God when he inaugurated and established a partnership between himself and man with a view to the realization of the great purpose for which he had created all things."[91]

"This definition of the covenant," he continues, "gives expression to a threefold truth: (1) It [the covenant] holds forth the astounding truth that the covenant brings about a *real partnership between God and man*, so that by it man is raised to the high office of being a co-worker with God in the realization of his divine program. (2) It brings home that this partnership and collaboration in God's great enterprise is a necessary partnership, and that man's position in it is indispensable if the purpose designed by God is to be realized. (3) It proclaims that this desired result, the glory of

83. William Hendriksen, *The Covenant of Grace* (Grand Rapids: Eerdmans, 1932).
84. Ibid., pp. 21–22.
85. Ibid., p. 60.
86. Ibid., pp. 70–84.
87. George W. Hylkema, *God's Covenant with Man* (Grand Rapids: Privately printed, 1944?).
88. Ibid., p. 1.
89. Ibid., p. 4.
90. Ibid., p. 7.
91. Ibid., p. 12.

God, is the direct and not the indirect object of the covenant. . . . Man's life and salvation are achieved in this process of co-laboring with God in the working out of the divine ideal."[92]

Hylkema goes on to say that God has bound himself to man and has made the fruitage of his vast creative work dependent on the choice, life, and service of man.[93] God, therefore, could never be glorified in the highest sense apart from the creation of man.[94] Man, thus, must be the mediator between creation and creation's God,[95] and must make God's purpose completely his own.[96]

Hylkema has given us a refreshing new slant on the meaning of the covenant of grace. His main emphasis is on man's responsibility as a partner with God in working out God's purpose with his creation.

We close this survey with a brief summary of a study of the covenant of grace by Andrew Kuyvenhoven, a minister in the CRC who is currently editor of its denominational weekly, *The Banner.* This booklet is entitled *Partnership*[97] and was published as a study guide for church groups by the Board of Publications of the CRC in 1974.

Kuyvenhoven holds that Reformed churches have always recognized that the Bible is essentially a history of the covenant of grace, and that in many respects this insight has been their strength.[98] He wishes to preserve the basic unity of the covenant throughout its various phases, without losing sight of the radical differences between the old covenant and the new.[99] By the old covenant, however, he does not mean the covenant with Abraham, but the covenant at Sinai.[100] He finds the contrast between the old and the new covenants particularly set forth in Jeremiah 31:31–34 and II Corinthians 3. What is specifically new about the new covenant is (1) the forgiveness of sins through the blood of Christ, and (2) the bestowal of God's Spirit, enabling man to live in a new obedience.[101] This second point, Kuyvenhoven avers, is often overlooked by writers on the covenant of grace.

The covenant of grace opposes all religious and spiritual individualism. In the covenant of grace God takes us to himself and reestablishes community among people.[102] Within this community, in which we learn to give

92. Ibid., pp. 12–13.
93. Ibid., p. 14.
94. Ibid., p. 15.
95. Ibid., p. 17.
96. Ibid., p. 19.
97. Andrew Kuyvenhoven, *Partnership,* A Study of the Covenant (Grand Rapids: Board of Publications of the Christian Reformed Church, 1974).
98. Ibid., p. 5.
99. Ibid., p. 6.
100. Ibid., p. 17.
101. Ibid., pp. 26–28.
102. Ibid., p. 46.

ourselves in the response of love, the individual personality is not destroyed but rightly developed.[103]

Kuyvenhoven insists that membership in the covenant of grace has many implications for the Christian life. Christians are not free to accept or support an educational system which is inconsistent with their covenantal views.[104] The blessings enjoyed in the covenant of grace are to be shared with all men. Therefore we must pray for the world,[105] and present the will of God to the world in our preaching and our testimony.[106] Spiritual separation from the world may never degenerate into physical isolation.[107]

It is evident from this survey that the doctrine of the covenant of grace has been an essential aspect of CRC doctrinal teaching throughout its history. It may be noted, however, that this doctrine is not as prominent in the theological reflection of the CRC today as it once was. Fred H. Klooster, Professor of Systematic Theology at Calvin Theological Seminary, in a recent article,[108] comments that the Reformed community has generally not been at the forefront of covenant study in recent years. "Fear of new divisions, embarrassment with past separations, and a general doctrinal lethargy appear to have contributed to the neglect of the covenant doctrines by many within the Reformed churches."[109] Klooster therefore pleads with the theological leaders of the CRC to give greater attention to the covenant teaching of Scripture.[110]

The Practical Value of the Doctrine of the Covenant

It may be helpful, in conclusion, to look at some of the practical values of the doctrine of the covenant of grace for the life and teaching of the church. First, what is the value of this doctrine in connection with the proclamation of the church? The doctrine of the covenant teaches us that the preaching of the Word which is addressed to the congregation must not be merely evangelistic in its purpose, but must seek to build up the people of God in the faith. The evangelistic note, however, must never be lacking even in the preaching which is addressed to covenant people, as it is not lacking in the prophets or epistles. The Bible clearly teaches that within the circle of the covenant there are always some who are not or not yet

103. Ibid., pp. 46–47.
104. Ibid., p. 54.
105. Ibid., p. 56.
106. Ibid., p. 58.
107. Ibid. Points similar to those just mentioned are made by Kuyvenhoven in a series of editorials entitled "The Covenant of Grace," *The Banner* 116 (July 20, 1981): 5–6, (July 27, 1981): 8, (August 3, 1981): 8. In the July 20 editorial he observes that whereas writers outside the CRC have in recent times been saying more about the covenant of grace than they did before, writers within the CRC seem to be saying less about the covenant than they did before.
108. Fred H. Klooster, "Covenant Theology Today," *The Messenger* 51 (January 1980): 6–9.
109. Ibid., p. 7.
110. Ibid., p. 8.

believers; these must be summoned to come to Christ in faith. A proper understanding of the doctrine of the covenant, therefore, will help the church stress both edification and evangelism in its preaching, and to keep these two in proper balance. Preaching within the church should emphasize both the promises of the covenant of grace and its requirements; both the privileges of covenant membership and its responsibilities.

Further, the doctrine of the covenant gives guidance to the church as it pursues its evangelistic outreach. A proper understanding of the covenant of grace is no hindrance but an incentive to missionary effort, since missions are but the recognition of the universal dimensions of the New Testament era of the covenant. The doctrine of the covenant has definite implications for the way in which the church should carry out its missionary and evangelistic task. When working with those who have never before come into contact with the gospel, the missionary should stress the significance of the covenant of grace for the life and conduct of the new convert, including his responsibilities toward his children. Covenantal evangelism and covenantal mission work, therefore, will seek to establish Christian homes, to foster family worship, to encourage the Christian training of the children, and to plant churches.

The covenant doctrine has valuable and important implications, moreover, for Christian ethics. The great motive for Christian ethics is the thankful response of the covenant member to God's covenant mercies. The covenant of grace requires man's full-orbed service of God as God's covenant partner. The covenant doctrine stresses the mutuality of the God-man relationship which is basic to Christian ethics. It teaches the priority of divine grace, which is the fountainhead of Christian living. But it also emphasizes the responsibility of man toward his covenant God.

The covenant of grace, further, does full justice to both the individual and social aspects of Christianity. Though the gospel comes first of all to a person as an individual, it comes to him or her within the matrix of the covenant community, and impresses on each covenant member his or her obligations not only toward other members of that community but also toward those who are outside of that community. Since the covenant is an instrument to promote the kingdom of God, each covenant member must live for God and for others, and must let his light shine in the entire world.

The covenant doctrine is also significant for the proper understanding of the family. The covenant of grace has as its material substratum the organization of the Christian society in terms of family groups. When an adult is converted, his or her family immediately becomes a covenant family (cf. I Cor. 7:14). When a child is born to or adopted by believing parents, such a child becomes a member of a covenant family. Since God promises to be the God of believers and their children, the Christian home is ordinarily the seedbed of true faith. A proper understanding of the covenant of grace, therefore, should lead to the recognition of the Christian home as the most crucially important unit of the Christian community, whose integrity and sacredness must be preserved at all costs. The Christian, whose home is to be a covenant home, is free to marry only "in the Lord." The Christian married couple will therefore recognize the God-ordained permanence of marriage and the sinfulness of divorce (barring exceptional cases), believing that marriage vows are sacred because they represent a covenant made not just with the other marriage partner, but with God.

The Christian home is not only the basic unit of the covenant community, but also a small-scale analogy of the covenant itself. All this has tremendous implications for our understanding of the Christian family. Since marriage is described in Scripture as a symbol of the union between God and his people (Old Testament) or between Christ and his church (New Testament), covenant parents must seek to reflect this kind of love in their life together. Such parents must therefore bring up their children in the training and instruction of the Lord, and covenant children are to obey their parents in the Lord. In the Christian home the covenant child will receive his or her first impression and undergo his first experiences of that fellowship with God and God's people which is the heart of the covenant of grace.

A word may finally be said about the significance of the covenant of grace for Christian education. The doctrine of the covenant implies that the children of believers are not to be considered religiously neutral, or merely objects of child evangelism, but are to be recognized as covenant children, who are therefore entitled not only to the seal of the covenant in baptism, but also to a distinctively Christian upbringing. This involves, first of all, Christian nurture in the home, in which parents conscientiously try to lead their children into genuine covenantal fellowship with God, pleading on the basis of God's covenant promise for the saving operation of the Holy Spirit in their hearts. This involves, further, Christian training in the church, including not merely instruction in Bible stories and Bible history but also instruction in the doctrinal heritage of the Christian faith. Thinking through the implications of the covenant of grace to the full, moreover, will lead to the recognition of distinctively Christian day school education as essential for the children of Christian parents, since the covenant child should be constantly surrounded by a covenant atmosphere, and should be taught to view all of life from a Christian point of view.

10

The Kingdom of God in the History of the Christian Reformed Church

Fred H. Klooster

H. Richard Niebuhr considered the kingdom of God to be the dominant idea in American Christianity. He concluded in 1937 that "the meaning and spirit of American Christianity" found "its center in the faith in the kingdom of God."[1] That conclusion is surprising; one would hardly consider faith in the kingdom of God characteristic of American Christianity today.

Niebuhr discovered three meanings of "kingdom of God," each characteristic of a specific period of American history. In the early period, when Calvinism was dominant, "kingdom of God" meant the "sovereignty of God." During the period of revivalism and the Great Awakening the basic meaning was the "reign of Christ." In the period preceding World War I, the idea of the kingdom of God was promoted by adherents of the social gospel and referred to a "kingdom on earth."[2]

How did the Christian Reformed Church in North America (hereafter CRC) fit into that kingdom pattern of American Christianity? How has the biblical doctrine of the kingdom of God fared in the history of this Reformed church? The fragile beginnings of the CRC go back to 1857, but prior to 1890 the church was so small that it was hardly noticed and it paid

---

1. H. Richard Niebuhr, *The Kingdom of God in America* (Chicago: Willett, Clark & Co., 1937), p. vii. This involved a significant change in Niebuhr's conclusions; in an earlier book he gave priority to social factors. Cf. H. Richard Niebuhr, *The Social Sources of Denominationalism* (New York: Henry Holt and Co., 1929).
2. Ibid., p. x.

little attention to its American environment.[3] By the end of the nineteenth century, however, the CRC reached a size of some consequence and began to show some concern for its American surroundings. By then American Christianity had moved into the social gospel stage of its history and the kingdom was viewed in a liberal context. Besides, premillennialism and dispensationalism were advancing in evangelical circles where the kingdom was intimately linked to millennial views.

This historical survey will take 1890 as its starting point. A decade earlier the CRC numbered only two thousand families, twelve thousand members, thirty-nine congregations, and nineteen ministers. During the 1880s immigration from the Netherlands swelled the size of the CRC so that by 1900 the church increased by almost 500 percent in the number of families, members, and ministers. The increase in the number of congregations was, of course, less dramatic; many congregations simply grew in size, yet the total number increased more than three fold, from 39 to 144. Even so, almost one-third of those congregations were still without a regular minister in 1900.[4]

The history of the CRC's concern for the kingdom of God falls into three rather distinct periods, each roughly three decades long. During the first period, prior to World War I (1890–1920), kingdom interest was great and debates were intense. The second period extended from the end of the first great war to the end of the second (1920–1950); kingdom interest waned during that period. A third period began shortly after World War II and continues to the present (1950–   ); it began with considerable interest in the kingdom of God, but the present situation is somewhat clouded. The first part of this contribution will briefly review that history and the second part will examine three significant contributions to the doctrine of the kingdom of God which can challenge the church today. These contributions came from three leading theologians—Geerhardus Vos, Louis Berkhof, and Samuel Volbeda.

Prior to World War I (1890–1920)

During this period the social gospel rose to prominence in American Christianity, but the CRC was not aroused to its kingdom interest by indigenous forces. Its motivation came from Scripture and especially from the Calvinistic revival in the Netherlands.

Laissez-faire capitalism flourished in the United States in the half-century between the Civil War and World War I. In Paris the Eiffel Tower of

3. Henry Zwaanstra, *Reformed Thought and Experience in a New World,* A Study of the Christian Reformed Church and its American Environment 1890–1918 (Kampen: J. H. Kok, 1973), p. 295.

4. Ibid., p. 323. See *Jaarboekje* voor de Hollandsche Christelijke Gereformeerde Kerk, voor het Jaar 1881 (Grand Rapids: D. J. Doornink, 1881), pp. 31–32; *Jaarboekje* ten Dienste der Christelijke Gereformeerde Kerk in Noord Amerika, voor het Jaar 1900 (Grand Rapids: J. B. Hulst, 1900), p. 42.

1889 symbolized the heights of modern technology; a century earlier (1789) the French Revolution released forces that affected all the capitalistic, technologically advancing countries. These forces were also at work in the New World. Industry concentrated in the rapidly growing cities and workers moved from the country to the cities where poverty, misery, ignorance, vice, and crime increased. Conflicts between labor and industry were intense at the turn of the century. The destructive railway strike of 1877, the Haymarket Riot of 1886, and a whole series of strikes in the early 1890s shocked American church leaders into an awareness of the social implications of the gospel. The social conscience of the American churches was awakened to the evil side effects of industrial progress. Gradually the "kingdom of God" became the biblical rallying point for a new socioeconomic-political address to the problems of urbanized, industrialized society. Walter Rauschenbusch became the leading spokesman for the social gospel in America.[5]

The chief impetus for CRC discussions on the kingdom of God came, however, from the Netherlands. During the final decades of the nineteenth century a dynamic revival of Calvinism took place there. Under the dramatic leadership of Abraham Kuyper, many came to recognize the demands of Christ on all of life; the kingdom of God required Christian obedience in every sphere of life. Kuyper's establishment of the Free University of Amsterdam in 1880 was symbolic of this renewed Calvinistic world and life view. In 1886, the year of Walter Rauschenbusch's ordination, Kuyper led the Doleantie, a reformatory movement within the national church. A merger in 1892 brought the secession movements of 1834 and 1886 together to form the Gereformeerde Kerken in Nederland. Eventually Christian organizations for labor, politics, and other areas of life were formed to promote the kingdom of God in human society. Many of the immigrants who swelled the size of the CRC after 1880 brought this renewed kingdom perspective with them. In 1898 Kuyper visited North America to present the Stone Lectures on Calvinism at Princeton University.[6] Then he made a triumphal tour of Dutch-American communities in Michigan, Illinois, Iowa, and Ohio.

The convergence of the Kuyperian influence from the Netherlands and the awakened social conscience in the United States and Canada stirred vigorous debate within the small but growing CRC. Unfortunately, the members of the church lacked a common mind on the issues. The tragedy of that lack of unanimity during this period as well as in subsequent CRC history was that kingdom practice was stalemated.

---

5. Robert T. Handy, "Introduction," in *The Social Gospel in America: 1870–1920*, Gladden, Ely, Rauschenbusch, Ed. Robert T. Handy, A Library of Protestant Thought (New York: Oxford University Press, 1966), p. 9.

6. Abraham Kuyper, *Lectures on Calvinism* (Grand Rapids: Eerdmans, 1931).

Three distinguishable viewpoints were present in the CRC prior to World War I. Henry Zwaanstra has submitted this period to careful historical analysis in his doctoral dissertation; he identified three parties whom he labeled "Confessional Reformed," "Separatist Calvinists," and "American Calvinists."[7] The first group largely reflected the mind of the Afscheiding of 1834 and lacked a kingdom vision; the other two groups differed on the means for promoting the kingdom in North America.

Representatives of the Confessional Reformed group were generally graduates of the Theological School at Kampen. Foppe M. Ten Hoor was their leader in the CRC. Their piety and doctrinal concern left little room for a clear-cut kingdom perspective that called for Christian action in all areas of life. They generally opposed Kuyper's views on the nature and task of the church and had no sympathy for his social and political activity. I think the standpoint of the Confessional Reformed group was somewhat reductionistic; they embraced the Calvinistic doctrines of the confessions but they lacked the kingdom vision of Scripture.

The other two parties in the CRC prior to World War I were kingdom oriented and sympathetic to Kuyper's views; they differed, however, on whether kingdom practice in North America called for separate Christian organizations. The Separatist Calvinists were committed followers of Kuyper. Led by Klaas Schoolland and John Van Lonkhuyzen, they called for establishing separate Christian organizations on the Dutch model. Between 1910 and 1918 they vigorously promoted their convictions in an effort to win the CRC to Kuyper's views.

The American Calvinists shared Kuyper's views but rejected the call for separate Christian organizations. Led by Henry Beets, John Groen, and B[arend] K. Kuiper, they were more open to the customs and institutions of American society and appealed to Kuyper's doctrine of common grace to promote their goals. The American Calvinists viewed Calvinism "primarily [as] a system of truths" and were more interested "in educating the Christian Reformed Church in Calvinism than in engaging in separate Calvinistic action."[8]

Prior to World War I the relatively small number of CRC people, mostly recent immigrants from the Netherlands, displayed considerable success in kingdom activity. Christian schools for covenant children were established by parent-run societies, and other Christian institutions were begun which continue today in greatly expanded form. Kingdom activity was also promoted in the areas of labor and society. But World War I brought hostility to ethnic diversity. The influence of the Separatist Calvinists began to decline; they were hurt by their insistence on the use of the Dutch language. They were unable to win the young people to their ideal of separate

7. Zwaanstra, *Reformed Thought and Experience*, pp. 69–70.
8. Ibid., p. 124.

kingdom organization. Their mouthpiece, *De Calvinist,* ceased publication in 1918. When the church did not embrace their views and their programs, "the party resorted to sarcasm and vitriolic criticism."[9] Their most resounding defeat came when the CRC decided to continue church control of Calvin College. It was ironic that the Separatist Calvinists lost that battle on practical grounds since the CRC continues to endorse the principle that it is not the church's task to run educational institutions other than a theological seminary.[10]

By the end of this first period the American Calvinists had become the dominant party within the CRC. They represented "the cutting edge of change and development" and "proved most effective in shaping the mind of the church"; their views prevailed in the debates on women's suffrage, prohibition, labor unions, and church control of Calvin College.[11] Then "World War I greatly facilitated the rise of the American Calvinists to a position of unchallenged predominance."[12] Zwaanstra summarizes what happened in the postwar period: "Throughout the period the church's faith in God remained undiminished; the principles did not fare quite so well. As the church was compelled to take the American situation in which it found itself seriously, the Reformed and Calvinistic principles for social and political life were accommodated to the exigencies and realities of American experience, and the earlier unlimited confidence in the principles gradually deteriorated."[13]

Between the Wars (1920-1950)

Kingdom interest, especially kingdom practice, waned during the three decades from the end of World War I to the end of World War II. The social gospel also went into eclipse during that period. There were striking parallels between the demise of the social gospel in North America and the waning kingdom interest in the CRC. Both floundered on disagreements concerning strategy on the part of their respective proponents. Furthermore, the enthusiasm for each was largely that of its leaders; the leaders were unable to transfer their enthusiasm to the members of their churches. The American Calvinists felt the need for educating CRC people in the principles of Calvinism; apparently they were not very successful in that project. Another parallel was the collapse of organizations set up to achieve

---

9. Ibid., p. 312.

10. *Acts of Synod 1957,* Centennial Year of the Christian Reformed Church, June 12 to June 26, 1927, at Calvin College, Grand Rapids, Michigan (Grand Rapids: Christian Reformed Publishing House, 1957), pp. 39–60 (Arts. 74, 80, 86, 91, and 99); *Acts of Synod 1967,* June 14 to 24, 1967, reconvened August 29 and 30, 1967, Calvin College, Grand Rapids, Michigan (Grand Rapids: Christian Reformed Publishing House, 1967), p. 97 (Art. 137).

11. Zwaanstra, *Reformed Thought and Experience,* pp. 315–316.

12. Ibid., p. 316.

13. Ibid., p. 297.

the goals of each program. The social gospel suffered greater loss on that score than did CRC kingdom projects. CRC periodicals and some organizations floundered, but Christian schools, institutions of mercy, and a struggling Christian Labor Association survived. The kingdom enthusiasm of previous decades was gone, however, and vigor was lacking to begin new projects.[14]

On the most important score, however, there was no parallel between the demise of the social gospel in North America and the loss of a dynamic kingdom vision in the CRC in the period between the wars. The liberal theology of the social gospel collapsed, but the biblical foundations for the CRC kingdom vision did not! Optimistic liberalism with its faith in man died in the face of the world at war. The "shaking of the liberal foundations of the social gospel was continued throughout the 1930s as neo-orthodox theology upset much of Protestant thinking" so that by the 1940s the social gospel as "a distinct, self-conscious movement with a clear sense of direction had largely disappeared."[15]

The decline of kingdom interest in the CRC during the same decades was not the result of the loss of its theological grounding. The Reformed confessions stood firm as did Reformed theology. The CRC faced the threats of liberalism in the Ralph Janssen and Frederick H. Wezeman cases of 1922 and 1937 and successfully withstood those threats. In 1924 the confessions were defended in the face of Herman Hoeksema's denial of common grace and the warning against worldliness that surfaced in that controversy became explicit in the decision of 1928.[16] While the Reformed faith remained firm in the CRC, Calvinism was nevertheless becoming a minority conviction in North America. At the time of the American Revolution, Calvinism was the majority position; between the wars it dwindled to minority status. When Clarence Bouma surveyed the state of Calvinism in American theology in 1947, he was able to point to only small pockets of authentic Calvinism remaining. Equally surprising is the fact that Bouma's article made no reference at all to the kingdom which was so basic to a virile Calvinism.[17] He was able to point only to remnants of "confessional or doctrinal Calvinism."

The three decades of CRC history between 1920 and 1950 have not yet received the careful historical analysis which they deserve. The "roaring twenties" were silenced by the depression of the thirties and the war of the forties. The energy and optimism of the first decade of the twentieth

14. See Handy, "Introduction," pp. 14–16 for factors leading to the demise of the social gospel.
15. Ibid., p. 15.
16. John H. Kromminga, *The Christian Reformed Church,* A Study in Orthodoxy (Grand Rapids: Baker, 1949), pp. 75–85. In 1918 and following years, Synod also took a stand against premillennial threats. Kromminga, *Christian Reformed Church,* pp. 72–75.
17. Clarence Bouma, "Calvinism in American Theology Today," in *Calvinism in Times of Crisis,* Addresses delivered at the Third American Calvinist Conference (Grand Rapids: Baker, 1947), pp. 77–95. Reprinted in *The Journal of Religion* 27 (1947):34–54.

century gave way to the struggle and pessimism of war, depression, and advancing totalitarianism in Germany, Italy, and Japan. The vision of the kingdom of God was not obliterated in CRC circles, but it was in eclipse. *The Calvin Forum*, a publication of the combined faculties of Calvin Seminary and Calvin College, under Clarence Bouma's leadership did promote world-wide Calvinism. Samuel Volbeda presented a series of four lectures at Westminster Theological Seminary in Philadelphia in 1939 which displayed a remarkable kingdom vision. Yet Volbeda did not awaken that vision in Calvin Seminary students. Those lectures will be examined below.

The decade of the 1940s was the period of my college, seminary, and graduate study. I studied at Calvin College, Calvin Theological Seminary, Westminster Theological Seminary, and the Free University at Amsterdam from 1940 until 1951. Not one of those historic Reformed institutions conveyed a dynamic kingdom vision to me. References to the kingdom were not absent, but they were not dominant; I was not molded by the kingdom perspective. Louis Berkhof's challenge to the church in 1913 to carry out its social responsibility was not incorporated into his *Systematic Theology*.[18] Geerhardus Vos' *Biblical Theology*,[19] available then only in a mimeographed syllabus, was required reading, but his book on the kingdom of God was not. The brilliant insights which Volbeda conveyed to a Westminster audience in 1939 were not shared with his Calvin Seminary students. Martin J. Wyngaarden's *Future of the Kingdom*[20] and Oswald T. Allis' *Prophecy and the Church*[21] helped to ward off the dispensational kingdom views, but they did not replace those erroneous views with a biblical view of the kingdom with its life-embracing demands. The kingdom perspective seems to have been something of a hobby, a subject for lectures on special occasions, for other campuses, or for articles in the church papers.[22]

The same was true to a surprising degree at Kuyper's Free University in the late 1940s. Kuyper's kingdom goals were still alive, especially among some of the Reformed people, but the Free University was no longer a strong advocate. Herman Dooyeweerd and Dirk H. Th. Vollenhoven developed Calvinistic philosophy "in Kuyper's line" and won many supporters, but the theologians were largely opposed to these developments. By the end of the 1940s Kuyper's followers were a minority in his seventy-year-old

18. Louis Berkhof, *Systematic Theology* (Grand Rapids: Eerdmans, 1938).

19. Geerhardus Vos, *Biblical Theology*, Old and New Testaments, ed. Johannes G. Vos (Grand Rapids: Eerdmans, 1948).

20. Martin J. Wyngaarden, *The Future of the Kingdom in Prophecy and Fulfillment*, A Study of the Scope of "Spiritualization" in Scripture (Grand Rapids: Zondervan, 1934).

21. Oswald T. Allis, *Prophecy and the Church*, An Examination of the Claim of Dispensationalists that the Christian Church Is a Mystery Parenthesis Which Interrupts the Fulfillment to Israel of the Kingdom Prophecies of the Old Testament (Philadelphia: Presbyterian and Reformed, 1945).

22. Louis Berkhof, for example, wrote a long series of articles on the kingdom in *De Wachter* from 1919 to 1920. For bibliographical references see Peter De Klerk, *A Bibliography of the Writings of the Professors of Calvin Theological Seminary* (Grand Rapids: Calvin Theological Seminary, 1980), Section 2, pp. 5–6.

university. Students were enamored by the German theologians and often scoffed at Kuyper and Herman Bavinck. The effect of Kuyper's work was still evident in the various organizations he helped to organize, but there, too, decline was evident. The impact of Karl Barth's theology also contributed to the break down of Christian organizations. Growing secularism in postwar Europe hit the Netherlands as a "blitzkrieg." The Kuyper-house in the Hague was rich in memories, but it was already becoming a museum of the kingdom vision and practice of earlier years. What had once come from the Netherlands to stimulate the immigrant CRC was now in decline on both sides of the Atlantic!

After World War II (1950-1980)

Shortly after World War II animated discussions concerning the kingdom of God again took place within the CRC. One is reminded of the decade before World War I when the Separatist Calvinists and the American Calvinists debated similar issues. The debates again focused on kingdom strategy: were separate Christian organizations on the Kuyperian model required or should Christians penetrate existing "neutral" organizations?

The debates within the CRC were occasioned, at least in part, by H. Evan Runner and his students. Runner studied philosophy at the Free University and became an enthusiastic disciple of Vollenhoven and Dooyeweerd. His appointment to Calvin College was aimed at providing the new Calvinist philosophy a fuller hearing there. Runner's enthusiastic support of Kuyper, Vollenhoven, and Dooyeweerd soon led to sharp conflict, especially from those who did not consider separate Christian organizations feasible in American society. Runner gained considerable support from Canadian students, many of whom had come from the Netherlands after the war to swell the ranks of the CRC in Canada. The Groen Club was organized at Calvin College for promotion of the kingdom vision. In 1956 an Association for Reformed Scientific Studies was organized in Canada with the aim of eventually establishing a Christian university. Several student conferences were held during the late 1950s and early 60s. In 1967 the Institute for Christian Studies was opened in Toronto, Ontario; the support society then changed its name to the Association for the Advancement of Christian Scholarship.

During the same decades kingdom practice was advancing in Canada with members of the CRC taking the lead. The Christian Labor Association of Canada and other organizations vigorously promoted kingdom action in areas where disinterest still marked the situation south of the Canadian border. Again the CRC mind was divided, as it had been at the dawn of the century. Writing in *The Reformed Journal* a year after the publication of Henry Zwaanstra's doctoral dissertation, Nicholas P. Wolterstorff also distinguished three groups in the CRC; he used the labels of "pietism," "doctrinalism," and "Kuyperianism."[23] Although he acknowledged the weakness of such labels, Wolterstorff applied them to the entire history of the CRC. Those whom Zwaanstra referred to as Confessional Reformed were now distinguished by the terms *pietism* and *doctrinalism*. Furthermore, Zwaanstra discovered two kinds of Kuyperians in the earlier decades; something similar is evident in the present period. Yet it was a new type of pietism that developed within the CRC after the 1950s; fundamentalism, evangelicalism, and neo-Pentecostalism were making inroads into CRC circles. That pietism differed from the pietism of the Afscheiding which was marked by Reformed confessional convictions.

Again it seems more accurate to me to note a certain reductionism evident in such groups within the CRC. Authentic Kuyperianism displays a rich kingdom vision coupled both with doctrinal sensitivity and genuine piety. Not all Kuyperians, of course, reflect all three characteristics, especially not during the decades under consideration. The doctrinalist, however, generally lacks a kingdom perspective, and the pietist lacks both a kingdom and a doctrinal concern. To a certain degree these different emphases contributed to the conflicts concerning the kingdom of God, and kingdom practice was again thwarted as a result of the conflicts.

Opposition to Runner and the North American Dooyeweerdians, as they were generally called, came from several sources—from fellow faculty members at Calvin College and Seminary, from *The Banner* editors, from Westminster Seminary, and from elsewhere. Supporters were more numerous in Canada than in the United States. Many, myself included, shared the kingdom perspectives, but often disagreed on procedures followed. For sympathetic critics, however, there was hardly room; dialogue was difficult.

Wolterstorff provides a vivid picture of the resistance that developed to Runner and his followers: "From one quarter pietists and doctrinalists resisted this new surge of Kuyperianism; from another old Kuyperians resisted this new version of Kuyperianism. And part of the resistance was by Dooyeweerdian Kuyperians to specific personalities and policies among themselves. It all became very confused, and in the confusion each party was ready to tar all others with the same brush."[24] The attacks upon Runner and his followers led to public counterattacks: "It became pronouncedly anti-Calvin College and anti-Calvin Seminary. It tended to write off the entire Christian Reformed Church with one stroke. It became defensive and paranoid, harshly condemnatory of those it disagreed with, often suggesting that their disagreement was an indication of deficiency in their Christian faith. It used hysterical, sometimes even offensive and vulgar, language."[25]

23. Nicholas P. Wolterstorff, "The AACS in the CRC," *The Reformed Journal* 24 (December 1974):9–16.
24. Ibid., p. 11.
25. Ibid., p. 12.

There was fault on all sides. Runner and his supporters were received by the CRC establishment "with undisguised hostility" which only "evoked aggressive paranoia" and "fed the hostility." The tragic result was that "little genuine discussion of issues took place. The parties shouted at each other and condemned each other; but discuss they did not. . . . The violence and acrimony of the public statements of the Dooyeweerdian Kuyperians in the 1950s was easily matched by the violence and acrimony of the private language of their opponents in the 1950s. Again, each must be seen as a judgment on the other."[26]

Again the result was loss for the kingdom. When the violence of the 1960s broke loose, the CRC was no more ready to take up the challenge than were most American churches. Serious Christian young people were inquiring about the social, economic, and political relevance of the gospel, but they heard very little about the kingdom message of God's Word. Hair length and life-style received priority; major issues were largely ignored.

I realize, of course, that I am indicting myself as I write these lines. Yet historical accuracy requires this account. The golden opportunity of revitalizing the kingdom vision during the 1950s was squandered; the "sarcasm and vitriolic criticism" that marked the end of the first period again characterized the opening of the present period. One of the disastrous results was the missed opportunity of the 1960s. And, as often happens after violent controversy, disinterest replaces debate. The present decade provides an opportunity for renewal.

It would be an exaggeration to say that the CRC has lost the biblical vision of the kingdom. Several different meanings would be suggested, however. The CRC certainly lacks a united mind on this crucial subject. The official decisions of the church have generally reflected an authentic kingdom perspective. Yet it is surprising that in recent years most of these have originated in the Reformed Ecumenical Synod or arisen from other cooperative ventures; they have not arisen from the bosom of the CRC itself.[27] Since this contribution is written from the perspective of one who

---

26. Ibid.

27. Note, for example, the 1958 RES decisions on Christian Organizations, *Acts* of the Fourth Reformed Ecumenical Synod of Potchefstroom, South Africa, August 6–13, 1958 (Grand Rapids: Reformed Ecumenical Synod, 1958), pp. 24–25 (Art. 28); the 1968 RES decisions on Race Relations, *Acts and Reports* of the Reformed Ecumenical Synod, Amsterdam, August 13–23, 1968 (Grand Rapids: Reformed Ecumenical Synod, 1968), pp. 60–66 (Arts. 154 and 162), pp. 339–341 (Suppl. 22); the 1976 RES decisions on the Church and its Social Calling, *Acts* of the Reformed Ecumenical Synod, Cape Town, 10–26 August 1976 (Grand Rapids: Reformed Ecumenical Synod, 1976), pp. 38–41 (Arts. 58 and 62), pp. 102–111 (Suppl. 1A and B); and *The Church and its Social Calling* (Grand Rapids: The Reformed Ecumenical Synod, 1981), a 102-page booklet prepared by a RES study committee which was approved by the RES, at Nimes, France in 1980, *Acts* of the Reformed Ecumenical Synod, Nimes, July 15–25, 1980 (Grand Rapids: Reformed Ecumenical Council, 1980), pp. 60–70 (Arts. 63 and 68), pp. 81–82 (Art. 81), pp. 221–225 (Suppl. 7). See also the Evangelism Manifesto of 1977 drawn up by a joint committee of CRC and RCA members, *Acts of Synod 1977*, June 14 to 24, 1977, Calvin College, Grand Rapids, Michigan (Grand Rapids: Board of Publications of the Christian Reformed Church, 1977), p. 32 (Art. 32), pp. 638–643

wants to see the biblical vision of the kingdom revived within the CRC, the second part of this contribution focuses upon three significant works that can challenge the members of the church to revitalization. Perhaps we can go forward by taking a brief look back.

Significant Kingdom Views

Geerhardus Vos (1862-1949)

A very significant study on the biblical doctrine of the kingdom of God was published by Geerhardus Vos at the turn of the century. Vos came to the United States from the Netherlands in 1881 when his father accepted the call to the First CRC, Grand Rapids. After graduating from Calvin Theological Seminary in 1883, Vos pursued graduate studies at Princeton Theological Seminary and the Universities of Berlin and Strasbourg, receiving his Ph.D. degree from the latter in 1888. Before he completed his doctoral work, Vos was invited to teach Old Testament studies at the Free University, which Kuyper established a few years earlier. Vos was inclined to accept that invitation, but he bowed to the wishes of his parents and began teaching at his *alma mater* in Grand Rapids in September, 1888.

In 1891 Vos delivered the rectoral address at Calvin Seminary on *De Verbondsleer in de Gereformeerde Theologie.*[28] He remained at the Seminary for only five years; in 1893 he accepted the second call to Princeton Theological Seminary and was ordained in the Presbyterian Church in the United States of America. Kuyper wrote Herman Bavinck that Vos probably went too far in becoming a Presbyterian but indicated that it would have been "academic suicide" if Vos had remained in Grand Rapids.[29] Vos spent the rest of his academic life at Princeton teaching biblical theology. He retired in 1932 and spent the final years of his life in Grand Rapids where he died in 1949. In spite of his long tenure at Princeton, the CRC regarded Vos as one of her own sons and it is appropriate to refer to Vos' important work on the kingdom in this article.

(Report 43). Compare the latter with the Statement of Mission Principles of the CRC in 1977 which lacks a kingdom perspective, *Acts of Synod 1977,* pp. 90–94 (Art. 61), pp. 614–637 (Report 42). Note also the editor of *The Banner,* Lester R. De Koster's negative evaluation of the Evangelism Manifesto: "When one reflects, however, on how vague and indefinite the concept 'kingdom of God' has become after repeated generations of discussion, the committee's suggestion may turn out to be a little like resolving a mystery by means of an enigma, or multiplying the unknown by the more unknown," *The Banner* 111 (February 13, 1976):6.

28. Geerhardus Vos, *De Verbondsleer in de Gereformeerde Theologie,* Rede by het Overdragen van het Rectoraat van de Theologische School to Grand Rapids, Michigan (Grand Rapids: "Democrat" Drukpers, 1891).

29. Rolf H. Bremmer, *Herman Bavinck en zijn tijdgenoten* (Kampen: J. H. Kok, 1966), pp. 81, 291. See also Geerhardus Vos, *Redemptive History and Biblical Interpretation: The Shorter Writings of Geerhardus Vos,* ed. Richard B. Gaffin (Phillipsburg, NJ: Presbyterian and Reformed, 1980), p. xi.

Vos published two short articles on "The Kingdom of God" in 1900.[30] Three years later he expanded that material and published *The Teaching of Jesus Concerning the Kingdom of God and the Church*.[31] Vos' careful biblical exposition was a major Reformed contribution to the subject of the kingdom dominated in his day by Albrecht Ritschl and Walter Rauschenbusch. Kuyper could have used that biblical exposition to strengthen the foundations of his own kingdom vision. One wonders whether Rauschenbusch ever came upon Vos' book when he was searching for a "theology for the social gospel."[32]

Vos began his book with the observation that "the references to the kingdom of God occupy a prominent place" in Jesus' teaching. Luke 4:43 even indicates that the main purpose of Christ's mission was to preach the good news of the kingdom of God. The kingdom of God stood at the beginning, middle, and end of Jesus preaching; it appears in the beatitudes, the parables, and other high points of his teaching. The subject of the kingdom of God was second to no other subject in Jesus ministry. Vos linked Jesus' teaching on the kingdom with the Old Testament, considered its present and future phases, distinguished his view from current misconceptions, and attempted to outline a comprehensive view of the kingdom. A provocative chapter deals with the relation of the church and the kingdom.

Since the CRC lacks a clear doctrinal statement on the kingdom, Vos' succinct summary of his book provides an excellent overview of the subject and a good start for further study:

In the first place, the kingdom-conception involves the *historic unity* of Jesus' work with the Old Testament work of God. These two constitute one body of supernatural revelation and redemption.

Secondly, the doctrine of the kingdom stands for the principle that the Christian religion is not a mere matter of subjective ideas or experiences, but is related to a *great system of objective, supernatural facts and transactions*. The kingdom means the renewal of the world through the introduction of supernatural forces.

Thirdly, the kingdom-idea is the clearest expression of the principle that in the sphere of objective reality, as well as in the sphere of human consciousness, everything is *subservient to the glory of God*. In this respect the kingdom is the most profoundly *religious* of all biblical conceptions.

Fourthly, the message of the kingdom imparts to Christianity, as Jesus proclaims it, the professed character of a *religion of salvation*, and of salvation not primarily by man's own efforts but by the power and grace of God.

---

30. Geerhardus Vos, "The Kingdom of God," *The Bible Student* n.s. 1 (1900):282–289, 328–335.

31. Geerhardus Vos, *The Teaching of Jesus concerning the Kingdom of God and the Church*, Second edition, revised (New York: American Tract Society, 1903). Reprint entitled *The Kingdom of God and the Church* (Nutley, NJ: Presbyterian and Reformed Publishing Co., 1972). The pages of the 1972 edition are added in parenthesis.

32. Walter Rauschenbusch, *A Theology for the Social Gospel* (New York: Macmillan, 1917).

The kingdom represents the specifically *evangelical* element in our Lord's teaching. The same principle finds subjective expression in his teaching on faith.

Fifthly, Jesus' doctrine of the kingdom as both inward and outward, coming first in the heart of man and afterwards in the external world, upholds *the primacy of the spiritual and ethical* over the physical. The invisible world of the inner religious life, the righteousness of the disposition, the sonship of God are in it made supreme, the essence of the kingdom, the ultimate realities to which everything else is subordinate. The inherently ethical character of the kingdom finds subjective expression in the demand for repentance.

Sixthly, that form which the kingdom assumes in the church shows it to be inseparably associated with *the person and work of Jesus himself.* The religion of the kingdom is a religion in which there is not only a place but in which the central place is for the Saviour. The church form of the kingdom rightly bears the name of *Christianity,* because in it on Christ everything depends.

Finally, the thought of the kingdom of God implies the subjection of the entire range of human life in all its forms and spheres to the ends of religion. The kingdom reminds us of *the absoluteness, the pervasiveness, the unrestricted dominion,* which of right belong to all true religion. It proclaims that religion, and religion alone, can act as *the supreme unifying, centralizing factor* in the life of man, as that which binds all together and perfects all by leading it to its final goal in the service of God.[33]

At times Vos' language might imply that the kingdom was primarily "spiritual" or "invisible." Perhaps he was searching for language that could counter the exclusively earthly view of the kingdom of Ritschlianism. Yet the last three points of Vos' summary indicate that for him the kingdom manifested itself in this world. The believer's recognition of the supremacy of God as king had to manifest itself in the world. Vos also saw the church as a visible manifestation of the kingdom, but not the only one. He was convinced that "the kingship of God, as his recognized and applied supremacy, is intended to pervade and control the whole of human life in all its forms of existence" as the parable of the leaven plainly teaches.[34] Then, in words that reveal his kinship with Kuyper, Vos added that "these various forms of human life have each their own sphere in which they work and embody themselves. There is a sphere of science, a sphere of art, a sphere of the family and of the state, a sphere of commerce and industry."[35] Furthermore, "Whenever one of these spheres comes under the controlling influence of the principle of the divine supremacy and glory, and this outwardly reveals itself, there we can truly say that the kingdom of God has become manifest."[36]

33. Vos, *Teaching of Jesus,* pp. 191–194 (pp. 102–103).
34. Ibid., p. 162 (p. 87).
35. Ibid., pp. 162–163 (p. 87).
36. Ibid., p. 163 (pp. 87–88).

Vos recognized that Jesus seldom made "explicit reference to these things" himself. Jesus "contented himself with laying down the great religious and moral principles which ought to govern the life of man in every sphere. Their detailed application it was not his work to show."[37] Yet Vos was convinced that Jesus' "doctrine of the kingdom was founded on such a profound and broad conviction of the absolute supremacy of God in all things, that he could not but look upon every normal and legitimate province of human life as intended to form part of God's kingdom."[38] That did *not* mean that all human life was subject to the church; the kingdom is broader than the church; the church is one manifestation of the kingdom.

Louis Berkhof (1873-1957)

A second example of a challenging kingdom vision came from Louis Berkhof in 1913. Berkhof was born in Emmen, the Netherlands, and came to the United States at an early age. He was educated at Calvin Theological Seminary and Princeton Theological Seminary. After six years in the pastorate, he began a thirty-eight year career at Calvin Seminary. He taught both Old and New Testament exegesis and from 1926 to his retirement in 1944 was Professor of Systematic Theology, serving for many years as president of the Seminary as well. In 1920–1921 Berkhof delivered the Stone lectures at Princeton Seminary on the kingdom of God but they were not published until 1951.[39] Our concern here is a lecture Berkhof presented at Calvin in 1913 on *The Church and Social Problems*.[40]

Students who know Louis Berkhof only from his *Systematic Theology* are often completely surprised to discover this small booklet. Zwaanstra called it "the most significant work to appear in the Christian Reformed Church on the task of the church in society."[41] Berkhof presented this lecture to the combined student bodies of what was then known as "The Theological School and Calvin College." His aim was to "promote the proper activity of the church along social lines" so that it might "lead to an ever increasing establishment of God's rule in every sphere of life."[42]

Today Berkhof's opening line almost sounds like the words of a liberation theologian: "The greatest liberating force in the world is the gospel of Jesus Christ."[43] He pointed to the momentous changes in society and

---

37. Ibid., (p. 88).
38. Ibid., pp. 163–164 (p. 88).
39. Louis Berkhof, *The Kingdom of God*, The Development of the Idea of the Kingdom, Especially Since the Eighteenth Century. (Grand Rapids: Eerdmans, 1951).
40. Louis Berkhof, *The Church and Social Problems* (Grand Rapids: Eerdmans-Sevensma Co., 1913).
41. Zwaanstra, *Reformed Thought and Experience*, p. 196.
42. Berkhof, *Church and Social Problems*, p. 2.
43. Ibid., p. 3.

history brought about by the gospel during its early years and during Reformation times. He emphasized that he and his students were heirs of those blessings. From that perspective he approached the subject of the church's social responsibility.

In 1913 the church was under attack for neglecting its social task. The indictment reads like a page from the 1960s. Berkhof traced the need for social reform to four main causes: the radical break with the past occasioned by the French Revolution, the introduction of the machine and the Industrial Revolution, the reaction to individualism promoted by the Socialist Revolution, and the Educational Revolution which popularized education and opened peoples' eyes to the prevalence of social injustice.[44]

While he rejected socialism, Berkhof approved of the positive social contributions of the labor movement, the trade unions, social settlements, recreation centers, and similar attempts to promote social justice. He quoted Walter Rauschenbusch's *Christianity and the Social Crisis*[45] a couple of times to illustrate the social problems. The church was reaching only the comfortable middle class; it did not affect the rich and did not reach the poor. An English writer, Henry Carter, expressed the paradox: "Within her borders, loss; beyond her borders, gain for the Kingdom of God."[46] The church was charged with indifference to the great social problems and insensibility to the glaring socio-economic injustice in society.

Berkhof listed seven frequently mentioned causes for the church's failure. 1) The church apparently sanctioned the existing social order, favored the rich, and was instrumental in capitalism's subjection of the working class. 2) The church preached a gospel of contentment while the laboring world cried out for justice. 3) The church held herself aloof from the masses, did not minister to them, and brought them no hope or comfort. 4) The church moved to the suburbs and abandoned the inner city. 5) The church discouraged reform movements and criticized those who intruded upon her domain and did the work which she neglected. 6) The church was concerned only for individual salvation and ignored the renewal of society. 7) Finally, the church preached an "other-worldly" gospel which did not touch the realities of every day life. Berkhof concluded: "To the hungry poor she preaches that the righteous shall live by faith; to the homeless that God is the eternal dwelling-place for all His people. It seems like mockery to many."[47] That startling catalog of

44. Ibid., pp. 5-7.
45. Walter Rauschenbusch, *Christianity and the Social Crisis* (New York: Hodder & Stoughton, 1907).
46. Berkhof, *Church and Social Problems*, p. 10.
47. Ibid., p. 12.

complaints from 1913 reminds us of the 1960s and is still heard in the 1980s!

To what extent was the church actually guilty of such charges? In addressing that question Berkhof contrasted the views of Anabaptists, Roman Catholics, and Social Gospel Protestants. The spiritual sons of John Calvin, he insisted, could not be satisfied with such views of the church; every dualism between nature and grace, natural and supernatural, body and soul, must be rejected. Whether one views the church as a "social organism" or as "an institution," the church has a social responsibility; the deacon's office alone was clear proof of that. Berkhof argued further that all facets are aimed at establishing "God's rule on earth."[48] That did not imply an endorsement of the social gospel; Berkhof distinguished the present and the future, the already and the not-yet, of the kingdom. Therefore we must look for the manifestation of God's kingdom already on this earth; that is involved in the prayer that God's will be done on earth as it is in heaven. Berkhof thought Calvin may have gone a little too far in Geneva,[49] but Calvin, John Knox, and Kuyper were on the right track.

Berkhof suggested a far-reaching six-point program whereby the institutional church could promote the kingdom of God through social action. First, the church must be "the nursery of true, healthy, virile spiritual life." This is basic because society can not be renewed without changing individuals. The social gospel was wrong in thinking that individuals could be reformed by changing their environment, but evangelical neglect of the church's social task was also wrong.[50] Second, the church must proclaim the social message of Scripture and seek the realization of the kingdom of God on earth. While the pulpit must not become a sociology platform, biblical directions for social life and principles for social reform must be clearly and fearlessly preached. An exclusively otherworldly preaching was illegitimate. There should be no dilemma between preaching the cross or the kingdom: "the Cross of Christ [is] the pulpit's message" but "on the Cross the kingdom is to be founded."[51]

Third, Berkhof urged the church to exemplify the gospel in her own social life, for actions speak louder than words. Social injustice, social sin, and social misery should have no place in Christ's church. "O what a different world this would already be," Berkhof sighed, "if all the members of the Church of Christ lived conscientiously according to the precepts of their heavenly Lord!"[52] Fourth, the church may not neglect the inner city and the ghetto. Foreign missionaries reported that conditions in American cities were often worse than those found in pagan lands. "What a terrible

48. Ibid., pp. 16–17.
49. Ibid., pp. 17–18.
50. Ibid., p. 18.
51. Ibid., pp. 18–19.
52. Ibid., p. 19.

indictment against our boasted civilization;" Berkhof exclaimed, "but also, what a fearful charge against the Church; what an imperative call to duty!"[53]

The fifth part of Berkhof's program was the appointment of a competent committee to study social problems and suggest biblical solutions to the church. And he recommended a course on social ethics for seminary students to alert them to their kingdom responsibilities.[54] Finally, Berkhof recommended that the church should encourage its members to promote separate Christian organizations to advance the kingdom of God. In this way Christians would be "the leaven permeating the lump, God's spiritual force for the regeneration of the world, His chosen agents to influence every sphere of life, and to bring science and art, commerce and industry in subjection to God."[55]

At the conclusion of the lecture Berkhof returned to the question of the churches' guilt. Some of the charges, he thought, were exaggerated, but no church should have a clear conscience. He referred approvingly to the social platform recently approved by the Federal Council of Churches. While some churches had lost sight of the true nature and task of the church, especially those gripped by the liberal social gospel, Berkhof thought the CRC had not moved fast enough. Hence he urged the church to work along the lines of his six recommendations; that would mean that the CRC would become a little more Calvinistic than it had been, certainly not less so. Perhaps the momentous significance of Calvinism in the past could be recaptured. ". . . Calvinism also contains the principles and forces that make for industrial democracy, for the establishment of God's rule in every sphere of life, for the introduction of a better social day, and for an ever increasing fulfillment of the Church's constant prayer: 'Thy will be done on earth as it is in heaven.'"[56] Is that challenge any less relevant today than it was in 1913?

Samuel Volbeda (1881-1953)

A third significant perspective on the kingdom of God in CRC history comes from Samuel Volbeda in the period between the wars. Volbeda was born in Winsum, the Netherlands. He came to the United States at the age of five in 1886—the year of Kuyper's Doleantie in the Netherlands and Rauschenbusch's ordination in New York. Barth and Paul Tillich were born in that year also. Volbeda graduated from Calvin Theological Seminary in 1904 and served two CRC churches before going to the Free University in 1911. He received his doctorate in 1914 and returned to teach church history at the Seminary. When William W. Heyns retired in 1926, Volbeda

---

53. Ibid.
54. Ibid., p. 20.
55. Ibid.
56. Ibid., p. 23.

moved to the chair of practical theology in which he continued until his retirement in 1952. In 1944 he succeeded Berkhof as president of the Seminary.

Volbeda presented four lectures to the alumni of Westminster Theological Seminary in August, 1939, on the subject of practical theology. The lectures were never published, but the hand-written manuscript is among the Volbeda Papers in the Colonial Origins Collection of Calvin College and Seminary Library.[57] The lectures were typically Volbedian—rich vocabulary, broad perspectives, brilliant insights. His subject did not suggest a kingdom theme. The unexciting question he addressed was: *"What* is the *practice* referred to in [practical] theology?"[58] In answering that question Volbeda explained the interrelations of covenant, church, and kingdom. In doing so, he went beyond the insights of Vos and Berkhof described above. The profundity of his 1939 conclusions provide an excellent starting point for us today in furthering the vision of God's Kingdom.

According to Volbeda, covenant, church, and kingdom are three strands of one cord—the people of God. The one people of God constitutes the unity within this triplicity. There is but one people of God and that one people is organized covenantally in the family, in the church ecclesiastically, and in a kingdom fashion in human society.[59] Normally every one of God's children sustains all three of these relations.

The covenant is first and basic. Volbeda referred to the 1891 rectoral address of Vos on the covenant as the indispensible traveling companion (*vademecum*) of every minister.[60] Volbeda did not develop the redemptive-historical stages of the covenants; he simply defined the covenant of grace as it pertains to New Testament believers. The covenant is "the relation of God to His people in pursuance of which God through His Spirit for Christ's sake bestows upon those predestined thereto the gift of eternal and spiritual life."[61] Hence "a covenant-minded Christian will be ecclesiastically loyal and zealous for God's kingdom."[62]

The relation between covenant and kingdom is intimate. "The covenant of God's grace is the matrix of spiritual or regenerate life and . . . the kingdom of God is the field of the believer's service to His heavenly Father"; the spiritual life which is generated within "the precincts of the covenant, is the power that enables us to do the work of the kingdom of God."[63]

57. Samuel Volbeda, "Studies in Practical Theology." I am indebted to my colleague, Richard R. De Ridder, for calling my attention to these lectures several years ago. Page references are to the hand-written manuscript in the Colonial Origins Collection of Calvin College and Seminary Library, pages 1–137.

58. Ibid., pp. 1, 92.
59. Ibid., p. 60.
60. Ibid., p. 34; see footnote 28 above.
61. Ibid., p. 12.
62. Ibid., p. 34.
63. Ibid., p. 31.

Volbeda insisted that spiritual life or true piety is never an end in itself; it should always be directed to the kingdom of God. "Covenantal life and kingdom service are related as one root and flower or fruit. No other flower can blossom on covenant soil than the cultivation of God's world to the praise of His glorious Name."[64] Volbeda considered the divorce of kingdom service *from covenant life* to be a typical worldly vice. On the other hand, a vice deeply entrenched in Christian circles is to dissociate covenant life *from kingdom service*. The spiritual life of the covenant is not an end in itself (a *Selbtszweck*); it must always be a means to the goals of God's kingdom. Volbeda expressed that in the figurative language for which he was famous: "The waters of their spiritual life descend from the highlands of God's covenant of grace. After passing through the reservoir of their soul, they inundate the wide fields of God's world in which they live, and make them wave with abounding harvest of glory to God and delight to God's angels and happiness for themselves."[65]

How did Volbeda visualize the *structures* of covenant and kingdom? He saw the family as the covenantal structure. Covenant structure is therefore simple, natural, and constant. What about the structure of the kingdom? The kingdom can not be simply spiritual, invisible, or amorphous. The kingdom comes to structural expression in the social forms that naturally arise out of life. Like the covenant structure, such kingdom structures are ordinary rather than special. Society, however, is a compound and its structural forms are arbitrary, artificial, and variable to a degree. While the state is universal, its morphology is varied both now and in the past. The same is true of schools. As redemptive history has moved through the patriarchal, the theocratic, and the first advent stages, and awaits Christ's second advent, so the temporal advance of the kingdom of God moves through progressive stages. Therefore, "instead of crystallizing in an institution definitely its own and by that token distinctive, the kingdom of God steals, spirit-like, into existing institutions and social structures, and leaven-like influences their life and activity in the direction of its own specific character."[66] The kingdom of God cannot possibly be amorphous since it is "the rule of God over men of flesh and blood living their life in a material world; . . . if it receives no embodiment in forms of its *own*, it must—and it does—seek expression structurally in the existing forms of society."[67]

How then is the church related to covenant and kingdom? In contrast to covenant and kingdom, Volbeda viewed the church as a special organization. In contrast to the natural structures of covenant and kingdom, the church's structure is artificial, mechanical, and imposed from without. Establishment of the church was a matter of expediency in Volbeda's

64. Ibid., pp. 31–32.
65. Ibid., p. 45.
66. Ibid., pp. 56–57.
67. Ibid.

judgment. He presented an insightful historical review to show why an institutional church was necessary to replace theocratic Israel in the post-Pentecost situation when the gospel was destined to permeate the Gentile nations of the world.[68] This does not denigrate the church; Volbeda emphasized its strategic significance in relation to covenant and kingdom.

The church is defined as "a divine agency instituted for the purpose of training God's covenant people for kingdom service through the cultivation of their spiritual life by means, pre-eminently, of the administration of the Word of God. It is a pedagogical institute; it is a school of Christ."[69] Therefore "our ecclesiastical relation to God cannot be rightly, and certainly not *fully* understood, unless it be clearly seen in the perspectives of the *alpha* of the covenant relation and the *omega* of the *basileion* relation to God."[70] A church that is not vital with covenant life becomes a mere organization, a dead mechanism. The ecclesiasticism of a lifeless church is lamented in these picturesque words:

> It is more than time that all concerned clearly realize that a church without a covenant foundation is a veritable aircastle, but not a house built upon a rock. It is not a tree planted in fertile and well-watered soil, but a post set in the ground. It is a soulless body; it is a steamless boiler; it is a dead wire. It may have the name that it lives, but in very deed it is dead.[71]

And if the church is not oriented to the *kingdom*, another evil form of ecclesiasticism develops:

> As soon as a church begins to live unto itself instead of being a feeder for the kingdom and a stimulus to kingdom-activity, it develops the mortal malady of ecclesiasticism. Mortal I say, because the covenant life that is not conducted *through* the church, pipe-line like, but shut up, reservoir-like, *in* the church, will cease to flow, back up, so to say, and will find other channels and outlets. Then we perceive the *un*ecclesiastical-mindedness, the *carentia sensus ecclesiastici*, that marks sectarianism and is fast becoming the vogue today in this fair land of ours.[72]

Volbeda did not minimize the significance of the church. He was simply indicating its practical subordination to covenant and kingdom. He therefore warned both against making the church an end in itself and confusing the church with the kingdom. Roman Catholicism confused the church with the kingdom on principle; Volbeda saw the same thing happening in practice by more or less orthodox churches and he thought the social

68. Ibid., pp. 20–22.
69. Ibid., p. 83.
70. Ibid., p. 51.
71. Ibid., pp. 13–14.
72. Ibid., p. 52.

gospel found ready entrance into such churches because of that confusion. When the church confuses itself with the kingdom, "one of the most pernicious and lamentable consequences" is "the *neglect* precisely of what is the divinely-ordained work of the church."[73] Avoidance of such ecclesiastical aberrations demands an understanding of the church's relation to both covenant and kingdom.

Volbeda waxed eloquent when he reflected on what happens when the church really carries out its covenantal-kingdom task. The three strands of the one cord should never be at odds; "members of the covenant and citizens of the kingdom are in duty bound to attend the *ecclesiastical training school* which Christ has founded, exactly in pursuance of their covenant membership and kingdom citizenship."[74] The church can be called "the light and power-house of the kingdom of God"; "where the church fails, the covenant declines and the kingdom decays."[75] History provides abundant proof of that! On the other hand, when the church performs her God-given task the covenant will flourish and the kingdom advance. Volbeda saw tremendous kingdom-building, kingdom-extending, kingdom-defending energies released when the people of God assemble on the Lord's day. The heart-felt emotion of this professor of preaching spilled over in this description of the kingdom-significance of Sunday worship: "It is manna to renew their strength, sparkling water to refresh their spirit, balm of Gilead to heal their wounds, the sword of the Spirit wherewith to put their enemies to flight, light to dispel their darkness, music to cheer them on their way, a chart to indicate a path through the wilderness, a program to execute in their life, a beacon to warn them of impending dangers."[76]

Even such words failed to express what he really wanted to say: "It is quite impossible to analyze completely the practical significance of the Word of God as administered to God's people on God's Day by those ordained to perform this momentous and sublime task."[77] "It need hardly be added," he continued, "that if God's people and their ministers were always mindful of the enormous kingdom-serving power in . . . preaching on the day when heaven bows down to earth and earth rises to meet heaven's embraces, there would be more consecrating prayer for the Day that the Lord hath made, more intense application to public worship while it is in progress, more trailing clouds of devotion after the gates of the temple have been closed, more heavenly mindedness during the six-day period of earthly labors, more thought of eternity as the clock ticks off the wearisome hours of time."[78]

73. Ibid., p. 76.
74. Ibid., pp. 84–85.
75. Ibid., pp. 85–86.
76. Ibid., p. 90.
77. Ibid.
78. Ibid., pp. 91–92.

That is an impressive, moving description of the relations of covenant, church, and kingdom. It is tragic that Volbeda did not share those rich insights with the general public. The need for hearing that perspective is urgent today! The people of God need to consider these biblical insights on covenant, church, and kingdom. Volbeda was right: together they flourish, divided they fail.

Is the CRC today ready to move forward in promoting the biblical vision of the kingdom of God? If it is ready, the seeds planted in past years must have taken root. If it is not yet ready, a careful review of the insights of Berkhof, Volbeda, and Vos will surely prove fruitful.

11

Mission Zeal in the Christian Reformed Church: 1857–1917

Harvey A. Smit

Through much of its history, the Christian Reformed Church in North America (hereafter CRC) has had an uneasy sense of having failed in obedience to one of Jesus Christ's direct commands. The risen Lord instructed his disciples, "Go into all the world and preach the good news to all creation" (Mark 16:15, NIV). The CRC has recognized this as a marching order it is duty bound to obey. Yet during the first sixty years or more of its existence, the church has lived with a disquieting awareness that it was not adequately carrying out that mission order.

The fact of this failure has been seldom disputed. Rather, church leaders have charged in repeated articles and editorials that the denomination has shown a singular lack in this area and have urged the church to remedy this failing.

An example will give the flavor of these urgings. In 1907 *The Banner* editor, Henry Beets, wrote on our lack of mission zeal.[1] He quoted an editorial from *The Leader* [a periodical of the Reformed Church in America (hereafter RCA)][2] which charged the CRC with this lack: "A little mission among the American Indians, and that of recent origin, and to which they contribute less than ten thousand dollars a year, is all that they are doing, as a Church to bring the light of the gospel to those who are in utter darkness."[3] Beets accepted this as a merited rebuke. The CRC had not been

1. Henry Beets, "Our Lack of Zeal for Missions," *The Banner* 42 (1907):2–3.
2. Evert J. Blekkink, "A better Day in a Sister Church," *The Leader* 1 (1906/07):137.
3. Beets, "Lack of Zeal for Missions," p. 2.

as active in evangelism as it should and could have been. More steward-ship and systematic giving was needed. Beets offered some reasons for this negligence: the small number of members; the need to build parsonages, churches, and a theological school; and the effort required to develop and support free Christian primary schools. But these reasons, he admitted, were not valid excuses.[4]

Beets intended the title of his editorial to reflect what he believed was the true failure: lack of mission zeal. The spirit was weak, so the flesh failed. The inner impulse toward evangelism was absent or faltering, so the church had not done this task well.

Through the first six decades of the CRC, those within it who were concerned for evangelistic outreach experienced frequent, often bitter, disappointments. Offerings for missions were neglected or so small as to be downright embarrassing—in 1905, an average of two cents per family per week.[5] Even after official approval was given and funds were available for mission, despite passionate pleadings there were often no volunteers to do the work.[6] When work finally was begun it sometimes showed such sparse results that it was discontinued.[7]

These and similar disappointments in the church's mission enterprise were rather regularly attributed to a *lack of zeal*. This rather amorphous phrase seemed to cover, if not excuse, a multitude of shortcomings—in offerings, in prayers, in interest, in volunteers, in participation, in enthusi-asm. This *lack of mission zeal* seems to have meant a weakness in the sort

---

4. Ibid., pp. 2–3.

5. Note, for instance, the complaint of elder Steven Lukas of Graafschap, Michigan, concerning the lack of missions to the "Klassikale Vergadering Gehouden den 5 Februari 1862, te Graafschap," in *Minutes* of the Highest Assembly of the Christian Reformed Church 1857–1880 (Grand Rapids: Calvin Theological Seminary, 1937), p. 19 (Arts. 5 and 6). (Mimeographed, and in the Dutch language); Henry Beets, "Over-zicht der Christelijke Gereformeerde Indianen Zending," *De Heidenwereld* 9 (August 1905):13; Henry Beets, "What We Give for Missions," *The Banner of Truth* 40 (1905):317–318.

6. For example, in 1874 the church decided to call a denominational home missionary, "an itinerant preacher for the church," in "Algemeene Vergadering Gehouden te Chicago den 3 Juny, 1874, en Volgende Dagen," see *Minutes 1857–1880*, pp. 146–147 (Art. 14). But it was not until 1879 that one was found, the Reverend Tamme M. Vanden Bosch. Within three years he asked to be released and when no replacement was found, in spite of repeated calls, Synod considered making it a condition for financial aid that theologi-cal students spend at least one year in home mission service, *Handelingen* van de Synode Vergadering der Hollandsche Christelijke Gereformeerde Kerk in de Vereenigde Staten van Noord Amerika, Gehouden te Grand Rapids, Michigan, den 9den Juni, en Volgende Dagen, 1886 (Holland: De Wachter Drukkerij, 1886), p. 29 (Art. 78); see also Henry Beets, *De Christelijke Gereformeerde Kerk in Noord Amerika*, Zestig Jaren van Strijd en Zegen (Grand Rapids: Grand Rapids Printing Co., 1918), pp. 192–193. Fortunately in 1886 a candidate, Marcusse J. Marcusse, volunteered for this work.

7. This was true of the work begun by Vanden Bosch in South Dakota among the American Indians in the Upper Brules region. He was installed on October 23, 1889, began working in South Dakota shortly thereafter, and was recalled (at his own request) on September 4, 1890; Richard R. De Ridder, "The Development of the Mission Order of the Christian Reformed Church," (M.A. thesis, Kennedy School of Missions, Hartford Seminary Foundation, 1956), p. 60. It was also true of the work among the Mormons in Utah. That work began in 1911. Results were so discouraging that work was later suspended, Beets, *Christelijke Gereformeerde Kerk*, pp. 348–349.

of evangelistic impulse or drive required to produce the needed sacrifices by the church and individuals in the church. The phrase was used to name the sickness underlying the varied symptoms.

But a *lack of zeal* also seemed to describe a sickness which supposedly could be healed by adequate ecclesiastical measures. Churchmen took the malady to be a curable illness, serious but in no sense deadly to the church's health.

Geert E. Boer, editor of *De Wachter* (1875–1878), spoke of a consciousness which must be awakened in the church.[8] Information about the pathetic plight of the poor heathen, recognition of our own pagan background from which we were delivered, examples of great missionaries and evangelists—all these were means to stir up interest and concern within the church.[9] Reflecting a similar understanding, Classes Grand Rapids East and West sent requests to the Synod of 1910, asking the synod to recommend to the churches certain means for awakening a mission spirit.[10] The underlying idea in such attempts was an awareness that the problem lay in a simple lack of interest in missions, a shortcoming that could be overcome by appropriate measures within the church. Just "stirring up the people" and "reminding them of their obligations" would solve the problem.[11]

In the minds of even the most enthusiastic supporters of missions, this *lack of zeal* did not appear to be a very serious problem, either spiritually or theologically. In the editorial cited above, Boer referred to an article in *De Bazuin* (A Dutch religious weekly) which contended that mission zeal is the pulsebeat of a church. It declared that, as in the human body, a weak pulse indicates a sick church. But Boer himself makes no judgment about the CRC's spiritual health from this criterion. Instead he urges the church to carry out this task for the King, asking itself not, "How much can we do?" but, "Are we doing what we can?"[12]

But what of historians and mission specialists? How have they evaluated this *lack of mission zeal?*

Beets, one of the earliest CRC historians and first secretary of foreign missions, blamed this lack on the fact that no systematic, persistent efforts had been made to instill and foster a mission spirit. The CRC, he observed,

---

8. Geert E. Boer, "De Zending de Polsslag der Kerk," *De Wachter* 11 (Mei 9, 1878):1.

9. Cf. John H. Bratt, "The Missionary Enterprise of the Christian Reformed Church of [sic] America," (Th.D. dissertation, Union Theological Seminary in Virginia, Richmond, 1955), pp. 68–73.

10. *Acta der Synode* van de Christelijke Gereformeerde Kerk, Gehouden van 15 tot 24 Juni, 1910, te Muskegon, Michigan (Grand Rapids: H. Verhaar Drukker, 1910), pp. 24–25 (Art. 39). These means included mission sermons, dealing with mission in catechism teaching, a mission lesson in each Sunday School quarter, a systematic study of mission in societies, formation of mission societies, a yearly mission day, area churches seeking to send out their own missionary, and systematic weekly giving for mission.

11. Henry Beets, "Reformed Mission Zeal—and Ours," *The Banner* 52 (1917):581.

12. Boer, "Zending de Polsslag der Kerk," p. 1; E. Douma, "School, Kerk en Zending," *De Bazuin* 26 (12 April 1878):5.

prided itself on its orthodoxy—well and good. But it should also have moved to join with other Christians in the greatest cause of all—making Christ known to the ends of the earth.[13]

Diedrich H. Kromminga stated that there was an interest in missions in the CRC from the beginning. The problem, he seemed to infer, was not *lack of zeal* but difficulty in determining how to direct and supervise mission work, a difficulty springing from the smallness and weakness of the church.[14]

John H. Kromminga, in his centennial history of the CRC, recognized an earlier lack of interest in mission and mentions that this had been blamed in the past to preoccupation with Christian education. If this were true in the past, he says it was less in the two decades, 1937–1957, during which there had been a significant rise in mission zeal. He attributed this to a number of factors, including incessant propagation of the mission cause by Beets and others who were directly involved in the missionary work, exposure of World War II veterans to other cultures, contacts with other denominations through The Back to God Hour, and, generally, to a breaking down of the CRC's traditional isolation.[15]

Henry Zwaanstra, another church historian, did not deal with this matter directly, but said that after 1870 there developed in the CRC a gradual awareness of its obligation to share its faith and to become a leaven in American society. He seemed to infer that the *lack of zeal* was a manifestation of the church's struggle to retain its faith while adapting to the American world.[16]

John H. Bratt made "the charge of a lack of missionary zeal and the presence of the spirit of evangelistic lukewarmness" the central theme of his doctoral dissertation.[17] In this historical study he recognized "considerable languor and apathy" until the 1910s.[18] But he appears to have found no clear cause or set of causes for this condition. Bratt contended that it was not rooted in theology or creedal beliefs, for Calvinistic doctrine is a stimulant, not deterrent, to the mission enterprise.[19] He saw a missionary consciousness as a gradually developing sense, based on growing knowledge of the need for evangelism, an impulse helped and hindered by a number of complex factors.[20]

---

13. Beets, "Reformed Mission Zeal," p. 581.

14. Diedrich H. Kromminga, *The Christian Reformed Tradition*, From the Reformation till the Present (Grand Rapids: Eerdmans, 1943), p. 126.

15. John H. Kromminga, *In the Mirror*, An Appraisal of the Christian Reformed Church (Hamilton: Guardian, 1957), pp. 138–139.

16. Henry Zwaanstra, *Reformed Thought and Experience in a New World*, A Study of the Christian Reformed Church and its American Environment 1890–1918 (Kampen: J. H. Kok, 1973), pp. 29, 33.

17. Bratt, "Missionary Enterprise," p. vi.

18. Ibid., p. 145.

19. Ibid., p. 47.

20. Ibid., p. 94.

In his master's thesis, Richard R. De Ridder concentrated on the development of the mission order of the CRC. In this context, he reviewed the first stages of mission work in the church and concluded that there was never a question about whether or not the church ought to do mission work. From the beginning it was committed to evangelism. But it struggled long over the questions of where and how.[21]

In a tenor strongly contrasting with most of these historians, Harold Dekker, Professor of Missions at Calvin Theological Seminary, contended that missionary spirit and activity in the CRC had been inhibited by a mistaken understanding of the doctrine of limited atonement.[22] Bad doctrine, he said, had been the cause of bad practice, of inept and ineffective evangelism in the CRC.

Dekker's articles[23] caused a furor in the church. The question of *lack of zeal* was almost lost in the resulting doctrinal controversy which centered in the Reformed teaching about God's love and limited atonement. Still this did become part of the mandate of the study committee appointed by the Synod of 1964.

Reporting in 1966, the study committee admitted there was indeed a lack of missionary zeal and activity in the CRC, "especially in the past." But it found the cause "not in our thoroughly scriptural doctrines of the saving and irresistible grace of God and the particular atonement; but in many other things which have tended to impair our missionary spirit and activity."[24] These "other things" included spiritual apathy due to material prosperity, "a feeling of inferiority and fear to speak to others," a lingering "immigrant mentality," weariness because of poor results in evangelizing, not enough individual prayer for the unconverted, and a preoccupation with theological correctness during the twenties, which hindered compassionate interest in people outside the church.[25]

Dekker replied that the committee was confusing symptoms with sickness, effects with causes. They had dealt with a practical issue in theoretical terms, not recognizing that their theory, in this case, didn't fit the practice. They had stated, "the doctrines of election and limited atonement need not in any way dampen our zeal for missions," but they had recognized, said Dekker, that these doctrines do indeed have precisely that dampening effect.[26]

21. De Ridder, "Development of the Mission Order," p. 58.

22. Harold Dekker, "God So Loved—All Men!" *The Reformed Journal* 12 (December 1962):7; Harold Dekker, "Limited Atonement and Evangelism," *The Reformed Journal* 14 (May–June 1964):22.

23. Dekker wrote seven articles on God's love and limited atonement in *The Reformed Journal* from December 1962 through May–June 1964.

24. *Acts of Synod*, June 8 to June 16, 1966, at Central College, Pella, Iowa (Grand Rapids: Christian Reformed Publishing House, 1966), p. 504 (Suppl. 42).

25. Ibid.

26. *Acts of Synod 1967*, June 14 to 24, 1967, Reconvened August 29 and 30, 1967, at Calvin College, Grand Rapids, Michigan (Grand Rapids: Christian Reformed Publishing House, 1967), pp. 490–491 (Suppl. 40).

Since the Synod of 1967 made no declaration or decision regarding this issue, the matter remained unresolved. Little, if anything, has been written about it in the last fifteen years. Yet this question of mission zeal deserves further study and discussion. It is of historical interest, and it illumines the CRC's past understanding of why and how it should be active in evangelistic outreach. Of special interest in the period between 1857 and 1917, when relatively little was being done in evangelism, what was done came at great cost, and accusations of lack of missionary spirit were most common.

The CRC came into existence in 1857 when a number of churches, made up of recent immigrants from the Netherlands, seceded from Classis Holland of the RCA. During the first few decades, this new denomination struggled for its very existence. Yet already during the very first year, at the second meeting of the new church body, one of the congregations (Graafschap) proposed that each church hold a monthly prayer meeting for the extension of God's kingdom and at that meeting take up a collection for Bible distribution.[27] It is true that several years later some congregations needed to be reminded of that decision and that one elder, Steven Lukas of Graafschap, complained to the classis of negligence in collecting money for missions.[28] Still it is remarkable that such a small, barely surviving group already recognized the necessity of evangelistic outreach.

The obvious fact—often forgotten—is that this was a new church, but not a church of new Christians. These immigrant people had been born of the strenuous Afscheiding in the Netherlands. They came to North America bearing their earlier experiences as Christians and also an interest in missions.

Through earlier revivals, the nineteenth-century churches in Europe and North America had gained a strong spirit of outreach, a powerful feeling of obligation to bring the gospel to the ends of the earth. The first half of this century was an exciting period in Christian evangelism. New mission societies sprang up in Great Britain, North America, and also in the Netherlands. Missionaries were sent to begin work in China, East Africa, Japan, and other distant lands. Reports flowed back to the churches, interest was high, and enthusiasm was great.

The Afgescheidene Kerk in the Netherlands (from which these immigrants came) seems not to have engaged in mission work as a denomination until somewhat later, but many of its members supported the new mission societies. They were also children of the revival spirit. They shared in the enthusiasm generated by the great mission events of the era, and their zeal is reflected in the reasons the emigrants gave for their decision to leave their homeland. Originally—so the leaders of the movement wrote—

---

27. "Classiekale Vergadering Gehouden den 7 October 1857, te Vriesland, Staat Michigan," in *Minutes 1857–1880*, p. 1 (Art. 9).

28. "Klassikale Vergadering Gehouden den 5 Februari 1862, te Graafschap," p. 19 (Art. 5 and 6).

they had considered forming a colony in Java. The main aim of this colony would have been to serve as a mission center for work among the twenty-five million unbelievers in that land. But on discovering that the governmental opposition they were experiencing in the Netherlands would extend to Java and might even be intensified under the autocratic rule of the Dutch governor-general, they had resolved instead to go to North America. In that land of religious freedom and economic opportunity, they hoped to establish strong, free churches. As God gave opportunity, they intended to bring the gospel of Jesus Christ to native American peoples.[29]

Even though it was customary for emigrant groups to include some mission purpose in their charter—this was often a formal indication that they were moving to the new land for something more than mere economic advantage—this band of immigrants appeared to have had a genuine missionary spirit. Other writings by the same leaders mentioned missionary movements overseas, urged the sending of missionaries and Bibles throughout the entire world and expressed an earnest desire to share in this evangelistic task.[30]

Obviously all the immigrants did not share equally in such a mission vision, but certain of the leaders and some of the members did display enthusiasm for the mission of the church. It would be an error, therefore, to suppose that since this denomination was newborn, interest in mission outreach also had to develop from zero and naturally needed time to grow. Concern for evangelism was present in the CRC from the very beginning.

Characteristic of these early decades of CRC history was a sense of frustration in trying to find some adequate outlet for the evangelistic impulse. Mission was conceived as reaching unbelievers, heathen, and pagans in distant lands or distant parts of North America, with the gospel. Various ways to share in such work, despite limited resources, were discussed and weighed. Helping Christians in Syria was rejected since they were Roman Catholic.[31] Cooperative work with the RCA or another American group seems not to have been considered, probably because of insurmountable theological barriers. The CRC was too weak to do independent work. The only outlets were to send money to the Afgescheidene Kerk in the Netherlands to aid in their work of Bible distribution and to help a Reformed pastor in South Africa in similar work.[32] With so little

29. Anthony Brummelkamp and Albertus C. van Raalte, *Landverhuizing*, of Waarom Bevorderen wij de Volksverhuizing en wel naar Noord-Amerika en niet naar Java? (Amsterdam: Hoogkamer & Compe, 1846), pp. 22–23.

30. Anthony Brummelkamp, Johannes W. ten Bokkel, and Albertus C. van Raalte, *Nog is er Hulpe!* Een Woord aan al het Godvrezend Volk (Amsterdam: Hoogkamer & Compe, 1844), pp. 7–8.

31. "Classicale Vergadering Gehouden te Grand Rapids, den 6 February, 1861," in *Minutes 1857–1880*, p. 14 (Art. 7).

32. "Klassikale Vergadering Gehouden op den 6 Juny 1866, te Holland," in *Minutes 1857–1880*, p. 66 (Art. 18); "Klassikale Vergadering Gehouden te Vriesland, 12 December, 1866," in *Minutes 1857–1880*, p. 73 (Art. 17).

direct participation possible, it is little wonder that interest flagged and giving declined.

Some of the concerns and thinking regarding mission in the CRC at this time were reflected in the polemical writing of Frederikus Hulst.[33] This was part of the ongoing polemic between the CRC and the RCA, a reply to a critical evaluation of the CRC written three years earlier.[34]

Hulst expressed deep suspicions about the sort of evangelism carried on by the RCA. Even before the secession, some churches had objected to the circulation in the churches of the Dutch version of Richard Baxter's *A Call to the Unconverted*,[35] by Albertus C. Van Raalte and other ministers. Classis Holland had refused to accept these objections, replying that it found nothing unreformed in this evangelistic book. Yet Hulst argued that it was clearly Remonstrant, Socinian, and Pelagian.[36] Baxter would have his readers say to unbelievers, "The eternal God, who created you for eternal life, has saved you through his only Son." To Hulst, this was clearly unreformed. It even implied that people can save themselves if they so wish.[37]

In a later conversation Hulst answered a charge that the CRC does no mission because they lack in love and consider evangelism unrighteous. He denied this. The case of the CRC, he said, is like that of the Afgescheidene Kerk in the Netherlands during the first twenty years of its existence—the church was too small and weak to carry on mission work; its hands were too full with its own tasks for it to serve others. But at that time the CRC had begun both home and foreign missions.[38]

Characteristic of this earliest period of the CRC was an admitted obligation to be active in mission outreach. However, circumstances in the church had prevented such activity. The means were lacking, but not necessarily the concern. There was also a strong desire to be thoroughly Reformed in evangelism and to avoid any contamination from other methods and approaches. If concern for theological purity had hampered mission activity, it seemed not to have done so directly—at least there are no clear indications of this. But indirectly perhaps, by ruling out local

---

33. Frederikus Hulst, *Zamenspraak tusschen Jan, Pieter en Hendrik* over de "Brochure" der Ware Hollandsch Gereformeerde Kerk en de "Stemmen" van de Leeraren de Beij en Zwemer (Holland: C. Vorst, 1874), p. 19.

34. Bernardus de Beij and Adrian Zwemer, *Stemmen van de Hollandsch-Gereformeerde Kerk in de Vereenigde Staten van Amerika* (Groningen: G. J. Reits, 1871).

35. *Classis Holland, Minutes 1848–1858*, tr. by a Joint Committee of the Christian Reformed Church and the Reformed Church in America (Grand Rapids: Grand Rapids Printing Co., 1943), p. 144 (Art. 9), pp. 181–182 (Art. 13); Richard Baxter, *A Call to the Unconverted* (Philadelphia: Presbyterian Board of Publication, 1825). Dutch version entitled *Roepstem tot de Onbekeerden*, om Zich te Bekeeren en te Leven (New York: Amerikaansche Traktaat-Genootschap, no date).

36. Hulst, *Zamenspraak tusschen Jan, Pieter en Hendrik*, p. 19; Hendrik Algra, *Het Wonder van de 19e Eeuw*, Van Vrije Kerken en Kleine Luyden, Rev. ed. (Franeker: T. Wever, 1966), pp. 195–196, says there was a tendency to label anything that smelled bad, Remonstrant, and if it smelled particularly bad, Socinian.

37. Hulst, *Zamenspraak tusschen Jan, Pieter en Hendrik*, pp. 19–20.

38. Ibid., p. 110.

cooperative mission and limiting outreach to gifts for work carried on by others far away, this concern may have thwarted mission zeal.

Beginning in the third decade of its existence, the CRC began to take steps to initiate its own mission program. These first steps were faltering and often misguided. But while unsteady, the movement forward was persistent. There was a discernible drive in the church toward an independent, church-controlled outreach program.

In 1879 the first home missionary (itinerant preacher) was appointed. His work was among scattered Dutch immigrants. In 1880 a committee for foreign missions was organized. In 1889 the first CRC missionary to the heathen was installed (since this work was to be among American Indians, the designation *foreign* was changed to *heathen*). In 1892 Jewish missions began. In 1898 the decision was made to do home missions among "Americans"—if work among the Dutch people allowed. In 1911 a mission was started among Mormons in Utah. In 1912 the first urban evangelism began in Paterson, New Jersey. In 1918 Synod decided to open a foreign (overseas) mission field. And in 1920 the first three missionaries were sent to China.

Reading through church literature of this period, one is struck, first of all, by how much was being written about missionary activity. *De Wachter, The Banner, De Heidenwereld* (later, *The Missionary Monthly*) are full of stories of missionary experiences in Arabia, India, Africa, China, and Japan, or accounts of progress of work in these lands. Much of this was being done by the RCA and other denominations, but as the CRC work grew, accounts of its own work and letters from missionaries also increased. If interest is a criterion of mission zeal, and if writing in church periodicals is a sign of interest, then mission zeal was definitely not lacking. It could have been that such enthusiasm was limited to certain segments of the denomination, but if church periodicals are any indication, these segments were no minority.

Second, there appeared to be one persistent answer given to the perennial question, "Why should we do mission work?" That answer was, "Because Christ commanded it."[39] It is our duty to obey our Lord's clear directive. He sends us, so we must go. We pray with our lips, "Thy Kingdom come." We must certainly also work to bring in that kingdom of Christ throughout the entire world.

Other reasons for mission were given. Love should constrain us to feed these hungry souls. We should be sensitive to the millions going to eternity without hope of salvation.[40] Like the good Samaritan in Jesus' parable, we must have a heart for the suffering unfortunates and reach out a helping hand to them.[41]

39. Roelof Duiker, "Predik het Evangelie aan alle Creaturen," *De Wachter* 16 (Maart 22, 1883):3.

40. Ibid.

41. Berend J. Bennink, "Wat Moet Ons Dringen tot de Christelijke Zending?" *De Wachter* 12 (September 25, 1879):2–3.

But the primary reason which church leaders gave again and again was Christ's command and our obligation to obey it. Clearly that struck the most responsive chord. That was the motive for evangelism that seemed most fitting, most in keeping with Reformed theology and teaching.

The third general impression one receives is of frustration. Beginning its own work, the CRC encountered organizational difficulties and knotty questions. Who calls missionaries to their work, a local consistory or a board? Who supervises the missionaries' work? How are board members to be chosen? The church struggled through three different attempts to write a satisfactory mission order; the first in 1888,[42] the second in 1898,[43] a revision in 1902,[44] and the third order in 1912.[45]

The lack of volunteers for work was another major frustration. Whether because of halting English, a reluctance to leave the Dutch immigrant communities, or the lesser honor given missionary work in comparison to the pastorate, very few ordained men were willing to serve in a missionary capacity. At times, because of this lack, money given for missions had to be temporarily invested—a matter of some irritation to those who had contributed the funds. Overall the outreach program seldom progressed as planned, and even when evangelistic work was done, the response of those who heard the gospel was disappointingly slight.

Not surprisingly, these disappointments seems to have blunted mission zeal for a time. The later part of the nineteenth century and the first decade of the twentieth were comparatively low times in mission enthusiasm. Then, from 1910 on, there seems to have been a marked increase in interest, especially in overseas mission, an interest at the grassroots level that brought a bombardment of classical requests to synod. By 1916 Classes Grand Rapids East, Grand Rapids West, Holland, Muskegon, Ost Friesland, Hackensack, Hudson, and Zeeland all overtured synod to open a foreign field.[46] Synod appointed a committee, and four years later approved China as the new mission field.[47]

That decision was the culmination of long and varied discussion as to where the CRC should do mission work. The Synod of 1888 decided to begin work among the American Indians.[48] But when this work in South Dakota ran aground, suggestions were made to work among Negroes in

42. De Ridder, "Development of the Mission Order," pp. 42–58.

43. Ibid., pp. 59–75.

44. Ibid., pp. 76–80.

45. Ibid., pp. 88–99.

46. *Acta der Synode 1916* van de Christelijke Gereformeerde Kerk, Gehouden van 21 tot 30 Juni, 1916, te Grand Rapids, Michigan (Holland: Holland Printing Co., 1916), pp. 18–19 (Art. 25).

47. *Acta der Synode 1920* van de Christelijke Gereformeerde Kerk, Gehouden van 16 tot 30 Juni, 1920, te Grand Rapids, Michigan (Grand Rapids: M. Hoffius, Printer, 1920), pp. 49–51 (Art. 34).

48. *Synodale Handelingen* der Hollandsche Christelijke Gereformeerde Kerk in Amerika, Gehouden te Grand Rapids, Michigan, 13 Juni, en Volgende Dagen, 1888 (Holland: De Wachter Drukkerij, 1888), pp. 14–15 (Art. 39).

the south, or in Persia, and in conjunction with the United Presbyterian Church.[49] Other questions were raised and other possibilities discussed. Should we work among the Jews? How do we determine priorities in our mission? The discussions were often passionate and intense.

The Lord had commanded his disciples to preach his name "beginning at Jerusalem" (Luke 24:47). Classis Hudson took this to mean we must begin work among American Indians rather than overseas.[50] Beets argued that this passage means we should work among the Jews.[51] Later a supporter of home missions contended this phrase clearly indicates that we must resist the lure of the strange and unknown (foreign mission fields) and concentrate on working in North America, in the neighborhoods of our own congregations.[52]

In view of this considerable confusion, it is not surprising that there were some who were apathetic toward the mission program of the church.[53] Surprising is the swell of enthusiasm for an overseas field that pushed those in ecclesiastical authority into complying and beginning work in China.

The character and source of this enthusiasm, as well as some of the resistance to it, is quite clearly portrayed in an extended discussion about mission zeal found in the *Calvin College Chimes* in the years 1910 and 1911.

John E. Luidens, a college student and the so-called "organization editor" of the *Calvin College Chimes*, initiated the discussion. In his comments about various school activities, Luidens regretted the meager attendance at a recent lecture given by an RCA missionary from Japan. It seemed that only 44 students and 8 professors had been present (out of a student body of 160 and a faculty of 13). This indicated, said Luidens, what a marked decrease there was in enthusiasm for heathen evangelism at Calvin. Four years earlier there had been three mission societies on campus, with over 60 members. In 1910 there was only one society with a scant 12 members. Clearly, the spirit of mission at Calvin College was dying.[54]

The next issue of *Calvin College Chimes* had a letter from a recent seminary graduate, Lee S. Huizenga. From the medical school where he was preparing himself for possible missionary service, Huizenga applauded

---

49. De Ridder, "Development of the Mission Order," pp. 64–65.

50. *Acta der Synode* van de Christelijke Gereformeerde Kerk in Amerika, Gehouden te Grand Rapids, Michigan, June 17 tot 31, 1896 (Grand Rapids: Verhaar & Keukelaar, Drukkers, 1896), pp. 59–61 (Art. 125).

51. Henry Beets, "Waarom Doen Wij aan de Jodenzending?" *De Heidenwereld* 19 (September 1915):2–3.

52. J. Koert, "Waarom Inwendige Zending?" *De Wachter* 57 (3 September 1924):7–8; Abel J. Brink, "Onze Inwendige Zending," *De Wachter* 45 (1 Mei 1912):2, stated that some maintain that we should work among the heathen rather than scattered Hollanders, because heathen are in total darkness. But Brink argued that according to Romans 1:21 the pagan have some true knowledge which they have forsaken. The plight and guilt of covenant breakers is worse; they have had greater light, so now their state is more desperate for they receive a greater condemnation.

53. Bratt, "Missionary Enterprise," p. 96.

54. John E. Luidens, "Mission Meanderings," *Calvin College Chimes* 4 (1910):149–151.

the fact that someone at Calvin College had finally discovered how lacking the school was in mission zeal. This lukewarmness, he wrote, was directly attributable to the absence of mission study classes and lack of zeal among faculty and students. What was needed was mission study as a part of the regular curriculum, four missionary speakers scheduled each year, visits by faculty to the mission field, and earnest prayer for a revival of the mission spirit.[55]

But the next fall a dissenting voice came from one of the seminary students, Karl Wm. Fortuin. He criticized Luidens for making no clear distinction between the American mission spirit (with its dollar standard and methodistic ideas of why and how we should do evangelism) and the biblical approach (best expressed in Reformed principles). The difference between these two versions came to explicit expression in the motto trumpeted at recent evangelism conferences, "The Evangelization of the Whole World in This Generation." That motto, contended Fortuin, is a purely human fabrication, quite unscriptural. It is not framed in terms of the evangelistic command of the Lord to his dearly bought church; it is a methodistic, emotional urging of us to win souls for Jesus. It stresses not the Lord's command but the need of poor, blind heathen. Many students, said Fortuin, refuse to support such evangelism.

Finally, he added, one must remember that a true mission spirit comes not by human effort but as a gift of God's Spirit. We should not grasp at every method to instill such zeal. Instead we should pray God to send it to us.[56]

Luidens replied in the same issue. He inquired why Fortuin judged methodist evangelism to be entirely unscriptural and whether this meant that all their mission work was valueless. Does not obedience to Christ's command go paired with sensitivity to human wretchedness and need? Why did Fortuin contrast these? Why did he oppose the American missionary spirit to a biblical one?[57]

The next month Fortuin answered Luidens. The organization editor, Fortuin said, wrote from an anthropological standpoint. Consequently, he failed completely to grasp what was written from a theological (biblical) standpoint. This principial difference between them made a discussion like measuring potatoes in a gallon measure and oil in bushel baskets. There was no common ground for talking.

Evangelism, continued Fortuin, must be based on Jesus' command, and mission zeal must be measured by the degree of obedience to that command. Methodism talks of "winning souls for Jesus." But that is to read God's Word differently from the way in which the Reformed have learned

55. Lee S. Huizenga, "Mission-Symposium," *Calvin College Chimes* 4 (1910):204–206.
56. Karl W. Fortuin, "Zendingsgeest," *Calvin College Chimes* 4 (1910):257–260.
57. John E. Luidens, "Reply to 'Zendingsgeest,'" *Calvin College Chimes* 4 (1910):270–273.

to read it. All methodist missions are not valueless—God uses even the worst methods. But this difference in understanding does mean that we who are Reformed should not join with those who do evangelism in a methodistic way. The ends do not justify the means. Our evangelism must be done biblically, in the light we have received as Reformed people.

Fortuin admitted that some people ask, "How is it possible for church groups with little doctrine or virtue, in which religion is little more than socials, aid societies, and sabbath schools, to bring up the most mission dollars?" The answer must be that if they don't give out of a scriptural mission impulse, they do so for other reasons; to be high on the list of mission donors or to cover a lack in their own spiritual lives. No good fruit comes from dry trees.

True mission zeal, said Fortuin in conclusion, springs only from a soul that says, "This must be done for it is God's will." The purpose must not be "converting souls" but "obeying the Savior's command." True mission spirit comes only from the Lord's Spirit; else we wade in Pelagian waters.[58]

The following month, the *Calvin College Chimes* editor, Rienk B. Kuiper, entered the discussion. The widespread mission enthusiasm of this age, he said, is exemplified by the Student Volunteer Movement and the Laymen's Missionary Movement. These movements and the enthusiasm they generated has influenced also the CRC. Still, he added, "Everybody admits that our students on the whole do not manifest the zeal for the expansion of God's kingdom that might justly be expected of them." This is a sad state of affairs. "It is a patent fact then that we do not have as much mission zeal as we ought to have." He said this cannot be understood otherwise than as a lamentable disobedience of Christ's final command, "Go ye. . . ."

Our proper course, said Kuiper, is to pray God to arouse true mission interest among us. Yet that should not be one-sided. We must make use of every opportunity. We should both pray and work (*ora et labora*). Thus we need to form mission societies, study mission principles, invite outside speakers, in a word, do everything possible to arouse mission zeal in our school.[59]

Typically, the final word in this discussion came from a minister. The Reverend John Hiemenga's speech at the school was recorded in the *Calvin College Chimes* several months later. He began by quoting Herman Bavinck: "The twentieth century is already and will more and more become the age of mission." That spirit, said Hiemenga, has also entered our circles.

True, the Lord's command, "Go out into all the world," remains unchanged. And by God's providence we Calvinists have received the purest understanding of the gospel of Christ. This means, said Hiemenga, that we

58. Karl W. Fortuin, "Weder-antwoord," *Calvin College Chimes* 4 (1910):293–298.
59. Rienk B. Kuiper, "The Mission-Zeal Problem," *Calvin College Chimes* 4 (1910):339–342.

must do evangelism as Calvinists, for no one else should have more mission zeal and love.

On the other hand, we need to recognize that Calvin lived and wrote in a polemic age of strife with the Roman Catholics, a time of unrest. This led later to a dead orthodoxy against which Methodism reacted. We may never deny that Methodism in fact restored life to many dead branches. We must be honest in our criticisms.

Hiemenga quoted as examples of false criticism a teacher who, on being invited to the Laymen's Missionary Movement, said, "We must be careful to remain Reformed," and a brother who, during a discussion about arousing mission spirit at the last synod, remarked, "Careful, this matter comes from a dangerous source, the Laymen's Missionary Movement." But Bavinck, Hiemenga told the students, calls that movement a triumphant journey of the gospel.

We as Calvinists, continued Hiemenga, need not fear enthusiasm or a true spirit. To call anyone with zeal a methodist is to lose the holy fire of love and become lukewarm, like the church of Laodicea. Remember how the disciples were filled with the Holy Spirit and went out with zeal and love.

Hiemenga assured the students that no system of Christian thought is more powerful than Calvinism. If we are lukewarm, it is because we're not Calvinistic enough.

Yet it is a fact that of the 150 ministers who have graduated from the CRC's Theological School, only two are on the mission field. It is a fact that for years the board had searched for a third missionary and found no one. It is a fact that young people have been invited to train for mission work at denominational expense, and no one has volunteered. The reason may be that we are too Calvinistic in our own eyes, too Calvinistic in theory.

Calvinism, said Hiemenga, begins with God's sovereignty. If the Lord reigns, he rules also over heathen lands. We, as Calvinists, should see how the Lord has been opening up the whole world for the proclamation of his gospel. And we should, as obedient subjects of that Lord, be zealous to make him known and bring everyone into subjection to him.

Some label the present missionary spirit anthropological and warn against the Arminian goal of rescuing souls. They say, "We Calvinists have a higher goal—God's glory." But in actual fact, said Hiemenga, God is glorified when sinners are saved. And we Calvinists, if we are serious about directing all to God's glory, should proclaim the gospel to the whole world. We should do this with greater certainty than the Methodists because we know God rules over the whole world and that the outcome is assured.

The noticeable growth in mission interest within the CRC during the last two years, declared Hiemenga, is directly attributable to the Laymen's Missionary Movement and the Student Volunteer Movement. Their influence has led us to organize more mission societies, celebrate mission days, and give more for missions. Now, if we as a denomination would only put as much energy into mission as we do into lesser matters, if we would truly concentrate on fulfilling the Lord's command and going forth as he directed, we could accomplish much. The command is clear. The need of the heathen world is great. Our task is to respond as true Calvinists.[60]

This lengthy, frank exchange in the *Calvin College Chimes* helps one see several factors in this *lack of zeal* matter.

First, the new enthusiasm for mission originated outside the CRC. Contacts with other groups, with the missionary movements sweeping the American Christian scene, moved the CRC to show interest, give money, produce volunteers, and begin mission overseas. As in the early nineteenth century, so also in the early 20th, an enthusiasm moving through the Christian world also excited CRC people. They may have contended that the Reformed Christian should be most zealous for mission, that out of obedience to their Lord, Calvinists should be on the forefront of any evangelistic endeavors, but as a matter of fact the mission spirit came from outside the CRC.

One consequence of this outside source of zeal was that those in the CRC most "American," best at English, more open to contacts beyond the church community, tended also to be most infected with the new mission zeal. Those least "American," most Dutch in language and outlook, more limited in their contacts with broader Christian groups were least influenced. Although it proves nothing, it is perhaps indicative that in the *Calvin College Chimes* discussion those favoring greater mission zeal wrote in English, those opposed in Dutch.

Second, there appears to be a comparative factor in this mission zeal. Earlier this took the form of a contrast between RCA zeal and CRC lukewarmness. Beets, and other church leaders, used such a comparison to shame the church members into giving more for missions. Around 1910 the comparison was with the new missionary movements and the work being done overseas by various American denominations.

Some charged that such comparisons made for bad motives. As the Israelites demanded a king like the nations about them, so some in the CRC demanded a foreign mission field like other churches.[61] But this does seem to have been an undeniable part of the church's developing drive toward doing mission work.

Third, it is clear that this missionary impulse was quite emotional. It was enthusiasm, a burning interest, a consuming concern. Those possessed by this zeal showed little patience with those who did not share their feelings.

Fourth, the resistance by men like Fortuin was not against the missionary enterprise itself—at least not visibly so; how could it be when this was

---

60. John J. Hiemenga, "Calvinisme en Zending," *Calvin College Chimes* 5 (1911):122–132.
61. John C. De Korne, "The Missionary Impulse," *The Banner* 68 (1933):935, 942.

Christ's command—but against the methodistic enthusiasm of the missionary movements. Yet no clear theological arguments are presented against this enthusiasm. The resistance seemed to come from a distrust, a suspicion, an unwillingness to commit themselves to a movement with origins outside the Reformed tradition.

Viewing this entire period from 1857 to 1917 from a modern mission perspective, one is struck, above all, by the then current understanding of the church's mission task. The evangelistic outreach of the church appeared to be a secondary thing, almost peripheral to the true being of the church.

It was a zeal, an enthusiasm. Such mission zeal should grow out of the Christian faith, but it seems not to have been seen as intrinsic to that faith. It was a feeling added to faith, secondary to faith. It was a spirit in addition to the Holy Spirit, an extra gift of God's Spirit given to some. The church is urged to pray for mission zeal as if it were some added dimension, not an inseparable part of the Pentecost Spirit which empowered and irresistibly drove the church to proclaim the gospel of Christ.

At first consideration such emotionally conceived zeal seems poorly matched with the insistence that mission must be done in obedience to Christ's command. But a closer examination shows that the insistence on the centrality of the command of Christ enforces this same secondary rating of evangelism. Not to do mission is to lack in obedience, but it is not a failing in faithfulness to the Lord. First the CRC must be the true, the pure, the real church of Christ. It must hold and teach the truth God has revealed. Then it must obey Christ's directives. But not obeying (at least this mission directive) seems not to have put in question the truth, purity, and reality of the church's teaching. Not to go and disciple was evidently an excusable lack, an understandable shortcoming in the eyes of most CRC people.

The reason generally given for the very limited mission efforts of the CRC during its first sixty years is *lack of mission zeal.* This was the answer of most writers of the time and has been accepted by many modern commentators. Of course, other factors played a role in this slow development of the CRC's mission and in directing it overseas rather than toward neighborhood evangelism. But the most striking factor, if one were to be singled out, seems to be not *lack of zeal* but the common view of the church and its mission task. To be a true church meant to preserve correct teaching. Witnessing to unbelievers, both near and far, was a far second to this task of self-maintenance. It was such an understanding of the church and its mission task, rather than *lack of zeal*, that seems to have been the main deterrent to the CRC becoming more active in evangelistic outreach.

12

Observations on the Concept of the Antithesis[1]
Henry Stob

The Term

The term *antithesis,* derived from *anti* (against) and *tithemi* (to set) refers to two entities, moments, or principles that are set over against each other. The term connotes the idea of "opposition," and it embraces within its signification the whole range of polarities that stretches from "complementation" through "contrariety" to "contradiction."

I do not know who first employed the term in theoretical discourse, but it entered philosophy no later than Immanuel Kant, who used it to name the negative member of the antimonies of reason. The term was subsequently employed by Georg F. W. Hegel to name the second phase of the dialectical process through which the absolute comes eventually to full expression. According to Hegel, the logico-historical world process begins with the establishment of a thesis which, because of its limitations, evokes an "anti-thesis" which in its turn, since it too is limited, elicits the emergence of a "syn-thesis" wherein the partial truths of the thesis and antithesis are blended and transcended. The achieved synthesis then becomes a new thesis, from which the dialectical process mounts through an ensuing

1. This contribution, prepared for this Festschrift, was, while awaiting publication, presented as a lecture under the sponsorship of the Calvin College Philosophy department in Gezon Auditorium on March 23, 1982. In this contribution Henry Stob discusses the concept of the antithesis and its application in the Reformed tradition, particularly as discussions influenced the Christian Reformed Church and elicited debate within its own circle. Stob does not engage, therefore, in a description and analysis of the concept of the antithesis in other Christian or non-Christian traditions. Eds.

antithesis to a still higher synthesis, until at last the full truth is attained and the all-encompassing absolute is reached.[2]

The use of the term *antithesis* in theological discourse dates, as far as I can determine, from the post-Hegelian era. It appears not to have been used by John Calvin or by his seventeenth- and eighteenth-century disciples. It came into prominence, however, with the so-called Neo-Calvinism that arose in the Netherlands during the latter half of the 19th century. Guillaume Groen van Prinsterer and Abraham Kuyper popularized the term, but they did not accept its Hegelian connotations. Lifting it out of its correlation with an overarching synthesis, they used it, not in concert with, but against the then regnant idealism. They discerned that this harmonizing monism tended to reduce all contradictions to simple contrarieties, to erase all boundaries, and to reconcile all differences. Against it they posited the view that a vast gulf exists between Jerusalem and Athens, and that a commitment to Christ cannot be harmonized with a purely humanistic outlook on life. At an early age Kuyper entered the lists against the synthesizing modernism of his teacher Johannes H. Scholten and the ethicism of the mediating theologians, and he proclaimed with word and deed that a radical antithesis exists between those who do and those who do not live their lives out of obedience to Jesus Christ. And in so doing he believed himself to have the support of the gospel and also of the classical Christian tradition.

And so indeed he did. Even though the term *antithesis* was not at all, or only scarcely, employed by theologians before his time, the thing to which the term is applicable had been in the purview of religious thinkers for ages. Known to Christians from apostolic times was the fact that since the fall an unrelenting cosmic struggle has been going on between the forces of good and the forces of evil. For these Christians the source of their intelligence was the Bible. From the Sacred Scriptures they had learned that there is a real and uncompromising, although uneven, contest being waged between God and Satan, between Christ and antichrist, between the seed of the woman and the seed of the serpent, between the church and the world. As St. Augustine saw it, arrayed against each other in the world are two spiritual kingdoms whose mutual opposition is the very theme and keynote of the historical process. This it is that Kuyper recognized, and this it is which Reformed Christians standing in his tradition have since continued to affirm.

To understand the nature of this antithesis it is important to know how it arose. I propose, accordingly, to consider its origin.

---

2. I am indebted for some of these phrases to Thomas Greenwood, "Antithesis," in *The Dictionary of Philosophy*, ed. Dagobert D. Runes (New York: Philosophical Library, 1942), p. 14.

The Origin

John Milton, not without scriptural warrant, traced the antithesis back to a primeval insurrection on the part of rebellious angels. The Bible, however, is chiefly concerned with God in his dealings with mankind, and when it wishes to inform us of the origin of intracosmic strife it tells of a confrontation in an earthly garden. The drama is depicted in the third chapter of Genesis.

It is customary to focus on verse 15 of this chapter, and there are those who on the basis of this text declare that God is the author of the antithesis, since it is he who is there depicted as the sower of enmity among his creatures. Now, it is of course true that when God said to Satan (symbolized in the narrative by a serpent), "I will put enmity between you and the woman," he initiated a kind of offensive. But what is to be noticed is that he did not start the war; he launched a counter-offensive. His was a reactive move evoked by a prior attack on the part of his creatures. And what is especially to be noticed is that this counteroffensive was salutary, full of grace and mercy.

To read Genesis 3:15 aright, one must recall that in the beginning there was no enmity at all; a universal concord reigned. There was no estrangement, hostility, or dislocation. Part did not threaten part, the seamless fabric of life lay unrent, and the undivided cosmos knew nothing of antithesis.

The enmity that marred and fragmentized the world, and set up those evil oppositions and conflicts which are still a pervasive feature of our life was introduced not by God but by proud Beelzebub and by disobedient man. When the creature took up arms against the Lord, the universe was split and a cosmic discord reigned, a discord born of and marking the presence of sin. In that situation God stood on one side, and on the other stood the demons and the fallen human race indulging a vain and self-defeating hostility to the Lord of all. The creature warred against the creator, evil against goodness, darkness against light.

From this basic war there flowed, of course, a legion of lesser oppositions and tensions. Alienated from God, man soon found himself alienated from himself and from his fellows. Yet these disruptions, playing as it were on the surface of human life, did not obscure and could not destroy the deeper unity of the fallen race. On the surface mankind was at war with itself; underneath mankind was undivided in its hostility to everything divine. Its ranks were closed under Satan's unifying banner. A demonic cohesion held all its members together. Men were one in their bondage to Satan, one in their enmity to God.

It was then that God came into the forfeited garden and spoke the words that became the hope of the world. He said, "I will create a division between the Prince of Evil and the Mother of Men." These two had joined their lives and they neither could nor would disjoin them. With arms locked and hands clasped in the grip of death, they stood inseparable in their opposition to God, awaiting their doom. But then God came, and he said: "I will separate the inseparable. I will unclasp those frozen hands. I will unlock those interlocking arms. I will separate the mother of men from the prince of evil. The bond that unites mankind with evil I will loosen. I will shatter the solidarity of my fallen creatures. I will cause a division among them. I will assault the bastions of opposition and I will take captives for righteousness. Out of the united forces of evil I will recruit forces of goodness. I will pour out my Spirit upon men and call into being a new humanity to fight against the arch perverter. I will set righteousness against sin, light against darkness, love against hate, my Son against the father of lies. I will shatter sin with my grace. I will cleave and divide the mass of perdition with the rod of my mercy."

This promise God has kept. In the fulness of time he sent his Son. On Christmas day Christ came, and he came splitting and splintering the world, alienating men from Satan's kingdom and organizing them into a kingdom of his own that stands for everything good and true.

Now, the mystery of evil is great and by us impenetrable. I shall therefore make no attempt to solve the issue of its origin in terms of an eternal divine determination, an inexplicable and implacable fate, the presence of nonbeing in creaturely existence, or a limitless human freedom. Nor shall I attempt to solve the issue of its continuance in terms of Zoroastrian dualism, an eternal reprobative decree of God, or the supposed invincibility of the human will. But the fact is that, while some members of the human race have succummed to the blandishments of God and entered through grace into life, others refuse to heed God's peaceful overtures, and in continued alliance with the perverter remain steadfast in their alienation and rebellion.

And so it happens that the world of men stands in the token of antithesis. Across every natural distinction of race, color, sex, age, and position, there is a cleavage that separates men into two different and opposing camps. There are (as yet) the children of light and the children of darkness, the sons of Christ and the sons of Satan. There are two cities: the city of God and the city of the world, and they stand in basic opposition, for they serve different gods—the one, the true God, the other, the pretender. And that the pretender's claims are challenged—also by men—is God's gracious doing.

Let it then be said that the God of the Bible is the God of love who, though involved in the antithesis, is nevertheless out to banish strife and opposition and to secure unity, peace, and harmony. The good creation is God's thesis. The Satan-provoked fall of our first parents is humanity's antithesis to God's thesis. The gift of Christ and the gospel of redemption is God's move, not toward a Hegelian synthesis of thesis and antithesis but toward a reassertion and reestablishment of an historically enriched original thesis.

From a consideration of its origin it may therefore be concluded that the antithesis is for Christians less a principle to be applauded than a factor to be banished. To be with God is to be at bottom thetic, and to seek to remove from the world all that is antithetic. The antithesis, in short, is what the gospel is out to destroy.

Having indicated its origin, I now proceed to consider the locus of the antithesis, its seat in mankind.

The Locus

Man as Differentiated

The antithesis is rightly described as taking place between God and Satan, between Christ and antichrist, between angelic and demonic forces, or more abstractly between grace and sin. But however well Christians know that centrally it is the force of God's invincible grace that overcomes the world, and however much they appreciate the involvement of the heavenly hosts in the fight against depravity and sin, they are aware that they themselves must function as active and responsible participants in the ongoing struggle between good and evil. And they know that they must conduct the battle not only within themselves, where both the new and the old man have their seat, but also in the social arena where men and women of flesh and blood present themselves as adversaries of the gospel.

From these adversaries the Christian is separated by a unique and exclusive religious commitment. But he is also linked with them by natural ties, and he is involved with them in Adam's fall. Differing in their basic allegiances, Christian and non-Christian are indifferently creatures and sinners. This complex fact gives rise to several questions, two of which—one concerning differences and the other concerning identity—I shall consider.

The first question is: Under what aspect must the participants in the antithetical struggle be contemplated? How shall the parties to the strife be named, and by what terms shall they be differentiated?

First, it is possible to construct the antithesis in terms of election and reprobation, and a number of Reformed theologians are disposed to do so—among them such formative thinkers as Herman Hoeksema and Cornelius Van Til. By them the cleavage within mankind is conceived as being the result of a divine decree, and the opposing human groups are held to be best described as consisting of those who have and those who have not been divinely chosen for life and beatitude. This construction has the appearance of simplicity. A line is drawn that is anything but fuzzy; it is straight and clear, if for no other reason than that it is drawn, or thought to be drawn, by God himself. By it the race of men is cut cleanly— even absolutely—in two.

But in our attempt to construe the antithesis, are election and reprobation the most fruitful categories to employ, and can we by the use of them really sustain the biblical vision upon the human predicament? I hazard the opinion that we cannot.

The traditional doctrine of double predestination is itself a complex theological construct, the biblical basis of which is not clear at all. Of course, every Reformed person asserts that he owes his salvation to the elective love of God. He thereby clearly and gratefully acknowledges that he is saved by grace alone through faith. But he is not by this heartfelt profession bound to declare that God's redemptive love is restricted to such as he. And as for reprobation, a biblically oriented Reformed person will find it possible to believe that God, at long last, lets the unresponsive and recalcitrant sinner remain in his selfimposed exile; but he will find it impossible to deny God's loving and patient concern for the welfare of every sinner and his wellmeant offer of salvation to all.

Further, within the social arena which is the scene of the antithesis we are considering, the existential bearing and practical utility of the doctrine of double predestination is minimal at best. The terms *elect* and *reprobate* as traditionally defined have no verifiable denotation. They are oriented to the secret counsel of God and refer to people who are not identifiable. We do not know who the elect and reprobate are, and therefore cannot recruit them for concrete historical tasks. Moreover, considered simply under the aspect of election and reprobation, people have no specifiable characteristics. These terms refer to timeless decisions or attitudes of God, but not to creative or recreative acts that bring something into existence or alter what does exist in some ascertainable way. To construe the antithesis in terms of double predestination is, therefore, to give to that doctrine an abstract and unreal cast, and to put it within a framework in which no actual problems can arise.

Finally, when the antithesis is placed exlusively between elect and reprobate, one loses sight of the fact that the struggle takes place also within the Christian himself, for the old Adam in the Christian's bosom still wages war against the implanted and developing new creature in Christ.

Second, to call the classes between which the antithesis exists the regenerate and the unregenerate, as Kuyper was wont to do, is to view the matter less abstractly. It is to leave the eternal realm of the divine decrees and to enter the world of history, for regeneration, like the fall, does actually take place in time. Only, and this keeps regeneration from being in the fullest sense historical, it stands, as it were, on the border of time; it impinges vertically on only a single moment of it, or so at least Kuyper thought. It is, in his view, an instantaneous act, and not a process. It takes place once and for all, and that completely. Moreover, it does not happen, or does not necessarily happen, on the conscious level of existence. It is not essentially an experience. It normally takes place below the threshold of awareness. This means that until in repentance, conversion, and profession intimations are given of its occurrence, we do not know who is regenerate and who is not; we cannot tell with whom we have to do.

Third, it would seem better, therefore, to say that the antithesis is between believer and unbeliever, between those who have and those who have not, in fact, responded affirmatively to the gospel and to the Christ who is its center. By so doing we make the doctrine of the antithesis concrete and existential. We posit an antithesis, not between ideal or potential, but between real, individual, and therefore identifiable persons, who moreover, are yet in process and full of possibilities. This is, no doubt, a gain. It is a gain because, while losing nothing, we have seized upon a dimension of man's existence which may not be ignored. Nothing is lost, for there is preserved as cause and background of faith the instantaneous act of divine recreation and the mysterious counsel of God, while yet man is secured in his concrete actuality.

It must be observed that to regard the antithesis as existing between believers and unbelievers is to preclude the possibility of ever speaking of the antithesis as absolute without qualification. There is an absolute element in the antithesis indeed; of this election and regeneration are witness. But there is a relative element in it too; of this man's actuality is proof. In the concepts "believer" and "unbeliever" these two elements are inextricably combined.

On the one hand, to contemplate the believer merely as someone who happens to believe, and the unbeliever as one who happens to disbelieve, is to fail to see the absolute dimensions of human existence. It is to fail to see that Christian faith emerges, not as the actualization of a human possibility, but as the result of a divine operation in the heart; that this operation is effectual only in those who confess to have been smitten to their knees by a lover whose charms they were unable to resist; and that those so smitten are, in regeneration, radically renewed, and in that renewal differentiated at the very core of their being from those who do not yet believe.

On the other hand, to contemplate the believer merely as elect is to contemplate an abstraction. It is to hide from view, not only his remaining sin, but also the historical decision for Christ and the subsequent growth in this commitment without which he is not an actual Christian. By the same token, to contemplate the unbeliever under the aspect of reprobation is to contemplate one who is by definition beyond amendment, and to be under constant temptation to say things about him which cannot be said of any concrete individual, namely, that he exists outside the love of God, and is therefore without hope.

This brings us to the second question concerning the parties aligned in the antithesis: What do those who differ as believers and unbelievers have in common? Are there kinships and affinities between them? Although they are not of one mind and heart, is there that which yet binds them together in human solidarity?

Man as Undifferentiated

I do not know of any Christian who denies all affinity between believer and unbeliever, but I do know of some who deny that they can occupy neutral territory or hold something in common. The antithesis, in their view, excludes neutrality of any and every kind. I cannot endorse this view, but I can develop sympathy for it, because in its neighborhood lies a truth that no biblically-informed person would wish to deny, namely, that no one is, or can be, neutral with respect to Christ. One is either for him or against him, either joined to him or alienated from him. There is here no middle ground. The man in Christ must always and everywhere maintain his spiritual identity and give expression to it. By the same token the man outside of Christ is ineluctably involved in, though not necessarily locked into, his antithetical stance.

Yet this is not the whole story, for it seems plain that no antithetical confrontation or engagement can take place except in a common field and by the employment of similar resources. Since the devil is only a destroyer and not a creator, the cosmic arena and the human equipment required for the moral struggle between Christian and non-Christian must be provided for the rival combatants by none other than the Creator-God himself. And this is the fact that I now wish to discuss.

To understand man at all we must understand that it is not merely the fall, nor merely redemption, but also the creation that has gone into his making. By creation he is constituted man, by the fall he becomes a sinner, and by redemption he becomes a son of God. But through all the vicissitudes of time and history he remains a man. Although sin changes his direction, alters his affections, and perverts his values, it does not cancel his humanity. Conversely, grace pardons and renews the sinner and by perfecting his increated and residual nature resettles him upon his true and original self. This is but to say that underlying the antithesis, and making it possible at all, is a nature or constitution which is held in common and fully shared by the parties which are set against each other in the cosmic struggle. The physical, psychological, and mental powers given to man in God's creative act, and preserved by his common grace, are distributed indifferently to all, and neither belief nor unbelief significantly diminishes or enhances these natural powers, or alters their common operations.

Neither apostasy nor conversion alters the size, weight, or contours of the body. Nor do they affect the amount of its physical energy, the quality of its biological life, or the degree of its nimbleness and dexterity. Moreover, on the physical plain Christian and non-Christian are nourished by the same food, made ill by the same diseases, made well by the same medicines, sheltered by the same houses, clothed by the same fabrics, and the like. It is for this reason that they have a common stake in, and a shared concern for, the development of agriculture, medicine, architecture, and all the rest.

It is equally true that on the psychological level they respond to similar impulses, are moved by similar passions and affections, and are activated by similar attractions and repulsions.

The solidarity of human kind extends also into the realm of mind, where a shared reason makes it possible for Christians and non-Christians to engage each other in intelligible address, and to conduct meaningful dialogues and debates.

It has often been said that natural or unredeemed reason is perverted and depraved, and incapable of arriving at truth. There is a level on which such an assertion must be affirmed, but there are other levels on which it must be disallowed. The unregenerate mind is quite evidently not bereft of all truth, even though the truth it holds may be embraced within a false perspective. But that is not my point at the moment. I am particularly concerned at this juncture to declare that human thought processes are not uniquely affected by a change in the quality or status of the heart. Such a change does not alter a person's capacity for thought, his aptitude for analysis and synthesis, or his ability to follow an argument. We discover, accordingly, that the unbeliever can think, and think straight, for he is bound to and employs the established canons of logic. Both the Christian and the non-Christian regulate their thought and speech, and signify their intentions, by the same rules. They may thus be said to share a common reason.

Does the antithesis, then, neither affect the mind nor significantly qualify reason? The answer to that question is both Yes and No, depending on what is meant by "reason."

To get the actual situation in focus it is necessary to distinguish between ontological and technical reason. Ontological reason may be defined as a grasping and shaping organ that must conform to and be shaped by its object—the real. Ontological reason is a possession of each and every human being, but its grasp is not the same in all. By the conscientious use of this reason the unbeliever can be authentically informed with the proximately real. In spite of the fall, and in the absence of saving grace, mundane truths are within his reach. To acknowledge this one need only to observe the vast range of knowledge that unregenerate men have attained concerning intra-cosmic entities and relations. But there is a dimension of truth that is beyond his grasp, and there is an aspect of reality that either escapes his notice or is falsely conceived. He is unable adequately to know transcendent truth.

In the case of the Christian, however, ontological reason can be, and by grace is, informed by the ultimately real, i.e., by God and his special disclosures. God, in this case, insinuates Himself into the regenerate mind and heart through the spirit-induced human posture of humble receptivity called faith. The ontological reason of the "natural" man is unable to receive and be informed by this saving disclosure of the divine, since the natural man is by his as yet uncanceled fall alienated from God and faithlessly unopen to God's redemptive incursions. It must therefore be declared that natural reason, in the ontological sense, is unable—outside of regeneration and renewal—rightly to apprehend and assess the manifestations of God, since in its ultimate reaches it ineluctably (for want of faith) misconceives and misconstrues the really real. This is what is meant when it is said that natural reason is depraved and cannot reach or receive transcendent truth.

But there is beside the ontological reason which is directed toward being and the real, a human capacity called technical reason, which is directed toward the formation and ordering of ideas, and which enables man to think. It is the capacity to form concepts (S, P, Q), to relate these concepts to each other in intelligible propositions (S is P), and so to compose these propositions as to produce a valid argument (All S is P; M is S; therefore M is P). This capacity to proceed logically is native to mankind and is shared by men of the most diverse religious persuasions.

Being increated, and being chiefly concerned with formal validity as contrasted with material truth, technical reason has remained relatively unaffected by the spiritual condition of its possessors.[3] It can not rightly be characterized as depraved, for it is serviceable to good ends as well as bad. Like most aptitudes and skills it is neutral relative to the fundamental issues that divide mankind. As such it provides the common ground upon which Christian and non-Christian can meet in order, through rational discourse, to challenge each other's antithetical claims. Upon this shared ground radical differences of orientation and outlook can be fruitfully expressed and evaluated, for undergirding the discussion is the mutual agreement that, to be taken seriously, all rival claims must satisfy the formal canons of reason, that is, be internally consistent and externally coherent. Without this agreement no meaningful discussion can take place, and the antithesis cannot be articulated.

Remembering that ontological reason is oriented to truth, it may not be amiss at this juncture to note that in religious inquiries, and elsewhere as

---

3. "The formal process of thought has *not* been attacked by sin, and for this reason palingenesis works no change in this mental task. There is but one logic, and not two." Abraham Kuyper, *Encyclopedia of Sacred Theology*, Its Principles, tr. J. Hendrik De Vries (New York: Scribners, 1898), p. 159.

well, truth cannot be fully attained when reason is divorced from faith. In such inquiries faith both precedes reason and directs it toward true understanding in accordance with the well-known dictum, *Credo ut Intelligam.* On the level of technical reason, however, the roles of belief and understanding are, in one respect at least, reversed. Here understanding precedes belief, and is the precondition for its occurring at all. A statement to be believed must first be rationally intelligible. No one can believe a putative proposition which, in whatever language, is by the arbitrary juxtaposition of words or vocables unintelligible, as, for example, "'T was brillig and the slithy toves did gimble in the wabe," or "The ergwhat quanifles somewhat on the kumquat." Linguistic philosophers are right, as St. Augustine was before them, when they declare "We can't believe what you say until we know what you mean." Here, too, the antithesis rests upon the basis of a nonantithetical, universally shared, increated, and common grace supported rationality.

I have in this section been concerned, not to soften the sharp edges of the antithesis, but to indicate that in the society of men it is contextually conditioned by a residual solidarity, that it takes place within a common humanity, and that it is articulated within a shared universe of discourse. The fact is that the antithesis, at bottom, is between sin and grace. But sin and grace are adjectival; they modify creation. And the structures of creation persist. It is only as these structures remain intact and support and accommodate the clash of rival forces, that these forces can possess both the room and the instruments to exercise themselves against each other.

Why and how the creational structures and ordinances remain intact is a matter of some disagreement among Christians, and I shall here not enter into the dispute, except to remark that Roman Catholic thinkers tend to regard created nature, both human and non-human, as integrally exempt from the ravages of sin, and to restrict the effect of sin to the loss of the super-natural endowments (the *superadditum*) with which the human head of the created cosmos was originally engraced. Hoeksema, as I understand him, ascribes the continuance of the creation structures to the gracious providence of God, who preserves the world, not because he is in any sense gracious to the reprobate, but because the ingathering of the elect requires that history proceed apace. Most Reformed theologians hold that death and negation—the threatened consequences of the fall—were averted by the decision of God to be gracious, not only savingly to those who were effectually led to believe, but also culturally to the entire human race. While some Reformed theologians ground this common grace in the Christ event, others ground it in the loving nature and disposition of God which precedes the giving of his Son. Without entering into all the intricacies of this disputed issue, I range myself with the proponents of common grace.

Having considered the locus of the antithesis in the human agent, I now proceed to consider the setting of it.

The Setting

The Spatio-Temporal World

The setting of the antithesis—the context in which it expresses itself—is two-fold: the spatio-temporal environment by which human beings are surrounded, and the human community in which they are incorporated. In the next section I shall hazard a brief address to one issue arising out of the social complex. Here and now I wish to consider the world of things, not indeed as such—in all its complexity and specificity—but only in its relation to minds caught up in the antithesis. In focus here is the epistemological question: How and to what extent does the presence or absence of Christian faith affect the knowing process? Restricting the question even farther, I am wishing to inquire whether believer and unbeliever hold facts in common. This issue arises because some Reformed scholars—Van Til in particular—have contended that all known facts are interpreted facts, and thus subjectively qualified by the knower's categorical apparatus. Observing that Christians and non-Christians employ differing categories of interpretation, Van Til concludes that the facts they apprehend are importantly dissimilar.

To get a hold on this issue it is necessary to step back and inquire whether it is really true that believer and unbeliever differently interpret the world and differently construe the facts it presents. Let it be said then that I share with Kuyper, Herman Dooyeweerd, Van Til, and many other Christian thinkers the view that all knowledge is embraced at its edges by an all-encompassing *Weltanschauung*. This means that all apprehension and reflection takes place within a global perspective in terms of which the data of experience are thought-molded and fitted into a frame. I also agree that the shape of this philosophical perspective or totality-view is determined by what one regards or evaluates as crucially significant or most real. I further agree that this judgment and evaluation is made before the cognitive process properly begins. The point of view from which the world is surveyed is not theoretically determined: it is chosen. And, what is more, the choice reflects a religious decision. It is an act of faith.

It should be noted, too, that there are fundamentally only two choices available to man. One can view the cosmos from some point within the cosmos, or from some point outside it. To take one's stand within the cosmos is to absolutize the cosmos, more particularly some aspect of it. Here, as Dooyeweerd points out, are the origin of all the "isms" of immanentistic philosophy and the ground for their mutual incompatibility. To take one's stand outside the cosmos is, however, to see it for what it is—a creature made and framed by God and dependent for its being and meaning on his continuing care and governance. But to stand outside the cosmos, really to transcend it, is possible to creatures such as we are only as we are incorporated into Christ, the God-Man, and only as we allow ourselves to be instructed by his word.

The upshot of all this is that, philosophically speaking, Christian and non-Christian view, interpret, and understand the world in radically different ways. Because of perspectival differences the antithesis extends deep into the intellectual realm and significantly affects all theory.

What, then, of facts? Can they be held in common by the parties to the antithesis? Are facts shareable and shared, or are they not? As I have already indicated, Van Til, at least in some of his expressions, thinks that they are not, and I shall here set forth his view as best I can.

Van Til draws a line between two sets of people—the elect and the reprobate—and then allows the principles that control these people—the principles of grace and sin—to penetrate without reserve into the depth of every fact, so that no commonness is left and an absolute antithesis is set up within the confines of the minutest fact.

He begins his argument theologically. Christian belief, he points out, though it is born in a personal confrontation with the living Christ through the Holy Spirit, is also a wholehearted assent to certain propositions, and the firm embracement of certain ideas. Chief of these is the idea of a self-contained triune God, who has created all things according to an eternal preconceived plan, and who holds all those things in the grasp of his mind. Every fact, process, law, event in the world is therefore known by God. Every fact, process, law, event is also related to every other in a pattern of wholeness increated by God, maintained by his providence, and comprehended by his mind. No one of these things exists in isolation. None is out of relation. All are caught up into a vast system rooted in and held together by the infinite mind of God.

Does a man now wish to know a fact? The only fact he can possibly wish to know is a real fact, which means a fact within the God-ordained system, for there is no other fact. There are no brute facts. There are only God-interpreted facts, God-systematized facts. To know truly a fact, therefore, is to know it in that system. To regard the fact in abstraction from that system is not to know the fact at all, because its very factness is constituted by its existence in that system.

But to see the fact in that system one must know God, for God is the source, or the keystone of that system. To know God, however, as he requires to be known, demands special grace and special revelation. But this only the believer has. Only he possesses the key to the system. He does not, indeed, possess the whole system—for then he would be God—but he does have the key to it, and thus in principle he can know the facts as they are.

The unbeliever, on the other hand, does not know God as he requires to be known. And, not knowing God, he is a stranger to the system in which each fact lies imbedded, and by which it is defined. And, not knowing the system, he does not know the fact whose very factness the system constitutes and guarantees. The unbeliever, therefore, does not know any fact. If it appears that he does—if it appears, for example, that he know the color of grass, or that two times two is four—then that is appearance only. He does not mean by these expressions what the Christian means by them.

I find this construction somewhat too metaphysical for my taste, and I think that the conclusions drawn from it are insufficiently nuanced, but I am able to engender sympathy for Van Til's intention and to put a tolerable face upon his construction. If we grant, as I think we must, that Christians and non-Christians survey the world from radically different standpoints and consequently have antithetical totality views, can we consistently maintain that the facts as they are grasped and understood by each are nevertheless the same? Is it not rather the case that perspectival differences significantly qualify every fact? Do different perspectives not give quite different meanings to facts? Surely, we cannot assert that a given perspective is false and then allow that the facts embraced by it are correctly apprehended in their ultimate bearing; the perspective cannot but affect the reading of every fact within it.

This point is of particular significance for apologetics. Suppose I grant that an unbeliever can understand a given fact or phenomenon in its ultimate bearing, not indeed with completeness (which no man can) but yet with essential correctness. What follows? What follows is that I am left without any good reason for urging him to abandon his perspective. I then implicitly acknowledge either that there are not a number of different perspectives, which is false; or that among the various perspectives his is an accredited one, which is to betray the Christian claim. What follows, furthermore, is that the unbeliever is given every right to demand that whatever fact I further propose for his acceptance conform to the facts as he has interpreted them, that is, I have acknowledged the competency of the natural mind to be the judge of all truth.

What, then, shall be our verdict about facts? Are we to abandon the notion of objective factuality or facticity? I think not. We may confidently declare with Van Til that all apprehended facts are interpreted facts. We may grant that, as held, they are embraced and ordered within some perspective. But we will want to add that facts—particularly empirical facts—can be disengaged from their perspectival ties and transferred across perspectival lines. If this were not the case how could Christian and non-Christian learn from one another, and how could dictionaries, encyclopedia, and scientific textbooks be informative to all? To use a popular expression, facts are facts, and they are the common stuff with which every theorist deals. Basic assumptions and presuppositions doubtless affect the selection of facts, the arrangements of facts, the significance assigned to facts, and they even disclose facts otherwise hidden or obscure, but they do not create facts or in any way modify them. Facts constitute the currency of the realm of knowledge, and they are both distinguishable from and separable from the interpretative context in which, in any concrete instance, they are inserted.

I suspect that this escapes Van Til's notice because he consistently thinks in terms of a total system, and neglects or depreciates the role of scientific abstractionism. But it must surely be admitted that there are many systems arranged, as it were, concentrically, within any total system. A fact that falls within one or another of these smaller systems may be defined in terms of that smaller system, and when it is so defined it acquires a meaning from it which leaves unaffected the larger meaning which the fact has, or acquires, in the larger system.

Two and four, for example, are entities falling within the number system. They are defined by that system. By reference to that system their meanings may be determined. Two, for example, means: integer standing between one and three. Now, the only thing men have to do in order to acquire commonness of meaning is to refer a fact to a common system; and this is what we do in arithmetic, and this is why, in arithmetic, the Christian and the non-Christian always agree. In terms of the system two times two cannot but be four.

This does not mean that the Christian cannot, and ought not, refer two and four also to a larger system—the totality system which he has through grace—but it does mean that he is then interpreting the proposition not mathematically, but philosophically, in terms of the larger context which is the true locus of the antithesis.

What is true of numbers is true also of grass. What do we mean when we say that it is green? One may answer: When the believer says green, he means: God-created. When the unbeliever says "green," he means: self-existent or chaos-occasioned. True. But the unbeliever also means, when he says green: color which stands in a definite and specifiable place in the color spectrum, or: color which reflects light waves of a precisely determinable length. And this is what the Christian also means when he says green. This meaning the Christian and the non-Christian have in common because the phenomenon is referred to the same system for definition.[4]

And this referral is, I contend, both christianly permissible and cognitively necessary. It is only as the believer and unbeliever dispute about the same facts that they can dispute at all. Here, as elsewhere, all differences are grounded on agreements.

---

4. "... they [the Christian and the non-Christian] cooperate daily in even the most technical scientific research without pleading two sets of figures, two columns of data, and two separate truth-systems." Edward J. Carnell, *An Introduction to Christian Apologetics*, A Philosophic Defense of the Trinitarian-Theistic Faith (Grand Rapids: Eerdmans, 1948), p. 211.

There remains a word to be said about the antithesis as this has come to expression in the social thought and action of the Reformed community here and abroad. This being in itself a very large subject, and my present discourse having already reached the limits set for me, I shall comment, and that as briefly as possible, on only one of the many issues arising out of the Christian's involvement in the life of society. That issue concerns the effort to institutionalize the antithesis through the establishment of separate Christian power organizations.

Human Society

Kuyper taught that the antithesis bore directly upon the scientific enterprise, and he not only proclaimed this fact: he implemented it. In concert with scholarly colleagues he established next to the state-controlled seats of learning an independent Christian university in which evangelical insights could direct the pursuit of knowledge. But Kuyper was no academic recluse. He threw himself into the public life of the Netherlands, and believing with Groen van Prinsterer that the regnant ideas in contemporary culture stemmed from the atheistic and humanistic French Revolution, he and his associates launched an antirevolutionary movement which, set against the rising tide, aimed to reestablish Dutch society upon its ancient Calvinistic foundations. To this end he gathered his followers together in a Christian political party in which the gospel could be integrated with statecraft. He also fostered the creation of a Christian labor union in and through which the Marxist class struggle could be dampened or eliminated. He seems to have felt, moreover, that to maximize the Christian impact upon society separate organizations were needed in many other departments of life. His followers, accordingly, withdrew enmasse from existing institutions, and in course of time consolidated their forces in everything from Christian agricultural and cattlebreeding associations to Christian garden and checker clubs.

This concretizing of the antithesis, and the consequent polarization of society, was from the beginning opposed by segments of the Dutch evangelical community, and it was severely criticized in later years by Karl Barth and Emil Brunner, who thought it impious to identify the gospel with a humanly conceived and implemented social program. On the broad and populous North American continent there was also little disposition to follow the Netherlands experiment. The persistence of the Puritan tradition had minimized the impact of modern paganism upon American culture, and an embracement of the Judaeo-Christian value system in large segments of the population made unattractive an antithetically oriented compartmentalization of social existence. In the Christian Reformed Church the pietistically inclined children of the Afscheiding were generally disinclined to adopt Kuyper's method of articulating the antithesis, and those who had their roots in the Doleantie, after an abortive attempt to establish a Christian political party, were able to put into place no more than a small, weak, and generally ineffective labor union.

The influx of Dutch immigrants into the CRC after the World War II elicited a renewed interest in the cultural mandate, and the accompanying plea for concerted Christian action within the social arena brought again into focus the issue of separate Christian organizations. Around this issue a generally friendly, though sometimes animated, debate took place in the fifties and sixties. Into all the ramifications of this debate, which has fortunately run its course and come to rest, I shall not now enter. It should be remarked, however, that though some people in the church questioned the utility of antithetical organizations, no one, as far as I know, was in principle opposed to them.

I myself was drawn into the debate at one point only. I entered the discussion when I was confronted with the extraordinary thesis that it is Christianly impermissible to be a member of any social organization which in its constitution declines to profess the universal lordship of Christ and in its behavior gives scant heed to evangelical imperatives. Advanced in support of this surprising thesis were two claims: the culturo-historical claim that since the renaissance every non-Christian organization in the occident is the very embodiment of religious apostasy and thus pervasively anti-Christian; and the biblical claim that, since Christians are forbidden to sit in the seat of the scorners and join in the councils of the wicked, they are bound to eschew all organizational fellowship with non-Christians, and be institutionally separate everywhere.

My reply to the proferred thesis, and to the assertions advanced in its support, is on record and need not here be repeated.[5] I shall only remark that though persons, in keeping with the principle of the antithesis, are either for or against the Christ, and thus unable to escape into some neutral area, organizations can be, and in the West usually are, neutral with respect to religious commitments. Most of them are nonideological constructs established to achieve generally human goals. They are indeed not specifically Christian, but neither are they anti-Christian; they are simply non-Christian. They, like the entire planet on which they exist, provide a shared arena in which common human ends can be pursued from within different personal perspectives and out of different personal motivations. Into them Christians may blamelessly and fruitfully enter.

---

5. Henry Stob, "Christian Organizations," (As we see it) *The Reformed Journal* 13 (October 1963):4; Henry Stob, "Christian Organizations: Power and Strategy," *The Reformed Journal* 14 (March 1964):7–10; Henry Stob, "The Christian and neutral Organizations," *The Reformed Journal* 14 (May– June 1964):14–17. Shortened versions of these three above mentioned articles are entitled "Social Strategy: Christian power Organizations," in *Ethical Reflections*, Essays on Moral Themes (Grand Rapids: Eerdmans, 1978), pp. 196–206.

A word in conclusion will bring this presentation to an end.

In summation let it be said that I have attempted in the foregoing to indicate only two things: first, that though the Christian is by grace involved in the antithesis, it is his hope that by that same grace the antithesis will eventually be overcome; and second, that underlying the antithesis is a structured reality which is shared by all, and without which the spiritual struggle can not be carried on.

By way of exhortation I should like to remind myself and others that the grace-induced struggle that Christians are engaged in leaves no room for pride. It licenses no attitudes and sentiments other than humility, gratitude, and compassion. It demands, furthermore, that we do not lightly judge the allegiance of others. It also demands that we do not, in the illusion of self-sufficiency, separate ourselves from all intercourse with the rest of mankind and refuse to carry on with them the necessarily common business of our common world. It demands, above all, that we do not interpret the "enmity" that God has put as something calling for hate. Love is the rule of the kingdom, and it is by this alone that the divine thesis can and will be reestablished.

PART THREE

Studies in Ecumenicity

13

Ecumenicity in the American Setting

The Christian Reformed Church and the North American Presbyterian and Reformed Council

John H. Bratt

Although the isolationist mentality was strong in the early years of the history of the Christian Reformed Church in North America (hereafter CRC) the ecumenical spirit was not thereby excluded. In fact it was present very early. From the outset the conviction was present that there were other *bona fide* churches of Jesus Christ and it was our obligation to pursue close relationships with them. In 1884, only twenty-seven years after the founding of the CRC, the synods of the CRC and the Reformed Church in America (hereafter RCA) met in Grand Rapids at the same time. Fraternal greetings were exchanged and the delegate from the RCA speaking to the CRC synod expressed the hope that eventually those of Reformed principles on the American continent would unite.[1] The CRC responded favorably to the idea, union discussions ensued, and in 1888 the CRC agreed to unite with the western segment of the RCA. The latter refused to break with its eastern segment, however, and the negotiations were terminated.[2]

1. *Handelingen van de Synode,* Synodale Vergadering, Gehouden te Grand Rapids, Michigan, Juni 11–17, 1884 (Holland: De Wachter Drukkerij, 1884), p. 6 (Art. 11). *The Acts and Proceedings* of the Seventy-eighth Regular Session of the General Synod of the Reformed Church in America, Convened at Grand Rapids, Michigan, June, 1884 (New York: Board of Publications of the Reformed Church in America, 1884), pp. 460–461 (Art. V).
2. *Synodale Handelingen* der Hollandsche Christelijke Gereformeerde Kerk in Amerika, Synodale Vergadering, Gehouden te Grand Rapids, Michigan, Juni 13–21, 1888 (Holland: De Wachter Drukkerij, 1888), pp. 15–16 (Art. 40).

The CRC also had contact from 1888 on with the United Presbyterian Church of North America (hereafter UPCNA), a church which originated in a secession from the Presbyterian Church of Scotland in part at least because of government domination. Contact was natural not only because of similarities of origin but also because the UPCNA subscribed to the Reformed doctrinal standards. In 1888 the fraternal delegate of the UPCNA to the CRC synod, the Reverend W. T. Meloy, pleaded for union.[3] As a result each denomination named an exploratory committee. The UPCNA named her committee from members of the Presbytery of Detroit. Before the committees had even met, the UPCNA committee members with the entire Detroit Presbytery left the UPCNA on account of their disagreement with UPCNA handling of Freemasonry.[4] Union discussions were carried on, however, into the next decade, reaching their peak between 1894 and 1896.[5] These discussions finally broke down in 1898.[6] Throughout the discussions the UPCNA has been very cordial to the CRC. Its Lafayette College in Easton, Pennsylvania, granted a D.D. degree to Geerhardus Vos in 1893,[7] and its Westminster College in New Wilmington, Pennsylvania, granted a D.D. degree to Hendericus Beuker in 1897.[8] Long after the ecumenical contacts ended, the Muskingum College in New Concord, Ohio, gave a LL.D. degree to Henry Beets in 1911. This degree was largely bestowed in recognition of his services on the Psalm Revision Committee.[9]

One organic union, however, was effected. In 1890 the classis of the True Reformed Dutch Church united with the CRC.[10] This church had originated in 1822 when Solomon Froeligh and four ministers led a secession out of the RCA. By 1824 the True Reformed Protestant Dutch Church had two classes, Union and Hackensack. Gradually the two classes drifted apart. After some negotiations Classis Hackensack united with the CRC, thereby adding 13 churches, 5 pastors and 508 families to the rolls of the CRC.[11] In 1908 Classis Hackensack severed the connections, while three congregations stayed with the CRC.[12]

---

3. Ibid., pp. 8–10 (Art. 19).

4. Diedrich H. Kromminga, *The Christian Reformed Tradition,* From the Reformation till the Present (Grand Rapids: Eerdmans, 1943), p. 123.

5. John H. Kromminga, *The Christian Reformed Church,* A Survey in Orthodoxy (Grand Rapids: Baker, 1949), p. 107.

6. *Acta van de Synode* der Christelijke Gereformeerde Kerk in Amerika, Gehouden te Grand Rapids, Michigan van 15 tot 24 Juni 1898 (Grand Rapids: Verhaar & Keukelaar, 1898), p. 78 (Art. 99).

7. William D. Vander Werp, "Memorial Articles on Pioneer Teachers and Deceased Faculty Members," in *Semi-Centennial Volume,* Theological School and Calvin College, 1876–1926 (Grand Rapids: The Semi-Centennial Committee, Theological School and Calvin College, 1926), p. 98.

8. Ibid., p. 100.

9. John W. Brink, "A Recognition of Worth," *The Banner* 46 (1911):408.

10. *Synodale Handelingen,* der Hollandsche Christelijke Gereformeerde Kerk in Amerika, Gehouden te Grand Rapids, Michigan van 4 tot 12 Juni, 1892 (Grand Rapids: J. B. Hulst, 1890), pp. 14–15 (Art. 49).

11. "Classis Hackensack," in *Jaarboekje* voor de Hollandsche Christelijke Gereformeerde Kerk in Noord Amerika voor het Jaar 1891 (Holland: De Grondwet Boekdrukkerij, 1890), p. 28.

12. *Acta* der Synode van de Christelijke Gereformeerde Kerk, Gehouden van 17 tot 26 Juni, 1908, te Muskegon, Michigan (Grand Rapids: H. Verhaar, 1908), pp. 45–46 (Art. 67).

In the twentieth century, the CRC effected four ecumenical connections, two of which are still operative today. In 1918 it joined the Federal Council of the Churches of Christ in America (the predecessor of the National Council of the Churches of Christ in the United States of America). It did so for pragmatic reasons. The Federal Council of Churches was the only church body authorized by the government to place chaplains and camp pastors among the American soldiers engaged in World War I. The CRC was forced to join in order to be able to provide its quota.[13] Connections were terminated in 1924 on the ground that the Federal Council of Churches was dominated by liberal churchmen.[14] In 1943 the CRC joined the National Association of Evangelicals.[15] This was a loosely organized conservative association. It had a seven-point doctrinal basis with which the CRC could find itself in agreement. But when the National Association of Evangelicals began to assume prerogatives which the CRC attached only to the established church (e.g., engaging in revivals), and finding itself uncomfortable with the fundamentalist leadership, the CRC withdrew. This occured in 1951.[16]

In 1946 the CRC was instrumental in forming the Reformed Ecumenical Synod, an international synod which meets every four years.[17] In 1975 it played a key role in forming an association of five Reformed churches on American soil called the North American Presbyterian and Reformed Council (hereafter NAPaRC).

The formation of NAPaRC cannot be understood except against the background of the birth of the Presbyterian Church in America (hereafter PCA). The movement toward the forming of that new denomination began as far back as 1941 with the founding of *The [Southern] Presbyterian Journal,* a religious periodical which became the mouthpiece and the rallying point for conservatives within the Presbyterian Church in the United States (hereafter PCUS; Southern Presbyterian Church). Associated with the publication was the organization in 1942 of a loosely knit body called the "Committee for a Continuing Southern Presbyterian Church." It was concerned with the invasion of liberalism and erosion of basic doctrines within the PCUS, and dedicated its efforts to opposing union with the northern Presbyterian Church, the United Presbyterian Church in the USA

13. *Acta der Synode 1918* van de Christelijke Gereformeerde Kerk, Gehouden van 19 tot 29 Juni, 1918 te Grand Rapids, Michigan (Grand Rapids Christelijke Gereformeerde Kerk, 1918), pp. 40–43 (Art. 41).

14. *Acta der Synode 1924* van de Christelijke Gereformeerde Kerk, Gehouden van 18 Juni tot 8 Juli, 1924 te Kalamazoo, Michigan (Grand Rapids: Grand Rapids Printing, 1924), pp. 111–112 (Art. 95).

15. *Acts of Synod 1943* of the Christian Reformed Church in Session from June 9 to June 18, 1943 at Grand Rapids, Michigan (Grand Rapids: M. Hoffius, 1943), pp. 132–137 (Art. 202).

16. *Acts of Synod 1951* of the Christian Reformed Church in Session from June 13 to June 26, 1951 at Grand Rapids, Michigan (Grand Rapids: Christian Reformed Publishing House, 1951), pp. 77–79 (Arts. 147 and 151).

17. Occasionally voices were raised in the CRC agitating for joining the World Council of Churches. These voices never reached crescendo proportions. John H. Kromminga has written extensively on the World Council of Churches, exhibiting acuteness of analysis and penetration of insight.

(hereafter UPCUSA). As the possibility of that union seemed to fade, this organization disbanded and it was succeeded by a layman-inspired group, the "Concerned Presbyterians." It was organized largely through the effort of Kenneth Keyes and lay members on the board of *The Presbyterian Journal.* This was followed by the formation in 1969 of "Presbyterian Churchmen United," a group of conservative ministers within the PCUS who felt compelled to stand up and be counted as opponents of what they took to be alarming trends within the PCUS denomination.

The Presbyterian Churchmen United, concerned about continuation of historic Presbyterianism and faithfulness to ordination vows, issued in 1969 a "Declaration of Commitment" signed by five hundred minsters and called a rally in which one thousand more ministers signed the Declaration vowing to "strive to preserve a confessional Church, thoroughly Reformed and Presbyterian."[18] That rally also gave rise to the formation of an affiliate organization, the National Presbyterian and Reformed Fellowship (hereafter NPRF) in which some fifty conservative leaders in the Presbyterian and Reformed traditions banded together to "join for encouragement and mutual assistance those who seek in our time the unity of a pure witness to the Word of God and the testimony of Jesus Christ."[19]

Also connected with the movement towards formation of a new denomination was the "Presbyterian Evangelistic Fellowship," a dozen or so men who were engaged in evangelistic ministries. Four men from the latter group along with four each from Concerned Presbyterians and Presbyterian Churchmen United and four from the the board of *The Presbyterian Journal* (which took the initiative in this regard) constituted the "steering committee" for the formation of the new denomination. They met on "Journal Day," August 25, 1971, at Weaverville, North Carolina, and, despairing of reforming the PCUS, laid plans for a new church.[20] These plans crystallized in February of 1973, when the proposed Plan of Union between the PCUS and the UPCUSA was amended to remove an original provision which would have permitted conservatives to continue what they took to be a "pure" church. Then it was that representatives of the four groups voted to establish a new denomination that year. "The vote was taken in an atmosphere of prayer, and when the unopposed action was announced, there was much weeping mingled with quiet rejoicing. There was no turning back."[21]

The first General Assembly of the newly-formed National Presbyterian Church (the name was changed one year later to the PCA) was held in Birmingham, Alabama, December 4–7, 1973. Present at that first assembly were 338 commissioners representing some 260 churches and 40,600

18. "Declaration of Commitment," *The Presbyterian Journal* 28 (October 8, 1969):12–13.
19. "New Conservative Fellowship is Formed," *The Presbyterian Journal* 29 (January 27, 1971):4.
20. "Plans for Continuing Church Announced," *The Presbyterian Journal* 30 (August 25, 1971):4–5.
21. Paul G. Settle, "God's Instrument for Revival," *The Presbyterian Journal* 34 (May 14, 1975):7–8.

members.[22] In keeping with the confessionalism of the Reformed tradition, the Westminster Confession of Faith and the unamended Westminster Larger and Shorter Catechisms were adopted as doctrinal standards.[23]

Ecumenical outreach was projected early. At the second General Assembly held in Macon, Georgia, September 17–20, 1974, the interchurch committee of the PCA was instructed to establish "fraternal relations with the following churches, if the way be clear: the Associate Reformed Presbyterian Church (hereafter ARPC), the Christian Reformed Church, the Orthodox Presbyterian Church (hereafter OPC), the Reformed Presbyterian Church of North America (hereafter RPCNA) and the Reformed Presbyterian Church Evangelical Synod (hereafter RPCES)."[24] The committee carried out its mandate with dispatch, and representatives of the interchurch committees of these churches named met in Pittsburgh, October 25–26, 1974. Out of this meeting came a decision to the effect that the interchurch committees of each denomination name a delegation of two and "prepare a plan for cooperation and relationship of the respective churches and report to the joint committee within six months for possible recommendation to the parent bodies."[25] Less than a month later, these subcommittees met in Chicago. John H. Kromminga and John H. Bratt represented the CRC. It was decided to go the conciliar route and the CRC delegation proposed a structural model for NAPaRC, which was adopted in substance. That led to a plenary session held in Philadelphia, January 22–23, 1975, involving all interchurch committee members of all the churches (except the ARPC). Here some details were refined and the resultant plan was adopted. It was submitted to the parent bodies in June of 1975. The CRC[26], the OPC[27], the PCA[28], and the RPCNA[29] adopted the new ecumenical structure without reservations and the RPCES[30] adopted it on

22. *Minutes* of the First General Assembly of the National Presbyterian Church, Birmingham, Alabama, December 4–7, 1973 (Montgomery: The Committee on Christian Education and Publications, 1974), pp. 11, 235.

23. Ibid., p. 31.

24. *Minutes* of the Second General Assembly of the Presbyterian Church in America, Macon, Georgia, September 17–20, 1974 (Montgomery: The Committee for Christian Education and Publications, 1975), p. 76.

25. *Minutes* of the Forty-second General Assembly of the Orthodox Presbyterian Church Meeting at Geneva College, Beaver Falls, Pennsylvania, May 29–June 5, 1975 (Philadelphia: The Orthodox Presbyterian Church, 1975), p. 152.

26. *Acts of Synod 1975*, June 10 to 20, 1975, at Calvin College, Grand Rapids, Michigan (Grand Rapids: Board of Publications of the Christian Reformed Church, 1975), p. 24 (Art. 30).

27. *Minutes of OPC 1975*, p. 156.

28. *Minutes* of the Third General Assembly of the Presbyterian Church in America, Jackson, Mississippi, September 9–12, 1975 (Montgomery: The Committee for Christian Education and Publications, 1976), p. 114.

29. *Minutes* of the One Hundred and Forty-sixth Synod of the Reformed Presbyterian Church of North America, Geneva College, Beaver Falls, Pennsylvania, May 31–June 6, 1975 (Pittsburgh: Reformed Presbyterian Church of North America, 1975), p. 86.

30. *Minutes* of the 153rd General Synod, Reformed Presbyterian Church Evangelical Synod Held at Geneva College, Beaver Falls, Pennsylvania, May 30–June 5, 1975 (Lookout Mountain: Reformed Presbyterian Church Evangelical Synod, 1975), p. 171.

a provisional basis (later opting for full membership). Thus, NAPaRC was born in 1975.

The charter members of this newly-formed council are churches in the Calvinistic tradition which have a history of secession in their background, similar church polity, and kindred confessions. The largest of them, the CRC, with its 286,321 members and 688 churches,[31] was founded in 1857, and traces its roots to two 19th century secessions from the state church in the Netherlands for reasons of government intrusion in the affairs of the church and religious liberalism in the church. The second largest, the PCA, with 60,134 members, 21 Presbyteries, and 393 churches,[32] began, as noted above in 1973 as a protest against creeping liberalism in the PCUS. The third largest, the RPCES, with its 16,853 members and 141 churches,[33] is the result of a merger in 1965 of two other denominations, the Reformed Presbyterian Church of North America (General Synod) and the Evangelical Presbyterian Church, both of which had come into being as protest against encroaching liberalism in parent denominations. The fourth largest, the OPC, with its 15,098 members and 123 churches,[34] was founded in 1936 under the leadership of J. Gresham Machen and others in protest against the liberalism infiltrating the Presbyterian Church in the USA (now the UPCUSA). The smallest of the five, the RPCNA, with its 22,274 members and 159 churches,[35] which dates its beginnings in North America in 1952, is of Scottish Covenanter stock and had its background in the church's struggle for freedom from government domination in Scotland in the eighteenth century. All five churches in NAPaRC hold kindred confessions, the Presbyterians subscribing to the Westminster Confession with the Westminster Larger and Shorter Catechisms, while the CRC holds to the continental symbols of the Heidelberg Catechism, the Belgic Confession, and the Canons of Dort.

This similarity in backgrounds and the virtual synonymity of polity and doctrine makes for a distinct homogeneity that characterizes this quintet of churches. Allowing for such minor differences as are occasioned by the English rootage as opposed to the continental and minor differences that spring from reactions to the American environment, there is a unanimity of attitude and outlook that enables them to forge close bonds and work effectively for the advancement of the kingdom of God in North America.

---

31. *1975 Yearbook* of the Christian Reformed Church (Grand Rapids: Board of Publications, 1975), p. 84.

32. *1975 Yearbook* of the Presbyterian Church in America (Clinton: Office of the Stated Clerk, 1975), p. 195.

33. *Minutes of RPCES 1975*, p. 268.

34. *Minutes* of the Forty-second General Assembly, the Orthodox Presbyterian Church at Beaver Falls, Pennsylvania, May 29–June 5, 1975 (Philadelphia: The Orthodox Presbyterian Church, 1975), p. 214.

35. *Minutes* of the 152nd General Synod, Reformed Presbyterian Church Evangelical Synod held at Elizabethtown College, Elizabethtown, Pennsylvania, May 24–30, 1974 (Lookout Mountain: Office of the Stated Clerk, 1974), p. 236.

The formation of NAPaRC illustrates the "concentric circle" ecumenical pattern exemplified by John Calvin in the 16th century, that of negotiating with those closest to you in doctrine and in polity before approaching those who are further distant from you.

NAPaRC held its first meeting on October 31–November 1, 1975, in Pittsburgh. All five charter member churches were represented. In addition, the ARPC and the Reformed Churches in the US (Eureka Classis) sent observers. A constitution and set of bylaws was adopted. The purposes of the new organization were spelled out as follows:

1. Facilitate discussion and consultation between member bodies on those issues and problems which divide them as well as on those which they face in common, and by the sharing of insights "communicate advantages to one another" (*Institutes*, IV, 2, 1);
2. Promote the appointment of joint committees [later on the word *conferences* was added, JHB] to study matters of common interest and concern;
3. Exercise mutual concern in the perpetuation, retention, and propagation of the Reformed faith; and
4. Promote cooperation wherever possible and feasible on the local and denominational level in such areas as missions, relief efforts, Christian schools, and church education.[36]

The independence of the participating denominations was safeguarded by the statement: "It is understood that all actions and decisions taken are advisory in character and in no way curtail or restrict the autonomy of the member bodies."[37]

At the first annual meeting of NAPaRC held in Pittsburgh, October 31–November 1, 1975, a doctrinal basis was adopted affirming "... full commitment both to the Scriptures of the Old and New Testaments as the infallible Word of God and to their teachings as set forth in the Reformed standards."[38] In response to some requests for a strengthening of this basis, delegates to the second annual meeting held in Grand Rapids, October 29–30, 1976, made a few emendations and the new basis now reads "... full commitment to the Bible in its entirety as the Word of God written, without errors in all its parts, and to its teachings as set forth in the Heidelberg Catechism, the Belgic Confession, the Canons of Dort, the Westminster Confession of Faith, and the Westminster Larger and Shorter Catechisms."[39]

---

36. *Acts of Synod 1975*, pp. 353–354 (Report 14; Art. III of NAPaRC Constitution).

37. Ibid., p. 354 (Report 14; Art. IV of NAPaRC Constitution).

38. Ibid., 353 (Report 14; Art. II of NAPaRC Constitution).

39. *Acts of Synod 1977*, June 14 to 24, 1977, at Calvin College, Grand Rapids, Michigan (Grand Rapids: Board of Publications of the Christian Reformed Church, 1977), pp. 36, 375 (Report 14). It should be noted that the third annual meeting was held in St. Louis on October 28–29, 1977. See *Acts of Synod 1978*,

One of the early fruits of the formation of NAPaRC was greater knowledge of and deeper appreciation on the part of the member churches for each other as Reformed bodies. Prior to this point, very little (except for the OPC and the CRC) was known of each other and virtually no contact was experienced. Contributing to these new fruits of contact were the conferences and joint meetings of denominational agencies sponsored by NAPaRC.

The "Home Mission Agencies" of the five denominations met in Pittsburgh on May 12, 1977; in St. Louis on November 10 and 11, 1977; in Lookout Mountain, Tennessee, on April 12 and 13, 1978; in Grand Rapids on November 20 and 21, 1978; in Philadelphia on March 19 and 20, 1979; in Pittsburgh on April 29 and 30, 1980; and in St. Louis on April 23 and 24, 1981. The "Mission Executives Seminar" met three times in Pittsburgh, on November 28 and 29, 1977; on November 20 and 21, 1978; and on November 24 and 25, 1980. The "Foreign Missions Agencies" met twice in Pittsburgh, on November 22 and 23, 1976; and on November 28 and 29, 1977. Conferences on "Diaconal Ministries" were held in Pittsburgh on October 21 and 22, 1976; in Grand Rapids on October 6 and 7, 1977; in Lookout Mountain on October 4 and 5, 1978; and in Atlanta on October 2 and 3, 1979. A conference on "Race Relations" was held in Grand Rapids on March 24 and 25, 1977; a conference on "Theological Education" was held in Philadelphia on October 13 and 14, 1978, and a conference on "Offices in the Church" was held in Pittsburgh on October 20 and 21, 1977.[40]

In 1980 the Council commissioned a ten-man study committee, two men from each denomination, to make a thorough study of hermeneutics, the science of interpreting the Bible. It is expected to issue its completed report in 1983.[41] A *Denominational Studies Index*[42] was authorized by the second annual meeting of NAPaRC in 1976, in order to enable fellow members to take advantage of studies on crucial issues already made and a study of

---

June 13 to 22, 1978 at Calvin College, Grand Rapids, Michigan (Grand Rapids: Board of Publications of the Christian Reformed Church, 1978), p. 311 (Report 14). The fourth meeting was held in Philadelphia on October 27–28, 1978. See *Acts of Synod 1979*, June 12 to 22, 1979, at Calvin College, Grand Rapids, Michigan (Grand Rapids: Board of Publications of the Christian Reformed Church, 1979), p. 356 (Report 14). The fifth meeting was held also in Philadelphia on October 26–27, 1979. See *Acts of Synod 1980*, June 10 to 18, 1980, at Calvin College, Grand Rapids, Michigan (Grand Rapids: Board of Publications of the Christian Reformed Church, 1980), p. 318 (Report 14). The sixth annual meeting was held again in Philadelphia on October 24 and 25, 1980. See *Acts of Synod 1981*, June 9 to 19, 1981, at Calvin College, Grand Rapids, Michigan (Grand Rapids: Board of Publications of the Christian Reformed Church, 1981), p. 280 (Report 14). The seventh meeting was held in Philadelphia on October 23, 1981. See *Acts of Synod 1982*, June 8 to 17, 1982, at Calvin College, Grand Rapids, Michigan (Grand Rapids: Board of Publications of the Christian Reformed Church, 1982), p. 363 (Report 13).

40. The minutes of these committees are on file in the office of the Stated Clerk of the CRC, 2850 Kalamazoo Avenue, S.E., Grand Rapids, Michigan 49560.

41. *Acts of Synod 1981*, p. 281 (Report 14). Two study meetings were held, the first one in St. Louis on February 18–19, 1981, and the second one in Beaver Falls on August 17–18, 1981. See *Acts of Synod 1982*, p. 365 (Report 13).

42. *Acts of Synod 1977*, p. 374 (Report 14).

church orders of the five denominations was undertaken by Richard R. De Ridder of Calvin Theological Seminary. There is cooperation in various areas and more are in the planning stage. The PCA is engaged in a joint venture with the OPC in the use of the Great Commission publications for the Sunday School; the RPCES is sharing in the Christian Reformed World Relief Committee effort of the CRC; and the PCA and the RPCES hold joint administration of Covenant College, Lookout Mountain, Tennessee.

The most visible highlight of NAPaRC thus far has been the five-fold concurrent synods/assemblies held June 12–23, 1978, on the campus of Calvin College and Seminary. Two of the member denominations (the CRC and the OPC) had classical or presbyterial representation, while the other three had "grassroots" or congregational representation. Some 1,200 delegates were officially registered.

Even though each denomination conducted its own ecclesiastical business separately, there was ample occasion for Christian fellowship, conversational interchange and the forging of new friendships along with renewal of old ones. All in all, it was a tangible demonstration of the unity of the Church of Jesus Christ. In addition to the intermingling at meals, in the dormitories, and at the dessert socials on the campus lawn, there was interchange of speakers at the various denominational devotionals, and there was participation by members of all five denominations at the Sunday afternoon organ recital by John E. Hamersma, Professor of Music, Calvin College; at the women's luncheon meetings; on the scheduled tours to various places of local interest; at the NPRF breakfast meeting with John Perkins as speaker; and especially at the joint praise and prayer service held on June 19, 1978, with Joel H. Nederhood, The Back to God Hour radio speaker of the CRC, speaking on "The Christ-filled Church." An offering for world hunger was taken at that service. At the conclusion of this worship service, which was televised by The Back to God Hour for nationwide viewing, the moderators of the five major assemblies brought greetings from their respective denominations.[43] The success of this venture led to a decision to hold similar joint meetings in 1982.

The second of the concurrent synods/assemblies of NAPaRC was held June 15–18, 1982, again on the campus of Calvin College and Seminary. Some 1,800 commissioners and delegates, with the CRC and the OPC having Classis and Presbytery delegates and the other three "grassroots" representation, were officially registered.[44]

Two joint meetings were held. One highlighted the mission work of the five denominations on the North American continent and featured James Montgomery Boice of the Tenth Presbyterian Church of Philadelphia as speaker.[45] The second meeting reported the findings of a Hermeneutics

43. *Acts of Synod 1979*, pp. 354–356 (Report 14).
44. *Acts of Synod 1982*, pp. 365–366 (Report 13).
45. *New Horizons* 3 (August–September 1982):1, 3.

Study Committee that had been appointed a few years before. It had become apparent in the contacts of the five denominations that different approaches were being employed in seeking to get at the basic meaning of Scripture and that a unified approach would be a *desideratum.* The progress report showed substantial agreement in interpreting the Bible but also identified points of difference that merited further exploration.[46]

There were two significant actions and decisions taken at this second NAPaRC concurrent synods/assemblies. One, no doubt promoted by the interchurch contacts, was the organic union of two of the NAPaRC churches, the PCA and the RPCES. The process, called "Joining and Receiving," had been initiated by the PCA in 1980. Its General Assembly issued an invitation to the OPC, the RPCES, and the RPCNA to join with them in organic union.[47] The last-named, with its exclusive Psalms and no-instrument tradition, expressed continued interest in close ties but did not see fit to consider the invitation to organic union at this time.[48] The other two, through their broadest assemblies, gave initial approval.[49] The proposal had to be settled first on the presbytery level of the denominations involved. Majority votes were secured by both the PCA and the RPCES. The final decision now rested with the broadest assemblies of the two involved. Such was not the case however with the OPC. Its presbyteries did secure a majority vote but the proposal failed in the presbyteries of the PCA and that automatically terminated the negotiations between them.[50]

The other negotiations reached an affirmative terminal. In an historic meeting on June 13, 1982 the RPCES by a 78 percent vote at its 160th Synod relinquished its separate identity and decided to merge with the PCA.[51] Francis Schaeffer, a proponent of the merger, addressed the combined churches in a service of thanksgiving.[52] The RPCES brought in 187 established churches, 34 mission churches, 480 ministers, and 25,728 communicant members so that the expanded Presbyterian Church in

46. A. James Heynen, "Hermeneutics in the Heat," *The Banner* 117 (June 28, 1982):27; "Hermeneutics Report Leaves Questions," *The Presbyterian Journal* 41 (June 30, 1982):14–15.

47. *Minutes* of the Ninth General Assembly of the Presbyterian Church in America, June 15–19, 1981, Ft. Lauderdale, Florida (Decatur: The Committee for Christian Education and Publications, 1981), pp. 304–309 (Appendix M).

48. *Minutes* of the One Hundred and Fifty-second Synod of the Reformed Presbyterian Church of North America, Geneva College, Beaver Falls, Pennsylvania, June 6–12, 1981 (Pittsburgh: The Reformed Presbyterian Church of North America, 1981), p. 108.

49. *Minutes* of the Forty-eighth General Assembly of the Orthodox Presbyterian Church meeting at Beaver Falls, Pennsylvania, May 28–June 4, 1981 (Philadelphia: The Orthodox Presbyterian Church, 1981), p. 165; *Minutes* of the 159th General Synod of the Reformed Presbyterian Church Evangelical Synod held at Covenant College, Lookout Mountain, Tennessee, May 22–28, 1981 (Lookout Mountain: Office of the Stated Clerk, 1981), p. 65.

50. *New Horizons* 2 (December 1981):14.

51. "In Convincing Vote, RPCES joins PCA," *The Presbyterian Journal* 41 (June 23, 1982):4–5.

52. "It Was a New Beginning for the PCA," *The Presbyterian Journal* 41 (June 30, 1982):4–5.

America in 1982 registered 706 churches and 117,564 communicant members.[53]

The second significant event was the enlargement of NAPaRC by the accession of two denominations, the Associate Reformed Presbyterian Church and the Korean American Presbyterian Church. The former, which had originated in 1782 by union of American elements in the Associate church and emigrants from the Reformed Church in Scotland and now numbers 109 churches and 32,000 members, sponsoring Erskine College and Seminary as its educational institutions, had applied for membership shortly after NAPaRC was founded. Its application had been tabled due to tension within the denomination on views of Scripture and when that had been clarified and a high view of the Bible had been reasserted, it was voted by the charter members of NAPaRC to membership.[54]

So, too, the Korean American Presbyterian Church. This is a denomination of recent origin, consisting of emigrants from Korea and having its headquarters located in California. It has experienced phenomenal growth, starting in 1978 with 39 churches and 55 ministers and totaling 81 churches, 101 ministers, and 5300 members by 1982. It had sought fellowship with the NAPaRC churches since its inception and its application to membership in NAPaRC was approved by all of the charter members of the latter organization.[55]

This concludes the history of this young ecumenical organization which now comprises six denominations (including 1,949 churches and 470,983 members) that are committed to working together for the perpetuation and propagation of the Reformed faith. It has experienced the Lord's blessing and it bids fair to be a fruitful and rewarding avenue of ecumenical activity for the Christian Reformed Church in North America.

---

53. "RPCES Was Healthy Going into Merger," *The Presbyterian Journal* 41 (June 30, 1982):9; Cf. *The Presbyterian Journal* 41 (June 30, 1982):3.
54. *The Presbyterian Journal* 41 (June 30, 1982):7; *Acts of Synod 1982*, p. 364 (Report 13).
55. Ibid.

14

The Future of a Distinctive Dutch/American Theology in the Reformed Church in America and the Christian Reformed Church

I. John Hesselink, Jr.

Dear John: I am not a futurist by nature or inclination and heretofore have only lectured or written in this vein when requested to do so. The topic I am addressing here, however, is one which increasingly both concerns and fascinates me, and one which, I suspect, is of special interest to you. Hence I am initiating what I hope will be a dialogue on a subject of mutual concern even though I recognize how hazardous this kind of venture is, especially when I seek to analyze, evaluate, and prognosticate concerning theology on your side of the fence.

There is a certain virtue, however, in having outsiders—especially when the outsider is a close relative—evaluate one's situation, for they often bring a refreshing innocence or insouciance to the scene which delights and surprises, even if the judgments are sometimes superficial or one-sided.[1] An added peril is that even when I write about more familiar

---

1. I am thinking here of the fascinating series, "As Others See Us," run in *The Banner.* Martin E. Marty, "By a Lutheran Churchman," *The Banner* 114 (May 4, 1979):4–6; Duncan Littlefair, "By a Liberal Minister," *The Banner* 114 (June 1, 1979):8–9; Harvie M. Conn, "By an Orthodox Presbyterian Minister," *The Banner* 114 (July 6, 1979):4–6; Howard G. Hageman, "By an RCA Observer," *The Banner* 114 (September 7, 1979):4–5; Waldir Berndt, "A Brazilian Looks at the CRC," *The Banner* 114 (October 5, 1979):16; John M. Perkins, "President, Voice of Calvary Ministries," *The Banner* 114 (November 9, 1979):8; Cornelius Lambregtse, "By an Author-Designer and Bookstore Manager," *The Banner* 115 (May 9, 1980):10–11.

territory, i.e., theology in the Reformed Church in America (hereafter RCA), I am strictly on my own. I do not pretend to represent a consensus or even the considered judgment of my own colleagues at Western Theological Seminary (hereafter WTS). They represent probably as much diversity as you have on your own faculty, even though all of them—your colleagues and mine—are self-consciously Reformed and committed to the standards of unity which we have in common.

Before proceeding further, it may be helpful to define my terms. By "future" I do not intend to predict so much as to conjecture as to what the prospects are for a distinctive Dutch/American theology. Yet I admit a bias as well as a hope that such a theology will not only persist but also flourish. I assume that you share this concern even if not always in the same way and on the same terms. That assumption is based both on my personal perception of your lifelong work and efforts and also on your work, *In the Mirror,* your appraisal of the Christian Reformed Church in North America (hereafter CRC) on the occasion of its centennial.[2] You are not uncritical of your denomination and the way it has expressed its theology, but you come to the task with an obvious love for your heritage.

Another of your books, *All One Body We,*[3] deals primarily with the World Council of Churches but it also reveals your broader concern for the whole church of Christ.[4] Neither of these studies called for a discussion of the RCA or its theology, except in passing,[5] but my hope is that you share my desire for a more intentional common pursuit—more of a joint venture, if you will—of a uniquely Dutch/American theology which will be largely a product of the constituencies we represent.

It is much more difficult to define the larger and more difficult phrase: "a distinctive Dutch/American theology." Some people, above all those from within our constituencies, would deny there is such a thing. (More about that later.) Yet I maintain that despite all the diversity between and within our respective theological traditions, there is a discernible shape of a theology that finds its locus in Western Michigan. There are representatives of this theology in other geographical areas and places: in particular, New Jersey, Iowa, and the Toronto and Chicago areas; but the center of this theology is, and will probably continue to be, the Grand Rapids-Holland, Michigan area. This may appear to be an arrogant and parochial

---

2. John H. Kromminga, *In the Mirror,* An Appraisal of the Christian Reformed Church (Hamilton, Ontario: Guardian Publishing Co., 1957). As you note, however, in the first chapter on page 9, you do not attempt to give a history of your denomination but rather focus on "the events and developments of . . . the last decade of its first century."

3. John H. Kromminga, *All One Body We,* The Doctrine of the Church in Ecumenical Perspective (Grand Rapids: Eerdmans, 1970).

4. See Kromminga, *In the Mirror,* pp. 65–99, the third chapter entitled "One and Many."

5. References to the RCA, in fact, are almost nonexistent even in the earlier work. One of the few is found on pp. 136–137 in connection with the centennial celebration. The reason for this may be that the focus is on the last decade and also on the relationship of the CRCs in Canada.

judgment, but the fact remains that the complex of Calvin College, Calvin Theological Seminary (hereafter CTS), Hope College and Western, plus the heavy concentration of RCA-CRC churches in this area and the fact that the two denominational journals, *The Church Herald* and *The Banner*, are both published in Western Michigan—all this, as well as having the CRC headquarters in Grand Rapids, adds up to an impressive and formidable concentration of educational, ecclesiastical, and theological power in a very limited area.[6]

The result, I maintain, is a discernible *Weltanschauung*, if not a theology, which, despite all its limitations and vagaries, frequently elicits the unsolicited admiration of theologians from other areas and traditions who have visited this area and have experienced this theological/ecclesiastical ethos. It may be impossible to define in precise terms but it can be perceived, yea, even felt!

Many years ago, for example, the prominent Southern Presbyterian theologian, William Childs Robinson, exclaimed after spending some time at WTS, "You have no idea what power you have here."[7] More recently Professor Thomas F. Torrance of Edinburgh, after a week's visit in this area in which he had contact with both college and both seminary faculties, commented: "Nowhere else in Europe or North America have I found such a consistent theological concern which so thoroughly informs all aspects of your thinking."[8] The late Calvin scholar, Ford Lewis Battles, also testified to the joy and stimulus he found in working at CTS, a new environment for him shortly prior to his untimely death in 1979.[9]

I have experienced similar reactions in most varied circumstances. Two illustrations should suffice. When I first started teaching at Tokyo Union Theological Seminary in Japan in 1961, the president at that time, Hidenobu Kuwada, approached me soon after my arrival and said, "You Dutch Reformed missionaries have a great tradition here in Japan. I knew many of your prewar missionaries; they were conservative, sound, and able."[10]

6. One should also not overlook the impact of the three major publishing firms in Grand Rapids: Baker Book House, Wm. B. Eerdmans Publishing Co., and Zondervan Publishing House, in addition to Kregel Publications. Although the first three of these firms were founded by CRC laymen, their editorial policies range from fundamentalist to ecumenical. Nevertheless, all of them in varying degrees have favored and promulgated CRC–RCA writers and projects. An auxiliary enterprise of Eerdmans, viz., the publication of *The Reformed Journal*, also exerts an influence far beyond its modest subscription list.

7. During an informal colloquy at M. Eugene Osterhaven's home in 1955.

8. Introductory remark made before his final lecture at WTS, March 19, 1981.

9. Ford Lewis Battles, a Congregationalist (United Church of Christ), who had taught at Hartford Theological Seminary and Pittsburgh Theological Seminary prior to coming to CTS as a visiting professor of Church History together with his wife Marion, joined the CRC shortly before his death in November 1979. He testified earlier to some of his colleagues at Calvin that coming to Grand Rapids was like a homecoming and gently chided his CRC friends for appreciating far too little the riches of their heritage as he experienced it in the scholarly community at Calvin College and Seminary and in the quality of preaching and worship in local churches. See John H. Kromminga, "Ford Lewis Battles: An Appreciation," *The Banner* 114 (December 28, 1979):6.

10. Hidenobu Kuwada was too young to have known well some of the first RCA missionary giants

Exactly ten years later when I first met the late John T. McNeill, for many years the dean of American Calvin scholars, in the library of the University of Chicago Divinity School, I received a similar response. After identifying myself and mentioning that I had studied under M. Eugene Osterhaven (who had assisted him in the publication of John Calvin, *Institutes of the Christian Religion* in the Library of Christian Classics series, he responded: "O yes, I know your church and Western Seminary. You people have something very special and solid which I admire."[11]

It may be difficult to describe adequately what these people admire in us, some of which is not theological as such but more of a type of commitment or life style. Nevertheless, I shall attempt this later in this contribution. Here I simply want to point out that we have something in this area, something common to both our traditions, which I am convinced is worth preserving and perpetuating, and that something is at bottom more theological than ethnic, although the latter is no small factor.

In order to facilitate what I hope will be an ensuing dialogue and discussion and in order to sharpen the issues I shall develop my theme by stating and elaborating six theses. Some of these are major, others, minor; but I shall not distinguish between them. The first three deal with the past and present; the last three portray a possible future scenario. There is a certain natural order in the progression—at least in my mind. I may have missed some important factors, but this should at least spark some discussion and no doubt some dissent as well. The theses are as follows:

1. There is a distinctive Dutch/American Reformed theology which has its roots in Western Michigan.
2. There always has been and will continue to be a theological pluralism within this Calvinistic context.
3. This distinctive theological approach cannot be separated from its ethos and piety.
4. The shape of this theology will continue to be nourished and influenced by its Dutch Reformed theological roots and heritage but it will increasingly address itself to ecumenical and American issues and concerns.

---

such as Guido F. Verbeck, nor would he have had much contact with the great Albertus Pieters, whose career in Japan was spent on the southern island of Kyushu, but he did have extended contact with many of the RCA missionaries who taught at Meiji Gakuin University in Tokyo and Ferris Girls School in Yokohama prior to World War II.

11. The great work of John T. McNeill, *The History and Character of Calvinism* (New York: Oxford University Press, 1954), was written before he knew Osterhaven of WTS. He refers briefly to the founding of New Brunswick Theological Seminary, New Brunswick, New Jersey (p. 350), but neither WTS nor CTS are mentioned. He does note, however, that Abraham Kuyper and Herman Bavinck had their CRC followers in this country, viz., Louis (mistakenly called D.) Berkhof and Cornelius Van Til (p. 430); and among English periodicals which espouse the Reformed viewpoint he cites, *The Calvin Forum* (1935–1956) which presents "what is regarded as an undeviating Calvinism" (p. 432).

5. The character of this distinctive Reformed theology will be more classical and evangelical and less parochial and polemic than in the past.
6. If a distinctive Dutch/American theology is to flourish and be influential in the coming decades, there must be increasing dialogue and interchange between CRC and RCA scholars and institutions.

Thesis 1

There is a distinctive Dutch/American Reformed theology which has its roots in Western Michigan.

At the outset it may be necessary to remind my readers that "Western Michigan" here refers primarily to the Reformed academic institutions which are located in Holland and Grand Rapids: Hope College and Western Theological Seminary in Holland, Calvin College and Calvin Theological Seminary in Grand Rapids.[12] Much theologizing, of course, in both the RCA and CRC takes place outside these institutions, so this thesis does not intend to suggest that this distinctive theology can be limited to a specific locale. Rather, the designation "Western Michigan" should be viewed as representative of a certain type of Reformed theology which both denominations have in common. Hence it might be better to call this a "neo-Dutch/American theology," since it transcends geographical boundaries.

This thesis would be challenged by some people who would maintain that theologically our diversity is greater than our unity and that it is unrealistic to speak of one theology which we have in common. There is indeed great diversity, of which we are both painfully aware, and this will be dealt with in my next thesis. Nevertheless, I think a strong case can be made for not only a common basic theology which our two traditions

---

12. To those who are not familiar with the Western Michigan scene it should be pointed out that the relationship between Hope College and WTS is a much looser one than that which exists between CTS and Calvin College. The former two, after a brief period of coexistence following their founding in 1866, have been completely separate institutions though on adjoining campuses. Both are related to the RCA but the college is not under the direct control of the church as is the seminary. Moreover, roughly since the end of World War II over half of the students have been from non-RCA backgrounds and the professors represent a wide variety of ecclesiastical backgrounds. In addition, there have been two other RCA colleges, Central College, Pella, Iowa, and Northwestern College, Orange City, Iowa, the former being almost as old as Hope, and thus RCA influence was more fragmented than in the CRC which until fairly recently had only one college and one seminary, both of which are operated by one board. Dordt College, Sioux Center, Iowa, was founded in 1955, Trinity Christian College, Palos Heights, Illinois in 1958, The King's College, Edmonton, Alberta, in 1979, and Redeemer College, Hamilton, Ontario, in 1982, thereby diverting a portion of CRC students who in years past would in most cases have gone to Calvin. It should be kept in mind that WTS's impact on the RCA does not quite correspond to that of CTS's in the CRC because again there is more decentralization. I am referring to our older sister, New Brunswick, which will celebrate its 200th anniversary in 1984 (the oldest theological seminary in North America with a continuing history). New Brunswick, though older, is also smaller—and attracts a more ecumenical student body. Consequently, currently approximately two-thirds of the active ministers are WTS graduates.

share but also a certain outlook, a *Weltanschauung,* a world and life view, which we have in common.

This should not be too surprising in view of certain givens which are incontrovertible. The first of these is our common historical and theological heritage. We both trace our roots to the Reformed Churches in the Netherlands. The plural—"churches"—is important because many people in both denominations—to the extent that they are aware of our ties with the Netherlands—assume that the RCA has its origins in and principle ties with the Nederlandse Hervormde Kerk, often considered the liberal state church, whereas the CRC exclusively relates to the Gereformeerde Kerken in Nederland (hereafter GKN), Herman Bavinck, Abraham Kuyper, and the Free University at Amsterdam.

What is often overlooked is that the immigrants who settled in Holland, Michigan, (and Pella, Iowa) were in many cases also the sons of the schism in the Netherlands.[13] Although the CRC came to tie its fortunes more and more exclusively with the GKN[14] and the Free University, both have contributed in various ways to the life and thought of the RCA, particularly in the Midwest. The GKN also regards the RCA as a sister church and the Free University has official ties with WTS.[15]

More important, from the beginning until the present we have shared the same three confessional standards: the Belgic Confession, the Heidelberg Catechism, and the Canons of Dort. Although the forms of subscription vary slightly, in both churches those seeking ordination must affirm their adherence and loyalty to these three standards of unity. I realize that many CRC ministers and lay people think that we do not take these standards very seriously, but I suspect that gap (to the extent that there is one) is narrowing, at least in the Midwest. Not only that, I counter the occasional criticisms of some of our (i.e., Western Seminary's) conservative critics that we no longer teach and promote our standards as seriously as in the alleged "good old days" with the contention that in recent years there has been more stress on Calvin, our standards, and our Reformed heritage than when I was a student at Western (1951–53) or when my father attended Western (1921–24)! Consequently, whatever the differences in emphasis and accent may have been in the first half of our century, today

13. See Arie R. Brouwer, *Reformed Church Roots,* Thirty-five Formative Events (New York: Reformed Church Press, 1977), pp. 110–118.

14. With the formation of the Reformed Ecumenical Synod in 1946, certain official ties were established, apart from direct church to church relationships. The RCA and the Nederlandse Hervormde Kerk, on the other hand, were linked together through their membership in the World Alliance of Reformed Churches.

15. This is not to deny that until very recently the ties between CTS and the theological faculty of the Free University have not been much closer. Whereas the RCA has had only two of its theologians receive their doctorates from the Free University (Winfield Burggraaff in 1928 and William Goulooze in 1950), while many graduates of CTS have done graduate work at the Free University.

the graduates of both our institutions share a similar training in the same confessions.

We are also inheritors of a common piety, both in its Dutch origins and in its contemporary Americanized modified form. Those early immigrants who settled in Western Michigan, in Iowa (especially the Pella area), and later in Illinois (the Chicago area), Wisconsin and further west represented various strains of Dutch church life and thought, but many of them were pietists[16] and some of this distinctive Dutch piety continues to influence our theology today despite the inroads of American evangelical piety. Here is a piety which is quiet and subdued, usually hesitant and restrained in speaking of one's faith, but at the same time warm, confident and caring. This is combined with a profound reverence for God, a delight in worship, a love of the Scriptures and of good theology. At its worst it degenerates into a virtual fatalism and legalism, but at its best it produces that fidelity and solidity so often admired by others.

A new type of evangelical piety, secularism (some would say Americanization!), a dispersion of once fairly solid ethnic enclaves, and the acids of modernity (e.g., Sunday afternoon professional football games) have made inroads, but something of the old Dutch/American Calvinistic piety perseveres and this colors our theologizing more than we may realize.

Thus far few people would deny a common heritage and outlook, but I submit that there is much more that we have in common. Because of space limitations I shall simply list twelve such characteristics (in addition to the Calvinistic Dutch heritage and three confessional standards held in common):

1. A deep piety without the usual trappings of pietism.
2. A theological approach to life and an appreciation of doctrine, the life of the mind, and education.
3. A growing appreciation for our liturgical roots.
4. A reverence for the Lord's Day and a loyalty to the church (despite difficulties with the evening service).
5. A high view of preaching and a love of solid doctrinal preaching, although popular evangelical piety is taking its toll here (witness the big crowds that turn out on Sunday nights to hear the leading Christian vocalist or ensemble in the area!).
6. A strong sense of God's sovereignty and providential care (with an increasing questioning of decretal theology and double predestination).
7. A high regard for the law—especially its third use, as a norm and guide for the Christian—with a diminishing legalism.

16. See Eugene P. Heideman, "The Descendants of Van Raalte," *The Reformed Review* 12 (March 1959):33–42. On the nature of this Dutch pietism see further M. Eugene Osterhaven, "The Experiential Theology of Early Dutch Calvinism," *Reformed Review* 27 (1973/74):180–189.

8. An evangelical commitment and concern which extends to the cause of Christ around the world.
9. A concern not only for the church but also for the wider causes of the kingdom including social justice.
10. A continuing appreciation for the confessions without an attendant confessionalism.
11. A hermeneutical approach to the Scriptures which hinges on the key of the one covenant of grace.
12. A due regard for the Reformation principle of *sola Scriptura* along with a concern for *tota Scriptura*.[17] (Thanks to its hermeneutical approach, the unity of Scripture and the significance of the Old Testament are esteemed as in few other traditions.)

The person who has no personal knowledge of our tradition may find it difficult to ascertain what makes this list of characteristics so distinctive. However, it is in the combination of these characteristics, together with many intangibles, that this theology/ *Weltanschauung* is unique and different from an Orthodox, Southern, or United Presbyterian approach.

Thesis 2

There always has been and will continue to be a theological pluralism within this Calvinistic context.

When I speak of a theological pluralism I am referring not only to separate strains and distinctive emphases which divide our two communions, but also to those varieties and types within the CRC and RCA. Henry Zwaanstra, for example, in his very helpful dissertation *Reformed Thought and Experience in a New World*,[18] distinguishes between "three distinct minds or mentalities" which were present in the CRC from 1890 to 1918. The first of these he designates the Confessional Reformed mind. This group was critical of Kuyper's theology and particularly his social and political activity in the Netherlands. A second group is called the Separatist Calvinists. Their distinguishing mark was "their unqualified conviction that under any and all circumstances Christian and Calvinstic principles demanded separate Christian organizations and independent action in all areas of life."[19] These separate Calvinists were the most Kuyperian of the

17. See Fred H. Klooster, "The Uniqueness of Reformed Theology, a Preliminary Attempt at Description," *Calvin Theological Journal* 14 (1979):32–54. ". . . the question of *sola scriptura* calls for attention to *tota Scriptura* at the same time; not only 'Scripture alone' but also 'the whole of Scripture,' the entire canon, is at stake" (p. 39).
18. Henry Zwaanstra, *Reformed Thought and Experience in a New World*, A Study of the Christian Reformed Church and Its American Environment 1890–1918 (Kampen: Kok, 1973).
19. Ibid., p. 69.

three groups. The third group were the American Calvinists. They wanted to remain loyal to Calvin's principles but on American terms. According to Zwaanstra, at the end of this period they were the dominant party in the church.[20]

It would be foolhardy for me to try to describe the various mentalities or types of Calvinism that exist within the CRC today. From my knowledge of the denomination I would guess that instead of three different types or minds it would be possible to distinguish a half dozen or more. This, in any case, is also true of the RCA.

In the first edition of a syllabus for a mini-course entitled "On Being Reformed,"[21] in which I deal with this theme by considering twelve misunderstandings of what it means to be Reformed, I point out in passing that even within the RCA it is not at all easy to decide what it means to be Reformed today. I then point out that I perceive approximately ten different types within the Reformed Church, all of whom would claim the title "Reformed." Examples of these types are: traditional orthodox, i.e., scholastic Reformed; neo-Calvinist, i.e., those who are particularly influenced by Kuyper; "classical" Reformed, i.e., those who go back to the confessions and skip for the most part the developments of later Presbyterian orthodoxy or Dutch neo-Calvinism; Calvinian, i.e., those who find their inspiration primarily in Calvin rather than in the confessions; neo-Orthodox, i.e., those who interpret the Reformed confessions through the eyes of Karl Barth and other more recent so-called "neo-Orthodox" theologians; the van Ruler school; the Latitudinarians, i.e., those who are not confessionally minded but still appreciate Reformed polity and the Reformed tradition broadly interpreted; and the political activists, i.e., those whose concerns are not so much doctrinal as ethical and practical. This does not exhaust the list because the RCA has within it its own special American brand of Calvinism in the person of and approach of Robert H. Schuller, minister of the Garden Grove RCA, Garden Grove, California!

Some of these types are obviously to be found in both communions, but some I have just listed are peculiar to the RCA. On the other hand, a certain type of Kuyperianism has always been much stronger in the CRC than in the RCA and more recently the influence of Herman Dooyeweerd and the Association for the Advancement of Christian Scholarship (hereafter AACS) have grown in the CRC to the extent that now Toronto can be said to be one of the theological bases of the CRC.

I know the CRC situation well enough to know that the AACS was very divisive at Trinity Christian College and later at Dordt College. I also recall vividly the devastating attack by the editor of *The Banner,* Lester R.

---

20. Ibid., p. 70.
21. To be published later this year by Servant Books in Ann Arbor, MI.

De Koster.[22] I have the impression, however, that a more irenic spirit now prevails and that gradually and quietly the influence of this movement—perhaps with some necessary modifications—has found growing acceptance not only in the CRC in Canada but also at Calvin College. One evidence of this is the growing influence of Professor H. Evan Runner, partial evidence thereof being the Festschrift recently contributed in his honor, *Hearing and Doing,* Philosophical Essays Dedicated to H. Evan Runner.[23]

You also have within your church your more progressive wings and the impatient young Turks (and some not so young!) as well as the traditionalist die-hards and those who are convinced that the foundations have been irreparably shaken, if not destroyed. Thus within our respective denominations as well as between our two traditions there are countless shades and varieties of Calvinism and understandings of what it means to be Reformed. All this pluralism and variety notwithstanding, there is still, I maintain, a fairly solid and discernible main core of Reformed understanding and belief. It is on this centrist position, much of which is common to both of us, we must build, and therein, I feel, lies our mutual hope.

Thesis 3

This distinctive theological approach cannot be separated from its ethos and piety.

The fact that I describe this distinctive theology or tradition as Dutch/American and sometimes located in Western Michigan in particular indicates that the ethos and theology cannot be separated. I have also tried to describe the piety which is characteristic of Dutch/American Calvinists, particularly those whose origins are in the Midwest.

Some would bemoan the fact that there is this peculiar and limited ethos and piety. In our circles we sometimes hear the charge or complaint that we are too insular or parochial; and some of our more "progressive" types feel that they must be liberated from the constraining influence of

22. Lester R. De Koster, "Tour of Cosmonomia," *The Banner* 109 (February 22, 1974):4–5; Lester R. De Koster, "Bird's-eye View of Cosmonomia," *The Banner* 109 (March 8, 1974):4–5; Lester R. De Koster, "Who Starts the Fire?" *The Banner* 109 (March 15, 1974):4–5; Lester R. De Koster, "'Spheres' Anyone?" *The Banner* 109 (March 22, 1974):4–5; Lester R. De Koster, "Sphere-sovereignty Ideology: Neither Biblical nor Reformed," *The Banner* 109 (March 29, 1974):4–5; Lester R. De Koster, "And Now, 'So What?'" *The Banner* 109 (April 19, 1974):4–5; Lester R. De Koster, "Ideology and the Law," *The Banner* 109 (April 26, 1974):4–5; Lester R. De Koster, "Tour's End . . . ?" *The Banner* 109 (May 3, 1974):4–5; Lester R. De Koster, "A Summing up and Turning Forward," *The Banner* 109 (August 30, 1974):4–5. Cf., the more irenical evaluation by Nicholas P. Wolterstorff, "The AACS in the CRC—Will It Guide Us or Divide Us?" *The Banner* 110 (January 3, 1975):13–15, (January 10, 1975):18–20, (January 17, 1975):12, 21.

23. John Kraay and Anthony Tol, eds., *Hearing and Doing,* Philosophical Essays Dedicated to H. Evan Runner (Toronto: Wedge Publishing Foundation, 1979). In 1981 a second Festschrift was presented to him entitled *Life is Religion,* Essays in Honor of H. Evan Runner, ed. Henry Van der Goot (St. Catharines, Ontario: Paideia Press, 1981).

Western Michigan Calvinism. Some of this is understandable. Nor is this spirit limited to Western Michigan. Many of the same attitudes and customs can be found in Pella and Sioux Center, Iowa, or in Lynden, Washington! I should also add immediately that I do not condone or enjoy the petty legalisms and the denominational smugness and arrogance that is all too pervasive in certain areas where the two Reformed churches dominate.

Nevertheless, there is a strength here and that indefinable solidity which have given birth to and continue to inspire this distinctive Reformed theological understanding and approach. I seriously doubt whether the theology and churchmanship which has evoked admiration from so many different quarters would flourish without this kind of environment and support system. If so, one cannot help but conjecture as to what CTS would be like if it were located in Denver and WTS in Cleveland.

One must also face the fact that Grand Rapids may not always be "Jerusalem" for the CRC. What has happened to the RCA in the East could well happen to both the RCA and CRC in the Midwest. We see evidences of this already in what has transpired in Chicago where areas like Englewood and Roseland once supported large and strong RCA and CRC churches, where hardly one congregation exists today. The change that has taken place in Grand Rapids is not yet as radical; but just as the majority of RCA and CRC churches fled from Chicago to areas like South Holland, Illinois, and points further south and west, there may well be a similar exodus from Grand Rapids as RCA and CRC churches locate in towns like Jenison and Hudsonville, Michigan.

What this will mean for our denominations I dare not say, but it does mean that certain power centers will be broken up and the locus of power and influence may move from places that are now considered bastions of Dutch/American Calvinism. My contention is, however, that if the ethos and piety which have characterized our area for over a century become so diluted that they cannot be distinguished from the general American spirit—whether evangelical or liberal—it will be difficult to sustain a distinctive theology.

Thesis 4

The shape of this theology will continue to be nourished and influenced by its Dutch Reformed theological roots and heritage but it will increasingly address itself to ecumenical and American issues and concerns.

If this theology which I extol and promote is to continue, flourish, and make a real impact upon the American scene, it must not cut itself off from its distinctive Dutch heritage. That means in the first place continuing to plumb the riches—though not uncritically—of our Dutch confessions, viz., the Heidelberg Catechism, the Belgic Confession, and the Canons of Dort. Too often they have been used as apologetic battering rams against foes, imagined or real, both within and without. If we truly believe that our confessions must always be subservient to Scripture then we will continue to raise questions about certain expressions, if not even certain points of doctrine that are found in our confessions.

This will mean on occasion a gravamen such as the one recently submitted by Harry R. Boer in relation to the doctrine of reprobation as found in the Canons of Dort.[24] Or the questioning may take a quieter form as is found in "Our Song of Hope," the contemporary confessional statement in the RCA written by Eugene F. Heideman.[25] As Heideman himself puts it: "'Our Song of Hope' has also given much attention to the use of the words 'election' and 'righteousness' in the Old Testament. As a result, one can feel considerable tension between 'Our Song' and the Canons of Dort in the understanding of 'election' and between 'Our Song' and the Heidelberg Catechism in the use of the word 'righteousness'"[26] Interestingly, among the various criticisms which have been leveled against "Our Song of Hope," no one to my knowledge has taken up this challenge seriously. It should be pointed out in passing that Heideman is indebted to his former Professor of Old Testament, Lester J. Kuyper, for his understanding of righteousness, and that in the CRC an attack on the traditional understanding of predestination, as devastating if not more so than Boer's, has been produced by James Daane, the CRC scholar who retired from teaching homiletics at Fuller Theological Seminary, Pasadena, California, and recently passed away. I am referring to his book, *The Freedom of God.*[27]

Above all, we should maximize the use of that "jewel of the Reformation" which is also a part of our heritage, namely, the Heidelberg Catechism. Although this theological classic is German, not Dutch, in its origin, it is utilized and appreciated more in Dutch Reformed circles than anywhere else. However, it did receive considerable attention in Germany on the occasion of its 400th anniversary in 1963.

Ironically, in the United States more was done to commemorate this anniversary in the RCA and in churches of German Reformed background than in the CRC. In the RCA a special commemorative commentary was

24. Harry R. Boer, "Confessional-Revision Gravamen," in *Acts of Synod 1977,* June 14 to 24, 1977, at Calvin College, Grand Rapids, Michigan (Grand Rapids: Board of Publications of the Christian Reformed Church, 1977), pp. 665–679.

25. *Our Song of Hope,* A Provisional Confession of Faith of the Reformed Church in America, with Commentary and Appendixes by Eugene P. Heideman (Grand Rapids: Eerdmans, 1975). "Our Song of Hope" was adopted by the 1978 General Synod of the RCA as an approved contemporary statement of faith but one lacking the authority of the catholic creeds or three standards of unity, see The *Acts* and Proceedings of the 172nd Regular Session of the General Synod, Reformed Church in America, Convened at Columbia University, New York, New York, June 12–16, 1978 (Grand Rapids: Dickinson Press, 1978), pp. 36–37.

26. Heideman, *Our Song of Hope,* p. 87.

27. James Daane, *The Freedom of God, A Study of Election and Pulpit* (Grand Rapids: Eerdmans, 1973). One of the sharpest critiques of this book came from Daane's long-time friend, Osterhaven. He felt that Daane went overboard in rejecting decretal theology and in effect undercut the whole doctrine of predestination. See Osterhaven's review in *Reformed Review* 27 (1973/74):151–154. A less critical review written by Philip C. Holtrop is found in *Calvin Theological Journal* 10 (1975):208–220.

commissioned and published by the denominational headquarters, *Guilt, Grace and Gratitude,* edited by Donald J. Bruggink.[28] The nine contributors are all RCA ministers and professors, six of whom eventually taught at WTS.

Bard Thompson, a church historian who formerly taught at Lancaster Theological Seminary, Lancaster, Pennsylvania, was instrumental in collecting and publishing *Essays on the Heidelberg Catechism.*[29] The four contributors were Thompson himself, Hendrikus Berkhof of the Nederlandse Hervormde Kerk, Eduard Schweizer of the Swiss Reformed Church, and Howard G. Hageman of the RCA. The United Church Press also published a new translation of the Heidelberg Catechism in 1963, this being a joint effort by Allen Miller of Eden Theological Seminary, St. Louis (also of German Reformed background), and Osterhaven of WTS.[30] In addition, the United Church Press published the English translation of a French Swiss Reformed pastor-scholar André Péry.[31] During the celebration year the efforts of the CRC were rather modest.[32] The most significant contributions were a collection of sermons on the Heidelberg Catechism written by a number of Canadian CRC ministers and a new translation of that catechism by a synodically appointed committee which was approved by the CRC Synod of 1975.[33]

Recently, however, the CRC has made up for any previous lack in this regard by publishing the splendid study of the Reformed creeds and confessions designed for lay people, namely, *A Place to Stand,* by Cornelius Plantinga, Jr.[34] Here for the first time all three of our standards are considered together and in a way which is both understandable and relevant to lay Christians. This is also a model of relating our specific Dutch

28. Donald J. Bruggink, ed., *Guilt, Grace, and Gratitude,* A Commentary on the Heidelberg Catechism Commemorating Its 400th Anniversary (New York: The Half Moon Press, 1963).

29. *Essays on the Heidelberg Catechism,* by Bard Thompson, e.a. (Philadelphia: United Church Press, 1963).

30. *The Heidelberg Catechism.* 400th Anniversary Edition, 1563–1963. Tr. from original German and Latin texts by Allen O. Miller and M. Eugene Osterhaven (Philadelphia: United Church Press, 1962).

31. *The Heidelberg Catechism with Commentary.* 400th Anniversary Edition, 1563–1963. The Commentary is a translation by Allen O. Miller from French edition by André Péry (Philadelphia: United Church Press, 1963).

32. See Thea B. Van Halsema, *Three Men Came to Heidelberg* (Grand Rapids: Christian Reformed Publishing House, 1963); Edward J. Masselink, *The Heidelberg Story* (Grand Rapids: Baker, 1964). These are both brief, popular accounts.

33. *Sermons on the Heidelberg Catechism* (Grand Rapids: Board of Publications of the Christian Reformed Church, 1970); "The Heidelberg Catechism," in *Ecumenical Creeds and Reformed Confessions* (Grand Rapids: Board of Publications of the Christian Reformed Church, 1979), pp. 7–63.

34. Cornelius Plantinga, Jr., *A Place to Stand,* A Reformed Study of Creeds and Confessions, Bible Way (Grand Rapids: Board of Publications of the Christian Reformed Church, 1979). This volume is a part of the Bible Way series. A most helpful sequel to this volume was published in the same series, Cornelius Plantinga, Jr., *Beyond Doubt,* A Devotional Response to Questions of Faith (Grand Rapids: Board of Publications of the Christian Reformed Church, 1980). Here Scripture and Confession are joined together in the context and personal issues and dealt with in a devotional manner. Another contribution to this cause has been a fresh translation of all three standards.

Reformed heritage to American issues and concerns. It should be noted in passing that this book has found almost as much of a response in RCA churches as in CRC, as is true of many of the other publications in the Bible Way series.

When I speak of our theological roots, however, I am thinking not only of our three confessional standards but also of the great theological tradition that is part and parcel of our theological makeup in the United States. Pride of place must be given to those two theological greats who so dominated the theological landscape in the Netherlands in the late nineteenth and early twentieth centuries, Herman Bavinck and Abraham Kuyper. Kuyper's name and fame have been duly recognized, particularly in the CRC, whereas Bavinck has still not come into his own.

In fact, it would be interesting to pursue the thesis that one of the major theological distinctives of the RCA and CRC churches is that the former reflects more the theology and spirit of Bavinck, the latter more that of Kuyper. Originally the influence of Kuyper in the RCA was direct and considerable. He had personal contacts and corresponded with many of the followers of Albertus C. Van Raalte, the founder of Holland, Michigan, and an influential pioneer RCA minister, as well as with many of Van Raalte's followers. WTS professors such as Henry E. Dosker and Nicholas M. Steffens knew Kuyper personally and corresponded with him,[35] and during that period at least two portraits of Kuyper were hung in the halls of WTS.

Kuyper's works, such as the Princeton Stone Lectures, *Lectures on Calvinism*,[36] and *The Work of the Holy Spirit*[37] were also read widely in RCA circles. Yet neither Van Raalte himself nor his descendants in the RCA could be considered Kuyperian.[38] Moreover, there was never an attempt in the RCA to try to apply Kuyper's views of sphere sovereignty in the United States (and later in Canada) as there was in the CRC, albeit unsuccessfully.[39]

Bavinck, however, though not cited so frequently in RCA circles or periodicals as in the CRC, was the subject of two studies by RCA ministers,[40] one a doctoral dissertation and the other a master's thesis, and has been

35. See Elton J. Bruins, "From Calvin to Van Raalte: The Rise and Development of the Reformed Tradition in the Netherlands, 1560–1900," in *The Impact of John Calvin on France, Switzerland, Germany and the Netherlands*, ed. Donald J. Bruggink (Holland: Western Theological Seminary, 1978), p. 14.

36. Abraham Kuyper, *Lectures on Calvinism*, Six Lectures delivered at Princeton University (1898) under Auspices of the L. P. Stone Foundation (Grand Rapids: Eerdmans, 1953).

37. Abraham Kuyper, *The Work of the Holy Spirit* (New York: Funk & Wagnalls, 1900).

38. See Bruins, "From Calvin to Van Raalte," p. 15, who contends against Gordon Spykman, *Pioneer Preacher: Albertus Christiaan Van Raalte, A Study of His Sermon Notes*, Heritage Hall Publications, 2 (Grand Rapids: Calvin College and Seminary Library, 1976), that Van Raalte was a Kuyperian.

39. Zwaanstra, *Reformed Thought*, pp. 306–307.

40. Bastian Kruithof, "The Relation of Christianity and Culture in the Teaching of Herman Bavinck" (Ph.D. dissertation, University of Edinburgh, 1955); Jerome B. De Jong, "The Ordo Salutis as Developed by the Dutch Theologian Herman Bavinck" (Th.M. thesis, Union Theological Seminary in New York, 1947).

indirectly influential in the RCA through two of its leading theologians, M. Eugene Osterhaven and his pupil and former colleague, Eugene P. Heideman. Even a cursory reading of the former's *The Spirit of the Reformed Tradition*[41] reveals the spirit of Bavinck, even though the citations are few. The same is true of his recent work, *The Faith of the Church*.[42] (At the same time it should not be overlooked that Osterhaven's contemporary in systematic theology at CTS, Anthony Hoekema, did his doctoral dissertation on Bavinck's doctrine of the covenant, and also at Princeton Theological Seminary.[43] The positions of Osterhaven and Hoekema are similar, although they have written in different areas.)

Heideman wrote his doctoral dissertation on *The Relation of Revelation and Reason in E. Brunner and H. Bavinck*[44] at the University of Utrecht, the Netherlands, under the direction of Arnold A. van Ruler. Heideman, in many ways, reflects more the theology of van Ruler, his mentor, and Osterhaven is influenced greatly by Calvin and Gerrit C. Berkouwer, but the spirit and approach of Bavinck are a significant influence in the RCA theological outlook. This has been further enhanced by the wide reading of Berkouwer's works at WTS for more than a quarter of a century; and Berkouwer, it would be generally acknowledged, is more a disciple of Bavinck than of Kuyper.

In the CRC, on the other hand, Kuyperianism in the variant form of Dooyeweerd's philosophy of law, has been a potent force in the last quarter century, but not so much in CTS as in Calvin College (H. Evan Runner, Gordon Spykman, and Henry Vander Goot), and at times at Trinity Christian College in Palos Heights, Illinois, and Dordt College in Sioux Center, Iowa. The center of the movement, however, is in the Institute for Christian Studies (AACS) in Toronto.

Further evidence of the vitality of Kuyperianism in the CRC, although today a minority movement, is in the publication of *The Kuyper Newsletter*, published roughly three times a year since 1980 by the department of philosophy of Calvin College.

It is a conundrum to me that Bavinck's classic, the *Gereformeerde Dogmatiek*,[45] has never been translated into English. For some strange reason the aborted attempt to translate this four-volume work ended in the translation of Volume II alone, *The Doctrine of God*,[46] and that in a strangely

41. M. Eugene Osterhaven, *The Spirit of the Reformed Tradition* (Grand Rapids: Eerdmans, 1971).

42. M. Eugene Osterhaven, *The Faith of the Church, A Reformed Perspective on Its Historical Development* (Grand Rapids: Eerdmans, 1982).

43. Anthony A. Hoekema, "Herman Bavinck's Doctrine of the Covenant" (Th.D. dissertation, Princeton Theological Seminary, 1953).

44. Eugene P. Heideman, *The Relation of Revelation and Reason in E. Brunner and H. Bavinck*, Van Gorcum's Theologische Bibliotheek, 32 (Assen: Van Gorcum & Co., 1959).

45. Herman Bavinck, *Gereformeerde Dogmatiek*, 4 vols. Third ed. (Kampen: Kok, 1918).

46. Herman Bavinck, *The Doctrine of God*, Tr., ed. and outlined by William Hendriksen (Grand Rapids: Eerdmans, 1951). We owe a great debt to the late Henry Zylstra for his magnificent translation of

edited version by William Hendriksen. Despite the reverence for Bavinck in the CRC, was it felt that the *Dogmatiek* was too dangerous to be translated in its entirety?

It is only recently that Bavinck's helpful view of the authority and inspiration of Scripture has been properly recognized in North America[47] and that by a scholar who is of neither CRC nor RCA background! I am referring to the works of Jack Rogers and particularly the monumental study, *The Authority and Interpretation of the Bible*, by Jack B. Rogers and Donald K. McKim.[48] In this response to Harold Lindsell's *Battle for the Bible*,[49] Rogers and McKim submit that there is a middle way between liberalism and the Reformed scholastic approach typified by the old Princeton school of which Charles Hodge and Benjamin B. Warfield were the principle figures. That middle way, they propose, is found in Dutch Calvinism as represented by Kuyper and Bavinck, particularly the latter. We had to be reminded of the possibilities within our own heritage by two United Presbyterians of Scottish background!

The riches of our Dutch heritage, however, have not been exhausted by any means in the persons of Kuyper and Bavinck. That should be only the beginning! There are other worthies of our own time, some of whom have received little attention and who could greatly enrich our Dutch/American theology such as Kornelis H. Miskotte, Theodorus L. Haitjema, Gerrit C. van Niftrik, and Oepke Noordmans, to name only four of the leading Nederlandse Hervormde Kerk theologians of a past generation. From the GKN side there are theologians like Andries D. R. Polman, the conservative Klaas Runia, and the controversial Harminus M. Kuitert. There are also biblical theologians such as Herman N. Ridderbos and Marinus de Jonge, and world renowned mission theologians such as Johannes Verkuyl, Johannes Blauw, the late Hendrik Kraemer, and the late Johannes C. Hoekendijk, who finished his teaching career at Union Theological Seminary in New York. One could go on and on with influential historians and ecumenical leaders such as the late Gerardus van der Leeuw and Willem A. Visser 't Hooft.[50] The point is that we have not yet begun to tap the rich reserves of our great heritage.

Herman Bavinck's popular one-volume dogmatics, *Magnalia Dei*, Onderwijzing in de Christelijke Religie naar Gereformeerde Belijdenis (Kampen: Kok, 1909), and entitled *Our Reasonable Faith* (Grand Rapids: Eerdmans, 1956). The only regrettable thing about this publication is the misleading English title: *Our Reasonable Faith*. The original title, which is Latin, not Dutch, could be translated as "The Mighty Works of God!"

47. Gerrit C. Berkouwer, *Holy Scripture*, Studies in Dogmatics (Grand Rapids: Eerdmans, 1975), represented in many ways only an elaboration of Bavinck's view.

48. Jack B. Rogers and Donald K. McKim, *The Authority and Interpretation of the Bible*, An Historical Approach (New York: Harper & Row, 1979). See especially pp. 329–330 and 388–393. Cf. An earlier work, ed. by Jack B. Rogers, *Biblical Authority* (Waco: Word Books, 1977), pp. 41–44.

49. Harold Lindsell, *The Battle for the Bible* (Grand Rapids: Zondervan, 1976).

50. I have discussed briefly all of these theologians in an essay, I. John Hasselink, Jr., "Contemporary

At the same time, it must be stressed that these resources must first be thoroughly digested, integrated, and evaluated before they are presented in American/Canadian dress. Otherwise we will repeat the failures of the past and simply adopt and often only barely adapt Dutch theological thought for North American consumption. Their culture, milieu, and issues are not ours—at least not in the same form—and hence this evolving theology must be more *American* than Dutch, even though it is continually nourished and renewed by sources from across the Atlantic.

Thesis 5

The character of this distinctive Reformed theology will be more classical and evangelical and less parochial and polemic than in the past.

By "classical" I mean two things: first, that this theology, though not neglecting its Dutch roots and heritage, will increasingly peel off the layer of neo-Calvinism and get back to its even deeper roots in the Reformation; secondly, that it will not limit itself to Dutch American or denominational concerns but will also seek to address the larger critical issues of each age and thereby make an impact beyond its boundaries. In regard to both aspects I am encouraged by recent developments, but the successes are limited and partial.

Whereas our fathers and forefathers knew the Heidelberg Catechism and were steeped in Kuyper, Bavinck, Hodge, Augustus H. Strong, and later, Louis Berkhof—or professors' lectures which were based on the above—they knew little of Calvin and the reformers. At least my father and father-in-law, both pastors who graduated from WTS over half a century ago, have told me this was the case when they were students at Western. I suspect the situation at CTS was not much different. Calvin's *Institutes* played only a minor role at best in their theological education, and his commentaries were not recommended and hence not purchased. Subsequently, several RCA scholars did doctoral dissertations on Calvin,[51] and

---

Protestant Dutch Theology," *Reformed Review* 26 (1972/73):67–89. The focus of my essay, however, is on what I have dubbed "the big three" of Dutch theology, viz., Berkouwer, van Ruler, and Hendrikus Berkhof. The remainder of this issue is devoted to the late van Ruler.

51. M. Eugene Osterhaven, "Our Knowledge of God according to John Calvin" (Th.D. dissertation, Princeton Theological Seminary, 1948); Leroy Nixon, "John Calvin's Teachings on Human Reason and Their Implications for Theory of Reformed Protestant Christian Education; a Problem in Philosophy of Religion Studied for Its Possible Implications for Theory of Religious Education" (Ph.D. dissertation, New York University, 1960); Justin Vander Kolk, "A Re-examination of Calvin's Doctrine of Scripture Based on Reading in his Commentary" (Ph.D. dissertation, University of Chicago, 1951); Victor L. Nuovo, "Calvin's Theology: a Study of Its Sources in Classical Antiquity (Ph.D. dissertation, Columbia University, 1964); Garret A. Wilterdink, "Irresistible Grace and the Fatherhood of God in Calvin's Theology" (Ph.D. dissertation, University of Chicago, 1974); John R. Walchenbach, "John Calvin as Biblical Commentator: an Investigation into Calvin's Use of John Chrysostom as an Exegetical Tutor" (Ph.D. dissertation, University of Pittsburgh, 1974); I. John Hesselink, Jr., "Calvin's Concept and Use of the Law" (Th.D. dissertation, Universität Basel, 1961).

with the advent of Osterhaven as Professor of Systematic Theology at WTS in 1952 that situation soon changed. The same has been true at Hope College since World War II where courses on Calvin's theology are taught regularly.

This is also true, I gather, at Calvin College where John H. Bratt has been a leader in Calvin studies. In addition to courses and numerous published articles about Calvin, he also promoted and edited the Heritage Hall Lectures, 1960–1970, published under the title *The Heritage of John Calvin.*[52] A remarkable Festschrift of essays on Calvin was published in his honor on the occasion of Bratt's retirement in 1976.[53] I say "remarkable" because all nine essays are substantial, scholarly studies of various aspects of Calvin's thought and all are by his colleagues at Calvin College, two of them now teaching at CTS.

In the modern era there have also been doctoral dissertations on Calvin by CRC scholars[54] although not so many as by their counterparts in the RCA. In four ways, however, Calvin College and CTS have made a signal contribution to Calvin studies in recent years: 1) by being the prime movers in organizing and hosting the colloquia of the Calvin Studies Society; 2) by bringing the distinguished Calvin scholar, Ford Lewis Battles, to the campus in 1978. (Unfortunately, his death, late the following year, cut short a very fruitful and promising relationship.);[55] 3) by initiating and continuing the most comprehensive Calvin bibliography ever attempted, edited by Peter De Klerk;[56] and 4) by the establishment of a Calvinism Collection in the Calvin Library, enlarged in 1982 to become the H. Henry Meeter Center for Calvin Studies. Here is housed the finest contemporary collection of Calvin studies in the world, in addition to an excellent collection of original and early publications of Calvin's works.

In addition, the theological journals of CTS and WTS—the *Calvin Theological Journal* and the *Reformed Review*—continue to publish solid and helpful essays on Calvin, probably as many as can be found in any theological journals in the world including distinguished journals like *Theology*

---

52. *The Heritage of John Calvin,* Heritage Hall Lectures 1960–1970, ed. John H. Bratt, Heritage Hall Publications, 2 (Grand Rapids: Eerdmans, 1973).

53. *Exploring the Heritage of John Calvin,* Essays in Honor of John H. Bratt, ed. David E. Holwerda (Grand Rapids: Baker, 1976).

54. Quirinus Breen, *John Calvin:* A Study in French Humanism (Grand Rapids: Eerdmans, 1931)— Breen was later disciplined because of a minor doctrinal difference; Lester R. De Koster, "Living Themes in the Thought of John Calvin: a Bibliographical Study" (Ph.D. University of Michigan, 1964); and Marvin P. Hoogland, *Calvin's Perspective on the Exaltation of Christ in Comparison with the Post-Reformation Doctrine of the Two States* (Kampen: Kok, 1966).

55. See John H. Kromminga, "Calvin Seminary's Encounter with Ford Lewis Battles," *Calvin Theological Journal* 15 (1980):158–159; James O'Brien, "Ford Lewis Battles: 1915–1979, Calvin Scholar and Church Historian Extraordinary," *Calvin Theological Journal* 15 (1980):166–189. This November issue is dedicated to the memory of Battles.

56. This has generally appeared annually in the November issue of the *Calvin Theological Journal* (with one exception) since 1972 and is scheduled for publication as a book in 1985.

Today, Scottish Journal of Theology, Theologische Zeitschrift, or *Nederlands Theologisch Tijdschrift.*

All this notwithstanding, until quite recently we were far better known for our neo-Calvinism than for our Calvin studies. In the CRC, for example, there were the fierce debates over common grace, and both denominations in recent years have had to concentrate their exegetical and theological efforts on internal struggles about women in ecclesiastical office and the interpretation of the first three chapters of Genesis.

Thus, despite our contributions to Calvin scholarship, the Reformed scholarship which emanates from Grand Rapids and Holland tends to be ingrown, parochial, and generally irrelevant to the American theological scene as a whole. There are, to be sure, some exceptions: Louis Berkhof's *Systematic Theology* is still known and used in conservative circles; and contemporaries like Hoekema, Osterhaven, Boer, Fred H. Klooster, Henry Stob and Heideman are known and recognized in limited evangelical or Reformed/Presbyterian circles, but their names would not be recognized in the average Protestant denominational seminary today, let alone Roman Catholic schools. The same would be true of our biblical and mission scholars who have recently published major studies or commentaries: James I. Cook, Lester J. Kuyper, Marten H. Woudstra, John H. Piet and Richard R. De Ridder. The best-known biblical scholar from our circles among conservatives would be William Hendriksen, largely because of his New Testament commentaries.

The best known Dutch/American Reformed scholars, however, do not teach at CTS or WTS but at Calvin College—Richard J. Mouw[57] and George M. Marsden[58]—and Fuller Theological Seminary—James Daane[59] (recently deceased) and Lewis B. Smedes.[60] Hope College and WTS professors have been fairly prolific in recent years, but most of them are known only in limited academic circles outside of the RCA-CRC orbit.[61] Actually,

57. Through his lectures, articles, and three books: Richard J. Mouw, *Political Evangelism* (Grand Rapids: Eerdmans, 1973); Richard J. Mouw, *Politics and the Biblical Drama* (Grand Rapids: Eerdmans, 1976); Richard J. Mouw, *Called to Holy Worldliness* (Philadelphia: Fortress Press, 1980).

58. Principally through his two highly acclaimed historical studies: George M. Marsden, *The Evangelical Mind and the New School Presbyterian Experience,* A Case Study of Thought and Theology in Nineteenth-Century America, Yale Publications in American Studies, 20 (New Haven: Yale University Press, 1970); George M. Marsden, *Fundamentalism and American Culture,* The Shaping of Twentieth Century Evangelicalism, 1870–1925 (New York: Oxford University Press, 1980).

59. Originally known for his critiques of Cornelius Van Til, also of CRC background, and more recently for his study of election and preaching, James Daane, *The Freedom of God,* A Study of Election and Pulpit (Grand Rapids: Eerdmans, 1973); James Daane, *Preaching with Confidence,* A Theological Essay of the Power of the Pulpit (Grand Rapids: Eerdmans, 1980).

60. See Lewis B. Smedes, *All Things Made New,* A Theology of Man's Union with Christ (Grand Rapids: Eerdmans, 1970); Lewis B. Smedes, *Love Within Limits,* A Realist's View of I Corinthians 13 (Grand Rapids: Eerdmans, 1978); and Lewis B. Smedes, *Sex for Christians, The Limits and Liberties of Sexual Living* (Grand Rapids: Eerdmans, 1976).

61. Recent authors at Hope College: Wayne G. Boulton, Robert J. Palma, Dennis N. Voskuil, and Henry Voogd as well as two of their colleagues, Elton J. Bruins (cited above) and Allen Verhey (a Calvin

the fame of Calvin College rests particularly with its philosophers such as Alvin Plantinga, now at Notre Dame University, South Bend, Indiana, and Nicholas P. Wolterstorff, and a host of other distinguished former students of the late W. Harry Jellema. Probably the best-known RCA theologian (and preacher) is Howard G. Hageman, an Easterner, who is the product of a quite different milieu—New York State University, Harvard University, and New Brunswick Theological Seminary.[62] It should be noted that many of the above named CRC scholars are fairly widely known through the stimulating and engaging monthly *The Reformed Journal*, begun in 1952. This is probably the best advertisement for Dutch/American theology there is, at least of a more progressive CRC variety, although there are a few contributing editors from other backgrounds. I should probably also add the name of the best known personage of all, Robert H. Schuller, a product of Hope College and WTS, who although primarily known as a TV evangelist, has entered the theological arena with his recently published book *Self Esteem*.[63]

It might be argued that a distinctive Reformed theological approach will never have a general appeal on most university or seminary campuses, nor will it ever be welcomed widely by American pastors who tend to be practical and pragmatic. A realistic aspiration, however, is that our efforts and impact would be felt in the larger Reformed world both here and abroad. If so, our inspiration and resources must come not only from Reformed theologians of Dutch background, whether Dutch or American, but also from other great Reformed theologians of our time beginning with Barth, however, one may feel about certain aspects of his theology. Any serious

---

College and CTS product) who have published frequently; at WTS, in addition to the prolific Heideman, who has recently left the seminary in order to become the secretary for the world mission program of the RCA, and Osterhaven, already cited: John H. Piet, Lester J. Kuyper, Stanley A. Rock, James I. Cook, and Christopher B. Kaiser. Another significant author from the RCA is the Dutch-American theologian Isaac C. Rottenberg, best known for his writings on the Christian-Jewish question. A disciple of van Ruler, his first major work received little attention, viz., Isaac C. Rottenberg, *Redemption and Historical Reality* (Philadelphia: The Westminster Press, 1964), but his most recent book is being well received, Isaac C. Rottenberg, *The Promise and the Presence*, Toward a Theology of the Kingdom of God (Grand Rapids: Eerdmans, 1980).

62. In addition to several smaller works, Howard G. Hageman, *We Call This Friday Good* (Philadelphia: Muhlenberg Press, 1961); Howard G. Hageman, *Lily Among the Thorns* (New York: Half Moon Press, 1953) and Howard G. Hageman, *Predestination*, a Fortress Book (Philadelphia: Fortress Press, 1963); his best known book is Howard G. Hageman, *Pulpit and Tablet*, Some Chapters in the History of Worship in the Reformed Churches (Richmond: John Knox Press, 1962), the Princeton Seminary Stone Lectures concerning worship in the Reformed tradition. While Hageman is recognized in the United States of America as its foremost scholar of Reformed liturgics, Donald J. Bruggink, church historian at WTS, must certainly take pride of place as the foremost authority in the country in the area of Reformed architecture, Donald J. Bruggink and Carl H. Droppers, *Christ and Architecture*, Building Presbyterian/Reformed Churches (Grand Rapids: Eerdmans, 1965), and Donald J. Bruggink and Carl H. Droppers, *When Faith takes Form*, Contemporary Churches of Architectural Integrity in America (Grand Rapids: Eerdmans, 1971).

63. Robert H. Schuller, *Self-esteem*, The New Reformation (Waco: Word Books, 1982).

theology, especially that which claims to be Reformed, must work through the challenges Barth poses; he cannot be avoided. If our theology is to be deepened and avoid parochialism, we must also learn from Reformed theologians from other countries and cultures, such as Thomas F. Torrance, recently retired from a long and distinguished career at New College, Edinburgh, and the late Otto Weber, the highly regarded German Reformed theologian whose famous *Grundlagen der Dogmatik*[64] is now available in English under the title *Foundations of Dogmatics*.[65]

One final comment in regard to this thesis: We must write for other than our own periodicals and journals. Again there are exceptions, i.e., people who write essays and reviews for *Christianity Today, The Christian Century, Interpretation, Theology Today*, etc., but an inordinately high percentage of our publications (other than books) appear in our house journals. A perusal of Peter De Klerk's voluminous work, *A Bibliography of the Writings of the Professors of Calvin Theological Seminary*[66] bears out this contention, and the same is generally true of WTS professors.[67]

If our theology is worth doing at all, it should be communicated to and be in dialogue with the larger Christian world.

Thesis 6

If a distinctive Dutch/American theology is to flourish and be influential in the coming decades, there must be increasing dialogue and interchange between Christian Reformed and Reformed scholars and institutions.

Here, too, this is already being accomplished in a minimal way, but the meager efforts leave much to be desired. Our annual Calvin-Western faculty gatherings are pleasant but do not contribute to serious scholarship. The same is true of the annual meetings of the Hope and Calvin College religion faculties. Granted, it is difficult even to get scholars within our campuses to collaborate on projects, but in an age of increasing specialization some sharing or dialogue at a preliminary level could be highly beneficial.[68]

---

64. Otto Weber, *Grundlagen der Dogmatik*, 2 Band, (Neukirchen Kreis Moers: Verlag der Buchhandlung des Erziehungsvereins, 1955).

65. Otto Weber, *Foundations of Dogmatics*, vol. 1 (Grand Rapids: Eerdmans, 1981). Vol. 2 scheduled for publication in 1983.

66. Peter De Klerk, *A Bibliography of the Writings of the Professors of Calvin Theological Seminary* (Grand Rapids: Calvin Theological Seminary, 1980).

67. John Muether, librarian at WTS, is about to prepare a similar bibliography of the writings of WTS professors.

68. The disciples of Arnold A. van Ruler in the RCA (more in the CRC) are few but able and influential. In addition to Heideman and Rottenberg, cited earlier, the name of Paul Fries should be added. A WTS graduate who teaches at the New Brunswick Theological Seminary, New Brunswick, New Jersey, Fries began his doctoral work under van Ruler at Utrecht, the Netherlands but had to finish it under his successor, J. M. Hasselaar because of van Ruler's untimely death. See Paul R. Fries, *Religion and the Hope for a Truly Human Existence*, An Inquiry into the Theology of F. D. E. Schleiermacher and

You will recall that when we were your guests in the spring of 1982 at our annual seminary faculty gathering I proposed that our faculties—or, better perhaps, various fields of our faculties—ought to get together periodically for colloquies where subjects and papers of mutual concern could be discussed in a colloquy-type setting. This is one possibility.

Another idea that intrigues me is that of trying to get your Dooyeweerdians and our van Rulerians together. What they have in common is a modified version of the Calvinian-Kuyperian concern for a life and world view where the Christian faith is related to every aspect of our existence.

These suggestions are meager and modest, but hopefully they will stir some of our theological friends and colleagues to bolder and more creative possibilities. Perhaps now that you are about to be relieved of major administrative responsibilities, you may have the time to be a facilitator of new and fruitful cooperative ventures. The world won't notice much if we fail to do more in this regard, but our churches and the church at large will be diminished if the distinctive theological heritage and contributions that are ours are not encouraged and enriched.

In concluding, I want to speak to the danger of a "Reformed elitism," an issue raised by Marlin Van Elderen in an essay in *The Reformed Journal* dealing with the theme, "On Being Reformed."[69] Here he addresses a broader problem, namely, the ethnic and denominational temptation to move from "parochialism to elitism, even arrogance." This arrogance takes various forms, one of which is theological. So Van Elderen warns, "In the Reformed community, the price of taking our faith seriously is too often taking ourselves—our community and its institutions and its theology— even more seriously."[70]

This is indeed a danger for any group that takes its confessional stance or some non-confessional position (such as Southern Baptists) very seriously. The CRC, being more zealous in this regard than the RCA, has been particularly prone to a superiority attitude not only against liberalism but also against Arminians and fundamentalists. This is amply documented in the fascinating Yale dissertation by a son of the CRC, James D. Bratt: "Dutch Calvinism in Modern America: The History of a Conservative Subculture."[71] Fundamentalism in the early decades of this century was viewed as "the opponent of the right"; modernism "the enemy on the left."[72]

A. A. van Ruler with Questions for America (Th.D. dissertation, Rijksuniversiteit Utrecht, 1979). (Privately printed).

69. Marlin J. Van Elderen, "A Chosen Race," *The Reformed Journal* 32 (March 1982):12–13, 16–18.

70. Ibid., p. 13.

71. James D. Bratt, "Dutch Calvinism in Modern America: The History of a Conservative Subculture" (Ph.D. dissertation, Yale University, 1978).

72. Ibid., pp. 267–276, 276–287. Cf. The reference to "Arminian odors" is on page 271.

In general there was the feeling of the superiority of our (Calvinistic) view to "American religiosity."[73]

In the RCA of that era these feelings were not quite so pronounced, except in certain Midwestern pockets where the prevailing attitudes did not differ perceptibly from their sister denomination. Due to greater Americanization in the RCA there was generally less self-consciousness about their distinctive heritage and theology. However, John E. Kuizenga, a WTS professor who closed out his career at Princeton Theological Seminary, wrote a series of articles in the *Intelligencer-Leader* (predecessor of *The Church Herald*) in the 1920s in response to the modernist fundamentalist controversy of that time in which he portrayed the Reformed Confessions as an orthodox middle way.[74]

While such attitudes are less prevalent or at least muted today, and Pharisaic attitudes are never appropriate, it must be conceded that one characteristic of the Reformed position is its mediating role between the extremes of fundamentalism and liberalism. Yet we have much in common with conservative evangelicals and can carry on fruitful dialogue with chastened liberals or so-called neo-orthodox types. On social issues, for example, several of our people—Merold Westphal, Professor of Philosophy at Hope College, Richard Mouw of Calvin College, and Paul Henry—have been involved with evangelical social activists sympathetic to the stance of *Sojourners* and *The Other Side;* and people like yourself, Arie Brouwer, General Secretary of the RCA,[75] and Harvey Hoekstra,[76] long-time missionary and former president of the RCA, have in various ways made an impact on the World Council of Churches.

I have little fear of overconfidence or arrogance as our friends, colleagues, and those who succeed them continue to pursue theology in this Dutch/American Reformed milieu. For the most part, I believe our sins of this sort are largely a thing of the past: the petty legalisms, denominational pride and exclusiveness, a defensive, negative mentality, and a scholastic, doctrinaire approach to theology. What I fear, rather, is a timidity and a desire to be so respected in the larger academic community that we lose or water down those distinctives which are our contribution to the cause of theology: a comprehensive *Weltanschauung* (life and world view), God-centered piety and disciplined Christian life, a covenant and kingdom focused hermeneutic, a sense of God's sovereignty and providential leading,

---

73. Ibid., pp. 272–273.

74. Cited in Bratt, p. 277.

75. Brouwer has been an active representative at several important World Council of Churches conclaves and was one of the key representatives, along with Billy Graham, at the peace gathering in Moscow in the spring of 1982. For the most part, Brouwer has been a supporter of the World Council of Churches.

76. See Harvey T. Hoekstra, *The World Council of Churches and the Demise of Evangelism* (Wheaton: Tyndale House Publishers, 1979).

an appreciation for the third use of the law, and a strong ecclesial loyalty.[77]

If these distinctive characteristics of our heritage and theological perspective can be preserved, deepened, and enlarged, there is indeed a future for a distinctive Dutch/American theology—in the service of the whole church of Jesus Christ and to the glory of God. *Yours, John*

77. Another major concern and emphasis is a high view of the inspiration and authority of the Bible, but this is hardly a Reformed distinctive.

15

The Gereformeerde Kerken in Nederland and the Christian Reformed Church[*]
Doede Nauta

Introduction

It is not surprising that there is a close relationship between the Gereformeerde Kerken in Nederland (hereafter GKN) and the Christian Reformed Church in North America (hereafter CRC). Both churches have the same background. Not only are they generally characterized by the same Reformed Confessions and church order, but one can add to this that they both trace their origin to the same form which this church order took in the Netherlands in the sixteenth century. Moreover, those who in the nineteenth century contributed to the beginning of the CRC were virtually all from the Netherlands.

Although it is not necessary to enter into detail about the matter of Dutch descent, it is necessary nevertheless to mention briefly a few details if one wants to understand correctly the relation between the two churches.

The GKN in their present form date back to 1892. They are an amalgamation of two church organizations which existed earlier, both of which in the course of the nineteenth century had come into being as a result of a bitter struggle over the Confessions and the way the Confessions were adhered to by the Nederlandse Hervormde Kerk of the Netherlands, in which the church of the Reformation had taken shape in 1816. The one group of churches had come out of the Afscheiding of 1834, the other out

---

[*]This contribution was completed early in 1981.

of the Doleantie of 1886. The Afscheiding group had gone through a difficult period of internal conflicts. These conflicts, together with internal
separations, resulted in 1869 in the formation of the Christelijke Gereformeerde Kerk in Nederland (hereafter CGKN), one of the partners of the
union of 1892. The other partner was the Nederduitsche Gereformeerde
Kerk (Dolerende), established in 1886 as a result of a serious conflict in the
congregation in Amsterdam, a conflict with which the names of Abraham
Kuyper and Frederik L. Rutgers are intimately connected. Not all local
churches agreed with the 1892 decision and once again a secession took
place, although of smaller proportion.

Those who joined the Afscheiding of 1834 had from time to time to
endure a great deal of opposition in the Netherlands. At first, as a result of
certain legal measures, they were even subject to treatment that can justly
be called persecution. As time went on other unfavorable circumstances
(especially economic ones) made themselves felt, causing certain groups
among them at various times to emigrate to North America. Prominent
figures in this movement were Hendrik P. Scholte and Albertus C. van
Raalte. These immigrants looked for and in part found affiliation with the
Reformed Church in America (hereafter RCA), which was already established in the land. This denomination was part of the heritage of the colonial period of the seventeenth century, and with this new immigration was
extended to what was then referred to as the western parts of the United
States of America. As time went on, however, differences of opinion arose,
which in 1857 resulted in a separation and establishment of what is now
known as the CRC.[1]

During the period preceding 1892 this church maintained contacts with
the Netherlands, but in this contribution these cannot be dealt with further.
My review is limited to what happened after 1892. After all, the CRC is older
than the GKN to which it is my privilege to belong, and of which I, in
this contribution honoring John H. Kromminga, may be considered a
representative.

In this connection I would like to call attention to a remarkable phenomenon. In the speeches of the delegates of CRC to the general synod of
the GKN, it has happened more than once that our churches were referred
to as "our mother church." This term hardly agrees with the historical data
mentioned above. It would be more correct to think of a relationship
between sister churches. The CRC then appears as the older of the two,
even if in terms of membership she was considerably smaller, especially in
her formative years. To be sure, considerations of a different nature can be
advanced to show that there is good reason to speak of a mother-daughter
relationship. It should be clear, however, that since we have already

1. John H. Kromminga, *The Christian Reformed Church*. A Study in Orthodoxy (Grand Rapids:
Baker, 1949), pp. 30–39.

reached the latter years of the twentieth century, there really is no reason at all to speak any more in such terms.

This contribution is concerned with the treatment and characterization of a period of slightly less than a century. A book could be written about all the things that have happened in this period in both churches. As far as their mutual relationship is concerned, one finds little material available. When the *Acta* and other sources of the respective synods are consulted, one soon discovers that no matter how intimate the mutual contacts may have been, in actual practice the two denominations did not always succeed in sharing in each other's experiences and in dealing thoroughly with the difficulties and problems which presented themselves in each of the two churches.

1892–1910

Concerning the relationships between both churches, repeated mention has been made of the common ethnic origins and the common faith which characterized their members. Moreover, the Dutch language was kept in honor in the CRC when in the years following 1892 immigrants from the Netherlands kept reinforcing the ranks of the CRC. It is all the more puzzling, therefore, that during this first period (until approximately 1910) little evidence can be found of a vital and powerful cooperative effort. This is especially true concerning the GKN. I feel inclined to speak of a more or less apathetic attitude.

The CRC gave evidence of a different attitude. She did not fail to send delegates to the general synods of her sister church in the Netherlands. Qualified persons out of her midst were appointed for this purpose. Already at the first synod of the united churches (i.e., the GKN) which gathered in 1893 in Dordrecht, the Reverend Jan H. Vos was present on behalf of the CRC. He originally had come from Bentheim and had studied in Kampen. He had served as a minister in Grand Rapids since 1881 and occupied a prominent place among his colleagues. In his extensive address he, among other matters, expressed deep gratitude for the union achieved in 1892 according to the Word of God and so necessary for the areas concerned. At the CRC synod, which happened to be in session in Grand Rapids at exactly the same time, prayer had been offered every day for the good success of the union. He also gave an elaborate report of the situation in his own church. It was inevitable that he would devote a few words to the break of the CRC with the RCA in 1857.[2] The way in which he expressed himself in connection with the secession of the CRC raised the ire of the two delegates of the RCA, Professor Nicholas M. Steffens and the

---

2. Jan H. Vos, "Toespraak," in *Acta* der Generale Synode van de Gereformeerde Kerken in Nederland, Gehouden te Dordrecht in den Jare 1893 (Amsterdam: J. A. Wormser, 1893), pp. 66–67 (Art. 47).

Reverend Rense H. Joldersma, who were also present as guests at the GKN synod. Joldersma declared later that their silence after Vos' address should not lead to the conclusion that his church (the RCA) agreed with the accusations implied in the remarks of Vos.[3] Immediately following Vos' address, it was the task of the Reverend Johannes H. Donner, Director of Missions, to respond. He addressed the delegates of both churches of North America together and so with great wisdom avoided entering into the disputes that kept the RCA and CRC divided. He also noted that it was deplorable that as a consequence of emigration, North America had deprived the Netherlands of so many talented persons, in the church as well as in society.

Donner also noted that what had moved men like Van Raalte and others was their search for more than just earthly bread for the Hollanders; closest to their hearts was the spiritual and moral well-being of those who had emigrated with them. Donner considered it a blessing that in the years preceding 1892 the immigrants had been so warmly received and helped along. He then issued a call to the American brethren to remain faithful to Calvinistic principles which not only in the Netherlands but also in North America were meeting with strong opposition. According to him it was a divine calling to fight for the preservation of what one possesses, and also, if necessary, to show themselves once more as united churches. What had happened in the old country constituted a forceful appeal for imitation.[4]

At the following synod, which assembled in Middelburg in 1896, no delegate from North America was present. There was, however, an official letter sent on behalf of the sister church, the CRC, by the Reverend Gerrit K. Hemkes. The writer, who resided there since 1877, was professor at the Theological School in Grand Rapids. The official letter contained a defense of the address Vos had delivered in Dordrecht and presented objections against the RCA in connection with the upholding of the Reformed confessions. Eight cases were cited. The advisory committee which reported on this matter was of the opinion that the Synod of 1893 had been fully justified in its actions. It held that the only thing that had been decided on that occasion was that it is inappropriate for delegates of churches represented at the synodical level to bring accusations against each other. At the same time the committee presented an analysis of the eight cases that had been cited, which analysis intended to show that their value could really not be taken too seriously. The synod accordingly decided that the desired correction could not be made. It also expressed its wish for an exchange of delegations who would have an advisory vote, and this not only with the

---

3. *Acta 1893*, pp. 191–192 (Art. 203).
4. Johannes H. Donner, "Antwoord aan de Amerikaansche Afgevaardigden," in *Acta 1893*, pp. 67–68 (Art. 47).

CRC but also with the RCA.[5] It seems that with this action the matter was closed. Nothing more was heard about it.

At the Synod of Groningen in 1899 a CRC delegate was present. This time it was Professor Hendericus Beuker[6] who, after having spent a long time of service in the Netherlands, was now teaching at the CRC Theological School in Grand Rapids as Professor of Systematic Theology. According to Professor Douwe K. Wielenga, who was teaching in Kampen and who had the privilege of addressing him, the synod considered it a distinct privilege to meet one who had lived and served for so many years among them.[7] Beuker himself gave an elaborate address, in which he went far back into history and then proceeded to give a thorough description of the current situation in the CRC. In the process he showed himself to be a man of vision. In his opinion a transition to the use of the English language ought to take place in the CRC. He recognized that the process of Americanization could bring with it a tendency toward liberalism. In order not to lose its Calvinistic principles, it would be important that the support and influence of the church in the Netherlands be maintained. According to Beuker's opinion, the CRC had to be on guard against two extremes: a onesided subjectivism of the Methodist kind and a onesided objectivism of an assumed regeneration without concern for the appropriation of faith. A thorough effort, he said, ought to be made to maintain ecclesiastical correspondence.[8] In saying this Beuker had in mind correspondence with all the Reformed Churches in the world, and this was to take place under the leadership of the church in the Netherlands. Consultations about this, he said, should be begun as soon as possible.

The synod did not follow up on this interesting idea, but when the guest took his leave, the president gave the assurance that the former had not attended the synod only as an interested onlooker, but as a full-fledged co-worker. And he added: "You are one of those living bridges, those living lines of communication, which maintain the communion between the churches in North America and those in the old country."[9]

The Synod of Arnhem in 1902 was attended by two American delegates, leading figures in the CRC: the Reverends Jacob Noordewier and Henry Beets.[10] Concerning the next GKN Synod, meeting in Utrecht in 1905, the 1904 Synod of the CRC had judged that it was not necessary to send a

---

5. *Acta* der Generale Synode van de Gereformeerde Kerken in Nederland, Gehouden te Middelburg, van 11 Augustus to 4 September 1896 (Leiden: D. Donner, 1897), pp. 86–87 (Art. 132).

6. *Acta* der Generale Synode van de Gereformeerde Kerken in Nederland, Gehouden te Groningen, van 15 tot 30 Augustus 1899 (Leiden: D. Donner, 1900), p. 8 (Art. 14).

7. Ibid., pp. 11–12 (Art. 30).

8. Hendericus Beuker, "Toespraak," in *Acta 1899*, pp. 136–141 (Bijlage E).

9. Jan van Andel, "Afscheid van Beuker," in *Acta 1899*, p. 68 (Art. 137).

10. *Acta* der Generale Synode van de Gereformeerde Kerken in Nederland, Gehouden te Arnhem, van 12 Augustus tot 5 September 1902 (Leiden: D. Donner, 1903), p. 9 (Art. 8). See also the speeches by Noordewier en Beets, Ibid., pp. 156–161 (Bijlage Q1 and 2).

delegate because no business of common interest and of special importance would come up for discussion.[11] It was decided, however, to send a
cablegram to the Theological School in Kampen with congratulations on
the occasion of its fiftieth anniversary: "God bless 'OUR OWN SCHOOL.'"[12]
When later the synodical committee discovered the important matters
which would in fact be brought up in Utrecht, it took the liberty to appoint
the Reverend Klaas Kuiper as delegate to this synod after all. Kuiper, who
had undergone his classical examination in Utrecht in 1877 and resided as
a minister in North America since 1891, was planning to visit the Netherlands anyway.[13] He attended the synod only occasionally,[14] but in his
address he paid ample attention to Christian education and the work
accomplished by the missions on behalf of his church; he also touched
upon the matter of membership of secret societies. As for the theological
quarrels which were the order of the day in the Netherlands, Kuiper
reported that the same disputes had been imported into North America,
except fortunately for the issue of ministerial training. Kuiper expressed
the hope that this sad conflict might be brought to a good conclusion at the
synod.[15]

Kuiper gave an account of these various matters to the synod of the
CRC in June 1906. In addition, there was discussion of the doctrinal statements which had been decided upon in Utrecht. A proposal of the majority
of the advisory committee on this matter recommended that the synod
simply express general agreement without further involvement, but their
advice was rejected. As a result of thorough discussion, the matter was
considered to be of such importance that an independent judgment was
called for.[16] Such an assessment was indeed made by the following Synod
of 1908 in Muskegon. It officially and completely accepted the doctrinal
statements, and they were included in a supplement to the *Acts of Synod
1908*.[17]

Two months later the Synod of Amsterdam assembled in the Netherlands. Originally the Reverend Gabriel D. DeJong had been appointed as
the CRC delegate to this synod, but since he was appointed to a professor-
ship at Calvin Theological Seminary (successor to Hemkes), the Reverend
Peter J. Jonker, who had emigrated from the Netherlands in 1884, appeared

11. *Acta der Synode* van de Christelijke Gereformeerde Kerk, Gehouden van 20 tot 29 Juni, 1906, te
Holland (Grand Rapids: H. Verhaar, 1906), p. 70 (Bijlage I).
12. *Acta der Synode* van de Christelijke Gereformeerde Kerk, Gehouden te Holland, 15–24 Juni, 1904
(Holland: H. Holkeboer, 1904), p. 7 (Art. 10).
13. *Acta der Synode 1906*, p. 70 (Bijlage I).
14. *Acta* der Generale Synode van de Gereformeerde Kerken in Nederland, Gehouden te Utrecht
van 22 Augustus tot 7 September 1905 (Amsterdam: Höveker & Wormser, 1906), p. 44 (Art. 41), p. 62
(Art. 99).
15. Klaas Kuiper, "Toespraak," in *Acta 1905*, pp. 120–121 (Bijlage XXIV).
16. *Acta der Synode 1906*, pp. 54–55 (Art. 93).
17. *Acta der Synode* van de Christelijke Gereformeerde Kerk, Gehouden van 17 tot 26 Juni, 1908, te
Muskegon (Grand Rapids: H. Verhaar, 1908), pp. 40–41 (Art. 58), pp. 81–83 (Bijlage XII).

in his place. In his address he made mention of the decisions which had been taken by his own synod. He also sketched the situation in which his own church found itself: year after year an increase in growth had been recorded. He reported concerning the care and the responsibility which his synod had taken upon itself for the Gereformeerden in Argentina. It had responded to an appeal from the Reverend John Van Lonkhuyzen, who had been sent to Argentina from the Netherlands. Of great importance was the fact that Jonker emphatically expressed his regret that while in North America much concern was shown for the church in the Netherlands, the latter did not in equal measure inform itself of the life and work of its sister church, the CRC. Both churches, he said, had to fight one and the same struggle. It was not right for the GKN to restrict its contact simply to written correspondence. Jonker noted that it was high time for a delegate from the GKN to appear at a synod in North America.

In the same vein an urgent written invitation from the CRC had been addressed to the synod of the GKN. It reminded the GKN that more than once a delegate had been sent from North America, giving expression to the essential unity of our Reformed churches.[18]

Even if Professor Anthony G. Honig, who was shouldered with the task to respond to Jonker, could not without reason argue that in the Netherlands there was really no lack of sincere interest in the way things were going in the church across the ocean, the hard facts proved undeniably that the expressed complaint was fully justified. It was only too obvious that there was no way to avoid a radical change in behavior. To be sure, during the previous years visits to North America had been made by some prominent figures of the church in the Netherlands. In 1892 two professors from Kampen, Herman Bavinck and Douwe K. Wielenga, had been to North America and brought official greetings from the Christelijke Gereformeerde Kerk to fellow believers in that country, and more especially to ecclesiastical gatherings when the opportunity to do so offered itself. But the actual purpose of their voyage was different. Bavinck was supposed to speak to the Presbyterian Alliance in Toronto, Canada. A similar reason caused Bavinck to make the trip for a second time in 1908 when he gave the Stone lectures at Princeton Seminary. In 1898 these lectures had been given by Kuyper who on that occasion met a large number of people in diverse localities.[19] During the Synod of Groningen in 1899 Beuker had reminisced about that visit, how Kuyper had been received with standing ovations.[20] Nevertheless, during all these years the synods had neglected to send a delegate to show that the mutual relationship between the two churches was more than a purely formal one. After all, it was a matter of

18. *Acta der Generale Synode van de Gereformeerde Kerken in Nederland, Gehouden te Amsterdam van 18 Augustus tot 3 September 1908* (Goes: Oosterbaan & le Cointre, 1908), pp. 36–38 (Art. 42).
19. Ibid., p. 38 (Art. 42).
20. Beuker, "Toespraak," in *Acta 1899,* p. 140.

essential unity which was at stake. What was the reason for this strange course of action? The fact that a person was not delegated to each and every synod in North America was understandable. The custom there was to meet every other year, while in the Netherlands the synod met every three years. The only reason sometimes given was the objection of the cost involved in such a delegation. But this objection could hardly have been considered to be of decisive importance. Basically there must have been a lack of awareness of the need for an intimate relationship and expressions of genuine interest.

It was at the Synod of 1910 in Muskegon that for the first time a delegate from the Netherlands was welcomed. The delegate, Harm Bouwman, a professor at Kampen, later published a book with pictures and reminiscences of his trip to North America. He was accepted at the synod as an advisory member and he acquitted himself well in that capacity.[21] In the greetings from both sides kind expressions were exchanged. The Reverend Johannes Groen, who responded to the speech of Bouwman,[22] gave this assurance: "Without you we could never have become what we are." He added that year after year hundreds, yes, thousands, of immigrants had come from the Netherlands.[23]

1910-1940

At the Synod of Zwolle in 1911 Henry Beets,[24] the delegate from North America, gave an interesting speech. He gave the assurance that his church was still living and growing like a fruitful branch of a tree. His statement was further elucidated by a comparison of the situation in 1857 and that in 1910: from four small churches the number had risen to almost two hundred congregations. Beets elaborated his sketch of the CRC in detail. He gave a survey of the difficulties with which his church had to cope, citing no less than twenty examples. He referred to the character of the American people in the midst of whom his church had to move and try to find its own particular place. He pointed out the materialistic tendency, the growth of scepticism, the increase in the loss of church affiliation, the craving for all that is new, the influence of secret societies, the aversion against doctrinal and expository preaching, and other phenomena of a similar character, all against which positions had to be taken. He expressed the wish—and this was really the point of his elaborate argument—that the

---

21. *Acta der Synode* van de Christelijke Gereformeerde Kerk, Gehouden van 15 tot 24 Juni, 1910, te Muskegon (Grand Rapids: H. Verhaar, 1910), p. 7 (Art. 3).

22. Harm Bouwman, "Rede," in *Acta der Synode 1910*, pp. 150–154 (Bijlage XVIII).

23. Johannes Groen, "Antwoord op de Toespraak van H. Bouwman," in *Acta der Synode 1910*, pp. 155–158 (Bijlage XIX).

24. *Acta* der Generale Synode van de Gereformeerde Kerken in Nederland, Gehouden te Zwolle van 22 Augustus tot 1 September 1911 (Goes: Oosterbaan & le Cointre, 1911), p. 30 (Art. 38).

church and the people in the Netherlands would help in the execution of this task. It should be noted that in saying this he did not lose himself in generalities but presented very concrete suggestions. The most important ones he suggested concerned the need for the publication of good books on the burning questions of the day (especially in the area of principles), the editing of sound periodicals, such as *De Heraut* and *De Bazuin* (for which much appreciation was expressed), the sending of men to give lectures; a suitable arrangement in Kampen as well as in Amsterdam for post-graduate studies for graduates from North America; firm application of Reformed principles and theories; counsel and leadership concerning burning issues, such as was done by the Synod of Utrecht in 1905; the delegations of prominent men to the synods; the issue of a better Bible translation than that of the seventeenth century; the arrangement of the psalms which would be more suitable for singing; changes in a number of liturgical forms; the completion and correction of the church order; the improvement of the quality of the spiritual life of the congregation "so that those who emigrate from you to us may by their piety be of benefit to us in North America and may gain a good reputation for you and your works." Finally he requested an offering for the establishment of a seamen's home in Hoboken, New Jersey, so that emigrants from the Netherlands and seamen who came to North America could be properly welcomed.[25]

In the presentation of this program Beets showed that he had a clear and responsible insight into the calling of the church of those days. In the following years quite a few of the items on his list were realized, although not always in immediate connection with the suggestions he had made.

Beets was without doubt an inspiring figure. In a letter to the Synod of 's-Gravenhage in 1914 he urgently asked for better and more intimate ecclesiastical correspondence.[26] In later years he paid additional visits to the synods in the Netherlands. Although he had been appointed as delegate in 1920, he was not able to be present in Leeuwarden because it was just about that time that he received his appointment as Director of Missions.[27] But he was present in Utrecht in 1923[28] as well as in Middelburg in 1933.[29]

Of the delegates to the synod of the GKN who came from North America separate mention must be made of Professor Louis Berkhof. He was

25. Henry Beets, "Toespraak," in *Acta 1911*, pp. 97–100 (Bijlage XVI).

26. Henry Beets, "Schrijven van de Christian Reformed Church in N.A., Stated Clerk," in *Acta* van de Generale Synode der Gereformeerde Kerken in Nederland, Gehouden te 's-Gravenhage 16 Juli, 10 September en 17 October 1912 en van 27 October tot 6 November 1914 (Rotterdam: W. Zwagers, 1915), pp. 319–320 (Bijlage CXVI).

27. *Acta* der Generale Synode van de Gereformeerde Kerken in Nederland, Gehouden te Leeuwarden van 24 Augustus–9 September 1920 (Kampen: Kok, 1921), p. 262 (Bijlage XL A).

28. *Acta* der Generale Synode van de Gereformeerde Kerken in Nederland, Gehouden te Utrecht van 21 Augustus–14 September 1923 (Kampen: Kok, 1924), p. 82 (Art. 80), pp. 186–188 (Bijlage XVIIIc).

29. *Acta* der Generale Synode van de Gereformeerde Kerken in Nederland, Gehouden te Middelburg van 22 Augustus tot September 1933 (Kampen: Kok, 1933), pp. 11–12 (Art. 4), pp. 105–106 (Art. 194), pp. 224–227 (Bijlage XXXIX).

present at the Synod of Groningen in 1927. His fellow delegate, Van Lonkhuyzen, had to forego the opportunity.[30] Berkhof, too, gave an overview of
the situation in his church and could witness to the growth which was to
be seen all along the line. However, in full agreement with the remarks of
Beets, he too called attention to the internal troubles with which they had
to cope. He referred to the unpleasant conflicts concerning the denial of
common grace, of which some ministers were guilty. He added: "These sad
experiences have made it possible for us to have more sympathy for you in
the struggle in which you have been involved lately." Of much greater
significance, in Berkhof's opinion, was the struggle against the general
mentality in North America. To him preserving Calvinism and Reformed
principles in the process of Americanization was the most important challenge. In his opinion this would be easier to achieve in the Netherlands than
in North America. After all, Berkhof said, the Netherlands is a country with
a strong Reformed tradition where the Reformed people constitute a
much larger percentage of the population. In North America, according to
him, the prevailing mentality was not favorable to the development of
Calvinism. What was prevalent there was not abstract thought but practical action. Pragmatism, he said, always poses the question: Does it work?
Methodism, with its onesided pragmatism, he stated, had joined itself to
this strongly practical attitude. Things were no different with the social
gospel, which was less interested in what a person believes than in what he
does. All this promoted superficiality in the life of the Christian. For these
reasons Berkhof called on his fellow believers in the Netherlands for their
prayers, the results of their study, and their moral support in the coming
struggle.[31]

When Berkhof mentioned the conflict in which the churches in the
Netherlands had become involved, he referred to the Geelkerken matter
with which the special Synod of Assen had had to deal the previous year.[32]
In that year Professor Seakle Greijdanus attended the CRC synod held in
Englewood, Chicago, as representative of the GKN. He had provided the
necessary information concerning this matter and had explained how in
this matter the exegesis of Genesis 2 and 3 was at stake. In his speech he
also called attention to, among other things, the fact that since the emigration from the Netherlands was declining more and more, in a number of
decennia few would experience personal ties with the Netherlands, and
that the process of Americanization would continue, resulting in an increasing independence of the sister church in North America. There is no
indication whether he made any mention of his own church's orderly
objections against the way in which the Geelkerken matter had come to

30. *Acta* der Generale Synode van de Gereformeerde Kerken in Nederland, Gehouden te Groningen
van 16 Augustus tot 9 September en van 25 tot 27 October 1927 (Kampen: Kok, 1928), p. 9 (Art. 2).
31. Louis Berkhof, "Toespraak," in *Acta 1927*, pp. 26–28 (Bijlage XXVI).
32. Ibid.

the floor of Synod.[33] Anyway, in the mutual relations between the two churches this matter has not been dealt with, nor was the possibility of asking advice from North America brought up. The matter was finally dealt with in the Netherlands in a completely independent manner. This must have been done deliberately. However, it is difficult to reconcile this course of action with the agreements made already in 1914.

At the Synod of Roseland, Chicago, 1914, the judgment had been expressed that the existing correspondence between the two churches ought to be strengthened. Up to that point it had virtually limited itself to a polite exchange of greetings, which was in conflict with the spirit of the church order. Delegates thought changes ought therefore to be made in this situation. They felt the need for each other's support and advice.[34] At this synod it was decided to address a letter regarding this matter to the synod which was to assemble some months later in 's-Gravenhage. It was Beets who composed the letter.[35] Van Lonkhuyzen would personally present the letter as an official delegate of the CRC, since he was planning to make a trip to the Netherlands in August anyway. However, this plan was not realized because the synod concerned, in deviation from regular practice, did not meet in August but at the end of October. The only option Van Lonkhuyzen had was to bring the matter in question to the attention of the synod in a forceful way by means of a long letter in which he with great urgency talked about the unity which bound the two churches together. This unity, he wrote, ought to be given practical form by informing each other about important questions and opinions; by not making changes or additions in the ecclesiastical forms and other documents in use by both churches without mutual consultation; by consulting each other in case new ecclesiastical rules were established; by informing each other of important issues in sufficient time; and in general by always determining together what belonged to the common task of both churches—in regard to each other, in regard to "the truth," and in regard to any third party. The synod did indeed acknowledge that it considered itself obligated to watch over one another according to the Word of God in order to prevent aberrations in doctrine, practice, and discipline. However, concerning mutual consultation it saw many practical difficulties, such as the great distance between the two countries and the great difference in circumstances in both lands. Nevertheless, it did declare that mutual exchange in information should not be lacking, especially in the case of changes in the confessions and the liturgy that involved doctrine. In such instances, the synod of

33. Seakle Greijdanus, "Toespraak," in *Acta der Synode 1926* van de Christelijke Gereformeerde Kerk, Gehouden van 9 Juni tot 28 Juni 1926 te Englewood, Chicago (Grand Rapids: Grand Rapids Printing Co., 1926), pp. 339–344 (Bijlage XVIII).

34. *Acta der Synode 1914* van de Christelijke Gereformeerde Kerk, Gehouden van 17 tot 25 Juni, 1914 te Roseland, Chicago (Grand Rapids: Grand Rapids Printing Co., 1914), p. 15 (Art. 17).

35. Beets, "Schrijven van de Christian Reformed Church in N.A.," pp. 319–320 (Bijlage CXVI).

the GKN declared that mutual agreement in accordance with the Word of God would be necessary.[36] It cannot be denied that the church in North America did indeed deal seriously with the intended course of action described above. This can be seen in the fact that the same CRC Synod of 1914 issued a warning against the propaganda which at that time was being spread in the Netherlands by the Latter-day Saints. It was thought important to provide countermeasures against the danger posed by this sect.[37] At the Synod of Rotterdam in 1917 a number of documents from the CRC were presented concerning discipline after unlawful divorce, with the request for advice in this matter.[38] This led to the appointment of a committee of deputies who were mandated to write a report, but it was not until 1923 that a decision could be made. Even then it was left undecided if malicious desertion constituted a ground for discipline. Soon, however, the reality of the well-intentioned plan for mutual helpfulness lagged far behind the lofty ideal.[39] In the Netherlands evidence was also given of a willingness to consult the sister church in matters of a similar nature. The matter of the expansion of the confession had been on the delegates' credentials for many years, beginning with the Synod of Leeuwarden in 1920.[40] In that matter it was emphatically stipulated that overseas churches, which were based on the same foundation, would be consulted. The CRC, among others, fell into this category.

The Synod of Groningen in 1927 decided to investigate the need for a definitive statement concerning the doctrine of Holy Scripture. This need was felt for such a statement in connection with problems which arose in the modern era, since heresies in this area were evident and it was felt that Reformed theology could shed light on the matter.[41] In accordance with the policy of mutual consultation, the synod decided to seek advice from the CRC Synod of 1928, meeting in Holland, Michigan.[42] In actual fact, however, the way in which this matter was treated did not bring results of any consequence. In general it must be concluded that notwithstanding all the good intentions, in reality very little was achieved toward an intense mutual consultation on important issues of doctrine and life. It remained

36. Jan Van Lonkhuyzen, "Schrijven," in *Acta 1912 en 1914*, pp. 321–322 (Bijlage CXVIII).

37. "Verzoek van de Synode der Christian Reformed Church in Noord-Amerika," in *Acta 1912 en 1914*, p. 320 (Bijlage CXVII).

38. "Rapport van de Deputaten over de Correspondentie met Buitenlandsche Kerken," in *Acta der Generale Synode van de Gereformeerde Kerken in Nederland, Gehouden te Rotterdam van 20 Augustus–6 September 1917* (Kampen: Kok, 1918), pp. 246–247 (Bijlage LXV).

39. "Advies in Zake Punt I a, Echtscheiding," in *Acta 1923*, pp. 202–204 (Bijlage XXVI).

40. "Rapport van Zake Voorstellen der Particuliere Synodes Rakende de Belijdenis," in *Acta 1920*, pp. 152–154 (Bijlage VI).

41. "Rapport van de Deputaten Inzake den 'Uitbouw' van de Belijdenis," in *Acta 1927*, pp. 197–199 (Bijlage CXXI).

42. "Brieven, Gereformeerde Kerken in Nederland," in *Acta der Synode van de Christelijke Gereformeerde Kerk, 13–29 Juni 1928, Holland* (Grand Rapids: Christelijke Gereformeerde Kerk, 1928), pp. 310–313 (Bijlage XVIII).

limited to a mutual exchange of information concerning each other's problems and concerns. When it came to decisions by each of the two churches, these were mostly taken in complete independence.

For the Netherlands church it seemed to be a difficult assignment to send a delegation to its sister church in America from time to time. In 1920 Beets, on behalf of his own synod, urgently requested that the Synod of Leeuwarden, in accordance with the agreement that had been made earlier, send delegates to North America in a more regular fashion.[43] It was not, however, until 1926 that the first delegate, Greijdanus, was present.[44] After that time a marked improvement can be noticed in the sending of delegates. In 1928 the illness of two professors of the Free University prevented the presence of anyone.[45] In 1930 Professor Valentijn Hepp, who was lecturing in North America, was present at the CRC Synod.[46] In 1932 the Reverend Sietse O. Los served as delegate. This synod met in Grand Rapids, which from then on would become the regular meeting place of the synod. In his speech Los indicated his agreement with the words of the Reverend John De Haan, spoken in his capacity as delegate to the Synod of Arnhem in 1930.[47] What De Haan had said at that time had a bearing on the intimate, mutual relationship between the two churches. It was precisely in view of this matter that Los had now been delegated. He called himself a friend of Beets and made mention of the pending burning issues, such as the expansion of the confession, the degree-granting status of the Theological School in Kampen, and the addition to the collection of hymns. He also mentioned matters relating to missions and evangelism. Of utmost importance was the decision which had been taken in Arnhem concerning a Reformed Ecumenical Synod. The suggestion had come from de Gereformeerde Kerken van Suid Afrika, which were willing to convene such a synod. The church in North America was now being included in the consideration of this matter.[48] The establishment of this inter-church body was indeed realized in later years, even though it has never achieved the importance which was originally intended.

---

43. Henry Beets, "Rapport van den Deputant naar de Generale Synode der Gereformeerde Kerken in Nederland van de Christelijke Gereformeerde Synode, Orange City, Iowa," in *Acta der Synode 1920* van de Christelijke Gereformeerde Kerk, Gehouden van 16 tot 30 Juni, 1920 te Grand Rapids, Michigan (Grand Rapids: M. Hoffius, 1920), pp. 227–231 (Bijlage XI).

44. *Acta der Synode 1926*, p. 12 (Art. 12), pp. 339–344 (Bijlage XVIII).

45. *Acta der Synode 1928*, pp. 312–313.

46. Valentijn Hepp, "Address," in *Acta der Synode 1930* van de Christelijke Gereformeerde Kerk, Gehouden van 11 Juni tot 27 Juni, 1930), pp. 358–360 (Suppl. XV).

47. John De Haan, "Toespraak," in *Acta* der Generale Synode van de Gereformeerde Kerken in Nederland, Gehouden te Arnhem van 19 Augustus tot 19 September 1930 (Kampen: Kok, 1931), pp. 229–231 (Bijlage XXXIV).

48. Sietse O. Los, "Address," in *Acts of Synod 1932* of the Christian Reformed Church in Session from June 8 to June 23, 1932 at Grand Rapids (Grand Rapids: Grand Rapids Printing Co., 1932), pp. 288–293 (Suppl. XIII).

While Los was still present, the same synod decided to take up contact with the church in the Netherlands concerning the matter of the liturgical forms, of which a revision was being considered.[49] It was toward the end of the synod that Los, who concluded that both churches were confronted with the same problems, especially with those originating from an increase in worldliness, made an interesting remark. In South Africa he had been introduced to a system of delegation from the local consistories, directly to the synod, whereas in the Netherlands delegates were chosen at the particular synods. The experience Los now had with the sister church in North America, where classes elected delegates to the synod led him to say that in his opinion the method followed by the CRC constituted a happy medium.[50]

The year in which Los was the delegate of the GKN to the CRC Synod of 1932 was also the year in which the CRC celebrated the seventy-fifth anniversary of its founding. This gave occasion for reflecting on its Dutch heritage, which was still much in evidence. The Dutch language was used in the sessions of the 1932 Synod, and proceedings were partially published in Dutch. Shortly afterward, however, English was used exclusively.

It was not until 1939 that the next delegate from the GKN, Professor Gerhard Ch. Aalders, appeared before a CRC synod.[51] Aalders, who was fluent in both Dutch and English, had no problem communicating to the synod.

Aalders reported a few months later to the Synod of Sneek that he had made many personal contacts not only at the synod, but also in several congregations and at the seminary. He considered this to be a welcome reinforcement of the mutual relationships between the two churches. In his address he discussed, among other things, the difficulties in his own church, especially the differences in views concerning the doctrine of the church, without expressing any personal judgment in the matter. He limited himself to the expression of the hope that a decision would be taken which would promote the well-being of the churches and the honor of God. In the church in North America he had found an increasing Anglicanization, which in his opinion could not but influence the character of Reformed church life. All the more would there be a need to maintain close contact with Reformed church life in the Netherlands, for it would be deeply regrettable if the Anglicanization would lead church life to lose its Reformed character. Aalders considered it to be the task of the church he represented to lend all possible support in the effort to maintain this Reformed character.[52]

49. *Acts of Synod 1932*, pp. 121–122 (Art. 134).

50. Ibid., p. 190 (Art. 169).

51. Gerhard C. Aalders, "Address," in *Acts of Synod 1939* of the Christian Reformed Church, in Session from June 14 to June 23, 1939 at Grand Rapids, Michigan (Grand Rapids: M. Hoffius, 1939), pp. 17–18 (Art. 35).

52. Gerhard C. Aalders, "Rapport van den Afgevaardigde naar de Synoden van 'The Reformed

It is questionable whether Aalders' lofty claim, expressed in his report to the Synod of Sneek in 1939, was really generally shared by the sister church in the Netherlands. Already in 1930 at the Synod of Arnhem De Haan had called attention.to this process of Anglicanization and had mentioned that the works of Herman Bavinck and others were being translated into English.[53] If the awareness mentioned above had indeed been vitally present, it could have been expected that the GKN would at least have arranged for a regular delegation to be sent to the church in North America. That this did not happen in the case of every single synod is understandable, especially since from 1936 on the synod of the CRC met annually. Nevertheless it happened all too often that no delegation was sent. The CRC delegate to the Synod of Amsterdam in 1936 expressed his disappointment that since 1932 there had been no further delegation from the Netherlands. He, the Reverend Emo F. J. Van Halsema, who himself was born and brought up in the Netherlands and who still had many relatives there, made an elaborate and fervent plea for the exercise of a close communion in the interest of being truly Reformed in faith and practice.[54]

This appeal apparently touched a responsive chord, as can be seen from the delegation of Aalders in 1939 and the activity displayed by him on that occasion. Shortly after this two delegates from North America appeared at the Synod of Sneek: Beets for the umpteenth time and the Reverend Idzerd Van Dellen. The latter spoke, again emphasizing the need for the maintenance of a mutual relationship. Consultation and cooperation, not only with the church in the Netherlands but also with other churches of Reformed confession, were in his opinion more than ever a necessity. Thanks to technical progress, Van Dellen said, it would now be easier to realize such relationships, more so than in the past. The church in the Netherlands had a sacred calling to give leadership in the task concerned.[55] Due to the threatening international situation both men had to leave Europe earlier than they originally had intended. World War II, which erupted the following year, curbed for quite some time the exercise of mutual relationships.

Church in America' en van 'The Christian Reformed Church in North America,'" in *Acta* der Voortgezette Generale Synode van Amsterdam 1936 en der Generale Synode van Sneek 1939 van de Gereformeerde Kerken in Nederland, Gehouden te Amsterdam op 5 en 6 April 1938 en te Sneek van 29 Augustus tot 6 October 1939 (Kampen: Kok, 1940), pp. 266–267 (Bijlage XLIX c).

53. De Haan, "Toespraak," in *Acta 1930*, p. 230.

54. Emo F. J. Van Halsema, "Toespraak," in *Acta* der Generale Synode van de Gereformeerde Kerken in Nederland, Gehouden te Amsterdam van 25 Augustus tot 2 October 1936 (Kampen: Kok, 1937), pp. 153–158 (Bijlage VII).

55. Idzerd van Dellen, "Toespraak," in *Acta 1939*, pp. 143–145 (Bijlage I).

1940-1965

During the years of World War II, 1940–1945, contact between the CRC and GKN had to be completely suspended. In that period it proved to be virtually impossible to remain accurately informed about each other's experiences. The Netherlands especially had to be content with occasional and even then very limited reports which managed to get through from time to time. When, however, the frightful horrors of the war had passed, a tremendous turnabout in the right direction took place concerning the mutual relations between the churches.

After 1945 the mutual attachment manifested itself more intimately and more intensely than ever before. To a very significant degree it was the disposition evidenced by the church in North America during the war years as well as immediately thereafter which contributed to the renewal of consultation and cooperation. In many different ways the CRC showed warm sympathy for the church in the Netherlands. This happened by the assumption of certain tasks which could not possibly have been taken care of anymore from the Netherlands. I mention in particular the obligation in connection with the mission work in Indonesia,[56] as well as the payment of the pension owed to the widow of Van Lonkhuyzen.[57] Special mention should also be made of the exemplary provisions which were made in the form of food and goods of various nature in the context of War Relief which after the fearful and cruel experiences of the war years were received as a blessing of love. Deep gratitude for this made itself felt for many years afterwards. Delegates to the synods in North America, even many years later, could not refrain from expressing over and over again the gratitude for help given. The fact that during this period delegates appeared at the synods in North America with fair regularity is sufficient proof that the sense of attachment to the sister church in North America had increased and been intimately reinforced.

In later years a similar show of active support manifested itself. When in 1953 a part of the Netherlands was devastated by a flood, which claimed a large number of victims, benevolent activity was once more kindled in North America to provide help. In still other ways the two churches showed that they knew how to meet each other's needs which in the years after the war would make themselves felt a number of times. A stream of emigrants from the Netherlands was received by the CRC as they settled in North America (both in the United States of America and Canada).

56. For more than two decades the CRC received repeated requests from the GKN to send missionaries to Indonesia. During this period several calls were extended but no one felt the urge to accept it. In 1965 the CRC Synod decided to discontinue the calling of missionaries for Indonesia. Eds.

57. *Acts of Synod 1944* of the Christian Reformed Church in Session from June 14 to June 23, 1944 at Grand Rapids, Michigan (Grand Rapids: Christian Reformed Church, 1944), pp. 90–91 (Art. 127); *Acts of Synod 1945* of the Christian Reformed Church in Session from June 13 to June 22, 1945 at Grand Rapids, Michigan (Grand Rapids: Christian Reformed Publishing House, 1945), p. 116 (Art. 114).

Without the powerful and determined help on the part of a number of boards and agencies in the sister denomination, the CRC, this operation could not have run so smoothly. The important consideration that it would gain in membership must no doubt have played a role in this, because even those who settled in Canada became part of this church. In this way in the course of time a series of new, and I think I can say, flourishing, congregations were added to the denomination. An invitation which was received by telegram in January 1946 to be present at the sessions of a special synod in the Netherlands could not possibly have been accepted by the CRC. At that time it was still impossible to make arrangements for a trip overseas on such short notice.[58] However, later in the same year the regular synod assembled, this time in Zwolle. Two delegates from North America appeared in its midst, the Reverends H. Henry Meeter and Nicholas Monsma. Both addressed the synod. The one made mention of the willingness in his church to render help and to make sacrifices—more than a million dollars had been collected—as well as of the fact that a deep impression had been made in her midst by the courageous resistance against the occupying forces, which reminded them of the heroes of faith.[59] The other made special mention of the concern that had been felt in his church about the experiences felt during the years of occupation and the prayers that had been offered by her. He also contrasted the current situation with that prior to World War II, when so little evidence had been given of intimacy in relations. The Synod of Zwolle responded by deciding to reinforce the contacts with its sister church and to seek closer cooperation. As evidence of this, it was decided that two copies of all official decisions would from now on be sent to the CRC.[60]

During the war years a serious schism had taken place in the church in the Netherlands, due to the conflict that centered especially around Professors Klaas Schilder and Seakle Greijdanus. It goes without saying that the course of events in connection with the schism and the relations between the parties could not be closely followed in North America. When the CRC finally took note of the schism as an actual fact, it could only be with deep regret. There was no hesitation, however, in displaying an attitude of the greatest loyalty toward its sister church in the Netherlands. An invitation, which had been received early in 1946, to be present at the Synod of the "Vrijgemaakten," as that group was then called (in accordance with Article 31 of the Church Order) was rejected without any reservation,

58. "Reports of the Synodical Committee and of the Stated Clerk," in *Acts of Synod 1946* of the Christian Reformed Church in Session from June 12 to June 22, 1946 at Grand Rapids, Michigan (Grand Rapids: Christian Reformed Publishing House, 1946), pp. 125–126 (Suppl. 1–a).

59. H. Henry Meeter, "Toespraak," in *Acta* van de Generale Synode van de Gereformeerde Kerken in Nederland, Gehouden te Zwolle van 27 Augustus-2 October 1946 (Kampen: Kok, 1947), pp. 145–148 (Bijlage VI).

60. Nicholas J. Monsma, "Toespraak," in *Acta 1946*, pp. 148–151 (Bijlage VII).

and it was decided to send a delegation to the Synod of Zwolle, as noted earlier.[61]

Not again until 1949 did a delegate from the Netherlands appear at the CRC Synod, and this was in the person of the Reverend Luitsen Kuiper.[62] Since that time there has been a fairly regular delegation to the CRC synods in North America, sometimes even annually. One has to take into consideration that the synod of the CRC continues to meet every year during a number of weeks in June. The synod of the church in the Netherlands before 1955 met every three years; after 1955 it has met every other year, and then for longer period of time, often with some interruptions. As a rule prominent figures from the GKN were appointed as delegates: members of the executive committee of Synod or of a particular synodical committee, sometimes a professor from Kampen or Amsterdam, sometimes even an elder, among whom Abraham Warnaar[63] must be mentioned (1950). Their addresses to the synod are always reported in the *Acts* of Synod, but only in summary; the full text is only included in the Supplement to the *Acts* in those cases in which the address was given directly in the English language. English has clearly and fully become the regular language of communication. By far most of the American churches have become completely alienated from the Dutch language. Somewhat typical, as far as I am concerned, is the appointment of a committee for the translation of Dutch theological works, which is mentioned in the *Acts*.[64] Notwithstanding the change to communication in English, the mutual relations between the two churches was considerably strengthened. The interrelationship was not limited to the exchange of delegates to the respective synods. In indirect ways there were also meetings between these two churches in the context of the Reformed Ecumenical Synod, which had been established in the period under discussion and which will be dealt with in another contribution to this Festschrift.

Of great significance, however, was the fact that the churches began to involve each other directly in their own affairs. The church in the Netherlands made, as far as her relationship with other churches is concerned, a distinction between correspondence in a broad sense and correspondence in a strict sense. Along with other denominations the church in North America, with which we are dealing here, was placed in the latter category. The churches in this category were considered to be in complete unity of

---

61. "Reports of the Synodical Committee and of the Stated Clerk," in *Acts of Synod 1946*, p. 126 (Suppl. 1-a).

62. Luitsen Kuiper, "Address," in *Acts of Synod 1949* of the Christian Reformed Church in Session from June 8 to June 17, 1949, Grand Rapids, Michigan (Grand Rapids: Christian Reformed Publishing House, 1949), pp. 373–374 (Suppl. 42).

63. *Acts of Synod 1950* of the Christian Reformed Church in session from June 14 to June 24, 1950, Grand Rapids, Michigan (Grand Rapids: Christian Reformed Publishing House, 1950), p. 44 (Art. 116).

64. *Acts of Synod 1946*, p. 91 (Art. 119).

confession and of maintenance of this confession. This allowed the possibility of involvement in each other's affairs, in so far as readiness to do this had been mutually agreed upon. This readiness proved indeed to be there. To a much greater degree than before, for instance, a process of mutual consultation was developed concerning important issues which were brought to the floor of the respective synods. I mention especially the thorough revision of the Church Order, considered necessary in the Netherlands, as well as the changes brought about in the orders of the worship services and in the related ecclesiastical forms. In addition, the matter of the relationship between church and state in connection with the statements made in Article 36 of the Belgic Confession was raised. These matters have been dealt with in a good spirit of mutual understanding. This is not to say that this always resulted in decisions which were the same for both churches. As far as the revision of the Church Order is concerned, the church in North America stated in 1953 that the circumstances of both churches were of such a nature that a common revision could not be established; however, they would nevertheless be able to profit from the work which was achieved in this matter in the Netherlands. It is obvious that one can speak of a common course taken in a common commitment to one and the same cause.[65]

From both sides the churches gave evidence of a deep trust in each other. Ministers of the one church were not hindered by trouble or conditions in the other church when they visited each other. The same situation prevailed concerning those who came to pursue further studies in the Netherlands, be it at the Theological School at Kampen or at the Theological Faculty of the Free University at Amsterdam.

A question was indeed raised, however, concerning the ministers from the Netherlands who received a call to a congregation of the CRC. This question was raised at the Synod of 1956 in the presence of the delegate from the Netherlands, Professor Herman N. Ridderbos, for whom they had deliberately waited before dealing with this matter. The question concerned the colloquium doctum which such ministers had to sustain. The explanation was now given that this was not intended to be an examination in the full sense of the word. The idea was simply that the ministers concerned should express their agreement with a number of stipulations which had been adopted at some time in the past, and which were now obligatory in the CRC.[66] There was great appreciation for the works of a theological nature which were published in the Netherlands, for instance,

---

65. *Acts of Synod 1953* of the Christian Reformed Church in Session from June 10 to June 26, 1953, Grand Rapids, Michigan (Grand Rapids: Christian Reformed Publishing House, 1953), pp. 410–411 (Suppl. 27).

66. *Acts of Synod 1956* of the Christian Reformed Church, June 13 to June 26, 1956, Grand Rapids, Michigan (Grand Rapids: Christian Reformed Publishing House, 1956), pp. 38–39 (Arts. 65 and 68), pp. 485–493 (Suppl. 36).

those of Gerrit C. Berkouwer, Klaas Dijk, Frederik W. Grosheide, and Ridderbos. This appreciation was publicly stated at the Synod of Rotterdam in
1952. At the same synod the CRC delegates expressed disappointment that
Berkouwer had declined an appointment to Grand Rapids.[67]
For the remainder of this period there was no lack of concern for each
other's situation. If one takes note of the speeches given at the various
synods, one will easily be convinced of this. A special opportunity to give
expression to this concern offered itself in 1957 when the church in North
America had the privilege to commemorate a century of continuing
growth and increase. The Reverend Cornelis van der Woude, who later
became a professor at the Theological School at Kampen, was appointed
as the delegate from the Netherlands, and he shared in this occasion. He
reminded the synod of the close ties of history and doctrine which united
the two churches.[68]
In the long run, however, matters arose which contributed to some
degree of alienation in the relationship between the two churches. This
process began with the question of the eventual membership in the World
Council of Churches (hereafter WCC). Already at the Synod of 's-Gravenhage in 1949 the delegate from North America, Professor Clarence Bouma,
gave expression of a deep concern about the favorable mood which he
found toward the WCC; in his address he urgently pleaded for a deepening
of spiritual life.[69] Only many years later, however, the point was reached in
the Netherlands, that the objections, which even there were raised, were
overcome. After a tentative decision in 1963[70] in favor of the WCC, the
actual affiliation took place in 1969.[71] It was on that occasion that the
church in North America expressed its concern in a great variety of ways.
The GKN delegates to the synods of the sister church in North America
were given the mandate to do everything possible to remove the objections
which had been raised, or at least to weaken them. Such was the case in
1962 when Professor Hendrik Bergema expressed hope concerning the

67. Henry Baker, "Toespraak," in *Acta* van de Generale Synode van de Gereformeerde Kerken in Nederland, Gehouden te Rotterdam van 26 Augustus–6 November 1952 en 5 Januari–16 Januari 1953 (Kampen: Kok, 1953), pp. 263–264 (Bijlage I).
68. *Acts of Synod 1957* of the Christian Reformed Church, June 12 to June 26, 1957, Grand Rapids, Michigan (Grand Rapids: Christian Reformed Publishing House, 1957), pp. 36–37 (Art. 65).
69. *Acta* van de Generale Synode en van de Voortgezette Generale Synode van de Gereformeerde Kerken in Nederland, Gehouden te 's-Gravenhage van 23 Augustus–3 November 1949 en van 28 Februari–3 Maart 1950 (Kampen: Kok, 1950), pp. 73–74 (Art. 185).
70. *Acta* van de Generale Synode van Groningen 1963 en 1964 van de Gereformeerde Kerken in Nederland, Gehouden te Groningen-Zuid op 2 en 3 Mei 1963, van 27 Augustus 1963 tot 22 September 1963, Gehouden te Lunteren van 7 Januari 1964 tot 17 Januari 1964 en van 2 Maart 1964 tot 6 Maart 1964 (Kampen: Kok, 1964), pp. 412–414 (Art. 495).
71. *Acta* van de Generale Synode van Sneek 1969 en 1970 van de Gereformeerde Kerken in Nederland, Gehouden te Sneek op 13 Mei 1969, te Lunteren van 25 Augustus t/m 5 September 1969, van 27 t/m 31 Oktober 1969, van 24 t/m 28 November 1969, van 5 t/m 9 Januari 1970, van 2 t/m 6 Februari 1970, van 2 t/m 6 Maart 1970 en van 27 April 1970 te Utrecht op 19 Juni 1970 en te Sneek van 2 t/m 5 November 1970 (Kampen: Kok, 1971), pp. 162–165 (Art. 185).

mission work in Indonesia and South America, but who also made an effort to elucidate the stance of the GKN concerning the WCC.[72] The same thing was done in a more thorough manner in 1965 by Professor Jan T. Bakker, who in addition made mention of other objections which had been raised in North America concerning the turn of events in the Netherlands. He called attention to the difference in circumstances in which both churches found themselves and very urgently requested that notwithstanding these differences mutual trust would be in evidence as both churches placed themselves under the light of the Word of God.[73]

It can hardly be denied, however, that beginning with those years a certain distance has begun to be felt in the mutual relationship between the two churches. At the Synod of Middelburg in 1965–1966 the Reverend William Haverkamp, president of the CRC Synod which had just been held, spoke. He had been born and baptized in the Netherlands and had grown up there. He mentioned that an overture from a consistory in Canada to censure the churches in the Netherlands because of their attitude toward the WCC had been rejected by his synod. At the same time he made sure that he called attention to the serious concern which was felt in his churches in regard to this matter.[74]

1965-1980

The matter of affiliation with the WCC was not the only matter which raised concern in North America. Other phenomena observed in the church in the Netherlands contributed to the rise of this critical attitude. The decision to admit women to the ecclesiastical offices caused surprise in North America. The main causes of concern, however, were declarations and actions in connection with the doctrine and the confessions of the church. These were interpreted as failures to maintain ecclesiastical discipline. The course of action taken toward Herman Wiersinga and his views of the doctrine of the atonement attracted special attention.

It was inevitable that at the encounters at the respective synods the delegates would express themselves on these matters. Those who came from the Netherlands tried in their speeches to gain the necessary understanding for the way things were going in their church and they asked for patience and prayer in these matters. They called attention to other

---

72. Hendrik Bergema, "Address," in *Acts of Synod 1962*, June 13 to June 22, 1962, Grand Rapids, Michigan (Grand Rapids: Christian Reformed Publishing House, 1962), pp. 422–474 (Suppl. 41).

73. Jan T. Bakker, "Address," in *Acts of Synod 1965*, June 9 to June 17, 1965, Sioux Center, Iowa (Grand Rapids: Christian Reformed Publishing House, 1965), pp. 440–442 (Suppl. 43).

74. *Acta* van de Generale Synode van Middelburg 1965 en 1966 van de Gereformeerde Kerken in Nederland, Gehouden te Middelburg op 11 Mei 1965, te Utrecht op 24 Juni 1965, te Lunteren van 31 Augustus 1965 tot 24 September 1965, te Utrecht op 21 Oktober 1965, te Lunteren van 4 Januari 1966 tot 21 Januari 1966, en van 14 Maart 1966 tot 16 Maart 1966 en te Utrecht op 22 September 1966 (Kampen: Kok, 1967), pp. 47–48 (Art. 51).

phenomena in their midst, such as the fact that a struggle had begun against various new theologies and the willingness to bring about changes in earlier statements concerning the conflict which had led to the formation of the Liberated Church according to Article 31 of the Church Order. The CRC Synod of 1969 took grateful note of this willingness.[75] A year earlier the CRC Synod had rejected a letter from the Liberated Church, in which the GKN was accused of deviation in doctrine and confession, and in which the statement was made that it no longer gave evidence of the marks of the true church.[76] This action was taken on the ground that it was not correct "that we should convey judgment by one Christian church against another Christian church."[77] It was obvious that, notwithstanding the existing concern, a severing of the ties with the sister church in the Netherlands was not even considered. The CRC Synod of 1968 gave evidence of the same spirit when it did not adopt a proposal from Classis Hamilton which wished to dissuade graduate studies in theology at the Free University in Amsterdam because of the views of some of its professors.[78]

This attitude was different from that adopted by the Orthodox Presbyterian Church, for it decided, as was reported to the CRC Synod of 1969, to sever completely its relations with the church in the Netherlands.[79] The GKN delegate who was present at the CRC Synod, the Reverend Douwe van Swigchem, took note of this. In his speech he made mention of the changes which were taking place in his church and paid special attention to its view of Scripture. He referred to the declarations of his synod about the first three chapters of Genesis, which constituted a revision of the decisions of the Synod of Assen of 1926. The intention he said, was to deal further with Scripture and its authority.[80] Nevertheless the objections on the part of the church in North America could not be met so easily. At the Synod of Sneek of this same year, i.e., 1969, Professor Marten H. Woudstra spoke as delegate of the CRC. He recalled the upheaval caused by the decisions made in the Netherlands. He added that in North America the question had been raised whether or not changes should be made in the ecclesiastical correspondence.[81] This caused Pieter G. Kunst, the president of this synod, to declare that this statement caused him and all of the synod pain. The relationship between the two churches, he said, should be maintained. In 1974 a change was indeed made in the correspondence

---

75. *Acts of Synod 1969*, June 11 to 20, 1969, Grand Rapids, Michigan (Grand Rapids: Christian Reformed Publishing House, 1969), pp. 347–354 (Suppl. 33).

76. *Acts of Synod 1968*, June 12 to 22, 1968, Grand Rapids, Michigan (Grand Rapids: Christian Reformed Publishing House, 1968), pp. 316–318 (Suppl. 22–A).

77. Ibid., p. 95 (Art. 122).

78. Ibid., pp. 93–94 (Art. 122).

79. *Acts of Synod 1969*, p. 10 (Art. 16).

80. Douwe van Swigchem, "Address," in *Acts of Synod 1969*, pp. 478–481 (Suppl. 54).

81. Marten H. Woudstra, "Toespraak," in *Acta 1969 en 1970*, pp. 82–83 (Art. 84).

referred to, but it was much less radical than apparently had been feared. In essence the idea of a mother-daughter relationship was completely abandoned. In other words, the unique position which the church in the Netherlands had held was terminated. From now on it was placed on an equal level with a number of other churches of Reformed confession with whom a close relationship was maintained: a relationship of ecclesiastical fellowship. This new arrangement introduced the idea that the churches who were part of this fellowship accepted greater responsibility for each other and would more carefully watch what the others were doing; further, that a transition from one church to the other would not take place unconditionally but would be accompanied by a closer examination of doctrine and life.[82]

This certainly did not mean that the church in North America wanted everything to remain as it always had been. On the contrary, it too knew how to keep up with developments. It did not hesitate to bring about changes in church order and liturgy, and in other respects also much care was given to improve the life of the church. But the one thing it did not want was abandonment of the once accepted principles of Reformed Protestantism. The desire to preserve these principles also made it vigilant when it came to those churches with whom they had established this relationship. And it is especially during the period of time with which we are dealing that this was shown in a convincing manner. In the Netherlands there was no lack of understanding of this desire. This is evident from the fact that GKN deputies to the CRC, in their report to the Synod of Maastricht in 1975, spoke of the very intimate ties between the church in North America and the church in the Netherlands.[83] They emphasized that at the Synod of Haarlem in 1973 Professor John H. Stek had in an impressive way given expression to the deep concern which was felt in his church about the direction taken in the Netherlands, a direction which threatened to lead to a complete alienation between the churches.[84] The tenor of Stek's address had been to call attention to an important defect which had been present in the relationship between the two churches during the past period of time; the fact that there had been no meeting and consultation between delegations from both churches about pending questions.[85] To this it should be added, that when Stek reported to his own synod in 1974,

---

82. *Acts of Synod 1974*, June 11 to 21, 1974, Grand Rapids, Michigan (Grand Rapids: Board of Publications of the Christian Reformed Church, 1974), pp. 346–348 (Suppl. 14).

83. *Acta* van de Generale Synode van Maastricht 1975/76 van de Gereformeerde Kerken in Nederland, Gehouden te Maastricht op 13 Mei 1975, te Lunteren van 23 t/m 26 September 1975, van 9 t/m 11 Oktober 1975, van 18 t/m 22 November 1975, van 1 t/m 5 Maart 1976, van 29 Maart t/m 2 April 1976, op 25 en 26 Mei 1976, van 5 t/m 8 Oktober 1976, van 1 t/m 4 November 1976, van 22 t/m 26 November 1976 (Kampen: Kok, 1977), pp. 16–18, 27–28 (Bijlage 2).

84. John H. Stek, "Address of Professor John Stek to the 1973 Synod of Haarlem Gereformeerde Kerken, the Netherlands," *The Banner* 109 (August 16, 1974):13–15.

85. *Acts of Synod 1974*, pp. 347–348 (Suppl. 14).

he called attention to the fact that at the same Synod of Haarlem a common testimony of faith had been adopted, written by Berkouwer and Ridderbos, and this was in his opinion a good piece of work.[86]

The presentation by Stek was not without fruit. At following synods stronger delegations appeared and the opportunity was given to have an exchange of opinion with the delegates. It goes without saying that this did not remove the substance of the complaints. It was especially the course of action taken by the Synod of Haarlem, mentioned above, in the Wiersinga matter, which caused much dissatisfaction. In the serious address given by Professor John H. Kromminga at the Synod of Maastricht, this was expressed in an intense but sensitive way. He called attention to the meaning of ecclesiastical fellowship which now had been adopted as a guideline for mutual relationship. He further related a few matters regarding inter-church contacts as they were actually in existence. In describing the situation in his own church, he made it especially clear that it too did not exactly live up to its high calling and that its love was not as great and full of self-denial as the Lord demands from us. In his church there was a desire to look for communion with and help from those who shared with them one and the same heritage. It was in this very spirit, he said that he now addressed the church in the Netherlands, with which his church felt a very close relationship, more so than with any other church in the world. The essence of this unity was found, in his opinion, in subscription to a common confession in the same spirit. It was precisely at this point that concern had risen in his church concerning the course of action taken in connection with certain matters of doctrine. There were some who, because of this, wanted to make short shrift and cut off all relations. Before taking any action of such a nature, however, his synod was of the opinion that it was necessary to obtain a clear picture of the actual situation. At that particular moment it had already become clear to him that within the church in the Netherlands there certainly was no intention to be unfaithful to the confession. But this did not mean that there was no longer any reason to be deeply concerned. He formulated this in a few questions:

> Could it perhaps be possible that within the Gereformeerde Kerken in Neder-land one could say that theology had become detached from the firm anchor as it is found in the confession? Could it be that the fine points are being omitted when doctrinal matters are being dealt with, and could this perhaps have led to the fact that many are no longer able to recognize the seriousness of an important deviation? Could it be that secularization has already pene-trated into the church to such an extent that sound doctrine has ended in second place? Could it be that the church encourages such deviations because of her failure to take decisive measures when an important error has been recognized as such?[87]

86. Ibid., p. 55 (Art. 56).
87. John H. Kromminga, "Toespraak," in *Acta* 1975/76, p. 60 (Bijlage 4).

Kromminga stated that if there was a desire to deal with each other in a different way than was customary in the past when church discipline was exercised, this could, in his opinion, create serious dangers for the well-being of the church. "Has not the time arrived for the healing action of discipline—a discipline which can only be applied, to be sure, after ample consideration and with much patience, but in which determination may not be lacking because the credibility of the church is at stake?" The confessional character of the church, he stated further, brings with it confessional unity. Concern for the body as a whole should therefore be given more weight than the concern for the individual members of the body, which is the church of Christ. This leads to the question:

> Are all the members of the church, regardless of their position, willing to acquiesce in the judgment of the church as a whole? Or should we perhaps leave room for the possibility of an endless variation of individual opinions, even when the church speaks against the background of her most sacred convictions? This is not just a question of minor importance; it touches the very heart of the church. It is a matter which concerns every single member of the church, young and old, teacher and student, officebearer and those who are not officebearers.[88]

It would not be right to do violence to conscience, said Kromminga. Yet on the other hand, all members of the church should realize that they are members of a body of which Christ alone is the Head and that the Spirit of the Lord, who dwells in this body, leads into all truth. Liberty of doctrine in teaching results in divisions and brings confusion; it destroys the solidarity of the church, whose hallmark it is to follow her Head Christ in obedience to His Word.[89]

It is hard to verify to what extent the words spoken by Kromminga have influenced the actions of the synod in the Netherlands. For myself I do not hesitate to declare myself in full agreement with them. In fact the decisions of the Synod of Maastricht have been well received. In the following synod, which met in 1977 in Zwolle, the Reverend Tymen E. Hofman spoke on behalf of the delegates from North America. He gave assurance that the decisions of the Synod of Maastricht concerning the work of Christ in the reconciliation between God and man had been brought to the attention of his synod and that this synod had reacted favorably. She had regarded them as proof that the church in the Netherlands had taken steps "to maintain the confession of the church," and that she was also concerned "to maintain the unity of the church around this confession." Expression was given to the hope that in the future also, when dealing with these and eventually with other questions of doctrine, the GKN would remain faithful to this same principle of Reformed church life.

88. Ibid., p. 61.
89. Ibid., pp. 57–62.

In his speech, Hofman brought up yet another subject. it is important that I intentionally include a reference to it here. It had to do with the large number of emigrants who left the Netherlands after World War II to settle in Canada where they, as far as the church is concerned, became part of the CRC. The majority of these immigrants came from the church which, among others, is the subject of this contribution. It appears that in this way no less than 160 new congregations have come into being. Concerning the members and ministers of these churches we learn from the speech concerned that they were characterized by "sound theological insight and a powerful vision of and dedication to an integration of faith with life in all its facets, not only in the kingdom of God but also in the world." Their presence may initially have caused friction, but—so we are assured—slowly but surely "a new unity with greater diversity has grown" between the two sectors of the church. Because of this the danger of deterioration into fundamentalism has been averted and a new inspiration was gained in the struggle against secularism. That is why Hofman thought that he could justifiably speak of "a great gift from the hand of God's providence."[90]

Epilogue

In the midst of all that happened and changed, the relationship between the two churches has been maintained. It cannot be denied that there still are differences, notwithstanding the fact that in 1977 both could say that they had come closer together. And it is unlikely that these differences will be completely removed. Rather I cannot get rid of the thought that new ones will be added. The report on the nature of biblical authority which saw the light in the Netherlands in 1981 can no doubt add material for this. It does not make much sense, however, to enter into further speculations about these and other possible points of difference. One can only wish that on the part of both churches the sense of responsibility toward each other may manifest itself clearly and conscientiously and that a dedicated effort will be shown in examining all questions and problems which may be raised, seeking together for a reasonable solution in strict submission to the Word of God.

At the end of my review I believe I can justifiably say that at no time have the mutual relations between both churches been so serious and thorough as during the period last mentioned. In earlier periods they have, notwithstanding all the signs of friendliness and of a brotherly spirit, only too often lived alongside each other in a more or less loose fashion. An exception

---

90. Tymen E. Hofman, "Toespraak," in *Acta* van de Generale Synode van Zwolle 1977/1979 van de Gereformeerde Kerken in Nederland, Gehouden te Zwolle op 10 Mei 1977, te Lunteren van 10 t/m 13 Oktober 1977, van 14 t/m 18 November 1977, van 6 t/m 9 Maart 1978, van 3 t/m 6 April 1978, van 10 t/m 13 Oktober 1978, van 20 t/m 24 November 1978, van 9 t/m 10 Januari 1979 (Kampen: Kok, 1979), pp. 119–123 (Bijlage 22).

occurred in the period after World War II. The cordial solidarity which made itself felt during that time ought to be faithfully preserved in our memory. Yet the fact should not escape us that even then the idea of what it means to stand together in the world—also together with other churches, to be sure—as the church of Jesus Christ with the calling to witness in and to this world of his Lordship was too seldom brought to the fore. The same must be said for a comprehensive and thorough sense of responsibility for each other. It is no little thing when we claim to be the church of Christ and when we try to give account of this claim to one another. Together we will have to make an effort to understand what this implies. In all this it will be our constant task to watch diligently over one another and to be of service to each other in a spirit of humility and brotherly love. Only if this calling is rightly understood and realized will there be readiness on both sides to listen to each other, while the one considers the other more excellent than himself. If that is the case, one church will not easily let go of the other and leave her to her own fate. Instead, the mutual relations will remain and will be maintained as intimately and as faithfully as possible.

16

The Christian Reformed Church and the World Council of Churches

Klaas Runia

During the greater part of this century the Christian Reformed Church (hereafter CRC) has frequently been engaged in reflection on the ecumenical task of the church. At times the reflection issued in ecumenical affiliations. From 1918–1924 the CRC was affiliated with the Federal Council of the Churches of Christ in America (hereafter FCC). From 1943–1951 it was a member of the National Association of Evangelicals. In 1946 it participated in the preparatory meeting for the establishment of a Reformed Ecumenical Synod (hereafter RES) and since then it has actively supported the work of this synod. At no time, however, has it been a member of the World Council of Churches (hereafter WCC). The question of membership in the WCC has often been discussed. Both the *Acts* of various CRC synods and the periodical literature appearing within the community of the CRC bear this out.

It is fitting that this Festschrift for John H. Kromminga should contain an article on the relation between the CRC and the WCC, for he has not only written about the subject in various CRC periodicals,[1] but he also was one of the signatories of the important minority report for the 1967 Synod[2]

---

1. Not trying to be complete, I only mention the following articles: John H. Kromminga, "Ecumenics and Confessions," *The Calvin Forum* 20 (1954/55):103–109; John H. Kromminga, "World Council Assembly—Before and After," *The Banner* 110 (November 28, 1975):24; John H. Kromminga, "World Council Assembly," *The Banner* 111 (February 20, 1976):6–7, 27; John H. Kromminga, "Evangelical Influence on the Ecumenical Movement," *Calvin Theological Journal* 11 (1976):149–180; John H. Kromminga, "Ecumenicity . . . the World Council of Churches," *The Federation Messenger* 38 (1966/67):245–247. There is also Kromminga's book entitled *All One Body We*, The Doctrine of the Church in Ecumenical Perspective (Grand Rapids: Eerdmans, 1970).

2. *Acts of Synod 1967*, June 14 to 24, 1967, Reconvened August 29 and 30, 1967, at Calvin College, Grand Rapids, Michigan (Grand Rapids: Christian Reformed Publishing Co., 1967), pp. 444–485 (Suppl. 39-B).

and was present at the WCC Assembly in Nairobi in 1975 as an official observer of his denomination.[3] In other words, throughout his career Kromminga has been deeply involved in the process that determined and still determines the attitude of the CRC to the WCC.

To understand the attitude of the CRC it is necessary to give attention to two important developments, both of which took place before the establishment of the WCC itself.

The first is the CRC's experience with the FCC (the predecessor of the present National Council of Churches). The CRC joined this council in 1918 mainly for practical reasons, but its affiliation was of short duration.[4] A mere six years later it decided to terminate its membership. Three grounds were presented for this decision:

> 1. There is a burdening conviction in our churches that ecclesiastical alliances of any kind between orthodox and liberals are contrary to the Word of God; 2. Liberalism is strongly in evidence in the Council as is clearly seen from its emphasis on the social gospel and its humanitarian tendencies; 3. The Council stands committed to elaborate programs pertaining to industrial, national, and international affairs which our churches have never endorsed and should not endorse, even if we could fully agree with them, since they do not belong to the province of the church as an organization.[5]

This decision, together with its grounds, played an important role in the subsequent history of the CRC as far as its ecumenical relations are concerned. These same three arguments return again and again in later discussions and decisions concerning affiliation with the WCC. As late as 1958 these grounds were simply repeated in a synodical decision concerning the Alameda CRC which had joined the Alameda Council of Churches. As a matter of fact the 1958 decision was even more strongly worded than the original 1924 decision, for the first ground was restated to read: "Scripture forbids such association with unbelievers and with those who preach another Gospel. Cf. 2 Cor. 6:14–18 and Gal. 1:8–9."[6] In other words, the attitude of the CRC had hardened at this point and this contributed to the CRC's strong opposition to membership in the WCC. The two issues have influenced each other![7]

---

3. *Acts of Synod 1975*, June 10 to 20, 1975, at Calvin College, Grand Rapids, Michigan (Grand Rapids: Board of Publications of the Christian Reformed Church, 1975), p. 24 (Art. 36).

4. *Acta der Synode 1918* van de Christelijke Gereformeerde Kerk, Gehouden van 19 tot 29 Juni, 1918 te Grand Rapids, Michigan (Grand Rapids: M. Hoffius, 1918), p. 43 (Art. 41).

5. *Acta der Synode 1924* van de Christelijke Gereformeerde Kerk, Gehouden van 18 Juni tot 8 Juli, 1924 te Kalamazoo, Michigan (Grand Rapids: Grand Rapids Printing Co., 1924), p. 112 (Art. 95).

6. *Acts of Synod 1958*, June 11 to June 21, 1958, at Calvin College, Grand Rapids, Michigan (Grand Rapids: Christian Reformed Publishing House, 1958), p. 93 (Art. 151).

7. Cf. also John Vander Ploeg, "Why not in the World Council," *The Banner* 97 (January 12, 1962):8–9. Vander Ploeg, in his argumentation against affiliation with the WCC, appeals, among others, to the 1958 decision concerning the Alameda CRC. A decision that was reaffirmed, see *Acts of Synod 1959*, June 10 to

The second development to be mentioned here is the ecumenical policy statement the CRC adopted in 1944.[8] It is not possible to deal at great length with this important report nor is it necessary to quote in full the twelve-point summary given at the end of that report.[9] Only the main lines of argument need be mentioned. Two main points characterize the report. The first is a statement of principle. The report clearly stated that it will not do to declare that all non-Reformed churches are "non-churches." The report summarizes: "On the assumption that other churches than our own are Christian churches indeed, those churches and our own are closely related as being all and severally manifestations of the one and indivisible body of Christ."[10] The same idea, now specifically applied to non-Reformed churches, appears in point 8: ". . . the non-Reformed churches, whether Protestant or non-Protestant, are Christian churches indeed, even though they are defective enough."[11] Secondly, the 1944 decision also indicates a line of action. If the non-Reformed churches are seen as Christian churches, however defective, it follows that the CRC has a duty and task toward them. Point 8 of the summary also states that "surely the CRC, for one, should make it its business to labor with them in love in order to help them, by the blessing of God, to attain a more scriptural character."[12] In the body of the report the task is described even more clearly: "If we believe that all Christians should be Reformed—and this we profess to believe—then we should at least try, ecclesiastically as well as otherwise, to win them for the Reformed faith, and so pave the way for our eventual union with them, please God."[13] The means of doing so, according to the report, is that of "correspondence."[14]

It cannot be denied that this is an important statement. As far as the "principle" is concerned one can only agree wholeheartedly. It is not only fully in line with the Reformed tradition,[15] but it also reveals a truly ecumenical ecclesiology. As far as the suggested line of action is concerned, it falls far short of an acceptable ecumenical ecclesiology. First of all, the goal is narrow-minded: all other churches ought to become Reformed! There is no hint whatever that the goal of ecumenicity is much higher: a new

---

June 24, 1959, at Calvin College, Grand Rapids, Michigan (Grand Rapids: Christian Reformed Publishing House, 1959), p. 60 (Art. 127).

8. *Acts of Synod 1944* of the Christian Reformed Church, June 14 to June 23, 1944, at Grand Rapids, Michigan (Grand Rapids: Christian Reformed Church, 1944), pp. 330–367 (Suppl. 21).

9. Ibid., pp. 357–361. These twelve points are quoted in full in the 1967 minority report, *Acts of Synod 1967*, pp. 453–456; Cf. also the still shorter summary in *Acts of Synod 1967*, pp. 382–383 (Suppl. 39-A).

10. Ibid., p. 357.

11. Ibid., p. 359.

12. Ibid.

13. Ibid., pp. 349–350.

14. Ibid., pp. 350–351.

15. Cf. Andries D. R. Polman, *Onze Nederlandsche Geloofsbelijdenis*, Verklaard uit het Verleden Geconfronteerd met het Heden, 4 vols. (Franeker: T. Wever, 1948–53), 3:229–278.

church that transcends the onesidedness and shortcomings of all existing churches (including the Reformed churches) and that it "may have power, together with all the saints, to grasp how wide and long and high and deep is the love of Christ, and to know this love that surpasses knowledge" (Eph. 3:18–19, NIV). Second, the ecumenical methodology offered, "correspondence," is poor indeed. Taken literally, it means that it will suffice for the CRC to send letters to other non-Reformed churches, telling them where they are wrong and urging them to mend their ways. Is this really the way to fulfil one's ecumenical calling? Does a genuine ecumenical endeavor not require more? Does it not entail that at least one is willing to enter into face-to-face conversation and dialogue with the other churches?

Whatever our appreciation of the 1944 statement may be, it is an undeniable fact that this statement has been basic to all CRC ecumenical policy and determinative for its attitude toward the WCC.

We shall now proceed to summarize the decisions various synods have taken concerning the WCC. We shall concentrate on the synodical decisions and not on articles published in various periodicals because the former constitute the official position of the denomination. Whenever necessary or helpful, however, we shall refer to statements made by leaders in the CRC.

The first mention of the WCC is in the *Acts of Synod 1950*.[16] Prior to 1950 the WCC had been discussed several times in the denominations's related periodicals,[17] but apparently the establishment of the WCC in 1948 had not raised any particular question on the institutional level. At the 1950 Synod Clarence Bouma reported on his assignment as fraternal delegate to the Synod of 's-Gravenhage of the Gereformeerde Kerken in Nederland (hereafter GKN). He reported that he strongly warned the GKN synod against membership in the WCC.[18] At the RES of Amsterdam 1949, which had convened prior to the Synod of 's-Gravenhage, there appeared to be "a number of delegates and a few Dutch professorial advisers who were favorably disposed toward membership in the WCC."[19] Although they did

---

16. Clarence Bouma, "Report of Fraternal Delegate to the General Synod of 'De Gereformeerde Kerken in Nederland,' Held at the Hague, 1949" *Acts of Synod 1950* of the Christian Reformed Church, June 14 to June 24, 1950, Calvin College, Grand Rapids, Michigan (Grand Rapids: Christian Reformed Publishing House, 1950), pp. 432–433.

17. E.g., Peter Van Tuinen, "Catholic Views on the World Council," *The Banner* 83 (1948):712; Peter Van Tuinen, "Reformed Churches and the World Council," *The Banner* 83 (1948):958; Peter Van Tuinen, "The Churches and the World Council," *The Banner* 83 (1948):1006; Peter Van Tuinen, "Voices at Amsterdam," *The Banner* 83 (1948):1160; Henry J. Kuiper, "Some Thoughts on the World Council of Churches," *The Banner* 83 (1948):1348–1349; Jacob T. Hoogstra, "The World Council at Amsterdam," *The Calvin Forum* 13 (1947/48):239–241; Clarence Bouma, "Reformed Ecumenical Synod: Amsterdam, 1949," *The Calvin Forum* 15 (1949/50):35–37; Clarence Bouma, "Ecumenicity—Spurious and Genuine," *The Calvin Forum* 15 (1949/50):59–62. Nearly all of these articles are strongly negative. Bouma, for instance, in his first article expresses his amazement and concern about the favorable attitude of some of the Dutch leaders to joining the WCC. In his second article he declares that the liberals are in control of the WCC. As a matter of fact many (if not most) of the large Protestant denominations are either themselves apostate as a whole or are in control of an apostate leadership.

18. Bouma, "Report of Fraternal Delegate," p. 433.

19. Ibid., p. 432.

not carry the day at the RES, "this type of thinking . . . was strong enough that no vote of repudiation of the World Council took place, and a committee to study the matter was appointed."[20] Bouma apparently found such a committee entirely unnecessary and superfluous!

The *Acts of Synod 1954* contain three matters of interest. First, there is the report that the Home Missions Committee had delegated the Reverends Peter H. Eldersveld and Harold Dekker as observers to the coming Assembly of the WCC in Evanston. The *Acts of Synod* only record: "Received as information."[21] Secondly, Synod itself decided to approve the intent of the Committee of Ecumenicity and Inter-Church Correspondence to have an observer at Evanston.[22] The third item is found in the report of the delegates to the 1953 RES in Edinburgh. They reported concerning the RES decision to advise the member churches not to join the WCC as now constituted.[23] The 1954 CRC Synod itself took no action on this matter. The report was received as a "significant item of information."[24]

The two official observers to the Evanston Assembly, the Reverends Jacob T. Hoogstra and William H. Rutgers, reported to Synod of 1955.[25] It is evident that the WCC Assembly was better than they had anticipated.[26] It was a truly ecumenical forum and included fine studies oriented to God's Word. In their opinion it would be wrong to daub the WCC as the apostate church, although it could not be denied that there are strong elements of apostasy in it.[27] Some problem areas were mentioned such as, "Unity precedes the oneness in the truth," and, "There seems to be no heresies any more, only different insights into the truth."[28] Finally the observers stated: "All ecumenicity which receives our support must be based upon the confession of the inerrancy of Scripture."[29] It is clear that these observers could not recommend joining the WCC. On the contrary, they explicitly

20. Ibid., p. 433.

21. *Acts of Synod 1954* of the Christian Reformed Church, June 9 to June 19, 1954, Calvin College, Grand Rapids, Michigan (Grand Rapids: Christian Reformed Publishing House, 1954), pp. 40–41 (Art. 84).

22. *Acts of Synod 1954*, p. 50 (Art. 101). The reasons given by the Committee are: 1. We should view this movement by actual observation; 2. Thus we can keep the entire denomination fully informed, *Acts of Synod 1954*, p. 145 (Suppl. 6).

23. *Acts of Synod 1954*, pp. 549–550 (Suppl. 41). The RES adduced two grounds: "a. The World Council of Churches actually permits essentially different interpretations of its doctrinal basis, and thus of the nature of the Christian faith; b. The World Council of Churches represents itself as a Community of faith, but is actually not this, for Churches of basically divergent positions are comprised in the World Council of Churches." In addition, RES member churches "which are already members of the WCC are requested to reconsider their position in the light of the foregoing." Ibid., pp. 549–550.

24. Ibid., p. 82 (Art. 141).

25. Clarence Bouma, "Observer's Report on Three 1954 Ecumenical Assemblies," *Acts of Synod 1955* of the Christian Reformed Church, June 8 to June 18, 1955, Calvin College, Grand Rapids, Michigan (Grand Rapids: Christian Reformed Publishing House, 1955), pp. 279–282.

26. Cf. also the statement of Kromminga, "Ecumenics and Confessions," p. 103, that "Evanston was almost wholly attractive."

27. Bouma, "Three 1954 Ecumenical Assemblies," pp. 279–280.

28. Ibid., pp. 280–281.

29. Ibid., p. 281.

stated that the witness of the CRC should go through the RES rather than through the WCC. "From the point of expediency we would be a stronger witness without than within, considering the huge machinery of the WCC."[30]

The 1955 Synod also decided to include in its *Acts* the advice of the RES of Edinburgh 1953 pertaining to WCC membership.[31] This action was taken in view of a letter of the Reformed Churches of New Zealand, remonstrating against the fact that some RES member churches had joined the WCC immediately after Edinburgh.[32]

In its report to the 1956 Synod the Committee on Ecumenicity and Inter-Church Correspondence suggested that a special study should be made of the relationship of GKN to the WCC. It suggested that contact could be made with a similar study committee appointed by the GKN.[33] Synod answered by mandating the Committee on Ecumenicity to study the questions in the New Zealand letter regarding compatibility of membership in the WCC and the RES.[34]

The 1957 Synod received a report on the questions raised in the New Zealand letter.[35] The committee reported that it was not a matter of either-or/either: compatible or incompatible. Admittedly, Edinburgh made a clear decision, but it also respected the liberty of the member churches to determine their own affiliations. All member churches have subscribed to the Reformed faith, and as long as they maintain their Reformed character, they comply with the requirements of fellowship. Naturally, this does not mean that Edinburgh was indifferent as to what the churches do concerning ecumenical affiliations. It only conceded its limitations, at the same time expressing the hope that by persuasion all its members might adopt the same position.[36] The report closed with a recommendation that:

> Synod advised the Ecumenical Synod of 1958 to abide by the decision of the RES of Edinburgh of 1953 re membership in the Reformed Ecumenical Synod and the World Council of Churches 1. The RES of Edinburgh gave a positive testimony in urging its members holding membership in the WCC to

30. Ibid., p. 282. Kromminga, "Ecumenics and Confessions," p. 109, concludes that it is far better to stay outside the WCC. "This isolation, I believe, is not something to be ashamed of. . . . Our forefathers have bought the truth—bought it dearly in some cases. Now we are simply trying, despite reproach and isolation, to live out the other half of that scriptural exhortation concerning the truth—'and sell it not'"; cf. also his argument on page 108.

31. *Acts of Synod 1955*, pp. 31–32 (Art. 64).

32. Whether or not this inclusion was caused by the letter of the Reformed Churches of New Zealand cannot be assertained from the *Acts of Synod.* But there must have been a close connection.

33. *Acts of Synod 1956* of the Christian Reformed Church, June 13 to June 26, 1956, Calvin College, Grand Rapids, Michigan (Grand Rapids: Christian Reformed Publishing House, 1956), p. 251 (Suppl. 17).

34. Ibid.

35. *Acts of Synod 1957,* Centennial Year of the Christian Reformed Church, June 12 to June 26, 1957, Calvin College, Grand Rapids, Michigan (Grand Rapids: Christian Reformed Publishing House, 1957), pp. 301–303 (Suppl. 18).

36. Ibid., p. 302.

review their position. 2. The conditions for membership in the RES as stipulated in Art. IV of the Rules Pertaining to the Reformed Ecumenical Synod (cf. pp. 35–36 of Acts of RES) are sound and specific. These are not necessarily violated by a denomination which holds membership in the WCC, although we consider such membership highly inadvisable as the Edinburgh Synod also judged. 3. A matter of this kind should be approached through persuasion rather than through absolutistic rules.[37]

On one hand it strongly supported the Edinburgh decision. On the other hand it refused to make non-membership in the WCC a condition for membership in the RES. In other words, even though it preferred membership in the RES only, it did not rule out membership in both RES and the WCC.

What did Synod do with this recommendation? It is interesting to note that it adopted the whole recommendation with the exception of the second sentence in the second ground! This meant that Synod refused to declare itself on the matter of dual membership. It neither approved such dual membership, nor did it exclude it. At the same time it did retain the first part of ground 2 which stated that "the conditions for membership in the RES . . . are sound and specific."[38] But these conditions say nothing about membership in the WCC! We can only conclude that Synod was wary of approving dual membership. Yet it did not want (or dare) to forbid it either, as is proved by the third ground. As far as dual membership was concerned, the decision was plainly ambiguous.

In 1962 the Committee of Ecumenicity and Inter-Church Correspondence presented to Synod an appraisal of the GKN report, "Ecumenicity and Pluriformity." The committee was of the opinion that this report was weak and that in several respects the report did not complete the assigned mandate, noting among other matters that "The examining of the question whether, and to what extent, accordance of confession and maintenance of confession are necessary to be able to come to ecumenical cooperation. Such examination should, in our judgment, involve an evaluation of the strong influence of Barthianism in modern ecumenism; of the attitude of existing ecumenical councils toward world-wide Communism; of the practical reality of the liberal leadership in such organizations as the WCC and International Missionary Council; and whether our Reformed standards and the Word of God allow ecclesiastical fellowship with those who are not 'of like precious faith with us,'"[39] Synod decided to forward the proposed evaluations and other materials to the secretary of the Committee of Deputies for Ecumenicity of the GKN.[40]

37. Ibid., p. 303.
38. Ibid., pp. 102–103 (Art. 173).
39. *Acts of Synod 1962*, June 13 to June 22, 1962, at Calvin College, Grand Rapids, Michigan (Grand Rapids: Christian Reformed Publishing House, 1962), p. 391 (Suppl. 31).
40. Ibid., p. 42 (Art. 78).

A new situation arose when in 1964 the Synod of the GKN declared that there is "no decisive impediment for the Reformed Churches to join the WCC."[41] To be sure, the Dutch Synod at the same time decided not to proceed as yet to affiliation because there was still too much disagreement within the Dutch churches themselves. For the time being it did not go beyond asking its own churches to study the decision and inviting sister churches belonging to the RES to give their opinion.[42] The 1966 CRC Synod dealt with this request and appointed a study committee on the WCC.[43] The committee received a double mandate: a. to define the CRC position with respect to the WCC; and b. to prepare a statement that could serve as the CRC reply to the resolutions of the GKN.[44] Of special interest is the first ground: "Synod has never explicitly defined its position."[45] Apparently Synod was well aware of the fact that until that time the CRC had done little else but echo the RES!

The year 1967 was important as far as the CRC stance toward the WCC was concerned. For the first time in its history the church had before it a very substantial report on the matter. In fact, it received two substantial reports because the study committee could not present a united report.[46] Since both reports are very lengthy it is impossible to summarize them here. The most we can do is to indicate the main lines of thought. As was to be expected, both reports largely cover the same ground and mention the same facts while arriving at quite different conclusions.

1. Both reports deal explicitly with past synodical decisions concerning the ecumenical calling of the CRC. The synodical report of 1944 plays an important part in both reports. Likewise, the twelve point summary is reproduced in both (albeit in slightly different forms). It is striking to see, however, that both use the 1944 decision in quite a different way. As we have already noted, the 1944 decision contained both a statement of principle and a course of action. The former was an explicit recognition of other churches as manifestations of the one and indivisible body of Christ. The latter defined the duty to win other churches for the Reformed faith. The major means of fulfilling this duty was "correspondence."

The majority did not see its way clear to apply the statement of principle

41. *Acta* van de Generale Synode van Groningen 1963 en 1964 van de Gereformeerde Kerken in Nederland, Gehouden te Groningen-Zuid op 2 en 3 Mei 1963, van 27 Augustus 1963 tot 20 September 1963, Gehouden te Lunteren van 7 Januari 1964 tot 17 Januari 1964 en van 2 Maart 1964 tot 6 Maart 1964 (Kampen: Kok, 1964), p. 413 (Art. 495).

42. Ibid.

43. *Acts of Synod 1966*, June 8 to June 16, 1966, at Central College, Pella, Iowa (Grand Rapids: Christian Reformed Publishing House, 1966), pp. 59–60 (Art. 84).

44. Ibid., p. 60.

45. Ibid.

46. *Acts of Synod 1967;* the Majority Report was signed by Peter Y. De Jong, Henry Evenhouse, Fred H. Klooster, Joel H. Nederhood, Louis Praamsma, and Richard S. Wierenga; see pages 380–443 (Suppl. 39-A); the Minority Report was signed by Clarence Boomsma and John H. Kromminga; see pages 444–485 (Suppl. 39-B).

to the WCC. While it did not deny its truth, this truth was not regarded as applicable to the WCC. In fact, the latter's claim to be a fellowship of churches which confess Jesus Christ as God and Savior was strongly contested. It may be true that the so-called "Toronto Statement" indicated that "membership [in the WCC] does not imply that each Church must regard the other member Churches as Churches in the true and full sense of the word. But this important reservation does not solve our problem."[47] By joining the WCC one affirms that all member churches are churches of Christ, share the given unity in Christ, and now manifest this unity in the WCC.[48] This is impossible for a Reformed church that seeks to remain true to the Bible and the Creeds.[49] Only one way is left: to witness to the WCC by staying outside it! But what about the course of action advocated in 1944 and reproduced at great length in the majority report?[50] The majority adhered to this course of action. Its last recommendation was "that a copy of this report, a transcript of these decisions, and an appropriate cover letter be sent to the secretariat of the World Council of Churches,"[51] and in the second ground for this recommendation it is stated that this "might open the way to a mutual correspondence."[52]

The minority placed the emphasis on the statement of principle contained in the 1944 decision. In its discussion of the WCC's claim to be a "fellowship of churches" it emphatically and explicitly recalled that the 1944 decision recognized other churches as churches of Christ. It also quoted at length what the 1944 report said on this matter and pointed out that even the Oriental and Roman Catholic Churches were recognized as churches of Christ.[53] Consequently the minority members found "a remarkable agreement" between the CRC stance and the "Toronto Statement" of the WCC.[54] It is interesting to note that its approach to this statement was quite different from that of the majority report. While the majority started off with the restrictive statement ("membership [in the WCC] does not imply that each Church must regard other member Churches as Churches in the true and full sense of the word")[55] and then declared that this does not solve the problem (for joining the WCC still

47. Ibid., p. 418. The official title of the "Toronto Statement" is "The Church, the Churches and the World Council of Churches," with the subtitle: "The Ecclesiological Significance of the World Council of Churches." It was received by the Central Committee in Toronto in 1950 and was commended for study and comment in the churches. Till now it is the most explicit statement of the WCC about its own ecclesiological nature. For the full text, see *A Documentary History of the Faith and Order Movement 1927–1963*, ed. Lukas Vischer (St. Louis: The Bethany Press, 1963), pp. 167–176.

48. Ibid.
49. Ibid., p. 419.
50. Ibid., pp. 392–393.
51. Ibid., p. 443.
52. Ibid.
53. Ibid., pp. 463–464.
54. Ibid., p. 465.
55. Ibid., p. 418.

means a recognition of the given unity in Christ),[56] the minority expressed the opposite conclusion. It first quoted the affirmation: "The member Churches recognize that the membership of the Church of Christ is more inclusive than the membership of their own Church body."[57] This was the minority's basic affirmation and in this assertion it was certainly in line with the Synod of 1944. But this was not the whole truth, and so another, somewhat restrictive affirmation needed to be added: "Nevertheless, membership does not imply that each Church must regard the other member Churches as Churches in the true and full sense of the word."[58] The minority believed that these complementary affirmations show "a remarkable agreement" with the 1944 report. Its conclusion was: "Both reports stand on high ground when they recognize the vestiges of the Church in other groups as the work of Christ and the Spirit. Perhaps the term 'fellowship' is not above criticism. But we cannot deny all fellowship. To deny the given unity is to deny the work of Christ."[59]

2. Both reports also dealt extensively with the biblical data. Here, too, they both cover largely the same ground. Again, the differences are striking and result in quite different conclusions.

Dealing with the subject "true Christian fellowship" the majority referred to two main lines of thought in the New Testament.[60] In the first place, this fellowship is constituted by adherence to the apostolic doctrine. "What . . . binds them together in this fellowship is the apostolic word."[61] Second, there is the converse to this fellowship: the duty to withhold fellowship from the unbelieving and unfaithful. At this point a number of texts are mentioned, such as James 4:4; Ephesians 5:10–11; Matthew 17:17; 1 Corinthians 5:13; 2 Thessalonians 3:6; 2 Corinthians 6:14–18; 2 John 10:11; Galatians 1:7–9; etc.[62] The section closed with the conclusion, "From all this it is apparent that according to Scripture true church fellowship always includes a denunciation of error and ungodliness and a calling to those who would be faithful to Christ and his gospel to separate themselves from all who persist in these sins."[63]

The minority referred to three lines of thought in the New Testament. The first two are identical with the two mentioned in the majority report. (1) Unity is fundamental to the church. It is a unity because of Christ; a unity in the truth; a unity in love; a unity that creates fellowship.[64] (2) There is a constant threat to this unity. It is constantly imperiled by error and

56. Ibid.
57. Ibid., p. 464.
58. Ibid., p. 465.
59. Ibid., p. 466.
60. Ibid., p. 407.
61. Ibid., p. 408.
62. Ibid., pp. 409–410.
63. Ibid., p. 410.
64. Ibid., pp. 445–446.

heresy on the one hand, and by sin and lack of love on the other. "A unity which is not in Christ, not in the truth, not in love, is a false unity, which in fact destroys the true unity. Therefore to preserve and to maintain the true unity of the Church it is necessary for the Church to separate from unbelief and evil."[65] (3) The minority, however, did not stop there. It pointed out that in the New Testament separation is not simply the last word. Such separation is also "limited, provisional, and hopefully unto the restoration of true fellowship."[66] The report quotes a number of instances from the Pauline writings where the apostle urged the churches to preserve and promote fellowship with erring and weak members who in some sense are brethren and must not be considered enemies. It is of special relevance to note how churches which manifest varying degrees of faithfulness to the truth are dealt with in the Epistles of Paul. In spite of all his severe criticisms, Paul did not hesitate to recognize the churches of Galatia and of Corinth as churches of Christ, and he never suggested breaking off fellowship with them. Similarly the exalted Lord, who is very critical of the seven churches of Asia Minor, never disowned them but continued to recognize them as his churches.[67] The final conclusion of the minority was, "We have a responsibility to all churches of Christ in order that we may all be one in Christ, in truth, and in love, and that our fellowship with Christ and with His body may be perfect."[68]

3. In their appraisals of the WCC both reports differ considerably. Although there is hardly any difference in their description of the data, the conclusions are quite divergent. The majority was of the opinion that the WCC is far from Reformed in both its nature and its actions, and therefore should be shunned. The minority agreed that the WCC is not Reformed, but believed that it is Christian enough to have fellowship with it and that there were sufficient opportunities to pass our Reformed heritage on to the other churches.

The majority mentioned no less than nine problems concerning the WCC. (1) The WCC wrongly and improperly claims to be a fellowship of Christian churches. (2) Its basis is inadequate for ecclesiastical fellowship in view of the doctrinal errors within churches today. (3) The WCC does not maintain its basis in a meaningful way. (4) Many of the socio-political activities and declarations of the WCC do not belong to the responsibility of the church. (5) By joining the WCC a genuinely Reformed church endorses this methodology and thereby beclouds or relativizes its own witness. These five problems are the main reasons why a Reformed church cannot join the WCC. Four additional problems were added. (6) Joining the WCC may inhibit or stifle our mission work. (7) There are syncretistic tendencies

65. Ibid., p. 449.
66. Ibid.
67. Ibid., p. 452.
68. Ibid., p. 453.

within the WCC. (8) The present functioning of the WCC does not promote real unity of conviction concerning the central issues of the Christian faith. (9) Joining the WCC may seriously harm ecumenical fellowship with other Reformed churches.[69]

The minority assessed the WCC quite differently and mentioned the following: (1) Taking into account the purpose of the WCC, namely, to bring together in a tentative way all Christians, the present basis of the WCC must be judged as sufficient for this purpose. (2) The limited fellowship claimed in the basis is one which the CRC has in essence recognized. (3) The problems arising from the way in which the basis functions are not sufficient to constitute a decisive consideration against joining the WCC.[70] On the basis of this evaluation it is not surprising to read that the minority answered the question whether it is permissible for a Reformed church to join the WCC in the following way: "... membership in the World Council of Churches does not constitute a denial of the faith nor involve a failure in obedience to the Word or loyalty to the Reformed Confessions, and therefore must be judged permissible to a Reformed Church."[71] The minority, however, asked a second question: Is WCC membership advisable for the CRC? Here matters are somewhat different. It cannot be denied that there are "some ambiguities and uncertainties" which persist within the Council.[72] For instance, there was a lack of definite theological orientation which made the WCC itself an arena in which the various theologies of today wrestle with each other. There was no clear method of interpretation of Scripture within the WCC. There were tendencies within the WCC to claim for itself a present ecclesiastical character to which it has no right. Moreover, membership in the WCC might conceivably harm our present relationship with other Reformed churches. (Of course, the responsibility is twofold! Other Reformed churches should be careful to lay on their sister churches no burden which is not required by obedience to Holy Scripture and loyalty to the Reformed Creeds!) The CRC must also consider what effect membership in the WCC might have on younger churches which were looking to the CRC for guidance in ecumenical matters. Finally, the CRC itself did not appear ready for membership in the WCC for two reasons, namely: lack of sufficient information and lack of experience in ecumenical activities. The conclusion, therefore, was that the CRC should postpone any definitive answer to the question of membership in the WCC.[73]

4. From the foregoing it naturally follows that both reports presented synod with quite different sets of recommendations.

---

69. Ibid., pp. 414–439.
70. Ibid., pp. 461–474.
71. Ibid., p. 474.
72. Ibid., p. 476.
73. Ibid., pp. 476–483.

The majority recommended among other things: (1) that Synod declare with regret that major objections to joining the fellowship of the WCC must be registered (here the first five points mentioned before were reiterated); (2) that Synod express its deep concern about the practical consequences of joining the WCC (here the last four points mentioned before were reiterated); (3) that Synod send a copy of this report to the GKN, to the secretariat and all the member churches of the RES, and to the secretariat of the WCC.[74]

In its recommendations the minority took its starting point, first of all, in the scriptural teaching of the unity of the church, declaring that this ought to come to visible expression, and second, in the position of the Synod of 1944 which declared that the CRC has a responsibility to all other churches. It then recommended that synod adopt the following declarations:

1. Synod judges that the basis, nature, and purpose of the World Council of Churches, as defined by its Constitution, are such as to permit a Reformed Church to seek membership in it.
2. Synod recognizes weighty problems involved in World Council membership, with respect to the actual functioning of the Council, the trends within the Council, and the implications of council membership for relations with other churches.
3. Synod urges the Gereformeerde Kerken to give due consideration, before applying for membership in the World Council of Churches, to the following matters:
   a. The preservation of their own internal unity;
   b. The question whether their total witness to the world, singly or in conjunction with other Reformed Churches, will be aided or impeded by World Council membership;
   c. The implications of the actual functioning of the World Council, judged by the best information available.[75]

What did the Synod of 1967 do with these reports? From the *Acts of Synod 1967* it appears that the advisory committee at Synod was also divided! It also presented a majority and a minority report. Unfortunately, the *Acts* do not report the discussion at Synod. Article 124 only states that "a number of motions fail to gain majority support." The next article states that the adjournment of this evening session took place "past midnight"![76] The next morning Synod again dealt with the matter. This time the majority report of the advisory committee served as the starting point. This report presented a careful analysis of both study reports, indicating some of the differences in approach. The majority of the advisory committee recommended that Synod not adopt the position of the minority report but

74. Ibid., pp. 441–443.
75. Ibid., pp. 484–485.
76. Ibid., p. 87 (Arts. 124 and 125).

follow the line suggested by the majority report (without, however, adopting all the detailed statements proposed by this report).[77]

The final result was that Synod declared "with regret that it is not permissible for the Christian Reformed Church to join the fellowship of the World Council of Churches because of its present nature, its inadequate basis, the maintenance and functioning of that basis, its socio-political activities and declarations, and the implications of membership in this Council" (the first five points of the majority report).[78] Synod further decided to communicate the following response to the GKN: (1) "in view of the grave implications of membership in the WCC, it is not sufficient enough to state that there is 'no decisive impediment,'" but one has "to demonstrate convincingly that one is acting in obedience to Scripture and in line with the Confession"; (2) assist us by "working out a positive statement on our ecumenical calling, in the context of our common confession of Articles 27–29 of the Belgic Confession," which demand of us (a) "fellowship with all who confess and obey Jesus Christ," and (b) "separation from those who reject, deny or pervert the truth of the Gospel"; (3) joining the WCC gives recognition also to churches with a radically different interpretation of the Gospel, i.e., churches which actually should be evangelized by us! "Therefore, membership in the WCC, even if it were permissible, would be inadvisable."[79] Finally, Synod decided to send these decisions to the GKN, the member churches of the RES and the General Secretary of the WCC, and to send two observers to the coming Assembly at Uppsala in 1968.[80] Synod appointed the Reverends William Haverkamp and John Vriend as observers.[81]

The two observers reported to the Synod of 1969. They pointed out, first of all, that Uppsala emphasized the churches' concern for the poor, the underprivileged, and underdeveloped peoples of the world. Consequently human rights came in for a good share of attention. This raised two questions for the CRC reporters: a. Does this passion for the improvement of human life arise directly from obedience to Jesus Christ? b. Is it the duty of the church as institute to set up the machinery with which to meet the social, economic, and political needs of mankind?[82] As far as the basis of the WCC and its functioning were concerned, the observers reported that appeals to the basis and to the biblical authority enshrined in it were honored. Their conclusion was "that the degree to which the basis functions can be affected favorably by participation in the Council's deliberations of

---

77. Ibid., pp. 87–89 (Art. 130).
78. Ibid., p. 89.
79. Ibid., pp. 90–91.
80. Ibid., p. 91.
81. Ibid., p. 95 (Art. 134).
82. *Acts of Synod 1969*, June 11 to 20, 1969, at Calvin College, Grand Rapids, Michigan (Grand Rapids: Christian Reformed Publishing House, 1969), pp. 146–147 (Suppl. 4).

competent, well-prepared Evangelicals."[83] As far as the work of the six sectionals of Uppsala was concerned, the observers noted that at times the emphasis on the social dimensions of the Gospel was very one-sided and that in many sessions a deep sense of dependence on divine grace for the realization of the aims announced was missing.[84]

In 1975 Kromminga attended the Assembly of Nairobi as an observer for the CRC. Unfortunately his official report was not included in the *Acts of Synod 1976*. However, he did give a review of the assembly in *The Banner*,[85] a review that turned out to be quite positive. In his opinion "the assembly was more inclined toward biblical, confessional, and evangelistic concerns than the preparatory materials and the staff influence would have suggested."[86] He also noted that there is a unity in the WCC and that this unity can only be described as a Christian unity. This does not mean that all the objections of the CRC have been removed. At most one can say that "in some respects the World Council in Nairobi appears less objectionable than it did in 1967."[87] His final conclusion was: "There have been many changes in World Council direction. They are, in the main, in a good direction. But they are far from sufficient to overcome the objections to membership raised by the Synod of 1967."[88] The best course of action for the CRC would be to continue careful observation, including the sending of observers.

This is, as far as the official record goes, a full description of the decisions of the CRC concerning the WCC. It cannot be denied that it is a consistent picture. Throughout the years the CRC has kept its distance from the WCC. Throughout the years its objections to the WCC remained the same. Throughout the years it closely followed the stance taken by the RES.

Undoubtedly the position of the CRC was deeply influenced by its own history and by the ecclesiastical situation in North America. The CRC came into existence through separation from the RCA. For many, many years the CRC existed in "splendid isolation" from other denominations. When in 1918, mainly for practical reasons, the CRC joined the FCC,[89] it soon discovered that this Council was riddled with modernism. For this reason it decided in 1924 to sever its connection with this Council,[90] on the

---

83. Ibid., p. 147.
84. Ibid., p. 151.
85. Kromminga, "World Council Assembly," pp. 6–7, 27.
86. Ibid., p. 6. Cf. also Kromminga, "Evangelical Influence on the Ecumenical Movement." On page 178 he assesses the evangelical influence as follows: genuine on the issue of evangelism; cosmetic on the issue of syncretism; none at all on the issue of politicizing the gospel.
87. Ibid., p. 27.
88. Ibid.
89. *Acta der Synode 1918*, p. 43 (Art. 41).
90. *Acta der Synode 1924*, pp. 111–112 (Art. 95). The closing remarks of Kromminga, "Evangelical Influence on the Ecumenical Movement," p. 180, should also be noted: "There is at least some reason for

basis of the three grounds mentioned at the beginning of this contribution. These grounds contain objections which are virtually identical with the objections raised afterwards against the WCC. When in 1944 the CRC tried to outline an ecumenical policy, there were two lines of thought. On one hand, the 1944 decision recognized other churches (including even the Oriental and Roman Catholic Churches) as churches of Christ. On the other hand, the 1944 decision limited its ecumenical methodology to the obligation of winning the other churches for the Reformed faith. When after 1944 the WCC came into existence, the CRC in its evaluation of this new ecumenical organization followed the latter rather than the former line of thought. In fact, there was an increasing emphasis on the incompatibility between the Reformed character of one's own church and the "mixed" character of the other churches. In 1958 it was declared with regard to membership in a local council of churches that Scripture forbids any association with unbelievers and with those who preach another gospel. Reference was made to such Scripture passages as II Corinthians 6:14–18 and Galatians 1:8–9. In the negative decision concerning membership in the WCC taken by the Synod of 1967 the statement of 1958 was reiterated.[91] Undoubtedly the ecclesiastical situation in the United States of America played a decisive part in the definition of the CRC position. This appears quite clearly from what the 1967 Synod wrote to the GKN: "Synod requests its sister churches to bear in mind the situation from which we are speaking. On our Continent we are daily confronted by the blight of theological modernism, and by the fact that evangelical churches—which, for example, supply the largest number of missionaries—are generally opposed to the WCC."[92]

The major decision, of course, was that taken by the 1967 Synod. For the first and so far only time the CRC dealt at length and explicitly with the question of membership in the WCC. It is interesting to note that Synod virtually came to the same decision as the RES of Amsterdam a year later. The RES then decided again to advise its member churches not to join the WCC. However, it added a few significant words, which are missing in the CRC decision, namely, "in the present situation."[93] The RES did not close the door altogether; the CRC Synod of 1967 spoke explicitly: "not permissible."

The most interesting aspect of the 1967 Synod decision, however, was

---

gratification in the way in which the two groups, evangelicals and ecumenicals, addressed each other and listened to each other. Some commonness of purpose, despite all qualifications, emerged from their dealings with each other. If this kind of mutual respect and attention to each other continues, it can only serve to the enrichment of both parties."

91. *Acts of Synod 1967,* p. 90 (Art. 130).

92. Ibid.

93. *Acts and Reports* of the Reformed Ecumenical Synod, Amsterdam, August 13–23, 1968 (Grand Rapids: The Reformed Ecumenical Synod, 1968), p. 45 (Art. 95).

that there were two major reports, the one rejecting membership in the WCC altogether, the other stating that membership, though in itself permissible, is not advisable for various reasons. The fact that two reports were submitted is evidence that the CRC was not of one mind in this matter. This is also indicated by the fact that in the same year the official denominational periodical, *The Banner*, in one and the same issue published two articles, the one advocating membership in the WCC, the other rejecting it.[94] These differences were not new, having already become manifest before 1967. In the early 1950's two journals were launched within the CRC community. The one was *Torch and Trumpet* (since 1971 called *The Outlook*), in which articles highly critical of the WCC were published at regular intervals.[95] The other was *The Reformed Journal* in which Lewis B. Smedes and James Daane published several articles advocating affiliation with the WCC.[96] Daane in particular submitted the 1967 decision of the CRC synod to a crushing criticism.[97] It is questionable, however, whether he does justice to this decision. At the end of his article he interpreted the 1967 Synod as saying: "Since the WCC admits, in the judgment of the Synod, churches that preach a radically different Gospel (no church is named), the WCC is, in the judgment of this Synod, worthy of Paul's *anathema*. Let it be damned."[98] A little further he asked: "How could the 1967 Synod raise its anathema, its 'let it be damned,' against the WCC and its 232 constituent churches?"[99] But this, of course, had not been said by synod! Taking his clue from synod's assertion that "Scripture forbids such association with unbelievers and with those who preach another Gospel,

---

94. Jacob D. Eppinga, "WCC? Yes," *The Banner* 102 (April 28, 1967):4–5; Eugene Bradford, "WCC? No," *The Banner* 102 (April 28, 1967):6–7. Eppinga offers three arguments for joining the WCC: a. The nature of the church: "The church is not obedient to her Lord when she is not ecumenical" (p. 4). b. The dividedness of the church is a hindrance for the world to accept Christ. c. The state of the world requires it. Bradford basically brings forward one main argument against joining the WCC: the latter does not really accept the Scriptures as the inspired Word of God and as the one infallible rule to which every one can appeal in seeking the resolution of their differences.

95. E.g., in 1962, volume 12 of *Torch and Trumpet* carried a series of articles on the historical development, the objectives and the basis of the WCC, the WCC and foreign missions, the WCC and the sixteenth-century Reformation. When the GKN declared in 1964 that there is "no decisive impediment" for the GKN to join the WCC, the then editor, Peter Y. De Jong, wrote a series of editorials opposing the GKN declaration. Again in 1967 De Jong wrote a long series of articles, while in the same year the volume contained three more major articles against affiliation with the WCC.

96. We mention the following articles: Lewis B. Smedes, "A Word for the World Council," *The Reformed Journal* 13 (July-August 1963):6–8; Lewis B. Smedes, "Another Word for the World Council of Churches," *The Reformed Journal* 13 (November 1963):5–6; Lewis B. Smedes, "The Dutch and the World Council," *The Reformed Journal* 14 (October 1964):5; James Daane, "Orthodoxy is not enough," *The Reformed Journal* 15 (March 15, 1965):4–5; James Daane, "The CRC and the WCC," *The Reformed Journal* 19 (January 1969):6–10; James Daane, "Reformed Church Joins WCC," *The Reformed Journal* 20 (January 1970):5; James Daane, "St. Paul and the World Council of Churches," *The Reformed Journal* 20 (January 1970):19–21.

97. Daane, "CRC and the WCC," pp. 6–10.

98. Ibid., p. 10.

99. Ibid.

Cf. 2 Cor. 6:14–18 and Gal. 1:8–9,"[100] Daane imposed upon his own synod a logic which Synod neither explicitly stated nor intended to state. Synod did not condemn the entire WCC and its 232 member churches as a group of unbelievers or false prophets, worthy of the Pauline anathema, but only stated that within the membership of the WCC there are churches with a radically different interpretation of the Gospel. Concerning such churches it stated that association was not permitted.

Even so, Synod's assessment of the WCC was very negative. In my opinion it was too negative. The more I study the phenomenon of the WCC, the more I realize that the WCC is a very complex entity which has a nature all its own.[101] If one simply compares it with or measures it by one's own ecclesiology, for instance the Reformed ecclesiology as outlined in the Belgic Confession Articles 27–29, one is forced to conclude that the WCC does not live up to this standard. But is this the correct approach? Does one use the right yardstick? I believe that the minority report of 1967 showed a more correct approach. It did not ask whether the WCC simply conformed with our Reformed ecclesiology but formulated the question as follows: "Would a Reformed Church be guilty of a denial of the faith it it undertook membership in the World Council? Would such membership involve an abandonment of loyalty to the Scriptures and to the Reformed Confessions?"[102] After a lengthy discussion of the basis of the WCC and its functioning, grounded on the interpretation of this basis as given by the WCC in its "Toronto Statement" and comparing it with the ecclesiology expounded by the 1944 CRC Synod, the minority report concluded that membership in the WCC does not mean a denial of the faith, disobedience to Scripture, or disloyalty to the Reformed confessions. Membership in the WCC must therefore be judged permissible to a Reformed church.[103] I believe that this is correct and does justice both to Reformed ecclesiology and to the ecclesiology underlying the WCC. A different matter, of course, is whether a particular Reformed church should actually join the WCC. The minority report was very cautious at this point. Rightly it pointed out that such a decision is determined by a number of factors, such as one's appraisal of the doctrinal position and of the activities and trends of the WCC, the impact affiliation with the WCC would have on one's relation with other Reformed churches and with so-called younger churches as well as the situation in one's own denomination.[104] The last factor in particular moved the writers of the minority report to state the inadvisability of membership in the WCC for the CRC. But this was not a statement of principle but of

100. *Acts of Synod 1967,* p. 90 (Art. 130).
101. Cf. "Toronto Statement."
102. *Acts of Synod 1967,* p. 461 (Suppl. 39–B).
103. Ibid., p. 474.
104. Ibid., pp. 476–482.

expediency.[105] In his important book, *All One Body We,* Kromminga himself favored the strategy of "maintaining contact with the World Council of Churches short of full membership."[106] He also suggested that conservative churches might participate "in such activities as may appear to be mutually desirable,"[107] and engage in some form of dialogue, especially on the level of Faith and Order conferences. This, to me, seems to be a fruitful approach which in the long run would be profitable both to the conservative churches themselves and to the WCC. For whether we like it or not, the WCC is there, and Reformed churches cannot ignore its existence. They can remain separated from the WCC, but this does not absolve them from their ecumenical responsibility towards the churches that are members of the WCC and towards the WCC itself. A purely negative attitude will not do. The RES, which has consistently advised its member churches not to join the WCC, was aware of this and therefore has through its Interim Committee entered into conversation with the WCC. I am convinced that some time in the future the CRC will also have to reconsider its present attitude. In some form or other it will have to exercise its ecumenical responsibility towards the WCC in line with the ecumenical ecclesiology so well formulated by the 1944 Synod.

105. Cf. Kromminga, *All One Body We.* On page 209 Kromminga describes the attitude of some conservative churches which have joined the WCC as follows: "They have an equal love for Christ and the Bible, an equal distaste for radical restructuring, and even a similar dislike for some council actions and utterances. But they are convinced that their place is in the council. This is a question of attitude and strategy, not of faith or nonfaith."

106. Ibid., p. 212.

107. Ibid. A suggestion made by the WCC itself. Cf. *The New Delhi Report,* The Third Assembly of the World Council of Churches 1961, ed. Willem A. Visser 't Hooft (New York: Association Press, 1962), p. 42.

17

The Christian Reformed Church and the Reformed Ecumenical Synod

A Comparative Study in Ecumenical Relations

Paul G. Schrotenboer

The Christian Reformed Church in North America (hereafter CRC) and the Reformed Ecumenical Synod (hereafter RES) both hold to the teachings of the classical Reformed confessions and cherish the Reformed heritage. The history of the CRC has been called a study in orthodoxy; the RES may be characterized as a venture in confessional ecumenism. Both have steered free from affiliation with the world ecumenical movement and from connection with the International Council of Christian Churches. Both have stressed unity among churches that are confessionally similar.

The RES is an affiliation of some thirty-five churches on all continents with a total membership of about five and a half million. The RES member churches may be classified roughly into three groups: those of Dutch origin, those of Presbyterian character, and churches in the third world planted by the Reformed Churches of the Western world.

The CRC, with just under 300,000 members, is a charter member of the RES and maintains a close affiliation with the RES church family. This comes in large part from the vast CRC network of mission activities which have resulted in close relations with other churches, both in the first and third worlds.

To our knowledge, the first reference to the need for a body such as the RES was voiced in 1898 at the Synod of the CRC. At that time a committee

345

reported to the synod, that it "would also . . . rejoice if soon a General Synod or Council of Reformed Churches would meet with the definite purpose of eliminating all foreign elements in the various Reformed Churches of our times, and of everywhere furthering sound development."[1]

When the goal of such an assembly was realized and the RES was established in 1946, it occurred on invitation of the CRC and was held in Grand Rapids, Michigan, where the CRC's denominational institutions are concentrated. It is apparent from this one fact alone that the histories of the RES and the CRC are closely intermixed.

This contribution is a comparative study of one aspect in the life of the CRC and the RES, that of the ecumenical calling of the church. Closely connected with this calling is the social task of the church. On that a worthwhile comparative study might also be made. It would not be possible however to discuss the latter within the scope of this contribution. Hence we confine our comments to the views and actions of the two bodies on ecumenical relations.

There are three areas in ecumenical relations which we will explore: 1) relationships with other Reformed churches, 2) with evangelical churches of other traditions, and 3) the ecumenical movement as expressed in the World Council of Churches (hereafter WCC).

In a number of ways the CRC has taken what may be called a "centrist position" in the RES. To understand what *centrist* means in this context we need to bear in mind that the impulse to form the RES has arisen largely from Dutch churches and churches with a Dutch background. For example, all three charter members, the Christian Reformed Church in North America, de Gereformeerde Kerken in Nederland (hereafter GKN), and die Gereformeerde Kerk van Suid-Afrika are united by this ethnic tie.

It should be added forthwith, however, that the strongest bond among RES churches is not ethnicity, but confessional agreement, for not all Dutch churches and churches with a Dutch background are RES members. Moreover, a large number of churches from the third world have become members and exert an increasing influence. In both respects, the ethnic and the confessional, the CRC has been able to function in a mediating role.

To explain this a bit further, we should be aware that differences have arisen that touch upon the confessional integrity of one charter RES church, namely, the GKN. The CRC, with its historical ties, has been able to understand the changes in that church more easily than other Western churches and young churches from the third world. Moreover, the influence of the GKN upon the CRC, especially through the Canadian churches which were formed since World War II, has been considerable. It was thus

---

1. *Acts of Synod 1944* of the Christian Reformed Church in Session from June 14 to June 23, 1944 at Grand Rapids, Michigan (Grand Rapids: Christian Reformed Church, 1944), p. 332 (Suppl. 21).

not only the information which the CRC had about the GKN but also a certain sympathy with the views of the GKN that afforded the CRC its mediating role.

In comparing the CRC and the RES, we shall first look at the former (which is older), and then the latter, which is in part a product of the former.

In 1898 the CRC was forty-one years old, having been formed of persons who had emigrated from the Netherlands with the intent of preserving their ecclesiastical heritage. In the Netherlands these people had seceded from the Nederlandse Hervormde Kerk and were wary of entering into any alliance in the new world that would endanger the stance and freedom that they attained in this secession.

It should also be noted that the relation with the Dutch churches, in both language and theology was strong. This, coupled with a "colony" situation in Western Michigan and Central Iowa, tended to preserve strong ethnic ties as well as theological and confessional unity.

When in 1898 the CRC, for the first time, reflected as a body on its relation to other churches, both the confessional and the ethnic emphases played a significant role. The concern was to have unity with Reformed churches, and for all intents and purposes, in those years this meant primarily with the GKN.

At the time inter-church relations were promoted in the form of "church correspondence." This meant more than simply corresponding, i.e., communicating with other churches. Correspondence as it was traditionally understood was first of all an affirmation of a correspondence or similarity between the churches. On the basis of this correspondence (or likeness), correspondence (communication) should be held.

This correspondence was conceived of in both a narrower and wider sense. In the narrower sense it was with sister churches which, except for the obstacles afforded by territory or language, would be organizationally one. In the wider sense, it was with churches which did not agree on all the essential points of the faith but were still churches of Jesus Christ.

In 1898 the CRC Synod reflected on the fact that in 1571 at the Synod of Emden, Germany; in 1618–1619 at the Synod of Dort, the Netherlands; in 1648 at the Synod of Westminster, England; and in 1559 at the Synod of Paris, France, inter-church correspondence operated "strong and beneficially."[2] Later, this correspondence deteriorated and it was said. "Every one withdrew into his own denomination".[3]

The 1898 Synod said that church correspondence should consist of:

2. Ibid., p. 331.
3. Ibid.

a. the sending of delegates to the major assemblies with advisory vote;
b. the exercise of mutual watchfulness against departures from the Reformed principles in doctrine, worship, and discipline;
c. common consultation on the question of the proper attitude toward third parties;
d. giving one another information and enlightenment, especially in questions of revision of the creed, Church Order, and Liturgy.[4]

With this in mind, the synod wanted to effect a "well defined correspondence between sister-churches of the Reformed family."[5]

When in 1944 a study committee of Synod surveyed the history of CRC inter-church relations, it had to admit that the program and proposal of corresponding churches never met with much success.[6] The was true of American churches as well as churches in the Netherlands.[7]

In an apt illustration the 1944 committee compared the Synod of 1898 to the blind man whose sight Jesus restored. When the man first began to see, he saw men as trees walking. The synod's vision was not clear enough to see any task toward the non-Reformed sections of the holy Catholic church,[8] nor did they see the need to correspond with American Reformed churches, for they should continue their own separate denominational existence.[9]

The 1944 committee set its strategy position by saying, "There is no warrant in the word of God for the radical doctrinal, canonical and liturgical varieties of ecclesiastical life that meet us in the world."[10] A distinction should be made, following John Calvin, between fundamental and non-fundamental articles of beliefs, and churches "have no right to be, that is, to deviate from God's truth and will as regards doctrine, polity, and liturgy."[11] Thus it issued a condemnation on principle of the "so-called pluriformity of the churches." The kinship binding sister churches together "asserts itself in their consciousness and becomes a categorical imperative in their consciences."[12]

The committee categorized other churches as 1) Reformed Churches that differ so as to make them qualitatively different from the CRC, 2) non-Reformed Protestant churches, and 3) the Roman Catholic and Oriental churches. Among the Reformed churches with a qualitative difference, a distinction was made between churches which are officially very similar

---

4. Ibid., p. 332.
5. Ibid.
6. Ibid., p. 333.
7. Ibid., p. 334.
8. Ibid., p. 354.
9. Ibid.
10. Ibid., pp. 340–341.
11. Ibid., p. 341.
12. Ibid., p. 339.

but differ in respect to the actualities of ecclesiastical life and those churches which differ both officially and in practice.

The task of the CRC toward other churches the committee formulated as follows.

> If the matter called correspondence comes down in the last analysis to this, that the Christian Reformed Church is the keeper of its sister-churches, of *all* its sister-churches in principle, surely of all its Protestant sister-churches, and very definitely of all its Reformed sister-churches, then it should make the conformity of all these sister-churches to the Scriptural pattern of the institutional church of Christ its practical concern and exercise this concern faithfully by all manner of means available when and as long as opportunity presents.[13]

Further, the committee said we should not tone down the categorical imperative to act as one church, short of formal Presbyterian connections and implied centralized authority.[14]

The committee also stated that this call to oneness should be practiced in regard to Reformed denominations not only with Dutch churches but also with those that are territorially American: "It goes without saying, that all Reformed Churches in one and the same country ought to unite and constitute one single denomination."[15]

In applying this principle to the American situation, in the estimation of the committee there are, in fact, churches that are historically and professedly Reformed but not actually Reformed. The official stand of a church is often a far from reliable index of its true connection.[16] Hence the imperative mentioned above does not apply here: "It is out of the question, then, that the Christian Reformed Church should esteem un-Reformed Reformed Churches of the U.S. and Canada as parallels [correspondents] of itself."[17]

The imperative that does apply for unity amid the defection of American churches leads to the conclusion that the duty of the CRC is "to do all in its power to reclaim the nominally Reformed churches of America and Canada from doctrinal error and canonical and liturgical malpractice."[18] This means to be "admonitory and corrective" and that the exercise of this duty should have as its aim the paving of the way for union.

Further, the committee of 1944 recognized the extreme difficulty of the task and admitted that "we have not as much as an inkling of just how to go about" reclaiming un-Reformed Reformed churches,[19] "if only because

13. Ibid., p. 343.
14. Ibid., p. 346.
15. Ibid.
16. Ibid., p. 350.
17. Ibid., p. 347.
18. Ibid., p. 348.
19. Ibid., p. 356.

we are poorly, if at all, acquainted with the actual status quo of these sister-churches."[20]

With respect to non-Reformed churches, the committee stated that if we believe that all Christians should be Reformed, then we should try ecclesiastically to win them for the Reformed faith and to prepare the way for our eventual union with them also.[21] The committee of 1944 recognized that carrying on such a program of correspondence with such churches would require meekness, love, patience, and wisdom to labor in the Lord.[22] To carry on correspondence is worthless if it is not a labor of love.[23] The Synod of 1898 had not considered correspondence to be admonitory and corrective, but the committee of 1944 envisioned it to be both.

At the end of its exposition of the principles that should govern inter-church correspondence, the committee stated:

> Your committee would advise synod not to address itself to correspondence with other churches in the spirit of traditionalism, but from a deep and pervasive sense of duty at a time when, on the one hand, the Holy Catholic Church, as respects its organizational unity, is like a beautiful porcelain vase that has been shattered, and may still be porcelain but no longer a vase; and when, on the other hand, the Lord of this Church has been reminding his people for all of a half a century of the need of brethren dwelling in unity, by the ecumenical spirit that is surging through Christendom; and when finally, the totalitarian tendencies, not only of statesmen and economists, but of the enemies of the cross of Christ in every field of life and labor, are suggesting that the churches of Christ unite and pool their strength and cease to leave the impression that, as being hopelessly divided amongst themselves and badly embittered against one another, the professed idea of one kingdom of God, of one body of Christ, of one temple of the Holy Spirit, is a vagary and a delusion instead of a solid truth. If, then, the Church is in earnest, let it go forward under the banner of Him, Who prayed, that all who believe in Him may be one even as He and the Father are one. If it be half-hearted, let it, like all who did not belong to Gideon's band of the the the three hundred, "go every man to his place."[24]

In regard to the ecumenical movement, the CRC has joined or considered joining several inter-church organizations: the Federal Council of the Churches of Christ in America (which later became the National Council of Churches of Christ in the United States of America), the National Association of Evangelicals, the World Alliance of Reformed Churches, the World Council of Churches. Of none of these is the CRC presently a member.

20. Ibid.
21. Ibid., pp. 349–350.
22. Ibid., p. 352.
23. Ibid., p. 356.
24. Ibid., p. 357.

The reason for withdrawing in 1924 from the Federal Council of Churches after joining in 1918 was perhaps best expressed in an observation that came from Classis Grand Rapids West: "We are convinced that ecclesiastical alliances of any kind between orthodox and liberals are contrary to the Word of God."[25]

The CRC joined the National Association of Evangelicals (hereafter NAE) in 1943 in a choice between it and the American Council of Christian Churches.[26] By means of this affiliation, the CRC felt that it could exercise influence among evangelicals in the United States of America. Nevertheless in 1951, after three years of study and several reports, the CRC terminated its membership in the NAE.[27] Among the reasons for withdrawal were the method of mass evangelism practiced by the NAE, the looseness of the organization which allowed denominations, congregations, groups of Christians and individuals to become members, and the manner in which NAE business was conducted. Delegates to the NAE 1951 convention complained that at the assembly resolutions were adopted of which no one except the chairman had copies.

The CRC did not at any time join the WCC but gave the question of affiliation with it more serious consideration than with any other body. The 1967 Synod mandated a committee to "define our position with respect to the World Council of Churches."[28] The occasion for this mandate was a request for advice on joining from the GKN which had informed the synod that it found no "decisive impediment" to joining the WCC. A year later the church had to choose between two lengthy reports, a majority report rejecting affiliation,[29] and a minority report permitting it but advising not to join.[30]

The 1967 advisory committee to Synod listed three convictions that underlie the statements on ecumenical relations:

that there is only one Church of Jesus Christ and that the Church's unity should come to visible expression;

that the Christian Reformed Church has a responsibility with respect to all Christian churches;

that we want to obey the Lord, both in seeking fellowship with all those who

25. John H. Kromminga, *The Christian Reformed Church*, A Study in Orthodoxy (Grand Rapids: Baker, 1949), p. 114.

26. *Acts of Synod 1943* of the Christian Reformed Church in Session from June 9 to June 18, 1943 at Grand Rapids, Michigan (Grand Rapids: Christian Reformed Church, 1943), pp. 132–137 (Art. 202). See also pp. 151–154.

27. *Acts of Synod 1951* of the Christian Reformed Church in Session from June 13 to June 26, 1951 at Grand Rapids, Michigan (Grand Rapids: Christian Reformed Publishing House, 1951), p. 79 (Art. 151). See also pp. 77–78, 432–435, 436–438.

28. *Acts of Synod 1967*, June 14 to 24, 1967, Reconvened August 29 and 30, 1967 at Calvin College, Grand Rapids, Michigan (Grand Rapids: Christian Reformed Publishing House, 1967), p. 380 (Suppl. 39).

29. Ibid., pp. 380–443.

30. Ibid., pp. 444–485.

confess Jesus Christ, and in separating ourselves from those who reject, deny or pervert the truth of the Gospel.[31]

The synod took the advice of the majority study report and decided not to affiliate with the WCC. It stated as its reasons: 1) "The ecclesiological character of the WCC is ambiguous and is regarded differently by various member churches"; 2) The WCC basis is inadequate for ecclesiastical fellowship because it does not assure the excluding of radically unbiblical interpretations of the Gospel. It rather "admits to membership in the WCC such churches with which we may not have ecclesiastical fellowship (koinonia)."[32]

The 1967 Synod further judged that the WCC Basis does not function in a meaningful way because the WCC does not judge whether member churches are faithful to the Basis. Moreover, the socio-political pronouncements and activities of the WCC, the synod said, are not the immediate responsibility of the church and are frequently an embarrassment to a Reformed church.[33]

The CRC early considered membership with what is now the World Alliance of Reformed Churches (hereafter WARC, formerly the World Presbyterian Alliance). Here was a church body holding since 1877 to the Presbyterian system of church government. But although attention was given to it in the CRC already in 1898[34] and membership was considered in 1930,[35] 1959,[36] and 1960,[37] and the 1972[38] Synod asked that membership again be studied, the CRC has not taken the step. The reasons the 1960 Synod gave for not joining the World Presbyterian Alliance (what is now the WARC) were that it was closely affiliated with the WCC and its constituency was theologically mixed.[39]

One development worth noting is that the CRC has for many years appointed a representative to meet with the theological commission of the North American and Caribbean Council of the WARC. This has been, to our knowledge, the first sortie into official ecumenical dialogue. Although this participation has not produced much tangible fruit, it means that a

31. Ibid., p. 89 (Art. 130).
32. Ibid., pp. 89–90.
33. Ibid., p. 90.
34. *Acta van de Synode* der Christelijke Gereformeerde Kerk in Amerika, Gehouden te Grand Rapids, Michigan, van 15 tot 24 Juni, 1898 (Grand Rapids: Verhaar & Keukelaar, 1898), p. 43 (Art. 58).
35. *Acta der Synode 1930* van de Christelijke Gereformeerde Kerk, Gehouden van 11 Juni tot 27 Juni, 1930 te Grand Rapids, Michigan (Grand Rapids: Grand Rapids Printing Co., 1930), pp. 103–105 (Art. 93).
36. *Acts of Synod 1959*, June 10 to June 24, 1959 at Calvin College, Grand Rapids, Michigan (Grand Rapids: Christian Reformed Publishing House, 1959), pp. 266–272 (Suppl. 19).
37. *Acts of Synod 1960*, June 8 to 21, 1960 at Calvin College, Grand Rapids, Michigan (Grand Rapids: Christian Reformed Publishing House, 1960), pp. 106–107 (Art. 165). See also p. 379.
38. *Acts of Synod 1972*, June 13 to 23, 1972 at Calvin College, Grand Rapids, Michigan (Grand Rapids: Board of Publications of the Christian Reformed Church, 1972), p. 75 (Art. 59). See also pp. 290–291.
39. *Acts of Synod 1960*, pp. 106–107 (Art. 165).

beginning has been made, for it is in this area, usually called "bilateral conversations," where the most significant advances toward unity in theology and confession are being made. It has yet to be explained satisfactorily why a church which avers that its ecumenical task includes the "admonitory and corrective" elements does not more actively enter into the arena where this can be done.

There is one other ecclesiastical affiliation which the CRC has considered, that with the North American Presbyterian and Reformed Council (hereafter NAPaRC). Here the story is different, for the CRC became a charter member of NAPaRC when it was organized in 1975.[40]

NAPaRC is an affiliation of five confessionally-oriented Presbyterian and Reformed churches in North America. In size, the CRC is twice that of all the rest together. Here, in this theologically compatible group, the CRC has from the start played a formative role. Ecumenism, like charity, begins at home. In 1978 five concurrent synods met at Calvin College and Seminary campus in Grand Rapids and again in 1982. Here material concerns, such as world diaconate programs, evangelism and missions, and theological issues such as biblical hermeneutics, are jointly considered.

A moment's reflection on this history of the CRC's ecumenical affiliations will lead to the conclusion that the CRC has given much and increasing attention to the churches with which it has a confessional affinity, but less and decreasing attention to non-Reformed evangelical churches. With the mainstream Protestant churches and the Roman Catholic and the Oriental (Orthodox) churches, the CRC has had almost no official contact.

Before leaving the topic of the CRC and its inter-church affiliations, we should note a recent significant change in its perception of its relation to its sister churches.

The 1973 Synod asked its Inter-Church Relations Committee to study the problem of sister church relations to determine the validity of the designation "sister churches" and "other denominations" and to redefine the system of the process of correspondence "as will promote most fully the fellowship of the true church of Jesus Christ and will work most effectively to maintain and restore the true unity of the churches."[41]

The committee in its report to the 1974 Synod noted that the church had an official position "which in application we were not ready to accept fully nor to reject."[42] There were, in other words, no churches anywhere with which the CRC would ipso facto be organizationally one were it not for territorial distance and language difference. The committee therefore proposed a redefinition of the "system of correspondence which would take

---

40. *Acts of Synod 1975*, June 10 to 20, 1975 at Calvin College, Grand Rapids, Michigan (Grand Rapids: Board of Publications of the Christian Reformed Church, 1975), p. 24 (Art. 30). See also pp. 346–347.

41. *Acts of Synod 1974*, June 11 to 21, 1974 at Calvin College, Grand Rapids, Michigan (Grand Rapids: Board of Publications of the Christian Reformed Church, 1974), p. 342 (Suppl. 14).

42. Ibid., p. 343.

into consideration the realities of our present ecclesiastical situation, world-wide, would insure adequate safe-guards for our doctrinal integrity and would enable us as a church to work fully and freely for the unity of the church of Jesus Christ in the truth of Scripture and creedal statement."[43]

The synod decided, in agreement with the advice of this committee, to replace the existing "sister church" and "corresponding church" relations with one relationship to be called "churches in ecclesiastical fellowship." This new category was seen to be not only realistic and flexible, but one that would strengthen rather than weaken inter-church bonds. The receiving of churches into ecclesiastical fellowship would involve 1) the exchange of fraternal delegates at major assemblies, 2) occasional pulpit fellowship, 3) inter-communion (i.e., fellowship at the table of the Lord), 4) joint action in areas of common responsibility, 5) communication on major issues of joint concern, 6) the exercise of mutual concern and admonition with a view to promoting the fundamentals of Christian unity.[44]

It may be said that in the few years that the new relationship has been in effect it has functioned well. In times of increasing polarization among churches of the same tradition, such as at the present, it allows for loosening instead of breaking the bond. It frees the church from an all-or-nothing situation to move in one in which the extent of fellowship may be determined by the degree of affinity or correspondence.

We have been looking at a church which is, on one hand, self-assured that its heritage is the best and that its position is true. At one time (1898) its synod seemed to imply that to deviate from the faith of this church was to deviate from God's truth. Its 1944 committee claimed that all churches should be Reformed. On the other hand, it is a church which has a somewhat discouraging history in broader ecumenical relations. The CRC was and still is fully assured that it is sound in doctrine. Accordingly, it has given little or no evidence that mutual consultation with other churches (non-Reformed or Reformed, except those with which it was very extensively in agreement) might change and enrich the outlook of the CRC.

On one hand it has come to greater clarity on how it should relate to like-minded churches of its own tradition. On the other hand it has done little to consult with other churches, either evangelical or ecumenical, nor has it entered into any significant bilateral conversations in which churches with differing confessions enter into dialogue with each other.

Although the 1944 CRC report said that it is a mistake to think, as has been done, that Reformed churches, our own for instance, should concern themselves only with members of their own, that is Reformed family,[45] the

---

43. Ibid.
44. Ibid., p. 57 (Art. 62).
45. *Acts of Synod 1944*, p. 354 (Suppl. 21).

CRC has not shown in this respect any great evidence of change. It has a stronger sense of having been Reformed (*reformata est*) than of the continuing need to be Reformed (*semper reformanda*).

What now of the RES and the role of the CRC in it? The RES joins together churches which are confessionally and theologically similar, and all of them subscribe to (some of) the historic creeds of the Protestant Reformation. This question is especially pertinent because the CRC played a lead role in the formation of the RES and also because the ecumenical council of Reformed Churches envisaged by the CRC already in 1898 was seen to be a means to implement and extend the system of "churchly correspondence."

The RES should be judged both on its Basis and Purpose, as they are constitutionally defined, and its actions. We should first look at the Constitution. As revised in 1972 the RES Constitution has taken as its Basis

> the Holy Scriptures of the Old and New Testament as interpreted by the Confessions of the Reformed faith, namely, the Gallican Confession, the Belgic Confession, the Heidelberg Catechism, the Second Helvetic Confession, the Thirty-nine Articles, the Canons of Dordt, and the Westminster Confession. The Scriptures, in their entirety as well as in every part thereof, are the infallible and ever-abiding Word of the living Triune God absolutely authoritative in all matters of creed and conduct; and the Confessions of the Reformed faith are accepted because they are in accordance with the divine truth as revealed in Scripture.[46]

The Purpose of the Synod is described as follows:

1. To express the Church's oneness in Christ and to promote the unity of the churches which profess and maintain the Reformed faith.
2. To give united testimony to the Reformed faith in the midst of the world living in error and groping in darkness, and to the churches which have departed from the truth of God's Holy Word.
3. To confer together, as far as advisability or necessity may require, regarding missionary work of the churches at home and abroad.
4. To advise one another regarding questions and problems of import pertaining to the spiritual welfare and the Scriptural government of the churches.
5. To strive to attain a common course of action with respect to common problems, likewise to issue joint resolutions regarding movements, practices, or dangers when joint statements are deemed necessary.[47]

46. *Acts* of the Reformed Ecumenical Synod, Sydney, Australia, August 15–25, 1972 (Grand Rapids: The Reformed Ecumenical Synod, 1973), pp. 62–63.
47. Ibid., p. 63.

When the RES was instituted it was deliberately called a synod. That word gave expression to an ideal that was only partially realized. That ideal was to form a synod in the full sense of the term, an extension of the synods or general assemblies of the member churches, with binding authority upon the member bodies.

The Constitution stated that the churches should confess and maintain the Reformed faith, in other words, be in full confessional agreement. This requirement for membership, it should be noted, displays an obviously western approach. It reflects the reaction of evangelical, conservative churches toward the encroachment of theological liberalism into the churches of the western world, such as those from which a number of RES churches seceded, at the time when only western churches were represented. The membership clause does not reflect the situation found in those churches in the third world whose brief history is indeed a secession of sorts, however, not from other churches but directly from paganism. Their knowledge of the western creeds is relatively scant and their dynamics are much different from those in North America or Europe. If the RES membership clause were to be re-written today and adequate account were to be taken of the context of the member churches in the third world, the formulation would be different. As it was, the synod to which membership was thus limited was to be an extension of the existing churches.

On the score of attitude toward the WCC, there has been a close similarity between both CRC and RES. In 1968, one year after the CRC stated its position toward the WCC, the RES advised its member churches not to join the Council.[48] (Actually, the RES had done so already in 1953, but not on the basis of extensive study.) The reasons for this advice were similar to those of the CRC for not seeking membership in the WCC:

Re: The Nature of the W.C.C.

The W.C.C. claims to represent the given unity in Christ, but this is an illegitimate claim, because the W.C.C. does not unitedly and unconditionally acknowledge the authority of Christ, the Head of the Church, as He speaks in the infallible Word, accordingly it does not unequivocally reject that which is contrary to the Gospel of Jesus Christ, nor does it warn its member churches against the false gospel that has a recognized place in many of these churches.

Re: The Basis of the W.C.C.

Although the words of the Basis are in themselves a summary of the gospel and include a reference to the Scriptures, this is inadequate as a basis or starting point for an ecumenical movement, because when understood in the light of history and in the context of contemporary theological discussion it is

---

48. *Acts* and Reports of the Reformed Ecumenical Synod, Amsterdam, The Netherlands, August 13–23, 1968 (Grand Rapids: The Reformed Ecumenical Synod, 1969), p. 45 (Art. 95).

open to various unbiblical interpretations; and in effect the World Council does permit such essentially different interpretations.[49]

While the actions taken by the CRC and the RES in regard to WCC membership were similar, the effects were not identical. In the CRC there has been no recent agitation for membership in the WCC. In the RES the admission to WCC membership of the GKN in 1969 has become a bone of contention and a major reason why a number of small Presbyterian churches have terminated their membership in the RES.

In 1981 and 1982 an international committee once again faced this issue and has reported its findings, based on its own study and upon input from regional conferences to the next RES Synod. The committee has rightly observed that the RES has concentrated its attention on the first purpose mentioned in the Constitution, namely "to express the Church's oneness in Christ and to promote the unity of the churches which profess and maintain the Reformed faith."[50] It also correctly stated that the RES "has done very little to promote the wider ecumenical responsibility set forth in the Constitution as the second purpose of the RES, namely "to give united testimony to the Reformed faith in the midst of the world living in error and groping in darkness, and to the churches which have departed from the truth of God's Holy Word."[51] In regard to the nettlesome issue of dual (RES/WCC) membership the recommendation is: "That the RES, while reaffirming its advice against WCC membership, decides not to terminate the RES membership of those churches now holding WCC membership on that ground alone."[52] It is hoped that a resolution to the issue will be found at RES Chicago 1984. That assembly should decide whether dual RES/WCC membership is permissible or not.

In another respect also there has been a difference between the CRC and RES, namely in the way the two bodies here being compared have used their contact with the WCC to fulfill their ecumenical calling. The CRC has limited its official contact to the sending of observers to the 1968 (Uppsala)[53] and 1975 (Nairobi)[54] general assemblies of the WCC. The RES has done the same but more intensely. The RES General Secretary not only attended as an observer the Uppsala and Nairobi assemblies but also the 1979 meeting of the WCC Central Assembly and the 1979 Conference on Faith, Science and the Future at the Massachusetts Institute of Technology, Cambridge. He also participated in 1976 in a joint meeting in

49. Ibid., pp. 45–46.

50. *Report to RES Chicago 1984 on Ecumenical Relations* (Grand Rapids: The Reformed Ecumenical Synod, 1982), p. 55.

51. Ibid., pp. 55–56.

52. Ibid., p. 59.

53. The observers to the 1968 Uppsala meeting were the Reverends William Haverkamp and John Vriend, *Acts of Synod 1967*, p. 95 (Art. 134).

54. The observers to the 1975 Nairobi meeting were Dr. John H. Kromminga and the Reverend Ralph Baker, *Acts of Synod 1975*, p. 351 (Suppl. 14).

Montreux, Switzerland, of evangelical theologians and representatives of the WCC on the interpretation of Scripture.[55]

Besides this participation of the General Secretary, on four occasions the RES Interim Committee has held consultations with leading representatives of the WCC on issues of mutual concern and on areas of difference in viewpoint. One such meeting (1970) was devoted to the merits and disadvantages of WCC membership.[56] Another considered the authority of the Bible (1972).[57] A third dealt with the nature of the church and the role of theology (1975).[58] From this meeting a booklet containing the papers of the consultation was published jointly.[59] A fourth meeting (1979) centered on the social calling of the Church. The participants of this meeting issued a joint statement that sketched the similarities and differences between the two ecumenical bodies.[60] On the planning board is a fifth meeting on human rights, perhaps in 1983.

In reflecting on the relationship of member churches to the WCC the RES Cape Town 1976 formulated a test to judge the affiliation of churches with ecumenical organizations: "The RES cannot, on the basis of its constitution, rule on the affiliations RES churches make with other organizations unless such affiliations result in demonstrated unfaithfulness to the Reformed confessions."[61]

With this test the RES 1984 will have to come to terms and decide whether those RES churches which are also affiliated with the WCC have thereby in fact been led astray confessionally. It would appear at this point that the application of this test is no less difficult than it is necessary. Unless confessional unfaithfulness is demonstrated, or proved to be unavoidable, affiliation with the WCC cannot be disallowed.

In regard to the evangelicals, it should be noted that the RES has recently entered into a relation of consultation and cooperation with the World Evangelical Fellowship (hereafter WEF).[62] The 1976 consultation mentioned above between evangelical theologians and representatives of the WCC on interpreting the Bible was arranged by the WEF which had in its delegation two members from the RES Interim Committee.[63]

55. Paul G. Schrotenboer, "The Bible in the World Council of Churches," *Calvin Theological Journal* 12 (1977):144–163.

56. *Acts RES 1972*, pp. 109–110 (Suppl. 1). See also *RES News Exchange* 7 (August 25, 1970):622.

57. "RES Australia Holds All-day Conference on Authority of Scripture" *RES News Exchange* 9 (April 28, 1972):788.

58. *Acts* of the Reformed Ecumenical Synod, Cape Town, South Africa, August 10–20, 1976 (Grand Rapids: The Reformed Ecumenical Synod, 1976), p. 92 (Suppl. 1). See also *RES News Exchange* 12 (October 14, 1975):1115–1116.

59. *The Nature of the Church and the Role of Theology*, Papers from a Consultation Between the World Council of Churches and the Reformed Ecumenical Synod, Geneva, 1975 (Geneva: The World Council of Churches; Grand Rapids: The Reformed Ecumenical Synod, 1976).

60. *Acts* of the Reformed Ecumenical Synod, Nîmes, France, July 15–25, 1980 (Grand Rapids: The Reformed Ecumenical Synod, 1980), pp. 156–159 (Suppl. 1).

61. *Acts RES 1976*, p. 55 (Art. 92).

62. *Acts RES 1980*, pp. 160–173 (Suppl. 1).

63. Schrotenboer, "Bible in the World Council of Churches," p. 145 (footnote 6).

Since then the contacts have been strengthened through an exchange of fraternal delegates and through participation of the RES General Secretary in the WEF Theological Commission and the WEF International Theological Assistance Fund. Both are engaged in studies on human rights[64] and may consult together on this topic in 1983.

Among the other ecumenical organizations with which the RES maintains regular contact is the annual meeting of secretaries of Christian World Communions (hereafter CWCs) (formerly World Confessional Families). The RES has sent representatives to these annual meetings for the last several years.[65] These meetings bring together churchmen who represent the widest spectrum of Christianity today. It includes not only the WCC but also the Roman Catholic Church and a number of other organizations not otherwise affiliated.

From these annual meetings have come a number of significant ecumenical documents, such as the booklet that surveys bilateral conversation, *Confessions in Dialogue*,[66] and "Models of Unity," a paper considered by the WCC in Nairobi. These documents have exerted influence on the general understanding of confessional affiliation.

One "confessional family" that has taken a lead role in the CWCs is the WARC. It, like the RES, represents churches in the Reformed tradition. It is older, larger, and theologically more diverse. In its early stages it stressed the Presbyterian church system rather than doctrine. At one time in its early history the Alliance attempted to form a statement of faith but after a number of years abandoned the attempt. The Alliance now has among its members not only churches holding the Presbyterian system of church polity but also Congregational churches and United churches. It is bound together not by a narrow and exclusive statement of doctrine but by a certain ethos, a kind of thinking and doing. This reflects a shift from church polity and doctrine to ethics.

The WARC is presently about ten times as large as the RES. Approximately a third of the RES churches are also members of WARC and belong to those WARC churches which are more conservative and evangelical.

Between the WARC and the RES there have been numerous informal contacts and an exchange of fraternal delegates at the major assemblies. An earlier effort by the RES Interim Committee to initiate talks with representatives of the WARC did not receive a warm reception from the WARC secretariat. A more recent attempt by the RES has received a favorable response. It would appear to be in line with the policies of both the CRC

---

64. *Acts RES 1980*, pp. 44–47 (Art. 50), pp. 97–98 (Art. 95).

65. Ibid., pp. 40–41 (Art. 42), pp. 139–140 (Suppl. 1).

66. Nils Ehrenstrom, *Confessions in Dialogue*, A Survey of Bilateral Conversations Among World Confessional Families 1959–1974, by Nils Ehrenstrom and Gunther Gassmann, third rev. and enl. edition, Faith and Order Papers, 74 (Geneva: World Council of Churches, 1975).

and the RES, namely, to stress the need to advance ecumenical relations with those which share the same tradition, that more substantial contacts be made between the RES and the WARC.[67]

The dynamics within the RES churches during recent years has, on the one hand, produced an outreach to other ecumenical organizations. This outreach has not been conducted on a basis of a least common denominator of cooperation but with the intention of bearing witness to the biblical faith in the best tradition of the Calvinist heritage.

At the same time we have witnessed a drawing back by a number of Presbyterian churches from the RES itself. In one instance (the Reformed Church in Africa), this was related to the alleged failure of the RES to assume a stronger profile against views on race relations held by Afrikaans-speaking churches in South Africa.[68] But the other five withdrawals have been taken on the basis of dissatisfaction that the last two RES assemblies have not taken a stronger stand against WCC membership and have not expressed a stronger disapproval of the theological developments within the GKN.[69] There has thus been a concurrent effort to carry out the ecumenical calling as outlined in 1968 and a withdrawal of churches because of dissatisfactions within the RES family.

In the RES there has been, as an aftermath to the tensions that have developed, an impulse similar to that in the CRC, namely, to loosen the bond among the churches in order to lessen the strain on the tie that binds them in synodical affiliation. At the present time consideration is being given to change the RES from a synod to a council or even a conference. The intention of those who propose this change is not to remove the ecclesiastical character of the body but to diminish the obligation to engage in mutual oversight on doctrine and life. This issue also will be faced in 1984.

This development means that instead of progressing from a synod in a limited sense to a synod in the full sense, the movement in the RES is now toward some form of affiliation that is less than a limited synod but still an ecclesiastical gathering.

The developments described in this contribution, both in the CRC and the RES, will elicit a feeling of some disappointment among those who desire a world-wide affiliation of evangelical Reformed churches. The goal of a body that would manifest that confessional oneness fully has not been realized. This does not mean that the CRC's system of correspondence caused the rift between it and the GKN. Nor does it imply that the formation and functioning of the RES has increased the differences among its

67. *Acts RES 1980*, pp. 100–102 (Art. 101).
68. *RES News Exchange* 17 (December 2, 1980):1610.
69. The five churches which withdrew over the last few years from the RES are Evangelical Presbyterian Church of Northern Ireland, Free Church of Scotland, Presbyterian Church of Eastern Australia, Reformed Presbyterian Church of Ireland (Covenanter) and Reformed Presbyterian Church of North America.

member churches. What has happened is that other, centrifugal developments within the family of Reformed churches outpaced the efforts to draw them together.

There is no doubt that the last two decades have seen the loss of a single perspective among these churches. This is true both of doctrinal and confessional issues as well as affiliation with other ecumenical bodies. It is true even more of social issues, primarily race relations in South Africa. More and more nontheological influences have affected the churches.

It should be recognized that a meaningful, unity-promoting affiliation must take account of the existing differences among the affiliated bodies. To do less is to be unrealistic, to ignore the divisive factors. This means that if the term "sister church" is a label that does not cover the cargo, it should be replaced. This means also that the structure of the RES should be tailored not only to the Reformed heritage and conviction but also to the present situation. If its synodal character causes churches to withdraw, consideration should be given to another form. It would appear to the writer that it is advisable to loosen the tie here also if the alternative is the breaking of the bond.

More and more the conviction grows that unity among churches cannot be attained only by considering what are strictly ecclesiastical issues. The reason is that the nontheological and nonecclesiastical issues exert an increasing pressure upon the church. And when these forces differ from culture to culture, the differences between the church of one culture and the church of another culture cannot but widen.

However, built into the purpose and functioning of the organization should be the impulse toward greater unity. This unity should be not only one of confessional correspondence, but also a unity in the mission of the church. In other words, it should be a working unity: in theological education, in world diaconal enterprises, in evangelism and missions, and in facing the great social issues such as human rights, technology, and race relations. Here the aim should be to speak with one voice and to strive together for the faith of the Gospel (Phil. 1:27).

When we now try to draw up a balance sheet on the ecumenical relation of the CRC and the RES, we should say that in terms of relationships with other Reformed Churches, both have given this aspect of the ecumenical task very much attention. Here both have made meaningful contributions. Among those churches where there already is a correspondence, the cooperation has increased. The recent efforts of the CRC, for example, to function in an "admonitory and correcting" way with the GKN has truly been impressive. Nevertheless, in terms of the task of calling churches back to their true confession and mission, neither the CRC nor the RES can claim much success. The 1944 Committee of the CRC openly admitted this when it said, "We have not as much as an inkling of just how to go about it" (reclaiming un-Reformed churches).[70]

The RES constitution mentions the task of "giving united testimony . . . to the . . . churches which have . . . departed from the truth of God's Holy Word."[71] But the closest thing to carrying out this purpose has been the consultations with representatives of the WCC. For at these meetings at least it was clearly stated why RES churches are not able to join the WCC, namely, the toleration of theological liberalism in some WCC member churches.

Such inter-ecumenical consultations were not at all in the mind of the founders of the RES in 1946. When mention was then made of churches that had departed from the truth, the denominations in the west were meant. The question may be asked whether, after decades of not having accomplished anything significant in an official way, the church or ecumenical organization really takes this task seriously. It is as valid today as in 1944 when it was said in the report to the CRC Synod, "It is one of the most serious problems of any faithful church, what to do about the unfaithfulness of ecclesiastical sisters."[72]

With regard to evangelical churches not of the Reformed tradition, it must be said that the CRC today is less active officially than it was two decades ago. At the same time, it must be recognized that on an unofficial level this affiliation and cooperation has increased. For instance, there was participation in the 1981 Festival of Evangelism in Kansas City. Approximately 70 persons from the CRC participated. It should also be said that the Christian Reformed Board of World Missions holds membership in the Evangelical Foreign Missions Association (EFMA) to facilitate its worldwide program of evangelism. The same may be said of the Christian Reformed World Relief Committee, which cooperates, as the need arises with, e.g., the Mennonite Central Committee. But with all this, there has been no synodical affiliation with evangelical bodies.

Although the RES has made a beginning in its recent closer relations with the WEF, this is only a beginning. In a number of areas the opportunity for mutually helpful cooperation is being explored, especially in theological education and in the approach to the social issues.

When the CRC celebrated its centennial in 1957 the theme was "God's Favor Is Our Challenge." Among the benefits of God's favor is the Calvinist heritage. And part of that heritage is the example of John Calvin who said he was ready to cross ten seas to advance the unity of the church. To follow his example is our challenge today.

---

70. *Acts of Synod 1944*, p. 356 (Suppl. 21).

71. *Acts* of the Reformed Ecumenical Synod, Grand Rapids, The United States of America, August 7–16, 1963 (Grand Rapids: The Reformed Ecumenical Synod, 1963), p. 190 (Suppl. 10).

72. *Acts of Synod 1944*, pp. 354–355 (Suppl. 21).

18

The Christian Reformed Church and the Christelijke Gereformeerde Kerken in Nederland

Willem van 't Spijker

Introduction

In a valuable essay about Calvin and ecumenicity John H. Kromminga pointed to the lasting significance of John Calvin for the subject of church unity.[1] Scholars often misrepresented the intentions of the Reformer. Neither Calvin the absolutist nor Calvin the uncritical enthusiast of ecumenicity can be located in history. According to the Professor of Church History and President of Calvin Theological Seminary: "The Calvin of the Reformation age would rebuke those who have no interest in the unity of the church, who are so stubborn as to refuse to yield one small point to others, or who deny the validity of ecumenical discussions. But on the other hand, he would most certainly insist that it is the truth, ultimately defined by Scripture, which must be sought, so that it may be indeed the church of Christ which is brought to unity."[2] We recall that Calvin pleaded

---

1. John H. Kromminga, "Calvin and Ecumenicity," in *John Calvin: Contemporary Prophet,* A Symposium, ed. Jacob T. Hoogstra (Grand Rapids: Baker, 1959), pp. 149–165.
2. Ibid., p. 165. We find the same conclusion in Willem Nijenhuis, *Calvinus Oecumenicus,* Calvijn en de Eenheid der Kerk in het Licht van Zijn Briefwisseling, Kerkhistorische Studiën, 8 ('s-Gravenhage: Martinus Nijhoff, 1959), pp. 293–305; cf. Günter Gloede, "Calvinus Oecumenicus: Weg und Werk des Reformators," in *Johannes Calvin 1509–1564,* eine Gabe zu seinem 400. Todestag, hrsg. von Joachim Rogge (Berlin: Evangelische Verlagsanstalt, 1963), pp. 9–26.

for such unity in fundamental matters.[3] If the members of Christ's Church would have to agree with one another in every respect, there would soon be no church left.[4] On the other hand, the truth must remain central. "For Calvin the Word of God, the gospel of Christ, the 'pure and sound doctrine,' was the essential mark of the Church and the basis of its unity."[5] Calvin strove for church unity in crucial matters, a unity which is strong and for that reason can make exceptions on less vital issues.

It is this unity that in the past determined the relationship between the Christian Reformed Church in North America (hereafter CRC) and the Christelijke Gereformeerde Kerken in Nederland (hereafter CGKN). The unity of the church is a great treasure. This ideal has often been under attack. The question as to what this requires has not always been answered in the same way, neither today nor in the past. This lack of consensus caused tension in the mutual relationship between the churches in North America and those in the Netherlands. Did the Dutch families who emigrated to North America broaden the truth? Or did they take along with them the ecclesiastical divisions peculiarly associated with the Netherlands? Naturally, not everyone gave the same answer. This caused tension between the churches of the old and the new world.

The tension did not always surface in the extant letters by countless immigrants.[6] Very often we recognize in them the identical expressions of Reformed piety: dependence and trust. As far as that is concerned, nothing changed. The questions concerning the nature of ecclesiastical fellowship and what form this must take were much more difficult. The principle of the Afscheiding was good. The consistory members of Ulrum, Groningen, declared on October 13, 1834, that they seceded from those who did not belong to the church and that "they would no longer have fellowship with de Nederlandse Hervormde Kerk until the latter returned to the genuine service of the Lord. They declared, further, that they wished to have fellowship with all members of truly Reformed persuasion and that they wished to unite with every group founded on God's infallible Word wherever *God* brought the same together. . . ."[7]

---

3. John Calvin, "For not all the articles of true doctrine are of the same sort. Some are so necessary to know that they should be certain and unquestioned by all men as the proper principles of religion. . . . Among the churches there are other articles of doctrine disputed which still do not break the unity of faith," *Institutes of the Christian Religion*, ed. John T. McNeill, tr. Ford Lewis Battles, The Library of Christian Classics, 20–21 (Philadelphia: The Westminster Press, 1960), IV.1.xii.

4. Calvin, "First and foremost, we should agree on all points. But since all men are somewhat beclouded with ignorance, either we must leave no church remaining, or we must condone delusion in those matters which can go unknown without harm to the sum of religion and without loss of salvation," *Institutes*, IV.1.xii.

5. Nijenhuis, *Calvinus Oecumenicus*, p. 301.

6. Pieter R. D. Stokvis, *De Nederlandse Trek naar Amerika 1846–1847* (Leiden: Universitaire Pers, 1977); Johannes Stellingwerff, *Amsterdamse Emigranten*, onbekende Brieven uit de Prairie van Iowa 1846–1873 (Amsterdam: Buijten & Schipperheijn, 1975).

7. Hendrik de Cock, *Acte van Afscheiding of Wederkeering, en Toespraak en Uitnoodiging aan de Geloovigen en Ware Gereformeerden in Nederland* (Groningen: J. H. Bolt, 1834), pp. 5–6.

In his "Toespraak en Uitnodiging aan de Gelovigen en Ware Gereformeerden in Nederland" which was published simultaneously with the *Acta*
of the Afscheiding, the Reverend Hendrik de Cock and the elders and
deacons of his church stated that they extended the hand of fellowship to
all those who place themselves under the yoke of Christ.[8] That was an
ecumenical ideal not easily realized in the Netherlands. But how must one
extend the hand of fellowship to those who are truly Reformed across the
ocean, and could the hand of fellowship be maintained with those who had
moved away?

Not all seceders thought alike about that issue, neither in North America
nor in the Netherlands. Hendrik P. Scholte objected to joining the Reformed Church in America (hereafter RCA). He could not join with a
synodically organized system.[9] Albertus C. Van Raalte, on the other hand,
did not object and joined the RCA.[10] Displeasure about this step led to a
division within the churches in the Holland, Michigan, colony in 1857. The
churches of Graafschap, Noordeloos, Grand Rapids and Polkton, followed
by others, severed ties with the RCA. They decided instead to follow in
North America the direction of the Afscheiding, just as they had done in
the Netherlands.[11] In this way, the bond of unity between the CGKN and
the CRC became subject to tension, a tension which has persisted to the
present day. In the remainder of this contribution we shall attempt to
describe this strain between the two denominations by referring to a
number of visits made to the CGKN by representatives of the CRC.

1857-1892

Immediately after the secession from the RCA in 1857, the CRC sought
to establish contact with the CGKN. The CGKN Synod of 1857 held at
Leiden received a letter from North America, signed by the Reverend H. G.
Klyn, as president, and the Reverend Koene Van den Bosch, as clerk of the
CRC Synod, who stated that the CRC was "seeking unity with de Christelijk
Afgescheidene Gereformeerde Kerk in Nederland."[12] The synod listened to

---

8. Ibid., p. 13.

9. Hendrik P. Scholte, "The Dutch Reformed people urged me to such an extent that I should join
their synod. I told them that I was not inclined thereunto, because I could not accept the synodical
system. I believe that Van Raalte will do so," from a letter of Scholte to A. A. V. Schuyt, dated May 14, 1847,
in Stellingwerff, *Amsterdamse Emigranten*, p. 78. Cf. Hendrik P. Scholte, *Tweede Stem uit Iowa* ('s Bosch:
H. Palier en Zoon, 1848). English version entitled "A Place of Refuge," ed. with an Introduction by Robert
P. Swieringa, *Annals of Iowa* 39 (1967/69):321–357.

10. Henry E. Dosker, *Levensschets van Dr. A. C. Van Raalte* (Nijkerk: C. C. Callenbach, 1893), pp.
112–146; Diedrich H. Kromminga, *The Christian Reformed Tradition*, From the Reformation till the
Present (Grand Rapids: Eerdmans, 1943), pp. 102–106.

11. Dosker, *Van Raalte*, pp. 261–270.

12. *Handelingen* van de Synode der Christelijk Afgescheidene Gereformeerde Kerk in Nederland,
Gehouden van den 3 den tot den 17 den Junij 1857 te Leijden (Kampen: S. van Velzen, 1857), p. 64 (Art.
139). (Rev. H. G. Klyn who seceded from the RCA in April 1857 but was back in the fold by the Classis
meeting of RCA in September 1857, Eds.).

the letter but did not react with great enthusiasm. The delegates discussed the matter extensively. According to the *Handelingen:* "Concerning the first point, i.e., the request from Klijn and Van den Bosch, the Assembly answers that it received their request as information, but that on account of conflicting reports from North America it can neither approve nor disapprove the mentioned secession, and for that reason advises the brethren in North America to act cautiously and in accordance with God's Word."[13] Apparently, the synod was of the opinion that it was more prudent not to choose sides in this conflict. It did not wish to act as an arbitrator. The remark "to act cautiously and in accordance with God's Word" made it look very much like a dead issue. The delegates were afraid to choose in favor of either group, no doubt thereby expressing the tension within the Dutch church of the Afscheiding itself. Van Raalte had exercised a great deal of influence on the churches of the Afscheiding. In 1837 he played the role of a mediator in the conflict between de Cock and Scholte, but at the synod held in 1843 objections were made against his preaching.[14] Now these conflicts and tensions continued making their effect felt, also as regards the position chosen vis-à-vis the churches abroad. For that reason, it was a wise decision that those living in the Netherlands answered those in North America: "We cannot judge concerning the division in North America. Act cautiously and in accordance with God's Word."

The synod itself was cautious and believed that it had acted according to the Word of God. The members of the CRC did not, however, consider the case closed. In 1860 they made another presentation to the synod in the Netherlands by means of a letter from North America, signed again by Van den Bosch, in which he pressed for recognition in the Netherlands of the Michigan CRCs and in which he complained about their stepsisterly treatment in the old country. The synod responded saying "that it recognized all churches that have and adhere to Reformed doctrine and church government."[15] Three years later another letter arrived at the synod, this time signed by the Reverends Wilhelmus H. Van Leeuwen and Van den Bosch, who urged, in the name of Classis Zeeland, that the brethren in the Netherlands "recognize the churches abroad."[16] Once again the synod intended to maintain its adopted standpoint, namely, that it would not make a pronouncement concerning the legitimacy or illigitimacy of the existence of the CRC.

What was the basis of their fear to speak out on this matter? Perhaps we

---

13. *Handelingen 1857,* p. 65 (Art. 139).

14. The unpublished portions are located in the archives of the Gereformeerde Kerken in Nederland.

15. *Handelingen* van de Synode der Christelijke Afgescheidene Gereformeerde Kerk in Nederland, Gehouden van den 6 den tot den 19 den Junij 1860, te Hoogeveen (Kampen: S. van Velzen, 1860), p. 48 (Art. 125).

16. *Handelingen* van de Synode der Christelijk Afgescheidene Gereformeerde Kerk in Nederland, Gehouden van den 12 den tot den 25 sten Augustus 1863, in Franeker (Amsterdam: P. Groenendijk, 1863), p. 62 (Art. 151).

can answer this question by taking note of what the *Acta* of the Synod have to say concerning the visit of Van Raalte to the synod of the Christelijke Afgescheide Gereformeerde Kerk in Nederland in 1866. It must have been an event of great significance. After thirty years one of the founding fathers of the Afscheiding was present at a synod. Introduced by the Reverend Anthony Brummelkamp, Van Raalte handed the president a letter from Classis Holland (RCA) which read:

To the Esteemed Synod of the Christelijke Afgescheidene Gereformeede Kerk in Nederland:

Esteemed Brethren:

While in the way of God's blessed providence our beloved brother, Dr. A. C. Van Raalte, decided to pay a visit to the old country, Classis Holland makes use of this opportunity of conveying through him its Christian greetings and prayer for protection. We still feel tied through bonds of love and fellowship to our Dutch brethren with whom at one time most of us suffered and struggled. We are and shall remain one with you in spirit, in dedication to doctrine, discipline, and service of the Gereformeerde Kerk. We wish to persist with you in adhering to the confession of truth, exactly as this is expressed in the [Three] Forms of Unity of our church. We gladly take note of the fact that your denomination actively promotes the spread of the Gospel among the heathen as well as supports the education of those desiring to preach the Word and defend the truth in the Netherlands. Though deeply convinced of our own imperfection and aware of our dissimilarity, we nevertheless confess to the glory of God's grace that it is our heart's desire to stand firm for the Lord and His cause. May the Lord bless you in your activities and grant that the deliberations of your assembly may lead to the salvation of Zion! Receive, dear brethren, the assurance of our love and fellowship. We commend you to God and to the Word of his grace.

Classis Holland,
Reverend Seine Bolks, President

Holland, April 18, 1865   Reverend Christian Van der Veen, Clerk[17]

After the letter was read to the delegates of the synod, the president, the Reverend Jan H. Donner, welcomed Van Raalte. Van Raalte expressed his joy about the meeting, and declared that "the purpose of his coming was to strengthen the ties of Christian love and unity between the brethren in the Netherlands and in North America. The great distance between us should not make us forget that we have the same origin. We must maintain our unity by means of mutual correspondence and communal cooperation."[18]

---

17. *Handelingen* van de Synode der Christelijk Afgescheidene Gereformeerde Kerk in Nederland, Gehouden van den 30 Mei tot den 8 Junij 1866, te Amsterdam (Kampen: S. van Velzen, 1866), pp. 11–12 (Art. 6).

18. Ibid., p. 12 (Art. 6).

The synod requested that Van Raalte remain with it in the capacity of an advisory member. At the close of their assembly, the delegates thanked him profusely. He was asked to express his thoughts about the possibility of closer fellowship.[19] Van Raalte believed that this would be no problem to the present generation. A more intimate relationship would be needed for future generations. He also gave information about joining the RCA and about the "ecclesiastical secession" which constituted the beginning of the CRC. He defended the right of joining the RCA, and ascribed the ecclesiastical secession to "diverse elements which had moved from here [the Netherlands] to North America and to various other reasons, though not to heterodoxy."[20]

Finally, the delegates shook hands with Van Raalte. The synod declared that it was prepared to "maintain where possible fellowship with the RCA and to confirm it in practice."[21]

It is clear that Van Raalte's point of view weighed heavily on the synod. He was unable to accept the separate existence of the CRC. It is a well-known fact that he ascribed it to the desire of those in North America who all too strongly wished to perpetuate the Dutch situation.[22] In 1869 another delegate from the RCA was present at the synod[23] as an official representative of the RCA "in order to maintain the fellowship founded between said denomination and ours."[24] An overture was received by the same assembly, requesting it to investigate whether or not the "secession in North America was legitimate."[25] Classis North Holland (the Netherlands) had presented the overture. Once again the synod refused to issue a statement about the matter confronting the brethren across the ocean. "We are unable to make a judgment in this matter," the synod declared. We sincerely hope that the brethren in North America "would come to understand that our denomination gladly unites itself with all Christians abroad who declare themselves in agreement with the old Gereformeerde Kerk in doctrine, discipline and worship."[26] In 1872 delegates, Jan Gelock and Jacobus De Jonge, of the Ware Hollandse Gereformeerde Kerk (CRC) were present. Though they lodged several objections against the RCA, they were admitted. The members of the assembly declared that they would make no pronouncement concerning the secession in North America. In the words described in the *Handelingen:* "The Assembly . . . judges that it should receive the delegates

---

19. Ibid., pp. 61–62 (Art. 142).

20. Ibid., p. 62 (Art. 142).

21. Ibid., p. 63 (Art. 142).

22. Dosker, *Van Raalte*, pp. 261–276.

23. *Handelingen* van de Synode der Christelijk Afgescheidene Gereformeerde Kerk in Nederland, Gehouden van den 16 den tot den 23 sten Juni 1869, te Middelburg (Kampen: S. van Velzen, 1869), pp. 10–11 (Art. 14).

24. Ibid., p. 11 (Art. 14).

25. Ibid., p. 42 (Art. 75).

26. Ibid., p. 44 (Art. 78).

from North America while this should not be considered as making a pronouncement on the ecclesiastical question in North America or deciding in favor of the objections contained in the mandate handed to Synod."[27]

As they left, the American delegates declared that it was their wish to remain united with the mother church in the Netherlands. Once again they expressly stated that the "secession in North America was not the fruit of enmity or schism, but rather one of love for the maintenance of Reformed principles."[28] The president still refused to express himself about the American controversy. "We love you for the sake of your principles, together with all who love them."[29] In this way the synod of the CGKN attempted to maintain unity both with the RCA and with the CRC. It received delegates from both denominations[30] or wrote letters to both.[31]

In 1879, however, a report mentioned the subject of "secret societies,"[32] a subject which prompted the Synod of 1882 to ask penetrating questions of the delegates of the CRC.[33] The Reverends Roelof T. Kuiper and Leendert Rietdyk defended the right of existence of the CRC: "It (CRC) was entirely one with the CGKN. Among all the sister churches no other is known to which such close ties are felt."[34] Judging from the questions presented to the brethren, it appears that the assembly wanted to come to some judgment concerning the conditions in North America.[35] Thus, the situation at that moment was as favorable as ever for favorable recognition of the CRC. In fact, four particular synods requested revision of the relationship with the RCA in connection with the issue of Freemasonry. The preliminary advisors strongly agreed: strong resistance had to be shown in this matter against the RCA.[36] It is true that the Dutch brethren did not wish to speak

27. *Handelingen* van de Synode der Christelijke Gereformeerde Kerk in Nederland, Gehouden van 5 tot 20 Junij 1872, te Groningen ('s-Gravenhage: S. van Velzen, 1872), pp. 11–12 (Art. 16).

28. Ibid., p. 65 (Art. 147).

29. Ibid.

30. See for example, the speeches of the two delegates: Roelof Pieters, "President!" in *Handelingen* van de Synode der Christelijke Gereformeerde Kerk in Nederland, Gehouden van 26 Mei tot 5 Juni 1875 te 's-Hertogenbosch (Kampen: G. Ph. Zalsman, 1875), pp. 70–72 (Bijlage III); Johannes Gezon, "President en Broeders!" in *Handelingen 1875*, p. 72 (Bijlage IV).

31. *Handelingen* van de Synode der Christelijke Gereformeerde Kerk in Nederland, Gehouden van 14 tot 23 Augustus 1877, in het Kerkgebouw der Christelijke Gereformeerde Gemeente te Utrecht (Kampen: G. Ph. Zalsman, 1877), p. 70 (Art. 168).

32. *Handelingen* van de Synode der Christelijke Gereformeerde Kerk in Nederland, Gehouden van 19 tot 30 Augustus 1879, in het Kerkgebouw der Christelijke Gereformeerde Gemeente te Dordrecht (Delfzijl: Jan Haan, 1879), pp. 34–35 (Art. 42).

33. *Handelingen* van de Synode der Christelijke Gereformeerde Kerk in Nederland, Gehouden van 15en tot 30en Augustus 1882, in het Kerkgebouw der Christelijke Gereformeerde Gemeente te Zwolle (Kampen: G. Ph. Zalsman, 1882), pp. 48–50 (Art. 60). The delegates of the RCA had sent a written excuse, *Handelingen 1882*, p. 19 (Art. 9). A portion of their letter contains extensive information about Freemasonry including the controversial expression: "What God hath cleansed that call not thou common or unclean," with which the ministers accepted Freemasonry, *Handelingen 1882*, pp. lxxxiii–lxxxiv (Bijlage XI).

34. Ibid., pp. 46–47 (Art. 60).

35. Ibid., p. 51 (Art. 63).

36. Ibid., pp. 65–66 (Art. 84).

of an apostate false church with which all fellowship was forbidden. Apparently the assembly had difficulty in formulating a single stance. The issue was extensively discussed. There was a clear difference of opinion. Finally, the assembly decided to appoint a committee of four members among whom the disagreements were the most pronounced. At this juncture the CGKN openly revealed a lack of unity within its own ranks which would show itself towards those outside its fellowship.[37]

The majority of the assembly did not as yet favor an actual break in their contacts with the RCA. A minority, including some members of the committee, wanted to "cut off the fellowship immediately."[38] The majority wanted to express a warning to those about to leave for North America.[39] Synod once again did not wish to make a pronouncement about the ecclesiastical entanglements that had caused the CRC to come into being.[40] And yet it cannot be denied that a turning point had been reached at this synod. The struggling brethren abroad received encouragement. Already in 1885 a proposal came to synod from the Province of Gelderland requesting a breaking off of all contact with the RCA. The RCA had not answered the letter sent by the previous Dutch synod.[41] The admonition of 1882 was once again repeated. But when Donner replied to the address given by the Reverend Geert H. Hoeksema, who represented the CRC, he could not pass up the opportunity of expressing his gladness about the growth of the CRC in the western states, because there was a place for the CRC to labor. According to the *Acta* of 1885, "We cannot watch your expansion in the Eastern states with 'unadulterated pleasure,' because it takes place there alongside of and partly at the expense of one denomination with which our denomination still maintains ties."[42] The entire issue was taken up once again in an extensive discussion. Of the three proposals the one advising consistories no longer to give membership certificates to congregations of the RCA was finally adopted.[43] Though perhaps the tone was a bit more friendly than that of previous letters, the same message was repeated in 1888. The president, in fact, called the relationship with the RCA tense.[44] In

---

37. Ibid., pp. 69–70 (Art. 91).

38. Ibid., p. 82 (Art. 122).

39. Ibid., pp. 82–83 (Art. 123): "The exact moment at which you break therewith, we ourselves will feel compelled to have the consistories point the members departing from here to your denomination to the dangers threatening them in your flock, through said cancer, and to have them interrogate the ministers and the members from your denomination joining ours."

40. Ibid., p. 81 (Art. 121).

41. *Handelingen* van de Synode der Christelijke Gereformeerde Kerk in Nederland, Gehouden van 18 Augustus tot 3 September 1885, in het Kerkgebouw der Christelijke Gereformeerde Gemeente te Rotterdam (Leiden: D. Donner, 1885), pp. 15–16 (Art. 27).

42. Ibid., p. 38 (Art. 52).

43. Ibid., p. 56 (Art. 87).

44. *Handelingen* van de Synode der Christelijke Gereformeerde Kerk in Nederland, in de 25 Zittingen door Haar Gehouden te Assen, van 14–30 Augustus 1888 (Leiden: D. Donner, 1888), p. 32 (Art. 36).

reality, however, the decision had been made. It was not clear that it signi-fied closer relationship with the CRC.[45]

Why did it have to take so long before the Dutch brethren recognized the brethren of the CRC as their own "flesh and blood?" Was it easier for people to adopt an attitude of ecumenicity and broadmindedness abroad than for the CGKN to do so in their native country? Or was it the case that the Dutch Christians no longer wholeheartedly supported the principle that the American brethren had employed as the basic principle for their Afscheiding?[46]

These considerations possibly played a role in this issue. Nevertheless, it must be openly stated that there were noticeable tensions within the Dutch Afscheiding. After all, Van Raalte was not in every respect considered a pure, Reformed person by all seceders in the Netherlands.[47] Brummel-kamp introduced him to the Synod of 1886. The Reverend Simon van Velzen pleaded strongly in favor of the brethren in North America who looked upon the RCA as de Nederlandse Hervormde Kerk in the Nether-lands. I believe that the inner tension within the churches of the Afscheid-ing was the deepest cause for the rather indecisive attitude toward the CRC. Years later history would repeat itself but in the opposite direction.

1892–1940

Those present at the Utrecht Assembly of the members of the Christelijke Gereformeerde Kerken (July 20, 1892) decided to voice their disapproval over the action of the Christelijke Gereformeerde Synode (Amsterdam, June 1892), which had brought about the reunion between the "Afge-scheidenen" and the "Dolerenden." They left the association into which they were incorporated "in a violent manner" and wished to remain (June 17, 1892) the "legitimate continuation of the old Gereformeerde Kerk in Nederland (CGKN). One of the first decisions was to "notify Her Majesty, the Queen-regent, about this decision and to acquaint the Christelijke Gereformeerde Kerk abroad, especially in North America, with the course of events for the purpose of continuing in fellowship with these churches."[48]

Before the delegates from the various congregations had a chance to

45. See the summaries in Henry Beets, *De Christelijke Gereformeerde Kerk in Noord-Amerika; Zestig Jaren van Strijd en Zegen* (Grand Rapids: Grand Rapids Printing Co., 1918), pp. 136–142, 186–189.

46. See the arguments with which the people severed the ties with RCA, Beets, *Christelijke Gerefor-meerde Kerk*, pp. 79–99; Dosker, *Van Raalte*, pp. 240–276; Albert Hyma, *Albertus C. Van Raalte and his Dutch Settlements in the United States* (Grand Rapids: Eerdmans, 1947), pp. 212–224; Kromminga, *Christian Reformed Tradition*, pp. 107–111.

47. Against his preaching there were, here and there, the same objections as against that of Anthony Brummelkamp. In 1866 he preached in the Netherlands, and was ready to consider a call, but in vain, Hyma, *Van Raalte*, p. 225.

48. *Notulen* van de Synodale Vergaderingen der Christelijke Gereformeerde Kerk, Gehouden in 1893 en 1894, en *Verslag der Vergadering van 20 Juli 1892* (Utrecht: G. Renkema, 1894), p. 4.

speak, this decision was taken. This decision was proof that it actually expected to receive the support of the American sister church. No doubt the members remembered the difficulties the CRC had endured in order to be recognized by the churches before the Union. Now there was a feeling that they could depend on understanding not only, but on the hand of fellowship as well. That this conviction was also present in the churches is evident from the question raised by the church of Zaandam in 1894 whether correspondence with the CRC was possible.[49] The Reverend Jacobus Wisse reported that the brethren in North America were already informed of the situation in the Netherlands. The Reverend J. R. Kreulen took it upon himself to correspond concerning this matter with a few ministers in North America. The synod also decided to invite delegates from North America to the next synod "at their own expense." Regarding the membership certificates from the CRC, every church could act according to its own judgment.[50] It would not be until 1911, however, before a delegate from North America would come to the synod of the CGKN.

Meanwhile, reports about North America appeared occasionally in *De Wekker*. Wisse wrote that the ecclesiastical situation in the Netherlands was similar to that of the CRC. Both experienced the growing influence of the theology of Abraham Kuyper. Wisse urged the Americans to read *De Wekker*, in addition to so many other publications.[51] Wisse was especially annoyed with a statement in *De Wachter* by Hendericus Beuker: "Our CRC has absolutely no connection with the existing CGKN." In order to avoid misunderstanding, he added, it would be more appropriate to speak of the "Nieuwe Christelijke Gereformeerde Kerk."[52] Mockingly Wisse replied, "If the Gereformeerde Kerk *is* the sister church, then there is in the Netherlands a sister church "A" and another "B," "beside a Christelijke Gereformeerde Kerk with which the brethren in North America have no relationship."[53]

At the same time, it was apparent that not every one in North America appreciated the increasing influence of Kuyper. In 1900 the Reverend I. Contant, together with part of his congregation at Lodi, New Jersey, separated from the CRC. According to the version of this minister, the CRC honored the same Kuyperian opinions as those which had gained momentum in the GKN. Therefore, Contant and his congregation sought to establish their own contacts with the synod of the CGKN.[54] For several reasons this was an interesting experiment. It tells us something about the circumstances in North America at the turn of the century. Contant wrote

49. Ibid., p. 55 (Art. 14).
50. Ibid.
51. Jacobus Wisse, "Aan Broeder B. in Noord-Amerika!" *De Wekker* 7 (27 Juli 1894):2–3.
52. Jacobus Wisse, "Een Weinige Correctie" *De Wekker* 8 (28 Juni 1895):2–3.
53. Ibid.
54. Beets, *Christelijke Gereformeerde Kerk,* p. 337.

extensively about this in *De Wekker*. It also demonstrated a lack of a sense of reality on the part of Contant and his supporters who requested an investigation by the synod of the CGKN in order "to be adopted as a congregation of the CGKN, e.g., as a congregation of Classis Amsterdam, or to be incorporated into whatever classis the synod wished. As soon as we are accepted regular labor among other equally misled Christelijke Gereformeerden in this vicinity can begin, and when new congregations have been started, we ourselves can form our own classis and send delegates to the synod in the Netherlands."[55] The issues which Contant raised were dear to the CGKN: the doctrines concerning baptism, justification, and others.[56] Perhaps the reaction to the letter from Lodi is even more interesting, because it showed to what extent the synod desired to enter into genuine contact with the CRC in North America.

Immediately there was a proposal to send one of the ministers to North America. Wisse proposed something quite extraordinary: they should gather written information and, in addition, they should ask the church at Lodi "whether it had any objection to writing in *De Wekker* concerning the ecclesiastical situation at Lodi and in this way acquaint the Dutch public with North America. Should some result come from such correspondence, would its members be willing to delegate Rev. Wisse, who had made himself available for this, to North America in order to inform the Dutch Christians there and to decide as he saw fit."[57] This proposal would have an adverse effect, however. Contant was, indeed, invited to write in *De Wekker*, but his letters were not well received. Though he appeared to be an ardent anti-Kuyperian, even in that respect he was not completely trusted,[58] for he had spoken to Kuyper during his visit to North America and had sung the praises of the distinguished visitor from the Netherlands. Contant defended his action by stating that he had treated Kuyper merely as a Hollander, not as a Professor of the Free University, even less as a minister of the GKN.[59] But would a genuine anti-Kuyperian do such a thing? When Contant gave a rather detailed explanation of his ecclesiastical entanglements, many a

---

55. *Notulen* van het Verhandelde in de Zittingen der Synode van de Christelijke Gereformeerde Kerk in Nederland, Gehouden te Utrecht, in het Kerkgebouw der Christelijke Gereformeerde Gemeente Aldaar, op 24 en 25 Juli 1900 (Leeuwarden: Jan van der Veen, 1900), pp. 9–12 (Art. 18). The letter of the Reformed Congregation of Lodi was signed by nearly all those who were members of the Christelijke Gereformeerde Kerk (before 1892) in the Netherlands.

56. Ibid., p. 10 (Art. 18).

57. Ibid., p. 12 (Art. 18). Indeed the synod decided to delegate Wisse, who would depart in May 1901. The cost to his denomination would not be more than two hundred guilders. He himself would pay the rest. Wisse was accustomed to do something for the denomination, for the editing of *De Wekker* cost him personally a considerable amount of money.

58. Jacobus Wisse, "Correspondentie," *De Wekker* 13 (14 September 1900):3.

59. I. Contant, "Aan de Redacteur en de Lezers van 'De Wekker,'" *De Wekker* 13 (7 December 1900):2–3.

reader of *De Wekker* must have given a sigh. Wisse even wrote: "We are glad that we are at the end of those boring explanations."[60]

Matters became worse, however, when Contant began writing articles concerning baptism, confession, and the Lord's Supper, the "hot potatoes" of the churches of the Afscheiding. This made Wisse ask Contant how he believed he was able to avoid Labadism.[61] Contant could assert that he "wanted to say the opposite of de Labadie,"[62] but he had, in fact, spoiled it for himself. The readers of the magazine were able to conclude from other articles as well that the manner in which Contant landed outside of the CRC could be viewed in another way. The Reverend Jacob Manni from Passaic, New Jersey, wrote an account in *De Wekker* about the true state of affairs at Lodi.[63]

When the Synod of 1901 met in Utrecht, it had to make a decision about this matter. Its decision turned out to be negative. Some of the delegates had stumbled over the writings in *De Wekker*. It appeared that Contant, though an old friend of Wisse since their student years, had a rather poor reputation among the earlier Dutch congregations. While Wisse still declared that the delegates could have expected presumably favorable results from "sending a feeler to a part of the church in North America,"[64] the synod decided not to acquiesce to the request from the church at Lodi,

1. on account of church order difficulties;
2. because under the circumstances no classical representation, church visiting, etc., can be realized;
3. because of the things Contant had written in *De Wekker*.[65]

The Reverend Frederik P. L. C. van Lingen revealed that it was he who had held Wisse back from going to North America. Why? Because someone else would have to assume giving his lectures and had to take upon himself the editorship of *De Wekker*. But who was qualified for such a task? He had withheld his cooperation regarding Wisse's journey to North America especially because "a stay in North America could become a temptation."[66] In this van Lingen possessed practical insight. For how many ministers went to North America and never returned?

Thus, Wisse continued to write in *De Wekker*. He answered Contant,

60. Jacobus Wisse, "Den Weleerw. Heer Ds. J. Contant de Lodi N.J. V.S.," *De Wekker* 13 (18 Januari 1901):2–3.
61. Jacobus Wisse, "Een Enkele Opmerking," *De Wekker* 13 (29 Maart 1901):2.
62. I. Contant, "Aan de Redacteur en de Lezers van 'De Wekker,'" *De Wekker* 13 (3 Mei 1901):3.
63. Jacob Manni, "Is Ds. J. Contant 'Uitgetreden' uit de Holl. Christ. Ger. Kerk in Amerika?" *De Wekker* 13 (12 October 1900):1–2.
64. *Notulen* van het Verhandelde in de Zittingen der Synode van de Christelijke Gereformeerde Kerk in Nederland, Gehouden te Utrecht, in het Kerkgebouw der Christelijke Gereformeerde Gemeente aldaar op 23 en 24 Juli 1901 (Utrecht: Renkema, 1901), p. 23 (Art. 37).
65. Ibid., pp. 23–24 (Art. 37).
66. Ibid., p. 22 (Art. 37).

from whom very little was heard after the decision of synod in 1901.[67] The exchange of letters gave Wisse an opportunity to formulate his opinions about the relationship between the churches in the Netherlands and those in North America. Among other things he noted that the churches in North America were nearly identical in character with the GKN.[68] In his own words: "And where they cannot possibly be one both with the Gereformeerde Kerken and with the Christelijke Gereformeerde Kerken in Nederland, it is a rather forgone conclusion that we in the Netherlands are in the same relationship to the Christian Reformed Church in North America as to the 'Gereformeerde Kerken in Nederland.' We have many objections to Kuyper, but that is no reason for breaking ecclesiastical ties."[69] At the same time Wisse did not place the CRC on a par with the GKN. He believed that they differed regarding the working out (of the principles) of neo-Calvinism.[70] From the private exchange of letters he knew that "there were still genuine sons and daughters of the Afscheiding who frowned upon the ideas of the Doleantie."[71] More than once he spoke about the necessity of having someone go to North America in order to provide accurate information about the CGKN.

That such a proposal was not superfluous became apparent from the pronouncement made by the Synod of the CRC in 1902 concerning the question of Classis Hudson, "whether membership certificates from the CGKN are valid in the CRC in North America." The synod declared that it wanted to have the same rule applied as the one "followed with regard to people coming with membership certificates from churches of less correct formation."[72] This Kuyperian formulation must have been difficult for the members of the CGKN to accept.[73] Wisse, at least, wrote in explanation of this pronouncement that the CRC clearly agreed with the GKN.[74] Somewhat bitterly he remarked: "We on our part have taken no official steps to establish a direct relationship with that denomination in North America."[75]

In 1910 a change in direction was noticeable. There was a request at the Synod of the CRC concerning starting correspondence with the CGKN "without admitting or expressing anything concerning the legality of the

---

67. Contant wrote more than thirty "Letters from America" in *De Wekker* between August 3, 1900 and July 26, 1901.
68. Jacobus Wisse, "De Christelijke Gereformeerde Kerk in Nederland en de Christelijke Gereformeerde Kerk in N. Amerika," *De Wekker* 13 (7 December 1901):2.
69. Ibid.
70. Ibid.
71. Wisse, "Den Weleerw. Heer Ds. J. Contant," p. 2.
72. *Acta der Synode* van de Christelijke Gereformeerde Kerk in Amerika, Gehouden te Holland, Michigan van 18 tot 27 Juni, 1902 (Holland, H. Holkeboer, 1902), p. 67 (Art. 128).
73. Cf. Abraham Kuyper, *Tractaat van de Reformatie der Kerken van de Zonen der Reformatie Hier te Lande op Luthers Vierde Eeuwfeest* (Amsterdam: Höveker & Zoon, 1884).
74. Jacobus Wisse, "De Christ. Geref. Kerk in Noord-Amerika," *De Wekker* 15 (25 Juli 1902):2–3.
75. Ibid.

existence of this church."[76] Synod decided "to begin such correspondence along this line." The same synod considered a request from Classis Illinois to the effect that synod make a pronouncement about the question as to which churches must be considered "churches of less justifiable origin." It replied as follows: "Members coming from churches not belonging to sister churches but which nonetheless maintain the Reformed Confession and are pure in doctrine and in life, will be accepted upon submission of a membership certificate as long as they promise to submit to the supervision and the discipline of the local consistories. This also applies to members of the present Christelijke Gereformeerde Kerken in Nederland."[77] Quietly, the characterization of the CGKN as "of less justifiable origin" had, in this way, disappeared.

Thus, room was also made for a brotherly visit by the Reverend Henry Beets to the Synod of 1911 of the CGKN. Beets was warmly welcomed. He was a good acquaintance of Professor Pieter J. M. de Bruin and for many consecutive years he had sent him the *Yearbook* and the *Acts of Synod* of the CRC. De Bruin, in turn, paid attention to these works in *De Wekker.* Beets addressed the synod as a representative of a denomination "that extends a sisterly hand to you and wishes to correspond with you."[78] Beets represented the CRC in such a way that the brethren in Utrecht were compelled to respond. He stated that "we in North America are the old seceded church of the Netherlands, both in doctrine and in discipline. We still preach the old way: the three divisions of the Heidelberg Catechism. We cannot do without them."[79] In his response, the president, the Reverend Hector Janssen, spoke of the similarity between the CGKN and the CRC in birth and development, in struggle and misunderstanding. But later in the questions which followed, the unity in doctrine came to the fore: did or did this not exist? Had the CRC not adopted the decisions of Utrecht? And had the CRC not gotten itself into difficulties by sending delegates to the synod of the CGKN as well as to the synod of the GKN?[80]

Beets' answer was recorded at length in the minutes:

> The Esteemed brother indicates that there is a minority within the Christian Reformed Church which endorses the teachings of the neo-Calvinists. In 1905 agitation swept through the Theological School in Grand Rapids; seemingly one of the professors taught something to that effect. The next year the synod of the Christian Reformed Church recorded in its minutes the decisions of the synod of the Gereformeerde Kerken in Nederland in order

76. *Acta der Synode* van de Christelijke Gereformeerde Kerk, Gehouden van 15 tot 24 Juni, 1910, te Muskegon (Grand Rapids: H. Verhaar Drukker, 1910), p. 60 (Art. 67).
77. Ibid.
78. *Notulen* van het Verhandelde in de Zittingen der Synode van de Christelijke Gereformeerde Kerk in Nederland, Gehouden te Utrecht, op 25, 26 en 27 Juli 1911 (Utrecht: G. Renkema, 1911), p. 15 (Art. 32).
79. Ibid.
80. Ibid., p. 16 (Art. 32).

thereby to bind the minority. The Synod of 1910 emphatically stated that the Christian Reformed Church left the differences between the Gereformeerde Kerken in Nederland and the Christelijke Gereformeede Kerken in Nederland to the brethren. It abstained from deciding on historical issues. It requested correspondence—correspondence, not union.[81]

After an extended discussion, in which both protagonists and opponents spoke, the Dutch synod declared that

> . . . it gladly agreed to the offered correspondence. In view of the doctrinal differences existing both between us and the Gereformeerde Kerken in Nederland, as well as in the Christian Reformed Church, however, it could not proceed to mutual recognition of membership certificates.[82]

In his words of farewell to Beets the president remarked: "We as a synod believed that we should and could decide nothing other in view of our position,"[83] meaning in view of the position of CGKN vis-à-vis the GKN.[84] To what extent the conflict with the GKN determined the situation appeared from the reaction to Beets' visit. People deduced from it that the CRC, though it did not wish to make a pronouncement regarding the situation in the Netherlands, did not look upon the CGKN as a schismatic denomination. That was the basis for the conclusion drawn by the members of the GKN: they thought that they alone were "the church of Christ in our country and had to consider every outside group as a sect, an erring church, or a church of less solid formation. Our American brethren 'don't give a cent' for this claim."[85]

In 1912 the synodical committee of the CRC noted that the CGKN could not proceed to "such correspondence as would include an exchange of membership certificates."[86]

For the time being, Beets' visit had completed another round of attempts at establishing contacts between the two denominations. Meanwhile, the Dutch brethren watched with interest the course of events in North America. Professor de Bruin, then still called an instructor, especially zeroed in on the CRC; Beets supplied him with materials. As everywhere else, personal

---

81. Ibid., p. 17 (Art. 32).

82. Ibid., p. 31 (Art. 54).

83. Ibid., p. 44 (Art. 73). Beets apparently felt very much at home at the synod. He gave advice concerning missionary matters and wrote a letter entitled "Waarde Broeder" about his experiences in *De Wekker* 35 (15 December 1922):3. He also advised the synod about the United Presbyterian Church in America. De Bruin had written that this church was according to Beets "Calvinistic," indeed the best denomination in North America with the exception of the Christelijke Gereformeerde Kerk, *De Wekker* 24 (11 Augustus 1911):2.

84. According to de Bruin's report of the synod, *De Wekker* 24 (25 Augustus 1911):2–3.

85. Thus Hector Janssen, "In de Weg der Scheuring?" *De Wekker* 24 (1 September 1911):2–3.

86. *Acta der Synode* van de Christelijke Gereformeerde Kerk, Gehouden van 19 tot 27 Juni, 1912, te Roseland, Chicago, Illinois (Holland: Holland Printing Co., 1912), p. 63 (Bijlage 1).

relations appeared to help, though in this case they did not imply that de Bruin presented an uncritical stance.[87]

In the early 1920s the Reverend Jan W. Geels, who in 1932 would become a professor, asked whether or not it was getting to be time that ecclesiastical ties ought to be established between the two denominations.[88] The affairs of the CRC were being eagerly watched, which events Geels and de Bruin designated as a crisis.[89] But nothing really happened! Neither the visit of the Reverend Idzerd van Dellen to the Synod of 1934 nor the visit of Janssen to the Synod of 1936 (in Grand Rapids) brought about a change. Van Dellen visited the Netherlands in the centennial year of the Afscheiding. He acted with a measure of reserve and said that he believed that the CGKN had refused to enter into correspondence with the CRC. He then made the following statement: "Blood goes where it cannot go."[90] As a result of his visit, it was decided in committee to send a delegate to North America in 1936 if at all possible.[91] Geels clarified this decision in *De Wekker.* If in a previous issue he had written that "beside the unity in name there is no relationship whatsoever between the two denominations,"[92] he now wrote that in terms of church polity not a single objection could be leveled against the legitimate existence of the CRC.[93] His conclusion was: "And when in our opinion the Christian Reformed Church, the fruit of the Afscheiding, is the legitimate church of the Lord in North America, then it is obvious that our members who move to North America must be referred to that denomination.[94] I do not shrink back from worthwhile correspondence . . . including an exchange of membership

---

87. Under the heading, "Buitenland" de Bruin wrote an account to the decision of the CRC not to acquiesce to a peace-manifesto [see *De Heraut* No. 2073 (14 October 1917):3], because "our country belongs to the warring nations"; "We deem it extremely objectionable that a Christian church, even one within a nation at war, sets aside a peace manifesto, and we judge that the church of Christ must at all times be zealous of peace. Further, we believe that this synod should have issued a rather urgent petition regarding the termination of the awful bloodshedding, the more so because the suffering of the nations has increased due to the United States of America joining the war. Though a voice of blood calls forth from the earth, it does not seem to find resonance in the consciences of the delegates of that synod." *De Wekker* 31 (8 November 1918):2. It is remarkable to note the statement of Janssen that the World War contributed to a large extent to the Americanization of the CRC, *De Wekker* 49 (7 Augustus 1936):2.

88. Jan W. Geels, "Vragenbus," *De Wekker* 35 (18 Augustus 1922):3–4.

89. Ibid., p. 4. "Within that denomination a struggle has started against the neo-Calvinistic idea of the covenant . . . the same struggle which is being fought here within the Christelijke Gereformeerde Kerk." In his column, "Buitenland" de Bruin gives detailed information (received from Beets?) about the crisis in the CRC, *De Wekker* 35 (25 Augustus 1922):2.

90. *Acta* van de Generale Synode der Christelijke Gereformeerde Kerk in Nederland, Gehouden te Zwolle van 4–6 September 1934 (Apeldoorn: Christelijke Gereformeerde Kerk, 1934), p. 23 (Art. 42). See also Idzerd Van Dellen, "Toespraak," Ibid., pp. 94–96 (Bijlage XIV), and Pieter J. M. de Bruin, "Antwoord," Ibid., pp. 97–98 (Bijlage XV). De Bruin wrote: "May it lead under the blessing of the Lord to closer ties of friendship," p. 98.

91. *Acta 1934,* p. 37 (Art. 84).

92. Jan W. Geels, "Synodalia," *De Wekker* 47 (11 Januari 1935):3.

93. Jan W. Geels, "Synodalia," *De Wekker* 47 (18 Januari 1935):3.

94. Jan W. Geels, "Synodalia," *De Wekker* 47 (1 Februari 1935):3–4.

certificates."[95] A week later, however, Geels retracted more or less his earlier statement.[96] This situation was characteristic of the atmosphere in which Janssen went to North America in 1936. Somewhere someone inexplicably published that Professor Gerard Wisse would be the delegate before van der Schuit announced in *De Wekker* that Janssen would go.[97] While Janssen reported extensively about his travels, mentioning a myriad of details, he gave only a summary treatment about his visit to the synod of the CRC.[98] When, finally, a rumor reached the Netherlands that he had touched the subject of possible correspondence with the CRC—concerning which issue the synod of the CGKN had decided as early as 1911, several church magazines mentioned that he had gone too far. But van der Schuit urged that they should at least wait for the report of Janssen to be given at the Dutch synod.

In his address to the CRC Janssen stated that his own denomination had delegated him "with the mandate" to petition the CRC to decide during its present assembly to initiate correspondence with the CGKN as "was the case previously between the 'Christelijke Gereformeerde Kerk' in North America (the CRC) and in the Netherlands. We in the Netherlands sincerely hope that now such correspondence will become a fact."[99]

The 1936 Synod of the CRC appointed a committee to prepare a proposal.[100] Synod then said it was willing to start correspondence with the CGKN if this gesture of cooperation would mean at least more than a merely formal exchange of greetings. Above all, it had to be clear that such a relationship would not signify that the CRC had made a decision regarding its relationship to the GKN.[101]

---

95. Ibid., p. 3.

96. Jan W. Geels, "Stemmen uit Amerika," *De Wekker* 47 (12 April 1935):3, (26 April 1935):3.

97. Jakob J. van der Schuit, "Naar Amerika," *De Wekker* 48 (20 Maart 1936):2.

98. Hector Janssen, "Indrukken en Ervaringen," *De Wekker* 49 (26 Juni 1936):2, (3 Juli 1936):2–3, (10 Juli 1936):2–3, (17 Juli 1936):2, (24 Juli 1936):2–3, (31 Juli 1936):2, (7 Augustus 1936):2, (28 Augustus 1936):1–2, (4 September 1936):1–2, (11 September 1936):1–2, (25 September 1936):3, (2 October 1936):2, (9 October 1936):2, (16 October 1936):2, (23 October 1936):2, (30 October 1936):2, (6 November 1936):2, (13 November 1936):2, (20 November 1936):1.

99. Hector Janssen, "Rede," *Acts of Synod 1936* of the Christian Reformed Church in Session from June 9 to June 26, 1936, at Grand Rapids, Michigan (Grand Rapids: Christian Reformed Church, 1936), pp. 268–273 (Suppl. XIII).

100. *Acts of Synod 1936*, pp. 24–25 (Art. 57).

101. Ibid., p. 97 (Art. 143), "That this correspondence, however, is not to consist only in an exchange of greetings and formal calls, but also:

1. In sending delegates to each other's major assemblies that there they may have an advisory vote;
2. In taking mutual heed lest there be deviation from Reformed principles in doctrine, worship, or discipline;
3. In mutual counsel what attitude to assume towards others;
4. In serving each other with advice, especially in case of proposed revision of the Confession, and of the Liturgy in so far as doctrine is concerned.

Furthermore, this synod wishes it to be clearly understood that the Christian Reformed Church of America by seeking such correspondence does not commit itself with respect to the relation between the

Finally, the synod asked Janssen to convey its decision to the synod of his own denomination.[102] Janssen presented his report to the Synod of Hilversum. It, in turn, replied laconically that the matter of correspondence between the two denominations had not as yet been decided.[103] The deputies for correspondence with higher authorities would look more carefully into this matter. The outbreak of World War II, however, swept the matter under the carpet. History had repeated itself, except that this time it happened in the reverse. Before 1892 the CRC made the petition; now the CRC refused to made a declaration. Soon another occasion would present itself at which the CGKN would be required to answer the question whether it would be oriented toward the CRC or the Old Christian Reformed Church.

1947-1980

The last period can and must be treated briefly. The synod of the CGKN, which met in Utrect in 1947, discussed intensively the matter of the unity of the church. It thoroughly discussed a report stating that "its general advice had to be that our negative attitude must be abandoned and be changed into a positive one in which necessary contact be established with all those accepting the Reformed confession." The delegates spoke of a prophetic calling of the church which had to be vigorously pursued.[104] At the same synod, however, the delegates for correspondence with other denominations reported that a petition requesting correspondence has been received from the Rehoboth Reformed Church in Grand Rapids, Michigan, founded in 1943 mainly from members of churches corresponding with the Gereformeerde Gemeenten in the Netherlands (Rev. Gerrit H. Kersten). Two ministers from the CGKN had preached in Grand Rapids, and the members felt a kinship with the churches in the Netherlands.[105]

After correspondence was initiated with these churches the Reverend G. A. Zijderveld accepted the call to become its minister in October 1948. Emigrants to the United States of America or to Canada were requested to

---

Reformed Churches of the Netherlands, nor with respect to our own relation towards the Reformed Churches in the Netherlands.

Finally to entrust this expression of the desire and willingness of our Synod to the Reverend Hector Janssen, delegate of the Christian Reformed Churches to our Synod, to deliver the same to his churches."

102. Ibid.

103. *Acta* van de Generale Synode der Christelijke Gereformeerde Kerk in Nederland, Gehouden te Hilversum van 31 Augustus–2 September 1937 (Apeldoorn: Christelijke Gereformeerde Kerk, 1937), p. 30 (Art. 75).

104. *Acta* van de Generale Synode der Christelijke Gereformeerde Kerken in Nederland, Gehouden te Utrecht van 9–18 September 1947 (Apeldoorn: Christelijke Gereformeerde Kerken, 1947), p. 25 (Art. 75).

105. "Rapport Deputaten voor Correspondentie met andere Kerken" in *Acta 1947,* pp. 72–74 (Bijlage IV).

have their membership certificates forwarded to this congregation because "we are the only Christelijke Gereformeerde Gemeente in Noord America."[106]

Simultaneously, however, another current began to gain momentum. Many persons emigrated to the United States of America and Canada, where they received assistance from the CRC. A number of ministers from the CGKN accepted calls to churches of the CRC. Near the close of the Synod of 1947 an overture was received requesting the CRC to send another petition to the CGKN in order to initiate correspondence. The deputies in the Netherlands inquired into the meaning of the decision of the 1905 Synod of the GKN as far as the CRC was concerned.[107] They received the answer that the CRC had adopted this decision and no change had to that time been made concerning this. This issue would repeatedly surface in future correspondence, but that did not prevent the deputies from advising the 1950 Synod of the CGKN to proceed to initiate "correspondence in a broader sense."[108] Synod, on the other hand, wanted to continue using the word "contact";[109] it also wanted to follow the same course with regard to the CRC as with regard to the GKN.

The entire matter came more concretely before the synod in the discussion of the report of deputies for emigration. On the advice of van der Schuit the deputies recommended the following policy: emigrating members would be advised to join the church nearest to them which was in closest agreement with the Reformed confession. At any rate, the members had to look for a church home, because their children would otherwise become unchurched."[110] Clearly, the deputies knew that they should adopt another point of view from that of the Old Christian Reformed Church in Grand Rapids.

In another respect the relationship with this local church became less firm. When members of this Grand Rapids church vigorously began to promote church growth and organization in Canada, a break took place between the Old Christian Reformed Church and the Free Christian Reformed Church in 1953,[111] a break which did not fail to have its effect felt in the Netherlands. This was undoubtedly one of the factors that made

106. A. Lindhout, "Amerika," De Wekker 58 (12 November 1948):3.

107. "Rapport van Deputaten voor Contact met de Gereformeerde Belijdenis," in Acta van de Generale Synode van de Christelijke Gereformeerde Kerken in Nederland, Gehouden te 's-Gravenhage, 5–7 en 12–13 September 1950 (Apeldoorn: Christelijke Gereformeerde Kerken, 1950), pp. 199–201 (Bijlage XLIV).

108. Ibid., p. 203 (Bijlage XLIV).

109. Ibid., p. 44 (Art. 123).

110. "Rapport van Deputaten inzake Emigratie," in Acta 1950, pp. 244–245 (Bijlage LVI).

111. Cf. Jacob Tamminga, Om de Waarheid (Privately printed); G. A. Zijderveld, Kort Rapport over Ds. J. Tamminga van de Tijd van Zijn Komst naar Canada tot Zijn Uittreden uit de Old. Chr. Ref. Church (Privately printed). Eds.' note: In 1961 the two churches (the one in Canada and the other in the United States) united and adopted the names, Free Christian Reformed Church of Canada and Old Christian Reformed Church of America. Their Synod of 1974 voted to adopt the name of the Free Reformed Church of North America.

discussion concerning the significance of the synodical decision of 1908 urgent for the CRC. This discussion caused much misunderstanding and difficulty, misunderstanding over the terms "correspondence" and "contact" (which were differently interpreted in North America and in the Netherlands), as well as misunderstanding concerning the extent of the decision of 1908.

The visit of the Reverend Bastiaan Nederlof to the Synod of Hilversum helped clarify the 1908 decision. He spoke as a delegate of the CRC and simultaneously as a good friend of a number of Dutch churches which he had served as pastor. He could not be suspected of Kuyperianism.[112] He informed the assembly that the synod of the CRC no longer considered the conclusions of the Synod of Utrecht binding.[113] By this action, he observed, the road had now been cleared of a serious obstacle lying in the way of recognizing each other as sister churches.[114] On the other hand, the information of the Reverend Jacob Tamminga, a delegate of the Free Christian Reformed Church, weighed heavily on the same synod. Therefore, Synod decided to declare that on its part not all objections had been removed, issues about which it wanted to correspond. Yet, all too often it had heard in the past that the CRC agreed with the GKN. All too well it remembered the reply: there is agreement in name only. Thus, it is not surprising that it took some time before the CGKN began to realize that the CRC intended to go its own way in faithfulness to the Reformed confession.

That the CRC took its own path became especially apparent in the way it sought to shape its contacts with other denominations. It now exchanged the former term ("sister church") for the new concept of "ecclesiastical fellowship" by which it saw an opportunity for improving its contacts with other Christians. That was the sense in which the Synod of Hoogeveen understood[115] and accepted it in principle.[116] In close consultation with the Free Reformed Church of North America, the synod of the CGKN proposed a ruling. At the 1980 Synod of Amersfoort, in the presence of the delegates of both the CRC and the Free Reformed Church of North America, it was emphasized once again that the tie with the Free Reformed Church of North America remained completely intact, while the relationship would be maintained with the CRC in a new and unique way. When, with respect to this difficult matter the decision was finally made, the president mentioned that a historic moment had been reached in which

112. As appeared from numerous articles in the *Kerkblad voor Friesland*, the official organ of Classis Leeuwarden of CGKN.

113. *Acta* van de Generale Synode van de Christelijke Gereformeerde Kerken in Nederland, Hilversum, 26 Augustus 1968–9 Januari 1969 (Dordrecht: D. J. van Brummen, 1969), p. 48 (Art. 128).

114. Ibid.

115. *Acta* van de Generale Synode van de Christelijke Gereformeerde Kerken in Nederland, Hoogeveen, 16 Augustus–23 September 1977 (Naarden: Drukkerij "Naarden," 1977), p. 43 (Art. 106).

116. Ibid., p. 49 (Art. 114).

"in no way was a choice made between the Christian Reformed Church in North America and the Free Reformed Church of North America. The Christelijke Gereformeerde Kerken in Nederland wanted to maintain this kind of ecclesiastical relationship in that great country of North America."[117]

No choice was made.

Three times now this had happened.

Between 1857 and 1892 the CGKN refused to choose between the RCA and the CRC. The CRC, in turn, did not wish to choose between the CGKN and the GKN between 1892 and 1947. Finally, the CGKN refused to take sides between the CRC and the Free Reformed Church in North America.

Is this refusal a sign of weakness or a symbol of strength and love? I believe it was the latter. For those standing in this strength and love, will like Calvin, the Calvin to whom Kromminga pointed, not be absolutists, but neither will they abandon God's truth. In this way the Christian church, which has experienced the Reformation, will have a future both in Europe and in North America.

---

117. *Acta* van de Generale Synode van de Christelijke Gereformeerde Kerken in Nederland, Amersfoort, 19 Augustus–3 Oktober 1980 (Naarden: Drukkerij "Naarden," 1980), pp. 32–33 (Art. 67).

A Bibliography of John Henry Kromminga

Peter De Klerk

Abbreviations

Art	After Recess Topics	NGTT	Nederduitse Gereformeerde
Awsi	As we see it		Teologiese Tydskrif
Ban	The Banner	Outl	The Outlook
CalCon	Calvinist Contact	PG	The Presbyterian Guardian
CCC	Calvin College Chimes	RefRev	The Reformed Review
CF	The Calvin Forum	RESNE	The Reformed Ecumenical
ChiCal	Chicago Calvinist		Synod. News Exchange
ChrCyn	Christian Cynosure	RESTB	The Reformed Ecumenical
CHS	Christian Home and School		Synod. Theological Bulletin
CLH	Christian Labor Herald	RevRef	La Revue Réformée
CT	Christianity Today	RJ	The Reformed Journal
CTJ	Calvin Theological Journal	RT	Revista Teologica
FM	The Federation Messenger	Sem-Alum	Sem-Alum
Fts	From the Scriptures	Stro	Stromata
GN	The Good News	TaS	Trowel and Sword
Herald	The Herald	TT	Torch and Trumpet
JES	Journal of Ecumenical Studies	Wach	De Wachter
Kerkb	Die Kerkblad	WTJ	The Westminster Theological
LD	The Listeners Digest		Journal
MM	Missionary Monthly	YC	The Young Calvinist

1947

"A call to savoriness" (Matthew 5, 13) in *Unsearchable riches*. Vol. 6. Grand Rapids: Christian Reformed Publishing House, 1947. Pp. 47–57.

"Our youth and the future" *Ban* 82 (1947) 359, 367.

Ed. "Leading questions answered by leading men" *ChiCal* 1 (April 1947) 8, 10, (May 1947) 12–13, (June 1947) 13–15, (October 1947) 17, (November 1947) 11, (December 1947) 17–18, (January 1948) 16, (February 1948) 16; 2 (April 1948) 13–14, (June 1948) 18, (September 1948) 12–13, 20.

"Thoughts on conformity" *YC* 28 (April 1947) 3, (May 1947) 5, (June 1947) 7, (July 1947) 6.

"Albertus Christiaan Van Raalte, 1811–1876" *CF* 12 (1946/47) 211–213, 238–240.

1948

The Christian Reformed Church. A study in orthodoxy. Th.D. dissertation. Princeton: Princeton Theological Seminary, 1948. 301 leaves. Published under same title, Grand Rapids: Baker Book House, 1949.

"The young calvinist in action in the church" in *A call to action.* Vital issues. Grand Rapids: The Young Calvinist Federation, 1948. Pp. 16–25.

"Strength through service" *Ban* 83 (1948) 263.

None so blind. (Psalm 36, 9) Radio message delivered August 1, 1948. Chicago: The Back to God Hour, 1948.

All the comforts of home. (Psalm 111, 10) Radio message delivered August 8, 1948. Chicago: The Back to God Hour, 1948.

No cause for shame. (Romans 1, 16) Radio message delivered August 15, 1948. Chicago: The Back to God Hour, 1948.

"Scotland's reformation hero" *Ban* 83 (1948) 1255, 1270.

"More opinions on secret societies" *ChrCyn* 81 (1948/49) 113.

1949

John Calvin, the life and significance of the Genevan reformer. Grand Rapids: The Back to God Hour Tract Committee, 1949(?). Also entitled "The life and significance of John Calvin" *GN* 11 (1953) 69, 77, 85, 93, 101, 109, 117, 125, 133, 141, 149, 156–157, 165, 173, 181, 189, 197, 204–205, 213, 221, and also entitled "The life and significance of the Genevan reformer" *Herald* 48 (April 1959) 4–10.

"From the scriptures" (Matthew 5, 6) (Fts) *CLH* 10 (January 1949) 5.

Review of *The Martin Luther Christmas book.* With celebrated woodcuts by his contemporaries. By Martin Luther. Tr. and arranged by Roland Herbert Bainton. Philadelphia: The Westminster Press, 1948. *Ban* 84 (1949) 22.

Review of *A handbook of organizations.* By Theodore Graebner. St. Louis: Concordia Publishing House, 1948. *ChrCyn* 81 (1948/49) 148–150.

"Not by bread alone" (Matthew 4, 4) (Fts) *CLH* 10 (February 1949) 3.

"Great power for little things" (Zechariah 4, 6) (Fts) *CLH* 10 (March 1949) 3.

"No compromise" (Psalm 1, 1) (Fts) *CLH* 10 (April 1949) 5.

"Witnesses of the resurrection" (Acts 1, 8b) (Fts) *CLH* 10 (May 1949) 5.

"The amalgamated silversmiths of Ephesus" (Acts 19, 27) (Fts) *CLH* 10 (June 1949) 7.

"Whatever is right" (Matthew 20, 4b) (Fts) *CLH* 10 (July 1949) 3.

"Not in fashion, but in favor" (Romans 12, 2) (Fts) *CLH* 10 (August 1949) 3.

"Faith of our fathers" *ChiCal* 3 (September 1949) 14–15, (October 1949) 18–19.

"The road to labor peace" (Leviticus 19, 18) (Fts) *CLH* 10 (September 1949) 7.

Review of *Wilfred Grenfell, Labrador's dogsled doctor.* By Basil Miller. Grand Rapids: Zondervan Publishing House, 1948. *MM* 54 (1949) 240–241.

"Manual labor is honorable" (Ephesians 4, 28) (Fts) *CLH* 10 (October 1949) 3.

"What are we working for?" (John 18, 36) (Fts) *CLH* 10 (November 1949) 3.

"How to honor Calvin" *Ban* 84 (1949) 1383.

"God save our homes" *CHS* 28 (December 1949) 20–23.

"Who is my neighbor?" (Luke 10, 29) (Fts) *CLH* 10 (December 1949) 7.

1950

"Our family circle, A.D., 1949" in *Yearbook of the Christian Reformed Church.* Grand Rapids: Christian Reformed Publishing House, 1950. Pp. 174–183.

"What is my time worth?" (Matthew 12, 36) (Fts) *CLH* 11 (January 1950) 7.

"Is the closed shop Christian?" (Philippians 2, 5) (Fts) *CLH* 11 (February 1950) 7.

"Am I my brother's keeper?" *CLH* 11 (February 1950) 7.

"The social gospel is not THE gospel" (Galatians 1, 6–7) (Fts) *CLH* 11 (March 1950) 8.

"Toward a broad Christian witness" *ChrCyn* 82 (1949/50) 180–181.

"The gospel is a social gospel" (James 1, 22) (Fts) *CLH* 11 (April 1950) 8.

Review of *Service for peace.* By Melvin Gingerich. Akron, Pennsylvania: The Mennonite Central Committee, 1949. *CF* 15 (1949/50) 223.

"The rich man's problem" (James 5, 1) (Fts) *CLH* 11 (May 1950) 8.

"Fight communism: how?" *ChrCyn* 83 (1950/51) 20–22.

"Clean hands for prayer" (Isaiah 1, 15–17) (Fts) *CLH* 11 (June 1950) 8.

"Knowledge of the word" *FM* 21 (1949/50) 245–251.

"Revivals in the light of American history" *Ban* 85 (1950) 775.

Review of *Christianity and class struggle.* By Abraham Kuyper. Grand Rapids: Piet Hein Publishers, 1950. *Ban* 85 (1950) 787.

"Gambling" *ChrCyn* 83 (1950/51) 36–37, 68–69, 95–96.

"We will if God will" (James 4, 13–16) (Fts) *CLH* 11 (July 1950) 8.

"History with an ax to grind" *Ban* 85 (1950) 839, 847.

"The epistle to the Philippians" in The Back to God *Family Altar,* August 1950. Chicago: The Back to God Hour, 1950.

"One gospel" (Luke 3, 8) (Fts) *CLH* 11 (August 1950) 5.

"No easy tasks" (Luke 3, 8, 14) (Fts) *CLH* 11 (September 1950) 3.

"Christian labor and a world at war" *CLH* 11 (October 1950) 2–3.

"Not by bread alone" (Matthew 4, 4) (Fts) *CLH* 11 (October 1950) 8.

"Problems facing the [Christian Reformed] Church" *YC* 31 (October 1950) 12, (November 1950) 10, (December 1950) 9; 32 (1951) 9, 47, 91,* 127, 167. *Also in *LD,* Summer 1953, pp. 12–13.

"Luther as a preacher" *Ban* 85 (1950) 1287, 1302.

"The value of being definite" *ChrCyn* 83 (1950/51) 106–108.

"The social message of the Old Testament" (Micah 6, 8a) (Fts) *CLH* 11 (November 1950) 7.

"Only one Christ" *ChrCyn* 83 (1950/51) 121–122. Also in *ChrCyn* 91 (1958/59) 36–37.

"Justice—kindness—humility" (Micah 6, 8b) (Fts) *CLH* 11 (December 1950) 8.

Review of *The imitation of Christ.* By Gerard Zerbolt of Zutphen (1367–1398) teacher of Thomas à Kempis. Tr. for the first time and ed. by Albert Hyma. Grand Rapids: Wm. B. Eerdmans Publishing Co., 1950. *Ban* 85 (1950) 1559.

1951

"The evangelist's message" (Luke 3, 1–20) in *Book of Sermons, No. 7.* Grand Rapids: Christian Reformed Publishing House, 1951. Pp. 65–75.

"Our family circle, A.D., 1950" in *Yearbook of the Christian Reformed Church.* Grand Rapids: Christian Reformed Publishing House, 1951. Pp. 205–214.

"Theology and the economic question; invitation to discussion" *CF* 16 (1950/51) 119–120.

"Christ our greatest need" (Romans 13, 14) (Fts) *CLH* 12 (January 1951) 8.

"Requirements of the times" *ChrCyn* 83 (1950/51) 150–151.

"Sunday labor and the national emergency" (Romans 13, 1–3a) (Fts) *CLH* 12 (February 1951) 8.

Review of *The Brethren of the Common Life.* By Albert Hyma. Grand Rapids: Wm. B. Eerdmans Publishing Co., 1950. *Ban* 86 (1951) 147.

Review of *The Apostolic Fathers: an American translation.* By Edgar J. Goodspeed. New York: Harper & Brothers, 1950. *CF* 16 (1950/51) 172.

"Can God punish America?" (Deuteronomy 28, 45) (Fts) *CLH* 12 (March 1951) 8.

Review of *The cultural concept of Christianity.* By Arthur Wallace Calhoun. Grand Rapids: Wm. B. Eerdmans Publishing Co., 1950. *Ban* 86 (1951) 275.

Review of *Power by the spirit: a study of the Prophet Micah.* By Benjamin A. Copass and E. Leslie Carlson. Grand Rapids: Baker Book House, 1950. *CF* 16 (1950/51) 198.

"Human effort and the kingdom" (John 18, 36a) (Fts) *CLH* 12 (April 1951) 8.

"We have only one king" (Psalm 2, 6) (Fts) *CLH* 12 (May 1951) 8.

"'The immortal dreamer of Bedford jail'" *Ban* 86 (1951) 551.

"Thoughts on national corruption" (Deuteronomy 30, 17–18) (Fts) *CLH* 12 (June 1951) 8.

"Labor unto rest" (Hebrews 4, 9–11) (Fts) *CLH* 12 (July 1951) 8.

Review of *The church in history.* By Barend Klaas Kuiper. Grand Rapids: Wm. B. Eerdmans Publishing Co., 1951. *Ban* 86 (1951) 851.

"From whom do blessings flow?" (James 1, 17a) (Fts) *CLH* 12 (August 1951) 8.

"Know your heritage" *Ban* 86 (1951) 999.

"Always with us" (John 12, 8a) (Fts) *CLH* 12 (September 1951) 8.

"The history of the Christian church" (Art) *FM* 23 (1951/52) 22–24, 51–54, 83–85, 120–122, 145–148, 176–178, 204–206; 24 (1952/53) 23–25, 54–56, 83–85, 115–117, 146–148, 179–181, 204–206; 25 (1953/54) 21–23, 54–56, 82–84, 114–116, 147–149, 178–180, 205–207; 26 (1954/55) 59–61, 93–95, 132–134, 166–168, 194–196, 222–224; 27 (1955/56) 28–30, 61–63, 92–94, 126–128, 159–161, 196–199, 224–226; 28 (1956/57) 22–24, 53–55, 80–82, 110–112, 145–147, 182–184, 206–208.

"The Christian ideal of service" (Mark 10, 43–44) (Fts) *CLH* 12 (October 1951) 8.

"A prayer for power" (Ephesians 3, 14–16) (Fts) *CLH* 12 (November 1951) 8.

"I work and I worship" (A tableau—especially prepared to conclude the West Michigan Young Calvinists rally) *YC* 32 (1951) 402–403.

"A prayer for growth" (Ephesians 3, 17–19) (Fts) *CLH* 12 (December 1951) 8.

1952

"Our family circle, A.D., 1951" in *Yearbook of the Christian Reformed Church.* Grand Rapids: Christian Reformed Publishing House, 1952. Pp. 178–189.

"Christian provocation" (Hebrews 10, 24) (Fts) *CLH* 13 (January 1952) 8.

"Do it with all thy might" (Ecclesiastes 9, 10) (Fts) *CLH* 13 (February 1952) 8.

"L'église chrétienne réformée d'Amérique" *RevRef* 3 No 9 (1952) 34–42.

"On being a real Christian" (Acts 4, 13) (Fts) *CLH* 13 (March 1952) 8.

"God's fast" (Isaiah 58, 3–6) (Fts) *CLH* 13 (April 1952) 8.

"Honesty and affection" (Ephesians 4, 15) (Fts) *CLH* 13 (May 1952) 5.

Review of *The story of Van Raalte.* By Marian Schoolland. Grand Rapids: Wm. B. Eerdmans Publishing Co., 1952. *Ban* 87 (1952) 691.

"Jesus and the kingdom" (Matthew 13, 3) (Fts) *CLH* 13 (June 1952) 8.

"Unfruitful soil" (Matthew 13, 19–21) (Fts) *CLH* 13 (July 1952) 8.

"Thorns or fruit" (Matthew 13, 22–23) (Fts) *CLH* 13 (August 1952) 8.

"The parable of the tares" (Matthew 13, 24–25, 27–30, 37–39) (Fts) *CLH* 13 (September 1952) 8, (October 1952) 8.

"The growth of the kingdom" (Matthew 3, 31–32) (Fts) *CLH* 13 (November 1952) 8.

"The church and the truth" *Ban* 87 (1952) 1383, 1399.

"The nations under God's protection" (Matthew 13, 31–32) (Fts) *CLH* 13 (December 1952) 8.

1953

"Our family circle, A.D., 1952" in *Yearbook of the Christian Reformed Church.* Grand Rapids: Christian Reformed Publishing House, 1953. Pp. 194–203.

"The kingdom as leaven" (Matthew 13, 33) (Fts) *CLH* 14 (January 1953) 8, (February 1953) 8, (March 1953) 8.

"Two parables compared" (Matthew 13, 44–46) (Fts) *CLH* 14 (April 1953) 8.

"Christian charity past and present" *Ban* 88 (1953) 423.

"The treasure in the field" (Matthew 13, 44) (Fts) *CLH* 14 (May 1953) 8.

"The precious pearl" (Matthew 13, 45–46) (Fts) *CLH* 14 (June 1953) 8.

"Thoughts on patriotism" (Romans 13, 5–7) (Fts) *CLH* 14 (July 1953) 8.

Review of *Foxe's Christian martyrs of the world.* From the celebrated work by John Foxe and other eminent authorities. Newly revised and illustrated. Chicago: The Moody Press, 1953. *Ban* 88 (1953) 853.

"Special retribution" (Amos 3, 1–2) (Fts) *CLH* 14 (August 1953) 8.

"How we got our New Testament" *Ban* 88 (1953) 999.

"Parting advice" (Deuteronomy 4, 39–40) (Fts) *CLH* 14 (October 1953) 8.

"Reflection on the life of Calvin" *Ban* 88 (1953) 1319, 1330.

"Thanksgiving has its day" (Psalm 107, 8–9) (Fts) *CLH* 14 (November 1953) 8. Also entitled "Gratitude to God" *LD,* Autumn 1954, pp. 8–10.

"Ecumenicity: the calling and the problem of the church" *RJ* 3 (November 1953) 1–3, (December 1953) 6–7; 4 (January 1954) 3–4.

Review of *Reformation writings.* Vol. 1, *The basis of the protestant reformation.* By Martin Luther. Tr. with introduction and notes from the definitive Weimar edition by Bertram Lee Woolf. New York: Philosophical Library, 1953. *WTJ* 16 (1953/54) 55–57.

"Christmas faith for today" *CF* 19 (1953/54) 75–77. Also entitled "In the fullness of time" *LD,* Winter 1954–1955, pp. 1–7.

"The parting of the ways" (Luke 2, 34–35) (Fts) *CLH* 14 (December 1953) 8.

1954

You shall be my witnesses. A challenge to bashful Christians. Grand Rapids: Wm. B. Eerdmans Publishing Co., 1954.

"Our family circle, A.D., 1953" in *Yearbook of the Christian Reformed Church.* Grand Rapids: Christian Reformed Publishing House, 1954. Pp. 215–224.

"The prospering word" (Isaiah 55, 10–11) (Fts) *CLH* 15 (January 1954) 8.

"Centennial expectations" *Ban* 89 (1954) 203.

"Paul and Apollos and Cephas" *RJ* 4 (April 1954) 1–4.

"Principles and practise in Christian labor" *Ban* 89 (1954) 743, 755.

Review of *The dilemma of church and state.* By G. Elson Ruff. Philadelphia: Muhlenberg Press, 1954. *Ban* 89 (1954) 786.

Review of *Calvijn.* Door Louis Praamsma. Wageningen: Zomer & Keuning, 1954. *Ban* 89 (1954) 854–855.

Review of *Wesleys at Oxford.* By Paul F. Douglass. Philadelphia: Bryn Mawr Press, 1953. *Ban* 89 (1954) 892.

Review of *J. Gresham Machen: a biographical memoir.* By Ned Bernard Stonehouse. Grand Rapids: Wm. B. Eerdmans Publishing Co., 1954. *Ban* 89 (1954) 1426.

"We are American" *CF* 20 (1954/55) 76–79.

1955

"Back to God Hour" and "Christian Reformed Church in America" in *Twentieth century encyclopedia of religious knowledge.* An extension of *The new Schaff-Herzog encyclopedia of religious knowledge.* Ed. by Lefferts A. Loetscher. Grand Rapids: Baker Book House, 1955. Vol. 14, pp. 103, 241. Reprinted in 1967.

"Characteristics of the American environment" (First and second lectures delivered at Minister's Conference, June 1955) in *Christian Reformed Minister's Institute.* Grand Rapids: Christian Reformed Minister's Institute, 1955. Pp. 1–7; 1–9. Also published under title "American religious characteristics" *RJ* 5 (July–August 1955) 6–9, (September 1955) 4–7.

"The dilemma in communication" (Third lecture delivered at Minister's Conference, June 1955) in *Christian Reformed Minister's Institute.* Grand Rapids: Christian Reformed Minister's Institute, 1955. Pp. 1–8. Also in *RJ* 5 (October 1955) 3–6.

"As we look northward" (Fourth lecture delivered at Minister's Conference, June 1955) in *Christian Reformed Minister's Institute.* Grand Rapids: Christian Reformed Minister's Institute, 1955. Pp. 1–8. Also published under title "Problems and opportunities in Canada" *RJ* 5 (November 1955) 4–7. Dutch version entitled "Problemen en kansen in Canada" *CalCon* 12 (February 10, 1956) 5, (February 17, 1956) 2, (February 24, 1956) 2, (March 2, 1956) 2.

"Our family circle, A.D., 1954" in *Yearbook of the Christian Reformed Church.* Grand Rapids: Christian Reformed Publishing House, 1955. Pp. 222–233.

"Ecumenics and confessions" *CF* 20 (1954/55) 103–109.

"All one body we" *CF* 20 (1954/55) 123–127.

Review of *A history of the ecumenical movement, 1517–1948.* Ed. by Ruth Rouse and Stephen Neill. Philadelphia: The Westminster Press, 1954. *CF* 20 (1954/55) 163–164.

Review of *Katherine, wife of Luther.* By Clara S. Schreiber. Philadelphia: Muhlenberg Press, 1954. *Ban* 90 (1955) 307.

Review of *Lutheran cyclopedia.* Ed. by Erwin L. Lueker. St. Louis: Concordia Publishing House, 1954. *Ban* 90 (1955) 407.

"Senior farewell" *RJ* 5 (June 1955) 1–4.

Review of *Ecumenism and the Bible.* By David Hedegard. Amsterdam: The International Council of Christian Churches, 1954. *Ban* 90 (1955) 1111.

Review of *Masters of the English reformation.* By Marcus L. Loane. London: Church Book Room Press, 1954. *WTJ* 18 (1955/56) 85–88.

Glory in God alone. (Jeremiah 9, 23–24) Radio message delivered November 6, 1955. Chicago: The Back to God Hour, 1955.

God save our homes? (Deuteronomy 6, 6–7) Radio message delivered November 13, 1955. Chicago: The Back to God Hour, 1955.

"Orthodoxy's task" *PG* 24 (1955) 152–153, 158–159, 172–173.

Recipe for thanksgiving. (I Timothy 6, 3–10) Radio message delivered November 20, 1955. Chicago: The Back to God Hour, 1955.

What has God to do with education? (Psalm 111, 10) Radio message delivered November 27, 1955. Chicago: The Back to God Hour, 1955.

Review of *Christianity in the apostolic age.* By George T. Purves. Grand Rapids: Baker Book House, 1955. *CF* 21 (1955/56) 61.

"Christ builds his church—1957—centennial of the Christian Reformed Church" *Ban* 90 (1955) 1478–1479. Dutch version in *Wach* 88 (1955) 781–782.

Review of *Netherlanders in America.* By Henry S. Lucas. Ann Arbor: The University of Michigan Press, 1955. *Ban* 90 (1955) 1560.

Review of *Een monument der Afscheiding.* Door W. de Graaf. Kampen: J. H. Kok, 1955. *Ban* 90 (1955) 1593.

1956

"Amerika" in *Christelijke encyclopedie.* Red. van Frederik Willem Grosheide en Gerrit Pieter van Itterzon. Kampen: J. H. Kok, 1956. Vol. 1, Pp. 167–171.

"Our family circle, A.D., 1955" in *Yearbook of the Christian Reformed Church.* Grand Rapids: Christian Reformed Publishing House, 1956. Pp. 234–243.

"Revival in the church" in *Revive us again*. Vital issues. Grand Rapids: The Young Calvinist Federation, 1956. Pp. 17–23.

Review of *Attrition and contrition at the Council of Trent*. By Gordon J. Spykman. Kampen: J. H. Kok, 1955. *TT* 5 (March 1956) 18–19, 23.

"Doing the work of the Lord" *Ban* 91 (1956) 1161, 1180–1181.

1957

In the mirror. An appraisal of the Christian Reformed Church. Hamilton, Ontario: Guardian Publishing Co., 1957.

"Christian Reformed Church" in *Christelijke encyclopedie*. Red. van Frederik Willem Grosheide en Gerrit Pieter van Itterzon. Kampen: J. H. Kok, 1957. Vol. 2, Pp. 192–193.

"1956 in retrospect" in *Yearbook 1957 of the Christian Reformed Church*. Grand Rapids: Christian Reformed Publishing House, 1957. Pp. 8–17.

"Our first hundred years" in *Centennial facts and background*. Grand Rapids: Centennial Committee of the Christian Reformed Church, 1957. Pp. 27–41.

"Our first hundred years" in *One hundred years in the new world*. The story of the Christian Reformed Church from 1857 to 1957: its origin, growth, and institutional activities; together with an account of the celebration of its anniversary in its centennial year. Grand Rapids: Centennial Committee of the Christian Reformed Church, 1957. Pp. 9–66.

"Calvin Seminary in the life of the church" in *One hundred years in the new world*. The story of the Christian Reformed Church from 1857 to 1957: its origin, growth, and institutional activities; together with an account of the celebration of its anniversary in its centennial year. Grand Rapids: Centennial Committee of the Christian Reformed Church, 1957. Pp. 69–78.

"Een man des volks" *Stro* 2 (March 1957) 1–2.

Be a church-goer. (Hebrews 10, 22–25) Radio message delivered April 7, 1957. Chicago: The Back to God Hour, 1957.

"Working and resting" *Stro* 3 (September 1957) 3–4.

"The nature of the unity we seek" *RJ* 7 (October 1957) 7–10.

"What kind of man is the minister?" *Ban* 92 (November 22, 1957) 16.

1958

Comp. *Thine is my heart*. Devotional readings from the writings of John Calvin. By John Calvin. Grand Rapids: Zondervan Publishing House, 1958.

"1957 in retrospect" in *Yearbook 1958 of the Christian Reformed Church*. Grand Rapids: Christian Reformed Publishing House, 1958. Pp. 262–270.

"Bon voyage" *Stro* 3 (Summer 1958) 1–2.

"The Reformed Ecumenical Synod—historical background and nature" *Ban* 93 (June 20, 1958) 4.

"Aspects of the race problem in South Africa" *Stro* 4 (September 1958) 3–5.

"A continent in need" *Ban* 93 (October 10, 1958) 4–5.

1959

"Calvin and ecumenity" in *John Calvin contemporary prophet*. A symposium. Ed. by Jacob Tunis Hoogstra. Grand Rapids: Baker Book House, 1959. Pp. 149–165. Spanish version in *Juan Calvino profeta contemporáneo*. Antología ordenada por temas. Ed. por Jacob Tunis Hoogstra. Grand Rapids: TSELF, 1973. Pp. 151–168.

"1958 in retrospect" in *Yearbook 1959 of the Christian Reformed Church*. Grand Rapids: Christian Reformed Publishing House, 1959. Pp. 282–290.

"Henry Schultze (1893–1959): the teacher" *CCC* 53 (March 13, 1959) 3.

"Professor Henry Schultze—1893–1959: as teacher and colleague" *Ban* 94 (March 27, 1959) 7.

"*Stromata* and infallibility" *Ban* 94 (May 1, 1959) 19.

"'Be men of God'" *Ban* 94 (June 19, 1959) 7.

"Calvinism in the light of its current revival" *Ban* 94 (August 28, 1959) 9.

"John Calvin—man of God—his influence" *FM* 31 (1959/60) 37–43.

"Lessons from Calvin" *RJ* 9 (September 1959) 7–10.

1960

"Foreword" in *Calvin's dying bequest to the church*. A critical evaluation of the commentary on Joshua. By Marten Hendrik Woudstra. Calvin Theological Seminary, Monograph Series, 1. Grand Rapids: Calvin Theological Seminary, 1960. P. 3.

"1959 in retrospect" in *Yearbook 1960 of the Christian Reformed Church*. Grand Rapids: Christian Reformed Publishing House, 1960. Pp. 287–297.

"Meditation; Memorial service address" [Re: Jacob R. Rip] *Stro* 5 (March 23, 1960) 5–6.

"Protestant council on Roman Catholicism" *Stro* 5 (May 1960) 2–3.

"Why study church history?" *Ban* 95 (May 6, 1960) 9, 25, (May 27, 1960) 9, (June 17, 1960) 9, 25.

"The protestant approach to Roman Catholicism" *RefRev* 14 (September 1960) 9–18.

"A fitting memorial" *Ban* 95 (November 4, 1960) 17, 19.

"The church at the crossroads" *Ban* 95 (December 30, 1960) 16–19.

1961

"Foreword" in *Calvin's doctrine of predestination*. By Fred H. Klooster. Calvin Theological Seminary, Monograph Series, 3. Grand Rapids: Calvin Theological Seminary, 1961. P. 3.

"Foreword" in *Man before God's face in Calvin's preaching*. By Carl Gerhard Kromminga. Calvin Theological Seminary, Monograph Series, 2. Grand Rapids: Calvin Theological Seminary, 1961. P. 3.

"Church and state in historical perspective" (Lecture delivered at Minister's Institute, June 1961) in *Christian Reformed Minister's Institute*. Grand Rapids: Christian Reformed Minister's Institute, 1961. Pp. 30–41.

"1960 in retrospect" in *Yearbook 1961 of the Christian Reformed Church*. Grand Rapids: Christian Reformed Publishing House, 1961. Pp. 305–313.

"A note of gratitude from the seminary faculty" *Ban* 96 (May 12, 1961) 6–7.

Review of *God's mission—and ours*. By Eugene L. Smith. Nashville: Abingdon Press, 1961. *CT* 5 (1960/61) 1002.

"Darkness and light" *RJ* 11 (December 1961) 3.

1962

"The Christian Reformed Church: a brief survey of its history and life" in *Doctrinal Standards of the Christian Reformed Church*. Consisting of The Belgic Confession, The Heidelberg Catechism, and The Canons of Dort. Grand Rapids: Publication Committee of the Christian Reformed Church, 1962. Pp. i–v.

"1961 in retrospect" in *Yearbook 1962 of the Christian Reformed Church*. Grand Rapids: Christian Reformed Publishing House, 1962. Pp. 321–329.

"Clarence Bouma, Th.D." *Ban* 97 (September 14, 1962) 19.

Review of *The spreading flame*. By Frederick Fyvie Bruce. Grand Rapids: Wm. B. Eerdmans Publishing Co., 1961. *CT* 7 (1962/63) 250.

1963

Teaching theology in an era of change. Inaugural address delivered in Calvin Seminary chapel. Grand Rapids: Calvin Theological Seminary, 1963.

"1962 in retrospect" in *Yearbook 1963 of the Christian Reformed Church*. Grand Rapids: Christian Reformed Publishing House, 1963. Pp. 333–344.

"Calvin Seminary: progress and problems" *RJ* 13 (January 1963) 14–15.

"What good is a sabbatical?" *Ban* 98 (May 17, 1963) 14.

"Inaugural ceremony at Calvin Seminary" *Ban* 98 (December 27, 1963) 10–11.

1964

"The churches seek co-operation and union" in *The church in history.* By Barend Klaas Kuiper. Grand Rapids: The National Union of Christian Schools; Grand Rapids: Wm. B. Eerdmans Publishing Co., 1964. Pp. 393–397.

"1963 in retrospect" in *Yearbook 1964 of the Christian Reformed Church.* Grand Rapids: Christian Reformed Publishing House, 1964. Pp. 321–332.

Review of *The layman in Christian history.* Ed. by Stephen Charles Neill and Hans-Reudi Weber. Philadelphia: The Westminster Press, 1963. *CT* 8 (1963/64) 607–609.

1965

"Common grace" *Ban* 100 (March 12, 1965) 16–17.

"The person of Christ" *Ban* 100 (March 26, 1965) 16–17.

"Inaugurations of two professors" [Re: Anthony Andrew Hoekema and Carl Gerhard Kromminga] *Ban* 100 (April 30, 1965) 11.

"The hard way is the right way" (Awsi) *MM* 70 (1965) 132, 139–140.

Review of *The Second Vatican Council and the new catholicism.* By Gerrit Cornelis Berkouwer. Grand Rapids: Wm. B. Eerdmans Publishing Co., 1965. *RJ* 15 (July–August 1965) 23–24.

"Why support theological education in Korea?" *Ban* 100 (November 12, 1965) 4–5.

"The marks of the church" *Ban* 100 (December 17, 1965) 14–15.

"Word and sacrament" *Ban* 100 (December 24, 1965) 20–21.

1966

"1965 in retrospect" in *Yearbook 1966 of the Christian Reformed Church.* Grand Rapids: Christian Reformed Publishing House, 1966. Pp. 330–340.

Review of *Ministry.* By Robert S. Paul. Grand Rapids: Wm. B. Eerdmans Publishing Co., 1965. *Ban* 101 (March 11, 1966) 24–25.

"Why we speak" *CTJ* 1 (1966) 5–10. Also in *NGTT* 23 (1982) 311–316.

Review of *The English reformation.* By Arthur Geoffrey Dickens. New York: Schocken Books, 1964. *CTJ* 1 (1966) 90–93.

Reviews of *Christ's church: evangelical, catholic and reformed.* By Bela Vassady. Grand Rapids: Wm. B. Eerdmans Publishing Co., 1965, and *A church for these times.* By Ronald E. Osborn. Nashville: Abingdon Press, 1965. *CTJ* 1 (1966) 128–132.

Review of *Christianity in world history.* By Arend Th. van Leeuwen. New York: Charles Scribner's Sons, 1966. *CT* 10 (1965/66) 1004.

Review of *Wildfire: church growth in Korea.* By Roy E. Shearer. Grand Rapids: Wm. B. Eerdmans Publishing Co., 1966. *Ban* 101 (October 14, 1966) 24.

"De verhouding Rome—reformatie" *Wach* 99 (25 October 1966) 5, 13.

Review of *Papal infallibility: its complete collapse before a factual investigation*. By J. B. Rowell. Grand Rapids: Kregel Publications, 1963. *CTJ* 1 (1966) 237–239.

Review of *Churches in North America*. By Gustave Weigel. New York: Schocken Books, 1965. *CTJ* 1 (1966) 247–249.

1967

"1966 in retrospect" in *1967 Yearbook of the Christian Reformed Church*. Grand Rapids: Christian Reformed Publishing House, 1967. Pp. 346–356.

"The great brotherhood; John Calvin . . . and the unity of the church" *YC* 48 (January 1967) 10–12.

"Ecumenicity . . . the World Council of Churches" *FM* 38 (1966/67) 245–247.

Review of *Henry VIII and the lutherans*. By Neelak Tjernagel. St. Louis: Concordia Publishing House, 1965. *CTJ* 2 (1967) 89–91.

Review of *The congregational way*. By Marion L. Starkey. Garden City, New York: Doubleday & Co., 1966. *CTJ* 2 (1967) 102–104.

Review of *Your Bible*. By Louis Cassels. Garden City, New York: Doubleday & Co., 1967. *CT* 11 (1966/67) 873–874.

"Lutherane in die Verenigde State van Amerika" *Kerkb* 70 (25 Oktober 1967) 15–16.

"Justification by faith; Protestant reformation—450th anniversary" *Ban* 102 (October 27, 1967) 4–5.

Review of *The seminary, protestant and catholic*. By Walter D. Wagoner. New York: Sheed and Ward, 1966. *CTJ* 2 (1967) 226–227.

Review of *Fundamentalism and the Missouri Synod*. By Milton L. Rudnick. St. Louis: Concordia Publishing House, 1966. *CTJ* 2 (1967) 240–242.

Review of *John Hus at the Council of Constance*. By Matthew Spinka. New York: Columbia University Press, 1965. *CTJ* 2 (1967) 257–258.

Review of *The ecumenical vanguard: the history of the Una Sancta movement*. By Leonard Swidler. Pittsburgh: Duquesne University Press, 1966. *CTJ* 2 (1967) 269–270.

Review of *Church cooperation: dead-end street or highway to unity?* By Forrest L. Knapp. New York: Doubleday & Co., 1966. *CTJ* 2 (1967) 271–272.

1968

"1967 in retrospect" in *1968 Yearbook of the Christian Reformed Church*. Grand Rapids: Christian Reformed Publishing House, 1968. Pp. 347–358.

"De rol van *De Wachter* in het leven van de *Christian Reformed Church*" *Wach* 101 (6 Februari 1968) 7.

Review of *Francis Asbury.* By L. C. Rudolph. Nashville: Abingdon Press, 1966. *CTJ* 3 (1968) 51-52.

Review of *The indomitable baptists.* By O. K. Armstrong and Marjorie Moore Armstrong. New York: Doubleday & Co., 1967. *CTJ* 3 (1968) 68-70.

Review of *The ecumenical mirage.* By C. Stanley Lowell. Grand Rapids: Baker Book House, 1967. *CTJ* 3 (1968) 70-73.

1969

"Kerken in Engeland" *Wach* 102 (18 Maart 1969) 12-13.

Review of *Paths to unity: American religion today and tomorrow.* By Ronald E. Modras. New York: Sheed & Ward, 1968. *CTJ* 4 (1969) 104-106.

Review of *Progress and decline in the history of church renewal.* Ed. by Robert Aubert. New York: Paulist Press, 1967. *CTJ* 4 (1969) 125-127.

"Changing times and conservative theology" *Ban* 104 (October 10, 1969) 16-19.

1970

All one body we. The doctrine of the church in ecumenical perspective. Grand Rapids: Wm. B. Eerdmans Publishing Co., 1970.

"1969 in retrospect" in *1970 Yearbook of the Christian Reformed Church.* Grand Rapids: Christian Reformed Publishing House, 1970. Pp. 375-384.

Review of *Luther: right or wrong?* By Harry J. McSorley. New York: Newman Press, 1969. *CTJ* 5 (1970) 81-87.

Review of *Erasmus of christendom.* By Roland Herbert Bainton. New York: Charles Scribner's Sons, 1969. *CTJ* 5 (1970) 87-88.

"The crisis in authority . . . the crisis in faith" *Ban* 105 (September 11, 1970) 4-5.

Review of *The ecumenical revolution.* By Robert McAfee Brown. New York: Doubleday & Co., 1969. *CTJ* 5 (1970) 197-201.

Reviews of *Dissent in and for the church: theologians and Humanae Vitae.* By Charles E. Curran and Robert E. Hunt. New York: Sheed & Ward, 1969, and *The responsibility of dissent: the church and academic freedom.* By John F. Hunt and Terrence R. Connelly. New York: Sheed & Ward, 1969. *CTJ* 5 (1970) 210-215.

1971

"1970 in retrospect" in *1971 Yearbook of the Christian Reformed Church.* Grand Rapids: Board of Publication, 1971. Pp. 387-394.

Review of *The Doukhobors.* By George Woodcock and Ivan Avakumovic. Toronto and New York: The Oxford University Press, 1968. *CTJ* 6 (1971) 74-77.

Review of *Professional education for ministry.* A history of clinical pastoral education. Nashville: Abingdon Press, 1970. *CTJ* 6 (1971) 93-96.

Review of *The Americanization of a congregation*. By Elton J. Bruins. Grand Rapids: Wm. B. Eerdmans Publishing Co., 1970. *CTJ* 6 (1971) 103–104.

"No time for division" (Awsi) *RJ* 21 (April 1971) 5.

"Symbols at the seminary" (1) *Ban* 106 (July 9, 1971) 16.

Review of *Ecumenicity and evangelism*. By David M. Stowe. Grand Rapids: Wm. B. Eerdmans Publishing Co., 1970. *RJ* 21 (October 1971) 23.

Review of *The evangelical mind and the new school Presbyterian experience*. By George M. Marsden. New Haven: Yale University Press, 1970. *CTJ* 6 (1971) 227–228.

Review of *Kerkelijke besluitvaardigheid*. Door J. Kamphuis. Groningen: De Vuurbaak, 1970. *CTJ* 6 (1971) 241–243.

1972

"1971 in retrospect" in *1972 Yearbook of the Christian Reformed Church*. Grand Rapids: Board of Publication, 1972. Pp. 404–413.

Review of *Thomas Becket*. By David Knowles. Stanford: Stanford University Press, 1971. *CTJ* 7 (1972) 112–114.

Review of *Western society and the church in the Middle Ages*. By R. W. Southern. The Pelican History of the Church, 2. Baltimore: Penguin Books, 1970. *CTJ* 7 (1972) 114–115.

Review of *The spirit of the reformed tradition*. By Maurice Eugene Osterhaven. Grand Rapids: Wm. B. Eerdmans Publishing Co., 1971. *CTJ* 7 (1972) 116–117.

"The shape of a new confession" *CTJ* 7 (1972) 146–157.

1973

"1972 in retrospect" in *1973 Yearbook of the Christian Reformed Church*. Grand Rapids: Board of Publication, 1973. Pp. 417–424.

"Mysticism" and "Renaissance" in *Baker's dictionary of Christian ethics*. Ed. by Carl Ferdinand Howard Henry. Washington, DC: Canon Press, 1973. Pp. 440–441, 576–578.

"Let's talk about confession" *Ban* 108 (January 5, 1973) 13.

Review of *Issues of theological warfare: evangelicals and liberals*. By Richard J. Coleman. Grand Rapids: Wm. B. Eerdmans Publishing Co., 1972. *CTJ* 8 (1973) 89–90.

Review of *A history of Christian thought*. Vol. 2, *From Augustine to the eve of the reformation*. By Justo L. Gonzalez. Nashville: Abingdon Press, 1971. *CTJ* 8 (1973) 94–95.

Review of *Christian reunion: historic divisions reconsidered*. By John S. Whale. Grand Rapids: Wm. B. Eerdmans Publishing Co., 1971. *CTJ* 8 (1973) 180–182.

Review of *God's statesman: the life and work of John Owen.* By Peter Toon. Grand Rapids: Zondervan Publishing House, 1973. *CTJ* 8 (1973) 228–230.

"Master of Divinity program at Calvin Seminary" By John Henry Kromminga, Harold Dekker, and Martin D. Geleynse. *Ban* 108 (November 2, 1973) 10–11.

1974

"Christian Reformed Church" in *The encyclopedia Americana.* New York: Americana Corporation, 1974. Vol. 6, p. 645.

"1973 in retrospect" in *1974 Yearbook of the Christian Reformed Church.* Grand Rapids: Board of Publications, 1974. Pp. 413–422.

"The catechism on distorting truth" *Ban* 109 (March 8, 1974) 13.

Reviews of *Liberation, development, and salvation.* By René Laurentin. Maryknoll, New York: Orbis Books, 1972, and *The message of liberation in our age.* By Johannes Verkuyl. Grand Rapids: Wm. B. Eerdmans Publishing Co., 1972. *CTJ* 9 (1974) 97–99.

"Calvino" *RT* 6 No. 22 (1974) 19–22, No. 23 (1974) 13–16, 23; 7 No. 24 (1975) 3–8, No. 25 (1976) 35–40.

"Church discipline as a pastoral exercise" *RJ* 24 (November 1974) 12–15; *Outl* 25 (April 1975) 2–4.

1975

"Abraham Kuyper (1837–1920)" in *A history of religious educators.* Ed. by Elmer L. Towns. Grand Rapids: Baker Book House, 1975. Pp. 288–296.

"New venture in ecumenical relations" *Ban* 110 (March 14, 1975) 24–25.

Review of *The mission of the church.* By Edward C. F. A. Schillebeeckx. New York: Seabury Press, 1973. *CTJ* 10 (1975) 60–63.

Review of *C. H. Spurgeon autobiography.* Vol. 2, *The full harvest.* By Charles H. Spurgeon. Rev. ed., originally compiled by Susannah Spurgeon and Joseph Harrald. Edinburgh: Banner of Truth Trust, 1973. *CTJ* 10 (1975) 63–66.

Review of *Is the day of the denomination dead?* By Elmer L. Towns. Nashville: Thomas Nelson, 1973. *CTJ* 10 (1975) 85–87.

Review of *Dealing with death—A Christian perspective.* By D. P. Brooks. Nashville: Broadman Press, 1974. *CTJ* 10 (1975) 90–91.

Review of *Frontiers for the church today.* By Robert McAfee Brown. New York: Oxford University Press, 1973. *CTJ* 10 (1975) 92–93.

"Unity in Christ" *Ban* 110 (May 30, 1975) 15.

Review of *Trumpeter of God: A biography of John Knox.* By William Stanford Reid. New York: Charles Scribner's Sons, 1974. *CTJ* 10 (1975) 220–223. Shortened version in *RESNE* 13 (1976) 1148.

"World Council assembly—before and after" *Ban* 110 (November 28, 1975) 24.

"How does the Reformed Church in America look to me?" *Ban* 110 (December 26, 1975) 6–7.

1976

"The threats to the Christian character of the Christian institution" in *Christian Higher Education. The contemporary challenge.* Proceedings of the First International Conference of Reformed Institutions for Christian Scholarship Potchefstroom, 9–13 September 1975. Wetenskaplike Bydraes van die P.U. vir C.H.O. Series F. Institute for the Advancement of Calvinism. F3, Collections No. 6. Potchefstroom: Institute for the Advancement of Calvinism, 1976. Pp. 57–68.

"Survival or service?" *Ban* 111 (January 2, 1976) 10–12.

"World Council assembly" *Ban* 111 (February 20, 1976) 6–7, 27.

"Response to Hendrik Bernard Weijland's 'Toward more effective church discipline'" *RESTB* 4 (March 1976) 18–19.

"The seminary future" *Ban* 111 (March 12, 1976) 14–15.

Review of *Memoirs.* By József Cardinal Mindszenty. New York: Macmillan Publishing Co., 1974. *CTJ* 11 (1976) 81–82.

"Milestone: to the graduates of Calvin Seminary 1976" *Ban* 111 (June 25, 1976) 13.

"Evangelical influence on the ecumenical movement" *CTJ* 11 (1976) 149–180.

Review of *The heritage of our fathers.* The Free Church of Scotland: her origin and testimony. By George Norman Macleod. Edinburgh: Lindsay & Co., 1974. *CTJ* 11 (1976) 294–295.

"NAPaRC meeting" *Ban* 111 (December 17, 1976) 23. Dutch version in *Wach* 109 (30 November 1976) 15.

1977

"Toespraak" in *Acta* van de Generale Synode van Maastricht 1975/76 van de Gereformeerde Kerken in Nederland, Gehouden te Maastricht op 13 Mei 1975, te Lunteren van 23 t/m 26 September 1975, van 9 t/m 11 Oktober 1975, van 18 t/m 22 November 1975, van 1 t/m 5 Maart 1976, van 29 Maart t/m 2 April 1976, op 25 en 26 Mei 1976, van 5 t/m 8 Oktober 1976, van 1 t/m 4 November 1976, van 22 t/m 26 November 1976. Kampen: J. H. Kok, 1977. Pp. 57–62 (Bijlage 4).

"Growing to maturity" *Ban* 112 (March 25, 1977) 6–7.

Review of *The anatomy of a hybrid.* A study in church-state relationships. By Leonard Verduin. Grand Rapids: Wm. B. Eerdmans Publishing Co., 1976. *CTJ* 12 (1977) 65–68.

Review of *A history of Christian thought.* Vol. 3, *From the protestant reformation to the twentieth century.* By Justo L. González. Nashville: Abingdon Press, 1975. *CTJ* 12 (1977) 93.

Review of *Gods of goodness*. The sophisticated idolatry of the main line churches. By Bruce Lothian Blackie. Philadelphia: The Westminster Press, 1975. *CTJ* 12 (1977) 97–98.

Review of *The inward pilgrimage*. Spiritual classics from Augustine to Bonhoeffer. By Bernhard Marinus Christensen. Minneapolis: Augsburg Publishing House, 1976. *CTJ* 12 (1977) 103–104.

"What's next?" (To the graduates of Calvin Seminary 1977) *Ban* 112 (June 24, 1977) 14.

"A confessional challenge" *TaS* 23 (September 1977) 5–7.

Reviews of *Ecumenical Testimony*. The concern for Christian unity within the Reformed and Presbyterian Churches. By John Thomas McNeill and James Hastings Nichols. Philadelphia: The Westminster Press, 1974, and *Study Draft*. A plan for union of the Presbyterian Church in the United States and the United Presbyterian Church in the United States of America to form the Presbyterian Church (USA). By the Joint Committee on Presbyterian Union. Atlanta: Materials Distribution Service, 1974. *JES* 14 (1977) 513–514.

"The church's vital signs" *Ban* 112 (November 4, 1977) 14–15.

1978

"Update on the Christian Reformed Church" in *Summary of proceedings*. Thirty-first annual conference, American Theological Library Association, Vancouver School of Theology, Vancouver, British Columbia, Canada, June 20–24, 1977. Philadelphia: Lutheran Theological Seminary at Philadelphia, 1978. Pp. 69–76.

Review of *Luther and the mystics*. A reexamination of Luther's spiritual experience and his relationship to the mystics. By Bengt Runo Hoffman. Minneapolis: Augsburg Publishing House, 1976. *CTJ* 13 (1978) 88–90.

Review of *Introduction to the reformed tradition*. A way of being the Christian community. By John Haddon Leith. Atlanta: John Knox Press, 1977. *WTJ* 40 (1977/78) 370–372.

"New Zealand en Australië" *Wach* 111 (4 April 1978) 10–11.

"Sri Lanka" *Wach* 111 (18 April 1978) 12–13.

"De Filippijnen" *Wach* 111 (2 Mei 1978) 10–11.

"Japan en Korea" *Wach* 111 (16 Mei 1978) 8–9.

"La function de las confesiones en la vida de la iglesia" *RT* 9 No. 31–32 (1978) 6–15.

Review of *The Cistercians: ideals and reality*. By Louis Julius Lekai. Kent, Ohio: The Kent State University Press, 1977. *CTJ* 13 (1978) 221–222.

Review of *The mindbenders*. A look at current cults. By John Sparks. Nashville: Thomas Nelson, 1977. *CTJ* 13 (1978) 260–261.

"Synod report unfair" *Outl* 28 (November 1978) 23.

"Just between us" (A response) [Re: Fraternal delegates] *Ban* 113 (December 22, 1978) 25.

1979

Review of *Anatomy of an explosion*. Missouri in lutheran perspective. By Kurt E. Marquart. Grand Rapids: Baker Book House, 1978. *CTJ* 14 (1979) 106–109.

Review of *The water that divides*. The baptism debate. By Donald Bridge and David Phypers. Downers Grove, Illinois: InterVarsity Press, 1977. *CTJ* 14 (1979) 130–131.

Review of *Contemporary perspectives on pietism*. Ed. by Donald W. Dayton. Chicago: Covenant Press of North Park Theological Seminary, 1976. *CTJ* 14 (1979) 131.

"The North American Presbyterian and Reformed Council" *WTJ* 42 (1979/80) 176–197.

"Perspective: an open letter from the president" *Sem-Alum* 1 No. 1 (1979/80) 1.

Review of *Profiles in belief*. The religious bodies of the United States and Canada. Vol. 2, *Protestant denominations*. By Arthur Carl Piepkorn. San Francisco: Harper & Row, 1978. *CTJ* 14 (1979) 242–244.

Review of *De wereldraad in discussie*. Door Klaas Runia. Kampen: J. H. Kok, 1978. *CTJ* 14 (1979) 249–251.

Review of *The gospel in America*. Themes in the story of America's evangelicals. By John D. Woodbridge, Mark A. Noll and Nathan O. Hatch. Grand Rapids: Zondervan Publishing House, 1979. *CTJ* 14 (1979) 267–268.

Review of *Lazarus Spengler*. A lay leader of the reformation. By Harold John Grimm. Columbus: Ohio State University Press, 1978. *CTJ* 14 (1979) 271–272.

Review of *The trial of Luther*. By Daniel Olivier. St. Louis: Concordia Publishing House, 1978. *CTJ* 14 (1979) 275.

"Perspective: presidential plaudits for patience" *Sem-Alum* 1 No. 2 (1979/80) 1.

"Ford Lewis Battles: an appreciation" *Ban* 114 (December 28, 1979) 5–7.

1980

Review of *The early Christians*. A sourcebook on the witness of the Early Church. By Eberhard Arnold. Grand Rapids: Baker Book House, 1979. *CTJ* 15 (1980) 132.

Review of *Profiles in belief*. The religious bodies of the United States and Canada. Vol. 3, *Holiness and pentecostal*. By Arthur Carl Piepkorn. San Francisco: Harper & Row, 1979, and *Profiles in belief*. The religious bodies of the United States and Canada. Vol. 4, *Evangelical, fundamentalist, and other Christian bodies*. By Arthur Carl Piepkorn. San Francisco: Harper & Row, 1979. *CTJ* 15 (1980) 139.

"Calvin Seminary's encounter with Ford Lewis Battles" *CTJ* 15 (1980) 158–159.

Review of *Die Zwinglische Reformation im Rahmen der europäischen Kirchengeschichte*. Von Gottfried Wilhelm Locher. Göttingen: Vandenhoeck & Ruprecht, 1979. *CTJ* 15 (1980) 280–282.

Review of *A religious history of the American people*. By Sidney Eckman Ahlstrom. New Haven: Yale University Press, 1979. *CTJ* 15 (1980) 305.

"What's ahead for the church in the 1980s?" *Ban* 115 (December 29, 1980) 16–17.

1981

Review of *A history of Christian doctrine*. In succession to the earlier work of George Park Fisher. Ed. by Hubert Cunliffe-Jones, assisted by Benjamin Drewery. Edinburgh: T. & T. Clark. *CTJ* 16 (1981) 81–84.

"Ecumenicity: practice reveals policy" *Ban* 116 (October 26, 1981) 14–15.

Review of *The lane rebels*. Evangelicalism and antislavery in Antebellum America. By Lawrence Thomas Lesick. Studies in Evangelicalism, 2. Metuchen, New Jersey: The Scarecrow Press, 1980. *CTJ* 16 (1981) 277–278.

"Foxholes of silence" (letter to ed.) *Ban* 116 (December 28, 1981) 4.

1982

"Quality control" *Ban* 117 (February 15, 1982) 9.

Review of *The mind of John Paul II*. Origins of his thought and action. By George Huntston Williams. New York: The Seabury Press, 1981. *CTJ* 17 (1982) 159–161.

"The shaping influence of a tradition" *CTJ* 17 (1982) 182–189.

Review of *Reformation and counter reformation*. By Erwin Iserloh, Joseph Glazik and Hubert Jedin. History of the Church, 5. A Crossroad Book. New York: The Seabury Press, 1980. *CTJ* 17 (1982) 265–267.

Review of *Eastern politics of the Vatican 1917–1979*. By Hansjakob Stehle. Athens: Ohio University Press, 1981. *CTJ* 17 (1982) 302–304.

1983

"Perspective" *Sem-Alum* 2 (1983) 1.

Review of *Acting in faith*. The World Council of Churches since 1975. By Lean Howell. Geneva: World Council of Churches Publications; New York: Friendship Press, 1982. *CTJ* 18 (1983) 82–83.